Children's Literature

A Guide to the Criticism

A
Reference
Publication
in
Literature

Rachel Fordyce,
Editor

"Children's Literature"

A Guide to the Criticism

LINNEA HENDRICKSON

G.K.HALL &CO.

70 LINCOLN STREET, BOSTON, MASS.

Library of Congress Cataloging-in-Publication Data

Hendrickson, Linnea.
  Children's literature, a guide to the criticism.

  (A Reference publication in literature)
  Includes indexes.
  1. Children's literature, English—History and criticism—
Bibliography.   2. Children's literature, American—History
and criticism—Bibliography.
I. Title.   II. Series.
Z2014.5.H46   1987   [PR990]   011'.62   86-19455
ISBN 0-8161-8670-7

This publication is printed on permanent/durable acid-free paper
MANUFACTURED IN THE UNITED STATES OF AMERICA.

This publication has been supported by the National Endowment for the Humanities, a federal agency that supports study in such fields as history, philosophy, literature, and languages.

for Jesse and Psyche

Contents

The Author

Linnea Hendrickson has been a reference librarian and a college instructor in English, social sciences, and humanities. She is coauthor, with Beverly Renford, of *Bibliographic Instruction: A Handbook*, and has presented papers on children's literature at professional conferences. She holds a degree in history from the University of Michigan and masters degrees in teaching, English, and library science from the University of Massachusetts and the University of Arizona. She currently resides in Albuquerque, New Mexico, with her husband, Ed Philips, and their children, Jesse and Psyche.

Preface

In recent years, children's literature has become an increasingly important area of literary scholarship. In 1973 the Children's Literature Association was founded and began publishing *Children's Literature*, a scholarly annual review now published by Yale University Press. In 1978 Roger Sale's *Fairy Tales and After* was published by Harvard University Press. In 1980 children's literature was raised to Division status by the Modern Language Association.

The number and quality of journals devoted to children's literature have also increased dramatically. Joining older journals such as *Horn Book* (1924) and *Junior Bookshelf* (1936), were *Bookbird* and *Interracial Books for Children Bulletin* in the 1960s, *Signal* and *Children's Literature in Education* in 1969 and 1970, followed by *Phaedrus* (1973), *Canadian Children's Literature* (1975), *Children's Literature Association Quarterly* (1976), *The Lion and the Unicorn* (1977), and *Advocate* (1981). In addition, increasing numbers of journals devoted to literary criticism have been accepting articles on children's literature, and entries under that subject heading in the *MLA Bibliography* have been increasing ever since the first appearance in 1976.

The traditional academic home of children's literature has been in departments of education and library science, but there has been a large increase in interest in English departments; and social scientists, psychologists, sociologists, historians, folklorists, and students of popular culture have all published articles relating to the field.

Purpose of this bibliography
The purpose of this bibliography is to draw together, for scholars and generalists, significant articles, books, and dissertations relating to children's literature criticism that have originated in disparate disciplines and been published in widely scattered popular and scholarly sources. The emphasis is on twentieth-century children's literature, although classics from earlier centuries have been included.

Definition of children's literature
For the purposes of this bibliography, literature is considered to be imaginative works such as fiction, drama, poetry, nonfiction of exceptional quality, and, in some cases, works of historical significance such as the Stratemeyer (Nancy Drew, Hardy Boys, et al.) series. Children's literature is defined as literature written for, or largely read by, children between the ages of one and sixteen, in format and style ranging from the picture book to the young adult novel.

Definition of criticism
Criticism involves defining, classifying, analyzing, and evaluating works of literature. It may be distinguished from "book reviewing" by its greater depth and scope. To quote Helen Haines, "A reviewer should tell what the author set

out to do, what he did and how he did it," whereas "the critic interprets in terms of intellectual or emotional analysis" (quoted by Elizabeth Nesbitt in "The Critic and Children's Literature," in *A Critical Approach to Children's Literature*, edited by Sara I. Fenwick [Chicago: University of Chicago Press, 1967], p. 121). A book review may, but does not necessarily, contain literary criticism.

The type of criticism emphasized in this bibliography is "explication," that is, it is concerned with interpreting the meaning or enhancing the understanding of a particular work. Although the usual method of explication is through close analysis of the text itself, criticism that places the work in a biographical, historical, or cultural context is also included. Articles interpreting the treatment of specific subjects or themes in children's literature, those examining the characteristics of particular genres, those surveying the status of the children's literature of a particular geographic area or of a particular time, and those on the nature, theory, and status of criticism of children's literature have been included.

Scope of the children's literature included

The critical works covered in this bibliography discuss children's literature originating in any language or time period, although the emphasis is on children's literature of the twentieth century. Since the criticism is limited to that written in English, however, the bulk of the literature covered has been written in or translated into English.

Genres of children's literature considered include picture books, wordless books, comics, periodicals, fairy tales, folklore and other traditional literature, series books and popular fiction, young adult fiction, drama, poetry, and nonfiction. Criticism of film, television, and textbooks has not been included. Author-illustrators and illustrators whose work is an integral part of a work have been included.

Coverage of criticism of such classic authors as Lewis Carroll, Mark Twain, Robert Louis Stevenson, J.R.R. Tolkien, Rudyard Kipling, and C.S. Lewis has been selective, concentrated on studies of their writings for children, and recent bibliographies and review articles.

An effort has been made to ensure coverage of authors of prize-winning books and authors featured in standard biographical and critical sources.

Scope of the criticism indexed

(1) Criticism of individual authors of and illustrators of children's books.

(2) Criticism centering on a particular subject or theme, for example, death, sex roles, war.

(3) Criticism centering on a particular genre, for example, poetry, historical fiction, fairy tales.

(4) Surveys of the literature or criticism originating in a particular country or geographic area, for example, studies of current scholarship or research in children's literature in the Soviet Union.

(5) Articles on the nature of the scholarship of children's literature, definitions of children's literature, discussions of trends, critical theory, and the status of children's literature.

(6) Books, including collections of essays. Individual chapters and segments are indexed separately as appropriate.

(7) Reviews of children's books are covered selectively. Winnowing substantial reviews from the vast number of primarily descriptive annotations was difficult, and numerous useful comments undoubtedly have been overlooked. Early reviews of important books are sometimes included for their historical

perspective. Lengthy and perceptive analyses in scholarly journals are included.

(8) Doctoral dissertations are included based on their abstracts in *Dissertation Abstracts International*. Unpublished masters theses and papers are not included.

(9) Biographical sketches of authors and published personal interviews and speeches are included only if they contain literary analysis or shed significant light on the background or creation of a work of literature.

(10) Criticism concerned with the censorship of specific titles and censorship of children's literature in general is included.

Criteria for selecting criticism

The chief criterion for each book or article selected for inclusion in this bibliography is: does it provide insight into the work or topic discussed? Does it say something significant or enlightening? Will it be helpful and worth the while of a person seeking fuller understanding of a particular work or topic? Some articles stand out immediately as first-rate criticism; others are borderline. The selector's biases, and even the circumstances under which the articles were indexed, have inevitably been reflected in the choices. In many cases articles have been included not for their critical excellence but because (1) they were the only ones about an important or controversial work, (2) they have generated many responses or much controversy, or (3) they offer a distinct or representative point of view.

Method of compiling the bibliography

The starting point for this bibliography was the critical sources, not a list of recommended works of children's literature. Periodicals central to the field of children's literature were examined issue by issue and cover-to-cover for appropriate articles. Other journals were accessed through periodical indexes and bibliographies. Books were accessed through bibliographies and indexes and through library catalogs. Numerous references came from reference notes in articles indexed. Lists of reference works consulted and periodicals central to the field are contained in the Appendix.

Subject headings

Subject terms were selected from terms used by the Library of Congress, *Sears List of Subject Headings*, the Wilson indexes, the ERIC system, and, in some cases, from terms recommended by the Council on Interracial Books for Children, which concerns itself with the treatment of the aged, the handicapped, and various minorities in children's books. Cross-references are provided in the Index of Authors, Titles and Subjects.

Annotations

The annotations are intended to be descriptive rather than evaluative, and to convey some of the flavor of the selections. A very few articles from the early issues of *Signal* and *Orana* were indexed on the basis of an examination of contents pages and the first pages of the articles, and are therefore not annotated.

Comparison with similar works

Children's Literature Review, published by Gale Research since 1976, is a serial publication that provides references to reviews and in-depth criticism, and also includes lengthy excerpts from them. It includes fewer authors than this bibliography and has no coverage of subjects, themes, or critical theory. *Children's Literature Abstracts* and *Phaedrus* are highly selective serial bibliographies that cover current criticism only.

Elva S. Smith's *History of Children's Literature* (Chicago: American Library Association, 1980) covers criticism of only those authors who wrote before the end of the nineteenth century. A 1977 bibliography by Irving P. Leif, *Children's*

Literature: A Historical and Contemporary Bibliography *(Troy, N.Y.: Whitson) is a somewhat limited and haphazard selection. Suzanne Rahn's* Children's Litera-ture: An Annotated Bibliography of the History and Criticism *(New York: Garland, 1981) has been of great help in compiling the present bibliography, but differs in several significant respects: (1) greater emphasis on older works of historical interest, (2) absence of a title index, (3) limited subject access, and (4) little or no coverage of many significant contemporary writers.*

Organization of the text and suggestions for use

The bibliography consists of two main parts: part A, "Authors and Their Works," and part B, "Subjects, Themes, and Genres." These two main parts are supplemented by two indexes, one for the names of critics, and one for the names of all authors of children's books, titles of children's books, and themes, genres, and topics discussed by the critics. Comments by one critic upon another have been included in the "Index of Critics."

A list of periodical title abbreviations and a full listing of books of criticism referred to in short form in the text will be found at the front of the volume, in the sections entitled "Periodical-Title Abbreviations" and "Books of Criticism Indexed." The appendix contains (1) a list of reference works related to chil-dren's literature that were used in compiling the bibliography and (2) a list of important journals concerned with children's literature.

In part A, "Authors and Their Works," entries whose main focus is the work of a particular author or illustrator are listed alphabetically under the name of the author or illustrator. Authors are listed under the names by which they are best known, whether these are pseudonyms or real names, and are cross-referenced in the "Index of Authors, Titles and Subjects."

Works listed under their titles rather than under an author's name will also be found interfiled in this section, for example, *St. Nicholas* magazine, and fairy tales such as "Snow White" and "Cinderella." When two or more authors are dis-cussed in one article, the listing has usually been included under only one, with additional references confined to the index. It is therefore imperative that the index be consulted for complete coverage of any author, illustrator or subject.

Part B, "Subjects, Themes, and Genres," contains discussions of the handling of certain themes or genres by more than one author. It also includes surveys of the literature of particular geographic areas, and discussions of such topics as the definition of children's literature, the nature of the criticism of children's literature, the role of the critic, censorship and issues approaches, and trends in children's literature and its criticism. Discussions of the nature and history of fairy tales, debates concerning their suitability for children, and discussions of particular themes or types of tales will be found, for example, under the heading "fairy tales" in part B, whereas discussions centering on the analysis of one particular tale will be found under the name of the tale or its author in part A. In any case, for all relevant discussions of any particular work, author, or topic, the author, title, and subject index must be consulted.

Availability of materials indexed

Some of the journals indexed are scarce, especially in their early issues. However, photocopies of single articles should be available through interlibrary loan. The volume and abstract numbers of doctoral dissertations located through *Dissertations Abstracts International* have been included in the citations to facilitate access to the more detailed abstracts and ordering information available there.

Acknowledgments

Without the help and support of many, this book would have been impossible. Rebecca Torres has been my faithful typist and right-hand assistant through numerous difficulties, detours, and tight places during the preparation of the manuscript.

Mona Bryant and Barbara Grady provided excellent assistance with library research. Dorothy Wonsmos and the interlibrary loan staff at the University of New Mexico Library helped with access to over one hundred articles and books. Carol Gay made available the complete published proceedings of the Children's Literature Association. Margaret N. Coughlan provided assistance with materials in the Children's Literature Center at the Library of Congress.

The resources of numerous libraries have been essential in compiling this work, notably those of the University of Arizona, the University of New Mexico, the Albuquerque Public Schools, and the Albuquerque Public Library.

At the very beginning of this project I received encouragement, support, and advice from Bruce Bonta and my fellow librarians at Penn State University, and from professor Harrison T. Meserole of Penn State's English Department. Later, Richard Van Dongen and the students I met through his courses in children's literature at the University of New Mexico broadened my perspectives of the field and provided me with firsthand experience of the needs of students and scholars.

Editors Janice Meagher and Rachel Fordyce have been patient, encouraging, and a source of expert advice. My husband, G. Edward Philips, has given personal support and assisted me with the complexities of computer hardware and software.

Finally, the financial support of the National Endowment for the Humanities has been invaluable, as was the encouragement and advice offered by grants officer Marcella Grendler on more than one occasion.

Periodical Title Abbreviations

CCL	*Canadian Children's Literature*
ChLAQ	*Children's Literature Association Quarterly*
CLE	*Children's Literature in Education*
EE	*Elementary English*
EER	*Elementary English Review*
Horn Book	*Horn Book Magazine*
IRBC	*Interracial Books for Children: Bulletin*
LA	*Language Arts*
L&U	*The Lion and the Unicorn*
NYRB	*New York Review of Books*
NYTBR	*New York Times Book Review*
SLJ	*School Library Journal*
TES	*Times Educational Supplement* (London)
TLS	*Times Literary Supplement* (London)
TON	*Top of the News*
WLB	*Wilson Library Bulletin*

Books of Criticism Indexed

A listing with full bibliographic information of books indexed and analyzed in more than one place in this bibliography.

ANDREWS, SIRI, ed. *The Hewins Lectures 1947-1962.* Boston: Horn Book, 1963, 375 pp.
  Contains the first fifteen Hewins Lectures, a series concentrating on "the writing and publishing of children's Books in New England's fertile years."

ASSOCIATION FOR LIBRARY SERVICE TO CHILDREN, comp. *Arbuthnot Lectures: 1970-1979.* Chicago: American Library Association, 1980, 203 pp.
  Reprints the first ten Arbuthnot Lectures, published annually in the June issue of *Top of the News.*

BADER, BARBARA. *American Picturebooks from Noah's Ark to the Beast Within.* New York: Macmillan, 1976, 615 pp.
  An immense, richly illustrated work that traces the development of American children's picture books. Many of the chapters on specific topics and individual illustrators have been indexed separately. The book is also rich in bibliographic notes and references.

BAMBERGER, RICHARD. *Reading and Children's Books: Essays and Papers, A Collection of Reprints.* Vienna: International Institute for Children's, Juvenile and Popular Literature, 1971, 108 pp.
  Includes numerous articles and addresses on children's literature and reading, many reprinted from *Bookbird.*

BARRON, PAMELA PETRICK, and BURLEY, JENNIFER Q., eds. *Jump Over the Moon: Selected Professional Readings.* New York: Holt, Rinehart and Winston, 1984, 512 pp.
  A collection of readings, reprinted from a variety of sources, on picture books and other books for children under the age of nine. Includes chapters on nursery rhymes, poetry, alphabet and counting books, wordless picture books, illustration, informational books, contemporary realistic fiction, folktales, storytelling, picture books, and controlled vocabulary books.

BATOR, ROBERT. *Signposts to Criticism of Children's Literature.* Chicago: American Library Association, 1983, 346 pp.
  Reprints a number of articles of children's literature criticism from recent specialized journals and from other sources.

BLISHEN, EDWARD, ed. *The Thorny Paradise: Writers on Writing for Children.* London: Kestrel Books, 1975, 176 pp.
Twenty-two writers discuss children's literature and their own work. Includes articles by Geoffrey Trease, Catherine Storr, John Gordon, Joan Aiken, C. Walter Hodges, Jill Paton Walsh, Nina Bawden, Russell Hoban, Jane Gardam, Leon Garfield, Ursula K. Le Guin, Rosemary Sutcliff, Ian Serraillier, Penelope Farmer, Helen Cresswell, Nicholas Fisk, K.M. Peyton, Mollie Hunter, Philippa Pearce, John Rowe Townsend, Barbara Willard, and Richard Adams.

BUTLER, FRANCELIA. *Sharing Literature with Children.* New York: McKay, 1977, 492 pp.
Combines excerpts and selections of children's literature with critical essays, grouped around themes of toys and games, fools, masks and shadows, sex roles, and circles. Several essays are reprints, some are original.

BUTTS, DENNIS, ed. *Good Writers for Young Readers.* St. Albans, England: Hart-Davis Educational, 1977, 144 pp.
Contains articles on Joan Aiken, Lucy Boston, Leon Garfield, Alan Garner, Cynthia Harnett, Russell Hoban, William Mayne, Mary Norton, Philippa Pearce, K.M. Peyton, Richard Adams, Ursula K. LeGuin, Ivan Southall, and Rosemary Sutcliff. Mostly reprinted from the British journal *Use of English* (see Appendix).

CADOGAN, MARY, and CRAIG, PATRICIA. *You're A Brick, Angela! A New Look at Girls' Ficton from 1839 to 1975.* London: Gollancz, 1976, 397 pp.
"We have tried here to relate each book discussed to the context of its own time, and also to indicate how it is regarded now."

CAMERON, ELEANOR. *The Green and Burning Tree: On the Writing and Enjoyment of Children's Books.* Boston: Little, Brown, 1962, 377 pp.
New and revised essays, many focusing on fantasy.

CARPENTER, HUMPHREY. *Secret Gardens: A Study of the Golden Age of Children's Literature.* Boston: Houghton Mifflin, 1985, 235 pp.
Examines major writers of children's literature from the 1860s to the 1930s and finds in them a common theme of rejection of grown-up values and society in favor of Arcadia, The Enchanted Place, Never Never Land, and The Secret Garden. Concentrates on Charles Kingsley, Lewis Carroll, George MacDonald, Louisa May Alcott, Richard Jeffries, Kenneth Grahame, E. Nesbit, Beatrix Potter, J.M. Barrie, and A.A. Milne.

CARR, JO, comp. *Beyond Fact: Nonfiction for Children and Young People.* Chicago: American Library Association, 1982, 224 pp.
Reprints articles on informational books for children.

CECH, JOHN, ed. *Dictionary of Literary Biography. Vol. 22, American Writers for Children, 1900-1960.* Detroit: Gale, 1983, 412 pp.
See annotation in Appendix.

CHAMBERS, NANCY, ed. *The Signal Approach to Children's Books.* Hammondsworth, Middlesex, England: Kestrel; Metuchen, New Jersey: Scarecrow, 1980, 352 pp.
A collection of articles from the first ten years of *Signal* (1970-80).

CHILDREN'S LITERATURE ASSOCIATION. *Proceedings of the Fifth Annual Conference.* Harvard University, 1978. Edited by Margaret P. Esmonde, and Priscilla A. Ord. Villanova, Pa.: Villanova University, 1979, 122 pp.

-----. *Proceedings of the Sixth Annual Conference.* University of Toronto, 1979. Edited by Margaret, P. Esmonde, and Priscilla, A. Ord. Villanova, Pa.: Villanova University, 1980, 203 pp.

-----. *Proceedings of the Seventh Annual Conference.* Baylor University, March 1980. Edited by Priscilla, A. Ord. New Rochelle, N.Y.: The Association, 1982, 174 pp.

-----. *Proceedings of the Eighth Annual Conference.* University of Minnesota, March 1981. Edited by Priscilla A. Ord. New Rochelle, N.Y.: The Association, 1982, 140 pp.

-----. *Proceedings of the Ninth Annual Conference: The Child and the Story: An Exploration of Narrative Forms.* University of Florida, March 1982. Edited by Priscilla A. Ord. Ruth K. MacDonald, Managing Editor. Boston: The Association, 1983, 157 pp.
    From the tenth annual conference in 1983, through the twelfth annual conference in 1985, the proceedings were published in the winter issues of the *Children's Literature Association Quarterly*, vol. 8-10. Vol. 8, no. 4 (Winter 1983) also contains an index to the first five separately published proceedings. Beginning with the 1986 conference, the proceedings will again be published separately.

COTT, JONATHAN. *Pipers at the Gates of Dawn: The Wisdom of Children's Literature.* New York: Random House, 1983, 327 pp.
    Contains articles on Dr. Seuss, Maurice Sendak, William Steig, Astrid Lindgren, Chinua Achebe, P.L. Travers, and Iona and Peter Opie.

CROUCH, MARCUS. *The Nesbit Tradition: The Children's Novel in England 1945-1970.* London: Ernest Benn, 1972, 239 pp.
    Traces the influences of E.Nesbit on recent British children's fiction, examining a number of writers at length.

CULPAN, NORMAN, and WAITE, CLIFFORD, eds. *Variety is King: Aspects of Fiction for Children.* Oxford: School Library Association, 1977, 173 pp.
    A collection of reprinted articles on children's fiction from a wide range of British journals. Topics include reading and child development, comic books, popular fiction, writing and illustrating children's books, young adult novels, and the reviewing of children's books.

DIXON, BOB. *Catching Them Young: Sex, Race, and Class in Children's Fiction.* London: Pluto Press, 1977, 176 pp.
    An issues approach to children's literature from a British perspective.

DONELSON, KENNETH, and NILSEN, ALLEEN PACE. *Literature for Today's Young Adults.* Glenview, Ill.: Scott, Foresman & Co., 1980, 484 pp.
    Combines original and reprinted essays.

DOOLEY, PATRICIA, ed. *The First Steps: Articles and Columns from the "Children's Literature Association Newsletter/Quarterly," Volume I-VI.* Lafayette, Ind.: Children's Literature Association Publications, 1984, 148 pp.
    Title on front cover reads: *The First Steps: Best of the Early Children's Literature Association Quarterly.* Contains excerpts from the first six years (1976-81) of the Children's Literature Association *Newsletter*, later called the *Quarterly*. A few of the articles have also been reprinted in *Children and Their Literature: A Readings Book*, edited by Jill May, and in *Festschrift*,

edited by Perry Nodelman.

EGOFF, SHEILA. *Thursday's Child: Trends and Patterns in Contemporary Children's Literature.* Chicago: American Library Association, 1981, 323 pp.

A survey, by genre and time period. Includes chapters on realistic fiction and the problem novel; the new fantasy; science fiction; historical fiction; folklore, myth, and legend; poetry; picture books; and European children's novels in translation.

EGOFF, SHEILA., ed. *One Ocean Touching: Papers from the First Pacific Rim Conference on Literature.* Metuchen, N.J.: Scarecrow, 1979, 252 pp.

The conference papers are divided into international and Canadian categories. Representatives from a number of countries touching the Pacific report on the literature of those countries and a number of Canadian authors, illustrators, and critics discuss their work and the status of Canadian children's literature.

EGOFF, SHEILA; STUBBS, G.T.; AND ASHELY, L.F., eds. *Only Connect: Readings in Children's Literature.* 1st ed. Toronto: Oxford University Press, 1969, 471 pp.

Gathers together from divergent sources a number of articles and essays on children's literature. See following entry for notes on changes in the second edition.

-----. *Only Connect: Readings on Children's Literature.* 2d ed. Toronto: Oxford University Press, 1980, 471 pp.

Reprints numerous essays on children's literature. The second edition deletes eleven articles from the first edition and adds nine new ones. Articles reprinted on the same pages in both editions have been listed without an edition number in this bibliography. Those found only in one edition or the other, or on different pages in each, include edition references.

ESCARPIT, DENISE, ed. *The Portrayal of the Child in Children's Literature: Proceedings of the Sixth Conference of the International Research Society for Children's Literature.* University of Gascony (Bordeaux, France), September 1983. Munich: K.G. Saur, 1985, 392 pp.

Includes 36 papers in French and in English, with summaries in the alternate language. Papers are grouped under the following topics: the child in national literature, the child in illustration, the child in minority groups, the child in literary genres, and individual visions of the child. Selected papers have been indexed under individual topics in this bibliography.

FENWICK, SARA INNIS, ed. *A Critical Approach to Children's Literature: The Thirty-First Annual Conference of the Graduate Library School, August 1-3, 1966.* University Graduate Library School Conference, 1966. Chicago: University of Chicago Press, 1967, 129 pp. (Also published in *Library Quarterly* 37 [1967]:1-130.)

Perhaps the first conference devoted to criticism of children's literature. Includes several influential papers.

FORD, BORIS, ed. *Young Writers, Young Readers: An Anthology of Children's Writing and Reading.* London: Hutchinson, 1960, 174 pp.

Includes articles on Enid Blyton, W.E. Johns, Robert Louis Stevenson, and Walter De la Mare.

FOX, GEOFF, et al., eds. *Writers, Critics, and Children: Articles from Children's Literature in Education.* New York: Agathon Press, 1976; London:

Heinemann, 1976, 245 pp.
Reprints many articles from the early years of *CLE*.

FOX, GEOFF, and HAMMOND, GRAHAM, eds. *Responses to Children's Literature: Proceedings of the Fourth Symposium of the International Research Society for Children's Literature.* New York: K.G. Saur, 1980, 141 pp.
Includes numerous papers, several concentrating on reader response criticism, and many concerned specifically with response to illustrations.

FRYATT, NORMA R., ed. *A Horn Book Sampler: On Children's Books and Reading, Selected from Twenty-Five Years of The Horn Book Magazine, 1924-1948.* Boston: Horn Book, 1959, 261 pp.
Reprints numerous *Horn Book* articles.

GERHARDT, LILLIAN, ed. *Issues in Children's Book Selection.* New York: Bowker, 1977, 216 pp.
Reprints twenty-nine articles from *School Library Journal.*

HAVILAND, VIRGINIA. *Children and Literature: Views and Reviews.* Glenview, Ill.: Scott, Foresman, 1973, 461 pp.
Primarily includes reprinted essays and selections, although some material has been revised, expanded, or written expressly for this volume. Chapters 1 through 4 concern the history of children's literature, 5 through 9 concentrate on major genres, chapter 10 is an international survey, and chapters 11 and 12 discuss children's literature criticism and awards.

-----. *The Openhearted Audience.* Washington, D.C.: Library of Congress, 1980, 198 pp.
Contains talks first given at the Library of Congress and published in *the Quarterly Journal of the Library of Congress* from 1967 to 1979. Contents include "Only Connect," by P.L. Travers, "Questions to an Artist Who Is Also an Author," by Maurice Sendak with Virginia Haviland, "Between Family and Fantasy: An Author's Perspectives on Children's Books," by Joan Aiken, "Portrait of a Poet: Hans Christian Andersen and His Fairy Tales," by Erik Christian Haugaard, "Sources and Responses," by Ivan Southall, "The Child and The Shadow," by Ursula K. Le Guin, "Illusion and Reality," by Virginia Hamilton, "Under Two Hats," by John Rowe Townsend, "Into Something Rich and Strange: Of Dreams, Art, and the Unconscious" by Eleanor Cameron, and "The Lords of Time," by Jill Paton Walsh.

HAZARD, PAUL. *Books, Children, and Men.* Translated by Marguerite Mitchell. 4th ed. Boston: Horn Book, 1960, 176 pp. (Fifth printing 1963.)
First translated into English in 1944, a highly influential classic of children's literature criticism.

HEINS, PAUL, ed. *Crosscurrents of Criticism: Horn Book Essays, 1968-1977.* Boston: Horn Book, 1977, 359 pp.
A collection of articles from *Horn Book.*

HEARNE, BETSY, and KAYE, MARILYN, eds. *Celebrating Children's Books: Essays on Children's Literature in Honor of Zena Sutherland.* New York: Lothrop, Lee, and Shepard, 1981, 244 pp.
Contains essays by a number of well-known children's authors, including Arnold Lobel, Jean Fritz, Lloyd Alexander, Susan Cooper, Paula Fox, John Rowe Townsend, Virginia Hamilton, E.L. Konigsburg, and Jill Paton Walsh.

HOFFMAN, MIRIAM, and SAMUELS, EVA, comps.   *Authors and Illustrators of Children's Books: Writings on Their Lives and Their Works.* New York: Bowker, 1972, 471 pp.

Authors and illustrators discussed in this collection of articles are Edward Ardizzone, Ludwig Bemelmans, Margaret Wise Brown, Clyde Robert Bulla, Virginia Lee Burton, Natalie S. Carlson, Ann Nolan Clark, Beverly Cleary, Elizabeth Coatsworth, Marguerite De Angeli, Meindert De Jong, Elizabeth Borton De Trevino, Roger Duvoisin, Ed Emberley, Marie Hall Ets, Genevieve Foster, Doris Gates, Theodor Seuss Geisel, Hardy Gramatky, Berta and Elmer Hader, Virginia Hamilton, Carolyn Haywood, Marguerite Henry, Holling C. Holling, Kristin Hunter, Clara Ingram Judson, Ezra Jack Keats, E.L. Konigsburg, Ruth Krauss, Robert Lawson, Lois Lenski, Julius Lester, C.S. Lewis, Astrid Lindgren, Leo Lionni, Robert McCloskey, Katherine Milhous, Mary Norton, Scott O'Dell, Leo Politi, Mariana Prieto, Margaret and H.A. Rey, Maurice Sendak, Kate Seredy, John R. Tunis, May McNeer and Lynd Ward, E.B. White, Brian Wildsmith, Maia Wojciechowska, and Elizabeth Yates.

HUNT, PETER, ed.   *Further Approaches to Research in Children's Literature.* Proceedings of the Second British Research Seminar in Children's Literature, Cardiff, September, 1981.   Cardiff: University of Wales, Institute of Science and Technology, Dept. of English, 1982, 129 pp.

Includes major papers and brief summaries of research in progress

HUNTER, MOLLIE.   *Talent Is Not Enough: Mollie Hunter On Writing for Children.* Introduction by Paul Heins. New York: Harper, 1975, 126 pp.

Collects a number of Hunter's previously published addresses and essays.

HÜRLIMANN, BETTINA.   *Three Centuries of Children's Books in Europe.* Translated and Edited by Brian W. Alderson.   Cleveland: World Publishing Co., 1968, 297 pp.

Surveys the contributions to children's literature of several outstanding European authors, and discusses the handling of various genres and themes by a number of writers.

INGLIS, FRED.   *The Promise of Happiness: Value and Meaning in Children's Fiction.* Cambridge: Cambridge University Press, 1981, 333 pp.

These essays tend to emphasize social theory rather than literary criticism. Inglis seeks to understand "the nature of popular culture, and the way these particular forms of the social imagination try to fix admired social values in a story."

JAN, ISABELLE.   *On Children's Literature.* Translated and edited by Catherine Storr.   Introduction by Anne Pellowski.   London: Allen Lane, 1973; New York: Schocken, 1974, 189 pp.

A classic attempt to define children's literature.

JONES, CORNELIA, and WAY, OLIVIA R.   *British Children's Authors: Interviews at Home.* Chicago: American Library Association, 1976, 176 pp.

A collection of interviews with British authors and illustrators.   Each interview includes biographical background, the subject's discussion of his or her philosophy and method of working, and an annotated bibliography of his or her works.   Those interviewed are Joan Aiken, Victor G. Ambrus, Edward Ardizzone, Ruth Arthur, Nina Bawden, Michael Bond, Lucy Boston, Pauline Clarke, Penelope Farmer, Joyce Gard, Alan Garner, Charles Keeping, Allan Campbell McLean, Margaret MacPherson, Kathleen Peyton, Barbara Leonie Picard, Rosemary Sutcliff, Brian Wildsmith, and Barbara Willard.

KINGSTON, CAROLYN T. *The Tragic Mode in Children's Literature.* New York and London: Teachers College Press, 1974, 177 pp.
Examines tragic moments in realistic fiction for eight to twelve year olds.

KOEFOED, INGERLISE, ed. *Children's Literature and the Child: Lectures and Debates.* From the International Course on Children's Literature, Loughborough Summer School 1972, Hindgoul, Denmark. Copenhagen: Danish Library Association-Scandinavian Library Center, 1975, 70 pp.

LANES, SELMA G. *Down the Rabbit Hole: Adventures and Misadventures in the Realm of Children's Literature.* New York: Atheneum, 1971, 239 pp.
Concentrates on books for children under seven.

LENZ, MILLICENT, and MAHOOD, RAMONA M., comps. *Young Adult Literature: Background and Criticism.* Chicago: American Library Association, 1980, 516 pp.
A wide-ranging collection of essays.

MacCANN, DONNARAE, and WOODARD, GLORIA, eds. *The Black American in Books for Children: Readings in Racism.* Metuchen, N.J.: Scarecrow, 1972, 223 pp.
A collection of essays and reprints of articles examining the portrayal of blacks in American children's books.

-----. *Cultural Conformity in Books for Children: Further Readings in Racism.* Metuchen, N.J.: Scarecrow, 1977.
A collection of essays and reprints of articles that examine the portrayal of various ethnic groups in children's books.

MacLEOD, ANNE S., ed. *Children's Literature: Selected Essays and Bibliographies.* Student Contribution Series, no. 9. College Park: University of Maryland, College of Library and Information Services, 1977, 153 pp.
Includes several substantial critical essays.

McVITTY, WALTER. *Innocence and Experience: Essays on Contemporary Australian Children's Writers.* Melbourne, Victoria, Australia: Nelson, 1981, 277 pp., bibl.
Discusses Mavis Thorpe Clark, Joan Phipson, Eleanor Spence, Patricia Wrightson, H.F. Brinsmead, David Martin, Colin Thiele, Ivan Southall.

MASON, BOBBIE ANN. *The Girl Sleuth: A Feminist Guide.* Old Westbury, N.Y.: Feminist Press, 1975, 145 pp.
Examines female roles in popular girls' series books.

MAY, JILL P., ed. *Children and Their Literature: A Readings Book.* West Lafayette, Ind.: Children's Literature Association Publications, 1983, 179 pp.
Includes reprinted articles, many from early Children's Literature Association *Proceedings.*

MEEK, MARGARET; WARLOW, AIDAN; and BARTON, GRISELDA, eds. *The Cool Web: The Pattern of Children's Reading.* London: Bodley Head, 1977.
Contains articles concentrating on several aspects of children's literature: the readers, the authors, approaches to criticism, and future directions for research.

NODELMAN, PERRY, and MAY, JILL, P., eds. *Festchrift: A Ten Year Retrospective.* West Lafayette, Ind.: Children's Literature Association

Publications, 1983, 79 pp.

Reprints articles from various publications from the Children's Literature Association's first ten years. Includes an index to the *Children's Literature Association Quarterly*, vols. 1-7.

NORTON, ELOISE S., ed. *Folk Literature of the British Isles: Readings for Librarians, Teachers, and Those Who Work with Children and Young Adults.* Metuchen, N.J.: Scarecrow, 1978, 263 pp.

Reprints a number of articles. Includes sources for additonal information and lists retellings of British folktales published for children.

PRAGER, ARTHUR. *Rascals at Large, or, The Clue in the Old Nostalgia.* Garden City, N.Y.: Doubleday, 1971, 334 pp.

Examines boys' series books.

REES, DAVID. *Marble in the Water: Essays on Contemporary Writers of Fiction for Children and Young Adults.* Boston: Horn Book, 1980, 211 pp.

Essays on Nina Bawden, Judy Blume, Jill Chaney, Beverly Cleary, Robert Cormier, Penelope Farmer, Paula Fox, Alan Garner, E.L. Konigsburg, Ursula K. Le Guin, Penelope Lively, Philippa Pearce, Doris Buchanan Smith, Rodie Sudbery, Mildred Taylor, Jill Paton Walsh, E.B. White, and Paul Zindel.

-----. *Painted Desert, Green Shade: Essays on Contemporary Writers of Fiction for Children and Young Adults.* Boston: Horn Book, 1984, 197 pp.

Rees attempts to "cast a retrospective light" on thirteen British and American writers for young people: L.M. Boston, M.E. Kerr, Betsy Byars, Ted Hughes, Jan Mark, Jane Langton, Katherine Paterson, John Rowe Townsend, Robert Westall, S.E. Hinton, Russell Hoban, Peter Dickinson, and Virginia Hamilton.

ROBINSON, EVELYN R., ed. *Readings About Children's Literature.* New York: David McKay, 1966, 431 pp.

Divided into sections on children and reading, the evaluation and selection of books, history and trends, illustrations, the young child, traditional and modern imaginative tales, fiction for older children, and nonfiction. Most of the articles are readily available in *Horn Book, Elementary English, Elementary School Journal, English Journal, Library Journal,* and *Top of the News.*

ROBINSON, MOIRA, ed. *Readings in Children's Literature: Proceedings of the National Seminar on Children's Literature.* Frankston, Victoria, Australia: Frankston State College, 1975, 293 pp.

Includes talks by Helen Oxenbury and John Burningham, Patricia Wrightson, Joan Phipson, Walter McVitty, Emily Neville, and others on various aspects of children's literature.

SALE, ROGER. *Fairy Tales and After: From Snow White to E.B. White.* Cambridge, Mass.: Harvard University Press, 1978, 280 pp.

Hailed as the first scholarly book on children's literature to be published by a university press, the book includes essays on Lewis Carroll, Beatrix Potter, Kenneth Grahame, Rudyard Kipling, L. Frank Baum, and E.B. White, among others.

SAYERS, FRANCES CLARKE. *Summoned By Books: Essays and Speeches.* Compiled by Marjeanne Jensen Blinn. Foreword by Lawrence Clark Powell. New York: Viking, 1965, 173 pp.

Reprints several of Sayer's speeches and essays, many concerning children's literature.

SCHMIDT, NANCY J. *Children's Fiction About Africa in English.* New York: Conch Magazine, 1981, 248 pp.
　　See annotation under Africa in Part B.

SCHWARCZ, JOSEPH H. *Ways of the Illustrator: Visual Communication in Children's Literature.* Chicago: American Library Association, 1982, 202 pp.
　　See annotation under picture books in Part B.

SMITH, LILLIAN H. *The Unreluctant Years: A Critical Approach to Children's Literature.* New York: Viking, 1953, 193 pp.
　　An early, now classic, examination of children's literature as literature. Uses Matthew Arnold's "touchstone" approach, comparing new literature to that which has stood the test of time.

TOWNSEND, JOHN ROWE. *A Sense of Story: Essays on Contemporary Writers for Children.* London: Longman, 1971, 216 pp.
　　Contains essays on the following writers: Joan Aiken, Lucy Boston, H.F. Brinsmead, John Christopher, Helen Cresswell, Meindert De Jong, Eleanor Estes, Paula Fox, Leon Garfield, Alan Garner, Madeleine L'Engle, William Mayne, Andre Norton, Scott O'Dell, Philippa Pearce, K.M. Peyton, Ivan Southall, Rosemary Sutcliff, and Patricia Wrightson.

-----. *A Sounding of Storytellers: New and Revised Essays on Contemporary Writers for Children.* New York: Lippincott, 1979, 218 pp.
　　A revised edition of *A Sense of Story*, adding seven new writers to seven previously discussed. Writers added are Nina Bawden, Vera and Bill Cleaver, Peter Dickinson, Virginia Hamilton, E.L. Konigsburg, Penelope Lively, and Jill Paton Walsh. Revised essays are on Paula Fox, Leon Garfield, Alan Garner, William Mayne, K.M. Peyton, Ivan Southall, and Patricia Wrightson.

TUCKER, NICHOLAS. *The Child and the Book: A Psychological and Literary Exploration.* Cambridge: Cambridge University Press, 1981, 259 pp.
　　Concentrates on the psychological aspects of chidren's literature for various age groups.

-----. *Suitable for Children? Controversies in Children's Literature.* London: Sussex University Press; Chatto & Windus, 1976, 224 pp.
　　Reprints essays grouped around controversial topics.

VANDERGRIFT, KAY E. *Child and Story: The Literary Connection.* New York: Neal Schuman, 1980, 340 pp.
　　Applies critical theory and literary criticism to the teaching of children's literature to children.

VARLEJS, JANA, ed. *Young Adult Literature in the Seventies: A Selection of Readings.* Metuchen, N.J.: Scarecrow, 1978, 452 pp.
　　Articles are grouped according to topics such as realism, censorship, minorities, and nonfiction.

WHITE, MARY LOU, ed. *Children's Literature: Criticism and Response."* Columbus, Ohio: Charles E. Merrill, 1976, 252 pp.
　　A collection of reprinted articles, designed to be used as a textbook.

WINTLE, JUSTIN, and FISHER, EMMA. *The Pied Pipers: Interviews with the Influential Creators of Children's Literature.* New York: Two Continents,

1975, 320 pp.

Twenty-four English and American writers of children's books are included, often with portraits and examples of illustrations from their works: Maurice Sendak, Edward Ardizzone, Charles Keeping, Richard Scarry, Laurent de Brunhoff, Charlotte Zolotow, Roald Dahl, Dr. Seuss, E.B. White, Richard Adams, Nicholas Stuart Gray, Joan Aiken, Scott O'Dell, Rosemary Sutcliff, Leon Garfield, Lloyd Alexander, Alan Garner, John Rowe Townsend, Madeleine L'Engle, K.M. Peyton, Lucy Boston, Rumer Godden, Maia Wojciechowska, and Judy Blume.

YOLEN, JANE. *Touch Magic: Fantasy, Faerie and Folklore in the Literature of Childhood*. New York: Philomel, 1981, 96 pp.

A collection of essays on folktale, fairy tale, and myth in children's literature.

Part A: Authors and Their Works
An Annotated Listing of Criticism

ACHEBE, CHINUA (1930-   )

A1   COTT, JONATHAN. "Chinua Achebe: At the Crossroads." In *Pipers*, pp. 161-92. (Also in *Parabola* 6, no. 2 [Spring 1981]:30-39.)
      Relates the themes and concerns of Achebe's works for adults to African storytelling tradition and to his four works for children, *Chike and the River*, "The Flute," *The Drum*, and *How the Leopard Got His Claws*. Includes an interview with Achebe about his work.

A2   MILLER, JAMES. "The Novelist as Teacher: Chinua Achebe's Literature for Children." *Children's Literature* 9 (1981): 7-18.
      Discusses *Chike and the River* and *How the Leopard Got His Claws* in terms of Achebe's developing concerns as a teacher.

A3   WELCHEL, MARIANNE. "Achebe's 'The Flute.'" In Butler, *Sharing*, pp. 248-51.
      Discusses Achebe's approach to folklore, particularly for children. Based partly on an interview Welchel conducted with Achebe in April 1976.

ADAMS, ADRIENNE (1906-   )

A4   SADOWSKI, ELOISE N. "Glimpses of an Artist: Adrienne Adams." *EE* 51 (October 1974):933-39.
      Discusses Adams's background and offers insights into techniques of book illustration. Includes a bibliography of books she has illustrated.

A5   WAUGH, DOROTHY. "Adrienne Adams, Illustrator of Children's Books." *American Artist* 29 (November 1965):54-59, 74-75.
      Concentrates on Adams's technique.

ADAMS, RICHARD (1920-   )

A6   ADAMS, RICHARD. "Some Ingredients of *Watership Down*." In Blishen, *Thorny Paradise*, pp. 163-73.
      Discusses briefly a number of writers and books that have influenced his own work.

A7   ANDERSON, CELIA CATLETT. "Troy, Carthage, and *Watership Down*." *ChLAQ* 8, no. 1 (Spring 1983):12-13.
      Finds resemblances in *Watership Down* to the *Aeneid* and, to a

lesser extent, the *Iliad*.

A8   FRITZ, JEAN. "An Evening with Richard Adams." *CLE*, n.s. 9, no. 2
      (Summer 1978):67-72.
          An acclaimed biographer provides insights into the personality
      and work of an acclaimed fantasist.

A9   GREEN, TIMOTHY. "Richard Adams' Long Journey from *Watership
      Down*." *Smithsonian* 10, no. 4 (July 1979):76-83.
          Discusses Adams's life, his writing, and his motivating concerns
      in this beautifully photographed account of a visit to the writer at
      his home on the Isle of Man.

A10   HAMMOND, GRAHAM. "Trouble with Rabbits." *CLE*, o.s., no. 12
      (September 1973):48-63.
          Explores and analyzes Adams's successes and failures in *Watership
      Down*. Letter in response from Joyce Stranger, a biologist and
      children's writer, in *CLE*, o.s., no. 14 (1974):70-72.

A11   INGLIS, FRED. *Promise of Happiness*, pp. 201-10.
          Sees *Watership Down* as a synthesis of "old heroics and new
      psychology," as "a way of learning to understand other cultures and
      modes of living things," and as an example of an effort to "maintain
      continuity across deep historical chasms. . . . A sprawling, immoder-
      ate, unreflective book."

A12   -----. "Spellbinding and Anthropology: The Work of Richard Adams
      and Ursula Le Guin." In Butts, *Good Writers*, pp. 114-28.
          Sees Adams in *Watership Down* and Le Guin in *Wizard of Earth-
      sea* as coinciding "with the dissident impulse in old and new frames
      of thought to celebrate and to understand without disenchantment the
      creative powers of natural life in all its forms."

A13   STONE, JAMES S. "The Rabbitness of *Watership Down*." *English
      Quarterly* 13, no. 1 (Spring 1980):37-46.
          Shows how "The fascination or enchantment of *Watership Down*
      stems from the way in which Richard Adams makes us enter the
      secondary world of the rabbits and experience it through their
      senses."

A14   THOMAS, JANE RESH. "Old Worlds and New: Anti-Feminism in
      Watership Down." *Horn Book* 50 (August 1974):405-8. (Reprinted in
      Heins, *Crosscurrents of Criticism*, pp. 311-14.)
          "The males are superhuman and the females sub-human." Main-
      tains that Adams reveals "an anti-feminism which deprives his female
      characters of the spiritual fruit of community." Letter in response in
      Horn Book 51 (February 1975):3, 93, from Jean Jordan. Jane Tho-
      mas replies, p. 94.

A15   WINTLE, JUSTIN, and FISHER, EMMA. *Pied Pipers*, pp. 32-46.
          Adams discusses his life and work in an interview.

ADELBORG, OTTILIA (1855-   )

A16   WERKMÄSTER, BARBRO. "Ottilia Adelborg: A Second Look at Her
      Role in Swedish Book Illustration." *Phaedrus* 9 (1982):11-16.
          Discusses the contribution of "Sweden's first important picture-

book artist representative of a Swedish art nouveau style adapted for children in a personal way."

ADKINS, JAN (1944-   )

A17   BAGNALL, NORMA. "Profile: Jan Adkins." *LA* 57 (May 1980): 560-66.
       Adkins discusses his life, his philosophy of writing, and his views on children's literature in this interview. Includes an annotated bibliography of books by Adkins.

AESOP (6th century B.C.)

A18   ADAMS, F.B., Jr. "The Codex Pithoeanus of Phaedrus." *Horn Book* 41 (June 1965):260-66.
       A history of versions of Aesop's "Fox and Crow," occasioned by the acquisition and public display of the Codex by the Pierpont Morgan Library.

A19   *AESOP: Five Centuries of Illustrated Fables.* Selected by John J. McKendry. New York: Metropolitan Museum of Art; distributed by New York Graphic Society, Greenwich, Conn., 1964, 95 pp.
       McKendry's introduction, pp. 5-10, provides a brief history of the fables, points out some of their salient characteristics, and traces the various styles and techniques that have been used to illustrate them. The main part of the book consists of reproductions of the illustrations, accompanied by contemporaneous texts.

A20   MINER, ROBERT G., Jr. "Aesop as Litmus: The Acid Test of Children's Literature." *Children's Literature* 1 (1972):9-15.
       Surveys versions of Aesop over the centuries and suggests that differences in versions may tell something about the times, cultures, and attitudes toward children of the societies that created them.

A21   PERKINS, AGNES, ed. "Special Section: The Five Hundreth Anniversary of Aesop in English." *ChLAQ* 9, no. 2 (Summer 1984):60-75.
       Includes an introduction by Agnes Perkins, pp. 60-62; "'Strange and Mervayllous Historyes': William Caxton, First English Printer," by Olivia Bottom, pp. 62-63, 72; "Tradition and the Individual Retelling," by Barbara Mirel, pp. 63-66, which compares retellings of "The Fox and Crow," by Ruth Spriggs, Joseph Jacobs, Eve Rice, Randolph Caldecott, Eric Carle, and Jack Kent; "To Instruct and Amuse: Some Victorian Views of *Aesop's Fables*," by Anita C. Wilson, pp. 66-68; "Tolstoy's Fables: Tools for a Vision," by Kristin Lehman, pp. 68-70; "Fables and Illustrations," by Joan Bush, pp. 70-72, which reviews John McKendry's *Aesop: Five Centuries of Illustrated Fables*; "The Modern Fable: James Thurber's Social Criticisms," by Ruth A. Maharg, pp. 72-73, which compares and contrasts the fables of Aesop and Thurber; and "Fables into Picture Books," by Pat Pflieger, pp. 73-75, 80, an overview of numerous modern picture-book versions. (References have been accidentally placed on p. 70.)

A22   PROVENZO, EUGENE FRANCIS, Jr. "Education and the Aesopic Tradition." Ph.D. dissertation, Washington University, 1976, 416 pp., ED 131 462.
       Describes the history and use of Aesop's fables as part of the Western pedagogical tradition, and to "demonstrate how the different

uses of the fables by different cultures reflect specific social, political, and economic concerns of the societies from which they are drawn.

A23   REINSTEIN, P. GILA. "Aesop and Grimm: Contrast in Ethical Codes and Contemporary Values." *CLE*, n.s. 14, no. (Spring 1983):44-53.
Explores differences in origins, content, and reader response. The fables "teach self-preservation" and portray a realistic world, while the folktales present a more idealized world where "wickedness is punished, and virtue rewarded."

A24   TAYLOR, MARY-AGNES. "The Literary Transformation of a Sluggard." *Children's Literature* 12 (1984):92-104.
Traces the variants and various literary treatments of the fable of the grasshopper and the ant through the centuries, including John Ciardi's poem *John J. Plenty and Fiddler Dan*, and Leo Lionni's *Frederick*.

AHLBERG, JANET (1944-   ), and AHLBERG, ALLAN (1938-   )

A25   CHAMBERS, AIDAN. "Letter from England: Two-in-One." *Horn Book* 58 (December 1982):686-90.
Praises *The Baby's Catalog* especially.

A26   NEUMARK, VICTORIA. "A Marriage of Words and Pictures." *TES*, 20 June 1980, pp. 42.
The Ahlbergs discuss their work in an interview.

AIKEN, JOAN (1924-   )

A27   AERS, LESLEY. "Writers for Children--Joan Aiken." *Use of English* 22 (Summer 1971):336-44. (Reprinted as "Joan Aiken's Historical Fantasies," in Butts, *Good Writers*, with an updated postscript, pp. 12-23.)
Traces Aiken's development in style and technique, including her use of fantasy, characterization, simplification, and exaggeration in *The Wolves of Willoughby Chase*, *Black Hearts in Battersea*, and *Nightbirds on Nantucket*.

A28   AIKEN, JOAN. "Between Family and Fantasy: An Author's Perspectives on Children's Books." *Quarterly Journal of the Library of Congress* 29 (October 1972):308-26. (Reprinted in Haviland, *Open-hearted Audience*, pp. 47-68.)
Discusses books that have influenced her writing and her views on realism and fantasy.

A29   -----. "Hope Is the Spur." *Signal* 45 (September 1984):146-51.
Points out ways in which hope has been a spur in her own life and in the lives of some of her fictional characters such as Dido Twite, and Felix in *Go Saddle the Sea* and *Bridle the Wind*.

A30   -----. "A Thread of Mystery." *CLE*, o.s., no. 2 (July 1970):30-47. (Reprinted as "Writing for Enjoyment," in Fox, *Writers, Critics, and Children*.)
Discusses influences on Aiken's writing, her preoccupation with the mystery and the past, significant books in her life, and her own writings, especially *The Wolves of Willoughby Chase* and its sequels,

Black Hearts in Battersea and *Nightbirds on Nantucket,* with their imaginary historical period.

A31 CADOGAN, MARY, and CRAIG, PATRICIA. *You're a Brick,* pp. 357-60.
Analyzes Aiken in terms of recent trends in children's books and links with the past, and discusses what she sees as successes and failures in the individual books.

A32 CROUCH, MARCUS. *The Nesbit Tradition,* pp. 38-39.
Although somewhat admiring, Crouch maintains that "Aiken lacks self discipline. Her stories gallop recklessly in all directions at once."

A33 ELLIS, ALEC. "Joan Aiken." *School Librarian* 18 (June 1970): 147-51.
Provides a good introduction to Aiken's work. "The well-documented narrative is gloriously shot through with fantasies both searing and side-splitting."

A34 INGLIS, FRED. *Promise of Happiness,* pp. 295-303.
Sees *Midnight Is a Place* as Dickensian and characterizes Aiken as a romantic. "She takes the traditional forms of popular Victorian drama and throws them into a new configuration," and she "has found the right language in which to tell the tale."

A35 JONES, CORNELIA, and WAY, OLIVIA R. *British Children's Authors,* pp. 3-10.
In an interview Aiken discusses her background, philosophy, and method of working. Includes an annotated bibliography of her works.

A36 TOWNSEND, JOHN ROWE. "Joan Aiken." *Signal* 5 (May 1971):72-77.
Earlier version of essay in a *Sense of Story.*

A37 -----. *Sense of Story,* pp. 17-27.
Comments on the Dickensian quality of Aiken's work, and calls her "one of the liveliest and most exuberant of today's writers for children." Works discussed include *The Wolves of Willoughby Chase, Nightbirds on Nantucket, Black Hearts in Battersea,* and *The Whispering Mountain.*

A38 USREY, MALCOLM. "America's Gift to British Children: The Tall Tales of Joan Aiken." *Proceedings of the Children's Literature Association* 6 (1979):196-202.
Finds similarities to traditional American tall tales with their mix of humor and solemnity and their outlandish and exaggerated plots in Aiken's *Wolves of Willoughby Chase, Black Hearts in Battersea,* and *Nightbirds on Nantucket.*

A39 WINTLE, JUSTIN, and FISHER, EMMA. *Pied Pipers,* pp. 161-70.
Aiken discusses her life and work in an interview.

ALCOTT, LOUISA MAY (1832-88)

A40 ALBERGHENE, JANICE M. "Alcott's Psyche and Kate: Self-Portraits, Sunny-Side Up." *Proceedings of the Children's Literature Association.* 8 (1981):37-43.
Makes biographical links between Psyche in "Psyche's Art" (which

is one of the three tales in the *Three Proverbs*), Kate in *An Old-Fashioned Girl*, and Alcott herself.

A41   -----. "Austen and Alcott or Matriarchy: New Women or New Wives?" *Novel* 10 (Fall 1976):6-26. (Reprinted in *Towards a Poetics of Fiction*. Edited by Mark Spilka [Bloomington, Ind.: Indiana University Press, 1977], pp. 266-86.)
Sees in Jane Austen's *Pride and Prejudice* and Alcott's *Little Women* "the passage of a bevy of sisters from the collective colony of women presided over by their mother to the official authority of masculine protection."

A42   AUERBACH, NINA. "Waiting Together: Two Families." In *Communities of Women: An Idea in Fiction*. Cambridge, Mass.: Harvard University Press, 1978, pp. 35-73.
Compares the matriarchal families of Jane Austen's *Pride and Prejudice* and Alcott's *Little Women*.

A43   BACON, FRANCES A. "Life in the 60s as Reflected in the Alcott Books." *EER* 9 (November 1932):231-32, 244.
Contains fascinating insights concerning the historical background of Alcott's books.

A44   BLACKBURN, WILLIAM. "Moral Pap for the Young? A New Look at Louisa May Alcott's *Little Men*." *Proceedings of the Children's Literature Association* 7 (1980):98-106.
Maintains that *Little Men* contains passages revealing depth and darkness behind the conventional morality, showing that Alcott was a true artist after all.

A45   BRAGG, MELVYN. "*Little Women*." *CLE*, n.s. 9, no. 2 (Summer 1978):95-100.
Identifies character as Alcott's chief concern.

A46   BROPHY, BRIGID. "A Masterpiece, and Dreadful." *NYTBR*, 17 January 1965, Children's Book section pp. 1, 44. (Reprinted in Haviland, *Children and Literature*, pp. 66-70.)
Describes Alcott's books as masterpieces of sentimentality.

A47   BURROWS, ALVINA TREUT. "A Critical Study of *Little Women*." *EE* 37 (May 1960):285-92.
Interprets the book as a biography of the Alcott family. Evaluates its style and technique, its combination of dialogue and action, and its universal themes, such as the conflict between idealism and materialism.

A48   CARPENTER, HUMPHREY. "Louisa Alcott and the Happy Family." In *Secret Gardens*, pp. 86-99.
In Alcott's work "we see clearly the questioning of parental authority which is hinted at by the English fantasy writers." Suggests the influence of Charlotte Yonge's *The Daisy Chain* on *Little Women*. Concludes that "Louisa Alcott had set out to be subversive, to describe her doubts about sexual stereotyping and the demands of family life, but she became a traitor to her destructive cause, and was in the end responsible for an act of construction, the creation of the Arcadian family novel."

A49 CURTIS, DAVID. "*Little Women*: A Reconsideration." *EE* 45 (November 1968):878-79.
Urges that *Little Women* be given more critical attention and argues that it has many qualities that make it deserving of its century of popularity.

A50 ELBERT, SARAH. *A Hunger for Home: Louisa May Alcott and "Little Women."* Philadelphia: Temple University Press, 1984, 278 pp.
Emphasizes Alcott's feminist concerns and the conflict of women's political, economic, and educational equality with the demands of domestic life. Views this conflict as central to Alcott's life and work and central to women today.

A51 GOLDMAN, SUZY. "Louisa May Alcott: The Separation Between Art and Family." *L&U* 1, no. 2 (Fall 1977):91-97.
Although Alcott herself succeeded in the artistic world, she never allowed her female characters to do the same, requiring them to choose marriage in a time when women were not allowed to combine marriage and art (or career).

A52 HAMBLEN, ABIGAIL ANN. "Louisa May Alcott and the 'Revolution' in Education." *Journal of General Education* 22, no. 2 (July 1970):81-92.
Explores the educational theories expressed in Alcott's fiction.

A53 HOLLANDER, ANNE. "Reflections on *Little Women*." *Children's Literature* 9 (1981):28-39.
Sees the book in terms of "how the feelings familiar in childhood are preserved in later days, and how individual character abides through life."

A54 *Horn Book* 44 (October 1968).
Includes Cornelia Meigs's introductions to centennial editions of *Little Women* and to her own *Invincible Louisa* and *Glimpses of Louisa*; an article by Lavinia Russ, "Not to Be Read on Sunday," which explores the long-lasting appeal of *Little Women* despite critical disparagement; and an article by Aileen Fisher and Olive Rabe about the writing of *We Alcotts*.

A55 JANEWAY, ELIZABETH. "Meg, Jo, Beth, Amy, and Louisa." *NYTBR*, 29 September 1968. (Reprinted in Egoff, *Only Connect*, 1st ed., pp. 286-90; 2d ed., 253-57.)
Why does this dated, sentimental, moralizing work endure? Because it is full of life and "was written by a secret rebel against the order of the world and woman's place in it, and all the girls who ever read it know it."

A56 KELLY, R. GORDON. "Human Nature in Three Late 19th Century American Children's Novels." In Escarpit, *Portrayal of the Child*, pp. 249-57.
Examines *Little Women*, Horatio Alger's *Ragged Dick*, and Mark Twain's *Adventures of Tom Sawyer* in terms of their views of human nature.

A57 KEYSER, ELIZABETH LENNOX. "Domesticity versus Identity: A Review of Alcott Research." *CLE*, n.s. 16, no. 8 (Autumn

1985):165-75.
   Includes comments on recent books on Alcott by Sarah Elbert, Joy A. Marsella, and Ruth MacDonald. Suggests Alcott deserves more consistent close reading than she has been given so far.

A58   -----. "Women and Girls in Louisa May Alcott's *Jo's Boys*." *International Journal of Women's Studies* 6 (November-December 1983):457-71.
   Explores Alcott's ambivalence about women's career aspirations as reflected in *Jo's Boys*.

A59   KINGSTON, CAROLYN T. *Tragic Mode*, pp. 130-32.
   Analyzes *Little Women* in terms of its treatment of loss in the form of death.

A60   KOLBA, ELLEN D. "Out on a Limb." *English Journal* 73 (November 1984):38-41.
   Examines Alcott's *Jack and Jill* and Susan Coolidge's *What Katy Did* as two "domestic romances" showing "an intelligent and active but headstrong young girl who must become an invalid in order to grow into a happy, productive woman."

A61   McCURRY, NIKI ALPERT. "Concepts of Childrearing and Schooling in the March Novels of Louisa May Alcott." Ph.D. dissertation, Northwestern University, 1976, 114 pp., DA 37:4356A.
   Argues that *Little Women*, *Little Men*, and *Jo's Boys* present the picture of an ideal upbringing and faithfully depict the educational philosophy and methods of Bronson Alcott.

A62   MacDONALD, RUTH K. *Louisa May Alcott*. Boston: Twayne, 1983, 111 pp.
   Concentrates on a close critical reading of Alcott's works for children and adults. Places the works for children within the context of Alcott's life and her works for adults. Includes a biographical sketch, one chapter devoted to the March family stories, another to the other juveniles, and a third to the works for adults. Also includes selected bibliographies of primary and secondary sources.

A63   -----. "The Progress of the Pilgrims in *Little Women*." *Proceedings of the Children's Literature Association* 7 (1980):114-19.
   Explores the reasons *Pilgrim's Progress* was so influential in American girls' books, particularly in *Little Women*.

A64   -----. "Recent Alcott Criticism." *Children's Literature* 9 (1981):210-13.
   Reviews eleven recent books and articles on Alcott and concludes that although recent criticism has extended Alcott's reputation beyond that as a writer of children's books, "We need a more sensitive reading of her children's books rather than a further diminution of her reputation as a writer for children."

A65   -----. Review. *ChLAQ* 9, no. 3 (Fall 1984):135.
   Reviews recent Alcott criticism, including Madelon Bedell's introduction to the Modern Library College Edition of *Little Women* and Joy A. Marsella's *The Promise of Destiny: Children and Women in the Short Stories of Louisa May Alcott*.

A66   MAY, JILL P. "Spiritual Females of the Nineteenth Century: Liberated

Moods in *Little Women*." *CLE*, n.s. 11, no. 1 (Spring 1980):10-20.
Sees in Alcott's women the forerunners of their twentieth-century sisters, "quietly beginning the march toward freedom within a marriage," and shows how they differ from the conventional nineteenth-century heroine.

A67 MEIGS, CORNELIA L. *Louisa M. Alcott and the American Family Story*. New York: Henry Z. Walck, 1971, 127 pp.
Relates Alcott's life to her writings, and places her books in the context of the American family stories of Jacob Abbott, Susan Coolidge, Laura E. Richards, Margaret Sidney, Kate Douglas Wiggin, and others.

A68 MONTEIRO, GEORGE. "Louisa May Alcott's Proverb Stories." *Tennessee Folklore Society Bulletin* 42, no. 3 (September 1976):103-7.
Examines Alcott's use of proverbs in her *Three Proverb Stories*, "Kitty's Class-Day," "Aunt Kipp," and "Psyche's Art."

A69 PAULY, THOMAS H. "*Ragged Dick* and *Little Women*: Idealized Homes and Unwanted Marriages." *Journal of Popular Culture* 9 (Winter 1975):583-92.
Examines the attitudes toward marriage portrayed by Alcott and Alger, maintaining that "The protagonists created by both authors become aligned with positions which militate against marriage, thus unwittingly undermining the very institution these writers are consciously striving to recommend."

A70 PAYNE, ALMA J. *Louisa May Alcott: A Reference Guide*. Boston: G.K. Hall, 1980, 87 pp.
The introduction to this bibliography of works by and about Alcott provides an excellent overview of available criticism. The annotated bibliography attempts "to include all scholarship of any substance on Louisa May Alcott." Includes many reviews but no foreign items unless translated into English.

A71 SALWONCHIK, MARIE. "The Educational Ideas of Louisa May Alcott." Ph.D. dissertation, Loyola University of Chicago, 1972, 150 pp., DA 33:1596.
Examines Alcott's educational ideas as expressed in her fiction.

A72 SHULL, MARTHA I. "The Novels of Louisa May Alcott as Commentary on the American Family." Ph.D. dissertation, Bowling Green University, 1975, 244 pp., DA 36:5304A.
Examines the matriarchal family system presented in Alcott's novels and uses it "as a mirror to comment on changes in the structure of the American family."

A73 SMITH, GROVER, Jr. "The Doll-Burners: D.H. Lawrence and Louisa Alcott." *Modern Language Quarterly* 19, no. 1 (March 1958):28-32.
Explores possible influences on D.H. Lawrence's *Sons and Lovers* of the doll-burning scene in Alcott's *Little Men*.

A74 STERN, MADELINE B. "Behind a Mask: The Unknown Thrillers of Louisa May Alcott." *SLJ* 21 (January 1975):13-17.
Explores Alcott's "gory, gruesome novelettes," and finds they "will disclose not only the nature of the creation, but also the nature of the creator," in this excerpt from the book of the same name, pub-

lished by William Morrow & Co, 1975.

A75   -----. "Louisa M. Alcott: An Appraisal." *New England Quarterly* 22, no. 4 (December 1949):475-98.
        Provides a perceptive overview of Alcott's career; suggests that her accurate depiction of domestic life and her studies of adolescent psychology have earned her a permanent place in literature.

A76   ULLOM, JUDITH C., comp. "Louisa May Alcott: A Centennial for *Little Women*." Washington D.C.: Library of Congress, 1969, 91 pp.
        Contains an extensive listing of various editions and translations of Alcott's works, including reprints of some of the illustrations and a brief listing of biocritical studies.

A77   "Views and Reviews on Louisa May Alcott." In Haviland, *Children and Literature*, pp. 64-65. (Reprinted from *Nation* 8 [May 20, 1869]:400; 21 [October 14, 1875]:250-51.)
        Two early reviews of Alcott's books, the second one attributed to Henry James.

A78   YELLIN, JEAN FAGAN. "From 'Success' to 'Experience': Louisa May Alcott's *Work*." *Massachusetts Review* 21 (1980):527-29.
        Explores Alcott's portrayal of a female in an untraditional role in her fictionalized autobiography *Work*.

ALDIS, DOROTHY (1896-1966)

A79   SARTAIN, HARRY W. "Dorothy Aldis: Poet Laureate of Young Children." *EE* 44 (May 1967):453-60.
        Considers Aldis's poetry for children to have the following essential qualities: (1) worthwhile ideas, (2) honesty, (3) uniqueness, (4) imagery, (5) musical quality, (6) rich mood, and (7) appeal to emotion. Includes a bibliography of Aldis's works.

A80   SEGEL, ELIZABETH. "In Biography for Young Readers, Nothing Is Impossible." *L&U* 4 (Summer 1980):4-14. (Reprinted in Carr, *Beyond Fact*, pp. 148-53.)
        Argues that the highly praised *Nothing Is Impossible: The Story of Beatrix Potter* glosses over the deep unhappiness of Potter's life and her major disappointments. "If ever there was a life which demonstrates that some things are not possible, it is Beatrix Potter's . . . . Dorothy Aldis, in screening out the pain, as too bleak for preadolescent readers, obscured the moving reality, and substituted for it a conventional formula."

ALEXANDER, LLOYD (1924-   )

A81   ALEXANDER, LLOYD. "The Flat-Heeled Muse." *Horn Book* 41 (April 1965):141-46.
        Explores the role of fantasy in his work, and its meaning for him.

A82   -----. "High Fantasy and Heroic Romance." *Horn Book* 47 (October 1971):508-11. (Reprinted in Norton, *Folk Literature of the British Isles*, pp. 162-70, and in White, *Children's Literature*, pp. 112-17.)
        Explores the nature of the classical hero as personified by Taran in the Prydain series.

A83   -----. "Notes on *The Westmark Trilogy*." *Advocate* 4, no 1 (Fall 1984):1-6.

Comments on the writing of the trilogy, especially the concluding volume, *The Beggar Queen*.

A84   CARR, MARION. "Classic Hero in a New Mythology." *Horn Book* 47 (October 1971):508-13. (Reprinted in White, *Children's Literature*, pp. 112-17.)

Applies Jan de Vries's definition of the traditional hero to Taran, hero of the *Chronicles of Prydain*, and finds that he fits eight of the ten motifs.

A85   GREENLAW, M. JEAN. "Profile: Lloyd Alexander." *LA* 61 (April 1984):406-13.

Alexander discusses his life and work in an interview.

A86   JACOBS, JAMES SWENSEN. "Lloyd Alexander: A Critical Biography." Ed.D. dissertation, University of Georgia, 1978, 684 pp., DA 39:3559A.

Focuses on "Alexander's life, the reception of his writing, and his perception of the world." Considers professional reviews and Alexander's own views of literature and himself.

A87   -----. "A Personal Look at Lloyd Alexander." *Advocate* 4, no. 1 (Fall 1984):8-18.

Based on the research for his doctoral dissertation, Jacobs relates Alexander's background and personality to various aspects of his work.

A88   WINTLE, JUSTIN, and FISHER, EMMA. *The Pied Pipers*, pp. 208-20.
Alexander discusses his life and work in an interview.

ALGER, HORATIO (1832-99)

A89   SCHARNHORST, GARY F. "Good Fortune in America: The Life and Works of Horatio Alger, Jr. and the Fate of The Alger Hero from the Civil War to World War II." Ph.D. dissertation, Purdue University, 1978, 389 pp., DA 39:2911A.

Examines Alger's life, writings, and critical reception in American culture between 1860 and 1947.

ALLEE, MARJORIE HILL (1890-1945)

A90   WINSLOW, AMY. "Marjorie Hill Allee." *Horn Book* 22 (May-June 1946):183-95.

A biocritical survey and appreciation, emphasizing Allee's convictions on social problems.

ALLEN, RICHARD

A91   BARDGETT, KEITH. "*Skinhead* in the Classroom." *CLE*, o.s., no. 8 (July 1972):56-64.

Proposes various approaches to *Skinhead* in the classroom.

A92   ELDERS, DEREK. "Top of the Charts: The Significance of *Skinhead*." *Use of English* 27, no. 3 (Summer 1976):44-48.

"The case against *Skinhead* is that no sane appraisal of sex and violence is possible in language as impoverished as that demonstrated in the foregoing extracts."

ALMEDINGEN, E.M. (1898-1971)

A93   ALDERSON, VALERIE. "E.M. Almedingen 1898-1971: An Appreciation." *Children's Literature Review* 1, no. 5 (October 1971):149-52.
An appreciative biocritical overview.

A94   RAY, SHEILA G. "E.M. Almedingen." *School Librarian* 21, no. 4
(December 1973):301-3.
Praises Almedingen's stories, set in old Russia, for the insights
they shed on that country today.

ALS, ROALD

A95   GORMSEN, JACOB. "An Interview." *Bookbird* 3-4 (1982):24-29.
In an interview Als discusses his approach to illustration.

AMBRUS, VICTOR G. (1935-)

A96   JONES, CORNELIA, and WAY, OLIVIA R. *British Children's Authors*,
pp. 11-20.
In an interview Ambrus discusses his background, philosophy, and
method of working. Includes an annotated bibliography of his works.

ANDERSEN, HANS CHRISTIAN (1805-75)

A97   BAYLEY, JOHN. "Duckling Among the Swans." *TLS*, 19 September
1975, pp. 1049-50.
Reviews Elias Bredsdorff's *Hans Christian Andersen: The Story
of His Life and Work, 1805-1875.*

A98   BREDSDORFF, ELIAS. *Hans Christian Andersen: The Story of His
Life and Work, 1805-1875.* New York: Charles Scribners & Sons,
1975, 376 pp.
Part 2 of this biography, pp. 308-58, surveys and classifies
Andersen's tales, analyzes his language and style and that of his
translators, and comments on the inspiration for, and origins of, a
number of tales. An extensive bibliography of primary and secondary materials is included on pages 366-72.

A99   DAL, ERIK. "Research on Hans Christian Andersen: Trends, Results
and Desiderata." *Orbis Litterarum* 17, nos. 3-4 (1962):166-83.
Provides a thorough survey of international Andersen research
before 1962.

A100   FELL, CHRISTINE E. "Symbolic and Satiric Aspects of Hans Andersen's Fairy Tales." *Leeds Studies in English* n.s. 1 (1967):83-91.
Examines structure, values, and the symbolic and satirical ways in
which Andersen conveys values in "The Snow Queen," "The Little
Mermaid," "Thumbelina," and "The Darning Needle."

A101   GRØNBECH, BO. *Hans Christian Andersen.* Twayne's World Author
Series, no. 612. Boston: Twayne, 1980, 171 pp.
Provides a biographical and critical overview of Andersen's life
and work. Chapter 3, "The Fairy Tales," pp. 88-133, provides background and analysis of a number of retold and original tales. Chap-

ter 4, "Criticism, Influence, Research," summarizes critical responses and Andersen research. Includes bibliographies.

A102 HAUGAARD, ERIK C. "Hans Christian Andersen: Twentieth Century View." *Scandinavian Review* 63 (December 1975):4-12.
Explores Andersen's handling of poverty and misfortune, his views of art and the artist, and his ability to mix realism and romanticism.

A103 -----. "The Poet Who Lives." *Horn Book* 51 (October 1975):443-48.
Examines the qualities of Andersen's tales that keep them alive. Andersen was able to identify with the heroes of fairy tales and regarded them as a guide by which to live.

A104 -----. Portrait of a Poet: Hans Christian Andersen and His Fairy Tales." In Haviland, *The Openhearted Audience*, pp. 69-81.
Reflects upon considerations in translating Andersen: his ideas, his qualities of style, and the nature of fairy tales.

A105 -----. "Random Thoughts by a Translator of Andersen." *Horn Book* 48 (December 1972):557-62. (Reprinted in Koefoed, *Children's Literature and the Child*, pp. 67-70, entitled "A Meeting with Erik Christian Haugaard," and in Heins, *Crosscurrents*, pp. 277-82.)
Discusses Andersen's basic beliefs in a Christian God, in the worth of literature, in souls for animals, plants, and even inanimate objects. Also explores his bitterness and his sense of pity, all of which are in evidence in his tales.

A106 HAZARD, PAUL. "Prince of Story Tellers." In *Books, Children and Men*, pp. 92-105. (Reprinted in *Horn Book* 19 [May-June 1943]:141-47.)
Calls him "the very prince of all story tellers." He was able "to penetrate the soul of both animate and inanimate things." Andersen is aware that there is much sorrow in the world, yet "Life finds its reasons for enduring."

A107 HEARN, MICHAEL PATRICK. "Afterword." In *Kate Greenaway's Original Drawings for "The Snow Queen" by Hans Christian Andersen*, pp. 53-58. N.Y.: Schocken, 1981.
Finds similarities in the personalities and biographies of Andersen and Greenaway, and concludes that Greenaway's unfinished sketches offer "an unusually sensitive interpretation" of the tale.

A108 HÜRLIMANN, BETTINA. *Three Centuries*, pp. 42-52.
A biocritical overview.

A109 JAN, ISABELLE. "Hans Christian Andersen or Reality." In *On Children's Literature*, pp. 45-55.
Sees Andersen as exploding the conventions of the folktale. "In him childhood and manhood merged."

A110 KUTTY, K. NARAYAN. "A Look at Andersen's 'The Shadow.'" In Butler, *Sharing*, pp. 251-56.
Provides an in-depth analysis of Andersen's short story.

A111 MISHLER, WILLIAM. "H.C. Andersen's 'Tin Soldier' in a Freudian Perspective." *Scandinavian Studies* 50 (Autumn 1978):389-95.

Concludes that "a psychoanalytic reading helps the reader to recognize the way in which the story contains its own interpretation."

A112   RUBECK, MARY ANN. "Annotations Documenting and Interpreting the Reflection of Hans Christian Andersen's Life in His Fairy Tales." Ph.D. dissertation, State University of New York at Buffalo, 1981, 260 pp., DA 42:1622A.
"The purpose of this study was to explore, document, interpret and to relate the parallelism between elements in the fairy tales and events in the life of Andersen."

A113   RUBOW, PAUL V. "Idea and Form in Hans Christian Andersen's Fairy Tales." In *A Book on the Danish Writer Hans Christian Andersen: His Life and Work*, edited by Svend Dahl and H.G. Topse-Jensen. Copenhagen: Det Berlingske Bogtrykkeri, 1955, pp. 97-135.
Discusses the tales within the context of the traditional fairy tale and Andersen's beliefs.

A114   SALE, ROGER. *Fairy Tales*, pp. 63-73.
Andersen marks the transition from fairy tales to later children's literature. His work is marred by the narrator's intruding voice. "The Little Mermaid" and "The Snow Queen" are analyzed in depth.

A115   SICHERMANN, RUTH. "Time To Tell An Andersen Tale." *TON* 30 (January 1974):161-68.
Comments upon several of Andersen's tales suitable for telling to children.

A116   WILLIAMS, ALAN MORAY. "Hans Christian Andersen." *Time and Tide* (February 1963):9-13. (Reprinted in Egoff, *Only Connect*, 1st ed., pp. 265-69; 2d ed., pp. 233-37.)
A brief biocritical overview.

ANDREW, PRUDENCE (1924-   )

A117   CROSS, GILLIAN. "Prudence Andrew: Fantasy in the Realistic Novel." *CLE*, o.s., no. 21 (Summer 1976):81-85.
Suggests that Andrew, instead of approaching social problems with a "watered-down adult view," attempts to examine them as children themselves might, especially in *Mr. O'Brien*. Also discusses *Una and Grubstreet* (*Una and the Heaven Baby*, U.S. version).

ANDREWS, J[AMES] S[IDNEY] (1934-   )

A118   TAYLOR, ANNE. "Travelling In Time--Towards a Project." *CLE*, o.s., no. 13 (1974):68-79.
A detailed analysis of *The Bell of Nendrum*, showing ways in which it was used with a group of students.

ANGLUND, JOAN WALSH (1926-   )

A119   BANNER, BARBARA A. "Authors and Editors: Joan Walsh Anglund." *Publishers Weekly* 199 (January 1971):35-36.
Discusses Anglund's background and the origins of some of her books.

A120   LANES, SELMA G. *Down the Rabbit Hole*, pp. 31-34, 37-42.

Compares Greenaway and Anglund.

ANNO, MITSUMASA (1920-)

A121 AOKI, HISAKO. "A Conversation with Mitsumasa Anno." *Horn Book* 59 (April 1983):137-45.
Discusses his background and the background of some of his books.

A122 FISHER, M.F.K. "Everywhere, Something Is Happening." *NYTBR*, 13 November 1983, Children's Book sec., pp. 39, 52.
Reviews *Anno's U.S.A.*

A123 MacCANN, DONNARAE, and RICHARD, OLGA. "Picture Books for Children." *WLB* 55 (January 1981):370.
A careful review of both text and illustrations.

A124 MATSUI, TADASHI. "The Art of Mitsumasa Anno." *Bookbird* 1-2 (1982):36-37.
Praises Anno's ability to represent difficult phase and space concepts pictorially.

A125 MORDOH, ALICE MORRISON. "Folklife in the Work of Mitsumasa Anno." *ChLAQ* 10 (Fall 1985):104-8.
Concentrates on Anno's accurate presentations of traditional cultural landscape and folk architecture.

APPLETON, VICTOR [Stratemeyer Syndicate pseudonym]

A126 MOLSON, FRANCIS. "Three Generations of Tom Swift." *ChLAQ* 10, no. 2 (Summer 1985):60-63.
Provides a detailed analysis of three separate series of *Tom Swift*.

A127 PRAGER, ARTHUR. "Peril: The Mother of Invention." In *Rascals at Large*, pp. 127-65.
Discusses the Tom Swift series. Later chapters examine the Tom Swift war books, pp. 191-93, and the Don Sturdy series, pp. 309-11 and 322-27.

A128 "Tom Swift Flies Again!" *Publishers Weekly* 164 (19 December 1953):2363-64.
An overview of the series on the occasion of the issuing of the first three titles in the new series, starring Tom Swift, Jr., and written by Victor Appleton II.

Arabian Nights

A129 KIRBY, W.B. "The Forbidden Doors of the Thousand and One Nights." *Folklore Journal* 5 (1887):112-24.
Examines five tales from the *Arabian Nights* based upon "(1) the existence of a door, which the hero is forbidden to open; and (2) his falling in love with a beautiful woman whom he sees from the housetop."

A130 WILSON, ANNE. "A New Arabian Nights." *Signal* 40 (January 1983):26-29.

Reviews Geraldine McCaughrean's *One Thousand and One Arabian Nights* (Oxford: Oxford University Press, 1982, 249 pp.), which she considers the most beautiful retelling in English.

ARDIZZONE, EDWARD (1900-79)

A131   ARDIZZONE, EDWARD. "About Tim and Lucy." *Horn Book* 14 (March 1938):88-90. (Reprinted in Fryatt, *Horn Book Sampler*, pp. 1-3.)
Tells how he came to create the Tim and Lucy books.

A132   -----. "The Born Illustrator." *Signal* 3 (September 1970):73-80.
Ardizzone's comments on illustration are preceded by a selection of "some favourite illustrations drawn by him for children," pp. 67-72.

A133   -----. "Edward Ardizzone: An Autobiographical Note." *Junior Bookshelf* 14, no. 2 (March 1950):39-45. (Reprinted in Hoffman, *Authors and Illustrators*, pp. 1-5.)
More biographical than critical; however, Ardizzone reflects on writing for children and the origins of some of his books.

A134   BELL, QUENTIN. "Edward Ardizzone." *Studio* 149 (May 1955):144-47.
Provides a critical analysis of Ardizzone as an illustrator, concentrating on his works for adults.

A135   CROUCH, MARCUS. "One Old, One New." *Junior Bookshelf* 34, no. 5 (October 1970):273-74.
A review of two books by Ardizzone. Brief but insightful comments on *Johnny's Bad Day* and the republished *Lucy Brown and Mr. Grimes*, "the famous book which offended the Puritan heart of America in the middle thirties."

A136   -----. "To Edward Ardizzone, with Thanks." *Junior Bookshelf* 43, no. 6 (December 1979):309-12.
Reviews Gabriel White's *Edward Ardizzone*, and adds his own reminiscences and appreciation of Ardizzone's work.

A137   HOGARTH, GRACE ALLEN. "Edward Ardizzone, 1900-1979: An Editor's View." *Horn Book* 56 (December 1980):680-86.
Reminiscences of Ardizzone over the years, primarily personal but with some interesting sidelights on his attitudes toward his books, their origins and publication history.

A138   JONES, CORNELIA, and WAY, OLIVIA R. *British Children's Authors*, pp. 21-30.
In an interview, Ardizzone discusses his background, philosophy, and method of working. Includes an annotated bibliography of his works.

A139   STONE, HELEN. "Artist's Choice." *Horn Book* 26 (May 1950): 210-11.
Analyzes the illustrations in *Tim to the Rescue*.

A140   TUCKER, NICHOLAS. "Edward Ardizzone." *CLE*, o.s., no. 3 (November 1970):21-29.

Discusses in detail the Tim series. "He writes for tough independent little kids who run away from home against good advice and do not faint at the sight of blood." Praises Ardizzone's pictures as a contrast to much of the "wretched" art to which children are subjected.

A141   WHITE, GABRIEL. *Edward Ardizzone: Artist and Illustrator.* New York: Schocken, 1980, 192 pp.
This study and pictorial record of Ardizzone's career as artist and illustrator devotes two chapters specifically to his books, pp. 121-52. Includes references.

A142   WINTLE, JUSTIN, and FISHER, EMMA. *Pied Pipers*, pp. 35-48.
Ardizzone discusses his life and his work in an interview.

ARMSTRONG, RICHARD (1903-   )

A143   ARMSTRONG, RICHARD. "Writing for Boys." *Junior Bookshelf* 13 (July 1949):73-76.
Expresses his views on writing for boys. Followed by an appreciative critical appraisal, "Richard Armstrong: Writer for Boys," by H.J.B.W., pp. 79-82.

A144   CROUCH, MARCUS. *The Nesbit Tradition*, pp. 187-92.
Singles out *Sea-Change* as his best work, and also comments on *Whinstone Drift*. "He is no great stylist. . . . It is in the exposition and analysis of character that Armstrong excels."

ARMSTRONG, WILLIAM (1914-   )

A145   KINGSTON, CAROLYN T. *Tragic Mode*, pp. 52-54.
Analyzes *Sounder* in terms of the theme of rejection.

A146   KUZNETS, LOIS R. "Some Issues Raised by the 'Issues Approach.'" *ChLAQ* 5 (Fall 1980):20.
Responds to Schwartz's analysis of *Sounder* (below).

A147   SCHWARTZ, ALBERT V. "*Sounder:* A Black or White Tale?" *IRBC* 3, no. 1 (1970). (Reprinted in MacCann and Woodard, *Black American,* pp. 89-93.)
Analyzes the book from the perspective of two questions raised by Julius Lester (see A1523): "Does it accurately present the black perspective?" and "Will it be relevant to black children?" Concludes that the answer to both questions is "No."

ARNOW, HARRIETTE (1908-   )

A148   McMAHAN, ELIZABETH. "Harriette Arnow's *The Dollmaker:* A Teacher's Lament." *English Journal* 72 (1983):55-58.
Focuses on the "teachable aspects" of the book, which she feels is "long overdue its rightful critical recognition." Summarizes and provides references to existing criticism.

ARTHUR, RUTH (1905-   )

A149   CROUCH, MARCUS. *The Nesbit Tradition*, pp. 201-3, 205-6, 218.
Analyzes *A Candle in Her Room* as a story of self-fulfillment

spread out over more than one generation, and *Requiem for a Princess* and *The Whistling Boy* as "mirror stories," the one dealing with adoption, the other with a stepmother.

A150   -----. "The Painful Art of Growing Up: The Novels of Ruth M. Arthur." *Junior Bookshelf* 42, no. 5 (October 1978):239-44.
Provides a detailed analysis of Arthur's work, identifying the development of common themes and techniques.

A151   JONES, CORNELIA, and WAY, OLIVIA R. *British Children's Authors*, pp. 31-40.
Arthur discusses her background, philosophy, and method of working. Includes an annotated bibliography of her works.

ARTZYBASHEFF, BORIS (1899-1965)

A152   BADER, BARBARA. *American Picturebooks*, pp. 187-96.
"Boris Artzybasheff brought to the making of books for children a special wit and polish and a total sense of style." Traces his relatively short but phenomenally successful career as a picture-book artist.

A153   BECHTEL, LOUISE S. "Boris Artzybasheff." *Horn Book* 42 (April 1966):176-80.
An appreciation touching on aspects of his life and art.

A154   COLUM, PADRAIC. "Boris Artzybasheff." *Horn Book* 4 (August 1928):38-40.
A brief discussion of the artist's style, accompanied by examples of his work and a list of his books.

A155   LOCKWOOD, BRUCE. "Boris Artzybasheff." *Creative Art* 12 (January 1933):11-18.
An early biocritical overview. Includes references and bibliographies.

A156   "*Seven Simeons* and Its Creator." *Junior Bookshelf* 2, no. 2 (December 1937):68-70.
An early review of this award-winning book.

A157   WATSON, ERNEST W. "The Art of Boris Artzybasheff." *American Artist* 5 (December 1941):11-15.
A brief biocritical overview.

ARUNDEL, HONOR (1919-73)

A158   BOYD, CELIA. "Growing Pains: A Survey of Honor Arundel's Novels." *Signal* 4 (January 1973):38-51.

A159   RUSSELL, J. "Honor Arundel." *Junior Bookshelf* 37 (December 1973):367-69.
A brief appreciation.

ASHLEY, BERNARD (1935-   )

A160   BRADMAN, TONY. "Children's Writers: 8 Bernard Ashley." *School Librarian* 30 (March 1982):6-12.

Compares and contrasts Ashley's work with Graham Greene's, and considers him one of the most talented writers in the field of children's literature at present.

ATWOOD, MARGARET (1939-   )

A161   BECKMAN, SUSAN. "Margaret Atwood: Can. Lit. to Kid Lit." *CCL* 12 (1978):78-81.
Reviews Atwood's first book for children, illustrated and hand-lettered by its author.

D'AULNOY, MADAME   (1650-1705)

A162   DeGRAFF, AMY VANDERLYN. "The Tower and the Well: A Study of Form and Meaning in Mme. d'Aulnoy's Fairy Tales." Ph.D. dissertation, University of Virginia, 1979, 242 pp., DA 40:888A.
Shows how "the application of psychological concepts to Madame d'Aulnoy's fairy tales can generate meanings as rich and complex as the structures that imply them."

A163   FILSTRUP, JANE. "Individuation in 'La Chatte Blanche.'" *Children's Literature* 6 (1977):77-92.
Compares d'Aulnoy's tale with "Rapunzel" and other tales from Grimm and from the *Arabian Nights* and Perrault, analyzing them in terms of birth and individuation.

A164   MITCHELL, JANE. "Thematic Analysis of Mme. D'Aulnoy's Contes De Fées." Ph.D. dissertation, University of North Carolina at Chapel Hill, 1973, 235 pp., DA 35:466A.
Examines the major themes of d'Aulnoy's fairy tales: her *Zeitgeist*, metamorphosis, and love.

A165   PALMER, MELVIN DELMAR. "Madame d'Aulnoy in England." Ph.D. dissertation, 1969, 236 pp., DA 31:396A.
Chronicles the history of Madame d'Aulnoy's works in English and explores the confusions concerning her biography.

A166   SALE, ROGER. *Fairy Tales*, pp. 54-58.
Describes "The Green Snake" as "masquelike and courtly, . . . far from the huts and castles in which fairy tales were told of old," but nevertheless "a beautiful tale."

A167   WILLIAMS, ELIZABETH DETERING. "The Fairy Tales of Madame d'Aulnoy." Ph.D. dissertation, Rice University, 1982, 297 pp., DA 43:465A.
Analyzes the themes, style, and structure of d'Aulnoy's fairy tales and places them within the historic context of the seventeenth century.

AVERY, GILLIAN (1926-   )

A168   BOWEN, NAOMI. "Gillian Avery: A Conversation." *School Librarian* 23, no. 3 (September 1975):205-8. (Reprinted in Culpan, *Variety is King*, pp. 102-5.)
In an interview Avery discusses *Childhood's Pattern* and her historical fiction, especially *The Warden's Niece*.

A169   BUTTS, DENNIS. "Writers for Children: 9 Gillian Avery." *School Librarian* 16, no. 2 (July 1968):153-57.
An introduction to Avery's historical fiction.

A170   CADOGAN, MARY, and CRAIG, PATRICIA. *You're a Brick*, pp. 361-64.
Analyzes Avery's approach to historical fiction, her handling of characters, and her approach to feminism in *The Warden's Niece*.

A171   CROUCH, MARCUS. *The Nesbit Tradition*, pp. 173-76.
Discusses *The Warden's Niece*, Avery's "most individual achievement," and *The Children of the House*, "a strong and authentic social document."

A172   INGLIS, FRED. *Promise of Happiness*, pp. 224-26.
Sees *The Warden's Niece* as an "inevitably personal" interpretation of history. "In less sensitive hands, the subject matter could far too easily have become a pale ontological project--how to do a spot of local history, using local resources. But the characters are too varied for a reader ever to lose sight of the livingness and contingent quality of full-blooded historical inquiry."

AWDRY, W., Rev. (1911-   )

A173   CHURCHER, JOHN. "Journey to the End of the Tunnel." *Junior Bookshelf* 41 (October 1977):267-69.
Discusses the appeal of Awdry's railway books.

BABBITT, NATALIE (1932-   )

A174   DE LUCA, GERALDINE. "Extensions of Nature: The Fantasies of Natalie Babbitt." *L&U* 1, no. 2 (Fall 1977):47-70.
Discusses Babbitt's first five novels and the way she maintains "a tension between the vulnerable and hopeful world of childhood and the more easily compromised world of adults."

A175   HIRSCH, CORINNE. "Toward Maturity: Natalie Babbitt's Initiatory Journeys." *Proceedings of the Children's Literature Association* 7 (1980):107-13.
Kneeknock Rise (1970), *Tuck Everlasting* (1975), and *The Eyes of the Amaryllis* (1977) explore "a common predicament by means of the initiatory journey of its young protagonist, who leaves the protected world of childhood to confront a fundamental human problem: the desire for security and concomitant need to take risks to achieve independence and involvement in life."

A176   LANES, SELMA G. "A Talk with Natalie Babbitt." *NYTBR*, 14 November 1982, Children's Book sec., pp. 44, 54.
An interview in which Babbitt discusses her work, particularly *Herbert Rowbarge*, which is also reviewed by Anne Tyler on these same pages.

A177   LYNCH, CATHERINE, M. "Winnie Foster and Peter Pan: Facing the Dilemma of Growth." *Proceedings of the Children's Literature Association* 9 (1982):107-11.
Suggests that both *Peter Pan* and *Tuck Everlasting* explore a conflict central to childhood experience: to grow up to adult respon-

sibilities or not to grow up at all. Argues that Babbitt deepens the Peter Pan myth by dramatizing the fact that embracing adulthood includes, of necessity, choosing death.

A178   MERCIER, JEAN F. "Natalie Babbitt." *Publishers Weekly* 208 (28 July 1975):66-67.
A brief biocritical overview.

A179   MOSS, ANITA. "A Second Look: *The Search for the Delicious.*" *Horn Book* 60 (December 1984):779-83.
Explores Babbitt's use of the quest romance "to show up human-kind's folly in failing to recognize elemental meanings and in cutting itself off from sacramental experience."

A180   WILDER, VIRGINIA. Review. *IRBC* 9, no. 1 (1978):17.
Faults *Phoebe's Revolt* on the basis of sexism.

BACON, PEGGY (1895-   )

A181   BADER, BARBARA. *American Picturebooks*, pp. 196-98.
Examines Peggy Bacon's illustrations for *Buttons*, text by Tom Robinson, in terms of their place in the evolution of a picture-book style.

BAGNOLD, ENID (1889-1981)

A182   KOLBA, ELLEN D. "Recommended: Enid Bagnold." *English Journal* 72 (October 1983):76-77.
A biocritical overview, concentrating on *National Velvet.*

BANK, CLAIR

A183   MASON, BOBBIE ANN. *The Girl Sleuth*, pp. 101-6.
Despite lacking the action and slick style of Stratemeyer books, the Beverly Gray college mystery series was popular because she was "one of the most adventurous and independent of the girl detectives."

BANNERMAN, HELEN [Brodie Cowan Watson] (1863-1946)

A184   BURKE, VIRGINIA M. "Mummy Didn't Mean No Harm." *LA* 53 (March 1976):272-75.
Summarizes the history of *Little Black Sambo*, especially critical reaction to it since 1972.

A185   DINNAGE, ROSEMARY. "The Taming of Teatime Tigers." *TLS*, 24 July 1981, p. 834.
Reviews Elizabeth Hay's *Sambo Sahib: "The Story of Little Black Sambo" and Helen Bannerman*, and comments on Marjorie McDonald's psychoanalysis of Sambo (see below).

A186   GARD, ELIZABETH. "Bits Strewn All Over the Page." *Books for Your Children* 5 (1970):4. (Reprinted in Tucker, *Suitable for Children?*, pp. 184-90.)
In an interview Bannerman's daughter discusses and exonerates *Black Sambo*, while admitting uneasiness about the violence in *Little Kettle Head.*

A187　HAY, ELIZABETH. *Sambo Sahib: "The Story of Little Black Sambo" and Helen Bannerman.* Edinburgh: Paul Harris; Totowa, N.J.: Barnes & Noble, 1981, 194 pp.

This highly sympathetic biography of Bannerman outlines the publishing history of *The Story of Little Black Sambo*, and attempts to correct several longstanding inaccuracies. Information on the writing, setting, and original publication of the book is included. The final chapter, "Sambo Blacked," concerns the charges of racism that have been leveled at the book.

A188　HILL, JANET. "Oh! Please Mr. Tiger." *TLS*, 3 November 1972, pp. 1315-16. (Reprinted in Tucker, *Suitable for Children?*, pp. 191-96.)

Explains why Hill has changed her opinion about *Little Black Sambo* and now feels it is time for it to be retired. Compares the attitudes in *Little Black Sambo* and *Little White Squibba* and finds them both condescending and patronizing. Concludes that Bannerman's books express "benevolent paternalism" and reveal "the deep roots of racism in our history, culture, and language."

A189　McDONALD, MARJORIE. "Little Black Sambo." *Pychoanalytic Study of the Child* 29 (1973):511-28.

Interprets the tale as a concealed primal scene story, and contrasts it with "Epaminondas," which has "little of psychoanalytic interest." Argues that "it is just this unconscious childhood sexuality that underlies *Sambo*'s racism."

A190　SCHILLER, J. "The Story of Little Black Sambo." *Book Collector* 23, no. 3 (Autumn 1974):381-86.

Provides a publication history of the book and argues that "If any negative stereotypes of the black child have come from *The Story of Little Black Sambo*, it was certainly not the intention of its author but rather the offspring of a conscience-ridden society."

A191　STOKES, HORACE W. *"Sambo and the Twins."* *Horn Book* 12 (1936):373-74.

This account of the origins of *Little Black Sambo* and one of its sequels is interesting primarily for the historical perspective so different from today's.

A192　YUILL, PHYLLIS J. *"Little Black Sambo:* A Closer Look." New York: Council on Interracial Books for Children, 1976, 52 pp. (Also available from ERIC Educational Document Reproduction Service, ED 123 308.)

Examines the origins of the story and traces its history in the United States through overlapping periods of popularity and controversy.

A193　-----. *"Little Black Sambo:* The Continuing Controversy." *SLJ* 22 (March 1976):71-76. (Reprinted in Gerhardt, *Issues in Children's Book Selection.*)

A survey and summary of responses to the book.

BARBOUR, RALPH HENRY (1870-1944)

A194　ERISMAN, FRED. "The Strenuous Life In Practice: The School and Sports Stories of Ralph Henry Barbour." *Rocky Mountain Social Science Journal* 7 (April 1970):29-37.

Explores Barbour's "dramatically intensified version" of the Progressive Era ideals of progress and moral values.

A195   PRAGER, ARTHUR. *Rascals at Large*, pp. 286-93.
Describes the typical Barbour book, complete with an example of a "grand heart-stopping moment." Considers Barbour one of the best writers of boys' books.

BARNE, KITTY (1883-1957)

A196   COLWELL, EILEEN. "Kitty Barne: An Appreciation." *Junior Bookshelf* 25 (October 1961):197-201.
A biocritical overview.

BARRIE, J[AMES] M[ATTHEW] (1860-1937)

A197   BLACKBURN, WILLIAM. "*Peter Pan* and the Contemporary Adolescent Novel." *Proceedings of the Children's Literature Association* 9 (1982):47-53.
Maintains that *Peter Pan*, like many contemporary adolescent novels, deals with the passage from innocence to maturity, but unlike many of them, also offers a consolation for the loss of innocence.

A198   CARPENTER, HUMPHREY. "J.M. Barrie and *Peter Pan*: 'That Terrible Masterpiece.'" In *Secret Gardens*, pp. 170-87.
Views *Peter Pan* as "a detailed map of the earthly paradise, the secret garden." Claims that Barrie "invokes religious belief in his creation only to dismiss it as childish nonsense. . . . At the heart of the sentimental dream is a cynical, mocking voice."

A199   EGAN, MICHAEL. "The Neverland of Id: Barrie, *Peter Pan* and Freud." *Children's Literature* 10 (1982):37-55.
Argues that Barrie unconsciously created a vast symbolic metaphor (Neverland) of the child's id, and populated it with archetypal characters engaged in Oedipal conflicts. Sees Freudian analysis as the key to interpreting Barrie's work.

A200   GREEN, MARTIN. "The Charm of Peter Pan." *Children's Literature* 9 (1981):19-27.
Compares the appeal and techniques of Barrie and Disney, and concludes they both represent the "end of the line" in popular culture in terms of sweetness and unreality.

A201   GREEN, ROGER L. *J.M. Barrie*. New York: Walck, 1961, 64 pp.
Outlines Barrie's career as a writer, commenting that "All of Barrie's life led up to the creation of Peter Pan." Concentrates on *Peter Pan*, but also discusses Barrie's other plays and books.

A202   GRIFFITH, JOHN. "Making Wishes Innocent: Peter Pan." *L&U* 3, no. 1 (Spring 1979):28-37.
Shows how Barrie used whimsy, wit, and fantasy to render the unthinkable harmless and innocent in what is basically the story of a child defeating his father (Captain Hook) and playing house with his mother (Wendy).

A203   KARPE, MARIETTA. "The Origins of Peter Pan." *Psychoanalytic Review* 43, no. 1 (January 1956):104-10.

Provides a psychoanalytic interpretation of Barrie's preoccupation with aging, death, eternal youth, and immortality, and his overwhelming appeal to international audiences.

A204　LURIE, ALISON. "The Boy Who Couldn't Grow Up." *New York Review of Books*, 6 February 1975, pp. 11-15.
Explores the biographical origins of *Peter Pan* and compares it to Barrie's *Mary Rose*.

A205　MEISEL, FREDERICK L. "The Myth of Peter Pan." *Psychoanalytic Study of the Child* 32 (1977):545-63.
Interprets *Peter Pan* as a fantasy or myth "which has as its center a self image that is of the opposite sex." Concludes that the story is "of a child's repair of injured narcissism," as well as a "cautionary tale" on the consequences of not growing up.

A206　RUSSELL, PATRICIA READ. "Parallel Romantic Fantasies: Barrie's *Peter Pan* and Spielberg's *E.T.: The Extraterrestrial*." *ChLAQ* 8 (Winter 1983):28-30.
Argues that there are many links between the two plays, but whereas "Barrie has created a tragedy of romanticism; Spielberg has made it into comedy."

A207　STEVENSON, LIONEL. "A Source for Barrie's *Peter Pan*." *Philological Quarterly* 8 (April 1929):210-14.
Argues that the structure of *Peter Pan* closely resembles that of George MacDonald's *Lilith*.

A208　TUCKER, NICHOLAS. "Fly Away Peter." *Signal* 37 (January 1982):43-40.
Examines the play's appeal to children by looking at "how the play came to be written in the first place," and providing a psychological interpretation of it. Response by Neil Philip in *Signal* 38 (May 1982):129-32.

BARSTOW, STAN

A209　HALL, BARBARA. Comment in "Teachers at Work II: Two Novels in the Classroom." *CLE*, n.s. 11, no. 3 (Autumn 1980):127-28.
Discusses her use of *A Kind of Loving* in a classroom of secondary students.

BARTHELME, DONALD (1931-　　)

A210　GATES, D. "A Highly Irregular Children's Story: The *Slightly Irregular Fire Engine*." *Virginia Quarterly Review* 52 (Spring 1976):298-308.
Provides a detailed analysis of Barthelme's children's story, showing how he uses the same techniques on a child's level that he uses in his extremely sophisticated fiction for adults.

BARTO, AGNIA

A211　KORKIN, VLADIMIR, and BARTO, AGNIA. "20th Century: Children and Books." *Soviet Literature* 4:141-47.
This Soviet children's poet discusses Soviet children's literature and his own writing in an interview.

BAUM, L[YMAN] FRANK (1856-1919)

A212 ABRAHM, PAUL M., and KENTER, STUART. "Tik-Tok and the Three Laws of Robotics." *Science-Fiction Studies* 5, no. 1 (March 1978):67-80.

Claims that Tik-Tok, Dorothy's companion in Oz, represents a perfect embodiment of Asimov's Three Laws of Robotics.

A213 *American Book Collector* 13, no. 4 (December 1962), 32 pp.

Special Baum issue articles include "L. Frank Baum--Shadow and Substance," by Russell P. MacFall, pp. 9-11; "'Utopia Americana' A Generation Afterwards," by Edward Wagenknecht, pp. 12-13; "Why Librarians Dislike Oz," by Martin Gardner, pp. 14-16; "How My Father Wrote the Oz Books," by Harry Neal Baum. There are several other items and a checklist of Baum's writings.

A214 *Baum Bugle.*

Published three times a year since 1957 by the International Wizard of Oz Club, 220 N. Eleventh St., Escanaba, Michigan 49829. Devoted to Baum scholarship and news.

A215 BECKWITH, OSMOND. "The Oddness of Oz." *Children's Literature* 5 (1976):74-91.

Provides a detailed psychoanalytical interpretation of the Oz books, comparing their appeal to young girls to that of *Alice*.

A216 BEWLEY, MARIUS. "The Land of Oz: America's Great Good Place." In *Masks and Mirrors: Essays in Criticism.* New York: Atheneum, 1970, pp. 255-67.

Finds similarities between Baum's style and themes and and those of Stephen Crane, Hawthorne, and other mainstream American writers.

A217 BROTMAN, JORDAN. "A Late Wanderer in Oz." *Chicago Review* 18, no. 2 (1965):63-73. (Reprinted in Egoff, *Only Connect*, pp. 156-69.)

Concludes that the Oz stories "have charm and variety and body enough to be real fairy tales." They also tell us much about the values and aspirations of the American people and their migration from the Middlewest to California.

A218 CATH, STANLEY H., and CATH, CLAIRE. "On the Other Side of Oz: Psychoanalytic Aspects of Fairy Tales." *Psychoanalytic Study of the Child* 33 (1978):621-39.

Examines common fairy tale themes, as exemplified in *The Wizard of Oz*, in psychoanalytic terms. Concludes, "Like all myths, dreams, and fables, *The Wizard of Oz* provides an age-appropriate mirror lighted by a distant and indirect source, filled with double messages and ambiguities. The final resolution is the protagonist's 'return home,' a little wiser, a little more tolerant, and a little more mature (one hopes)."

A219 ERISMAN, FRED. "L. Frank Baum and the Progressive Dilemma." *American Quarterly* 20 (Fall 1968):616-23.

Interprets the Oz books and the Aunt Jane's Nieces books in terms of Baum's solution to the progressive dilemma of reconciling and adapting rural ideals to an urban society.

A220   GARDNER, MARTIN. "John Dough and the Cherub." *Children's Literature* 2 (1973):110-18. (Also to be published as the introduction to a facsimile of first edition of *John Dough and the Cherub* [New York: Dover Publications].)

Provides an introduction and background to the work.

A221   -----. "Why Librarians Dislike Oz." *Library Journal* 88 (15 February 1963):834-36. (Reprinted from *American Book Collector*, December 1962.)

Suggests seven reasons why librarians have long refused to put *Oz* on their shelves.

A222   GARDNER, MARTIN, and NYE, RUSSELL B., eds. *The Wizard of Oz and Who He Was*. East Lansing: Michigan State University Press, 1957, 208 pp.

Contains an annotated version of the original 1900 edition of *The Wonderful Wizard of Oz*, including reproductions of numerous W.W. Denslow illustrations. Preceded by Gardner's essay "The Royal Historian of Oz," pp. 19-45, and Nye's "An Appreciation," pp. 1-18, a revised and expanded version of an article that first appeared in *Fantasy and Science Fiction*. Nye explores Baum's strengths and possible reasons for his critical neglect, while Gardner chronicles the history of Oz and suggests numerous areas for further study of the books. Also contains a bibliography of primary and secondary sources.

A223   GREENE, DAVID L. "The Concept of Oz." *Children's Literature* 3 (1974):173-76.

Argues that Baum's concept of Oz is more complex than the utopia most critics have considered it to be.

A224   GREENE, DOUGLAS G. "Introduction." *The Woggle Bug Book (1905): A Facsimile Reproduction*. Delmar, N.Y.: Scholars' Facsimiles and Reprints, 1978, pp. 5-7.

Points out that the *Woggle Bug Book*, while not of the quality of Baum's major works, is important "for the light it sheds on Baum's writing at an important period in his career."

A225   HAMILTON, MARGARET. "There's No Place Like Oz." *Children's Literature* 10 (1982):153-55.

Reflects on the significance of "home" to the popularity of the *Wizard of Oz*.

A226   HEARN, MICHAEL PATRICK. *The Annotated Wizard of Oz*. New York: Clarkson N. Potter, 1973, 384 pp.

Hearn's introduction, interspersed with numerous photographs and reproductions of illustrations, some in color, summarizes the book's publication history, its critical reception, and its increasing recognition as literature. Extensive annotations accompany the text. There is an appendix devoted to W.W. Denslow, and an annotated chronological checklist of Baum's writings. Also includes bibliographies of writings on Baum and Denslow.

A227   -----. "L. Frank Baum and the 'Modernized Fairy Tale.'" *CLE*, n.s. 10, no. 2 (Summer 1979):57-67.

Maintains that Baum consciously sought to alter many of the forms of traditional literature and through his experimentation "made a significant contribution to twentieth century juvenile literature."

A228   JONES, VERNON H.   "The Oz Parade." *New Orleans Review* 3 (1973):375-78.
        Summarizes Baum's career and his recently burgeoning critical recognition.

A229   LITTLEFIELD, HENRY M.   "The Wizard of Oz: Parable on Populism." *American Quarterly* 16, no. 1 (1964):47-58.
        Provides a detailed analysis of the first and most popular of the Oz books. Concludes that "Baum's fantasy succeeds in bridging the gap between what children want and what they should have," that he conveyed messages while keeping entertainment foremost.

A230   MANNIX, DANIEL P.   "The Father of the Wizard of Oz." *American Heritage* 16 (December 1964):108-9.
        Provides an illustrated overview of Baum's career and his popular and critical reception.

A231   PRENTICE, ANN E.   "Have You Been To See the Wizard?" *TON* 27 (November 1970):32-44.
        Provides background on Baum and surveys the history of the Oz books' reception by the public, librarians, and critics. Includes a bibliography of secondary sources.

A232   SALE, ROGER.   "Baum's Magic Powder of Life." *Children's Literature* 8 (1980):157-63.
        Reviews recent Baum research.

A233   -----.   "L. Frank Baum and Oz." In *Fairy Tales*, pp. 222-43.
        Sees Baum as a reflection of American optimism. "A good deal of the best of American children's literature is like this; it enchants by its ease, its unselfconsciousness, its naiveté.   And the first to achieve this, and still the best, is Baum." Examines *Ozma, The Road to Oz*, the *Tin Woodman*, and *Glinda*. "The essence of Baum is his restless, careless ease, his indifference to the complexities of life, his eagerness to describe what enchanted him without ever exploring or understanding it."

A234   -----.   "L. Frank Baum and Oz." *Hudson Review* 25 (Winter 1972-73):571-92.
        Provides insights into Baum's "rare gifts," analyzing the essence of his greatness and arguing that his "apparently crushing limitations are really only the defects" of his virtues.

A235   SCHUMAN, SAMUEL.   "Comic Mythos and Children's Literature--or, Out of the Fryeing Pan and into the Pyre." In *It's a Funny Thing, Humour*. Edited by Antony J. Chapman and Hugh C. Foot. Oxford: Pergamon, 1977, pp. 119-21.
        Finds evidence of Northrop Frye's archetypal comic pattern in L. Frank Baum's *The Wizard of Oz*, and in "Hansel and Gretel" and "Jack and the Beanstalk."

A236   SMYERS, RICHARD PAUL.   "A Librarian Looks at Oz." *Library Occurrent* 21 (December 1964):190-92.
        Examines librarians' objections to the Oz series, and the continuing and growing enthusiasm of Oz fans.

BAUMANN, HANS (1914-   )

A237   "Famous Authors of Literature for Youth." *Bookbird* 3 (1965):19-22.
A brief biocritical overview, including a bibliography of Baumann's books.

BAWDEN, NINA (1925-   )

A238   BAWDEN, NINA. "A Dead Pig and My Father." *CLE*, o.s., no. 14 (May 1974):3-13. (Reprinted in Fox, *Writers, Critics, and Children* pp. 3-14.)
Describes some of the experiences she has incorporated in her writing, maintaining "the only real difference between writing for adults or for children is whose eyes I'm looking through."

A239   -----. "The Imprisoned Child." In Blishen, *Thorny Paradise*, pp. 62-64.
Discusses why she writes for children.

A240   CHAMBERS, AIDAN. "Letter from England: Nina Bawden--Storyteller Argent, Children's Writer Proper." *Horn Book* 50 (June 1974):264-68.
Praises her "clean, uncluttered but well-sculptured style," her characterizations, and her skill in portraying relationships in *Carrie's War*.

A241   CROUCH, MARCUS. *The Nesbit Tradition*, pp. 46-47.
Characterizes *A Handful of Thieves* as coming "dangerously near to being a model children's novel."

A242   INGLIS, FRED. *Promise of Happiness*, pp. 267-70.
Praises *Carrie's War*, although he feels Bawden lacks "fight." The end of the book "creates, in its straight, workmanlike prose, the reality of what most threatens our children--that they will lose those they most love, uncomprehendingly destroy what they most cherish."

A243   JONES, CORNELIA, and WAY, OLIVIA R. *British Children's Authors*, pp. 41-48.
In an interview Bawden discusses her background, philosophy, and method of working. Includes an annotated bibliography of her works.

A244   MOSS, ELAINE. "Nina Bawden: An Author for Today." *Signal* 4 (January 1971):28-33.
An appreciative overview.

A245   REES, DAVID. "Making the Children Stretch: Nina Bawden." In *Marble in the Water*, pp. 128-40.
Traces Bawden's development as a writer, from *The Secret Passage* to *Carrie's War* and *Peppermint Pig*, which he considers her finest work. She demands much from children, but does not offer more than they can grasp.

A246   TOWNSEND, JOHN ROWE. *A Sounding*, pp. 18-29.
Traces Bawden's development as writer for children from "fictional cliché" to the "wholly admirable" *Carrie's War* (1973) and *The Peppermint Pig* (1975).

A247   TUCKER, NICHOLAS. *The Child and the Book*, pp. 147-51.
       Examines Bawden's treatment of the "misapprehensions" of her
       child characters, which "are always due to the romantic, sometimes
       superficial perception of things of younger children's thinking."

A248   -----. "Getting Used to Things as They Are: Nina Bawden as a Chil-
       dren's Novelist." *CLE*, o.s., no. 13 (1974):35-44.
       Suggests that the tension between realism and fantasy, present to
       some extent in all fiction, is "particularly evident" in Bawden's work.
       Attempts to show why this characteristic is especially relevant to the
       young.

BAYNES, PAULINE (1922-   )

A249   MOSS, ELAINE. "Pauline Baynes: Mistress of the Margin." *Signal* 11
       (May 1973):88-93.
       Reports on a visit to Baynes to discuss her life and work.

B.B. [Denys James Watkins-Pitchford] (1905-   )

A250   FISHER, MARGERY. "'B.B.' as a Writer for Young People." *Bookbird*
       5, no. 3 (1967):21-27.
       Provides an overview of B.B.'s wide-range of illustrations and
       writings, from fairy tales to animal stories to nature adventures.

A251   RYAN, J.S. "B.B.--Delineator of England's Natural Glories." *Orana* 19
       (February 1983):11-24.
          Provides an extensive critique of B.B.'s writings and praises his
       ability to make us "much more imaginatively aware of the myriad
       perceptions, sympathies, and intuitions available to each one of us."

"Beauty and the Beast"

A252   MINTZ, THOMAS. "The Meaning of Rose in 'Beauty and the Beast.'"
       Psychoanalytic Review 56, no. 4 (1969-70):615-20.
       Explores the symbolism of the rose in the context of "Beauty and
       the Beast."

BEHN, HARRY (1898-1973)

A253   BADER, BARBARA. *American Picturebooks*, pp. 485-87.
       Provides insight into the charm and unique character of the Peter
       Pauper Press book *All Kinds of Time*.

A254   BEHN, HARRY. *Chrysalis*. New York: Harcourt, Brace & World,
       1968, 92 pp.
       A study of childhood and poetry. Includes reminiscences and
       comments on children, the creative process, Haiku, and poetry for
       children.

A255   -----. "On Haiku." *Horn Book* 40 (April 1964):166-67.
       Comments on the nature of Haiku, with examples from his own
       translations.

A256   -----. "Poetry for Children." *Horn Book* 42 (April 1966):163-75.
       Expresses his views about poetry for children, illuminated by

examples from his own poetry.

A257   GROFF, PATRICK J.   "Children's Poetry of Harry Behn."   *EE* 38
        (November 1960):441-46.
            Evaluates Behn's poetry in terms of rhythm, sound, sense, and
        suggestion.

A258   RICHARDSON, CARMEN C.   "Harry Behn: Wizard of Childhood." *EE*
        51 (October 1974):975-76, 1002.
            This appreciative overview seeks the key to Behn's success in
        communicating both the innocent view of a child and the wisdom of
        a sage.

A259   ROOP, PETER.   "Profile: Harry Behn."   *LA* 62 (January 1985):92-94.
            Finds the key to understanding Behn's poetry for children in
        Chrysalis and *A Golden Hive.*

A260   RUMMEL, MARY KAY.   "Haiku Translations of Harry Behn."   *LA* 58
        (April 1981):431-36.
            Analyzes Behn's approach to Haiku for the classroom teacher.

BEISSEL, HENRY (1929-   )

A261   CARNEGIE, DAVID.   "All Things Have Their Season: Henry Beissel's
        Children's Drama."   *CCL* 8-9 (1977):74-83.
            Analyzes the Canadian author's children's and marionette plays.

BEMELMANS, LUDWIG (1898-1962)

A262   BADER, BARBARA.   "Ludwig Bemelmans."   *American Picturebooks*,
        pp. 47-51.
            Considers *Castle Number Nine* "Bemelmans's best story, and also
        his most interestingly illustrated book," despite the success of the
        Madeline stories.

A263   BEMELMANS, LUDWIG.   "Caldecott Award Acceptance."   *Horn Book*
        30 (August 1954):270-75.   (Reprinted in *Junior Bookshelf* 18, no. 6
        [December 1954]:284-89.)
            Tells of the origins of *Madeline.*

A264   -----.   "The Humor of Ludwig Bemelmans."   *Publishers Weekly* 134 (22
        October 1938):1508-10.
            A brief biocritical overview.

A265   -----.   "The Story of Bemelmans's *Madeline.*"   *Publishers Weekly* 178
        (14 November 1960):16-17.
            Tells of *Madeline*'s origins.

A266   GRAHAM, MARGARET BLOY.   "Artist's Choice."   *Horn Book* 31
        (December 1955):474-75.
            Reflections on *Parsley*, the pictures and text.

A267   GROFF, PATRICK J.   "The Children's World of Ludwig Bemelmans."
        EE 43 (October 1966):559-68.   (Reprinted in Hoffman, *Authors and
        Illustrators*, pp. 6-18.)
            Relates Bemelmans's life and childhood to his writing and art.
        Comments on the quality of his work and offers some interpretation.

A268   MASSEE, MAY. "Ludwig Bemelmans." *Horn Book* 30 (August 1954):263-69.
Mainly biographical background with an excerpt from *Father, Dear Father* (1953).

A269   ROOT, SHELTON L., Jr. "Ludwig Bemelmans and His Books for Children." *EE* 34 (January 1957):3-12.
Examines Bemelmans's own statements about his writing, interviews Bemelmans's editor, and studies the stories to trace the artist's development as an author-illustrator. Compares earlier efforts (*Hansi, The Golden Basket*) with some of his less successful books (*Parsley, The High World*) and the highly successful Madeline Books.

BENARY-ISBERT, MARGOT (1889-1979)

A270   BENARY-ISBERT, MARGOT. "An Author's Reflections." *Library Journal* 82 (15 May 1957):1329-34.
Talks about her writing, her childhood, and children and reading. Concludes that children need books about people who have struggled against all odds and won because they believed in something, and also about people who succumbed but kept their integrity, "even in defeat."

A271   -----. "The Need of Understanding in Our Shrinking World." *Horn Book* 31 (June 1955):167-76.
The author tells how and why her postwar experience led her to write for children, and how she has used some of her experiences in her books.

A272   CROUCH, MARCUS. *The Nesbit Tradition*, pp. 180-82.
Reviews *The Ark*. "Her finest achievement is in the character of Margret, who more than the others carries into peacetime the scars of war."

A273   KINGSTON, CAROLYN T. *Tragic Mode*, pp. 108-10.
Analyzes *The Ark* in terms of its handling of the theme of war.

BENÉT, LAURA (1884-1979)

A274   BENÉT, LAURA. "The Childhood of Genius." *Horn Book* 14 (January-February 1938):12-18.
The author describes her frustrating search for indications in the boy Shelley of the poet who was to come.

A275   GRAY, ELIZABETH JANET. "Ariel in the Making." *Horn Book* 14 (January-February 1938):7-10.
A highly favorable review of *The Boy Shelley*.

BENNETT, RAINEY (1907-   )

A276   VANDERGRIFT, KAY E. *Child and Story*, pp. 157-60.
Analyzes *The Secret Hiding Place* in terms of character and playful humor.

BERKOVÁ, DAGMAR (1922-   )

A277   STEHLÍKOVÁ, BLANKA. "Czech Artist Dagmar Berková." *Bookbird*

13 (1976):67-74.
A profile of the Czech illustrator, including lists of illustrations, exhibitions, and awards.

BERNA, PAUL (1913-   )

A278   CROUCH, MARCUS. *The Nesbit Tradition*, pp. 40-42.
Berna depicts a classless and sexless society in *A Hundred Million Franks*. "Not since *Emil* (Kästner) have children been depicted with such spirit and unsentimental affection." Considers it Berna's best.

A279   NORRIS, RALPH E. "In Search of a Head." *Junior Bookshelf* 42, no. 4 (August 1978):183-86.
Identifies the horse as a symbol for the gang in *A Hundred Million Franks*, and discusses the importance of the fact that both are headless.

BERTON, PIERRE (1920-   )

A280   SIGMAN, JOSEPH. "Pierre Berton and the Romantic Tradition." *CCL* 7 (1977):21-27.
Although Berton's *The Secret World of Og* is grounded in the conventions of the romantic tradition, Sigman points out that his outlook is essentially hostile to the romantic vision of childhood's dreams and magic.

A281   STOTT, JON C. "An Interview with Pierre Berton." *CCL* 23-24 (1981):4-19.
A wide-ranging interview that includes some comments on *The Secret World of Og*, said to be one of the most popular Canadian children's books of all times.

BESKOW, ELSA (1874-1953)

A282   ØRVIG, MARY. "Elsa Beskow Maartman, 1874-1953." *TON* 22 (April 1966):240-52.
Examines Beskow's work within the context of her life and times. Includes a bibliography of her books, indicating those that have been translated and lists material about Beskow in Swedish.

BEST, HERBERT (1894-1981)

A283   MacKENZIE, JEAN KENYON. Review of *Garram the Hunter*. *Horn Book* 6 (May 1930):155-61.
Favorable early review. "A full book, and the reading of it will give a boy a fine full feeling."

A284   SCHMIDT, NANCY. *Children's Fiction About Africa*, pp. 112-14.
"Although Garram, an African, is the hero of the novel, the perspective of the novel is Euroamerican." Points out that 1930s stereotypes of Africa are perpetuated in *Garram the Hunter*.

BILECK, MARVIN (1920-   )

A285   BADER, BARBARA. *American Picturebooks*, pp. 478-80.
Praises Bileck's distinctive style of illustration.

BISHOP, CLAIRE HUCHET

A286   KINGSTON, CAROLYN. *Tragic Mode*, pp. 10-11.
Analyzes *All Alone* in terms of its theme of rejection.

A287   -----. *Tragic Mode*, pp. 105-7.
Analyzes *Pancakes-Paris* in terms of the theme of war.

A288   LANES, SELMA. "A Case for *The Five Chinese Brothers*." *School Library Journal* 24 (October 1977):90-91.
Defends the book against Albert V. Schwartz's attack.

A289   SCHWARTZ, ALBERT V. "The *Five Chinese Brothers*: Time to Retire." *IRBC* 8, no. 3 (1977):3-7.
Condemns *Five Chinese Brothers* for peddling racism and misanthropy, and argues that it should be retired. Summarizes the book's reviewing history and quotes Asians who oppose the book.

BLAKE, QUENTIN (1932-   )

A290   BLAKE, QUENTIN. "Wild Washerwomen, Hired Sportsmen, and Enormous Crocodiles." *Horn Book* 57 (October 1981):505-13.
Comments on his illustrations, his philosophy of illustrating, and his way of working.

A291   MOSS, ELAINE. "Quentin Blake." *Signal* 16 (January 1975):33-39.
Discusses the contributions of the humorist to children's illustration.

BLAKE, WILLIAM (1757-1827)

A292   HEARN, MICHAEL PATRICK. "William Blake's Illustrations for Children's Books." *American Book Collector* 2, no. 2 (March-April 1981):33-43.
Examines Blake's illustrations for children's books, all of which "possess something of the Blakean spirit."

BLEGVAD, ERIK (1923-   )

A293   BLEGVAD, ERIK. *Self-Portrait*. Reading, Mass.: Addison-Wesley, 1979, 32 pp.
The Danish-born illustrator discusses his life and his work in this self-portrait.

BLUME, JUDY (1938-   )

A294   CHAMBERS, NANCY, and SALWAY, LANCE. "Endpapers." *Signal* 30 (September 1979):169-76, passim.
Chambers and Salway exchange lengthy comments on Judy Blume and Robert Cormier.

A295   COUNCIL ON INTERRACIAL BOOKS FOR CHILDREN. "Old Values Surface in Blume Country." *IRBC* 7, no. 5 (1976):8-10.
Argues that although Blume gives sex the "now" treatment, she depicts mostly traditional middle-class values concerning sex roles, competition, and racial and ethnic issues.

A296   DONELSON, KENNETH. *"Seventeenth Summer* and *Forever* as Love-Romances." In *Literature for Today's Young Adults*, pp. 214-15.
Analyzes *Forever* as a love-romance and compares it with Maureen Daly's *Seventeenth Summer*.

A297   EAGLEN, AUDREY. "Answers from Blume Country: An Interview with Judy Blume." *TON* 34 (Spring 1978):233-43.
In an interview Blume discusses many of the issues raised in the *IRBC* article "Old Values Surface in Blume Country" (A295). Donnarae MacCann responds in *TON* 35 (Fall 1978):33-38.

A298   GARBER, STEPHEN M. "Judy Blume: New Classicism for Kids." *English Journal* 73 (April 1984):56-59.
"The main character of a Judy Blume novel is an illustration of a problem." The books are classical in that they focus attention on the middle-class experience; they provide a pattern for life, but they offer only norms, not a transformation of reality.

A299   HAMILTON, LYNNE. "Blume's Adolescents: Coming of Age in Limbo." *Signal* 41 (May 1983):88-96.
Although sexual taboos have been lifted, "throughout Blume's novels the age-old image of the female, a dependent, ineffectual creature whose importance can only be derived from a man, remains drooped over its pedestal." Examines Blume's "demystifying" of potentially transforming crises in *Are You There God? It's Me, Margaret*; *Deenie*; *Tiger Eyes*; and *Forever*. "Her heroines adjust and cope; they do not suffer and change."

A300   HAUCK, ROSEANN PHILOMENA. "Judy Blume and Beyond." ERIC Educational Document Reproduction Service, 1982, 14 pp., ED 220 859.
Compares teachers' and students' responses to Judy Blume.

A301   -----. "The World of Judy Blume." Ph.D. dissertation, University of Oregon, 1981, 148 pp., DA 42:3414A.
Investigates the world as depicted in nine of Judy Blume's juvenile novels, concentrating on (1) the nature of the environment in the novels, (2) the major problems of the main character, and (3) the values presented.

A302   JACKSON, RICHARD W. "Books that Blume." *EE* 51 (September 1974):779-83.
Blume's editor provides insight into the editorial and writing processes.

A303   MAYNARD, JOYCE. "Coming of Age with Judy Blume." *New York Times Magazine*, 3 December 1978, pp. 80-86, 90, 92, 94.
Parents comment on Blume's books, particularly *Forever*.

A304   PORTE, BARBARA ANN. "Point of View: What Is It About Books by Judy Blume?" *Advocate* 2, no. 1 (Fall 1982):44-49.
Examines the appeal of Blume's books and concludes part of it lies in the fact that children, like adults, like to read about themselves.

A305   REES, DAVID. "Not Even for a One Night Stand." In *Marble in the*

Water, *pp. 173-84, Boston: Horn Book, 1980.*

A highly critical attack on Blume for trivial focus, poor quality language, and moral and social deficiencies. Especially critical of *Are You There God, It's Me, Margaret?* as "a bore and an embarrassment, a complete waste of one's time. . . . the ultimate in the read-it-and throw-it-away kind of book."

A306   ROBERSON, TERRI. "Judy Blume's *Forever*, and Other Novels: Are Teachers Ready for Them?" *Focus: Teaching English Language Arts* 3, no. 2 (Winter 1977):35-39. (Also available from ERIC Educational Document Reproduction Service, ED 157 082.)

Examines in terms of the problems and solutions in a number of Blume's novels.

A307   SAUNDERS, PAULA C. "Judy Blume as Herself." *Writer's Digest* 59 (February 1979):18-24.

In an extensive interview Blume discusses herself and her work.

A308   SIEGEL, R.A. "Are You There God? It's Me, Me, ME!: Judy Blume's Self-Absorbed Narrators." *L&U* 2 (Fall 1978):72-77.

The key to Blume's popularity lies in the way her narrative techniques "are used to communicate a style of experiencing and perceiving the self and the world and a definition of what it means to be a pre-adolescent child in suburban America." Concludes that her books are "poor nourishment for the imagination of children."

A309   WINTLE, JUSTIN, and FISHER, EMMA. *Pied Pipers*, pp. 308-20, Blume discusses her life and work in an interview.

BLYTON, ENID (1897-1968)

A310   BARKER, KEITH. "The Use of Food in Enid Blyton's Fiction." *CLE*, n.s. 13, no. 1 (Spring 1982):4-11.

Blyton "carried the use of food in her books to new heights (or, perhaps, depths) and in so doing demonstrated the manipulation of both her readers and her own subconscious creative forces."

A311   BLISHEN, EDWARD. "Who's Afraid of Enid Blyton?" *Where*, July 1967. (Reprinted in Culpan, *Variety Is King*, pp. 79-82.)

Argues that Blyton's banality dampens the imagination. He suspects that Blyton's supporters find "her bland insipid world, with its strict nursery basis, a comforting one."

A312   CADOGAN, MARY, and CRAIG, PATRICIA. *You're A Brick*, pp. 336-47.

Sees "a decline in the adventure story which culminates in the books of Enid Blyton." Analyzes Blyton's appeal to children and uses *Six Bad Boys* ("perhaps [her] nastiest story") as an example of her techniques and her use of the "happy family" motif.

A313   CULLINGFORD, CEDRIC. "Why Children Like Enid Blyton." *New Society* 9 (August 1979):290-91.

Maintains that "the attraction lies precisely in the predictability that teachers often so object to."

A314   DIXON, BOB. "The Nice, the Naughty and the Nasty: The Tiny World of Enid Blyton." *CLE*, o.s., no. 15 (1974):43-61. (Reprinted

in *Catching Them Young*, pp. 56-73.)
Examines Blyton's ideological basis, as pronounced in her prefaces and as exemplified in the Famous Five series. An editorial comment by Kenneth Sterck follows. Brian Alderson responds in *CLE*, o.s., no. 17 (Summer 1975):101-3.

A315 DOHM, JANICE. "The Work of Enid Blyton." In Ford, *Young Writers, Young Readers*, pp. 99-106. (Also in *Journal of Education* and reprinted in Culpan, *Variety is King*, pp. 83-88.)
Analyzes the reasons for Blyton's popularity.

A316 INGLIS, FRED. *Promise of Happiness*, pp. 186-91.
"No book which aims to deal ambitiously with children's reading can simply condemn the novels of Enid Blyton and have done with her. . . . Enid Blyton invites children to hold her hand on a walk through an adventure recounted with such flatness both of diction and of representation that any reader could be sure that no threat either to experience or to technique lurked in any sentence."

A317 McKELLAR, PETER. "Enid Blyton." In Meek, *Cool Web*, pp. 222-25. (Reprinted from *Imagination and Thinking: A Psychological Analysis* [London: Cohen & West, 1957].)
Blyton describes her writing process.

A318 RAY, SHEILA. *The Blyton Phenomenon*. London: Andre Deutch, 1982, 246 pp.
The first half of the book concentrates on the history of the public's reception and rejection of Blyton's books, whereas the second half examines the question of why children like her books and analyzes critical consideration of her Noddy and nursery stories, pp. 132-39; her fantasies, pp. 140-51; her holiday adventure stories, pp. 152-70; her detective fiction, pp. 171-77; her circus stories, pp. 178-84; her family stories, pp. 185-94; and her school stories, pp. 195-200. Includes a bibliography of criticism and Blyton's books.

A319 SHAVIT, ZOHAR. "The Portrayal of Children in Popular Literature. The Case of Enid Blyton." In Escarpit, *Portrayal of the Child*, pp. 315-32.
Finds that Enid Blyton and Carolyn Keene exemplify the way writers of popular children's literature manage to create temporary illusions of "an exclusive children's world."

A320 STONEY, BARBARA. *Enid Blyton*. London: Hodder & Stoughton, 1974, 252 pp.
Concentrates on biography rather than criticism.

A321 TINDALL, GILLIAN. Review. *New Statesman* (27 September 1974):434.
Reviews Barbara Stoney's biography of Enid Blyton, finding it "never quite gets to grips with the peculiar element of Enid Blyton's tractive but positively repulsive to many adults."

A322 TUCKER, NICHOLAS. "The Blyton Enigma." *CLE*, o.s., no. 19 (Winter 1975):191-97. (Reprinted in Culpan, *Variety is King*, pp. 72-78.)
Surveys reviews of Barbara Stoney's unflattering biography and takes up a cudgel in Blyton's defense. She was "on the child's side" and also "mastered her craft as a novelist." Explores other reasons

for her popularity with children despite critical disapproval.

A323   -----. *The Child and the Book*, pp. 105-16.
         Provides fascinating insights into Blyton's appeal for children:
         the child heroes, the reliance on cliché and simplification that allows
         the stories to "move at a truly spanking pace," her identification with
         the child's own "egocentric, quasi-magical views about life," the
         "theme of children having everything their own way." Maintains that
         Blyton was sometimes a "more skillful writer for children than she
         has been given credit for," and suggests further avenues of approach
         to her work.

A324   WELCH, COLIN. "Dear Little Noddy." *Encounter* 10, no. 1 (January
         1958):18-22. (Reprinted in *New Zealand Libraries* 21, no. 9 [1958].)
         A parent complains of lack of depth in the highly popular
         Noddy books. "In this witless, spiritless, snivelling, sneaking doll the
         children of England are expected to find themselves reflected."

A325   WOODS, MICHAEL. "The Uses of Blyton." *New Society*, 19 September 1974, pp. 731-33.
         Surveys teachers' views of Blyton's books. Finds hostility soften-
         ing.

A326   WRIGHT, PETER. "Five Run Away Together--Should We Let Them
         Back?" *English in Education* 14, no. 1 (Spring 1980):16-22.
         Argues that Blyton's books provide children with "a sense of
         security . . . a resting place," and that many of her questionable
         attitudes "are being defused by the passage of time."

BOND, MICHAEL (1926-   )

A327   BLOUNT, MARGARET. "Animals are Equal: A Bear in a London
         Family." In *Animal Land*, pp. 307-22.
         Analyzes Paddington as a bear who "has joined the human race
         without the transition really showing."

A328   BOND, MICHAEL. "Jumping in at the Deep End: On Writing for
         Children." *Horn Book* 56 (June 1980):335-39.
         The creator of Paddington Bear discusses his background, meth-
         ods, and goals in writing.

A329   JONES, CORNELIA, and WAY, OLIVIA R. *British Children's Authors*,
         pp. 49-54.
         In an interview Bond discusses his background, philosophy, and
         method of working. Includes an annotated bibliography of his works.

BONHAM, FRANK (1914-   )

A330   BONHAM, FRANK. "The World of Rufus Henry." *Horn Book* 42
         (February 1966):34-36.
         Tells of exploring the world of gangs as background for *Durango
         Street*.

BONTEMPS, ARNA (1902-73)

A331   BONTEMPS, ARNA. "The *Lonesome Boy* Theme." *Horn Book* 42
         (December 1966):672-80.
         Reflects upon the significance of the lonesome boy theme in his

own works.

A332   -----. "Sad-Faced Author." *Horn Book* 15 (January-February 1939):7-12.
        The story behind the *Sad-Faced Boy.*

BORLAND, HAL (1900-1978)

A333   BELL, LOREN C. "The Onion and *When the Legends Die.*" *English Journal* 73 (November 1984):56-57.
        Outlines eight layers in Tom Black's circular journey back to "the heart of things."

BORN, ADOLPH (1930-   )

A334   STEHLÍKOVÁ BLANKA. "Adolf Born and the Development of Czech Book Illustration for Children." *Phaedrus* 9 (1982):22-26.
        An in-depth discussion of Born's work within the context of the development of Czech book illustration.

BOSTON, LUCY M. (1892-   )

A335   BLATT, GLORIA. "Profile: Lucy M. Boston." *LA* 60 (February 1983):220-25.
        Reports on a visit to Boston at her home, with comments on the way its various elements have been worked into her stories. Includes photographs and a bibliography of works by Boston.

A336   BOSTON, LUCY M. "Christmas at Green Knowe." *Horn Book* 31 (December 1955):471-73.
        A description of Green Knowe, particularly of events in the music room at Christmas time, and how these helped to inspire Boston's fantasies.

A337   -----. "The Place That Is Green Knowe." *Junior Bookshelf* 26 (December 1962):295-302. (Reprinted in *Horn Book* 39 [June 1963]:259-64 and in Meek, *Cool Web*, pp. 216-21 as "A Message from Green Knowe.")
        Discusses her house, "which is the underlying symbol" in all her books, her conception of children's books as works of art, and a little of her background.

A338   CAMPBELL, ALASDAIR. "Children's Writers: 4. Lucy Boston." *School Librarian* 26 (September 1978):212-17.
        Attempts to convince librarians that Boston is "potentially a popular author, as well as an outstandingly good one."

A339   CHAMBERS, AIDAN. "Why the Children of Green Knowe?" In "The Reader in the Book." *Signal* 23 (May 1977):64-68. (Reprinted in Chambers, *Signal Approach*, pp. 267-75.)
        Applies the critical theory of the "implied reader" to *The Children of Green Knowe.*

A340   CROUCH, MARCUS. "Lucy Boston at 80." *Junior Bookshelf* 36, no. 6 (December 1972):355-57.
        Brief critical reflections on Boston's work.

A341 HOLLINDALE, PETER. "The Novels of L.M. Boston." In Butts, *Good Writers*, pp. 25-33.

Surveys Boston's dominant themes, the sense of place, of space, of time. Sees "continuity and change" as her most important themes, and "displacement" as a close second. Relates her fiction to her autobiography, *Memory in a House*.

A342 JONES, CORNELIA, and WAY, OLIVIA R. *British Children's Authors*, pp. 55-64.

In an interview Boston discusses her background, philosophy, and method of working. Includes an annotated bibliography of her works.

A343 MEEK, MARGARET. "A Private House." In Meek, *Cool Web*, pp. 325-30. (Also in *TLS*, 15 June 1973.)

Uses Boston's autobiography, *Memory In a House*, as a basis for examining her fiction.

A344 REES, DAVID. "Green Thought in a Green Shade--L.M. Boston." In *Painted Desert*, pp. 1-16.

Contends that *A Stranger at Green Knowe* and *An Enemy at Green Knowe* are the best of the Green Knowe books, and agrees with John Rowe Townsend that *The Sea Egg* is her best work. Concludes that it is "the power of a particular place" that distinguishes Boston and gives her work a richness.

A345 ROBBINS, SIDNEY. "A Nip of Otherness, Like Life: The Novels of Lucy Boston." *CLE*, o.s., no. 6 (1971):5-16.

Praises Boston's originality and depth. "Here is, surely, a 'classic' series of children's stories which, though hardly 'safe' in any superficial sense, will set free and extend the imagination and feeling of those children who are enabled to absorb them."

A346 ROSE, JASPER. *Lucy Boston*. New York: Henry Z. Walck, 1965, 71 pp.

Includes a biographical sketch and vivid personal impressions of Boston. Emphasizes her appeal to a wide range of ages, her skill and excellence as a writer, her plotting, her mysteriousness, and her affinities with the Victorians.

A347 ROSENTHAL, LYNNE. "The Development of Consciousness in Lucy Boston's *The Children of Green Knowe*." *Children's Literature* 8 (1980):53-67.

A Jungian analysis that sees the work in terms of its attempt to help children with the uncertainty of modern life by providing "images and processes by which they might recover lost wholeness." The recurring image of the ark and the theme of rescue are explored.

A348 STOTT, JON C. "From Here to Eternity: Aspects of Pastoral in the Green Knowe Series." *Children's Literature* 11 (1983): 145-55.

"Whereas most pastorals show the impossibility of escaping the destructiveness of time, the Green Knowe books imply that those who have fully experienced and completely committed themselves to the pastoral world will always remain part of it."

A349 TOWNSEND, JOHN R. *Sense of Story*, pp. 28-38.

Discusses Boston's house as the center for her tales, but praises the *Sea Egg*, which is dominated by the sea, not the house, as her finest book.

A350   TRAVERS, P.L. "World Beyond World." *Book Week*, 7 May 1967, pp. 4-5. (Reprinted in Haviland, *Children and Literature*, pp. 246-49.)
Discusses *The Sea Egg* and The Green Knowe Books. Points out that in Boston's work "one is never aware that any of the stories has either beginning or end, the point of view is always mature, and the characters are perfectly balanced and juxtaposed, like those in a fairy tale."

A351   WINTLE, JUSTIN, and FISHER, EMMA. *Pied Pipers*, pp. 277-84.
Boston discusses her life and work in an interview.

BOUTET DE MONVEL, MAURICE (1850-1913).

A352   HEARN, MICHAEL PATRICK. "Maurice Boutet de Monvel: Master of the French Picture Book." *Horn Book* 55 (April 1979):170-81.
An overview of the career, chief accomplishments, significance and influence of the French illustrator.

A353   LANES, SELMA G. "A Second Look: Joan of Arc." *Horn Book* 58 (February 1982):79-83.
Analyzes Boutet de Monvel's successful techniques of illustration in this review of a new edition of his classic *Joan of Arc*.

Boy's Own Paper

A354   MOYLES, R.G. "A *Boy's Own* View of Canada." *CCL* 34 (1984):41-56.
Discusses the images of Canada conveyed by *The Boy's Own Paper*.

BRADBURY, RAY (1920-   )

A355   DIMEO, RICHARD STEVEN. "The Mind and Fantasies of Ray Bradbury." Ph.D. dissertation, University of Utah, 1970, 236 pp., DA 31:3541A.
Explores "the opinions, characters, and central themes of Ray Bradbury for the autobiographical and psychological implications of his symbolism."

A356   DOMINIANNI, ROBERT. "Ray Bradbury's 2026: A Year with Current Value." *English Journal* 73 (November 1984):49-51.
Suggest approaches to *The Martian Chronicles*, particularly the short story "August 2026: There Will Come Soft Rains," for the secondary classroom.

BRANFIELD, JOHN (1931-   )

A357   McMAHON-HILL, GILLIAN. "John Branfield's Novels: 'Writing About Real Issues.'" *CLE*, o.s., no. 12 (September 1973):29-41.
Explores John Branfield's handling of "real issues" of contemporary settings in two novels for young adults, *Nancecuke* and *Sugar Mouse*.

BRAZIL, ANGELA (1869-1947)

A358 FREEMAN, GILLIAN. *The Schoolgirl Ethic: The Life and Works of Angela Brazil.* London: Allen Lane, 1976, 160 pp.
Traces interrelationships between Brazil's life and her books.

A359 MARSH, GEVEN. "Angela Brazil." *Junior Bookshelf* 12 (March 1948):27-31.
Points out ways in which Brazil stands apart from her imitators.

BRENNAN, NICHOLAS (1948-   )

A360 CHAMBERS, AIDAN. "Letter from England: Look Out for Olaf." *Horn Book* 51 (February 1975):26-30.
Praises Brennan's originality, his ablility to draw popular and contemporary sources together, to create a work entirely his own. Discusses *Jasper and the Giant*, *The Wonderful Potion and Other Stories*, and *Olaf's Incredible Machine*.

BRIDGERS, SUE ELLEN (1942-   )

A361 BRIDGERS, SUE ELLEN. "People, Families and Mothers." *ALAN Review* 9, no. 1 (Fall 1981):1, 36. (Also in ERIC Educational Document Reproduction Service, ED 208 419.)
The writer discusses her difficulty in telling people what her books are "about," notably *Home Before Dark*, *All Together Now*, and *Notes for Another Life*, and makes an attempt to do so.

BRIGGS, KATHERINE M. (1898-1980)

A362 HODGES, MARGARET. "Katherine M. Briggs: A Memoir." *CLE*, n.s. 12, no. 4 (1981):209-13.

A363 MOSS, ELAINE. "K.M. Briggs: Novelist." *Signal* 30 (September 1979):133-39.
Discusses the folklorist's novels *Hobberdy Dick* and *Kate Crackernuts*. These demonstrate "through story the important part played in the lives of the people in seventeenth-century England and Scotland by their belief in hobgoblins, ghosts, witchcraft, and devil worship."

A364 PHILIP, NEIL. "The Goodwill of Our Hearts: K.M. Briggs as Novelist." *Folklore* 92, no. 2 (1981):155-59.
Discusses *Hobberdy Dick* and *Kate Crackernuts*.

BRIGGS, RAYMOND (1934-   )

A365 BRIGGS, RAYMOND. "That Blooming Book." *Junior Bookshelf* 38, no. 4 (August 1974):195-96.
Tells of the origins of *Father Christmas*.

A366 CHAMBERS, AIDAN. "Letter from England: *Fungus*, Encore." *Horn Book* 56 (February 1980):88-90.
Chambers champions the controversial *Fungus the Bogeyman*, explaining why he thinks it one of the most significant children's books of the last ten years.

A367   FRITZ, JEAN. "The House That Jack Built." *Horn Book* 42 (December 1966):681-3.
        Describes the way in which Briggs's Mother Goose illustrations fulfill the images in her own mind and experience.

A368   MOSS, ELAINE. "Raymond Briggs: On British Attitudes to the Strip Cartoon and Children's Book Illustration." *Signal* 28 (January 1979):26-33.
        In an interview Briggs discusses the strip cartoon as a combination of two art forms--the narrative and the illustrative--and expresses dismay that the form is not given the critical attention and appreciation he feels it deserves. *Fungus the Bogeyman* and *Father Christmas* are also commented upon at length.

BRINK, CAROL RYRIE (1895-1981)

A369   BRINK, CAROL RYRIE. "*Caddie Woodlawn*; Newbery Medal Winner 1936: Her History." *Horn Book* 12 (July-August 1936):248-50.
        Excerpt from the Newbery Medal acceptance speech. The story behind *Caddie Woodlawn*.

A370   HADLOW, RUTH M. "*Caddie Woodlawn*." *EE* 37 (April 1960): 221-26, 237.
        An enthusiastic appreciation pointing out key incidents and strong points of the book.

A371   ODLAND, NORINE. "Carol Ryrie Brink and *Caddie Woodlawn*." *EE* 45 (April 1968):425-28, 451.
        Discusses the book's background and the methods used in writing it.

BRINSMEAD, H[ESBA] F[AY] (1922-   )

A372   BRINSMEAD, H.F. "How and Why I Write for Young People." *Bookbird* 7, no. 4 (1969):24-26.
        The author explains her motivation for writing and describes "how" she writes; includes an extended example from *Sapphire for September*.

A373   McVITTY, WALTER. "Hesba Fay Brinsmead: Truth and Romantic Vision." In *Innocence and Experience*, pp. 133-62.
        Sees Brinsmead's apparently realistic teenage fiction as actually representing a "fusion between truth and romantic vision." Includes a brief biographical sketch, Brinsmead's own comments, and a bibliography of her books.

A374   TOWNSEND, JOHN ROWE. *Sense of Story*, pp. 39-47.
        Praises Brinsmead's sympathy for the young people she writes about, her strongly realized settings, and her vitality, although he faults her sometimes unsatisfactory story structure and unmemorable male characters. Discusses *Beat of the City*.

BRISLEY, JOYCE LANKESTER (1896-1978)

A375   FACTOR, JUNE. "Joyce Lankester Brisley: An Appreciation." *CLE*, n.s. 10, no. 4 (Winter 1979):163-73.

A study of the Milly-Molly-Mandy stories that, despite their currently unpopular didacticism, retain an appeal. Classifies Brisley as a major "minor" writer.

BROOKE, L[EONARD] L[ESLIE] (1862-1940)

A376   BROOKE, HENRY. *Leslie Brooke and Johnny Crow.* London: Frederick Warne, 1982, 144 pp.
This biography and memoir by Brooke's son includes many comments on Brooke's illustrations and stories and their origins. Includes many reproductions and a checklist of books illustrated by Brooke.

A377   CROUCH, MARCUS S. "Homage to Leslie Brooke." *Junior Bookshelf* 16, no. 2 (July 1952):86-93.
Finds in Brooke's work both "painstaking technical ability and infinite personal kindliness." Ranks him among the very best.

A378   HOGARTH, GRACE. "A Second Look: *Johnny Crow.*" *Horn Book* 59 (February 1983):77-80.
Suggests that the key to Brooke's success continued to appeal to children may be that he was with his own children when he created his books.

A379   *Horn Book.* "L. Leslie Brooke." 17, no. 3 (May-June 1941).
Special Issue. Contains a variety of tributes and appreciations, including a biographical sketch by Anne Carroll Moore and a fine critical analysis by Lillian H. Smith. (Smith's article is reprinted as "A Canadian Tribute to Leslie Brooke" in Fryatt, *Horn Book Sampler*, pp. 224-27.)

A380   MOORE, ANNE CARROLL. "Leslie Brooke: Pied Piper of English Picture Books." *Horn Book* 1 (November 1924):10-13. (Reprinted in Fryatt, *Horn Book Sampler*, pp. 60-62.)
Primarily an appreciative overview.

BROOKS, NOAH (1830-1903)

A381   STREET, DOUGLAS. "*The Fairport Nine*, The American Boy's First Baseball Novel." *Proceedings of the Children's Literature Association* 8 (1981):91-97.
Argues that the one-hundred year old novel, the first to use the sport of baseball as its framework, is still worth reading because of "a remarkably vibrant quality about the writing."

BROOKS, WALTER R[OLLIN] (1886-1958)

A382   CART, MICHAEL. "Freddy, St. Peter, and Me." *CLE*, n.s. 14, no. 3 (Autumn 1983):142-48.
Reminisces about growing up with the Freddy books and examines the qualities they represented.

A383   SALE, ROGER. *Fairy Tales*, pp. 245-58.
Analyzes the Freddy books, especially *Wiggins for President.* Describes Brooks as an author "that anyone can carry around through one's days, because one's days have many situations in them very much like Brooks's."

BROWN, JAMIE

A384   BLACKBURN, WILLIAM. "The Metaphor or the Moral? Didacticism in Contemporary Adolescent Fiction." *CCL* 27-28 (1982):175-76.
    Suggests that with *Superbike!* Brown has arrived at a "way of teaching without moralizing or condescending."

BROWN, MARCIA (1918-   )

A385   BADER, BARBARA. "Marcia Brown." In *American Picturebooks*, pp. 313-22.
    Traces Brown's career and her development as an artist.

A386   BROWN, MARCIA. "Big and Little: Caldecott Award Acceptance." *Horn Book* 38 (August 1962):342-46.
    The story behind *Once a Mouse*. An account by Helen Adams Master of Brown's career in the years between 1955 and 1962 follows, pp. 347-52.

A387   -----. "Caldecott Award Acceptance." *Horn Book* 31 (August 1955):279-90.
    Tells about her background, her philosophy of illustrating children's books, and the background of some of her books. A biographical sketch by her editor, Alice Dalgliesh, follows, pp. 291-95.

A388   -----. "Caldecott Medal Acceptance." *Horn Book* 59 (August 1983):414-22.
    Analyzes the origins of *Shadow*, the techniques she used to create it, and the effect she wanted to achieve. A biographical sketch by Janet A. Lovanger follows, pp. 423-26.

A389   -----. "My Goals as an Illustrator." *Horn Book* 43 (June 1967):305-16.
    Discusses her goals, techniques, and the necessity of matching the illustration to the work. Also speaks of trends in illustration and three of her own works: *Once A Mouse*, *The Wild Swans*, and "The Story of Paka'a and His Son Ku."

A390   -----. "*Shadow*: The Voice of Illustration." *Advocate* 3, no. 1 (Fall 1983):12-18.
    Reviews the origins of *Shadow* and defends it against critics who see it as stereotyped.

A391   HOWARD, ELIZABETH F. "Shadows and Marcia Brown's *Shadow*." *Horn Book* 59 (October 1983):621-23.
    Discusses some of the controversial interpretations and accusations of racial stereotypes that have surrounded *Shadow*.

A392   KENT, NORMAN. "Marcia Brown: Author and Illustrator." *American Artist* 27 (January 1963):26-31.
    A brief biocritical overview.

A393   PAINTER, HELEN W. "Marcia Brown: A Study in Versatility." *EE* 43 (December 1966):841-55, 876.
    An overview of her life and work, stressing her versatility. Includes references.

A394   WILSON, GERALDINE. Review. *IRBC* 14, nos. 1&2 (1983):33-34.

Feels the book caricatures the religious life of another people in a stylized and disrespectful manner, and reinforces stereotypes of Africa and Africans that have been combatted in recent decades.

BROWN, MARGARET WISE (1910-52)

A395   BADER, BARBARA. *American Picturebooks*, pp. 215-29 passim, 252-64.
Discusses her contributions to the books published by the William R. Scott company on pages 215-29, and provides in-depth interpretations of her creations, particularly *Good-Night Moon*, in the latter section.

A396   BECHTEL, L.S. "Margaret Wise Brown: 'Laureate of the Nursery.'" *Horn Book* 34 (June 1958):172-86. (Reprinted in Hoffman, *Authors and Illustrators*, pp. 19-27.)
A brief bio-critical overview and personal recollection.

A397   BLIVEN, BRUCE, Jr. "Child's Best Seller." *Life* 21 (2 December 1946):59-66.
Brown discusses her life and work in this illustrated interview.

A398   HEINS, ETHEL L. "A Second Look: The Noisy Books." *Horn Book* 52 (December 1976):646-47.
Explores the appeal of The Noisy Books to the young child.

A399   MARCUS, L.S. "Legend of Margaret Wise Brown." *Publishers Weekly* 224 (22 July 1983):74-76.
Summarizes the enduring aspects of Brown's achievements. "No writer since . . . has achieved a voice and vision so knowlingly alert to the sensual immediacies and actual concerns of persons newly aware of the world beyond their toes."

A400   SAUL, E. WENDY. "Children's Literature: A View from the Great Green Room." *Advocate* 2, no. 1 (Fall 1982):16-24.
Applies techniques suggested by Aidan Chambers in "The Reader in the Book" to *Good-Night Moon*, and compares this interpretation with the responses recorded in two parent diaries.

A401   SENDAK, MAURICE. "Artist's Choice." *Horn Book* 31 (August 1955):296-97.
Analyzes the appeal of *The Two Little Trains*, this "miracle" of bookmaking.

BROWN, PALMER (1919-   )

A402   BADER, BARBARA. *American Picturebooks*, pp. 492-94.
Discusses the distinguishing characteristics of Brown's four books.

BROWN, ROY (1921-82)

A403   SHADIOW, LINDA. "The Author as Villain: The Treatment of Outsiders in Four Roy Brown Mysteries." *ALAN Review* 9 (Fall 1981):6-7. (Also in ERIC Educational Document Reproduction Service, ED 208 419.)
Accuses Brown of "adding to the fear, uneasiness, and misunderstanding many young adult readers already feel" toward the mentally

ill, the retarded, and other people characterized as "outsiders."

BROWNE, ANTHONY (1923-   )

A404   CHAMBERS, AIDAN.   "Letter from England."   *Horn Book* 56 (April 1980):211-14.

Praises Shirley Hughes and Anthony Browne as foremost representatives of a new wave of English picture-book making.

A405   -----.   "Letter from England: Making Them New."   *Horn Book* 57 (December 1981):703-8.

Analyzes Charles Keeping's illustrations for *The Highwayman* and Browne's for *Hansel and Gretel* as examples of revitalizing old tales.

A406   DOONAN, JANE.   "Talking Pictures: A New Look at *Hansel and Gretel*."   *Signal* 42 (September 1983):123-31.

Examines the way in which Browne's illustrations interpret the folktale.

A407   MARANTZ, SYLVIA, and MARANTZ, KENNETH.   "An Interview with Anthony Browne."   *Horn Book* 61 (November 1985):696-704.

The discussion ranges over Browne's work and the critical response it has received.

The Brownies' Book

A408   SINNETTE, ELINOR D.   "*The Brownies' Book*:   A Pioneer Publication for Children."   In *Black Titan, W.E.B. Dubois: An Anthology by the Editors of "Freedomways*. Boston: Beacon Press, 1970, pp. 164-75.

Describes *The Brownies' Book*, a periodical for children edited by W.E.B. Dubois, whose purpose was "To seek to teach universal love and brotherhood for all little folk, black and brown and yellow and white."

BROWNING, ROBERT (1812-1889)

A409   BLACKBURN, WILLIAM.   "Lifting the Curse of the Roman: Quintus Horatius Flaccus Meets The Pied Piper of Hamelin."   Paper presented at the 34th Annual Meeting of the Rocky Mountain Modern Language Association (Denver, Colorado, October 16-18, 1980).   ERIC Educational Document Reproduction Service, 1980, 23 pp., ED 195 998.

Finds similarities in *The Pied Piper of Hamelin* and Lewis Carroll's *Alice in Wonderland*, especially in the way immutable laws are rearranged in such a way "as to set logic, order, authority, or accepted standards of behavior slightly awry. . . . Both violate the reigning didactic premise that had been in existence since Horace."

A410   QUEENAN, BERNARD.   "The Evolution of the Pied Piper."   *Children's Literature* 7 (1978):104-14.

Traces the historical origins of the Pied Piper of Hamelin.

BRUCE, MARY GRANT (1878-1958)

A411   ALEXANDER, ALISON.   *Billabong's Author*. Sydney: Angus & Robertson, 1979, 150 pp.

This biography of Mary Grant Bruce contains sections on the

writing, and critical reception of the Billabong books. Includes bibliographies.

A412   NIALL, BRENDA. *Seven Little Billabongs: The World of Ethel Turner and Mary Grant Bruce.* Melbourne: Melbourne University Press, 1979, 219 pp.

Outlines the lives and literary careers of the two writers in part 1, and in part 2 concentrates on their novels' themes, characters, family patterns, and depiction of the Australian landscape.

BRUCKNER, KARL (1906-   )

A413   KINGSTON, CAROLYN. *Tragic Mode*, pp. 116-20.

Analyzes *The Day of The Bomb* in terms of its treatment of the theme of war.

BRUNHOFF, JEAN De (1899-1937), and
BRUNHOFF, LAURENT De (1925-   )

A414   DORFMAN, ARIEL. *The Empire's Old Clothes: What the Lone Ranger, Babar, and other Innocent Heroes Do to Our Minds.* New York: Pantheon, 1983, 225 pp.

Includes a lengthy and thoughtful critique of the Babar books as representative of new colonialism, pp. 17-64.

A415   GRAHAM, ELEANOR. "The Genius of De Brunhoff: The Creator of the Babar Books." *Junior Bookshelf* 5 (January 1941):49-56.

Praises Jean De Brunhoff's benevolence, inventions, and understanding of human nature. Also comments on the books' production.

A416   HASKELL, ANN S. *"Babar's Anniversary Album: Six Favorite Stories."* *NYTBR*, 15 November 1981, pp. 49, 68.

Reviews this new collection with its introduction by Maurice Sendak.

A417   HILDEBRAND, ANN M. "Jean De Brunhoff's Advice to Youth: The Babar Books as Books of Courtesy." *Children's Literature* 11 (1983):76-95.

Places the Babar books in the context of French society of the time and makes a convincing case for them as part of the courtesy-book tradition. Argues that they portray a system of behavior written by the absent father for the children who would have to grow up without him.

A418   HÜRLIMANN, BETTINA. "Jean De Brunhoff and the Benevolent Monarchy of King Babar." In *Three Centuries*, pp. 195-200.

Highly critical of Laurent with much praise for Jean.

A419   IMHOLTZ, AUGUST A. "Sanskrit Verses in a Babar Book." *CLE*, n.s. 12, no. 4 (1981):207-8.

Discovers the meaning of the "Song of the Elephants" in *Babar the King* in Sanskrit, and raises questions of possible Sanskrit connections in other Babar books.

A420   LEACH, EDMUND. "Babar's Civilization Analysed." *New Society* 1, no. 12 (20 December 1962):16-17. (Reprinted in Egoff, *Only Connect*, pp. 176-82.)

Suggests that Babar's appeal to adults lies in the carefully structured society of exotic animals, far enough from reality to be comfortable.

A421 MITCHELL, MARGUERITE MacKELLAR. Review. *Horn Book* 9 (February 1933):29-30.
First American review, highly favorable, of original French editions of the *Story of Babar* (*Histoire de Babar*) and *The Travels of Babar* (*Le Voyage de Babar*). "The reviewer admits, rather reluctantly, that these books are intended, probably, only for children." Praises the "dashing simplicity" of the illustrations and the "directness" of the storytelling.

A422 PAYNE, HARRY C. "The Reign of King Babar." *Children's Literature* 11 (1983):96-108.
Suggests that the longstanding appeal of the Babar books to both children and adults lies in their combination of childlike gratification and adult responsibility. Points out that Babar himself creates an "adult" civilized world, whereas most fantasies contain already created worlds ready for the characters to stumble into. "Brunhoff offers a vision of an elephant-child who grows up, in spite of obstacles, with ease, trust and initiative, and who nurtures a society that makes it easy for others to do the same."

A423 RICHARDSON, PATRICK. "Teach Your Baby to Rule." *New Society*, 10 March 1966 pp. 25-26. (Reprinted in Tucker, *Suitable for Children*, pp. 179-83.)
The earlier Babar stories "are a primer in power politics," a "parody reaction" to the dictatorships of the 1930s.

A424 SALE, ROGER. *Fairy Tales*, pp. 12-15.
Analyzes the style and illustrations in *Travels of Babar*.

A425 SENDAK, MAURICE. "Homage to Babar on His 50th Birthday." In *Babar's Anniversary Album*. New York: Random House, 1981, pp. 6-15.
"There is always an underlying emphasis on developing a child's (an elephant child's) personal freedom and individuality through self-control. . . . No one before, and very few since, has utilized the double-spread illustration to such dazzling, dramatic effect." Sendak shares his personal and professional reactions to the Babar books.

A426 WINTLE, JUSTIN, and FISHER, EMMA. *Pied Pipers*, pp. 77-86.
Laurent De Brunhoff discusses his life and work in an interview.

BRYAN, ASHLEY (1923-   )

A427 SWINGER, ALICE K. "Profile: Ashley Bryan." *LA* 61 (March 1984):305-11.
A brief biocritical overview.

BUCHAN, JOHN (1875-1940)

A428 BLACKBURN, WILLIAM. "John Buchan's *Lake of Gold*: A Canadian Imitation of Kipling." *CCL* 14 (1979):5-13.
A comparison with Kipling reveals that "in a fully successful work, the 'Canadian' quality of setting and background must express

itself through situations and characters having some more potent claim on our attention than that conferred by the accidents of geography and historical coincidence."

BUCK, PEARL S. (1892-1973)

A429   KINGSTON, CAROLYN. *Tragic Mode*, pp. 134-38.
Analyzes the theme of loss in *The Beech Tree* and *The Big Wave*.

BULLA, CLYDE ROBERT (1914-   )

A430   GRIESE, ARNOLD A. "Clyde Robert Bulla: Master Story Weaver." *EE* 48 (November 1971):766-78. (Reprinted in Hoffman, *Authors and Illustrators*, pp. 28-40.)
A fine overview of Bulla's work, dwelling on the breadth of his writing, his background, and his wide-ranging interests. Characterizes Bulla as a "master plot weaver," and comments on his empathy and style.

BURCH, ROBERT (1925-   )

A431   BURCH, ROBERT. "Stories from the Front Porch." *ChLAQ* 9, no. 4 (Winter 1984-85):164-67.
Discusses the influences of his rural southern background on his work.

A432   KINGSTON, CAROLYN. *Tragic Mode*, pp. 22-25.
Analyzes the theme of rejection in *Queenie Peavy*.

A433   OLIVER, JO ELLEN. "'Old' and 'New' Realism in Adolescents' Literature." *Journal of Reading* 21 (January 1980):335-38.
Considers *Skinny* an example of the 'old realism' as defined by R. Wald in "Realism in Children's Literature," *LA* (October 1975):938-41.

BURKERT, NANCY EKHOLM (1933-   )

A434   *ART OF NANCY EKHOLM BURKERT.* Edited by David Larkin. Introduction by Michael Danoff. New York: Harper & Row, 1977, 95 pp.
Danoff's introductory essay traces influences on Burkert's art and discusses her philosophy of art and illustration. The book contains numerous black and white and color reproductions of Burkert's illustrations, paintings, and sculptures.

A435   COCHRAN-SMITH, MARILYN. "The Art of Nancy Ekholm Burkert." *ChLAQ* 4, no. 3 (Fall 1979):1, 8-10. (Reprinted in May, *Children and Their Literature*, pp. 117-21.)
Stresses Burkert's sense of place, detail, and authenticity, and discusses the suitability of these elements to the works of fantasy she has illustrated. Includes references.

A436   GARDNER, JOHN. Review of *Snow White*. *NYTBR*, 5 November 1972), pp. 1, 18, 30.
Compares Burkert favorably to Doré and Tenniel, but has less respect for Jarrell's translation. Provides a fine analysis of Burkert's

illustrations for *Snow White* and for Lear's *Scroobious Pip*.

A437   ROSEN, BARBARA. Review of *Snow White and the Seven Dwarfs*. *Children's Literature* 2 (1973):224-25.
Discusses the balance between text and illustration.

BURNETT, FRANCES HODGSON (1849-1924)

A438   BIXLER, PHYLLIS. "Idealization of the Child and Childhood in Frances Hodgson Burnett's *Little Lord Fauntleroy* and Mark Twain's *Tom Sawyer*." In *Research About Nineteenth Century Children and Books: Portrait Studies*. Edited by Selma K. Richardson. Urbana: University of Illinois, Graduate School of Library Science, 1980, pp. 85-96.
Places the idealization of the child in the context of pastoral traditions in literature.

A439   -----. "The Oral-Formulaic Training of a Popular Fiction Writer: Frances Hodgson Burnett." *Journal of Popular Culture* 15, no. 4 (Spring 1982):42-52.
Examines Burnett's use of oral traditions and formulas.

A440   BIXLER, PHYLLIS, and AGOSTA, LUCIEN. "Formula Fiction and Children's Literature: Thornton Waldo Burgess and Frances Hodgson Burnett." *CLE*, n.s. 15, no. 2 (Summer 1984):63-72.
Applies John G. Cawelti's description of formula fiction to an analysis of the works of Thornton Burgess and Frances Hodgson Burnett.

A441   CADOGAN, MARY, and CRAIG, PATRICIA. "Rags To Riches and Riches to Rags." In *You're A Brick*, pp. 60-72.
Explores the "Cinderella quality" of Burnett's books, especially *That Lass O'Lowrie's*.

A442   CARPENTER, HUMPHREY. *Secret Gardens*, pp. 188-90.
Although the Secret Garden is the unifying theme of Carpenter's book he devotes only a few paragraphs to this "last book which uses the Arcadian image quite so confidently."

A443   CATE, DICK. "Uses of Narrative." *EE* 53 (Winter 1971):45-50. (Reprinted in Meek, *Cool Web*, pp. 24-31, as "Forms of Storying: The Inner and Outer Worlds.")
Shows how the various characters in *A Little Princess* use fictionalizing or make-believe on various levels and how this makes the book "realistic."

A444   GOHLKE, MADELON S. "Re-Reading *The Secret Garden*." *College English* 41 (April 1980):894-902. (Discussion in 43 [April 1981]:423-25.]
Examines the book through a combination of "personal reminiscence" and "more conventional literary analysis," and finds that "each side of the transaction illuminates the other."

A445   INGLIS, FRED. *Promise of Happiness*, pp. 111-13.
Highly praises *The Secret Garden* as "a pagan Garden of Eden for children where culture is detached from labour and returned to

creativeness." Links it with Philippa Pearce's *Tom's Midnight Garden*, written forty years later.

A446   KEYSER, ELIZABETH LENNOX. "Quite Contrary: Frances Hodgson Burnett's *The Secret Garden*." *Children's Literature* 11 (1983):1-13.
Argues that Mary's independence and contrariness make her appealing and memorable, but Colin's ascendence in the last third of the book is less successful, reflecting Burnett's own conflict about sex roles.

A447   KOPPES, PHYLLIS BIXLER. "Tradition and the Individual Talent of Frances Hodgson Burnett: A Generic Analysis of *Little Lord Fauntleroy*, *A Little Princess*, and *The Secret Garden*." *Children's Literature* 7 (1978):191-207.
Argues that in *Little Lord Fauntleroy* and *A Little Princess*, Burnett combined the genres of fairy tale and exemplum, and in *The Secret Garden* "she gave symbolic enrichment and mythic enlargement to her poetic vision by adding tropes from a pastoral tradition at least as old as Virgil's *Georgics*."

A448   LASKI, MARGHANITA. *Mrs. Ewing, Mrs. Molesworth, and Mrs. Hodgson Burnett*. London: A. Marhr, 1950, 121 pp.
Provides a critical analysis of Burnett's children's stories on pages 73-96.

A449   LEWIS, NAOMI. "The Road to Misselthwaite." *TLS*, 5 July 1974, pp. 711-12.
Reviews Ann Thwaite's *Waiting for the Party*.

A450   LURIE, ALISON. "Happy Endings." *NYRB*, 28 November 1974, p. 40.
Review of *Waiting for the Party: The Life of Frances Hodgson Burnett* by Ann Thwaite. Explores the reasons for the enduring popularity of *Little Lord Fauntleroy* and *The Secret Garden*.

A451   MacLEOD, ANNE SCOTT. "Ragged Dick and L.L.F.: A Curious Kinship." *Horn Book* 59 (October 1983):613-20.
Despite differences, Horatio Alger's Ragged Dick and Burnett's Little Lord Fauntleroy each represents his creator's idealized version of American boyhood and a "prototype of democratic character."

A452   ROXBURGH, STEPHEN D. "'Our First World': Form and Meaning in the Secret Garden." *CLE*, n.s., 10, no. 3 (Autumn 1979):120-30. (Also in *Proceeding's of the Children's Literature Association* 6 [1979]:165-77.)
Analyzes *The Secret Garden* in terms of Northrop Frye's mythic structures and archetypal modes, finding similarities with T.S. Eliot's "Burnt Norton."

A453   THREADGOLD, ROSEMARY. "*The Secret Garden*: An Appreciation of Frances Hodgson Burnett as a Novelist for Children." *CLE*, n.s., 10, no. 3 (Autumn 1979):113-19.
Attempts to find a key to the lasting popularity of the book through an analysis of its themes and style.

A454   WHITE, ALISON. "Tap-Roots into a Rose Garden." *Children's Literature* 1 (1972):74-76.

Finds parallels in the garden images of T.S. Eliot's "Burnt Norton" and Burnett's *Secret Garden.*

BURNFORD, SHEILA (1918-85)

A455   KERTZER, ADRIENNE E. "Animal Lessons: Correcting the Perspective." *CCL* 12 (1978):85-88.
Reviews *Bel Ria: Dog of War* and finds the animals more fully drawn than the humans.

BURNINGHAM, JOHN (1936-   )

A456   BURNINGHAM, JOHN, and OXENBURY, HELEN. "A Dialogue on Illustrating." In Robinson, M. *Readings in Children's Literature*, pp. 104-23.
Burningham and Oxenbury discuss the course of their careers, their approaches to illustration, and the backgrounds of a number of their books.

BURROUGHS, EDGAR RICE (1875-1950)

A457   FARMER, PHILIP JOSE. "Tarzan Lives." *Esquire* 77 (April 1972):127-31, 195.
An imaginary "interview" with the eighth duke of Greystoke.

A458   HOLTSMARK, ERLING B. *Tarzan and Tradition: Classical Myth in Popular Literature.* Westport, Conn.: Greenwood Press, 1981, 196 pp.
"This study, then, hopes to indicate the precise nature of the relationship of Burroughs' Tarzan to the classical prototypes, not because he needs more readers, but because he merits more serious attention than critics and academicians have hitherto given him."

A459   NESTEBY, JAMES RONALD. "The Tarzan Series of Edgar Rice Burroughs: Lost Races and Racism in American Popular Culture." Ph.D. dissertation, Bowling Green State University, 1978, 263 pp., DA 39:4347A.
Concludes that "Burroughs is a blatant racist who is also capable of satirizing through lost races and cultures his own and American ideas about the development and disintegration of races and cultures. Tarzan represents a rejection of twentieth-century American values, for the values he upholds are from the nineteenth century."

A460   -----. "Tenuous Vine of *Tarzan of the Apes.*" *Journal of Popular Culture* 13 (Winter 1979):483-87.
Explores possible precedents for Burroughs's Tarzan.

A461   ORTH, MICHAEL. "Tarzan's Revenge: A Literary Biography of Edgar Rice Burroughs." Ph.D. dissertation, Claremont Graduate School, 1974, 409 pp., DA 35:3002A.
"Tarzan denied all the values of the industrial, urban society in which Burroughs and his readers lived, and from which they consciously drew their ideals, and thus Burroughs had to deny the source of all his success."

A462   PENDLETON, THOMAS A. "Tarzan of the Papers." *Journal of Popular Culture* 12, no. 4 (Spring 1979):691-701.

Examines the way comic strip versions of Tarzan were able to overcome the literary difficulties inherent in continuing to present, challenge, and maintain interest in a hero with superhuman powers.

A463   PORGES, IRWIN. *Edgar Rice Burroughs: The Man Who Created Tarzan.* Provo, Utah: Brigham Young University Press, 1975, 820 pp.

Although this lengthy biography contains little critical evaluation, it provides extensive background on Burroughs, describes his methods of working, and contains extensive notes and references. Chapter 8, "Tarzan of the Apes," concentrates on the origins of the first of the Tarzan books, Burroughs's themes, and the early critical response.

A464   PRAGER, ARTHUR. "The Victory Cry of the Bull Ape." In *Rascals at Large*, pp. 19-43.

Discusses *Tarzan of the Apes*, outlines the standard Burroughs plot, and pokes fun at Buroughs's prose style. Prager also discusses *Tarzan the Untamed* in his chapter on World War I (pp. 180-86).

A465   SCHMIDT, NANCY. *Children's Fiction About Africa*, pp. 172-74.

Points out that the Tarzan series is full of stereotypes of Africa prevalent at the turn of the century.

A466   TOPPING, GARY. "The Pastoral Ideal in Popular American Literature: Zane Grey and Edgar Rice Burroughs." *Rendezvous* 12, no. 2 (Fall 1977):11-25.

Examines Grey and Burroughs as popular "wilderness cult" writers. Sees Tarzan as "a savage who is unhappy in civilization, yet he is a civilized man who is unhappy in the jungle."

BURTON, HESTER (1913-   )

A467   BURTON, HESTER. "How I Came to Write *Time of Trial.*" *Junior Bookshelf* 28 (July 1964):135-38.

BURTON, VIRGINIA LEE (1909-68)

A468   BADER, BARBARA. *American Picturebooks*, pp. 199-203.

Briefly discusses Burton's achievement as a picture-book artist with a narrative bent.

A469   BURNS, PAUL C., and HINES, RUTH. "Virginia Lee Burton." *EE* 44 (April 1967):331-35.

Relates Burton's books to her life and beliefs, and examines their appeal.

A470   BURTON, VIRGINIA LEE. "Making Picture Books." *Horn Book* 19 (July-August 1943):228-29.

Describes how she made *The Little House* and other books, and iterates her belief in the importance of books for children.

A471   -----. "Symphony in Comics." *Horn Book* 17 (July-August 1941):307-11.

Describes her experiment of working with her son to create *Calico the Wonder Horse or the Saga of Stewy Slinker* in comic-book style. Also analyzes the appeal of comics.

A472   COLBY, JEAN POINDEXTER. "A Book Production Story." *Horn Book* 24 (March-April 1948):110-18.
Depicts the painstaking process that went into producing the detailed design of *Song of Robinhood*, edited by Anne Malcolmson.

A473   KINGMAN, LEE. "Virginia Lee Burton's Dynamic Sense of Design." In *Horn Book* 46 (October-December 1970):449-60, 593-602. (Reprinted in Hoffman, *Authors and Illustrators*, pp. 41-55.)
Provides in-depth analysis of Burton's texts and art.

A474   MacCAMPBELL, JAMES C. "Virginia Lee Burton: Artist-Storyteller." *EE* 33 (January 1956):3-10.
Provides background on Burton's life and discusses her use of devices which appeal to children.

A475   STOTT, JON C. "Pastoralism and Escapism in Virginia Lee Burton's *The Little House*." *North Dakota Quarterly* 49, no. 1 (Winter 1981):33-36.
Sees in *The Little House* "a profound representation of two main aspects of American social history; the fear of spreading urbanization and the yearning for a return to a simpler, rural way of life."

BUSCH, WILHELM (1832-1908)

A476   TAYLOR, R. LORING. "The Ambiguous Legacy of Wilhelm Busch." *Children's Literature* 1 (1972):77-92.
Surveys and analyzes research on Busch, creator of the comic strip "Katzenjammer Kids." Includes a bibliography of German scholarship on Busch.

BYARS, BETSY (1928-   )

A477   BYARS, BETSY. "Beginnings, 'Human Things,' and the Magical Moments." *Proceedings of the Children's Literature Association* 8 (1981):4-8.
Comments on the origins of some of her books.

A478   -----. "Writing for Children." *Signal* 37 (January 1982):3-10.
Tells of the origins of her writings.

A479   CHAMBERS, AIDAN. "Letter from England: Arrows--All Pointing Upward." *Horn Book* 54 (December 1978):680-84.
Discusses changes in Byars's work "coming from her strengthening confidence about her attitudes toward childhood and what fiction can and should offer child readers." Focuses especially on *The Cartoonist* and *Pinballs*.

A480   HANSEN, I.V. "A Decade of Betsy Byars' Boys." *CLE*, n.s. 15, no. 1 (Spring 1984):3-11.
Analyzes Byars's skillful portrayals of small boys.

A481   KUZNETS, LOIS T. "Betsy Byars' Slice of 'American Pie.'" *ChLAQ* 5, no. 4 (1981):31-33.
A brief critical overview.

A482   REES, DAVID. "Little Bit of Ivory--Betsy Byars." In *Painted Desert*, pp. 33-46.

Maintains that Byars's novels all have similar structures, themes, and audience, and display "wit and good sense, a succinct prose style with tense, vivid perceptions and ironical observations of life." Like Jane Austen, Byars works on a "little bit (two inches wide) of ivory."

A483 ROBERTSON, INA. "Profile: Betsy Byars--Writer for Today's Child." *LA* 57 (March 1980):328-34.
A brief biocritical overview, including Byars's response to a questionnaire. Includes bibliographies of secondary materials and of children's books by Byars.

A484 SEGEL, ELIZABETH. "Betsy Byars: An Interview." *CLE*, n.s. 13, no. 4 (Winter 1982):171-79.
Touches on her life and childhood and briefly discusses many of her books, their technique and background.

A485 WATSON, KEN. "The Art of Betsy Byars." *Orana* 16 (February 1980):3-5.
Traces Byars's development of a more economical style and tighter plot construction.

CALDECOTT, RANDOLPH (1846-86)

A486 BODGER, JOAN H. "Caldecott Country." *Horn Book* 37 (June 1961):227-28.
Caldecott's pictures come alive for a family who visits the places where he lived.

A487 ENGEN, RODNEY K. *Randolph Caldecott: Lord of the Nursery.* London: Oresko, 1976, 104 pp.
A biocritical overview, followed by a well-illustrated catalog of Caldecott's work, including his books.

A488 HEARN, MICHAEL PATRICK. Introduction to *The Caldecott Aesop: Twenty Fables Illustrated by Randolph Caldecott.* Garden City, N.Y.: Doubleday, 1978, pp. 1-6.
Hearn comments on Alfred Caldecott's handling of the text and Randolph Caldecott's illustrations. He analyzes the publishing history of the fables and of this particular edition, first published in 1883.

A489 HUTCHINS, MICHAEL. "Caldecott's Gentle Art with Children." *Penrose Annual* 72 (1980):145-56.
Primarily a brief biographical account thath includes discussion and illustrations of the printing processes used to create the *Three Jovial Huntsmen*. Characterizes Caldecott as "a superb storyteller who could develop a narrative with spontaneous, witty drawings that delighted children and adults alike."

A490 LAWS, FREDERICK. "Randolph Caldecott." In Egoff, *Only Connect*, pp. 317-25. (Reprinted from *Saturday Book* #16.)
Analyzes Caldecott's technique as an illustrator, and his place in the history and development of book illustration.

A491 VAN STOCKUM, HILDA. "Caldecott's Pictures in Motion." *Horn Book* 22 (March-April 1946):119-25
Examines the way in which Caldecott achieves the effect of continuous movement in his illustrations.

CAMERON, ELEANOR (1912-   )

A492   CAMERON, ELEANOR. "Fantasy, Science Fiction, and the Mushroom Planet Books." *ChLAQ* 5, no. 1 (Winter 1981):5-9. (Reprinted in Bator *Signposts*, pp. 294-300.)

Discusses the background of her Mushroom Planet books and their links with science fiction and fantasy.

A493   -----. "Into Something Rich and Strange: Of Dreams, Art, and the Unconsious." *Quarterly Journal of Library of Congress*, April 1978, pp. 92-107. (Reprinted in Haviland, *The Openhearted Audience*, pp. 153-75.)

Examines the role of the dreams in all art, including her own. Comments also on the difference in her work before and after writing her book of critical essays, *Green and Burning Tree*.

A494   -----. "One Woman as Writer and Feminist." *ChLAQ* 7, no. 4 (1982):3-6.

Provides a feminist analysis of some of her own books.

A495   -----. "A Realm of One's Own." In *Green and Burning*, pp. 48-70.

Discusses how she wrote the Mushroom Planet books for her son David. In relating their origins to her son's love for *Doctor Dolittle*, also makes some insightful comments on Lofting's works.

A496   NODELMAN, PERRY. "Beyond Explanation; and Beyond Inexplicability, in Eleanor Cameron's *Beyond Silence*." *Children's Literature* 12 (1984):122-33. (Followed by Cameron's "A Response to Perry Nodelman's 'Beyond Explanation,'" pp. 134-46. A summary of Nodelman's paper also appears in *Proceedings of the Children's Literature Association* 9 [1982]:128-29.)

Nodelman suggests that although a Cameron story may seem to have many loose ends, "Cameron uses these apparent loose ends to achieve completeness."

A497   -----. "The Depths of All She Is: Eleanor Cameron." *ChLAQ* 4 (Winter 1980):6-8.

Finds Cameron's fiction and criticism expressive of herself as a human being.

CAMPBELL, JULIE

A498   MASON, BOBBIE A. "Just Plain Trixie." In *The Girl Sleuth*, pp. 91-98.

The *Trixie Belden* series, including some books written by Kathryn Kenny, is seen as portraying "one of the most liberating" of the girl sleuths.

CAMPBELL, MARIA (1940-   )

A499   STOTT, JON C. "A Conversation with Maria Campbell." *CCL* 31-32 (1983):15-22.

This Canadian Native American writer discusses her life and work in an interview.

CANIFF, MILTON (1907-   )

A500   ADAMS, JOHN; MARSHALL, RICK; and NANTIER, T. *Milton Caniff: Rembrandt of the Comic Strip.* Endicott, N.Y.: Flying Buttress, 1981, 62 pp.
Analyzes Caniff's skill as a comic-strip artist and storyteller. Includes many illustrations.

A501   MINTZ, LAWRENCE E. "Fantasy, Formula, Realism, and Propaganda in Milton Caniff's Comic Strips." *Journal of Popular Culture* 12, no. 4 (Spring 1979):653-80.
Attempts to analyze the success of Caniff's comic strip creations in terms of a formula combining fantasy and realism. Includes extensive references.

CARIGIET, ALOIS (1902-85)

A502   CARIGIET, ALOIS. "Acceptance Speech." *Bookbird* 4 (1966):7-9.
Hans Christian Andersen Award, 1966. Tells of the origins of the Ursli books.

A503   WERTH, KURT. "Artist's Choice." *Horn Book* 36 (February 1960): 26-27.
Praises the illustrations of *The Snowstorm* by Selina Chönz and provides a detailed analysis of one particular picture.

CARLE, ERIC (1929-   )

A504   KLINGBERG, DELORES R. "Profile: Eric Carle." *LA* 54 (April 1977):445-52.
A biocritical overview.

CARLSON, DALE (1935-   )

A505   CARLSON, DALE. "Girls Are Equal Too." *TON* 32 (April 1976): 269-77.
Discusses her *Girls Are Equal Too*, its evolution, and responses to it.

CARLSON, NATALIE SAVAGE (1906-   )

A506   CARLSON, JULIE McALPINE. "Family Unity in Natalie Savage Carlson's Books for Children." *EE*, February 1968, pp. 214-17. (Reprinted in Hoffman, *Authors and Illustrators*, pp. 56-61.)
Carlson's daughter discusses the theme of family unity in her books.

A507   McALPINE, JULIE CARLSON. "Fact and Fiction in Natalie Savage Carlson's Autobiographical Stories." *Children's Literature* 5 (1976):157-61.
Carlson's daughter compares her mother's autobiographical fiction with her real life.

CARNEGIE, ANDREW (1835-1919)

A508 GRISWOLD, JERRY. "Andy and the Beanstalk: *Andrew Carnegie's Own Story for Boys and Girls.*" *CLE*, n.s. 13, no. 4 (Winter 1982):180-87.

Demonstrates how the tale of "Jack and the Beanstalk" provides the framework for Carnegie's autobiography.

CARROLL, LEWIS [Charles Lutwidge Dodgson] (1832-98)

A509 AUDEN, W.H. "Lewis Carroll." In *Forewords and Afterwords*, pp. 283-93. New York: Random House, 1973.

Contrasts Alice with the American child-hero ("are there any American child-heroines?") who is a "Noble Savage, an anarchist," whereas Alice is a "'lady,'" reasonable and polite.

A510 BACON, DEBORAH. "The Meaning of Non-Sense: A Psychoanalytic Approach to Lewis Carroll." Ph.D. dissertation, Columbia University, 1950, 276 pp., DA 11:338A.

Attempts to "demonstrate, from the psychoanalytic point of view, a parallelism between the known character and life of Charles Lutwidge Dodgson and the latent meaning, symbolism, and intent in his literary creations."

A511 BLAKE, KATHLEEN. *Play, Games and Sport: The Literary Works of Lewis Carroll.* Ithaca: Cornell University Press, 1974, 216 pp.

Analyzes Carroll's works in terms of play, games and sports.

A512 -----. "The Play Theme in the Imaginative Writing of Lewis Carroll." Ph.D. dissertation, University of California, San Diego, 1971, 255 pp., DA 32:2082A.

Examines the role of play in Carroll's work.

A513 CARPENTER, HUMPHREY. "*Alice* and the Mocking of God." In *Secret Gardens*, pp. 44-69.

Provides comments on Carroll's life and the speculations of his biographers as well as offering insights into *Alice* as a mockery of religion and social conventions which Carroll later regretted.

A514 FLESCHER, JACQUELINE. "The Language of Nonsense in *Alice.*" *Yale French Studies* 43 (1969):128-44.

Examines the nature of the language of nonsense used by Carroll. Emphasizes the necessary balance of order and disorder, and concludes that full appreciation of nonsense requires "a willing suspension of disbelief." "The reader of the *Annotated Alice* has, in a sense, outgrown Wonderland."

A515 GABRIELE, MARK. "*Alice in Wonderland*: Problem of Identity-- Aggressive Content and Form Control." *American Imago* 39 (Winter 1982):369-90.

Argues that Alice "defines herself more from without than from within," that "she avoids contact with her own feelings, and looks toward rules to preserve her from threat."

A516 GARDNER, MARTIN. "An Anniversary for Alice: A Child's Garden of Bewilderment." *Saturday Review* 48 (17 July 1965):18-19.

(Reprinted as "A Child's Garden of Bewilderment," in Egoff, *Only Connect*, pp. 150-55.)

Contends that *Alice* is no longer a book for children, but should be given to those over age fifteen, while Baum's Oz books are more appealing to younger children.

A517   GRAY, DONALD J., ed. *Lewis Carroll's Alice in Wonderland.* Norton Critical Editions. New York: W.W. Norton, 1971, 434 pp.

Following the standard Norton Critical Edition format, this volume contains texts of *Alice's Adventures in Wonderland*, *Through the Looking Glass*, and *The Hunting of the Snark*, together with sections of background writings and critical essays. The critical essays include Gillian Avery's "Fairy Tales with a Purpose," and "Fairy Tales for Pleasure"; Peter Conveney's "Escape"; William Empson's "The Child As Swain"; A.L. Taylor's "Chess and Theology in the *Alice* Books"; Elizabeth Sewell's "The Balance of Brillig"; George Pitcher's "Wittgenstein, Nonsense, and Lewis Carroll"; Michael Holquist's "What Is a Boojum? Nonsense and Modernism"; Phyllis Greenacre's "Reconstruction and Interpretation of the Development of Charles L. Dodgson and Lewis Carroll"; and a "Selected Bibliography."

A518   GUILIANO, EDWARD FRANK. *Lewis Carroll: An Annotated International Bibliography, 1960-1977.* Charlottesville: University of Virginia Press, 1977, 253 pp.

Contains annotated listings of primary works, reference works and exhibitions, biography and criticism, and miscellaneous--including dramatic and pictorial adaptations and discussions of translations.

A519   -----. "Lewis Carroll: A Sesquicentennial Guide to Research." *Dickens Studies Annual* 10 (1982):263-310.

An extensive, recent bibliographic essay.

A520   -----. "Popular and Critical Responses to Lewis Carroll: A Comprehensive Survey of Publications Since 1960." Ph.D. dissertation, State University of New York at Stony Brook, 1978, 251 pp., DA 39:158687A.

Surveys and analyzes Carroll scholarship since 1960 in part 1, and in part 2 lists and annotates primary works (including translations), reference and bibliographical works and exhibitions, biography and criticism, and miscellaneous materials published between 1960 and 1976.

A521   HAZARD, PAUL. *Books, Children and Men*, pp. 135-40.

Uses *Alice* to define English character.

A522   HENTOFF, NAT. "Looking Backwards--and Ahead--with Alice." *WLB* 45 (October 1970):169-71.

Personal reflections about the influences of Alice upon his perception of life.

A523   HOLEŠOVSKY, FRANTIŠEK. "Contribution to the Lewis Carroll Jubilee By Illustrators of the BIB." *Bookbird* 1 (1984):52-55.

Surveys the approaches of four illustrators to *Alice*: Dagmar Berková, Markéta Prachatickà, Dušan Kállay, and Gennadij Kalinovskij.

A524   HOLQUIST, MICHAEL. "What is a Boojum? Nonsense and Modernism." *Yale French Studies* 43 (1969):145-64.

Examines the complex pattern of "resistances" in *The Hunting of the Snark*, and suggests the significance the pattern may have for readers of experimental modern fiction.

A525   HUDSON, DEREK. *Lewis Carroll: An Illustrated Biography.* 1954. Reprint. London: Constable, 1976, 272 pp.

This lavishly illustrated biography devotes considerable attention to Carroll's children's books and provides an antidote to the Freudian school of criticism.

A526   INGLIS, FRED. *The Promise of Happiness*, pp. 103-9.

Sees *Alice* as Victorian yet timeless. "If you celebrate courtesy *and* courage, calm good sense *and* dauntlessness, grace and candour, you can hardly do better than Alice." Like Twain, Carroll criticizes society. "Like Huck Finn, Alice is innocent and right."

A527   JOHNSON, P. "Alice Among the Analysts." *Hartford Studies in Literature* 4 (1972):114-22.

Concludes that "an approach to Alice based on Freud's insights can yield useful results, in an analysis not so much of the work in itself (still less the author via the work), but of the nature and value of our pleasure in it."

A528   JORGENS, JACK J. "Alice Our Contemporary." *Children's Literature* 1 (1972):152-61.

Summarizes some recent critical approaches to Carroll and describes an interpretation by the Manhattan Project (a theater group) directed by Andre Gregory.

A529   KELLY, RICHARD. *Lewis Carroll.* Twayne's English Author Series, no. 212. Boston: G.K. Hall, 1977, 163 pp.

Concentrates on Carroll's "mastery of the art of nonsense." Includes a bibliography of primary and secondary sources.

A530   KOLBE, MARTHA EMILY. "Three Oxford Dons as Creators of Other Worlds for Children: Lewis Carroll, C.S. Lewis, and J.R.R. Tolkien." Ed.D. dissertation, University of Virginia, 1981, 285 pp., DA 43:1532A.

Explores the motivations of the three men to compose fantasy works for children in the midst of their academic careers, and describes some of the unique qualities of the work of each.

A531   KUTTY, K. NARAYAN. "Nonsense As Reality." *Children's Literature* 5 (1976):286-87.

Reviews *Poems of Lewis Carroll*, selected by Myra Cohn Livingston.

A532   LEWIS CARROLL SOCIETY, founded in 1969, publishes a journal *Jabberwocky* and a newsletter *Bandersnatch*.

A533   MARCUS, LEONARD S. "*Alice's Adventures*: The Pennyroyal Press Edition." *Children's Literature* 12 (1984):175-84.

Reviews Barry Moser's illustrations for the Pennyroyal Press Edition (Berkeley: University of California Press/Pennyroyal Press, 1982), comparing them to those of Tenniel and others.

A534   MORTON, L. "Memory in the Alice Books." *Nineteenth-Century Fiction* 33 (December 1978):285-308.
Explores the role of memory and the past, and the golden haze of nostalgia with which Carroll surrounded the Alice stories, but points out that the stories themselves are not nostalgic.

A535   MORTON, RICHARD. "*Alice's Adventures in Wonderland* and *Through the Looking Glass.*" *EE* 37 (December 1960):509-13.
Suggests the tales be presented to children by emphasizing the whole rather than the individual parts.

A536   MULDERIG, GERALD P. "*Alice in Wonderland*: Subversive Elements in the World of Victorian Children's Fiction." *Journal of Popular Culture* 11 (Fall 1977):320-29.
Points out that *Alice* "does not simply depart from the major conventions of nineteenth-century juvenile literature, but rather ridicules and subverts them."

A537   NATOV, RONI. "The Persistence of *Alice.*" *L&U* 3, no. 1 (Spring 1979):38-61.
Praises Carroll's sense of the way children experience the world: the thinness of the line between dreams and the waking world of young children, the games, the incongruities, the dependable leitmotivs, the vitality of the characters, the jokes, the delight in the sounds of words, the irreverant spirit of the work, Alice's need to define, limit, and control chaos, her experience of being bossed around, and--for the older child--the preoccupation with identity and rebellion against the establishment, the difficulties of communication, and the awareness of uncertainty and ambiguity.

A538   OVENDEN, GRAHAM, ed. *The Illustrators of "Alice in Wonderland" and "Through the Looking Glass."* Introduction by John Davis, pp. 5-18. London: Academy; New York: St. Martin's, 1972, 88 pp.
Davis's introduction surveys the illustrators of Alice, beginning with Tenniel and Carroll. The remainder of the book reproduces illustrations by various illustrators for a number of scenes. Includes a bibliography of illustrated English-language editions of the books and a selected bibligraphy of works about Carroll.

A539   RACKIN, DONALD. "Corrective Laughter: Carroll's *Alice* and Popular Children's Literature of the Nineteenth Century." *Journal of Popular Culture* 1, no. 3 (Winter 1967):243-55.
Sees *Alice* as "the final flowering of a long development in children's books--a gradual movement toward stimulating, imaginative, completely undidactic stories for the young."

A540   SALE, ROGER. "Lewis Carroll." In *Fairy Tales*, pp. 100-125.
Links Carroll's writing to his interest in little girls, and concludes that while "Carroll's fragmentary view of life is a child's view" his books are not necessarily children's books. Includes a detailed discussion of "Jabberwocky," pp. 103-6.

A541   SUCHAN, JAMES. "Alice's Journey from Alien to Artist." *Children's Literature* 7 (1978):78-92.
Concentrates on the issue of identity. "The perplexing and crucial debate whether Alice is a 'monster,' a 'serpent,' a 'child judge,' or simply a little girl clearly reflects the ambivalent attitude that

Victorian adults held about children."

CARTER, PETER (1929-   )

A542   MORGAN, PEGGY. "A Prophetic Voice: The Writing of Peter Carter." *CLE*, n.s. 15, no. 1 (Spring 1984):47-57.
Provides an overview of Carter's work, examining his handling of complex moral themes and religious and social issues in six books.

CAUDILL, REBECCA (1899-   )

A543   BURNS, PAUL C., and HINES, RUTH. "Rebecca Caudill." *EE* 40 (November 1963):703-6.
Surveys Caudill's background and writings.

A544   CAUDILL, REBECCA. "Appalachian Heritage." *Horn Book* 45 (April 1969):143-47.
Comments on the importance of her Appalachian heritage in her life and work.

A545   -----. "Writing for Children." *Illinois Libraries* 39 (June 1957):200-207.

A546   KINGSTON, CAROLYN. *Tragic Mode*, pp. 89-92.
Analyzes *Tree of Freedom* in terms of its theme of sensitivity.

A547   TOOTHAKER, ROY. "Rebecca Caudill." *LA* 52 (October 1975):930-34, 982.
Caudill discusses her life and writing in an interview.

A548   -----. "Reminiscing with Rebecca Caudill." *TON* 28 (January 1972):179-88.
Relates Caudill's books to her life and Appalachian background. Includes a bibliography of her books and articles about her.

CAUSLEY, CHARLES (1917-   )

A549   BRADMAN, TONY. "Charles Causley: Nursery Rhymes of Innocence and Experience." *Junior Bookshelf* 45, no. 2 (April 1981):55-57.
Identifies Causley's theme as "this Painful turning of golden innocence into the ironic knowledge of experience . . . growing up."

A550   CHAMBERS, AIDAN. "Letter from England: Charles Causley and The Tail of the Trinosaur." *Horn Book* 51 (August 1975):406-10.
Praises *The Tail of the Trinosaur*, relates it to Causley's Cornish background, and compares his style and subject to Robert Browning's.

A551   -----. "Letter from England: Something Rich and Strange." *Horn Book* 55 (February 1979):111-15.
Praises Causley's skill as the anthologist of *The Puffin Book of Salt-Sea Verse*.

A552   COOK, STANLEY. "Modern Authors 11: Charles Causley." *School Librarian* 24, no. 4 (December 1976):304-5.
A brief critical overview.

A553 PHILIP, NEIL. "Magic in the Poetry of Charles Causley." *Signal* 39 (September 1982):139-52.
Provides a detailed, appreciative analysis of Causley's work. His poems "are real poems, full of transforming magic; real spells, in which the omission of a word would be fatal." Includes a bibliography of Causley's works.

CAVANNA, BETTY (1909-   )

A554 MASON, BOBBIE ANN. *The Girl Sleuth*, pp. 115-19.
Points out that the author of the *Connie Blair Mysteries*, Betsy Allen, is actually Betty Cavanna, whose young adult fiction has been praised. Mason compares the portrayals of sex roles in series books and the typical "junior miss" novel, and concludes that the series books allow more freedom.

A555 SCHMIDT, NANCY. *Children's Fiction About Africa*, pp. 121-22.
Calls *Mystery in Marrakech* "entirely American in perspective" and "full of contemporary girls' stereotypes of Africa."

CHALMERS, MARY (1927-   )

A556 BADER, BARBARA. *American Picturebooks*, pp. 487-92.
Feels Chalmers's books duplicate "the way the young child has been found to think." Discusses several of her books.

CHANEY, JILL (1932-   )

A557 RAY, SHEILA. "Children's Writers: 2. Jill Chaney." *School Librarian* 26, no. 1 (March 1978):11-16.
Examines Chaney's books for teenagers, those for younger children, and those about the woffle.

A558 REES, DAVID. "A Plea for Jill Chaney." *CLE*, n.s. 8, no. 2 (Summer 1977):85-93.
Considers her one of the most interesting writers of teenage fiction in England today. "She is unsurpassed among writers for the young in what it feels like to be fifteen or sixteen or seventeen and falling in love, happily or otherwise." Discusses *Half a Candle*, *Mottram Park*, and *The Buttercup Field* (1976).

A559 -----. "The Sadness of Compromise: Robert Cormier and Jill Chaney." In *Marble in the Water*, pp. 155-72.
Both novelists are "concerned with the essential sadness of the inevitable passing from innocence to experience." Discusses especially Chaney's *Mottram Park* and *Half a Candle*.

CHAPMAN, ALLEN [Stratemeyer Syndicate Pseudonym]

A560 PRAGER, ARTHUR. *Rascals at Large*, pp. 147-52, 186-91.
Discusses the Ralph Fairbanks and Radio Boys series.

CHARLIP, REMY (1929-   )

A561 BADER, BARBARA. "Remy Charlip." In *American Picturebooks*, pp. 530-37.
Discusses Charlip's creative, unconventional contributions to the

picture book.

A562   MONIGLE, MARTHA. "Remy Charlip's Children's Books." *Print* 20 (July-August 1966):42-47.
A biocritical overview.

CHARLOT, JEAN (1898-1979)

A563   BADER, BARBARA. "Jean Charlot." In *American Picturebooks*, pp. 265-76.
Provides a detailed overview of Charlot's contribution to the American picture book.

CHASE, RICHARD (1904-   )

A564   PAINTER, HELEN W. "Richard Chase: Mountain Folklorist and Storyteller." *EE* 40 (November 1963):677-86.
Reports on Chase's folktales, especially the Jack tales.

CHAUNCY, NAN (1900-1970)

A565   ALDERSON, BRIAN. "Properly Alive." *Children's Book News* 4, no. 2 (March-April 1969):64-66.
Points out Chauncy's strengths and weaknesses and praises her aliveness and "captivating warmth."

A566   CROUCH, MARCUS. "Half a World Away." *Junior Bookshelf* 29 (June 1965):135-40.
A brief critical overview.

A567   HARRINGTON, LYN. "World's End is Home for Nan Chauncy." *Horn Book* 45 (August 1969):441-45.
Describes a visit to Chauncy, her background, and its influence on her books.

CHÖNZ, SELINA

A568   HÜRLIMANN, BETTINA. *Three Centuries*, pp. 236-39.
Analyzes the Ursli books illustrated by Alois Carigiet, *A Bell for Ursli*, *Florina and the Wild Bird*, and *The Snowstorm*.

CHORPENNING, CHARLOTTE (1872-1955)

A569   BEDARD, ROGER LEE. "The Life and Work of Charlotte B. Chorpenning." Ph.D. dissertation, University of Kansas, 1979, 185 pp., DA 41:23A.
Chronicles the life and work of Chorpenning and assesses her impact on American children's theater. One chapter is devoted to a discussion of her writings, including her plays for children.

A570   RUBIN, JANET ELAINE. "The Literary and Theatrical Contributions of Charlotte B. Chorpenning to Children's Theatre." Ph.D. dissertation, Ohio State University, 1978, 384 pp., DA 39:5812A.
The first comprehensive study of Chorpenning, and the first to analyze her work from a literary point of view. Focuses on *Cinderella*, *Jack and the Beanstalk*, *Rumpelstiltskin*, and *Sleeping Beauty*.

CHRISMAN, ARTHUR (1889-1953)

A571   JORDAN, Mrs. ARTHUR M. "Arthur Chrisman--Newbery Medalist." *EER* 3 (October 1926):251, 267.
A thoughtful review of *Shen of the Sea.*

CHRISTOPHER, JOHN [C.S. Youd] (1922-)

A572   CRAGO, HUGH, and CRAGO, MAUREEN. "John Christopher: An Assessment with Reservations." *Children's Literature Review* 1, no. 3 (June 1971):77-79.
Concludes that Christopher, when viewed within the context of science-fiction writing for both adults and children, "lacks the depth that would make him either an original user of science fiction conventions or a first rate novelist."

A573   CROUCH, MARCUS. *The Nesbit Tradition*, pp. 50-52.
"John Christopher's stories are distinguished by excellent writing and keen, original and logical thinking." His most "consistently successful novel for young readers" is *The Guardians.*

A574   GOUGH, JOHN. "An Interview with John Christopher." *CLE*, n.s. 15, no. 2 (Summer 1984):93-102.
In a series of interview letters, Gough and Christopher discuss Christopher's work.

A575   TOWNSEND, JOHN. *Sense of Story*, pp. 48-55.
Sees Christopher's characters in both adult and children's books as "struggling to survive and make a comeback." Discusses the Tripods trilogy: *The White Mountains*, *The City of Gold and Lead*, and *The Pool of Fire.* Also mentions *The Lotus Caves* and *The Guardians.*

A576   WILLIAMS, JAY. "John Christopher: Allegorical Historian." *Signal* 4 (January 1971):18-23.
Views Christopher's work as closer to that of Samuel Butler and C.S. Lewis than to that of most science-fiction writers.

CHUKOVSKY, KORNEI (1882-1969)

A577   CHUKOVSKY, KORNEI. "Confessions of an Old Story Teller." *Horn Book* 46 (December 1970):577-91; 47 (February 1971):28-39.
Discusses his riddles and verses.

A578   LEIGHTON, L.G. "Homage to Kornei Chukovsky." *Russian Review* 31 (January 1972):38-48.
An overview of Chukovsky's career.

A579   MORTON, MIRIAM. "Kornei Chukovsky--The Pied Piper of Peredel-kino." *Horn Book* 38 (October 1962):458-68.
A survey of Chukovsky's work, with special attention to his children's tales and verses.

A580   ØRVIG, MARY. "A Russian View of Childhood: The Contribution of Kornei I. Chukovsky (1882-1969)." *Horn Book* 50 (October 1974):69-84. (Reprinted in Heins, *Crosscurrents*, pp. 261-74.)
Summarizes Chukovsky's life and work in children's literature, particularly his critical theories. Places him in the context of the

development of modern Russian children's literature.

CHURCH, RICHARD (1893-1972)

A581   HANNABUSS, STUART. "The Motive in the Actuality: Richard Church as Writer for Children." *Children's Literature Review* 2, no. 3 (June 1972):69-70.
Provides an overview of Church's seven children's books.

CHUTE, MARCHETTE (1909-   )

A582   CHUTE, MARCHETTE. "Shakespeare of London." *Horn Book* 31 (February 1955):28-35.
Describes the techniques of researching and writing her Shakespeare books.

CIARDI, JOHN (1916-   )

A583   GROFF, PATRICK J. "The Transformation of a Poet: John Ciardi." *Horn Book* 40 (April 1964):153-58.
Applies Ciardi's own standards to his poetry and finds both the standards and the poems lacking.

A584   ODLAND, NORINE. "Profile: John Ciardi." *LA* 59 (November-December 1982):872-76.
Discusses Ciardi's poetry for children and his beliefs about children and poetry.

"Cinderella"

A585   BINGHAM, JANE, and SCHOLT, GRAYCE. "The Great Glass Slipper Search: Using Folktales with Older Children." *EE* 51 (October 1974):990-98.
Examines twelve variants of the Cinderella story from various geographic areas as a means of introducing teachers and students to the study of folklore.

A586   COOK, ELIZABETH. "Cinderella's Sisters Get Ready for a Ball." In *The Ordinary and the Fabulous*, pp. 102-12. (Reprinted in Meek, *Cool Web*, pp. 272-83.)
Compares alternate versions of "Cinderella." "A reader who really knows Perrault and Wanda Gag's Grimm is most unlikely to go back to the anonymous modern versions I have been castigating."

A587   DUNDES, ALAN, ed. *Cinderella: A Casebook.* New York: Garland, 1982, 311 pp.
Contains eighteen essays on "Cinderella," reflecting a wide range of scholarly approaches. Includes reprints of three of the best-known versions of the tale: Basile's, Perrault's, and Grimms'; and extensive references and suggestions for further reading.

A588   HIEATT, CONSTANCE. "Responses . . . The Case of Cinderella." *CCL* 33 (1984):92-96.
In response to Nodelman's article on *Little Red Riding Hood* (*CCL* 20 [1980]:17-27), discusses a number of versions of and approaches to *Cinderella*.

A589   MARCUS, DONALD M. "The Cinderella Motif: Fairy Tale and Defense." *American Imago* 20, no. 1 (Spring 1963):81-92.
       Examines, in psychoanalytic terms, the use of the Cinderella motif by young girls to help solve Oedipal conflicts.

A590   PHILIP, NEIL. "Cinderella's Many Guises: A Look at Early Sources and Recent Versions." *Signal* 33 (September 1980):130-46.
       Examines many version of "Cinderella" from many times and countries within the context of folklore tale-type and motif indexes. Includes bibliographies for background and for current versions of the tale.

A591   SCHWARCZ, JOSEPH H. "Humiliation and Urgency in Two Key Scenes in *Cinderella*." In *Ways of the Illustrator*, pp. 106-19.
       Examines the ways in which fifty illustrators have approached variants of "Cinderella," in an attempt to learn what illustrators do with (and to) fairy tales, concentrating especially on the ways in which two scenes are depicted: Cinderella's humiliation by her stepmother and her sisters, and Cinderella's flight from the ball.

A592   WHALLEY, IRENE. "The Cinderella Story 1724-1919." *Signal* 8 (May 1972):49-62. (Reprinted in Chambers, *Signal Approach*, pp. 140-55.)
       Traces the history of various versions of the tale up to 1919. Includes bibliography.

A593   YOLEN, JANE. "America's Cinderella." *CLE* 8, no. 1 (Spring 1977):21-29.
       Traces origins and variants of the tale, emphasizing the distinctive characteristics that have developed in American retellings, including the Disney versions. Concludes that the mass-market Cinderellas have presented American children with the wrong dream. Extensive references.

CLARK, ANN NOLAN (1896-   )

A594   BISHOP, CLAIRE HUCHET. "Ann Nolan Clark." *Catholic Library World* 34 (February 1963):280-86, 333.
       A biocritical overview, concentrating on Clark's portrayal of Native Americans.

A595   CLARK, ANN NOLAN. *Journey to the People.* New York: Viking Press, 1969, 128 pp.
       This autobiographical account contains many sections expressing Clark's philosophy and discusses the inspiration for her writing.

A596   -----. "Newbery Award Acceptance." *Horn Book* 29 (August 1953):249-57.
       Tells of her background and its influence on her books.

A597   GRIESE, ARNOLD A. "Ann Nolan Clark--Building Bridges of Cultural Understanding." *EE* 49 (May 1972):648-58.
       Summarizes the two outstanding characteristics of Clark's work as (1) her theme of Indian traditions and world view as related to universal concerns and (2) her highly poetic prose style. Explores the relationship of her life to her work, and examines elements of her themes and style.

A598   WENZEL, EVELYN. "Ann Nolan Clark: 1953 Newbery Award Winner." *EE* 30 (October 1953):327-32. (Reprinted in Hoffman, *Authors and Illustrators*, pp. 62-69.)
Describes how Clark's writing grew naturally out of her work as a teacher and how she is able to communicate easily between cultures. Discusses *Secret of the Andes*.

CLARK, BILLY CURTIS (1928-   )

A599   BURNS, PAUL C. "Billy Curtis Clark--Appalachia's Young Novelist." *EE* 46 (October 1969):722-30.
Includes a biographical sketch, general assessment of Clark's writings, and separate brief reviews of eight of his books.

CLARK, CATHERINE ANTHONY (1892-1977)

A600   KEALY, J. KIERAN. "The Flame-Lighter Woman: Catherine Anthony Clark's Fantasies." *Canadian Literature* 78 (Autumn 1978):32-42.
Analyzes Clark's unique approach to fantasy, pointing out that its incorporation of Canadian, especially Indian, influences, makes it different from fantasy in the European tradition.

A601   MURRAY, HEATHER. "The Geography of the Imagination: The Fantastic Frontier of Catherine Anthony Clark." *ChLAQ* 8 (Winter 1983):23-25.
Examines Clark's work within the contexts of Canadian fantasy tradition, Canadian myth and folklore, and Canadian children's fiction. Responds to earlier critical assessments of Clark's work.

A602   SELBY, JOAN. "The Creation of Fantasy: The Fiction of Catherine Anthony Clark." *Canadian Literature* 11 (Winter 1962):39-45.
Explores Clark's synthesis of European and Indian folklore in her fantasies.

CLARK, LEONARD (1905-   )

A603   APSELOFF, MARILYN. "A Salute to Leonard Clark." *ChLAQ* 5, no. 2 (Summer 1980):1, 30-32, 34.
Provides an overview of Clark's career.

CLARK, MAVIS THORPE

A604   McVITTY, WALTER. "Mavis Thorpe Clark: Lover of the Sunburnt Country." In *Innocence and Experience*, pp. 8-35.
Concentrates on Clark's historical fiction and problem novels. Includes a brief biographical sketch, comments by Clark, and a bibliography of her books.

CLARKE, PAULINE (1921-   )

A605   CLARKE, PAULINE. "The Chief Genii Branwell." *Junior Bookshelf* 27 (July 1963):119-23.
A biocritical overview.

A606   JONES, CORNELIA, and WAY, OLIVIA R. *British Children's Authors*, pp. 65-76.
In an interview Clarke discusses her background, philosophy, and

method of working. Includes an annotated bibliography of her works.

CLEARY, BEVERLY (1916-   )

A607   BURNS, PAUL C., and HINES, RUTH. "Beverly Cleary: Wonderful World of Humor." *EE* 44 (November 1967):743-47, 752.
Surveys and evaluates Cleary's work from *Henry Huggins* through 1964, describes it as "pure Americana," and points out its humor.

A608   CLEARY, BEVERLY. "Newbery Medal Acceptance." *Horn Book* 60 (August 1984):429-38.
Cleary reflects upon her long career as a writer and offers insights into the origins of *Dear Mr. Henshaw.* Also reveals some children's responses to the book. A biographical sketch by David Reuther follows, pp. 439-43.

A609   -----. "Writing Books About Henry Huggins." *TON* 14 (December 1957):7-11.
Describes her background and the origins of her very first Henry and Ribsy books.

A610   NOVINGER, MARGARET. "Beverly Cleary: A Favorite Author of Children." *Southeastern Librarian* 18 (Fall 1968):194-202. (Reprinted in Hoffman, *Authors and Illustrators*, pp. 70-83.)
Discusses the Henry and Eileen books, books for teenaged girls, and books for young children. Concludes with excerpts from reviews of *The Mouse and The Motorcycle.* Includes references and bibliographies.

A611   REES, DAVID. "Middle of the Way: Rodie Sudbery and Beverly Cleary." In *Marble in the Water*, pp. 90-103.
Claims Cleary "writes for varying levels of response, and this reflects an immense skill." Gives examples from the Ramona books.

A612   ROGGENBUCK, MARY JUNE. "Profile: Beverly Cleary--The Children's Force at Work." *LA* 56 (January 1979):55-60.
Discusses Cleary's background and the responses of children to her work.

CLEAVER, ELIZABETH (1939-85)

A613   CLEAVER, ELIZABETH. "Picture Books as an Art Form." In Egoff, *One Ocean*, pp. 195-96.
The Canadian illustrator talks briefly about her life as an artist and her approach to her work.

A614   ELLIS, SARAH. "News from the North." *Horn Book* 62 (January 1986):100-103.
Provides a brief overview of Cleaver's career.

A615   HERBERT, NANCY D. "Elizabeth Cleaver." *Bookbird* 11, no. 1 (1973):66-73.
A profile with background information and technical notes, on the work of this Canadian illustrator.

CLEAVER, VERA (1919-   ), and CLEAVER, BILL (1920-81)

A616   CIANCIOLO, PATRICIA J. "Vera and Bill Cleaver Know Their Whys and Wherefores." *TON* 32 (June 1976):338-50.
Provides an extensive discussion of the Cleavers' themes of tenacity, mental retardation, death, divorce and alienation, and cultural heritage.

A617   KINGSTON, CAROLYN T. *Tragic Mode*, pp. 69-71.
Analyzes the theme of entrapment in *Where the Lilies Bloom*.

A618   TOWNSEND, JOHN ROWE. "Vera and Bill Cleaver." In *A Sounding*, pp. 30-40. (Also in *Horn Book* 55 [October 1979]:505-13.)
"Their gallery of fierce, determined heroines like Mary Call and Littabelle . . . their vividly drawn settings," and "the ordeals their young people have to face" are memorable.

CLIFTON, LUCILLE (1936-   )

A619   CLIFTON, LUCILLE. "Writing for Black Children." *Advocate* 1, no. 1 (Fall 1981):32-37.
Talks about her goals as a writer and her responsibilities to black children.

A620   SIMS, RUDINE. "Profile: Lucille Clifton." *LA* 59 (February 1982):160-67.
In this interview Clifton discusses her views on poetry, the inclusion of both black and white characters in her books, and the inspiration and background for her work. Includes a bibliography of Clifton's books.

COATSWORTH, ELIZABETH (1893-   )

A621   ABBOTT, BARBARA. "To Timbuctoo and Back: Elizabeth Coatsworth's Books for Children." *Horn Book* 6 (November 1930):283-89.
Briefly reviews *The Cat and the Captain*, *The Boy with a Parrot*, *Toutou in Bondage*, and *The Cat Who Went to Heaven*.

A622   COATSWORTH, ELIZABETH. "Upon Writing for Children." *Horn Book* 24 (September 1948):389-95.
Says she usually begins with "place." Discusses the origins of several of her books, standards for books, and details of the background for *Here I Stay*.

A623   KUHN, DORIS YOUNG. "Elizabeth Coatsworth: Perceptive Impressionist." *Elementary English* 46 (December 1969):991-1007. (Reprinted in Hoffman, *Authors and Illustrators*, pp. 84-107.)
Begins with an account of a meeting with Coatsworth, interspersed with quotations from her writings. Summarizes biographical and critical works about her, and concludes with a critical overview emphasizing style and themes. Includes extensive references and a bibliography.

A624   MEIGS, CORNELIA. "*Alice-All-By-Herself.*" *Horn Book* 14 (March 1938):77-80.
An appreciative appraisal.

A625 RICE, MABEL. "The Poetic Prose of Elizabeth Coatsworth." *EE* 31 (January 1954):3-10.
An overview of Coatsworth's life and writing and the relationship between the two.

A626 SCHMIDT, NANCY. *Children's Fiction About Africa*, pp. 178-79.
Points out stereotypes and lack of realism in Coatsworth's portrayal of Africa and Africans.

COHEN, BARBARA (1932-   )

A627 KARP, HAZEL B., and VEAL, SIBLEY. "Point of View." *Advocate* 1, no. 2 (Winter 1982):122-25.
The two discussants agree that Cohen's retelling of the biblical story of Joseph, *I Am Joseph*, illustrated by Charles Mikolaycak, is more suited to adults than to children.

COLLIER, CHRISTOPHER (1930-   ), and
COLLIER, JAMES LINCOLN (1928-   )

A628 MOIR, HUGHES. "Profile: James and Christopher Collier--More Than Just a Good Read." *LA* 55 (March 1978):373-78.
The author-brothers express their opinions on writing for children and on children's historical fiction.

A629 MOORE, OPAL, and MacCANN, DONNARAE. "Cultural Pluralism." *ChLAQ* 10, no. 4 (Winter 1986):201-3.
Reviews *Jump Ship to Freedom*. Faults the "thematic fuzziness and unconvincing treatment of Black protagonists," and argues for the relevance of cultural concerns and biases to literary criticism.

COLLIER, VIRGINIA MacMAKIN

A630 COLLIER, VIRGINIA. "A Modern Pilgrimage." *Horn Book* 10 (September 1934):277-84. (Reprinted in Fryatt, *Horn Book Sampler*, pp. 12-18.)
The author describes her journeys through the territory inhabited by Roland and Charlemagne as part of her research for the book.

A631 -----. "Why a New Story of Roland?" *EER* 13 (May 1936):174-76, 183.
An account of the research for *Roland the Warrior*.

COLLODI, CARLO [Carlo Lorenzini] (1826-1890)

A632 BACON, MARTHA. "Puppet's Progress: Pinocchio." *Atlantic Monthly* 225 (April 1970):88-90, 92. (Reprinted in Haviland, *Children and Literature*, pp. 71-77.)
Places *Pinocchio* in its historical and national context, provides biographical background on Collodi, and interprets the book as a children's story and also as "a political comment, an interpretation of history, a document of man's search for his soul, and a sign of the shape of things to come."

A633 CAMBON, GLAUCO. "*Pinocchio* and the Problem of Children's Literature." *Children's Literature* 2 (1973):50-60.
Places *Pinocchio* high in the canon of children's literature and

also within folk and classical (Homeric) traditions.

A634   GANNON, SUSAN. "A Note on Collodi and Lucian." *Children's Literature* 8 (1980):98-102.
Makes a case for the influence of second-century rhetorician and satirist, Lucian, on Collodi's *Pinocchio*.

A635   -----. "*Pinocchio*: The First Hundred Years." *ChLAQ* 6, no. 4 (Winter 1981-1982):1, 5-7. (Reprinted in Dooley, *First Steps*, pp. 131-33.)
Sees the vivid personality of the central character as a key to the book's long-lived success. See response by Morrissey below (A640).

A636   HAZARD, PAUL. *Books, Children and Men*, pp. 111-19. (Excerpted in *Horn Book* 19 [March-April 1943]:119-26. Translated by Marguerite Mitchell.)
Maintains that children recognize themselves in Pinocchio. He is not bad, but weak. Traces his origins in Italian theater, comments on the witticisms, and links the book to Italian history and national character.

A637   HEINS, PAUL. "A Second Look: *The Adventure of Pinocchio*." *Horn Book* 58 (April 1982):200-204.
Touches on the picaresque tradition, the use of improvisation and metamorphosis, and the sources of Collodi's characters.

A638   HEISIG, JAMES. "Pinocchio: Archetype of the Motherless Child." *Children's Literature* 3 (1974):23-35.
Explores the levels of universal meaning of *The Adventures of Pinocchio* as well as its concern with injustice, self-realization, and self-integration. Includes a bibliography of Italian criticism.

A639   KURZWEIL, ALLEN. "A Nose for Success." *TLS*, 25 November 1983, p. 1320.
Reviews two recent Italian critical editions of *Le Avventure di Pinocchio* by Ornella Castellani Pollidori (Pescia: Fondazione Nazionale Carlo Collodi, 282 pp.) and Fernando Tempesti (Milan: Arnoldo Mondadori, 254 pp.).

A640   MORRISSEY, THOMAS J. "Alive and Well But Not Unscathed: A Reply to Susan R. Gannon's *Pinocchio at 100*." *ChLAQ* 7, no. 2 (Summer 1982).
Argues that (1) *Pinocchio* has not emerged "relatively unscathed" and (2) "though there are some anomalies of plot, *Pinocchio* is a classic work of epic fantasy--not a lucky stab in the dark but a well-crafted epic journey in the tradition of Homer, Virgil, and Dante."

A641   MORRISSEY, THOMAS J., and WUNDERLICH, RICHARD. "Death and Rebirth in *Pinocchio*." *Children's Literature* 11 (1983):64-75.
Places *Pinocchio* in the tradition of the epic hero who experiences some form of death and resurrection. Many of Pinocchio's adventures have mythic significance. "It is Collodi's tribute to children that he chooses to depict their very real trials and triumphs in terms of mythic patterns ordinarily reserved for adults."

A642   SALE, ROGER. Review of the Marianne Mayer translation with illustrations by Gerald McDermott. *NYTBR*, 15 November 1981, pp. 49, 71.

A643   WUNDERLICH, RICHARD, and MORRISSEY, THOMAS J. "The Desecration of *Pinocchio* in the United States." *Proceedings of the Children's Literature Association* 8 (1981):106-18. (Edited version also in *Horn Book* 58 [April 1982]:205-12.)

Surveys and assesses changes in various versions of *Pinocchio* over the years as they reflect changing visions of childhood. The cruelest fate of a classic is "to be debased and trivialized and then remembered. . . . Such is the fate of *Pinocchio*." Includes a bibliography of translations, adaptations, and revisions, and plays.

COLUM, PADRAIC (1881-1972)

A644   BECHTEL, LOUISE S. "Padraic Colum: A Great Storyteller of Today." *Catholic Library World* 32 (December 1960):159-60.

More praise than criticism, Bechtel's article does attempt to touch on key characteristics of Colum's style.

A645   BOWEN, ZACK R. *Padraic Colum: Biographical-Critical Introduction.* Carbondale: Southern Illinois University Press, 1970, 162 pp.

Pages 122-48 are devoted to Colum's contribution to children's literature in the categories of world epics, folk romance, and stories for younger children.

A646   MYERS, ANDREW. "In the Wild Earth a Grecian Vase! For Padraic Colum (1881-1972)." *Columbia Library Columns* 22 (February 1973):11-21.

Provides a brief, laudatory overview of Colum's career, especially emphasizing his Columbia University connections.

COOLIDGE, OLIVIA (1908-   )

A647   COOLIDGE, OLIVIA. "Writing About Abraham Lincoln." *Horn Book* 51 (February 1975):31-35. (Reprinted in Heins, *Crosscurrents*, pp. 241-45.)

Describes the goals and techniques of her two books on Lincoln for young adults.

A648   HOLTZE, SALLY HOLMES. "A Second Look." *Horn Book* 56 (February 1980):88-90.

Characterizes *Come By Here* as ahead of its time in its extensive use of realism.

A649   LONG, SIDNEY, D. Review of *Gandhi*. *Horn Book* 47 (December 1971):597.

"Her gift for sorting out the many influences that shape a great man, and for showing how, in turn, events are shaped by him, has never been more apparent. . . "

COOLIDGE, SUSAN (1835-1905)

A650   DARLING, FRANCES C. "Susan Coolidge, 1835-1905." Eleventh Caroline M. Hewins Lecture. In Andrews, *The Hewins Lectures 1947-62*, pp. 251-64. (Shortened version in *Horn Book* 35 [June 1959]:232-46.)

A biocritical overview.

COONEY, BARBARA (1917-   )

A651   COONEY, BARBARA. "Caldecott Award Acceptance." *Horn Book* 35 (August 1959):310-14.
Provides background information on *Chanticleer and the Fox*, and offers keys to some of its details. Followed by a biographical sketch by Anna Newton Porter (her mother-in-law), pp. 315-19.

A652   -----. "The Spirit Place." *ChLAQ* 9, no. 4 (Winter 1984-1985):152-53.
Reflects on the way that early in her career Cooney was encouraged to concentrate on drawing children and animals, and only later in life did landscape and sense of place become important to her work.

A653   WATSON, ALDREN A. "Artist's Choice." *Horn Book* 36 (October 1960):386-87.
Critiques the pictures and also the sewing of the binding of *Chanticleer and the Fox*.

COOPER, PAUL FENIMORE (1900?-1970)

A654   DALPHIN, MARCIA. "I Give You the End of a Golden String." *Horn Book* 14 (May 1938):143-49. (Reprinted in Fryatt, *Horn Book Sampler*, pp. 133-35.)
Praises *Tal* as a "highly imaginative 'quest'" book.

A655   JONES, LOUIS C. "Paul Fenimore Cooper and *Tal*." *Horn Book* 26 (January 1950):30-32.
Describes background of Cooper's Albanian folktale retellings.

COOPER, SUSAN (1935-   )

A656   CARLSON, DUDLEY BROWN. "A Second Look: *Over Sea, Under Stone*." *Horn Book* 52 (October 1976):522-23.
Briefly analyzes the elements believed to account for the success of the book.

A657   COOPER, SUSAN. "Who Knows Where the Ideas Come From?" *Horn Book* 52 (September 1976):522-23.
Tells of the origins of her *Dark Is Rising* series.

A658   ELLIS, MARGERY. "A Second Look: *Dawn of Fear*." *Horn Book* 58 (August 1982):436-39.
Analyzes the story's themes and techniques.

A659   LEVIN, BETTY. "A Journey Through Mountain and Mist: *The Grey King*." *Horn Book* 52 (August 1976):443-45.
"What is important about Susan Cooper's *The Grey King* is the special use to which she has put recognizable elements of myth, her vital fusion of past with present, and not those elements themselves."

A660   PHILIP, NEIL. "Fantasy: Double Cream or Instant Whip?" *Signal* 35 (May 1981):82-90.
Attempts to "define the point where genre writing transcends genre and shades into the mainstream." Makes Susan Cooper his

example and concludes that of her books only *The Dark Is Rising* makes use of the "good/evil polarity" and only it will last.

A661 REES, DAVID. "Children's Writers: 11. Susan Cooper." *School Librarian* 32 (September 1984):197-205.

Rees agrees with Neil Philip's description of Cooper's *Dark Is Rising* series as "instant whip" cream. Argues that it has "little poetry and no scholarship at all: dull, safe, predictable narratives; cardboard thin characterisation; immense quantities of cliché; and its prose, apart from a few felicitous phrases . . . [is] undistinguished."

CORLETT, WILLIAM (1938-)

A662 CHAMBERS, AIDAN. "Letter from England: Looking Out for Yourself." *Horn Book* 54 (February 1978):86-88.

Discusses *Gate of Eden*, *The Land Beyond*, and *Return to the Gate*.

A663 CORLETT, WILLIAM. "After the Gates." *Signal* 32 (May 1980): 107-13.

Shares his responses to the televising of a play based on his *Gate of Eden*.

CORMIER, ROBERT (1925-)

A664 *ALAN Review* 12 (Winter 1985), 56 pp.

Special issue includes "The Pleasures and Pains of Writing A Sequel," by Robert Cormier; "Cormier and the Pessimistic View," by W. Geiger Ellis; "A Telephone Interview with Robert Cormier," by Judith Bugniazet; "Young Adult Books in the Classroom: Adolescent Initiation in Cormier's *After the First Death*," by Amelia M. Bell; an excerpt from *Beyond the Chocolate War*; and "Of Fish and Bears and Bumblebees: The Craft of Robert Cormier," by Betty Ann Fargnoli.

A665 CHAMBERS, AIDAN. "An Interview with Robert Cormier." *Signal* 30 (September 1979):119-32.

In an interview Cormier expresses his views on writing, and discusses influences on him, and the origins of some of his books.

A666 CLEMENTS, BRUCE. "A Second Look: *The Chocolate War*." *Horn Book* 55 (April 1979):217-18.

Compares the ending to the ending of *Hamlet*.

A667 CORMIER, ROBERT. "The Cormier Novels: The Cheerful Side of Controversy." *Catholic Library World* 50 (July-August 1978):6-7.

Reflects on the benefits of controversy for the writer and the reader.

A668 -----. "Forever Pedaling on the Road to Realism." In Hearne, *Celebrating Children's Books*, pp. 45-53.

Explains what he is trying to accomplish in his books, particularly in *The Chocolate War* and *After the First Death*.

A669 DE LUCA, GERALDINE, and NATOV, —a+21.6HRONI. "An Interview with Robert Cormier." *L&U* 2, no. 1 (Fall 1978):109-35.

In this lengthy interview Cormier reveals the incident involving his son that provided the seed for *The Chocolate War*, discusses the way the story developed, and analyzes some of his feelings and other people's responses to the book and its characters. Discusses *I Am the Cheese* in a similar fashion.

A670 DONELSON, KENNETH, and NILSEN, ALLEEN PACE. "*The Chocolate War* as a Problem Novel." In *Literature for Today's Young Adults*, pp. 186-90.
    Analyzes the book as "an example of the best modern realism for young adults."

A671 GALLO, DONALD R. "Robert Cormier: The Author and the Man." *ALAN Review* 9, no. 1 (Fall 1981):33-36. Based on a speech honoring Cormier at a reception commemorating the establishment of the Robert Cormier Collection at the Fitchburg State College Library, Fitchburg, Massachusetts, on 3 May 1981. (ERIC Educational Document Reproduction Service, 1977, ED 208 419.)
    Discusses *Chocolate War*, *I Am the Cheese*, *After the First Death*, and varying public critical reactions to them. "All good literature, in fact, makes people think, reflect, re-examine beliefs. Robert Cormier's books certainly do that."

A672 HEINS, PAUL. Review. *Horn Book* 53 (August 1977):427-28.
    Primarily a plot summary of *I Am the Cheese*, but concludes "Truly a novel in the tragic mode, cunningly wrought, shattering in its emotional implications."

A673 INGLIS, FRED. *Promise of Happiness*, pp. 276-79.
    What is wrong with *The Chocolate War* "is its grossness and indelicacy in telling its child-readers that heroism is, strictly, such a dead end."

A674 LENZ, MILLICENT. "A Romantic Ironist's Vision of Evil: Robert Cormier's *After the First Death*." *Proceedings of the Children's Literature Association* 8 (1981):50-56.
    In an attempt "to resolve some of the confusions and contradictions surrounding the world view in Cormier's work," Lenz examines Cormier's own statements about himself as an artist, and his use of irony in *After the First Death*.

A675 LUKENS, REBECCA. "From Salinger to Cormier: Disillusionment to Despair in Thirty Years." *ALAN Review* 9, no. 1 (Fall 1981):38-42. (Also available from Eric Document Reproduction Service, 1977, ED 208 419.)
    Feels Cormier "does not deal with the existential *angst* of humankind--the eternal issue" and "the skillfully portrayed reality of the particular evils in the 'now' produce terror in the reader. Like Salinger, Cormier disillusions the adolescent reader, but unlike Salinger, who offers discovery, Cormier offers only despair."

A676 MacLEOD, ANNE SCOTT. "Robert Cormier and the Adolescent Novel." *CLE*, n.s. 12, no. 2 (Summer 1981):74-81.
    Claims that Cormier's works are basically political novels, and that in this they break from tradition, an aspect of Cormier's work that hitherto has been ignored.

A677 MARCH-PENNY, ROBBIE. "From Hardback to Paperback: *The Chocolate War* by Robert Cormier." *CLE*, n.s. 9, no. 2 (Summer

1978):78-84.
An introduction to the book for teachers, with a list of suggestions for the classroom.

A678 MERTZ, MAIA PANK, and MERTZ, ROBERT J. "Adolescents against Society: Institutional Values in *The Chocolate War* and *The Magician*." *Focus* 3, no. 2 (Winter 1977):27-35. (Also ERIC Educational Document Reproduction Service, ED 157 082.)
Provides a detailed examination of the handling of the theme of individual versus society in Robert Cormier's *The Chocolate War* and Sal Stein's *The Magician*.

A679 MICHAELS, WENDY. "Heigh Ho, the Merry Oh, The Farmer in the Dell." *Orana* 18 (May 1982):57-58.
Comments on Cormier's narrative techniques in *I am the Cheese*.

A680 NODELMAN, PERRY. "Robert Cormier Does a Number." *CLE*, n.s. 14, no. 2 (Summer 1983):94-103.
Explores the narrative techniques Cormier uses to "do a number on" the reader, and thereby lead him or her to identify with the protagonist in *I Am the Cheese*.

A681 O'MALLEY, WILLIAM J. Review of *I Am the Cheese*. *Media and Methods* 14 (May-June 1978):24-28.
A highly favorable, in-depth review, followed by Frank M. McLaughlin's brief profile.

A682 PIEHL, KATHY. Letter to the Editors. *CLE*, n.s. 9, no. 4 (Winter 1978):198-201.
Examines Cormier's *Chocolate War* within the context of the school story tradition, and compares it to Kipling's *Stalky & Co..*

A683 REES, DAVID. "The Sadness of Compromise: Robert Cormier and Jill Chaney." In *Marble in the Water*, pp. 155-72.
Discusses *The Chocolate War* and *After the First Death*.

A684 SILVEY, ANITA. "An Interview with Robert Cormier." *Horn Book* 61 (March, May 1985):145-61, 289-96.
Focuses on *Beyond the Chocolate War*, his methods of writing, and the influences on his work.

A685 WESS, ROBERT C., and STEWART, CLAIRE L. "Robert Cormier's Underlying Vision in *The Chocolate War*." *Advocate* 4, no. 1 (Fall 1984):26-37.
Argues that by looking at Cormier's work as a whole and examining its deeper meanings, "students can pierce through the clouds of Robert Cormier's dark vision of the world to see as well some hopeful illumination breaking through."

COURLANDER, HAROLD (1908-   )

A686 SCHMIDT, NANCY. *Children's Fiction About Africa*, pp. 160.
Praises the author's careful use of oral folk history in *Son of the Leopard*.

A687 WOLKSTEIN, DIANE. "An Interview with Harold Courlander." *Library Journal* 99 (15 May 1974):1437-40 and *SLJ* 20 (May 1974):19-22.

In this interview Courlander discusses his work, his approach to folk-tale collecting and his philosophy.

COX, PALMER (1840-1924)

A688 CUMMINS, ROGER W. *Humorous But Wholesome: A History of Palmer Cox and the Brownies*. Watkins Glen, N.Y.: Century, 1973. 254 pp.
Includes a biography of Cox in the first three chapters, an account of the Scottish origins of the Brownies and their appearance in literature, a discussion of the writing of the books and their spin-offs, and finally a brief critical evaluation. Contains numerous illustrations, some reprints of rare material, and primary and secondary bibliographies.

CRAIG, JOHN (1921-82)

A689 FERNS, JOHN. "John Craig: An Under-Estimated Writer?" *CCL* 33 (1984):32-39.
Provides a critical overview of Craig's career, with special emphasis on *Ain't Lookin* (originally entitled *Chappie and Me*).

CRAMPTON, GERTRUDE

A690 RIESMAN, DAVID. "*Tootle*: A Modern Cautionary Tale." In *The Lonely Crowd: A Study of the Changing American Character*. New Haven: Yale University Press, 1950, pp. 107-111. (Reprinted in Margaret Mead and Martha Wolfenstein, eds., *Childhood in Contemporary Culture* [Chicago: University of Chicago Press, 1955], pp. 236-42.)
Interprets *Tootle the Engine*, illustrated by Tibor Gergely, as a story that preaches conformity and "other-directed" values.

CRANE, WALTER (1845-1915)

A691 CRANE, WALTER. "*Signal* Reprints: Notes on My Own Books." *Signal* 13 (January 1974):10-15. (Also reprinted in *Junior Bookshelf* 5, no. 1 [October 1940]:13-18.)
Describes the making of his children's books in this reprint of a 1913 essay.

A692 ENGEN, R.K. *Walter Crane as Book Illustrator*. London: Academy Editions; New York: St. Martin's, 1975, 105 pp.
An introduction, pp. 1-11, provides a critical overview. The remainder of the book consists of reproductions of plates from Crane's books and annotations.

A693 HEARN, MICHAEL PATRICK. "Nursery Aesthetics: Walter Crane and His Picture Books for Children." *American Book Collector*, n.s. 2, no. 4 (July-August 1981):19-33; no. 5 (September-October 1981):2-12.
Surveys Crane's career, his illustrations for children's books, and his place in history of children's book illustration.

A694 SPENCER, ISOBEL. *Walter Crane*. London: Studio Vista, 1975. 208 pp.
A detailed study of Crane as artist, craftsman, and creator of children's books. Includes references and bibliographies.

A695　WEINSTEIN, FREDERIC DANIEL. "Walter Crane and the American Book Arts, 1800-1915." Ph.D. dissertation, Columbia University, 1970, 275 pp., DA 32:468A.

Documents the influence of Walter Crane's book designs "upon the visual atmosphere of late nineteenth-century and early twentieth-century American book arts."

CRAWFORD, ISOBELLA VALANCY (1850-87)

A696　TIERNEY, FRANK M. "Isobella Valancy Crawford's *The Halton Boys*." *CCL* 22 (1981):15-26.

Provides a detailed analysis of this nineteenth-century boys' adventure story.

CREANGĂ, ION (1837-89)

A697　TAYLOR, R.L. "Romanian Folklore and Ion Creangă's *Recollections of Childhood*." *Children's Literature* 4 (1975):70-79.

Examines the distinguishing characteristics of the Romanian folktales collected by Creangă, comparing them to patterns in his autobiography.

CREDLE, ELLIS (1902-　)

A698　BADER, BARBARA. *American Picturebooks*, pp. 141-43, 375.

Surveys Credle's contributions to the picture book.

CRESSWELL, HELEN (1934-　)

A699　CRESSWELL, HELEN. "Ancient and Modern and Incorrigibly Plural." In Blishen, *Thorny Paradise*, pp. 108-16.

Cresswell comments upon her approach to writing.

A700　-----. "If It's Someone from Porlock, Don't Answer the Door." *CLE*, o.s., no. 4 (March 1971):32-39.

Shares her thoughts on writing fantasy, specifically on her *The Night Watchmen*.

A701　CROUCH, MARCUS. "Helen Cresswell--Craftsman." *Junior Bookshelf* 34 (June 1970):135-39.

Praises Cresswell's craftsmanship and calls *The Piemakers* her "most delightful book," in which she "blends most successfully her creative imagination and her acute observation."

A702　GREAVES, MARGARET. "Warm Sun, Cold Wind: The Novels of Helen Cresswell." *CLE*, o.s., no. 6 (July 1971):51-59.

"Helen Cresswell's books are largely concerned with three of the major experiences of childhood--the awareness of family, of miracle and ceremony." Praises her joyfulness.

A703　MAQUIRE, GREGORY. "A Second Look: *The Piemakers*." *Horn Book* 57 (April 1981):215-17.

An enthusiastic appreciation.

A704　TOWNSEND, JOHN R. *Sense of Story*, pp. 57-67.

"Miss Cresswell has written several books that are slight and some that are inferior. But her best is very good, and her slighter books have often shown true quality." Discusses *The Piemakers*. "It has all the qualities which should enable a children's book to last."

CROKER, THOMAS CROFTON (1798-1854)

A705   KAMENETSKY, CHRISTA. "The Irish Fairy Legends and the Brothers Grimm." *Proceedings of the Children's Literature Association* 9 (1982):77-86.
Attempts to reestablish the value of the *Fairy Legends and Traditions of the South of Ireland* as a milestone in the history of folklore research and children's literature. Based on correspondence between Croker and the Brothers Grimm within the context of prevailing romantic theories of folktale collections.

CROMPTON, FRANCES ELIZA (1866-1952)

A706   BRILL, BARBARA. "Frances Eliza Crompton." *Signal* 29 (May 1979):103-8.
Surveys and analyzes Crompton's work, describing it as "marked by a keen understanding of a child's mind, and by an awareness of the beautiful sound of the English language . . . full of detailed observations of the countryside" and "underlaid by a firm Christian faith." Includes a bibliography of Crompton's stories.

CROMPTON, RICHMAL [Richmal Crompton Lamburn] (1890-1969)

A707   CADOGAN, MARY, and CRAIG, PATRICIA. "William and Jane." In *You're a Brick*, pp. 206-26.
"In William, Richmal Crompton lumped together all the child characteristics which adults find most abhorrent, thereby assuring his appeal for a generation of English children." Discusses the William books and William's female counterpart, Jane, in the series of Jane books by Evadne Price.

A708   TUCKER, NICHOLAS. *The Child and the Book*, pp. 116-22.
Provides an in-depth analysis of William's character and appeal.

ČTVRTEK, VACLAV (1911-76)

A709   AMOR, STUART. "Rumiajs: A Modern Fairy-Tale Hero." *Signal* 27 (September 1978):150-62.
Discusses the modern Czech fairy tales that have been popularized by television throughout Europe, starring the hero Rumiajs. Includes Amor's own translation of "How Rumiajs the Cobbler Became a Robber."

CUMMINGS, E.E. (1894-1962)

A710   APSELOFF, MARILYN. "Children's Books by Famous Writers for Adults." *Children's Literature* 2 (1974):130-38.
Examines the children's books of five important twentieth-century writers: Aldous Huxley, James Joyce, Arthur Miller, William Faulkner, and E.E. Cummings.

A711   OSTROM, ALAN. "*Fairy Tales*: The Other Cummings." *L&U* 2, no.

1 (Spring 1975):65-72.
Asks why these tales are so unexceptional, when we expect so much more of Cummings. Suggests that without "the distance from innocence and the awareness of that distance that adultness offers, Cummings is unable to make full use of his remarkable gifts."

CUNNINGHAM, JULIA (1916-   )

A712   CUNNINGHAM, JULIA. "Dear Characters." *Horn Book* 43 (April 1961):233-34.
The author reveals the origins of the characters and title of her *Dorp Dead*.

DAHL, ROALD (1916-   )

A713   BOUCHARD, LOIS KALB. "A New Look at Old Favorites: *Charlie and the Chocolate Factory.*" *IRBC* 3, nos. 2-3 (1970):3, 8. (Reprinted in MacCann, *Black American*, pp. 112-15.)
Points out that the Oompa-Loompas are treated in terms of "time dishonored stereotypes, childishness and dependency upon whites."

A714   CAMERON, ELEANOR. "McLuhan, Youth and Literature." *Horn Book* 48 (October, December 1972):433-40, 572-79. (Reprinted in Heins, *Crosscurrents*, pp. 98-125.)
Considers *Charlie and the Chocolate Factory* "one of the most tasteless books ever written for children." Like candy it "leaves us poorly nourished." Contrasts it with *Charlotte's Web*, "one of the best" books ever written for children. Roald Dahl's "*Charlie and the Chocolate Factory*: A Reply," follows in *Horn Book* 49 (February 1973):77-78: "I believe that I am a better judge than Mrs. Cameron of what stories are good or bad for children."
Cameron responds to Dahl in 49 (April 1973):127-29, "A Reply to Roald Dahl." She maintains her position and emphasizes the depressing situation and lack of feeling shown toward the Oompa-Loompas. "Popularity in itself does not prove anything about a book's essential worth." Critics must think about books as well as respond with emotion.
The debate was also taken up in letters to the editor in in February, April, August, and October 1973, and in Paul Heins's editorials "In Protest" and "At Critical Cross-Purposes" in February and April.

A715   -----. "A Question of Taste." *CLE*, o.s., no. 21 (Summer 1976):59-63.
Further discusses and defends her opinion on *Charlie and the Chocolate Factory*, which generated such controversy in the 1972 *Horn Book* article (see above).

A716   CAMPBELL, ALASDAIR. "Children's Writers: 6. Roald Dahl." *School Librarian* 29 (June 1981):108-14.
Surveys the nine children's books Dahl wrote between 1960 and 1980. Finds his writing difficult to characterize but "marked by a powerful creative imagination and an instinctive understanding of the sort of themes and incidents that appeal to young readers."

A717   CHESTERFIELD-EVANS, JAN. "Roald Dahl: A Discussion and Comparison of his Stories for Children and Adults." *Orana* 19 (November 1983):165-68.

Compares Dahl's style in his writing for children and for adults.

A718   CORNER, CALLA. "The Weird Writing World of Roald Dahl." *Writers Digest* 60 (August 1980):40-42, 47.
Interviews Dahl about his life and his stories for children and adults.

A719   MERRICK, ANNE. "*The Nightwatchmen* and *Charlie and the Chocolate Factory* as Books to Be Read to Children." *CLE*, o.s., no. 16 (Spring 1975):21-30.
Examines *Charlie and the Chocolate Factory* and Helen Cresswell's *The Nightwatchmen* in an attempt to determine why they are received so differently by children and adults. After painstaking analysis concludes that "Cresswell's book is of greater literary merit" while "*Charlie* has the robust folk qualities that make its appeal much broader."

A720   SARLAND, CHARLES. "The Secret Seven vs. The Twits: Cultural Clash or Cosy Combination?" *Signal* 42 (September 1983):155-71.
Compares Dahl's *The Twits* and Enid Blyton's *Shock for the Secret Seven.*

A721   WEST, MARK I. "Regression and Fragmentation of the Self in *James and the Giant Peach.*" *CLE*, n.s. 16, no. 4 (Winter 1985):219-25.
"A psychoanalytic interpretation of this book indicates that it is considerably more than an exciting, transatlantic adventure story."

A722   WINTLE, JUSTIN, and FISHER, EMMA. *Pied Piper*, pp. 101-12.
Dahl discusses his life and work in an interview.

DALY, MAUREEN (1921-   )

A723   DONELSON, KENNETH. "*Seventeenth Summer* and *Forever* as Love-Romances." In *Literature for Today's Young Adults*, pp. 152, 214-15.
Analyzes the book as a love-romance and compares it with Judy Blume's *Forever.*

Dandy

A724   TUCKER, NICHOLAS. "Anti-Superman." In *Suitable for Children*, pp. 87-92. (Also in *TLS*, 6 June 1968.)
Analyzes the popular British comic strip.

DANZIGER, PAULA (1944-   )

A725   NODELMAN, PERRY. "'I think I'm Learning a Lot': How Typical Children Read Typical Books About Typical Children on Typical Subjects." *Proceedings of the Children's Literature Association* 7 (1980):146-52. (Reprinted in *CLE*, n.s. 12, no. 4 (Winter 1981):177-85 as "How Typical Children Read Typical Books.")
Uses Danziger's *The Cat Ate My Gymsuit* as typical of the type of story children identify with and contrasts it with Paula Fox's *Slave Dancer*, a story admired by many adults but not especially popular with children. Argues that we should not train children to read only about themselves because good writing is always about people different than ourselves.

DARINGER, HELEN FERN (1892-   )

A726   KINGSTON, CAROLYN T. *Tragic Mode*, pp. 39-41.
Analyzes theme of rejection *Adopted Jane*.

DAUGHERTY, JAMES (1889-1974)

A727   BADER, BARBARA. *American Picturebooks*, pp. 151-54.
Analyzes *Andy and the Lion*; maintains that of all of Daugherty's books it stands alone.

A728   *Imprint: Oregon* 2, no. 2 (Fall 1975):24 pp.
Special issue. Contains a "Note on James Daugherty," by Lynd Ward, a biographical overview, and a checklist of books illustrated by Daugherty.

A729   KENT, NORMAN. "James Daugherty, Buckskin Illustrator." *American Artist* 9 (March 1945):16-20.
A brief biocritical overview.

A730   TITZELL, JOSIAH. "James Daugherty, American." *Publishers Weekly* 116 (26 October 1929):2073-76.
A brief biocritical overview concentrating on Daugherty's artistic techniques.

A731   WARD, LYND. "A Note on James Daugherty." *Horn Book* 16 (July-August 1940):239-46.
High praise for Daugherty, especially for *Daniel Boone* and *Andy and the Lion*.

**D'AULAIRE, EDGAR (1898-   ), and
D'AULAIRE INGRI PARIN (1904-80)**

A732   BADER, BARBARA. "Ingri and Edgar Parin D'Aulaire." In *American Picturebooks*, pp. 42-46.
Evaluates the D'Aulaires' contribution to the history and development of the American picture book.

A733   CHILDREN LITERATURE REVIEW BOARD. Review. In MacCann, *Cultural Conformity*, pp. 144-45.
The 1940 Caldecott Medal winner, *Abraham Lincoln*, is attacked for unrealistic and stereotypical portrayals of blacks.

DE ANGELI, MARGUERITE (1889-   )

A734   BURNS, PAUL C., and HINES, RUTH. "Marguerite De Angeli: Faith in the Human Spirit." *EE* 44 (December 1967):833-39. (Reprinted in Hoffman, *Authors and Illustrators*, pp. 108-14.)
Categorizes De Angeli's work as family related, Philadelphia related, and history or minority group related.

A735   CHILDREN'S LITERATURE REVIEW BOARD. Review. In MacCann, *Cultural Conformity*, pp. 141-44.
Argues that the highly acclaimed *Bright April* "does a severe injustice to the Black experience and is not recommended for general reading."

A736   DE ANGELI, MARGUERITE. *Butter at the Old Price.* New York: Doubleday, 1971, 258 pp.

Revealing of De Angeli's background and personality, this autobiography contains chapters on her development as an illustrator and a writer, on the research processes for several of the books and on the origins of *Bright April.*

A737   -----. "Newbery Award Acceptance." *Horn Book* 26 (1950):252-62.

Describes the background of several of her books, especially *The Door in the Wall.* A brief biographical sketch by one of her children, Maury De Angeli, follows on pages 264-68.

A738   HOLLOWELL, LILLIAN. "Marguerite De Angeli--Writer and Illustrator for Children." *EE* 24 (October 1952):317-25, 358.

Primarily a summary of De Angeli's works up to 1952; offers some critical insights.

A739   KINGSTON, Carolyn T. *Tragic Mode*, pp. 32-34.

Analyzes *The Door in the Wall* in terms of its themes of rejection and physical disability.

DE BECK, BILLY (1890-1942)

A740   SAGARIN, EDWARD. "The Deviant in the Comic Strip: The Case History of Barney Google." *Journal of Popular Culture* 5 (Summer 1971):179-93.

Analyzes the Barney Google comic strip, concentrating on the relationship between Google and his horse Spark Plug.

DEFOE, DANIEL (1660-1731)

A741   HARDY, BARBARA. "*Robinson Crusoe.*" *CLE*, n.s. 24, no. 8 (Spring 1977):3-11.

Analyzes the continuing appeal of this classic to today's children.

A742   HAZARD, PAUL. *Books, Children and Men*, pp. 47-61.

Provides background on Defoe and explores the immense appeal of *Robinson Crusoe* for children.

A743   REEDER, KIK. "The Real *Robinson Crusoe*: A Classic Revisited." *IRBC* 5, no. 5 (1974):1-3.

Indicts the classic as imperialist and racist.

DE JONG, DOLA (1911-   )

A744   KINGSTON, CAROLYN T. *Tragic Mode*, pp. 95-98, 113-16.

Analyzes *The Level Land* and *Return to the Level Land* in terms of the theme of war.

DE JONG, MEINDERT (1906-   )

A745   BURGESS, ELEANOR. "Meindert De Jong, Storyteller." *EE* 32 (May 1955):267-76.

A biocritical overview of De Jong's work. "Here is an author who writes as he speaks" and incorporates many of the techniques of the storyteller.

A746   CARR, MARION GRUDIER. "Meindert De Jong and the World's Children." *TON* 27 (June 1971):395-402.
Primarily a listing of books by De Jong in English and their many translations into foreign languages.

A747   CIANCIOLO, PATRICIA JEAN. "Meindert De Jong." *EE* 45 (October 1968):725-30. (Reprinted in Hoffman, *Authors and Illustrators*, pp. 115-21.)
A brief biocritical overview. Includes a bibliography of De Jong's books.

A748   DE JONG, MEINDERT. "The Author has Something to Say: A Symposium." In *NYTBR*, 14 May 1961, Children's Book sec. p. 3. (Reprinted in Bator, *Signposts*, p. 45.)
The author has no message: "My sole mission is to tell the tale."

A749   -----. "The Cry of Creativity." *Bookbird* 1 (1965):5-13.
Hans Christian Andersen Medal Speech, 1962. Discusses sources of his creativity.

A750   -----. "For Love of the Word." *Horn Book* 60 (September-October 1984):569-77.
Recounts his career as a writer of children's books. A brief account by Betsy Hearne, highlighting some of his books, precedes, pp. 566-68.

A751   -----. "Newbery Award Acceptance." *Horn Book* 31 (August 1955):241-46.
Tells how he tries to write from the perspective of the inner child, from the unconscious. Followed by a biographical reminiscence by his brother David Cornel De Jong, pp. 247-53.

A752   GARD, ROGER. "Meindert De Jong's *Tower By The Sea*." *Use of English* 21, no. 3 (Spring 1970):221-23, 227.
Concentrates on the moral certainty and complexity of the work, and the ways in which its themes might be approached with children.

A753   KINGSTON, CAROLYN T. *Tragic Mode*.
Discusses death in *Shadrach* pp. 160-63, and *The Wheel on the School*, pp. 75-78.

A754   TOWNSEND, JOHN ROWE. *Sense of Story*, pp. 68-78.
Identifies De Jong's two most remarkable talents: "Achieving an extraordinary empathy with children and animals," and "expressing joy."

A755   "When Once A Little Boy. . . . " *TLS* 68 (4 December 1959):24. (Reprinted in Haviland, *Children and Literature*, pp. 277-80.)
Identifies excitement and De Jong's ability to recapture childhood memories as key characteristics of his work.

DE LA MARE, WALTER (1873-1956)

A756   AUDEN, W.H. "Walter De la Mare." In *Forewords and Afterwords*. New York: Random House, 1973, pp. 384-94.
Comments upon the distinguishing characteristics of De la Mare's poetry, paying special attention to his poetry for children.

A757   BARFIELD, O. "Poetry in Walter De la Mare." *University of Denver Quarterly* 8 (Autumn 1978):69-81.
        Attempts to draw attention to "certain qualities in his poetry," both for adults and children, which Barfield feels have been overlooked.

A758   BIANCO, MARGERY. "De la Mare." *Horn Book* 18 (May-June 1942):141-47.
        Praises De la Mare's poetry and his anthologies, emphasizing the way "reality and unreality interpenetrate."

A759   CLARK, LEONARD. *Walter De la Mare.* New York: Walck; London: Bodley Head, 1961, 81 pp.
        Argues that De la Mare "is the greatest writer of English lyrical poetry, (particularly for children) of the first half of this century. Provides biographical background and detailed examinations of his poetry and stories. Includes a bibliography of works by and about De la Mare.

A760   COOPER, SUSAN. "Nahum Tarune's Book." *Horn Book* 56 (October 1980):497-507.
        A personal response to *Come Hither*, placing it in the context of more recent fantasy for children. It captures the freshness of the child's vision of the world, and "the whole life of an artist."

A761   CROUCH, M.S. "Walter De la Mare and His Illustrators." *Junior Bookshelf* 17, no. 2 (March 1953):51-60.
        Comments upon De la Mare's various illustrators.

A762   DALPHIN, MARCIA. "I Give You the End of a Golden String." *Horn Book* 14 (May 1938):143-49. (Reprinted in Fryatt, *Horn Book Sampler*, pp. 133-34, 138-39.)
        Praises *The Three Mulla Mulgars* as a "highly imaginative 'quest'" book; "How one wishes that everyone might have his imagination kindled by it!"

A763   DEGAN, JAMES NERHOOD. "The Short Fiction of Walter De la Mare." Ph.D. dissertation, University of Iowa, 1982, 301 pp., DA 43:1150A.
        Examines De la Mare's short stories, the role of the child as visionary in particular, but pays little attention to his works for children.

A764   GRAHAM, ELEANOR. "The Riddle of Walter De la Mare: An Appreciation of His Work for Children." *Junior Bookshelf* 12 (July 1948):59-65.
        Sees De la Mare's stories as a treasure house full of secret places and "rooms he has cunningly furnished to rouse the curious."

A765   LATHROP, DOROTHY P. "Illustrating De la Mare." *Horn Book* 18 (May-June 1942):188-96.
        An illustrator's insights into the poet's work.

A766   McCROSSEN, DORIS ROSS. *Walter De la Mare.* Twayne's English Authors Series, no. 33. New York: Twayne, 1966, 170 pp.
        Concentrates on De la Mare's novels and works for adults, but

contains sections on his children's poetry, pp. 63-77, and *The Three Royal Monkeys* (originally published as *The Three Mulla Mulgars*), pp. 95-101.

A767   MÉGROZ, RODOLPHE L. *Walter De la Mare: A Biographical and Critical Study.* London: Hodder & Stoughton; New York: George H. Doran, 1924, 303 pp.
   Devotes chapter 3, "The Poetry of Childhood," pp. 50-84, to De la Mare's works for children.

A768   REID, FORREST. *Walter De la Mare: A Critical Study.* London: Faber & Faber, 1929, 256 pp.
   Discusses early poetry in "Songs of Childhood," pp. 27-52, and "The Three Mulla-Mulgars" and "Poems of Maturity," pp. 108-25; pp. 148-79 are devoted to *The Listeners* and *Peacock Pie*.

A769   WALSH, WILLIAM. "De la Mare's Small World." In Ford, *Young Writers, Young Readers*, pp. 107-14.
   Views De la Mare as a minor poet whose "retreat from reality back to the shelter of the dream" holds great appeal.

DE LARRABEITÉ, MICHAEL

A770   ZIPES, JACK. "The Adventure of Fantasy as Struggle for Survival." *Children's Literature* 7 (1978):242-47.
   Regards *The Borribles* as "one of the finest fantasy works in recent years."

DENSLOW, W. W. (1856-1915)

A771   *American Book Collector*, December 1964, pp. 10-21.
   Contains articles on Denslow and a checklist of his work.

A772   GREENE, DOUGLAS. "W.W. Denslow, Illustrator." *Journal of Popular Culture* 7, no. 1 (Summer 1973):86-96.
   Traces Denslow's career and provides insights into his style.

A773   GREENE, DOUGLAS, and HEARN, MICHAEL PATRICK. *W.W. Denslow.* Mount Pleasant, Mich.: Central Michigan University, Clarke Historical Library, 1976, 225 pp.
   A biographical overview and bibliography.

A774   HEARN, MICHAEL PATRICK. "W.W. Denslow: The Forgotten Illustrator." *American Artist* 37 (May 1973):40-45, 71-73.
   A biocritical overview.

DE PAOLA, TOMIE (1934-   )

A775   BERT, RITA ANN. "Tomie de Paola: Creator of Excellence in Children's Books." *Catholic Library World* 54 (February 1983):278-79.
   A brief biocritical overview.

A776   HEPLER, SUSAN INGRID. "Profile: Tomie de Paola: A Gift to Children." *LA* 56 (March 1979):296-301.
   Primarily an overview of de Paola's career with insight into his techniques and influences on him--especially those of Fra Angelico and Giotto.

DE TREVINO, ELIZABETH BORTON (1904-   )

A777   MacCANN, DONNARAE. "Racism in Prize-Winning Biographical Works." In *Black American*, pp. 101-6.
Analyzes racial stereotypes in the Newbery Award-winning *I, Juan de Pareja*.

DE VEAUX, ALEXIS (1948-   )

A778   MILLER, RICHARD H. "Three Musical Lives: Billie Holiday, Bessie Smith, and Mahalia Jackson." *L&U* 4, no. 1 (Summer 1980):71-82.
This comparative review of three biographies concludes that only Billie Holiday, in De Veaux's *Don't Explain: A Song of Billie Holiday*, emerges as a real person.

A779   VANDERGRIFT, KAY E. *Child and Story*, pp. 160-64.
Analyzes the pictures and layout as well as the words of *na-ni*, which is interpreted as a mood piece.

DHONDY, FARRUKH (1944-   )

A780   WHITCOME, BOBBIE. "East-West: The Divided Worlds of Farrukh Dhondy." *CLE*, n.s. 14, no. 1 (Spring 1983):35-43.
Discusses *Poona Company*, stories from *East End at Your Feet*, *Come to Mecca*, *Trip Trap*, and the novel *The Siege of Babylon*. Touches on the question of racism and the theme of illusion vs. reality.

DICKINSON, PETER (1927-   )

A781   CROUCH, MARCUS. *Nesbit Tradition*, pp. 50-52.
"Much of the interest of Dickinson's achievement comes from his examination of society, whether the embryo manorial system of *The Devil's Children* or its matured counterpart in *Heartsease*."

A782   GRIMSHAW, NIGEL. "Peter Dickinson's Children's Stories." *School Librarian* 22, no. 3 (September 1974):219-23.
Provides a critical evaluation of Dickinson's first six books.

A783   HEINS, ETHEL. Review. *Horn Book* 54 (April 1978):150.
Finds intimations of Poe and Dostoevski in the style and psychological impact of Dickinson's *Annerton Pit*.

A784   HUTCHINSON, JOANNA. "Peter Dickinson Considered, In and Out of the Classroom." *CLE*, o.s., no. 17 (Summer 1975):88-98.
Discusses the use of Peter Dickinson's books with students.

A785   REES, DAVID. "Plums and Roughage: Peter Dickinson." In *Painted Desert*, pp. 153-67.
Finds in Dickinson a refusal to take himself seriously which is both a strength and a weakness. Argues that he writes mainly to entertain, but there are "plums . . . messages, fine writing, original and profound comments on human nature" in the "roughage" if one chooses to seek them out.

A786   TOWNSEND, JOHN ROWE. *A Sounding*, pp. 41-54.

"For all their variety the books have much in common: strong professional storytelling, rapid action and adventure, continual invention, a proliferating interest in ideas, and an understanding of how things are done. Behind all this one glimpses an energetic, speculative mind with a leaning towards the exotic."

A787 WILLIAMS, JAY. "Very Iffy Books: An Interview with Peter Dickinson." Signal 13 (January 1974):21-29.
Discusses Dickinson's life and work.

DILLON, EILIS (1920-   )

A788 WHITEHEAD, WINIFRED. "Eilis Dillon and The Sense of Community." Use of English 30, no. 2 (Spring 1979):58-62.
Discusses Dillon's books for younger and older children, praising her sense of the child's place within the larger community and her ability to re-create rural Ireland.

DILLON, LEO (1933-   ), and DILLON, DIANE (1933-   )

A789 DILLON, LEO, and DILLON, DIANE. "Caldecott Award Acceptance." Horn Book 52 (August 1976):373-77.
Discusses the process and technique of illustrating Why Mosquitoes Buzz in People's Ears. Biographical sketch by Phyllis J. Fogelman follows, pp. 378-83.

A790 -----. "Caldecott Award Acceptance." Horn Book 53 (August 1977): 415-21.
Tells how they gathered background for their illustrations of Margaret Musgrove's folktale retelling of Ashanti to Zulu: African Traditions. Biographical sketches of each follow, pp. 423-26.

DISNEY, WALT (1901-66)

A791 BAILEY, ADRIAN. The Fantasy World of Walt Disney. New York: Everest House, 1982, 253 pp.
A highly favorable survey of Disney's fantasy creations, including numerous color plates and a text with details about the techniques used, Disney's goals, and critical responses to his work, including his interpretations of fairy tales and other classics of children's literature. Typical of Bailey's tone and approach: "Above all, Walt Disney was a great storyteller in the ancient tradition of the fairy tale--often as grim as Grimm, fanciful as Hans Andersen, fantastic as Lewis Carroll, sentimental as Charles Kingsley."

A792 BERLAND, DAVID L. "Disney and Freud: Walt Meets the Id." Journal of Popular Culture 15, no. 4 (Spring 1982):93-104.
Applies Freud's theories to Disney's created characters and to his interpretations of traditional literature.

A793 CHAMBERS, DEWEY W. "The 'Disney Touch' and the Wonderful World of Children's Literature." EE 43 (January 1966):50-52.
Argues that Disney takes advantage of "poetic license" in transforming books into movies, sometimes removing original symbolic and psychological meanings.

A794 DORFMAN, ARIEL, and MATTELART, ARMAND. How to Read

Donald Duck: Imperialist Ideology in the Disney Comics. *New York: International General, 1975, 112 pp. (First published as* Plata Leer al Plato Donald *in Chile in 1971.*

An extensive Marxist critique of Disney and the capitalist society he represents, through a detailed examination of the Donald Duck comics.

A795 FREEMAN, JAMES A. "Donald Duck: How Children (Mainly Boys) Viewed their Parents (Mainly Fathers), 1943-1960." *Children's Literature* 6 (1977):150-64.

Sees Donald as a father figure who appealed to children because he both resembled and parodied their fathers. Based on examination of *Walt Disney's Comics and Stories*, nos. 31-243 (April 1943-December 1960).

A796 HYUN, PETER. "Walt Disney Through the Looking Glass." *Bookbird* 5, no. 4 (1967):20-22.

Considers Disney's motion pictures and animated cartoons a misuse of forms and "a corruption of the best children's literature."

A797 MAY, JILL P. "Walt Disney's Interpretation of Children's Literature." *LA* 58 (April 1981):463-72. (Reprinted in Barron, *Jump Over the Moon*, pp. 461-72.)

A close look at Disney's animated productions reveals the values and American qualities promoted and criticized through his films. May examines Disney's handling of "Snow White," "Cinderella," *Pinocchio*, and *Bambi*.

A798 SAYERS, FRANCES CLARKE. "Walt Disney Accused." *Horn Book* 41 (December 1965):602-11.

Denounces Disney's "debasement of the traditional literature of childhood."

A799 SIDWELL, ROBERT T. "Naming Disney's Dwarfs." *CLE*, n.s. 11, no. 2 (Summer 1980):69-75.

Argues that not all of Disney's alterations of traditional tales despoiled them, but that some, such as the naming of the dwarfs in *Snow White*, fit into folktale tradition. Letter in response by Jill P. May (*CLE*, n.s. 11, no. 2 (Winter 1980):200-203) argues that Sidwell's defense of Disney does not answer Sayers's objection, or deny Disney's restructuring of the essence of the tale to reflect middle-class American values.

A800 SMITH, ROSEMARY. "Walt Disney's *Mary Poppins*." *EE* 44 (January 1967):29-31.

Argues that the Disney book and film destroyed "the remarkable personality of Mary Poppins herself and the meaning and magic of the individual stories."

DIXON, FRANKLIN W. [Stratemeyer Syndicate pseudonym]

A801 O'CONNOR, GERARD. "The Hardy Boys Revisited: A Study in Prejudice." In *Challenges in American Culture*. Edited by Ray B. Browne, et al., Bowling Green, Ohio: Bowling Green University Popular Press, 1970, pp. 234-41.

Analyzes racial and ethnic stereotypes and prejudices in the Hardy Boys series, and comments on recent revisions: "About as effective as putting a band-aid over a cancer."

A802   PRAGER, ARTHUR. "Rascals at Large." In *Rascals at Large*, pp. 99-123.
        Analyzes the Hardy Boys series.

DODGE, MARY MAPES (1831-1905)

A803   GRISWOLD, JEROME. "*Hans Brinker*: Sunny World, Angry Waters." *Children's Literature* 12 (1984):47-60.
        Unremitting cheerfulness and self-control in the face of emotionally disturbing situations are seen as key aspects of the book. Griswold concludes his detailed analysis by saying, "Dodge teases for tears but at the same time condemns tears as leaks, emotional adultery that jeopardizes not a marriage, but a family."

DONOVAN, JOHN (1928-   )

A804   GOLDMAN, SUZY. "John Donovan: Sexuality, Stereotypes and Self." *L&U* 2, no. 2 (Fall 1978):27-36.
        Argues that while Donovan handles the important theme of self-realization well, his books are marred by their somewhat bizarre sexual elements and stereotyped secondary characters. Discusses *Remove Protective Coating a Little at a Time*, *Wild in the World*, and *I'll Get There, It Better Be Worth the Trip*.

DU BOIS, WILLIAM PÈNE (1916-   )

A805   BADER, BARBARA. *American Picturebooks*, pp. 175-86.
        Traces William Pène Du Bois's development as a creator of picture books.

A806   BURKERT, NANCY EKHOLM. "A Second Look: *Lion*." *Horn Book* 56 (December 1980):671-76.
        Examines Du Bois's techniques and assesses their suitability to the picture book text, a celebration of "the creation of uniqueness" and "the uniqueness of creation."

A807   DU BOIS, WILLIAM PÈNE. "Animal History Will Bear This Out." In *Contents of the Basket and Other Papers on Children's Books and Reading*. New York: New York Public Library, 1960, pp. 35-39.
        Provides a lighthearted account of the origins of *Lion*.

DUBRAVSKÝ, VILIAM (1924-76)

A808   DUBRAVEC, ROBERT. "Viliam Dubravský." *Bookbird* 15, no. 2 (1977):60-64.
        A biocritical look at this Czechoslovakian artist-illustrator, including a chronological outline of his career.

DUNHAM, KATHERINE (1910-   )

A809   SCHMIDT, NANCY. *Children's Fiction About Africa*, pp. 158-60.
        Suggests Dunham's selectivity in presenting African culture in *Kasamance* "has been towards cultural complexity and positive aspects of African life."

DUNNING, STEPHEN N.

A810   HOFFECKER, FELICITY. "Reflections on a Gift of Watermelon Pickle." *English Journal* 72 (April 1983):19-20.

    The Felicity who made the original watermelon pickles featured in John Tobias's poem reflects upon the history and popularity of the poem and the anthology *Reflections on a Gift of Watermelon Pickle*, edited by Dunning. Edward Lueders and Dunning respond, pp. 21-22. Tobias himself responds in September 1983, p. 41.

DUVOISIN, ROGER (1904-80)

A811   BADER, BARBARA. "Roger Duvoisin." In *American Picturebooks*, pp. 128-39.

    Analyzes Duvoisin's style and technique, his development as a picture-book artist through his many books.

A812   CROUCH, MARCUS. "From Petunia, Veronica and Crocus--with Love." *Junior Bookshelf* 45, no. 1 (February 1981):5-7.

    An appreciative overview.

A813   DUVOISIN, ROGER. "*The Happy Lion* Finds a Welcome Everywhere." *Publishers Weekly* 181 (12 February 1962):82-83.

    Discusses the origins, development, and publishing history of *The Happy Lion*, illustrated by Duvoisin, written by Louise Fatio Duvoisin.

A814   KANE, RUTH E. "Roger Duvoisin--Distinguished Contributor to the World of Children's Literature." *EE* 33 (November 1956):411-19. (Reprinted in Hoffman, *Authors and Illustrators*, pp. 125-34.)

    An interview and biocritical summary of Duvoisin as writer and artist.

A815   UNWIN, NORA S. "Artist's Choice." *Horn book* 35 (April 1959): 110-11.

    Comments on *A for the Ark*'s design and technique.

A816   WAUGH, DOROTHY. "Roger Duvoisin as Illustrator for Children." *Horn Book* 24 (January-February 1948):11-22.

    Demonstrates how Duvoisin's illustrations have added to the atmosphere of the works he has illustrated.

EATON, JEANETTE (1886-1968)

A817   EATON, JEANETTE. "A Heroine of the French Revolution." *Horn Book* 5 (November 1929):22-29.

    Describes her research on Madame Roland for her *A Daughter of the Seine*.

EDMONDS, WALTER D. (1903-   )

A818   KINGSTON, CAROLYN T. *Tragic Mode*, pp. 63-65.

    Analyzes *The Matchlock Gun* in terms of the theme of entrapment.

EDWARDS, LEO [Stratemeyer Syndicate pseudonym]

A819 PRAGER, ARTHUR. *Rascals at Large*, pp. 251-64.
Discusses the Stratemeyer Syndicate's Jerry Todd series.

EICHENBERG, FRITZ (1901-   )

A820 EICHENBERG, FRITZ. "May Hill Arbuthnot Honor Lecture: Bell, Book, and Candle." *TON* 40 (Spring 1984):353-67.
Presented 6 April 1984. Tells the story of his life, discusses favorite childhood books, illustrations, philosophy, and dreams.

EIDRIGEVICIUS, STASYS

A821 KORSAKAITÉ, I. "On the Untrodden Paths of Fantasy." *Bookbird* 3 (1980):53-56.
Analyzes the work of this young Lithuanian illustrator.

EKWENSKI, CYPRIAN (1921-   )

A882 EMENYONOU, ERNEST. *Cyprian Ekwenski.* London: Evans, 1974, 137 pp.
Chapter 3, pp. 47-69, concentrates on Ekwenski's fiction for children. *Juju Rock* is seen as "an attempt to provide for the Nigerian reader something authentic that could be substituted for foreign adventure stories." Includes bibliographies.

A823 NDU, POL. "Urban Modality in Ekwenski's Juvenile Literature." *Conch Review of Books* 3, nos. 2-4 (1975):83-86.
Concentrates on *Juju Rock* and *The Rain Maker*.

A824 SCHMIDT, NANCY. *Children's Fiction About Africa*, pp. 128-35.
Suggests that Ekwenski presents "a realism based on details of Nigerian life which ordinarily seem to be taboo in children's fiction, such as illegal brewing of palm wine, highway robbery, death from diseases, being struck by lightning, or fights after a sports match." Analyzes *Juju Rock*.

ELIOT, T[HOMAS] S[TEARNS] (1888-1965)

A825 DOUGLASS, PAUL. "Eliot's Cats: Serious Play behind the Playful Seriousness." *Children's Literature* 11 (1983):109-24.
Argues that interpretations such as Hodge's (see below), which emphasize a message, are overly serious, and that the significance of *Old Possum's Book of Practical Cats* is in its playful and rhythmical prosody.

A826 HODGE, MARION C. "The Sane, The Mad, The Good, The Bad: T.S. Eliot's *Old Possum's Book of Practical Cats*." *Children's Literature* 7 (1978):129-46.
Provides a detailed critical discussion, concluding, "Eliot says much the same things to children in *Old Possum's Book of Practical Cats* as he says to adults in his other work."

EMBERLEY, ED (1931-   )

A827 EMBERLEY, ED. "Caldecott Award Acceptance." *Horn Book* 44 (August 1968):399-402.

Describes techniques used in creating the illustrations and interpreting *Drummer Hoff*'s theme. Biographical sketch by wife Barbara follows, pp. 403-16.

A828   "Meet Ed Emberley." *Library Journal* 88 (15 October 1963):3991-95 and *SLJ* 10 (October 1963):113-17.
         Primarily a portrait of Emberley and his family, with brief discussion of his art. Includes a bibliography of books he has written and illustrated.

A829   REYNOLDS, JEAN. "Ed Emberley." *Library Journal* 93 (15 March 1968):1287-88 and *SLJ* 15 (March 1968):113-14.
         Emberley's editor comments upon the design in his books, especially on the procedures used to create *Drummer Hoff* and *One Wide River to Cross*.

A830   WAUGH, DOROTHY. "The Meteoric Career of Ed Emberley." *American Artist* 30 (November 1966):54-61. (Reprinted in Hoffman, *Authors and Illustrators*, pp. 135-40.)
         Emphasizes his artistic technique.

ENGDAHL, SYLVIA (1933-   )

A831   ENGDAHL, SYLVIA. "Perspective on the Future: The Quest of the Space Age Young People." In Lenz, *Young Adult Literature*, pp. 425-33.
         Discusses several of her works, and expresses her belief that science fiction can help young people acquire "a perspective on the future" and assist in "the search for truth."

ENRIGHT, ELIZABETH (1909-68)

A832   CAMERON, ELEANOR. "The Art of Elizabeth Enright." *Horn Book* 45 (December 1969):641-51;46 (February 1970):26-30.
         Compares Enright with Katherine Mansfield and sees parallels between the short story form and the children's novel.

ESTES, ELEANOR (1906-   )

A833   ALTSTETTER, MABEL F. "Eleanor Estes and Her Books." *EE* 24 (May 1952):245-51.
         Provides insights into the way characters and family relationships are portrayed in the Moffat books.

A834   ESTES, ELEANOR. "Gathering Honey." *Horn Book* 36 (December 1960):487-94.
         Anecdotal accounts of events that found their way into her books.

A835   KINGSTON, CAROLYN. *Tragic Mode*, pp. 21-22.
         Analyzes the theme of rejection in *The Hundred Dresses*.

A836   RICE, MABEL R. "Eleanor Estes: A Study in Versatility." *EE* 45 (May 1968):553-57.
         Provides an overview of Estes's literary career and attempts to explain her enduring popularity.

A837 SAYERS, FRANCES CLARKE. "The Books of Eleanor Estes." *Horn Book* 28 (August 1952):257-60. (Reprinted in Sayers, *Summoned by Books*, pp. 116-21.)

Praises Estes's originality, immediacy, vitality, and humor. Estes's Newbery Acceptance speech follows.

A838 TOWNSEND, JOHN ROWE. *Sense of Story*, pp. 79-87.

"The quality of the three Moffat books which makes them exceptional is, I think, an unusual purity of the childish vision." Considers them her best.

ETS, MARIE HALL (1895-   )

A839 BADER, BARBARA. *American Picturebooks*, pp. 167-74.

Discusses the contributions of Ets to the development of the picture book.

A840 ETS, MARIE HALL. "Caldecott Award Acceptance Speech." *Horn Book* 36 (August 1960):275-77.

Provides background on the making of *Nine Days to Christmas*.

A841 HEINS, ETHEL L. "A Second Look: *Mr. T. W. Anthony Woo*." *Horn Book* 52 (February 1976):75.

A842 IRVINE, RUTH R. "Marie Hall Ets--Her Picture Story Books." *EE* 33 (May 1956):259-65. (Reprinted in Hoffman, *Authors and Illustrators*, pp. 141-48.)

Surveys Ets's early works, including *Mr. Penny*; *The Story of a Baby*; *In the Forest*; *My Dog Rinty*; *Oley, The Sea Monster*; *Little Old Automobile*; *Mr. T.W. Anthony Woo*; *Another Day*; *Play with Me*; and *Beasts and Nonsense*, which she does not like.

EYERLY, JEANNETTE (1908-   )

A843 MORGAN, DIANE. "The Popularity of Jeannette Eyerly's Novels." *Arizona English Bulletin* 14, no. 3 (April 1972):122-25.

Examines the reasons for Eyerly's popularity with teenaged girls.

FALKNER, J. MEADE (1858-1932)

A844 STIBBS, ANDREW. "Pernicious Nonsense: *Moonfleet* by J. Meade Falkner." *CLE*, o.s., no. 3 (November 1970):11-20.

Defends this book, often derided as nonsense, with a description of how the author has used it in the classroom.

FARBER, NORMA (1909-84)

A845 BAGNALL, NORMA. "Profile: Norma Farber." *LA* 58 (April 1981):481-86.

In an interview Farber discusses her work and expresses views on poetry for children. Includes an annotated bibliography of Farber's children's books.

A846 HELBIG, ALETHEA K. "Bravura and Skill Yield Kernels of Truth: Norma Farber's Poetry for the Young." *ChLAQ* 9, no. 2 (Summer 1984):79-80.

Points out the elements that make Farber's poems succeed.

FARJEON, ELEANOR (1881-1965)

A847 ANDREWS, SHERYL B. "A Second Look: *The Glass Slipper.*" *Horn Book* 53 (April 1977):193-94.
   Praises Farjeon's retelling of the Cinderella story as a fantasy that sensitively touches a real human problem.

A848 CAMERON, ELEANOR. "A Fine Old Gentleman." In *Green and Burning*, pp. 317-34.
   Cameron's personal response to Farjeon's works is linked to what is known of Farjeon's childhood.

A849 COLWELL, EILEEN. *Eleanor Farjeon.* New York: Walck; London: Bodley Head, 1962, 94 pp.
   Includes biographical material and discusses Farjeon's stories, poems, and retellings of classic and traditional tales. Includes a bibliography of British and American editions of her books.

A850 -----. "Eleanor Farjeon: A Centenary View." *Horn Book* 57 (June 1981):280-87.
   A biocritical overview and remembrance.

A851 FISHER, MARGERY. "Eleanor Farjeon: In Memoriam." *Bookbird* 4 (1965):3-10.
   A biocritical overview and evaluation of Farjeon's contribution to children's literature.

A852 GRAHAM, ELEANOR. "Eleanor Farjeon--A Study and an Appreciation." *Junior Bookshelf* 5 (July 1941):81-86.
   Maintains that despite its unevenness, Farjeon's work contains "the breath of real inspiration." An article follows on Farjeon's illustrator, Isobel Morton-Sale, by M. McLeish, pp. 87-89.

A853 GREENE, ELLIN PETERSON. "Eleanor Farjeon: The Shaping of Literary Imagination." *Proceedings of the Children's Literature Association* 9 (1982):61-70.
   Explores the relationship between Farjeon's childhood fantasy play in a "literary-theatrical-musical-milieu" and her choice of material and use of fantasy and daydream in her writing.

A854 -----. "Eleanor Farjeon: The Shaping of a Literary Imagination." Ed.D. dissertation, Rutgers University, 1979, 171 pp., DA 40:5858A.
   Explores the relationship between childhood fantasy play and the development of artistic creativity and the "shaping of a literary imagination" through a study of Eleanor Farjeon's published and unpublished writings and through interviews with her family, friends and colleagues. Concludes that "Farjeon's central theme is the wisdom of the 'wise child within,' and that her spiritual joy, emanating from her childhood sense of wonder, pervades all of her stories for children."

A855 *Junior Bookshelf* 29 (August 1965):195-208.
   Special issue. Reminiscences by Edward Ardizzone, Grace Hogarth, and Eileen Colwell.

A856 MORGAN, M.E. "Eleanor Farjeon: An Evaluation." *Junior Bookshelf* 18 (October 1954):175-79.

Considers Farjeon's musicality a key aspect of her ability to weave a spell around her readers.

A857 SAYERS, FRANCES CLARKE. "Eleanor Farjeon's Room with a View." *Horn Book* 32 (October 1956):335-44. (Reprinted in *Horn Book* 57 [June 1981]:337-46 and in Sayers, *Summoned By Books*, pp. 122-32.)
Examines the nature of Farjeon's writing with its blending of fantasy, romance, folklore, and scholarship with "an abounding, yea-saying joy in the experience of life."

FARMER, PENELOPE (1939-   )

A858 CRAGO, HUGH. "Penelope Farmer's Novels." *Signal* 17 (May 1975):81-90.
Sees her as "a realist trying to work within fantasy."

A859 ESMONDE, MARGARET P. "Narrative Methods in Penelope Farmer's *A Castle of Bone.*" *CLE*, n.s. 14, no. 3 (Autumn 1983):171-79.
Explores Farmer's use of Celtic myth in her "introvert fantasy."

A860 FARMER, PENELOPE. "Discovering the Pattern." In Blishen, *Thorny Paradise*, pp. 103-7.
Discusses her approach to form.

A861 -----. "Patterns on a Wall." *Horn Book* 50 (October 1974):169-76.
Describes how she writes, with *Castle of Bone* as a chief example. Tells how she arrived at its structure.

A862 JONES, CORNELIA, and WAY, OLIVIA R. *British Children's Authors*, pp. 77-84.
In an interview Farmer discusses her background, philosophy, and method of working. Includes an annotated bibliography of her works.

A863 McELDERRY, MARGARET K. "Penelope Farmer: The Development of an Author." *EE* 51 (September 1974):799-805.
Farmer's editor provides insights into her work.

A864 REES, DAVID. "*Marble in the Water*: Penelope Farmer." In *Marble in the Water*, pp. 1-13. (Also in *Horn Book* 52 [October 1976]:471-78.)
Suggests that Farmer uses the universal problems and ideas of fantasy in a personal way that realistic fiction could not.

A865 SALWAY, LANCE, and CHAMBERS, NANCY. "Book Post." *Signal* 25 (January 1978):49-55. (Also in "Book Post Returns," *Signal* 26 [May 1978]:92-98, with extended reply by Farmer.)

FARNSWORTH, DAVID

A866 RUBIO, GERALD. "Rejuvenating Out of Date Plays." *CCL* 8-9 (1977):144-51.
Discusses Farnsworth's *The King, the Sword, and the Dragon* as "one of the most perfectly conceived examples of participatory drama one is likely to find." However, suggests changes to eliminate the sexism and stereotyped treatment of stock characters.

FAULKNER, WILLIAM (1897-1962)

A867   BROWN, CALVIN S. "Faulkner's Rowan Oak Tales." *Mississippi Quarterly* 34 (1981 Summer):367-74.
    Provides a scholarly review of Dean Faulkner Wells's retellings of William Faulkner's ghost stories for children, *The Ghosts of Rowan Oak* (Oxford, Miss.: Yoknapatawpha Press, 1980, 63 pp.).

A868   DITSKY, JOHN. "William Faulkner's *The Wishing Tree*: Maturity's First Draft." *L&U* 2, no. 1 (Spring 1978):56-64.
    Analyzes the story's parallels to Faulkner's adult writings and its significance in his development as a novelist.

A869   GIDLEY, MICK. "William Faulkner and Children." *Signal* 3 (September 1970):91-102.
    Concentrates on *The Wishing Tree*.

FEELINGS, TOM (1933-   )

A870   FEELINGS, TOM. "Illustration Is My Form, The Black Experience My Story and My Content." *Advocate* 4, no. 2 (Winter 1985):73-82.
    Feelings expresses his views on the blending of political and social values and on the form of his work.

A871   -----. "The Artist at Work: Technique and the Artist's Vision." *Horn Book* 61 (November 1985):685-95.
    Discusses his life and his work. "The techniques I now work with and the ones I used in the past are so heavily influenced by my life experiences that it is difficult for me to separate, even now, the technique and its form from the content of the work and my subject matter."

FERRIS, JAMES CODY [Stratemeyer Syndicate pseudonym]

A872   PRAGER, ARTHUR. *Rascals at Large*, pp. 327-34.
    Discusses the Stratemeyer Syndicate's X Bar X Boys series, a Western version of the Hardy Boys.

FERRY, CHARLES (1927-   )

A873   KNIGHT, R. FAWN. "Interview with Charles Ferry." *CLE*, n.s. 16, no. 1 (Spring 1985):15-20.
    Provides an overview of Ferry's historical fiction for young people.

FIELD, RACHEL (1894-1942)

A874   FIELD, RACHEL. "How *Hitty* Happened." *Horn Book* 6 (February 1930):22-26.
    Describes her discovery of the doll Hitty in an antique shop and tells how the story developed from there. Dorothy Lathrop describes making the illustrations, pp. 27-30.

A875   *Horn Book* 18 (July-August 1942).
    Rachel Field memorial issue. Primarily remembrances and reminiscences.

A876 LANE, MARGARET. "Rachel Field and Her Contributions to Children's Literature." In Andrews, *The Hewins Lectures, 1947-1962*, pp. 343-75.

An extensive biocritical overview with lengthy bibliographies and references to articles and books by and about Field. Concludes that the best of Field's children's books will survive because "There is lilt, vitality, humor, vibrant action and integrity on every page."

A877 USREY, MALCOLM. "The Child Persona in *Taxis and Toadstools*." *ChLAQ* 7, no. 2 (Summer 1982):39-49.

Examines facets of the young female persona of Field's poems.

FINLEY, MARTHA FARQUHARSON (1828-1909)

A878 BROWN, JANET E. "The Saga of Elsie Dinsmore: A Study in Nineteenth Century Sensibility." *University of Buffalo Studies* 17, no. 3 (July 1945):75-131.

Provides a thorough examination of the Elsie books, their faults and their enduring charm. Attempts to account for the long-standing and overwhelming popularity of these tales of "virtues personified in a docile child, or struggling with a recalcitrant one," a theme that was far from new when Finley began writing. Includes a bibliography of biography and criticism and a chronology of the Elsie and Mildred books.

A879 JACKSON, JACQUELINE, and KENDALL, PHILLIP. "What Makes a Bad Book Good: *Elsie Dinsmore*." *Children's Literature* 7 (1978):45-67.

Probes the reason for the long and great popularity of *Elsie Dinsmore*.

A880 STERN, G.B. "Onward and Upward with the Arts: Elsie Reread." *New Yorker* 12 (14 March 1936):52-55.

Explores the long-lasting appeal of Elsie Dinsmore. Stern relishes perusing "for the hundredth time the snarling record of how dark-haired Lulu, in a fit of jealousy lest Papa should love the new little baby sister best, throws the golden-haired toddler lightly down a flight of stone steps, explaining that she thought it was only a dog. Papa whipped her for it, of course. Dear reader--which had the better time--Lulu or Papa?"

FINN, FRANCIS J., S.J. (1859-1928)

A881 MOLSON, FRANCIS J. "Francis J. Finn, S.J.: Pioneering Author of Juveniles for Catholic Americans." *Journal of Popular Culture* 11 (Summer 1977):28-41.

Examines the Catholic protagonists and settings of Finn's juvenile fiction.

FISCHER, HANS (1909-58)

A882 HÜRLIMANN, BETTINA. *Three Centuries*, pp. 239-43.

Provides an overview of Fischer's contributions to children's book illustration.

FISHER, A. HUGH (1867-1945)

A883   WHITMORE, ELIZABETH M. "A. Hugh Fisher: A Comrade for Children." *Horn Book* 4 (May 1928):47-54.
Praises illustrator and describes children's reactions to his pictures.

FISHER, AILEEN (1906-)

A884   KEVORKIAN, KATHLEEN D. "Aileen Fisher, Poet: An Overview." *ChLAQ* 5, no. 2 (Summer 1980):25-27.
Analyzes a number of Fisher's poems and collections.

A885   RAMSEY, IRVIN L., and RAMSEY, LOLA B. "Aileen Fisher: Like Nothing at All." *EE* 44 (October 1967):593-601.
Regards Fisher as prolific, versatile, realistic, perceptive and whole; and suggests these are why her poetry and nature picture books succeed.

FISHER, DOROTHY CANFIELD (1879-1958)

A886   MAGUIRE, GREGORY. "A Second Look: *Understood Betsy.*" *Horn Book* 55 (October 1979):558-60.
Praises Canfield's portrayal of character development and rural life.

A887   WASHINGTON, IDA H. *Dorothy Canfield Fisher: A Biography.* Shelburne Vt.: New England Press, 1982, 258 pp.
Discusses *Understood Betsy* and its relationship to Canfield's experiences with Montessori, pp. 79-81; the *Made-to-Order-Stories*, pp. 70-73.

FITZHUGH, LOUISE (1928-74)

A888   MOLSON, FRANCIS J. "Another Look at *Harriet The Spy.*" *EE* 51 (October 1974):963-70.
Although the book's realism has gained the most attention, Molson feels that Harriet's ambition to write and "the skill and insight with which Fitzhugh systematically presents Harriet's development as a writer," may be the most distinctive and enduring feature of the book. Provides a lengthy analysis.

A889   STERN, MAGGIE. "A Second Look: *Harriet The Spy.*" *Horn Book* 56 (August 1980):442-45.
Sees the book's theme as the balance of life. None of the early reviewers understood this. The book shows a progression from unawareness to awareness; "from order to chaos to new order."

A890   WOLF, VIRGINIA L. "*Harriet The Spy*: Milestone, Masterpiece?" *Children's Literature* 4 (1975):120-26.
Concludes that the novel is a "milestone and a masterpiece of children's literature--perhaps *the* masterpiece of the mid-twentieth century." At its deepest level "a celebration and exploration of the nature of love and development." Examines the novel's structure and the controversies surrounding it. The novel's implications are "rich and multiple" and can be seen in terms of Eliot's "objective correlative" and Pound's "vortex."

A891   -----. "A Novel of Children's Liberation." *Children's Literature* 5 (1976):270-72.
        A detailed critical review of Fitzhugh's last novel, *Nobody's Family Is Going to Change*. Concludes that "Message dominates at the expense of the heroine's credibility."

FLACK, MARJORIE (1897-1958)

A892   BADER, BARBARA, *American Picturebooks*, pp. 61-64.
        "Marjorie Flack drew, but not very well; she wrote, but she wasn't a writer; what she had was a feel for stories."

FLEISCHMAN, SID (1920-   )

A893   JOHNSON, EMILY R. "Profile: Sid Fleischman." *LA* 59 (October 1982):754-59, 772.
        A biocritical overview. Includes a bibliography of Fleischman's books.

FOORD, ISABELLE

A894   REANEY, JAMES S. "Components of Success in Foord's Plays." *CCL* 8-9 (1977):105-7.
        A brief discussion of Canadian children's playwright Foord's plays *A Dream of Sky People*, *Shaman*, *Junkyard*, and *Say Hi to Owlsey*. All published by Playwrights Co-op, Toronto.

FORBES, ESTHER (1891-1967)

A895   COLLIER, CHRISTOPHER. "Johnny and Sam: Old and New Approaches to the American Revolution." *Horn Book* 52 (April 1976):132-38. (Reprinted in Heins, *Crosscurrents*, pp. 234-40.)
        Compares the Collier approach to the historical background of the American Revolution in *My Brother Sam Is Dead*, with Esther Forbes's approach in *Johnny Tremain*.

A896   FORBES, ESTHER. "Newbery Medal Acceptance." *Horn Book* 20 (July-August):261-67.
        Explains how her biography of Paul Revere led her to create *Johnny Tremain*. Discusses her purposes in writing and the influences of World War II on the book.

FORD, FORD MADOX (1873-1939)

A897   LURIE, ALISON. "Ford Madox Ford's Fairy Tales." *Children's Literature* 8 (1980):7-21.
        Relates Ford's fairy tales, *The Brown Owl*, *The Feather*, *The Queen Who Flew*, and *Christina's Fairy Book*, to his life.

A898   -----. "Ford Madox Ford's Fairy Tales for Children." In *The Presence of Ford Madox Ford: A Memorial Volume of Essays, Poems, and Memoirs*. Edited by Sondra J. Stang. Philadelphia: University of Pennsylvania Press, 1981, pp. 130-42.
        Discusses *The Brown Owl* and *Christina's Fairy Book*.

FOSTER, GENEVIEVE (1893-1979)

A899   DAWSON, MITCHELL. "Genevieve Foster's World." *Horn Book* 28 (June 1952):190-95.
        Describes Foster's "world" books and also her Initial Biographies series. A biographical sketch of Foster by her daughter, Joanna Foster, follows.

A900   FENWICK, SARA INNIS. "Exploring History with Genevieve Foster." *EE* 31 (October 1954):315-21. (Also in Hoffman, *Authors and Illustrators*, pp. 149-56.)
        Discusses the nature, background, and use of the "world" books.

FOX, PAULA (1923-   )

A901   BACH, ALICE. "Cracking Open the Geode: The Fiction of Paula Fox." *Horn Book* 53 (October 1977):514-21.
        Suggests that Fox's integrity sets her above the run-of-the-mill young adult author.   Praises her writing style and her believability.

A902   COUNCIL ON INTERRACIAL BOOKS FOR CHILDREN. *"The Slave Dancer*: Critiques of This Year's Newbery Award Winner." *IRBC* 5, no. 5 (1974):4-6, 8. (Articles by Binnie Tate and Sharon Bell Mathis are reprinted in MacCann, *Cultural Conformity*, pp. 146-56.)
        Includes articles by Binnie Tate, Sharon Bell Mathis, Albert V. Schwartz, and Lyla Hoffman attacking the book on grounds of racism.

A903   HEINS, PAUL. "Paula Fox: Hans Christian Andersen Medal Winner." *Horn Book* 54 (October 1978):486-7.
        Summarizes Fox's outstanding characteristics: her range of subject matter and form, her theme of noncommunication, her dramatic presentations of character, her "chiseled style," and vivid imagery.

A904   INGLIS, FRED. *Promise of Happiness*, pp. 281-83.
        "She isn't quite enough of a novelist--that is, of an intellectual and artist--to create a structure which will carry her theme.   Her hero is *not* a victim, but being a child, is left only as an observer." He concludes that *The Slave Dancer* "remains at the level of humanities project resource."

A905   McDONNELL, CHRISTINE. "A Second Look: *The Stoned-Faced Boy*." *Horn Book* 60 (April 1984):219-22.
        Pays special attention to Gus's character.

A906   PARKER, PATRICIA ANNE FALSTAD. "Responses of Adolescents and Librarians to Selected Contemporary Fiction." Ph.D. dissertation, University of Minnesota, 1974, 145 pp., DA 35:5357A.
        Investigates responses of eighth graders and junior high school librarians to Paula Fox's *Blowfish Live in the Sea* and Jill Paton Walsh's *Fireweed*.

A907   REES, DAVID. "'The Colour of Saying': Paula Fox." In *Marble in the Water*, pp. 114-27.
        Highly praises Fox's style.   Summarizes distinctive characteristics and themes, and provides in-depth analysis of *The Slave Dancer*, which he calls a masterpiece.

A908   TOWNSEND, JOHN ROWE. "Paula Fox." In *A Sounding*, pp. 55-65.
Revises and updates the above essay on Fox from a *Sense of Story*, adding a discussion of the *Slave Dancer*, which he considers "her finest achievement."

A909   -----. *Sense of Story*, pp. 89-96.
Praises Fox's "striking quality" and says that although children may not like her books at first, "If they are read they will not be quickly forgotten." Concentrates on *How Many Miles to Babylon*.

FRANÇOIS, ANDRE (1915-)

A910   BADER, BARBARA. *American Picturebooks*, pp. 362-63.
Discusses François's illustrations for Isobel Harris's *Little Boy Brown*.

A911   BROWN, MARCIA. "Artist's Choice: *Little Boy Brown*." *Horn Book* 26 (January 1950):28-29.
Analyzes the illustrations by Andre François for Isobel Harris's *Little Boy Brown*.

FRANK, ANNE (1929-44)

A912   SCARLETT, GEORGE. "Adolescent Thinking and the Diary of Anne Frank." *Psychoanalytic Review* 58 (Summer 1971):265-78.
Points out cognitive aspects of adolescent behavior and thinking as reflected in Anne Frank's diary.

FRASCONI, ANTONIO (1919-)

A913   BADER, BARBARA. *American Picturebooks*, pp. 343-46.
Traces Frasconi's contributions to the art of the picture book.

A914   "Frasconi's Brio With A Book." *Horizon* 3 (March 1961):122-28.
Provides a brief, but well-illustrated look at some of Frasconi's art.

A915   GASSER, MANUEL. "Antonio Frasconi: *A Book of Many Suns*." *Graphis* 100 (March-April):208-17.
Explores Frasconi's use of the sun motif in works for children and adults.

FREEMAN, DON (1908-78)

A916   BADER, BARBARA. *American Picturebooks*, pp. 206-8.
A brief analysis of Freeman as picture-book artist. Feels that *Dandelion* is his best.

A917   -----. "Child of the Theater, Artist to Children." *NYTBR*, 30 April 1978, Children's Book section, pp. 26, 34.
An appreciative appraisal of Freeman's career, concentrating on his children's books. "His work is slow to date because, individual and unchanging, it was never fashionable."

A918   ZUCKERMAN, LINDA. "Don Freeman: An Editor's View." *Horn Book* 54 (June 1979):273-81.

More about Freeman's personality and methods of working than a critical appraisal, but does include Freeman's account of the origins of *Corduroy*.

FRENCH, HARRY W.

A919 KINGSTON, CAROLYN T. *Tragic Mode*, pp. 11-12.
Analyzes the theme of rejection in *The Lance of Kanana*.

FREUCHEN, PIPALUK

A920 KINGSTON, CAROLYN T. *Tragic Mode*, pp. 65-67.
Analyzes the theme of entrapment in *The Eskimo Boy*.

FRIERMOOD, ELISABETH HAMILTON (1903-   )

A921 FRIERMOOD, ELISABETH HAMILTON. "Where Did You Get *That* Idea?" *Horn Book* 41 (December 1965):655-61.
Answers that question in terms of several of her books.

FRITZ, JEAN (1915-   )

A922 AMMON, RICHARD. "Profile." *LA* 60 (March 1983):365-69.
A brief biocritical overview.

A923 CALIFF, JANE. Review. *IRBC* 6, no. 7 (1975):6.
Reviews *Where Was Patrick Henry on the 29th of May?*, pointing out the omission of any discussion of blacks and the role of slaves in Patrick Henry's life.

A924 FRITZ, JEAN. "Making It Real." *CLE*, o.s., no. 22 (Autumn 1976):125-27.
Explains her approach to biography and how she meets the challenge of compressing the essential facts plus a new perspective into 48 pages.

A925 -----. "On Writing Historical Fiction." *Horn Book* 43 (October 1967):565-70.
Describes her methods and techniques.

A926 -----. "Turning History Inside Out." *Horn Book* 61 (January 1985):29-34.
Address given at the Boston Globe-Horn Book Award Ceremony for *The Double Life of Pocahontas*, 1 October 1984. Discusses her approach to history and to the writing of the Pocahontas book in particular.

FROST, KELMAN

A927 SCHMIDT, NANCY. *Children's Fiction About Africa*, pp. 118-19.
"Many aspects of North African life are described in stereotyped terms" and, "in the end, European civilization triumphs."

FUJIKAWA, GYO (1908-   )

A928 KRANER, MADELINE R. "Gyo Fujikawa: An Illustrator Children Love." *Publishers Weekly* 199 (4 June 1971):45-46.

Discusses Fujikawa's background, her style, and her philosophy of illustration.

FULLA, LUDOVIT

A929 VESELY, MARIAN. "Slovak National Artist Ludovit Fulla." *Bookbird* 12, no. 4 (1974):73-79.
A biocritical overview. Includes a bibliography of Fulla's books.

FYLEMAN, ROSE (1877-1957)

A930 FYLEMAN, ROSE. "Writing Poetry for Children." *Horn Book* 16 (January-February 1940):58-66.
Describes her background and how and why she started writing poems, especially fairy poems.

A931 SHIPPEN, ELIZABETH P. "Rose Fyleman." *EE* 35 (October 1958):358-65.
A biocritical overview of the "poet of the fairies." Includes primary and secondary bibliographies.

GÁG, WANDA (1893-1946)

A932 BADER, BARBARA. "A Second Look: *Millions of Cats.*" *Horn Book* 54 (October 1978):536-40.
Examines Gág's masterpiece in its historical context.

A933 -----. "Wanda Gág." In *American Picturebooks*, pp. 32-37.
An overview of Gág's career and an analysis of her work. Includes references.

A934 CAMERON, ELEANOR. "Wanda Gág: Myself and Many Me's." In *Green and Burning*, pp. 295-315.
Primarily biographical, based largely on Gág's journals, this essay outlines how Gág found her way into children's literature and reveals much of the background and personality behind her work.

A935 COX, RICHARD W. "Wanda Gág: The Bite of the Picture Book." *Minnesota History* 44 (Fall 1975):238-54.
Points out the strong undercurrent of social concern, "a rejection of easy sentiment, and even a disenchantment with American values and institutions" in her drawings, prints, and children's books of 1920-40.

A936 CROUCH, MARCUS. "Through Peasant Eyes." *Junior Bookshelf* 26 (March 1962):51-55.
Finds in Gág's Grimm tales "the pure spring water of folk-tale, not the flat 'pop' which children are too often given in substitute."

A937 DUNN, NANCY E. *Wanda Gág: Author and Illustrator of Children's Books.* Charlottesville, N.Y.: SamHar Press, 1973, 32 pp.
A biocritical overview, devoting several pages to her children's books. Includes a bibliography of works by and about Gág.

A938 GÁG, WANDA. *Growing Pains: Diaries and Drawings for the Years 1908-1917.* St. Paul, Minn.: Minnesota Historical Society Press, 1984, 475 pp.

Karen Nelson Hoyle provides an overview of Gág's career in the introduction to this reprint of Gág's diaries and notebooks..

A939 HERENDEEN, ANNE. "Wanda Gág: The True Story of A Dynamic Young Artist Who Won't Be Organized." *Century* 116 (October 1928):427-32.

An early biocritical investigation. "All my life I shall look at objects differently for having seen how Wanda Gág saw them."

A940 *Horn Book* 23 (May-June 1947).

Special issue. Contains a biographical sketch by Alma Scott (pp. 159-69); an analysis of Gág as an artist by Carl Zigrosser (pp. 170-81); as a writer, by Ernestine Evans (pp. 182-88); as a fellow worker, by Rose Dobbs (pp. 189-93); and as a fellow artist, by Lynd Ward (pp. 194-97). Concludes with a selection of letters from children to Gág, selected and edited by Earle Humphreys (pp. 199-205). (Article by Evans reprinted in Fryatt, *Horn Book Sampler*, pp. 34-38.)

A941 HURLEY, BEATRICE J. "Wanda Gág--Artist, Author." *EE* 32 (October 1955):347-54.

Surveys Gág's talents, noting characteristics of her work.

A942 Review of *Tales from Grimm*. *Junior Bookshelf* 2, no. 1 (October 1937):26-28.

A substantial early review.

A943 SCOTT, ALMA. *Wanda Gág: The Story of An Artist*. Minneapolis: University of Minnesota Press, 1949, 235 pp.

This early biography written by Gág's high school friend comments on her writing and illustrating of children's books.

A944 ZIGROSSER, CARL, ed. "Wanda Gág." In *The Artist in America*. New York: Knopf, 1942, pp. 33-44.

Provides insights into Gág's art and personality.

GARD, JOYCE [Joyce Reeves] (1911-   )

A945 JONES, CORNELIA, and WAY, OLIVIA R. *British Children's Authors*, pp. 85-93.

In an interview Joyce Gard discusses her background, philosophy, and method of working. Includes an annotated bibliography of her works.

GARDAM, JANE (1928-   )

A946 GARDAM, JANE. "Mrs. Hookaneye and I." In Blishen, *Thorny Paradise*, pp. 77-80.

Comments on the writing process.

A947 -----. "On Writing for Children: Some Wasps in the Marmalade." *Horn Book* 54 (October, December 1978):489-96, 672-79.

Reflects upon Gardam's aims in writing and the influence of children's literature upon her, but provides little direct discussion of her own writing.

A948 INGLIS, FRED. *Promise of Happiness*, pp. 287-91.

Describes *A Long Way from Verona* as an affecting tale. Praises her ability to "recreate the rambling, directionless lines of conversation with the fidelity of Harold Pinter, and the much more satisfactory humour of Alan Galton, and at the same time give the scene its historical location. . . ."

GARDNER, JOHN (1933-82)

A949   DE LUCA, GERALDINE, and NATOV, RONI. "Modern Moralities for Children: John Gardner's Children's Books." In *John Gardner: Critical Perspectives.* Edited by Robert A. Morace and Kathryn Van Spanckeren. Carbondale: Southern Illinois University Press, 1982, pp. 89-96.
     Probes the reasons why Gardner's children's books are "partial failures."

A950   NATOV, RONI, and DE LUCA, GERALDINE. "An Interview with John Gardner." *L&U* 2, no. 1 (Spring 1978):114-36.
     Discusses Gardner's works for children and adults, especially *Dragon, Dragon*; *The King of the Hummingbirds*; and *The Suicide Mountain.*

GARFIELD, LEON (1921-   )

A951   CAMP, RICHARD. "Garfield's Golden Net." *Signal* 5 (May 1971):47-55.
     Praises Garfield's unity of content and form, which fit together like "body and soul."

A952   CROUCH, MARCUS. *Nesbit Tradition*, pp. 34-38.
     Argues that Garfield's craftsmanship, especially the "extraordinary evocative language all his own," is "what makes these absurd plots not merely acceptable but absorbingly fascinating." Pays particular attention to *Jack Holborn* and *Smith.*

A953   GARFIELD, LEON. "Bookmaker and Punter." In Blishen, *Thorny Paradise*, pp. 81-86.
     Garfield comments on his approach to writing.

A954   -----. "An Evening with Leon Garfield." In Egoff, *One Ocean*, pp. 110-20.
     Tells about his methods of writing and especially the genesis of *Jack Holborn.*

A955   -----. "And So It Grows," *Horn Book* 44 (December 1968):668-72. (Reprinted with slight changes from March-April 1968 *Children's Book News.*)
     Describes how he set about writing *Jack Holborn* .

A956   -----. "Writing for Childhood." *CLE*, o.s., no. 2 (July 1970):56-63.
     Tells why he writes books set in the eighteenth century; ponders why writers deny they write for children. Provides insight into his works.

A957   GARFIELD, LEON; BLISHEN, EDWARD; and KEEPING, CHARLES. "Greek Myths and the Twentieth Century Reader." *CLE*, o.s., no. 3 (November 1970):48-65.

The authors and illustrator describe the genesis of *The God Beneath the Sea* and some of the difficulties encountered in producing it. Includes illustrations and an extract from the book. (See also reviews of the book in this same issue, by Ted Hughes, pp. 66-67; and Alan Garner, pp. 69-71.)

A958   HOLLAND, PHILIP. "Shades of the Prison House: The Fiction of Leon Garfield." *CLE*, n.s. 9, no. 4 (Winter 1978):159-72.
Analyzes Garfield's fiction, concluding that he is "a master of mystery and a master of style."

A959   JONES, RHODRI. "Writers for Children--Leon Garfield." *Use of English* 23 (Summer 1972):293-99. (Reprinted in Butts, *Good Writers*, pp. 34-40, with an updating postscript, pp. 41-43.)
Provides an evaluation of several of Garfield's books, noting his reliance on intricate plots and heroes on their own. Compares Garfield to Dickens.

A960   NATOV, RONI. "'Not the blackest of villains. . . not the brightest of of saints': Humanism in Leon Garfield's Adventure Novels." *L&U* 2, no. 2 (Fall 1978):44-71.
Places Garfield in the tradition of Fielding, Smollett, and Dickens. "In his warmth and humor he urges an acceptance of humanity and a tolerance of ambivalence which is unique to the world of adolescent fiction." Examines *Jack Holborn, Devil-in-the-Fog, Smith, Black Jack, The Sound of Coaches*, and *The Prisoners of September*.

A961   PEMBERTON, CLIVE. "Aspects of *Treasure Island* and *Jack Holborn*." *Use of English* 23 (Winter 1971):113-17.
Finds both books stylistically excellent. Sees Stevenson's *Treasure Island* as the product of a writer of adult books of genius who attempted to write a book for children, and *Jack Holborn* as an attempt of a writer of juveniles to write for adults. In both there is something to appeal to both child and adult.

A962   SUCHER, MARY WADSWORTH. "Recommended: Leon Garfield," *English Journal* 72 (September 1983):71-72.
Provides an introductory overview of Garfield's work.

A963   TOWNSEND, JOHN ROWE. *Sense of Story*, pp. 97-107.
Calls Garfield the "richest and strangest" talent to have emerged in the 1960s. Comments on his eighteenth-century settings, and concludes that he has "livelier expectations from Leon Garfield than from anyone else whose work is being published on a children's list in England today."

A964   -----. *A Sounding*, pp. 66-80.
An updating and revision of the essay on Garfield in *Sense of Story*. Townsend feels Garfield has lived up to his expectations. Discusses newer works such as *The Strange Affair of Adelaide Harris* and *The Pleasure Garden*.

A965   WINTLE, JUSTIN, and FISHER, EMMA. *Pied Piper*, pp. 192-207.
Garfield discusses his life and work in an interview.

GARIS, HOWARD (1873-1962)
[Also author of the first thirty-five Tom Swift books under the pseudonym Victor Appleton]

A966   DOUGLAS, GEORGE H. "Howard R. Garis and the World of Uncle Wiggily." *Journal of Popular Culture* 8, no. 3 (Winter 1974):503-12.
Provides biographical background on Garis and analyzes the chief characteristics of the Uncle Wiggily stories.

A967   GARIS, ROGER. "My Father Was Uncle Wiggily." *Saturday Evening Post*, 19 December 1964, pp. 237-64, 266.
Describes his family's writing.

A968   STREET, DOUGLAS. "Howard Garis." In Cech, *Dictionary of Literary Biography*, 22:191-99.
Includes an extensive article and primary and secondary biboliographies.

GARNER, ALAN (1934-   )

A969   AERS, LESLEY. "Alan Garner: An Opinion." *Use of English* 22, no. 2 (Winter 1970):141-47, 153.
Argues that "Alan Garner's use of myths and folk-tales contributes little more than furniture to his novels." Discusses *The Weirdstone of Brisingamen*, *Moon of Gomrath*, *Elidor*, and *The Owl Service*.

A970   BARTLE, F.R. "Alan Garner." *Children's Libraries Newsletter* 8 (May 1972):38-47.
Analyzes four of Garner's books and compares him to William Mayne.

A971   BENTON, MICHAEL. "Detective Imagination." *CLE*, o.s., no. 13 (1974):5-12.
"*Red Shift* expresses the significance of place and the insignificance of time." Thoughtful reflections on the novel's construction, style, and theme. Jessica Kimball-Cook comments in *CLE*, o.s., no. 15 (1974):67-68.

A972   BLISHEN, EDWARD. "Ambiguous Triptych." *TES*, 12 October 1973, p. 22.
Reviews *Red Shift*. "How to begin to describe anything so intricate, finely wrought--in places, cunningly and even perversely enigmatic?" Questions Garner's need "to build a wall of erudite puzzles between himself and his readers."

A973   "Books of International Interest: Forum of Children's Books." *Bookbird* 6, no. 1 (1968):27-30.
Provides brief background information on Garner and surveys reviewers' responses to *Elidor*.

A974   BREWER, ROSEMARY. "Alan Garner: A Perspective." *Orana* 14 (November 1978):127-33.

A975   CADOGAN, MARY, and CRAIG, PATRICIA. *You're a Brick*, pp. 367-71.
Sees Garner's first five children's novels as a movement "towards

increased internal pressure and thematic compression."

A976   CAMERON, ELEANOR.   "The Owl Service: A Study."   *WLB* 44
(December 1969):425-33.   (Reprinted in White, *Children's Literature*,
pp. 191-202.)
Discusses Garner's development as a writer in books preceding
The Owl Service, and provides a detailed critical analysis of that
book.

A977   CHAMBERS, AIDAN.   "An Interview with Alan Garner."   In Chambers, *Signal Approaches*, pp. 276-328.   (Expanded version of interview originally published in *Signal* 27 [September 1978]:119-37.)
Based on ideas Chambers expressed in "The Reader in the Book"
(*Signal* 23 [May 1977]:64-87).

A978   -----.   "Letter from England: Literary Crossword Puzzle . . . or Masterpiece?"   *Horn Book* 49 (October 1973):494-97.   (Reprinted in Heins,
Crosscurrents, pp. 315-18.)
Suggests that with *Red Shift*, Garner has "given up any pretense
at writing for children and is now writing entirely to please himself
and those mature, sophisticated, literate readers who care to study his
work."   Discusses some of the difficulties and strong points of the
novel.

A979   -----.   "Letter from England: A Matter of Balance."   *Horn Book* 53
(August 1977):479-82.
Sees *Stone Book*'s subject as a balance "between head and heart,
the eternal and the momentary, the old ways and the new, the profound and the simple, the wide bright sky and the secret close spaces
of the earth, the folk tongue of the people and the language of
artifice and studio."

A980   FARRELL, JACQUELINE M.   "Recommended: Alan Garner."   *English
Journal* 70 (September 1981):65-66.
Suggests ways of using Garner's books with middle-school stu-
dents.

A981   GARNER, ALAN.   "Achilles in Altjira."   *CHLAQ* 8, no. 4 (Winter
1983):5-10.
Discusses the role of language and the role of the storyteller,
relating them to his background as a working-class child who
received schooling in standard English and classical languages.

A982   -----.   "A Bit More Practice."   *TLS*, 6 June 1968.   (Also in Meek,
Cool Web, pp. 196-200.)
Describes the background of his writing, especially of *The Owl
Service*.

A983   -----.   "Coming to Terms."   *CLE*, o.s., no. 2 (July 1970):15-29.
Interview in which Garner discusses his approach to writing and
comments on several of his books, notably *The Owl Service*.   Also
discusses his use of myth and fantasy, and makes brief autobiographical comments.

A984   -----.   "The Edge of the Ceiling."   *Horn Book* 60 (September-October
1984):559-65.
Reflects upon the influences of his childhood isolation and his

sense of place in his writing.

A985   -----. "Inner Time." In *Science Fiction at Large: A Collection of Essays, by Various Hands, About the Interface Between Science Fiction and Reality.* Edited by Peter Nichols. New York: Harper and Row, 1976, pp. 119-38.
    Discusses myth and time and reveals some of the painful central events of Garner's emotional life, which he relates to his art.

A986   GILLIES, CAROLYN. "Possession and Structure in the Novels of Alan Garner." *CLE,* o.s., no. 18, (Fall 1975):107-17.
    Argues that the plots of Garner's first five books are linked by two major concepts, possession and structure; and "gradually develop from pure children's reading into adult literature."

A987   GOUGH, JOHN. "Alan Garner, the Critic and Self-Critic." *Orana* 20 (August 1984):110-18.
    Examines Garner's criticism of himself and others and urges the reader to beware of accepting these comments at face value as criticism of Garner's work.

A988   HEINS, PAUL. "Off the Beaten Path." *Horn Book* 49 (December 1973):580-81. (Reprinted in *Crosscurrents,* p. 319.)
    Briefly discusses the blurring of the distinction between children's and adult books in terms of *Red Shift.*

A989   HELLINGS, CAROL. "Alan Garner: His Use of Mythology and Dimension in Time." *Orana* 15 (May 1979):66-73.

A990   INGLIS, FRED. *The Promise of Happiness,* pp. 242-45.
    Examines *Elidor,* finding "Garner's achievement is to have given magic a credibility in terms of modern science."

A991   JONES, CORNELIA, and WAY, OLIVIA R. *British Children's Authors,* pp. 94-100.
    In an interiew Garner discusses his background, philosophy, and method of working. Includes an annotated bibliography of his works.

A992   KOHLER, MARGARET. "Author Study: Alan Garner." *Orana* 16 (May 1980):39-48.
    Analyzes Garner's themes, characterizations, settings, structures, and style, and summarizes his development as a writer.

A993   McMAHON, PATRICIA. "A Second Look: *Elidor.*" *Horn Book* 56 (June 1980):328-31.
    Examines Garner's transformation of mythological sources so that they stand on their own.

A994   PEARCE, PHILIPPA. *The Owl Service.* In Meek, *Cool Web,* pp. 291-93. (From *Children's Book News* 2, no. 4 [July-August 1967]:164-65.
    Faults the difficulty of understanding and the failure of Garner to "make plain" what is happening in *Owl Service.*

A995   PHILIP, NEIL. *A Fine Anger: A Critical Introduction to the Work of Alan Garner.* London: Collins, 1981, 191 pp.
    Provides a serious critical analysis of Garner's work. "The vigour

of the oral tradition has been transfused into the sluggish bloodstream of the modern novel, and a new life imparted." The introduction contains an overview of Garner's work and his significance in modern English literature. Subsequent chapters are devoted to discussions of one or more of his books: *The Weirdstone of Brisingamen* and *The Moon of Gomrath*, pp. 21-44; *Elidor*, pp. 45-64; *The Owl Service*, pp. 65-75; *Holly from the Bongs* and *The Hamish Hamilton Book of Goblins*, pp. 76-85; *Red Shift*, pp. 86-109; *Potter Thompson*, *The Guizer*, and *The Lad of the Gad*, pp. 110-25; and *The Stone Book Quartet*, pp. 126-45. Includes an extensive bibliography of Garner's writings, Garner criticism, and background material.

A996   REES, DAVID. "Alan Garner: Some Doubts." *Horn Book* 55 (June 1979):282-89. (Revised version entitled "Hanging in Their True Shapes: Alan Garner," in Rees, *Marble in the Water*, pp. 56-67.)
Discusses Garner's development as a writer in *Elidor*, *Owl Service*, and *Red Shift*. Concludes his works are flawed masterpieces.

A997   SPRAGGS, GILLIAN. Review of Neil Philip's *A Fine Anger*. *Use of English* 33, no. 2 (Spring 1982):81-83.
Disagrees with Philip's claim for Garner's literary status and suggests that the influence of Garner's predecessors in the magical adventure story should have been considered.

A998   TOWNSEND, JOHN ROWE. *Sense of Story*, pp. 108-19.
"His stories have become less complicated but more complex, less crowded but more intricately ramified." Traces Garner's development as an author through *Weirdstone of Brisingamen*, *Moon of Gomrath*, *Elidor* and *Owl Service*.

A999   -----. *A Sounding*, pp. 81-96.
An updating and revision of Townsend's earlier essay in *A Sense of Story*, adding discussions of *Red Shift* and the quartet, *The Stone Book*, *Granny Reardun*, *The Aimer Gate*, and *Tom Fobble's Day*.

A1000   WALSH, ROBIN. "Alan Garner: A Study." *Orana* 13 (May 1977): 31-39.

A1001   WATKINS, TONY. "Alan Garner." In Butts, *Good Writers*, pp. 45-49.
Explores Garner's use of folklore and myth as the basis for his fiction. A postscript comments on *Red Shift*, pp. 48-49.

A1002   -----. "Alan Garner's *Elidor*." *CLE*, o.s., no. 7 (March 1972):56-63.
Explores Garner's use of the imagery of myth as a means of transcending various levels of experience.

A1003   WATSON, VICTOR. "In Defense of Jan: Love and Betrayal in *The Owl Service* and *Red Shift*." *Signal* 41 (May 1983):77-87.
Examines the two novels in terms of "choices and betrayals almost forced upon women by the violence and anger of men." Attempts to show that this theme, "worked out incompletely in *The Owl Service*, reappears brilliantly and triumphantly in *Red Shift*," especially in the character of Jan.

A1004   WHITAKER, MURIEL A. "'The Hollow Hills': A Celtic Motif in Modern Fantasy." *Mosaic* 13 (Spring-Summer 1980):165-78.
Examines the use of Celtic myths in the works of Alan Garner,

William Mayne, and Mary Stewart.

A1005 WINTLE, JUSTIN, and FISHER, EMMA. *Pied Pipers*, pp. 221-35.
Alan Garner discusses his life and work in an interview.

GARNETT, EVE

A1006 GARNETT, EVE. "The How and Why of the Ruggleses." *Junior Bookshelf* 2, no. 4 (July 1938):171-74.
Provides background information on the Ruggles stories.

GATES, DORIS (1901-   )

A1007 ALTSTETTER, MABEL F. "*Blue Willow*." *EE* 36 (October 1959):367-73.
Primarily a plot summary, revealing in its length, choice of incidents, and emphasis.

A1008 GATES, DORIS. "Along the Road to Kansas." *Horn Book* 31 (October 1955):382-90.
William Allen White Children's Book Award acceptance. Tells of her background and the background of some of her books.

A1009 KINGSTON, CAROLYN T. *Tragic Mode*, pp. 83-85.
Analyzes the theme of sensitivity in *Blue Willow*.

A1010 ROLLINS, CHARLEMAE. "The Work of Doris Gates." *EE* 31 (December 1954):459-65. (Reprinted in Hoffman, *Authors and Illustrators*, pp. 157-64.)
Biographical background and a review of Gates's books up to *Little Vic*.

A1011 STOTT, JON C. "The Artistry of *Blue Willow*." *EE* 50 (May 1973):761-65, 839.
Examines the basic structural patterns of this realistic novel in relationship to understanding the archetypal base of all fiction. Praises the artistry with which Gates handles structure, setting, and symbolism to transform "an interesting story into a meaningful and moving work of art."

GEORGE, JEAN CRAIGHEAD (1919-   )

A1012 GEORGE, JEAN CRAIGHEAD. "Newbery Award Acceptance." *Horn Book* 49 (August 1973):337-47.
Describes the background and research which went into *Julie of the Wolves*.

A1013 -----. "The Voice of Realism." *Advocate* 3, no. 1 (Fall 1983):20-26.
Discusses her approach to realism.

A1014 GEORGE, JEAN, and GEORGE, JOHN. "Introducing Children to Animals." *TON* 14 (March 1958):32-35.
The Georges describe their methods of writing about animals.

A1015 HOPKINS, LEE BENNETT. "Jean Craighead George." *EE* 50 (October 1973):1049-53.
A brief biocritical overview that includes many comments by

George about her work.

A1016　STOTT, JON C. "Jean George's Arctic Pastoral: A Reading of *Julie of the Wolves.*" *Children's Literature* 3 (1974):131-39.
Examines *Julie of the Wolves* in terms of the pastoral tradition.

GERGELY, TIBOR (1900-1978)

A1017　SCHREYER, ALICE D. "Scuffy, Tootle and Other Creations By Tibor Gergely." *Columbia Library Columns* 28 (February 1979):25-34.
Provides an overview of Gergely's art and career based on materials in the Tibor Gergely Collection in the Rare Book and Manuscript Library at Columbia University.

GILSON, JAMIE (1933-　)

A1018　JOHNSON, RICHARD. "Profile." *LA* 60 (May 1983):661-67.
Discusses Gilson's life and work. Includes a bibliography of her books.

GIPSON, FRED (1908-　)

A1019　HENDERSON, SAM H. *Fred Gipson.* Southwest Writers Series, no. 10. Austin, Texas: Steck-Vaughn, 1967, 52 pp.
A biocritical overview with extended discussion of *Old Yeller* and *Savage Sam.*

Girl's Own Paper

A1020　FORRESTER, WENDY. *Great Grandmama's Weekly: A Celebration of "The Girl's Own Paper" 1880-1901.* Guildford and London: Lutterworth Press, 1980, 176 pp.
Combines a history and discussion of the magazine with excerpts and reproductions of illustrations. Chapters include sections on health and beauty, the modern woman, fiction, dress, features, and domestic arts.

GOBLE, PAUL (1933-　)

A1021　STOTT, JOHN C. "Profile: Paul Goble." *LA* 61 (December 1984):867-73.
A brief biocrit ical overview.

GODDEN, RUMER (1907-　)

A1022　HINES, RUTH, and BURNS, PAUL C. "Rumer Godden." *EE* 44 (February 1967):101-5.
Discusses Godden's life and work."

A1023　SIMPSON, HASSELL A. *Rumer Godden.* Twayne's English Authors Series, no. 151. New York: Twayne Publishers, 1973, 160 pp.
Godden's children's books are mentioned mainly in passing as they relate to her adult novels. *In Noah's Ark* is analyzed, pp. 101-5. Includes a biography of Godden and bibliography of primary and secondary sources.

A1024　WINTLE, JUSTIN, and FISHER, EMMA. *Pied Piper*, pp. 285-94.

Rumer Godden discusses her life and work in an interview.

GOFFSTEIN, M.B. (1940-   )

A1025   PORTE, BARBARA ANN. "The Picture Books of M.B. Goffstein." *CLE*, n.s. 11, no. 1 (Spring 1980):3-9.
A critical analysis of key elements in Goffstein's texts and pictures.

A1026   SHANNON, GEORGE. "Goffstein and Friends." *Horn Book* 59 (February 1983):88-95.
Discusses the theme of shared feelings, dignity, and truth in five of Goffstein's books.

"The Golden Bird"

A1027   NODELMAN, PERRY M. "What Makes a Fairy Tale Good: The Queer Kindness of 'The Golden Bird'." *CLE*, n.s. 8, no. 3 (Autumn 1977):101-8. (Reprinted in Bator, *Signposts*, pp. 184-91.)
Argues that traditional literary criticism fails to account for the effect of the "Golden Bird," which is created through matter-of-fact telling of the astonishing. Concludes that this quality is, to a certain extent, characteristic of all good literature.

Golden Books

A1028   BADER, BARBARA. "Golden Books." In *American Picturebooks*, pp. 277-95.
Recounts the history of the Little Golden Books series, singling out some of the most successful volumes.

GOLDING, WILLIAM (1911-   )

A1029   CARTER, MARY RUTHE. "Peter Brueghel and William Golding." *English Journal* 73 (November 1984):54-55.
Finds numerous similarities in the paintings of Peter Brueghel and Golding's *Lord of the Flies*.

A1030   GOLDING, WILLIAM. "Fable." In *The Hot Gates and Other Occasional Pieces*. London: Faber & Faber, 1963. (Reprinted in Meek, *Cool Web*, pp. 226-40.)
Discusses *Lord of the Flies* in terms of fable and compares it with Ballantyne's *The Coral Island*.

GOODRICH, SAMUEL GRISWOLD (1793-1860)

A1031   MAXWELL, MARGARET. "'Higglety, Pigglety Pop!': or, The Man Who Tried to Murder Mother Goose." *Horn Book* 45 (August 1969):392-94.
Tells how the famous verse came to be written.

"The Goosegirl"

A1032   BOTTIGHEIMER, RUTH B. "Iconographic Continuity in Illustrations of 'The Goosegirl.'" *Children's Literature* 13 (1985):49-71.
Suggests that the continuity in illustrations of "The Goosegirl," like the continuity of its verses, is "responsible for the tale's

resistance to change during its oral and literary history."

GORDON, JOHN (1925-   )

A1033   BLISHEN, EDWARD. "The Bare Pebble: The Novels of John Gordon."
         Signal 8 (May 1972):63-73.
         Discusses *Giant Under the Snow* and *House on the Brink*, both
         concerned with tensions between credulity and incredulity.

A1034   -----. "The Slow Art of John Gordon." *Signal* 40 (January
         1983):12-17.
         A follow-up to Blishen's earlier article on Gordon, "The Bare
         Pebble" (*Signal*, May 1972), this one discussing his more recent books:
         The Ghost on the Hill, *The Waterfall Box*, and *The Spitfire Grave*.

GOREY, EDWARD (1925-   )

A1035   BADER, BARBARA. *American Picturebooks*, pp. 552-58.
         Discusses the nature of Gorey's art.

A1036   FILSTRUP, JANE M. "An Interview with Edward St. John Gorey at
         the Gotham Book Mart." *L&U* 2, no. 1 (Spring 1978):17-37.
         Gorey discusses his work, children's responses to it, and aspects
         of his life that have bearing on his books and illustrations.

GORMSEN, JAKOB

A1037   JENSEN, VIRGINIA ALLEN. "A Picture Book for the Blind--A Con-
         versation with Jakob Gormsen About the Book *What's That?*" *Book-
         bird* 1 (1980):7-12.
         Discusses the creation of this book designed for blind children.

GOUDGE, ELIZABETH (1900-   )

A1038   COLWELL, EILEEN H. "Elizabeth Goudge." *Junior Bookshelf* 11 (July
         1947):58-61.
         An appreciative overview. Goudge's "Today and Tomorrow," in
         which she comments on the importance of fairy tales, precedes, pp.
         53-57.

GRAHAM, LORENZ (1902-   )

A1039   GRAHAM, LORENZ. "An Author Speaks." *EE* 50 (February
         1973):185-88.
         Graham speaks about his purposes in writing, his background,
         and his desire to further cross-cultural understanding.

GRAHAME, KENNETH (1859-1932)

A1040   BRAYBROOKE, NEVILLE. "Kenneth Grahame--1859-1932: A Cente-
         nary Study." *EE* 36 (January 1959):11-15.
         "Music, magic, and beauty" distinguish Grahame's writing. Dis-
         cusses *Dream Days* and *The Golden Age* as well as *Wind in the
         Willows*.

A1041   -----. "A Note on Kenneth Grahame." *Horn Book* 46 (October
         1970):504-7.

Concise comments on Grahame's style and background. Similar to Braybrooke's earlier article in *EE* (see above).

A1042   CARPENTER, HUMPHREY. "Kenneth Grahame and the Search for Arcadia." In *Secret Gardens*, pp. 115-25.

Views Grahame as Richard Jeffries's follower in getting "inside the experience of childhood," but unlike Jeffries, Grahame was able to "communicate great excitement" to the reader. Concentrates on *The Golden Age*, with its Good Place and Golden City accessible through the imagination. Also points out the tension between "Wanderer" and "Home-lover" that dominates all of Grahame's work. Provides a detailed analysis of *Wind in the Willows* in a separate chapter, pp. 151-69, exploring the influences of Beatrix Potter and Richard Jeffries and the symbolism of the River and the Kitchen.

A1043   CRIPPS, ELIZABETH A. "Kenneth Grahame: Children's Author?" *CLE*, n.s. 12, no. 1 (Spring 1981):15-23.

Explores reasons why some parts of Grahame's work are more appealing to children than others, within the context of the continuing controversy over whether or not Grahame is a children's writer.

A1044   FADIMAN, CLIFTON. "Professionals and Confessionals: Dr. Seuss & Kenneth Grahame." In Egoff, *Only Connect*, 1st ed., pp. 316-22; 2d ed., pp. 277-80.

Suggests that while Grahame put "his deepest sense of the meaning of his own adult life" into *Wind in the Willows*, Dr. Seuss writes not as "self-revelation, but to please and entertain himself and his young readers."

A1045   GREEN, PETER. *Kenneth Grahame: A Biography*. Cleveland: World Publishing, 1959, 400 pp.

Traces the origins of various themes, elements, and characters in *Wind in The Willows*, on pages 272-86.

A1046   INGLIS, FRED. *Promise of Happiness*, pp. 117-23.

Finds *Wind in the Willows* one of the "shaping spirits of all that was to be written for children thereafter." Views Badger's kitchen as the embodiment of "continuity" and "home" and every child's "Hidey-hole."

A1047   KUZNETS, LOIS. "Toad Hall Revisited." *Children's Literature* 7 (1978):115-28.

"In this study I try to show that homesickness is not peripheral but central to *Wind in the Willows* and is buried deep in its structure, as it is in the word 'nostalgia.'"

A1048   LOWE, ELIZABETH COCHRAN. "Kenneth Grahame and the Beast Tale." Ph.D. dissertation, New York University, 1976, 230 pp., DA 37:5817A.

Studies *Wind in the Willows* as an example of the beast tale in transition--the animal characters exhibiting the major effects of romanticism, Darwinism, and the industrial revolution.

A1049   POSS, GERALDINE D. "An Epic in Arcadia: The Pastoral World of *The Wind in the Willows*." *Children's Literature* 4 (1975):80-90.

Grahame's epic and Arcadian themes are traced from their beginnings in his early stories to their fuller development in *Wind in the Willows* where Grahame has included "the gentler trappings of epic," but omitted "all aspects of the heroic life that might cause strife and pain and eventually death."

A1050   RAY, LAURA KRUGMAN. "Kenneth Grahame and the Literature of Childhood." *English Literature In Transition* 20 (1977):3-12.
Examines the portrayal of childhood in Grahame's *The Golden Age*.

A1051   RYAN, J.S. "The Wild Wood--Place of Dander, Place of Protest." *Orana* 19 (August 1983):133-40.
Examines the tradition of the forest or wild wood as a place of defiance and adventure in English literature, particularly in the work of Kenneth Grahame.

A1052   SALE, ROGER. "Kenneth Grahame." In *Fairy Tales*, pp. 164-93.
Includes a close reading of *Wind in the Willows*.

A1053   SHEPARD, ERNEST H. "Illustrating *Wind in the Willows*." *Horn Book* 30 (April 1954):83-86.
Briefly describes his meeting with Grahame and his exploration of the river bank in preparation for illustrating the book.

A1054   SMITH, KATHRYN A. "Kenneth Grahame and the Singing Willows." *EE* 45 (December 1968):1024-35.
Looks for the key to Grahame's genius in his biography and in his distinct writing style. Characterizes him as one of the "men whose ways with language let them convey their knowing in unforgettable ways."

A1055   STEIG, MICHAEL. "At the Back of *The Wind in the Willows*: An Experiment in Biographical and Autobiographical Interpretation." *Victorian Studies* 24 (Spring 1981):303-23.
Describes an approach to criticism that combines a history of the critic's own reading of the book (in the manner of David Bleich's *Subjective Criticism*) with biographical criticism.

A1056   STERCK, KENNETH. "*The Wind in the Willows*." *CLE*, o.s., no. 12 (September 1973):20-28.
Explores some of the themes of *Wind in the Willows* that have different appeal for children and adults.

A1057   TAYLOR, S. KEITH. "Universal Themes in Kenneth Grahame's *The Wind in the Willows*." Ed.D. dissertation, Temple University, 1967, 208 pp., DA 29:1216A.
Sees the book on two levels: (1) as a child's tale of adventure and, (2) as an adult's book--Grahame's letter to himself, heavy with symbolism. Concludes that the book is "a mine of universal themes to be uncovered, dug out, observed, and enjoyed by the probing literary miner."

A1058   TUCKER, NICHOLAS. "The Children's Falstaff." *TLS*, 26 June 1969. (Reprinted in *Suitable for Children?*, pp. 160-64.)
Sees the character and adventures of the "bad, low animal" Toad as the key to the book's appeal to children.

A1059 WATKINS, TONY. "'Making a Break for the Real England': The River Bankers Revisited." *ChLAQ* 9, no. 1 (Spring 1984):34-35.

Summarizes a number of recent critical interpretations (by Poss, Kuznets, and Zanger) of *Wind in the Willows* and the book's use in advertisements by the English Tourism Board. Reflects upon the ways in which the "meanings" of a work are influenced by its social context, and concludes that "Rereading *The Wind in Willows* in the context of nostalgia for the 'real England' may help us understand a little more about the space occupied by the category 'children's literature' in our culture."

A1060 WILLIAMS, JAY. "Reflections on *Wind in the Willows*." *Signal* 21 (September 1976):103-7.

Sees "cosiness" and "snugness" as keys to the book's charm.

GRAMATKY, HARDIE (1907-79)

A1061 BADER, BARBARA. *American Picturebooks*, pp. 203-4.

Finds elements of the Disney animator in Gramatky's *Little Toot*. Considers his formula less successful in subsequent books, however.

A1062 PAINTER, HELEN W. "*Little Toot*--Hero." *EE* 37 (October 1960):363-67. (Also in Hoffman, *Authors and Illustrators*, pp. 172-79.)

Analyzes the essence, style, and illustration of *Little Toot*. Concludes that the charm of Gramatky's books lies in machines taking on childlike, irrepressive character and becoming full-blown human personalities. Includes references.

GRAY, ELIZABETH JANET [Elizabeth Gray Vining] (1902-   )

A1063 GRAY, ELIZABETH JANET. "History is People." *Horn Book* 19 (July-August 1943):216-20.

Newbery Medal acceptance speech. Describes the background of *Adam of the Road*.

A1064 MASSEE, MAY. "Elizabeth Janet Gray." *Horn Book* 19 (July-August 1943):205-14.

Her editor discusses Gray's development as a writer during her "first twenty years."

A1065 PEASE, HOWARD. "Technically Speaking." *Horn Book* 12 (March/April 1943):90-97.

"In the field of the junior novel there are scarcely half a dozen authors" who reveal "deep knowledge of their craft." Uses Elizabeth Janet Gray's *Beppy Marlowe* as his primary example of excellent craftsmanship, with detailed analysis, and shows where other writers, notably E.C. Gaggin in *Down Ryton Water*, fail.

GRAY, HAROLD (1894-1968)

A1066 HAMAKER, GENE E. "Alla-Ca-Zaba! Gazah! Presto! Some Observations on the Role of the Orient in 'Little Orphan Annie' (1924-1968)." *Journal of Popular Culture* 9 (Fall 1975):331-40.

Examines American attitudes toward Asia and Asians and the ways in which these attitudes, and the changes in them, were reflected in *Little Orphan Annie* over the years. Includes extensive references.

A1067   YOUNG, WILLIAM H. "That Indomitable Redhead: Little Orphan
         Annie." *Journal of Popular Culture* 8, no. 2 (Fall 1974):309-16.
         Examines the conservative biases in Annie's and the other charac-
         ters' responses to the depression and World War II.

GRAY, NICHOLAS STUART (1922-81)

A1068   CROUCH, MARCUS. "Revels Ended." *Junior Bookshelf* 45, no. 3
         (June 1981):101-3.
         An appreciative overview of Gray's career as novelist, short story
         writer, and playwright.

A1069   WINTLE, JUSTIN, and FISHER, EMMA. *Pied Piper*, pp. 147-60.
         Gray discusses his life and work in an interview.

GREENAWAY, KATE (1846-1901)

A1070   ALDERSON, BRIAN. "Heavy Boots in the Marigold Garden: An
         Extended Comment on Current Kate Greenaway Literature." *Phaedrus*
         9 (1982):7-10.
         Calls for accurate information regarding Greenaway's published
         books, for an assessment of the history of her reputation, and for a
         good biography; then summarizes and critiques recent Greenaway
         scholarship in terms of these needs.

A1071   HEARN, MICHAEL PATRICK. "Mr. Ruskin & Miss Greenaway."
         Children's Literature 8 (1980):22-34.
         Explores the relationship between the two and Ruskin's influence
         on her work.

A1072   PARRISH, ANNE. "Flowers for a Birthday: Kate Greenaway, March
         17, 1846." *Horn Book* 22 (March 1946):97-108. (Reprinted in
         Fryatt, *Horn Book Sampler*, pp. 41-49.)
         Largely biographical with small bits of insight into her work.

A1073   *Under the Window*, 1971-.
         A quarterly journal published by the Kate Greenaway Society,
         devoted to Greenaway news and scholarship.

GREENBERG, JOANNE [Hannah Green] (1932-   )

A1074   CROSSLEY, BRIAN MILES. "The Last Frontier: Self-Destruction in
         Contemporary American Fiction." Ph.D. dissertation, State University
         of New York at Binghamton, 1981, 395 pp., DA 42:1633A.
         Chapter 3 concentrates on the literary technique of *I Never
         Promised You a Rose Garden* "in terms of the schizophrenia it so
         assiduously narrates."

A1075   WOLFE, KARY K., and WOLFE, GARY K. "Metaphors of Madness:
         Popular Psychological Narrative." *Journal of Popular Culture* 9
         (Spring 1976):895-907. (Reprinted in Lenz, *Young Adult Literature*,
         pp. 155-60.)
         Examines characterization, structure, style, imagery, and rhetoric
         in *I Never Promised You a Rose Garden.*

GREENE, BETTE (1934-   )

A1076   OSA, OSAYIMWENSE. "Adolescent Girls' Need for Love in Two Cultures--Nigeria and the United States." *English Journal* 72 (December 1983):35-37.
Compares the treatment of adolescent love in Bette Greene's *Summer of My German Soldier* and in Buchi Emecheta's *The Bride Price*.

GREENFIELD, ELOISE (1929-   )

A1077   GREENFIELD, ELOISE. "Something to Shout About." *Horn Book* 51 (December 1975):624-26.
Talks about what she wants for children, in her own books and those of others--to help children maneuver their way through the dangers of life.

A1078   KIAH, ROSALIE BLACK. "Profile: Eloise Greenfield." *LA* 57 (September 1980):653-59.
Kiah interviews Greenfield about her life and work, and comments on her responses.

GRICE, FREDERICK (1910-   )

A1079   BOARD, M.J. "Frederick Grice: A Sentimental Realist." *School Librarian* 23, no. 1 (March 1975):20-23.
Sees Grice as both a sentimentalist and a realist, and finds the two aspects of his work interdependent.

GRIMM, JACOB (1785-1863), and GRIMM, WILHELM (1786-1859)

A1080   ANNAN, GABRIELE. "Borne Along by Goblins." *TLS*, 20 September 1974, pp. 1008-9.
Reviews the Sendak-Segal-Jarrell *The Juniper Tree and Other Tales*.

A1081   CARSCH, HENRY. "Dimension of Meaning and Value in a Sample of Fairy Tales." Ph.D. dissertation, Princeton University, 1965, 161 pp., DA 27:827A.
Analyzes "agents of the supernatural as they are presented in Grimms' *Kinder und Hausmärchen*" as a dimension of culture. The findings are related to "salient characteristics of German National character and its ontogenesis."

A1082   CROUCH, MARCUS S. "Illustrating Grimm." *Junior Bookshelf* 14, no. 6 (December 1950):236-43.
Surveys the illustrators of Grimms' *Household Tales* and concludes that the tales "remain without their successful interpreter."

A1083   DAVID, ALFRED, and DAVID, MARY E. "A Literary Approach to the Brothers Grimm." *Folklore Institute* 1, no. 3 (1964):180-96.
Provides a readable introduction to the Grimms' own literary and historical approach to their material.

A1084   DEGH, LINDA. "Grimms' *Household Tales* and its Place in the Household: The Social Relevance of a Controversial Classic." *Western Folklore* 38 (April 79):83-103.

Examines the controversies surrounding the origins and the nature of the Grimms' tales from a folklore perspective.

A1085   ELLIS, JOHN M. *One Fairy Story Too Many: The Brothers Grimm and Their Tales.* Chicago: University of Chicago Press, 1983, 214 pp.

Argues that the Grimms deliberately falsified their tales and suppressed evidence of their origins; and furthermore, that scholars have been reluctant to question the reports the Grimms presented on their work. Provides variant texts of three tales: "The Frog Prince," "Sleeping Beauty," and "Hansel and Gretel."

A1086   FITZSIMONS, EILEEN. "Jacob and Wilhelm Grimms' *Irische Elfenmarchen.* A Comparison of the Translation with the English Original: *Fairy Legends and Traditions of the South of Ireland* by T. Crofton Croker." Ph.D. dissertation, University of Chicago, 1978, 326 pp., DA 39:3609A.

A1087   KAMENETSKY, CHRISTA. "The Brothers Grimm: Folktale Style and Romantic Theories." *EE* 51 (April 1974):379-83. (Reprinted in Barron, *Jump Over the Moon*, pp. 316-22.)

Explores the romantic theories that provided the framework for the Grimms' approach to folktale collecting.

A1088   LORRAINE, WALTER. "The Brothers Grimm Across Time and Space: A Side View of the Illustrators of the Grimm Tales." In *Children's Books International 1. Proceedings and Book Catalog.* Boston: Boston Public Library, 1976, pp. 16-21.

Briefly traces the publishing and illustration history of the Grimms' folktales, but the accompanying illustrations are not included in the proceedings.

A1089   MALLET, KARL-HEINZ. *Fairy Tales and Children: The Psychology of Children Revealed through Four of Grimms' Fairy Tales.* New York: Schocken, 1984, 213 pp.

Applies the methods of depth psychology and dream interpretations to "Hansel and Gretel," pp. 51-99, "Little Red Riding Hood," pp. 100-127, "The Boy Who Set Out to Learn Fear," pp. 128-75, and "The Goose Girl," pp. 176-205.

A1090   MARTHE, ROBERT. "The Grimm Brothers." *Yale French Studies* 43 (1969):44-56.

Finds in the Grimms' tales a combination of "grace and art" that are their "strongest protection against any disquieting undertakings that may come from science." Reflects upon differences between French and German versions of the tales.

A1091   SALE, ROGER. *Fairy Tales*, pp. 33-36.

Analyzes several motifs in the Lore Segal translation of "The Juniper Tree": the longing for a child, the wicked stepmother, and resurrection.

A1092   TATAR, MARIA. "Tests, Tasks, and Trials in the Grimms' Fairy Tales." *Children's Literature* 13 (1985):31-48.

Examines the male protagonists of the Grimms "to determine what character traits they share and to assess the extent to which the plots of their adventures possess a degree of predictability."

A1093   USSHER, ARLAND, and METZRADT, CARL von, eds. *Enter These Enchanted Woods: An Interpretation of Grimms' Fairy Tales.* Rev. ed. Dublin: Dolmen Press, 1966, 63 PP.

      Explores archetypal ideas found in a number of the Grimms' tales.

A1094   ZIPES, JACK. "Who's Afraid of the Brothers Grimm? Socialization and Politicization through Fairy Tales." *L&U* 3, no. 2 (Winter 1979-80):4-56.

      This lengthy scholarly article reviews the nature and history of the tales, the notion of socialization through fairy tales, and the revitalization and transformation of the tales for political purposes by West German writers such as Friedrich Karl Walchter, Andreas and Angela Hopf, Johannes Merkel, Janosch, Hans-Joachim Gelberg, Rosemarie Künzler, Irmela Brender, Doris Lerche, and O.F. Gmelin. Includes brief translations of some of the versions of the tales.

GRIPE, MARIA (1923-   )

A1095   GRIPE, MARIA. "A Word and a Shadow." *Bookbird* 12, no. 2 (1974):4-10.

      Discusses her writing and influences upon her, particularly those of Andersen's fairy tales.

A1096   MANNHEIMER, CARIN. "Maria Gripe." *Bookbird* 11, no. 2 (1973):24-34. (From an article in *Barn och Kultur*, 1971 no. 2.)

      Sees the basic motif of Gripe's books as "man's relation to his role in life." Divides the books into psychological/realistic ones, and mystic/romantic ones. Includes a bibliography of Gripe's books and their translations.

A1097   STANTON, LORRAINE. "Shadows and Motifs: A Review and Analysis of Works of Maria Gripe." *Catholic Library World* 51 (May 1980):447-49.

      "In her stories, realistic and fairy tales alike, Mrs. Gripe combines symbolism, humor, morality and the themes of loneliness and lack of communication with imaginative creativity."

GROVE, FREDERICK PHILIP (1879-1948)

A1098   *Canadian Children's Literature* 27-28 (1982):1-169.

      Almost an entire double issue is devoted to Grove's *Leonard Broadus,* which is reprinted here completely, with an "Afterword: Genesis of a Boys' Book," by Mary Rubio, pp. 127-57, and "The Publishing History of *Leonard Broadus,*" pp. 157-69.

GRUELLE, JOHNNY (1880-1938)

A1099   LANES, SELMA G. "Raggedy Ann to Riches." *NYTBR*, 1 May 1977, Children's Book sec., pp. 30, 39. (Reprinted in Butler, *Sharing Literature with Children*, pp. 70-74.)

      Explores the history of the Raggedy Ann stories. Comments on reasons for their appeal and on several new editions.

A1100   WILLIAMS, MARTIN. "Some Remarks on Raggedy Ann and Johnny Gruelle." *Children's Literature* 3 (1974):140-46.

Feels that although Gruelle was a hack who wrote too much, some of his work is very good and deserves more attention. Examines characteristics of Gruelle's work, pointing out his strengths, idiosyncracies, and shortcomings.

GUILLOT, RENÉ (1900-1969)

A1101   CROUCH, MARCUS. *The Nesbit Tradition*, pp. 39-40.
Considers Guillot "a superb story-teller" and *Companions of Fortune* a great book that can "haunt a reader for a lifetime."

A1102   SCHMIDT, NANCY. *Children's Books About Africa*, pp. 114-18.
Decries the entrenched stereotypes in Guillot's African stories, and his "negative views on the African environment, and the religion, animallike [*sic*] hunting abilities, and un-European appearance, work habits and values of its people."

GUY, ROSA (1928-   )

A1103   GUY, ROSA. "All about Caring." *TON* 39 (Winter 1983):192-96.
A moving personal statement that reveals much about Guy's books and her goals as a writer.

A1104   -----. "Young Adult Books: I Am a Storyteller." *Horn Book* 61 (March 1985):220-21.
Guy explains that in her storytelling she wants not only to entertain but to teach people about each other.

HADER, BERTA (1890-1976), and HADER, ELMER (1889-1973)

A1105   ALTSTETTER, MABEL F. "Berta and Elmer Hader." *EE* 32 (December 1955):501-6. (Reprinted in Hoffman, *Authors and Illustrators*, pp. 180-85.)
Discusses psychological aspects of the Haders' books.

HAGGARD, Sir HENRY RIDER (1856-1925)

A1106   GREEN, R.L. "Rider Haggard." *Junior Bookshelf* 20 (October 1956):179-85.
Argues that it is a feeling of higher romance, of "appeal to something more than mere excitement," that gives to Haggard's stories the quality which has kept them alive.

A1107   TURNER, ANN. "Bring Back Rider Haggard." *Use of English* 31, no. 3 (Summer 1980):28-36.
Argues that "Haggard's books have a simplicity and directness, a mythic grandeur and a lack of sentimentality that could make them popular classics for our children even today."

HAIG-BROWN, RODERICK (1908-76)

A1108   BIRKS, JOHN. "The Work of Roderick Haig-Brown." *Junior Bookshelf* 17, no. 3 (July 1953):95-102.
Compares Haig-Brown to Richard Armstrong in his sincerity and sympathy with adolescents, but finds him a more accomplished writer.

A1109   LUCAS, ALEC. "Haig-Brown's Animal Biographies." *CCL* 11 (1978):21-38.
Examines changes in Haig-Brown's technique from *Silver* to *Panther*, to *Return to the River*.

A1110   STOW, GLENYS. "A Conversation with Roderick Haig-Brown." *CCL* 1, no. 2 (Summer 1975):9-22.
An interview in which Haig-Brown discusses his animal stories and historical fiction, his aims, values, and several of his books, especially *Starbuck Valley Winter* and *The Whole People*.

HALE, KATHLEEN (1898-   )

A1111   MOSS, ELAINE. "Kathleen Hale and Orlando the Marmalade Cat." *Signal* 9 (September 1972):123-27.
Discusses the origins of the Orlando books.

HALE, LUCRETIA (1820-1900)

A1112   WANKMILLER, MADELYN C. "Lucretia P. Hale and *The Peterkin Papers*." Tenth Caroline M. Hewins Lecture. Shortened version in *Horn Book* 34 (April 1958):95-103, 137-47. (Complete version in Andrews, *The Hewins Lectures, 1947-1962*, pp. 235-49.)
A biocritical overview.

HALEY, GAIL (1939-   )

A1113   HALEY, GAIL E. "Everyman Jack and the Green Man: Keynote Address." *Proceedings of the Children's Literature Association* 9 (1982):1-19.
Author-illustrator Haley outlines her methods of researching her folklore characters, with examples from Everyman Jack and the Green Man.

HAMILTON, ELIZABETH (1906-   )

A1114   DOBBS, ROSE. "*The P-Zoo*: A Child's Book." *Horn Book* 21 (September-October 1945):357-61.
Tells the story behind the creation of this book, and also comments on the illustrations by Peter Hurd.

HAMILTON, VIRGINIA (1936-   )

A1115   APSELOFF, MARILYN. "A Conversation with Virginia Hamilton." *CLE*, n.s. 14, no. 4 (Winter 1983):204-13.
Hamilton discusses her life and work in an interview.

A1116   -----. "Creative Geography in the Ohio Novels of Virginia Hamilton." *ChLAQ* 8, no. 1 (Spring 1983):17-20.
Explores the ways in which Hamilton has creatively used actual landscapes surrounding Yellow Springs, Ohio, to establish mood and create the vividly real settings of her books.

A1117   DRESSEL, JANICE HARTWICK. "The Legacy of Ralph Ellison in Virginia Hamilton's Justice Trilogy." *English Journal* 73 (November 1984):42-48.
"To appreciate Hamilton's accomplishment in the trilogy, it is

important to understand the historical controversy surrounding Ellison's *Invisible Man* and to look at the novel itself." Concludes that there are many parallels between Ellison and Hamilton.

A1118   HAMILTON, VIRGINIA.   "Ah, Sweet Rememory!"   *Horn Book* 57 (December 1981):633-40.
Discusses her background and her ways of writing.

A1119   -----. "*Boston Globe-Horn Book* Award Acceptance."   *Horn Book* 60 (February 1984):24-28.
Reflects upon the process of writing *Sweet Whispers, Brother Rush*.

A1120   -----. "Changing Woman, Working."   In Hearne, *Celebrating Children's Books*, pp. 54-61.
Provides insights into her background, her methods of working, some of her characters, and the dreams and goals that permeate her work.

A1121   -----. "Illusion and Reality."   In Haviland, *The Openhearted Audience*, pp. 115-31.
Explores the nature of fiction, of illusion and reality, and comments on her use of eccentric characters, which she sees as reflective of the entire history of blacks in America. Concludes by discussing her biographies of Paul Robeson and W.E.B. DuBois and their connection with the eccentricities of black American history.

A1122   -----. "The Mind of the Novel: The Heart of the Book."   *ChLAQ* 8, no. 4 (Winter 1983):10-14.
Explores why and how she creates her fiction, providing background on *Sheema, Queen of the Road* and *The Magical Adventures of Pretty Pearl*.

A1123   -----. "Newbery Award Acceptance."   *Horn Book* 51 (August 1975):337-43.
Elucidates *M.C. Higgins, The Great*'s origins and symbolism. A biographical sketch by Paul Heins follows, pp. 344-48.

A1124   -----. "Portrait of the Author as a Working Writer."   *EE* 48 (April 1971):237-40, 302. (Reprinted in Hoffman, *Authors and Illustrators*, pp. 186-92.)
In this skillfully created "self-portrait" Hamilton shares her history as a writer, and speaks about some of her major themes and the characters Junior Brown, Zeely, M.C. Higgins, Mr. Pluto, and Jahdu.

A1125   HEINS, ETHEL L.   Review.   *Horn Book* 52 (December 1976):611.
Comments on the impressionistic, oblique, and elliptical style of *Arilla Sun Down*.

A1126   HEINS, PAUL.   Review.   *Horn Book* 48 (February 1972):81.
Praises *The Planet of Junior Brown* and Hamilton's "Dostoevskian intensity."

A1127   LANGTON, JANE.   "Virginia Hamilton, The Great."   *Horn Book* 50 (December 1974):671-73.
Enthusiastically praises *M.C. Higgins, The Great* and "the strength and rightness" of Hamilton's style.

A1128   MOSS, ANITA. "Frontiers of Gender in Children's Literature: Virginia Hamilton's *Arilla Sun Down*." *ChLAQ* 8, no. 4 (Winter 1983):25-27.
Argues that in *Arilla Sun Down*, as in *M.C. Higgins, The Great*, Hamilton reveals an "androgynous vision" of the self, and "endorses liberation from excessively rigid gender norms." She shows that "a spirit of reconciliation can help to heal gaps between cultures, races, and gender."

A1129   REES, DAVID. "Long Ride through a Painted Desert--Virginia Hamilton." In *Painted Desert*, pp. 168-84.
"Only two of her nine novels--*Zeely* and *M.C. Higgins, The Great*"--are one hundred percent successful. . . in all the others there is some major flaw that spoils the finished product." Discusses Hamilton's strengths and weaknesses.

A1130   SCHOLL, KATHLEEN. "Black Traditions in *M.C. Higgins, The Great*." *LA* 57 (April 1980):420-24.
Suggests that the folklore in the book provides "a key to understanding the characters and their belief systems upon which the conflict in the book is built."

A1131   TOWNSEND, JOHN ROWE. *A Sounding*, pp. 97-110.
"Even at their simplest, her stories are capable of extension; they contain more than is expressed in their words." Discusses *Planet of Junior Brown*, *M.C. Higgins, The Great*, and *Arilla Sun Down*, among others.

A1132   WILSON, GERALDINE. Review. *IRBC* 14, nos. 1-2 (1983):32.
Praises the construction, African American language, and emotional depth of *Sweet Whispers, Brother Rush*.

"Hansel and Gretel"

A1133   KROGNESS, MARG MERCER. "Viewpoints: From a Classroom Teacher." *LA* 58 (April 1981):408-9.
Role-playing in the classroom reveals fascinating insights about the folktale and awareness of human nature.

A1134   SCHUMAN, Elliot P. "A Psychoanalytic Study of Hansel and Gretel." *Journal of Contemporary Psychotherapy* 4 (Spring 1972):121-25.
Uses "Hansel and Gretel" to illustrate ways in which fairy tales are useful to both children and adults as a means of working through psychological problems.

HARDY, THOMAS (1840-1928)

A1135   BUTTS, DENNIS. *"Our Exploits at West Poley*: A Plea for Reprinting." *CLE*, o.s., no. 3 (November 1970):41-47.
Argues that Hardy's little-known and out-of-print book for children should be reprinted. Feels it would provide children with ideal preparation for later reading of Hardy's work for adults.

HARGREAVES, ROGER

A1136   BARKER, KEITH. "The Washing Powder Syndrome: An Examination of a Popular Children's Writer." *School Librarian* 31, no. 2 (June

1983):102-7.
Compares Hargreave's financially successful *Mr. Men* and *Little Miss* books with Enid Blyton's.

A1137   EVANS, DAVID. "The Family of *Mr. Men.*" *CLE*, n.s. 13, no. 3 (Autumn 1982):130-37.
Discusses the appeal of these popular books: size, simplicity, humor, repetition, echoes of parents' tricks, audience participation ploys, simple characters, and plot lines. Questions whether they encourage stereotyping and labeling and asks, "What do they lack?"

HARNETT, CYNTHIA (1893-1981)

A1138   COLWELL, E.H. "Cynthia Harnett." *Junior Bookshelf* 21 (March 1957):37-43.
Characterizes Harnett's approach to historical fiction as "an imaginative reconstruction in story form of the life of ordinary people."

A1139   CROUCH, MARCUS. *The Nesbit Tradition*, pp. 60-63.
"Of all the historical novelists writing for the young, Cynthia Harnett most resembles an architect, shaping a myriad of tiny details and fitting them together so that they all perform necessary functions and all contribute to an impressive and satisfying structure."

A1140   EDWARDS, TONY. *"Stories, Not History:* The Historical Novels of Cynthia Harnett." *CLE*, o.s., no. 9 (November 1972):24-32.
Examines Harnett's books from the perspective of history teaching rather than from the perspective of literary criticism.

A1141   HARNETT, CYNTHIA. "From the Ground Upwards." *Horn Book* 37 (October 1961):413-18.
Describes her methods of researching the life of the common people for her historical fiction.

A1142   PARROTT, PHYLLIS. "Cynthia Harnett--A Tribute on Her Eightieth Birthday." *Junior Bookshelf* 37, no. 4 (August 1973):233-34.
A brief appreciative analysis.

A1143   WHITEHEAD, WINIFRED. "Writers for Children--Cynthia Harnett." *Use of English* 25 (Summer 1974):301-6. (Reprinted in Butts, *Good Writers*, pp. 50-55.)
Discusses the appeal of Harnett's historical fiction for young children and examines her themes, style, and techniques.

HARRIS, AURAND (1915-   )

A1144   HARRIS, AURAND. *Six Plays for Children.* Austin: University of Texas Press, 1977, 378 pp.
Includes a foreword by Lowell Swortzell and a biography and play analyses by Coleman A. Jennings, as well as the texts of six plays.

A1145   JENNINGS, C. "The Dramatic Contributions of Aurand Harris to Children's Theatre in the United States." Ed.D. dissertation, New York University, 1974, 327 pp., DA 35:6848.
Includes biographical background on Harris, evaluation of all of

the scripts published from 1945 to 1972, and a detailed study of Harris's use of dramatic form in six plays: *Once Upon a Clothesline*, *Pinocchio and the Indians*, *Buffalo Bill*, *Androcles and the Lion*, *Rags to Riches*, and *Punch and Judy*. The bibliography consists of 223 entries relating to playwriting for children's theater.

HARRIS, CHRISTIE (1907-)

A1146 ELLISON, SHIRLEY, and MISHRA, MARY. "Author Portraits: The Award-Winning Canadian Author Christie Harris." *Bookbird* 4 (1981):19-22.
A brief biocritical overview.

A1147 HARRIS, CHRISTIE. "In Tune with Tomorrow." *CCL* 78 (Autumn 1978):26-30.
Discusses the origins of a number of her books.

A1148 -----. "The Shift from Feasthouse to Book." *CCL* 31-32 (1983):9-11.
Describes the painstaking process of rewriting Native American oral tales as literature.

A1149 RADU, KENNETH. "Canadian Fantasy." *CCL* 1, no. 2 (Summer 1975):73-79.
Places Harris in the context of Canadian fantasy. Points out weaknesses in *Secret in the Stlalakum Wild* and in the genre of Canadian fantasy itself but concludes that the book has real merit.

A1150 WOOD, SUSAN. "Stories and Stlalakums: Christie Harris and the Supernatural World." *CCL* 15-16 (1980):47-56.
Suggests that although Harris does not create worlds, as a fantasy writer, she does re-create "a world view in which spiritual, natural and human elements co-exist in harmony . . . her gift is to make us regard our own world through Indians' eyes, and with, perhaps, something of their reverence." Reviews of three of Harris's books also appear in this issue, pp. 98-105.

HARRIS, JOEL CHANDLER (1848-1908)

A1151 BICKLEY, R. BRUCE, comp. *Joel Chandler Harris: A Reference Guide*. Boston: G.K. Hall, 1978, 360 pp.
A chronological, annotated survey of English-language commentaries on Joel Chandler Harris published between 1862 and 1976. A preface summarizes the findings.

A1152 BURROUGHS, MARGARET. "Uncle Remus for Today's Children." *EE* 30 (December 1953):485-92.
Argues convincingly, by examining many variants of the Uncle Remus tales, that the stories should be made available in plain English.

A1153 LEA, JAMES. "Shadow at the Cabin Door: Implications of Reality in Joel Chandler Harris's Tales of Uncle Remus." Ph.D. dissertation, University of North Carolina at Chapel Hill, 1973, 140 pp., DA 35:460A.
Contents include a biography of Harris, discussion of his methods of collecting he tales, a detailed study of a body of the tales, and a study of Harris's knowledge of the deeper significance of the tales.

Concludes that the Uncle Remus tales are "powerful literary records of the nineteenth-century Southern Black experience."

A1154   LIGHT, KATHLEEN. "Uncle Remus and the Folklorists." *Southern Literary Journal* 7 (Spring 1975):88-104.
Explores the effect of folklore study on Harris's writings. "Not willing to cast himself as a champion of the Negro, he would not challenge the openly racist interpretations of the folklorists."

A1155   MIKKELSEN, NINA. "When the Animals Talked--A Hundred Years of Uncle Remus." *ChLAQ* 8, no. 1 (Spring 1983):3-5, 31.
Surveys the publishing history and varied critical responses to the Uncle Remus tales.

A1156   MUFFETT, D.J. "Uncle Remus Was a Hausaman?" *Southern Folklore Quarterly* 39 (January 1975):151-66.
Explores the possibilities that the Uncle Remus stories originated in Africa in the Hausa language, and suggests possible avenues for further exploration of the topic.

A1157   NICKELS, CAMERON C. "Early Version of the Tar Baby Story." *Journal of American Folklore* 94 (July-September 1981):364-69.
Reprints and analyzes an earlier version of the Tar Baby story retold by Harris.

A1158   RUBIN, LOUIS D., Jr. "Uncle Remus and the Ubiquitous Rabbit." *Southern Review* 10 (October 1974):787-804.
Surveys Harris life and work, exploring some of the depths and complexities of his attitudes toward blacks and Southern society.

A1159   STRICKLAND, W. "Joel Chandler Harris: A Bibliographical Study." Ph.D. dissertation, University of Georgia, 1976, 302 pp., DA 37:7755A.
The first descriptive bibliography of the literary writings of Joel Chandler Harris.

A1160   TURNER, ARLIN. "Joel Chandler Harris (1848-1908)." *American Literary Realism* 1, no. 3 (Summer 1968):18-23.
Provides an overview of Harris criticism, including information on bibliographies, the existence of manuscript collections, recent critical articles, and areas needing further study.

HARRIS, MARILYN (1931-   )

A1161   SEALE, DORIS. "Indians without Hope, Indians without Options --The Problematic Theme of *Hatter Fox*." *IRBC* 15, no. 3 (1984):7-10, 22.
Strongly criticizes this novel about a young Navajo woman, maintaining that it misrepresents reality and conveys some exceedingly questionable messages.

HARRIS, ROSEMARY (1923-   )

A1162   SCHMIDT, NANCY. *Children's Fiction about Africa*, pp. 157-58.
Faults Harris's improbabilities in re-creating ancient Egypt.

HASKINS, JIM (1941-)

A1163   HASKINS, JIM. "Writing Sports Biographies for Young Readers." *L&U* 4, no. 1 (Summer 1980):32-40.
This author of many sports biographies for young people discusses his purposes and techniques.

HAUGAARD, ERIK CHRISTIAN (1923-)

A1164   KUZNETS, LOIS R. "Other Poeple's Children: Erik Haugaard's '"Untold Tales.'" *CLE*, n.s. 11, no. 2 (Summer 1980):62-68. (Also in *Proceedings in the Children's Literature Association* 6 (1979):128-35.)
Suggests that, "throughout his works, Haugaard's choices of situation, character, narrator, and image are significant because they contribute not to glorification of the powerful but to the appreciation of the often neglected powerless." His "internationalism goes beyond most."

A1165   LAVENDER, RALPH. "Hans Christian Andersen and Erik Christian Haugaard." *School Librarian* 23, no. 2 (June 1975):113-19.
Evaluates Haugaard's translation of Hans Christian Andersen. "Is this particular version the one we need? The answer must, then, be a qualified yes."

A1166   NIST, JOAN. "*Places of Freedom*: Erik Christian Haugaard's Historical Fiction." *Advocate*, no. 2 (Winter 1985):114-20.
Explores Haugaard's approaches to history and historical fiction and examines some of his specific techniques.

A1167   ROOT, SHELTON L., and GREENLAW, M. JEAN. "Profile: An Interview with Erik Christian Haugaard." *LA* 56 (May 1979):549-61.
In an interview, Haugaard discusses his life and his work. Includes a bibliography of his books.

HAUTZIG, ESTHER (1930-)

A1168   HAUTZIG, ESTHER. "*The Endless Steppe*--For Children Only?" *Horn Book* 46 (October 1970):461-68.
Tells of writing the book and her struggles with editors.

A1169   REES, DAVID. "From Russia with Love? Esther and Deborah Hautzig." *School Librarian* 28 (December 1980):350-56.
Compares and contrasts Esther Hautzig's *Endless Steppe* with daughter Deborah's *Hey, Dollface!*

HAYWOOD, CAROLYN (1898-)

A1170   BURNS, PAUL C., and HINES, RUTH. "Carolyn Haywood." *EE* 47 (February 1970):172-75. (Reprinted in Hoffman, *Authors and Illustrators*, pp. 193-96.)
Discusses the Betsy and Eddie books and others and assesses Haywood's appeal for children.

A1171   SHAKEN, GRACE. "Our Debt to Carolyn Haywood." *EE* 32 (January 1955):3-8.
Explores reasons why children love Haywood's books.

HEINLEIN, ROBERT A. (1907-   )

A1172 CROUCH, MARCUS. *The Nesbit Tradition*, pp. 55-56.
"Heinlein. . . is a master of the art of painless indoctrination.
His secret is that he shows his characters learning their lessons, and
the reader shares in the educational experience."

A1173 SULLIVAN, C.W., III. "Heinlein's Juveniles: Still Contemporary after
All These Years." *ChLAQ* 10, no. 2 (Summer 1985):64-66.
Examines Heinlein's twelve novels aimed at a young adult
audience.

HELLÉ, ANDRE (1871-   )

A1174 AVERILL, ESTHER. "Andre Hellé." *Horn Book* 7 (August
1931):179-86.
A survey of the work of the French author/illustrator, with comments on his literary and artistic style. Includes a bibliography of
his works.

HENRY, MARGUERITE (1902-   )

A1175 HENRY, MARGUERITE. "Newbery Acceptance Paper." *Horn Book* 26
(January 1950):9-17.
Describes the background of *King of the Wind* and *Justin Mor-
gan Had a Horse*. "My Sister Marguerite Henry," by Gertrude B.
Jupp, follows, pp. 18-24.

A1176 -----. "A Weft of Truth and Warp of Fiction." *EE* 51 (October
1974):921-25.
Describes her writing career and the responses of children and
teachers to her books.

A1177 WILT, MIRIAM E. "In Marguerite Henry--The Thread That Runs So
True." *EE* 31 (November 1954):387-95. (Reprinted in Hoffman,
Authors and Illustrators, pp. 197-209.)
Considers Henry "the best author of children's horse stories in
this era, perhaps of all time." An overview, with favorable critical
comments of her work up to *Brighty of Grand Canyon*.

HENTOFF, NAT (1925-   )

A1178 HENTOFF, NAT. "Back to You, Nat: Hearing from the Teen-age
Reader." *WLB* 47 (September 1972):38-41. (Reprinted in Varlejs,
Young Adult Literature, pp. 151-55.)
Reflects upon the responses his readers have made to *Jazz Coun-
try*, *I'm Really Dragged But Nothing Gets Me Down*, and *In the
Country of Ourselves*.

A1179 -----. "Getting Inside *Jazz Country*." *Horn Book* 42 (October
1966):528-32.
Explores his intentions and didactic purposes for writing the
book.

HENTY, GEORGE ALFRED (1832-1902)

A1180 SCHMIDT, NANCY. *Children's Fiction About Africa*, 105-8.

Discusses Henty's depiction of Africa and Africans.

HERGÉ [Georges Remi] (1907-83)

A1181   APOSTOLIDES, JEAN-MARIE. *"Tin-Tin* and the Family Romance." *Children's Literature* 13 (1985):94-108.
Examines the recurrent structures of *Tin-Tin* in this article translated and adapted from several chapters of Apostolides's *Les Metamorphoses de "Tin-Tin"* (Paris: Laffont, 1984).

A1182   CUNNINGHAM, VALENTINE. "Xenophobia for Beginners." *TLS*, 25 November 1983, p. 1316.
Reviews *The Blue Lotus* and *The Making of Tintin.*

A1183   PEASE, NICHOLAS. "The Seriocomicstrip World of *Tin-Tin." L&U* 1, no. 1 (1977):54-61.
Explores the long standing appeal of *The Adventures of Tin-Tin* to "the tastes of those who take literature seriously."

A1184   RODENBECK, JOHN. "The *Tin-Tin* Series: Children's Literature and Popular Appeal." *Children's Literature* 1 (1972):93-97.
Describes and analyzes the comic strip series.

A1185   SCOTT, DOROTHY HAYWARD. "The *Tin-Tin* Saga: A Tribute to Herge." *Horn Book* 60 (April 1984):230-41.
History and description of the *Tin-Tin* series and its author.

HINTON, S.E. (1950-)

A1186   HINTON, S.E., et al. "Readers Meet Author." *TON* 25 (November 1968):27-39; (January 1969):194-202.
An extensive discussion by Hinton and a panel of high-school students of *The Outsiders* and issues it has raised.

A1187   REES, DAVID. "Macho Man, American Style--S.E. Hinton." In *Painted Desert*, pp. 126-37.
Maintains that while it is easy to understand the popularity of Hinton's works for young teenagers, it is hard to understand why she has won critical acclaim and acceptance in the classroom. Examines all of Hinton's books to date.

HOBAN, RUSSELL (1925-)

A1188   BADER, BARBARA. *American Picturebooks*, pp. 472-77.
Concentrates on the Frances books and *Herman The Loser.*

A1189   BLOUNT, MARGARET. *Animal Land*, pp. 186-88.
Examines *Mouse and His Child* in the context of animal toys in literature and what happens to them. "The path of every toy is always downwards."

A1190   BOWERS, JOAN A. "The Fantasy World of Russell Hoban." *Children's Literature* 8 (1980):80-97. (Also in *Proceedings of the Children's Literature Association* 6 (1979):86-93, entitled "From Badgers to Turtles: The Fantasy World of Russell Hoban.")
Relates Hoban's children's books to his adult books. Sees them as

"a unified aesthetic whole" and maintains that in both he "typically expresses his psychological and metaphysical concerns in fantasies involving animals." Traces his development as a writer.

A1191   BUTTS, DENNIS. "Riddley Walker and The Novels of Russell Hoban." *Use of English* 33, no. 3 (Summer 1982):20-27.
Relates *Riddley Walker* to *Mouse and His Child* and Hoban's adult novels.

A1192   HOBAN, RUSSELL. "Thoughts on a Shirtless Cyclist, Robin Hood, Johann-Sebastian Bach and One or Two Other Things." *CLE*, o.s., no. 4 (March 1971):5-23. (Reprinted in Fox, *Writers, Critics, and Children*, pp. 95-103.)
Describes his own creative processes, seeing in Robin Hood "the radical spirit of life" which society tries to tame and which may be expressed truly in fantasy.

A1193   -----. "Thoughts on Being and Writing." In Blishen, *Thorny Paradise*, pp. 65-76.
A highly personal statement that sheds light on Hoban's shifts in direction as a writer.

A1194   -----. "Time Slip, Uphill Lean, Laminar Flow, Place-to-Place Talking and Hearing the Silence." *CLE*, o.s., no. 9 (November 1972):33-47.
Hoban expresses his views on love, learning, experience, and literature. Also comments on Kipling.

A1195   INGLIS, FRED. *Promise of Happiness*, pp. 303-4.
Calls *Mouse and His Child* a "little masterpiece." Places Hoban, with Joan Aiken, in the Dickensian tradition. Also praises his exuberance, his prose which "moves you on," and "his carnal and vigorous eye for incongruity."

A1196   LENZ, MILLICENT. "Russell Hoban's *The Mouse and His Child* and the Search to Be Self-Winding." *Proceedings of the Children's Literature Association* 5 (1978):64-69.
Examines the symbolic and metaphoric meanings of the work that make it "an illumination of the human condition" as well as an exciting and satisfying story.

A1197   MacKILLOP, IAN P. "Russell Hoban: Returning to the Sunlight." In Butts, *Good Writers*, pp. 57-67.
Discusses *Mouse and His Child*, *Turtle Diary*, *Kleinzeit*, and *The Lion of Boaz-Jachin and Jachin-Boaz*.

A1198   McMAHON-HILL, GILLIAN. "A Narrow Pavement Says 'Walk Alone': The Books of Russell Hoban." *CLE*, o.s., no. 20 (Spring 1976):41-55.
Relates the stylistic qualities and themes of *Mouse and His Child*, as the first of Hoban's "mature writing," to three of his subsequent books for adults.

A1199   O'HARA, J. DONALD. Review of *Letitia Rabbit's String Song*. *Children's Literature* 2 (1973):234.
Takes a rather adult, tongue-in-check approach to the book.

A1200   REES, DAVID. "Beyond the Last Visible Dog--Russell Hoban." In *Painted Desert*, pp. 138-52.

Traces Hoban's career in children's literature from his beginnings as an illustrator, through the Frances books, to *Mouse and His Child*.

A1201 TOWNSEND, JOHN ROWE. "A Second Look: *The Mouse and His Child*." *Horn Book* 51 (October 1975):449-51. (Reprinted in Heins, *Crosscurrents*, pp. 330-32.)
Praises the book as a tale of adventure, and points out its wit, humor, and psychological depth.

HODGES, C. WALTER (1909-   )

A1202 CROUCH, MARCUS S. "Illustrated by C. Walter Hodges." *Junior Bookshelf* 15 (July 1951):79-84.
An appreciative overview of Hodges as an illustrator. Includes a bibliography of books he has illustrated.

A1203 HODGES, C. WALTER. "Adventures with a Problem." *Horn Book* 16 (September-October 1940):331-33.
Recounts his difficulties in completing the historical research behind *Columbus Sails*, and comments on the difficulties of presenting historical figures to children.

A1204 -----. "On Writing About King Alfred." *Horn Book* 43 (April 1967):179-82. Also in *Junior Bookshelf* 31, no. 3 (June 1967):159-63. (Reprinted in Norton, *Folk Literature of the British Isles*, pp. 67-70.)
Discusses writing *The Marsh King*.

A1205 LONG, SIDNEY. "A Second Look: *The Namesake*." *Horn Book* 53 (August 1977):477-82.
A second reading reveals flaws as well as virtues in the book.

HODGES, MARGARET (1911-   )

A1206 MATHEWS, H. JAMES. Review of *The Other World: Myths of the Celts*. *Children's Literature* 2 (1973):235.

HOFFMANN, HEINRICH (1798-1874)

A1207 BECKER, JÖRG. "*Struwwelpeter* Revised: New Versions Still Racist." *IRBC* 6, no. 2 (1975):2.
Examines racism in old and new versions of *Struwwelpeter*

A1208 FREEMAN, THOMAS. "Heinrich Hoffmann's *Struwwelpeter*: An Inquiry into the Effects of Violence in Children's Literature." *Journal of Popular Culture* 10, no. 4 (Spring 1977):303-20.
Summarizes the rationalizations of many critics and disagrees with their pronouncements that the book is not harmful to children. Concludes that *Struwwelpeter* can reinforce a troubled child's anxieties, fears, and violent tendencies. Includes extensive references.

A1209 HÜRLIMANN, BETTINA. *Three Centuries*, pp. 53-63.
Provides a detailed history and analysis of *Struwwelpeter* and defends it as presenting "a kind of symbolic hyper-reality which is far less dangerous for children than many of the photographic representations of similar happenings which they see daily in newspapers and magazines."

A1210   MOSHEIM, L. "*Struwwelpeter*: Yes Or No?" *Junior Bookshelf* 27 (December 1963):330-32.
    Points out arguments for and against *Struwwelpeter*, but concludes, "Everyone must decide for himself."

HOGROGIAN, NONNY (1932-   )

A1211   DURRELL, ANN. "Nonny Hogrogian." *Library Journal* 91 (15 March 1966):1594-95 and *SLJ* 13 (March 1966):128-29.
    Provides insight into the artist's methods and techniques.

A1212   WAUGH, DOROTHY. "Decorator of Books for Children." *American Artist* 30 (October 1966):52-57.
    A biocritical overview, concentrating on Hogrogian's woodblock-cutting technique.

HOLDEN, MOLLY (1927-   )

A1213   ALMA, ROGER. "The Novels of Molly Holden." *Signal* 25 (January 1978):16-24.
    Favorably discusses *The Unfinished Feud*, *A Tenancy of Flint*, *White Horse and Wanderer*, *Reivers' Weather*.

HOLLAND, ISABELLE (1920-   )

A1214   BROWN, LYNNE. "Isabelle Holland--Novelist for Adolescents." *Arizona English Bulletin* 18, no. 3 (April 1976):190-93.
    Praises Holland's ability to create characters with whom adolescents can identify.

A1215   HIRSCH, CORINNE. "Isabelle Holland: Realism and Its Evasions in *The Man Without a Face*." *CLE*, n.s. 10, no. 1 (Spring 1979):25-34.
    Criticizes Holland's "oversimplification and distortion of character and situation" in her "attempt to impose moral values on her adolescent readers." Argues that she evades the complex questions she raises by "lapsing into didacticism and melodrama."

HOLLING, HOLLING CLANCY (1900-1973)

A1216   ARMSTRONG, CLYDE, M. "Holling Clancy Holling." *Horn Book* 31 (April 1955):135-43.
    Primarily biographical background with some insights into Holling's work and ways of working.

A1217   RAMSEY, IRVIN, L. "Holling C. Holling: Author and Illustrator." *EE* 31 (February 1954):67-71. (Reprinted in Hoffman, *Authors and Illustrators*, pp. 209-16.)
    Surveys Holling's work, especially his writings about American Indians.

HOLM, ANNE (1922-   )

A1218   "Books of International Interest: Forum of Children's Books." *Bookbird* 2 (1966):43-45.
    Discusses varying critical responses to *David* (*North to Freedom*, U.S. version; *I am David*, British version).

A1219   CROUCH, MARCUS. *The Nesbit Tradition*, pp. 196-97.
        Calls *I am David* "one of the most profoundly disturbing of
        contemporary novels." Suggests that it is David's sense of identity
        that sustains him.

A1220   KINGSTON, CAROLYN T. *Tragic Mode*, pp. 110-13.
        Analyzes *North to Freedom* in terms of its handling of the theme
        of war.

HOLMAN, FELICE (1919-   )

A1221   HOLMAN, FELICE. "*Slake's Limbo*: In Which a Book Switches
        Authors." *Horn Book* 52 (October 1976):479-85.
        Tells about her decisions and problems in writing the book.

HOOVER, H.M. (1935-   )

A1222   ANTCZAK, JANICE. "The Visions of H.M. Hoover." *ChLAQ* 10, no.
        2 (Summer 1985):73-76.
        Characterizes Hoover as a writer who gives her readers a great
        deal to think about.

A1223   HOOVER, H.M. "Where Do You Get Your Ideas?" *TON* 39, no. 1
        (Fall 1982):57-61.
        Hoover tells how some of her books originated.

HOPE, ANTHONY [Sir Anthony Hope Hawkins] (1863-1933)

A1224   INGLIS, FRED. "Prisoner of Zenda." In *Promise of Happiness*, pp.
        152-54.
        "A really savory old-fashioned melodrama." Sees the book as
        providing a fantasy setting "Where the manly virtues could thrive
        without malodorous compromise."

HOPE, LAURA LEE [Stratemeyer Syndicate pseudonym]

A1225   COHEN, SOL. "Minority Stereotypes in Children's Literature: The
        Bobbsey Twins, 1907-1968." *Educational Forum* 34, no. 1 (November
        1969):119-25.
        Surveys the stereotyping of minority and ethnic groups in chil-
        dren's literature, concentrating on the *Bobbsey Twins* series.

A1226   MASON, BOBBIE ANN. "Bobbsey Bourgeois." In *The Girl Sleuth*, pp.
        29-47.
        Traces the developments and changes in the series over the years,
        and explores its appeal to the child.

A1227   PERRY, PHYLLIS J. "Looking Back on *The Bobbsey Twins*." *LA* 55
        (February 1978):202-3.
        Focuses on racism and misinformation about health in the series.

A1228   STARK, MARY KAY. "Bert & Nan & Flossie & Fred: The Bobbsey
        Twins Roll On." *IRBC* 6, no. 1 (1975):1, 5-6.
        Points out the racism in the long-continuing series, even through
        its revisions.

HOPKINS, ELISABETH

A1229   HOPKINS, ELISABETH. "The Sale of a Story." *Canadian Literature* 78 (Autumn 1978):22-25.
Discusses writing and illustrating *The Painted Cougar.*

HOSFORD, DOROTHY (1900-1952)

A1230   ARMSTRONG, HELEN. Review. *Horn Book* 23 (September-October 1947):367-69.
Praises Hosford's *By His Own Might: The Battles of Beowulf* for capturing the style and sense of importance of the original while simplifying the story for children.

HOUSTON, JAMES A. (1921-   )

A1231   STOTT, JON C. "An Interview with James Houston." *CCL* 20 (1980):3-16.
A lengthy interview in which Houston discusses his books portraying the Canadian Arctic.

A1232   SUTTON, WENDY K. "Profile: James Houston." *LA* 60 (October 1983):907-13.
Explores Houston's life and work, particularly his fascination with the arctic. Includes a bibliography of his books about the arctic.

HOVEY, TAMARA

A1233   ALBANESE-BAY, CAROL. "Nineteenth-Century Women for Twentieth-Century Teenagers: A Review of Recent Biographies of George Sand and Mary Shelley." *L&U* 4, no. 1 (Summer 1980):54-70.
This comparative review of Hovey's *A Mind of Her Own: A Life of the Writer George Sand* and Janet Harris's life of Mary Shelley analyzes why Hovey's work succeeds while Harris's fails, and in the process reveals "both the possibilities and the limitations of the adolescent biography as a literary form."

HUDSON, WILLIAM HENRY (1841-1922)

A1234   DALPHIN, MARCIA. "I Give You the End of a Golden String." In Fryatt, *Horn Book Sampler*, pp. 133-34, 136-38. (Also in *Horn Book* 14 [May 1938]:143-49.)
A Little Boy Lost "is far too little known. It is not everyday that a great naturalist and one of the greatest prose writers of his day writes a book for children, and we should be properly grateful."

HUGHES, MONICA (1925-   )

A1235   ELLIS, SARAH. "News from the North." *Horn Book* 60 (September-October 1984):661-64.
Explores the science fiction of Canadian writer Monica Hughes, especially her *Isis* trilogy.

A1236   HUGHES, MONICA. "The Writer's Quest." *CCL* 26 (1982):6-27.
Hughes talks about her writing and answers questions from an interviewer.

A1237   RUBIO, GERALD. "Monica Hughes: Overview." *CCL* 17 (1980):20-26.
   Briefly discusses all eight of Hughes's books published so far.

HUGHES, RICHARD (1900-1976)

A1238   PARKER, GEOFFREY. "Richard Hughes *The Spider's Palace and Other Stories*." *CLE*, o.s., no. 20 (Spring 1976):32-40.
   Analyzes Hughes's style, imaginative invention, and psychological understanding in this frequently overlooked collection of "consummately told tales."

A1239   -----. "*The Wonder-Dog*: The Collected Children's Stories of Richard Hughes." *CLE*, n.s. 8, no. 4 (Winter 1977):163-75.
   A detailed review of a newly published collection of Hughes's stories. Includes a reprint of Hughes's "Home," pp. 173-75.

HUGHES, SHIRLEY (1929-   )

A1240   CHAMBERS, AIDAN. "Letter from England: Hughes in Flight." *Horn Book* 56 (April 1980):211-14.
   Praises *Up and Up* and calls Shirley Hughes and Anthony Browne foremost representatives of a new wave of English picture-book making.

A1241   MOSS, ELAINE. "'Where's The Colours?': Shirley Hughes at Work." *Signal* 32 (May 1980):75-80.
   A brief biocritical overview concentrating on *Up and Up*.

HUGHES, TED (1930-   )

A1242   ADAMS, JOHN. "Dark Rainbow: Reflections of Ted Hughes." *Signal* 5 (May 1971):65-71. (Reprinted in Chambers, *Signal Approach*, pp. 101-8.)
   Discusses animals in Hughes's poetry, his attitudes toward poetry and children, his vitality, and his black and narrow views. See article in response by Morse (below).

A1243   BRADMAN, TONY. "The Giant Singer: The Children's Books of Ted Hughes." *Junior Bookshelf* 44, no. 4 (August 1980):163-65.
   Examines the theme of reconciliation in Hughes's work for children, a theme that he "worked so hard to achieve for adults in the sixties."

A1244   CHAMBERS, AIDAN. "Letter from England: Me or It." *Horn Book* 57 (June 1981):347-50.
   Recommends *Poetry in the Making* (*Poetry Is*, U.S. version) as "a statement about the nature of poetry and the art of writing it."

A1245   FOREMAN, STEPHEN H. Review of *The Tiger's Bones and Other Plays for Children*. *Children's Literature* 3 (1974):210-11.
   Maintains that "Ted Hughes must be given credit for attempting to create intelligent, imaginative, and gutsy plays for children," but he does not know how to construct a play.

A1246   HUGHES, TED. "Myth and Education." *CLE*, o.s., no. 1 (March 1970):55-70. (Reprinted in Fox, *Writers, Critics, and Children*, pp.

77-94.)
> Discusses "story" as related to "myth" and "imagination" as a powerful therapeutic force. Uses his *Iron Man: A Story in Five Nights* (*Iron Giant*, U.S. version) as an example.

A1247   INGLIS, FRED. *Promise of Happiness*, pp. 248-50.
> Describes *Iron Man: A Story in Five Nights* as "indisputably a great modern myth. . . . Hughes creates from nothing a new myth of industrial society."

A1248   MORSE, BRIAN. "Poetry, Children and Ted Hughes." *Signal* 6 (September 1971):102-13. (Reprinted in Chambers, *Signal Approach*, pp. 109-27.)
> Responds to Adams's article (see above). Maintains that art should be judged purely on its merits, not on whether it is "good" for children. Claims Adams has misread Hughes, and goes on to give his own readings. A lengthy reply, written by Adams in 1979, is appended to the reprint in *Signal Approach*.

A1249   REES, DAVID. "Hospitals Where We Heal--Ted Hughes." In *Painted Desert*, pp. 47-61. (Originally in *San Jose Studies*, July 1983, in slightly different form.)
> Maintains that the poet's best writing for children is in prose. Sees a concern with guiding, teaching, and directing children as the motivating force in all his work, although he is not "overtly didactic".

HUGHES, THOMAS (1822-96)

A1250   CHAMBERS, AIDAN. "Letter From England: A Tale of Two Toms." *Horn Book* 52 (April 1976):187-90.
> Compares Twain's Tom Sawyer and Hughes's Tom Brown.

A1251   HIBBERD, DOMINIC. "Where There Are No Spectators: A Rereading of *Tom Brown's Schooldays*." *CLE*, o.s., no. 21 (Summer 1976):64-73.
> Examines the values and attitudes behind this first of all school stories.

HUNT, IRENE (1907-   )

A1252   KINGSTON, CAROLYN T. *Tragic Mode*, pp. 120-23.
> Analyzes *Across Five Aprils* in terms of its theme of war.

HUNTER, MOLLIE (1922-   )

A1253   COOK, STANLEY. "Children's Writers: 3. Mollie Hunter." *School Librarian* 26 (June 1978):108-11.
> Provides a fine overview and critical introduction to Hunter. "The movement of Mollie Hunter's work is from the historical to the supernatural, to an old testament position where natural and supernatural come together."

A1254   DOOLEY, PATRICIA. "Profile: Mollie Hunter." *ChLAQ* 3, no. 3 (Autumn 1978):3-6.
> Characterizes Hunter's books as having either a historical setting or a traditional form, both using components of "past" and "story."

A1255   HICKMAN, JANET. "Profile: The Person Behind the Book--Mollie
        Hunter." *LA* 56 (March 1979):302-6.
        Discusses Hunter's Scottish settings, the folk culture basis for her
        fantasies, and the Scottish history and archaeology backgrounds of her
        historical fiction.

A1256   HOLLINDALE, PETER. "World Enough and Time: The Work of Mol-
        lie Hunter." *CLE*, n.s. 8, no. 3 (1977):109-19.
        Places Hunter in the Scottish tradition, stressing the depth and
        timelessness, and the international appeal of her historical fiction,
        fantasy, and autobiographical novels.

A1257   HUNTER, MOLLIE. "Folklore--One Writer's View." In Norton, *Folk
        Literature of the British Isles*, pp. 124-33.
        Explains some of the ways in which she has used traditional fol-
        klore in her writing. Hunter says she attempts to re-create the
        feeling of folktale in her work.

A1258   -----. "The Last Lord of Redhouse Castle." In Blishen, *Thorny Para-
        dise*, pp. 128-39. (Also in *Children's Books International* 1
        [1976]:26-32.)
        Dramatically traces the process by which she became a children's
        writer.

A1259   -----. "A Need for Heroes." *Proceedings of the Children's Literature
        Association* 6 (1979):52-66. (Reprinted in *Horn Book* 59 (April
        1983):146-57.)
        Discusses *The Haunted Mountain*, *The Ghosts of Glencoe*, and
        The Third Eye in terms of her concept of the hero as one who has
        "greatness of soul." Maintains that the young need to encounter such
        heroes.

A1260   -----. *Talent is Not Enough: Mollie Hunter On Writing for Children*.
        New York: Harper & Row, 1975, 126 pp.
        Contents: "Talent Is Not Enough," May Hill Arbuthnot Honor
        Lecture, 1975; "Shoulder the Sky," Anne Carroll Moore Lecture, 1975;
        "One World"; "The Other World"; and "The Limits of Language."
        These essays are also indexed and annotated separately in this bibli-
        ography under headings Criticism, Fantasy, Folklore, Historical
        Fiction, and Style.

A1261   KAYE, MARILYN. "Mollie Hunter: An Interview." *TON* 41 (Winter
        1985):141-46.
        Hunter answers questions about her methods of working, her
        theme of conflict, and her goals in writing.

A1262   RYAN, J.S. "The Spirit of Old Scotland: Tone in the Fiction of Mol-
        lie Hunter." *Orana* 20 (May 1984):93-101; (August 1984):138-45.
        Praises Hunter's ability to synthesize reality, history, fantasy, and
        a concern for the quality of life "as she ever seizes on the essential
        relationships." Includes references.

HUTCHINS, PAT (1942-   )

A1263   MOSS, ELAINE. "Pat Hutchins: A Natural." *Signal* 10 (January
        1973):32-36.
        Hutchins discusses her life and work in an interview.

A1264 THOMPSON, HILARY. "An Interview with Pat Hutchins." *ChLAQ* 10, no. 2 (Summer 1985):57-59.
Hutchins discusses her work in an interview.

HUTTON, WARWICK (1939-   )

A1265 HUTTON, WARWICK. "How *Jonah and the Great Fish* Began." *Horn Book* 61 (January 1985):35-37.
Discusses his approach to the book and his use of various techniques of illustration.

HYMAN, TRINA SCHART (1939-   )

A1266 FARRELL, DIANE. Review. *Horn Book* 51 (February 1975):36-37.
Highly favorable comments upon Hyman's *Snow White* illustrations as "passionate pictures which expose the basic human conflicts that give the tale its timeless universal appeal."

A1267 HEARN, MICHAEL P. "The 'Ubiquitous' Trina Schart Hyman." *American Artist* 43 (May 1979):36-43, 96-97.
Sees Hyman's greatest strength as lying in her sense of drama. Provides a good overview of Hyman's work and her background.

A1268 HYMAN, TRINA SCHART. "Caldecott Medal Acceptance." *Horn Book* 61 (July-August 1985):410-21.
Discusses her background, her approach to illustration, and especially her approach to Margaret Hodges's retelling of *Saint George and the Dragon*. A biographical sketch by daughter Katrin Hyman follows, pp. 422-25.

A1269 MAY, JILL P. "Illustration as Interpretation: Trina Hyman's Folk Tales." *ChLAQ* 10 (Fall 1985):127-31.
Argues that Hyman's illustrations of folktales succeed "because her personal interpretations of them unveil the universal conflicts of fidelity, trust, envy, and pride the tales contain." Discusses "Snow White," the "Sleeping Beauty," and "Little Red Riding Hood."

A1270 WHITE, DAVID E. "Profile: Trina Schart Hyman." *LA* 60 (September 1983):782-92.
A biocritical overview based on an interview in which Hyman discusses her work. A lengthy, but partial, bibliography of her publications is included.

ISH-KISHOR, SULAMITH (1896-1977)

A1271 KINGSTON, CAROLYN T. *Tragic Mode*, pp. 46-48.
Analyzes the theme of rejection in *A Boy of Old Prague*.

ISHII, MOMOKO

A1272 HÜRLIMANN, BETTINA. "Momoko Ishii and Her Place in Japanese Children's Literature Today." *Bookbird* 3 (1966):15-18.
Surveys the work of the Japanese writer, translator, and collector of folk and fairy tales for children.

"Jack and Jill" (nursery rhyme)

A1273   SMITH, WILLIAM H. "What They Didn't Tell You About Jack and Jill: An Aspect of Reading Comprehension." *Journal of Reading* 24, no. 2 (November 1980):101-8.

Applies linguistic theory to an interpretation of "Jack and Jill."

"Jack and the Beanstalk"

A1274   DESMONDE, WILLIAM H. "Jack and the Beanstalk." *American Imago* 8, no. 3 (September 1951):287-88. (Reprinted in White, *Children's Literature*, pp. 37-40.)

Offers a psychoanalytic interpretation of the tale.

A1275   WOLFENSTEIN, MARTHA. "Jack and the Beanstalk": An American Version." In *Childhood in Contemporary Cultures.* Edited by Margaret Mead and Martha Wolfenstein. Chicago: University of Chicago Press, 1955, pp. 243-45.

Examines the way in which the tale has been transformed in the American version "Jack and the Bean Tree," as told in the mountains of North Carolina and recorded by Richard Chase.

JACKSON, JACQUELINE (1928-   )

A1276   FITZGERALD, SHEILA. "Profile: Jacqueline Jackson." *LA* 58 (March 1981):347-52.

Reports on Jackson's life and work. Includes a bibliography of her children's books.

A1277   JACKSON, JACQUELINE. "Realism in Children's Stories." *TON* 16 (March 1960):62-63.

Describes how she handled children's realistic resistance to growing up in *Paleface Redskins.*

JACKSON, JESSE (1908-   )

A1278   LANIER, RUBY J. "Profile: Call Me Jesse Jackson." *LA* 54 (March 1977):331-39.

A brief biocritical overview.

JACKSON, SHIRLEY (1919-65)

A1279   BOGART, EDNA. "Censorship and 'The Lottery.'" *English Journal* 74 (January 1985):45-47.

Summarizes the history of popular and critical responses to this famous short story.

JAMES, WILL [Joseph Ernest Nephtali DuFault] (1892-1942)

A1280   CHRISMAN, ARTHUR BOWIE. "*Smoky, The Cowhorse.*" *Horn Book* 3 (August 1927):42-46.

A rather idiosyncratic review of this early Newbery Award winner.

JANOSCH [Horst Eckert] (1931-   )

A1281   KÜNNEMANN, HORST. "Janosch: Or An Excursion Into Fantasy In

the Modern Picture Book." *Bookbird* 11, no. 2 (1973):18-23.
Analyzes the distinguishing characteristics of Janosch's picture-
book fantasies. Includes a bibliography of Janosch's books and their
translations.

JANSSON, TOVE (1914-   )

A1282   BLOUNT, MARGARET. *Animal Land*, pp. 277-79.
Examines the Moomin tales as a type of animal story.

A1283   CROUCH, MARCUS. "Moomin-Sagas." *Junior Bookshelf* 30, no. 6
(December 1966):353-57.
Suggests Moomin humor arises from incongruity, "from a comic
view of life, a humour not of situation or even of character but of
being."

A1284   "Finnish Twilight." *TLS*, 22 October 1971, pp. 1315-16.
Reviews a number of Moomin books.

A1285   FLEISHER, FREDERIC, and FLEISHER, BOEL. "Tove Jansson and
the Moomin Family." *American-Scandinavian Review* 51, no. 1
(March 1963):47-54.
Provides an overview of the Moomins, and reports on a visit to
Jansson.

A1286   HUSE, NANCY L. "Equal to Life: Tove Jansson's Moomintrolls." *Proceedings of the Children's Literature Association* 8 (1981):44-49.
Argues that the Moomin books are worthy of more serious critical attention than they have so far received outside of Scandinavia.

A1287   JANSSON, TOVE. Hans Christian Andersen Award acceptance speech,
1966. *Bookbird* 4 (1966):3-6. (Also in *TON* 23 [April 1967]:234-39.)
Discusses her approach to writing and her attitudes toward children's literature. "In a book for children there should always be
something left unexplained and without any illustration."

A1288   WELSH, RENATA. "Toffle Seen Through Childish Eyes." *Bookbird* 5,
no. 2 (1967):37-38.
Compares children's and adults' criticism of Tove Jansson's *Who
Will Comfort Toffle?*

JARRELL, RANDALL (1914-65)

A1289   ADAMS, CHARLES M., comp. *Randall Jarrell: A Bibliography.* Chapel Hill: University of North Carolina Press, 1958, 72 pp.
Lists books, collections containing his work, poems, prose, book
reviews, and translations held by the Library of the Women's College
of the University of North Carolina.

A1290   ELLIS, SARAH. "A Second Look: *The Bat-Poet.*" *Horn Book* 57
(August 1981):453-55.
Sees the book as "the integrated vision of the poet and the child."

A1291   GETZ, THOMAS H. "Memory and Desire in *Fly By Night.*" *Children's Literature* 2 (1983):125-34.
Examines the juxtaposition of fantasy and reality as an invitation
to reader participation.

A1292   GRISWOLD, JEROME JOSEPH. "Mother and Child in the Poetry and Children's Books of Randall Jarrell." Ph.D. dissertation, University of Connecticut, 1979, 194 pp., DA 40:5442A.
Explores the mother and child theme of separation anxiety and its resolution in Jarrell's works for adults and children. An appendix includes a discussion with Maurice Sendak on his illustrations for Jarrell's children's books.

A1293   HOLTZE, SALLY HOLMES. "A Second Look: *The Animal Family*." *Horn Book* 61 (November 1986):714-16.
An "uncommon book for children" that "creates a cozy world in prose that is written with the craft of a poet."

A1294   HORN, BERNARD. "'The Tongue of Gods and Children': Blakean Innocence in Randall Jarrell's Poetry." *Children's Literature* 2 (1973):148-51.
Compares Jarrell's qualities of "innocence" with Blake's.

A1295   HOWELL, PAMELA R. "Voice Is Voice Whether a Bat or a Poet: Randall Jarrell's *The Bat-Poet*." *Proceedings of the Children's Literature Association* 9 (1982):71-76.
Sees *The Bat-Poet* as an exploration of the artist's dilemma in "maintaining his individuality in his work, of finding his voice, and yet reaching an audience."

A1296   NEUMEYER, PETER F. "Randall Jarrell's *The Animal Family*: New Land and Old." *Proceedings of the Children's Literature Association* 7 (1980):139-45.
Discusses *Animal Family* as "primordial, archetypal, mythopoeic," and reflective of Jarrell himself.

A1297   -----. "Randall Jarrell's *The Bat-Poet*: An Introduction to the Craft." *ChLAQ* 9, no. 2 (Summer 1984):51-53, 59.
Views *The Bat Poet* as Jarrell's treatise on poetry and poetry-writing "disguised as a children's story."

A1298   SALE, ROGER. *Fairy Tales*, pp. 84-90.
Sees the *Animal Family* partially as a critique of Hans Christian Andersen's values as expressed in "The Little Mermaid," but analyzes it mainly as the relationships between animals and the mermaid and between myth and realism.

A1299   TRAVERS, P.L. "A Kind of Visitation." In *Randall Jarrell 1914-1965*. Edited by Robert Lowell. New York: Farrar Straus & Giroux, 1967, pp. 253-56. (Reprinted from *NYTBR*, 21 November 1965.)
Reviews *The Animal Family*.

A1300   UPDIKE, JOHN. "Fly By Night." *NYTBR*, 14 November 1976, Children's Book sec., pp. 25, 36.
Reviews *Fly By Night*. Finds the poems less sharp than they should be, and prefers Jarrell's prose in *The Animal Family*.

A1301   ZANDERER, LEO. "Randall Jarrell: About and For Children." *L&U* 2, no. 1 (Spring 1978):73-93.
Compares the bleakness of vision in Jarrell's poems, with the life-filled, hopeful qualities of his children's stories: *The Bat-Poet*,

The Animal Family, and *Fly By Night*.

JEFFRIES, RICHARD (1846-87)

A1302   CARPENTER, HUMPHREY. "Bevis, the Pioneer." In *Secret Gardens*, pp. 103-14.
Sees *Bevis: The Story of a Boy* as pioneering the beginning of new values and a new kind of children's story written from the child's point of view.

A1303   JACKSON, BRIAN. "*Bevis*: A Lost Classic." *Use of English* 24 (Autumn 1972):3-10.
Argues that this long out-of-print book ranks with *Huckleberry Finn* and *Treasure Island*. Argues that it is a child's book, and points out some of its charms and distinguishing characteristics.

A1304   STOATE, GRAHAM. "The Unconscious Teaching of the Country--A Rereading of *Bevis: The Story of a Boy*." *CLE*, n.s. 8, no. 1 (Spring 1977):30-38.
Looks at the continuing appeal of the book and its "ageless celebration of individuality and self-determination."

JIMENEZ, JUAN RAMON (1881-1958)

A1305   MARCUS, LEONARD. "The Beast of Burden and the Joyful Man of Words: Juan Ramon Jimenez's *Platero and I*." *L&U* 4, no. 2 (Winter 1980-81):56-74.
Calls this Spanish classic one of the few acknowledged masterpieces of both children's literature and literature as a whole.

JOHNS, W.E. (1893-1968)

A1306   BARNES, D.R. "Captain Johns and the Adult World." In Ford, *Young Writers, Young Readers*, pp. 115-22.
Objects to the *Biggles* tales in terms of their unreality and objectionable morality.

A1307   BUSH, K.E. "These 'Biggles' Books." *Junior Bookshelf* 7, no. 2 (July 1943):55-59.
Winner of a *Junior Bookshelf* contest for the best appraisal of the Biggles books.

A1308   DAY, A.E. "Biggles: Anatomy of a Hero." *CLE*, o.s., no. 15 (1974):19-28.
Examines the origins and values of the Biggles books.

A1309   SALWAY, LANCE. "Biggles Breathes His Last." *Children's Book News* 4, no. 6 (November-December 1969):308-9.
Finds the posthumously published Biggles books, *Biggles and the Little Green God* and *Biggles and the Noble Lord*, "pale shadows of the adventures of earlier years."

JOHNSON, CROCKETT (1906-75)

A1310   BADER, BARBARA. "Crockett Johnson." In *American Picturebooks*, pp. 434-42.
Discusses the career of Johnson who "had inherently a child's

point of view," and created "quotable" dialogue and "showable" pictures full of visual puns and jests.

JONES, DIANA WYNNE (1934-   )

A1311   SPRAGGS, GILLIAN. "True Dreams: The Fantasy Fiction of Diana Wynne Jones." *Use of English* 34, no. 3 (Summer 1983):17-22.
Analyzes Jones's children's fantasies, especially *Cart* and *Cwidder*.

JOYCE, JAMES (1882-1941)

A1312   WHITE, ALISON. "The Devil Has a Dublin Accent." *Children's Literature* 2 (1973):139-41.
Discusses the influence of the children's literature Joyce knew as a child on *Dubliners*, and concludes with a brief discussion of *The Cat and the Devil*, Joyce's only book for children.

JUDSON, CLARA INGRAM (1879-1960)

A1313   JUDSON, CLARA INGRAM. "Writing Juveniles Isn't All Fun." *Library Journal* 72 (August 1947):1075-77.
Describes the processes of researching and writing her books.

A1314   ROLLINS, CHARLEMAE. "Clara Ingram Judson: Interpreter of America." *EE* 30 (December 1953):477-84. (Reprinted in Hoffman, *Authors and Illustrators*, pp. 220-29.)
Summarizes, with critical insights, works beginning with *Flower Fairies* (1915) through the "They came from" series and her biographies.

JUSTUS, MAY (1898-   )

A1315   BURNS, PAUL C., and HINES, RUTH. "May Justus: Tennessee's Mountain Jewel." *EE* 41 (October 1964):589-93.
An overview of Justus's writings.

KÄSTNER, ERICH (1899-1974)

A1316   KÄSTNER, ERICH. "The Natural History of the Author of Children's Books." *Bookbird* 2 (1965):3-8.
Hans Christian Andersen Medal Speech, 1960. Explores reasons why authors, including himself, write for children.

KATAEV, VALENTIN

A1317   RADO, DIANE F. "Valentin Kataev as a Children's Writer: An Analysis of *Volny Cernogo Morja*." Ph.D. dissertation, University of Michigan, 1977, 184 pp., DA 38:6762A.
Analyzes the appeal to children of Valentin Kataev's historical tetralogy. Also examines a large body of Soviet children's literary theory of the 1920s and 1930s.

KEATS, EZRA JACK (1916-83)

A1318   FREEDMAN, FLORENCE B. "Ezra Jack Keats: Author and Illustrator." *EE* 46 (January 1969):55-65. (Reprinted in Hoffman, *Authors and Illustrators*, pp. 230-42.)

A personal reminiscence and appreciation by one of Keats's high-school English teachers. Quotes extensively from Keats's Caldecott acceptance speech for *The Snowy Day.*

A1319   KEATS, EZRA JACK. "Caldecott Award Acceptance." *Horn Book* 39 (August 1963):361-63.
Describes in detail the techniques and process of creating *The Snowy Day.* A biocritical account by Esther Hautzig follows, pp. 364-68.

A1320   -----. "Dear Mr. Keats." *Horn Book* 48 (June 1973):306-10.
The author-illustrator shares his mail from young readers who have responded to his books.

A1321   LANES, SELMA G. "Ezra Jack Keats: In Memoriam." *Horn Book* 60 (September-October 1984):551-58.
An appreciative overview of Keat's career as a creator of picture books, pointing out his distinctive qualities and some of the techniques he employed.

A1322   PERRY, ERMA. "The Gentle World of Ezra Jack Keats." *American Artist* 35 (September 1971):48-53, 71-73.
A biocritical overview.

A1323   SCHWARCZ, JOSEPH H. "The Opus of the Author-Illustrator." In *Ways of the Illustrator*, pp. 183-88.
Examines the "distinctive themes, motifs, and stylistic features" of Keats's work as exemplified in his books about Peter, Willie, Amy, Archie, Roberto, and Louie.

KEENE, CAROLYN [Stratemeyer Syndicate pseudonym often used by Harriet Adams] (1894-1982)

A1324   AHRENS, R.C. "Nancy Drew Was Downright Sexy." *AB Bookman's Weekly* 68 (16 November 1981):3420-24. (Letter in response in 68 [21 December 1981]:4372.)
Explores the long-standing appeal of Nancy Drew. Concludes that "her charm endures" despite her naiveté and stodginess.

A1325   BROOKER-GROSS, SUSAN R. "Landscape and Social Values in Popular Children's Literature: Nancy Drew Mysteries. *Journal of Geography* 80 (February 1981):59-64.
Discusses landscape symbolism and the correspondence between social stereotypes and landscape stereotypes in the Nancy Drew series.

A1326   DONELSON, KENNETH. "History Re-Written: Nancy Drew and *The Secret of the Old Clock.*" *Catholic Library World* 52 (December 1980):220-25.
Analyzes and comments upon changes, some obvious, some puzzling, that have been made over the years in the Nancy Drew series.

A1327   FISHER, ANITA. "YA Detective Fiction: Nancy Drew and the Age of Technology." *ALAN Review* 11, no. 2 (Winter 1984):8-10.
Discusses the influence and transformations of Nancy Drew in a world dominated by science and computers.

A1328   JONES, JAMES P. "Nancy Drew, *WASP* Super Girl of the 1930s."

Journal of Popular Culture 6, no. 4 (Spring 1973):707-17.
An overview of the series.

A1329   -----. "Negro Stereotypes in Children's Literature: The Case of Nancy Drew." *Journal of Negro Education* 40, no. 2 (Spring 1971):121-25.
Shows, with impeccably documented examples, that as presented in Nancy Drew, "Negroes are menials who speak incorrect English. They are inclined toward crime, strong drink, and they 'shuffle.'"

A1330   KUSKIN, KARLA. "Nancy Drew and Friends." *NYTBR*, May 1975, pp. 20-21. (Reprinted in Varlejs, *Young Adult Literature*, pp. 350-52.)
Examines the longstanding appeal of the series.

A1331   MASON, BOBBIE ANN. "Nancy Drew: The Once and Future Prom Queen" and "Imposter Tea." In *The Girl Sleuth*, pp. 48-75, 726-39.
The first chapter concentrates on Nancy's character and appeal, the second examines recent changes in the series.

A1332 ' PRAGER, ARTHUR. "The Secret of Nancy Drew: Pushing Forty and Going Strong." In *Rascals at Large*, pp. 73-95. (Also in *Saturday Review* 52 (25 January 1969):18-19+.)
Compares Nancy Drew to Judy Bolton and the Dana Girls.

A1333   WERTHEIMER, BARBARA S., and SANDS, CAROL. "Nancy Drew Revisited." *LA* 52 (November-December 1975):1131-34, 1161.
Summarizes critical attacks on the series and some of Harriet Adams's responses. Concludes that although *Nancy Drew* provides entertainment, the series does not encourage critical reading or "imaginative sympathy."

A1334   ZACHARIAS, LEO. "Nancy Drew, Ballbuster." *Journal of Popular Culture* 9, no. 4 (Spring 1976):1027-38.
Analyzes the messages given about the role of the female in American society through the five major, recurring characters in the series.

KEEPING, CHARLES (1924-   )

A1335   JONES, CORNELIA, and WAY, OLIVIA R. *British Children's Authors*, pp. 101-13.
In an interview Keeping discusses his background, philosophy, and method of working. Includes an annotated bibliography of his works.

A1336   KEEPING, CHARLES. "Illustration in Children's Books." *CLE*, o.s., no. 1 (March 1970):41-54.
After some introductory remarks about the underrated position of illustration and the neglect of illustrations of picture books by book reviewers, Keeping discusses several of his own works.

A1337   -----. "The Illustration of Children's Books." In Keyse, *Loughborough 1983 Proceedings*, pp. 137-40.
Reflects upon the nature of illustration and discusses the origins of several of his books.

A1338   -----. "My Work as a Children's Illustrator." *ChLAQ* 8, no. 4 (Winter

1983):14-19.
Expresses his views on illustrating and describes the origins of many of his illustrations.

A1339 WINTLE, JUSTIN, and FISHER, EMMA. *Pied Pipers*, pp. 49-63.
Keeping discusses his life and work in an interview.

KEITH, HAROLD (1903-   )

A1340 PAINTER, HELEN W. "*Rifles for Watie*--A Novel of the Civil War." *EE* 38 (May 1961):287-91, 297.
A critical appraisal of the 1958 Newbery Award winner.

KELLOGG, STEVEN (1941-   )

A1341 LANES, SELMA G. "Bicentennial Bowdlerizing or the Rape of Yankee Doodle." *SLJ* 23 (Summer 1976):34-35.
Recounts the controversy surrounding the substitution of "folks" for "girls" in Steven Kellogg's version of "Yankee Doodle."

KELLY, ERIC P. (1884-1960)

A1342 DALPHIN, MARCIA. Review. *Horn Book* 6 (August 1930):222-27.
A detailed and favorable review of *The Blacksmith of Vilno*; suggests, however, that "the author's great love for his subject and his familiarity with it has made him overload it a bit."

A1343 KELLY, ERIC P. "The City of a Thousand Secrets." *Horn Book* 6 (February 1930):37-42.
Tells how he came to write *The Blacksmith of Vilno*.

A1344 -----. "The City That Sings." *Horn Book* 5 (February 1929):27-32. (Reprinted in *Horn Book* 16 [1940]:53-57, as "Krakow Is Still Singing.")
Describes the experiences behind the writing of *The Trumpeter of Krakow*.

KELLY, WALT (1913-73)

A1345 MISHKIN, DANIEL. "Pogo: Walt Kelly's American Dream." *Journal of Popular Culture* 12, no. 4 (Spring 1979):681-90.
Argues that "Kelly takes the usually secure world of the 'funny animal' comic strip and bristles its furry edges in an artistic examination of life around him."

A1346 WARDE, BEATRICE. "Homage to Walt Kelly as a Depicter of Conversation." *Penrose Annual* 55 (1961):46-51.
Explores the ways in which Walt Kelly has used the possibilities of the comic strip.

KEMP, GENE (1926-   )

A1347 CROSS, GILLIAN. "Children Are Real People: The Stories of Gene Kemp." *CLE*, n.s. 10, no. 3 (Autumn 1979):131-40.
Maintains that Kemp's books are funny and original and "based upon a deep and intimate understanding of the needs and feelings of children.

KENNEDY, RICHARD (1932-   )

A1348   NEUMEYER, PETER F. "Introducing Richard Kennedy." *CLE*, n.s. 15, no. 2 (Summer 1984):85-92.
Argues for wider appreciation of Kennedy's talents and originality.

KEPES, JULIET (1919-   )

A1349   BADER, BARBARA. *American Picturebooks*, pp. 350-53.
Traces Kepes's contributions to the art of the picture book.

KERR, M.E. [Marijane Meaker] (1932-   )

A1350   BERKLEY, JUNE. "Between Parents and Children: M.E. Kerr's Novels for Young Adults." *Focus* 3, no. 2 (Winter 1977):25-27. (Also in ERIC Educational Document Reproduction Service, ED 157 082.)
Explores parent-child relationships in *If I Love You Am I Trapped Forever?*; *Dinky Hocker Shoots Smack*; and *The Son of Someone Famous*.

A1351   KAYE, MARILYN. "Recurring Patterns in the Novels of M.E. Kerr." *Children's Literature* 7 (1978):226-32.
Examines *Dinky Hocker Shoots Smack*; *Gentlehands*; *If I Love You Am I Trapped Forever?*; *Is That You Miss Blue?*; *Love Is a Missing Person*; and *The Son of Someone Famous*.

A1352   KINGSBURY, MARY. "The Why of People: The Novels of M.E. Kerr." *Horn Book* 53 (June 1977):288-95.
Views Kerr's novels as outstanding attempts to clarify the "why" of people.

A1353   MATTER, ROXANA M. "Elkind's Theory of Adolescent Egocentrism as Expressed in Selected Characters of M.E. Kerr." *Adolescence* 17 (Fall 1982):657-66.
Finds that Kerr's characters realistically represent the unique and typical behaviors of egocentrism common to adolescents.

A1354   REES, DAVID. "Discreet Charm of the Bourgeoisie--M.E. Kerr." In *Painted Desert*, pp. 17-32.
Argues that Kerr is one of the most gifted writers for young adults of the past decade, but she lacks sensitivity to place and individual character. Her range is narrow, but she is one of few writers for young adults who puts adults at the center of her work.

A1355   SWEENEY, PATRICIA RUNK. "Self-Discovery and Rediscovery in the Novels of M.E. Kerr." *L&U* 2, no. 2 (Fall 1978):37-43.
Examines the theme of self-revelation in Kerr's first six novels, "the imprisonment of one's true self in a shell of one's own making."

KIMENYE, BARBARA (1940-   )

A1356   SCHMIDT, NANCY. *Children's Fiction About Africa*, pp. 186-88.
Describes the basic characteristics of the Moses stories (Ugandan school stories).

KINGMAN, LEE (1919-   )

A1357   HEINS, PAUL. "A Second Look: *The Year of the Raccoon.*" *Horn Book* 54 (February 1978):74-75.
Sees the book as antedating the new realism in American fiction for young people.

KINGSLEY, CHARLES (1819-75)

A1358   CARPENTER, HUMPHREY. "Parson Lot Takes a Cold Bath: Charles Kingsley and *The Water-Babies.*" In *Secret Gardens*, pp. 24-43.
Examines *The Water Babies* within the contexts of Kingsley's life and time and the history of children's literature. Argues that the book is a work of "destruction . . . written at a time when its author's religious faith had nearly crumbled," and that it shows that "'untrue' stories, despised ever since the days of John Locke, by those who regarded themselves as the guardians and censors of English children's literature, could be deeply true, and therefore of inestimable value."

A1359   JOHNSTON, ARTHUR. "*The Water-Babies*: Kingsley's Debt to Darwin." *English* 12 (Autumn 1959):215-19.
Sees in Tom's metamorphosis from chimney sweep to water-baby the beginnings of "moral Darwinism."

A1360   LEAVIS, Q.D. "*The Water Babies.*" *CLE*, o.s., no. 23 (Winter 1976):155-63.
Suggests uses of *The Water Babies* for modern children's education and defends "its innate literary justification for being kept in circulation."

A1361   UFFELMAN, LARRY K. "An Evolutionary Fantasy: *The Water Babies.*" In *Charles Kingsley.* Boston: Twayne, 1979, pp. 67-81.
Interprets *The Water Babies* as Kingsley's attempt to place "the nineteenth-century conflict between science and religion in the context of a fantasy designed to reconcile them by showing continuous development to be the creative principle at work in the world." He wanted to enable children "to accept the advance of science without losing their Christian faith."

KIPLING, RUDYARD (1865-1936)

A1362   ANDERSON, CELIA CATLETT. "'O Best Beloved'": Kipling's Reading Instructions in the *Just So Stories.*" *Proceedings of the Children's Literature Association* 9 (1982):33-39.
Investigates strategies from storytelling tradition (set phrases, asides to the reader, heavy repetition), poetic devices (refrains, rhyme, alliteration), and typographical clues that Kipling used to retain the original oral tone and emphasis of his tales.

A1363   BLACKBURN, WILLIAM. "Internationalism and Empire: *Kim* and the Art of Rudyard Kipling." *Proceedings of the Children's Literature Association* 6 (1979):78-85.
Argues that interpretations emphasizing Kipling's political views may have distorted critical perceptions of *Kim*'s success.

A1364   BLOUNT, MARGARET. "The Tables Turned at the Zoo: Mowgli and

Stuart Little." In *Animal Land*, pp. 226-44.

Examines, in depth, how Kipling's *Jungle Books* and E.B. White's *Stuart Little* portray animals befriended and rejected by humans and animals, outcasts "without any real place in the world."

A1365 CHAMBERS, AIDAN. "Letter from England: *Just So*." *Horn Book* 58 (October 1982):565-70.

Discusses newly illustrated versions of the *Just So* tales.

A1366 FEELEY, MARGARET P. "The *Kim* That Nobody Reads." *Studies in the Novel* 13, no. 3 (Fall 1981):266-81.

Shows that between a heretofore unknown working draft of *Kim* and the final manuscript "Kipling transcended his racism in several ways."

A1367 -----. "Kipling's *Kim*: Introduction and Additions." Ph.D. dissertation, City University of New York, 1976, 584 pp., DA 37:5140A.

"A three-part study of Kipling's *Kim*, consisting of a critical introduction, the text of the first English edition of *Kim*, and notes to this edition that explain obscure references and provide a selection of textual variants from other editions."

A1368 GREEN, ROGER LANCELYN. *Kipling and the Children*. London: Elek Books, 1965, 240 pp.

Concentrates on Kipling's children's books "by which he is best known, but about which relatively little has been written." Provides an account of Kipling's early years and discusses each of his children's books and stories.

A1369 -----, comp. *Kipling: The Critical Heritage*. New York: Barnes & Noble, 1971, 409 pp.

Includes reprints of early reviews of *Stalky & Co.* from *Atheneum* and *Academy*; a review of *Kim* from *Blackwood's Magazine*; G.K. Chesterton's review of *Just So Stories* from *Bookman* (1902); Agnes Deans Cameron on "Kipling and the Children" from *Anglo-American Magazine* (1902), plus additional articles on *Stalky & Co.*; an excerpt from Harvey Darton's *Children's Books in England* (1932); and Kipling's obituary in the *Times Literary Supplement* (1936). Also includes a bibliography and index.

A1370 HAINES, HELEN E. "The Wisdom of Baloo: Kipling and Childhood." *Horn Book* 12 (May-June 1936):135-41.

Considers *The Jungle Books* his masterpiece--"parables of human life in its strength, its weakness, its interrelationships."

A1371 HARRISON, JAMES. *Rudyard Kipling*. Twayne's English Authors Series. Boston: Twayne, 1982, 173 pp.

Concentrates on Kipling's fiction. In chapter 3, pp. 58-75, discusses the children's stories, including the *Just So Stories*, *The Jungle Books*, *Captains Courageous*, *Stalky & Co.*, *Puck of Pook's Hill*, and *Rewards and Fairies*. A discussion of *Kim*, pp. 47-57, concludes: "Certainly he never again gave expression to the duality of life so perfectly as he did in *Kim*." The book's final chapter attempts to sum up Kipling through a comparison with E.M. Forster and Joseph Conrad.

A1372 HAVHOLM, PETER. "Kipling and Fantasy." *Children's Literature* 4

(1975):91-104.
>Contrasts Kipling's failure to create a successful tragedy in *The Light That Failed* with his success in touching the emotions and providing "glimpses of joy" that even a child could understand in the "non-didactic" Mowgli stories and the *Jungle Books.*

A1373   HINDLE, ALAN. "Rudyard Kipling's *Rewards and Fairies.*" *School Librarian* 21, no. 4 (December 1973):295-300.
>Prefers *Rewards and Fairies* to *Puck of Pook's Hill* and examines it in depth.

A1374   INGLIS, FRED. *Promise of Happiness*, pp. 156-62.
>Kipling's "very best attributes" come out when he speaks to children "in a faultlessly sustained style." Praises the *Puck* stories most highly but concludes, "At its heart, the manliness which Kipling admires is hollow."

A1375   ISLAM, SHAMSUL. "Psychological Allegory in *The Jungle Books.*" *Kipling Journal* 40 (March 1973):9-12.
>Points out elements of psychological allegory in the *Jungle Books.*

A1376   KIMMEL, ERIC A. "A Second Look: *Captains Courageous.*" *Horn Book* 58 (October 1982):543-47.
>Questions why the book fails when it shares many of the same elements as Kipling's more successful books: concludes it lacks both a memorable character and a plot.

A1377   Kipling Society. Founded in 1927, it publishes *The Kipling Journal* four times a year.

A1378   MEYERS, JEFFREY. "The Quest for Identity in *Kim.*" *Texas Studies in Literature and Language* 12 (Spring 1970):101-10.
>Explores Kim's struggle for identity in his existence in between two worlds, the English and the Indian.

A1379   MOSS, ROBERT F. *Rudyard Kipling and the Fiction of Adolescence.* New York: St. Martin's, 1982, 165 pp.
>Traces the handling of adolescence in Kipling's works for children and adults in the years up to 1901. Concentrates on the *Jungle Books*, pp. 107-17, *Captains Courageous*, pp. 115-25, *Stalky and Co.*, pp. 125-27, and *Kim*, which is seen as "Kipling's triumph," pp. 128-41.

A1380   MUSGRAVE, P.W. "Kipling's View of Educating Children." *Australian Journal of Education* 25 (1981):211-23.
>Explores Kipling's views of the child and his education as portrayed in his books for children and for adults.

A1381   -----. "*Stalky and Co.* Re-Read: A Taste of Things to Come?" *CLE*, n.s. 10, no. 4 (Winter 1979):186-93.
>Points out similarities in use of "physical violence, psychological pressure, and the use by the religious staff of the informal school groupings for their own ends" in *Stalky & Co.* and Robert Cormier's *Chocolate War.*

A1382   NESBITT, ELIZABETH. "The Great Originator." *Horn Book* 29 (April 1953):106-14. (Excerpt from Meigs et al., *A Critical History of*

Children's Literature.)
A concise biocritical overview.

A1383 PARRY, G. "The Identity Quest in Kipling's *Kim.*" *Caliban* 14 (1977):55-60.

Argues that in *Kim*, Kipling's "finest and most spacious piece of fiction, he dramatises the conflicting claims exerted by India and England" on the young boy. Provides a detailed thematic and structural analysis.

A1384 ROSENTHAL, LYNNE M. "Boy Society in Rudyard Kipling's *Stalky & Co.*" *L&U* 2, no. 2 (Fall 1978):16-26.

Interprets the book in terms of the question of "how individuality might be retained in a world increasingly constrained by the pressure to conform."

A1385 SALE, ROGER. "Kipling's Boys." In *Fairy Tales*, pp. 194-221.

"The Kipling that has always been the most popular, and that will last longer than any of the rest, is the work done for children and growing boys." Finds the *Just-So Stories* condescending toward animals. Describes *Kim* as "such a seductive book because every detail is real, authentic, yet its aim is romance, excitement, adventure, a view of life so boyish that it sees nothing ugly, mean, or dull."

A1386 STEWART, JOHN I.M. *Rudyard Kipling.* New York: Dodd, Mead, 1966, 245 pp.

Chapters 8, pp. 136-51, and 9, pp. 152-71, are devoted to Kipling's children's books.

A1387 SUTCLIFF, ROSEMARY. "*Kim.*" *CLE*, n.s. 13, no. 4 (Winter 1982):164-70.

Admitting she has always loved the book so much she has difficulty judging how good it is, Sutcliff examines Kipling's craftsmanship and evaluates the book within the context of the Empire, the time, and Kipling's cultural and religious beliefs.

A1388 -----. *Rudyard Kipling.* New York: Walck, 1961, 61 pp.

Sutcliff's love and admiration for Kipling's work is evident throughout this biocritical analysis. She concentrates on those works she classifies as children's: *The Jungle Books, Captains Courageous, Stalky and Co., Kim,* the *Just So Stories, Puck of Pook's Hill,* and *Rewards and Fairies.*

A1389 TOMPKINS, JOYCE, M.S. *The Art of Rudyard Kipling.* 2d ed. London: Methuen, 1965, 277 pp.

Discusses *Kim*--comparing it to *Huckleberry Finn*--pp. 21-32, and *The Jungle Books, The Just so Stories, Puck of Pook's Hill,* and *Rewards and Fairies,* in chapter 3, pp. 55-84.

A1390 -----. "Kipling and Nordic Myth and Saga." *English Studies* 52 (April 1971):147-57.

Suggests that Kipling's early knowledge of Nordic myths and sagas provided "forms for his imagination and emotion in his later years."

A1391 WILSON, ANGUS. "*Kim* and the Stories." In *The Strange Ride of*

Rudyard Kipling. New York: Penguin, 1977, pp. 122-33.
Analyzes *Kim* and the *Jungle Books*, calling *Kim* "the best thing he ever wrote."

KLEIN, NORMA (1938-   )

A1392   AGEE, HUGH. "The Illegitimate Heroine and the Theme of Change in Two Adolescent Novels." *Focus: Teaching English Language Arts* 3, no. 2 (Winter 1977):39-42. (Also in ERIC Educational Document Reproduction Service, ED 157 082.)
Discusses the theme of change in two novels featuring protagonists whose mothers are unmarried: Norma Klein's *Mom, the Wolfman and Me*, and Katie Letcher Lyle's *I Will Go Barefoot All Summer for You.*

A1393   DONELSON, KENNETH. "Norma Klein's Adolescent Novels: The Reversal of the Usual." *Focus* 3, no. 2 (Winter 1977):15-24. (Also in ERIC Educational Document Reproduction Service, ED 157 082.)
Examines four of Klein's early books but feels that the more recent *Taking Sides* and *What It's All About* are "trendy" and "eminently forgettable."

A1394   KLEIN, NORMA. "Growing Up Human: The Case for Sexuality in Children's Books." *CLE*, n.s. 8, no. 2 (Summer 1977):80-84.
Discusses her background and interests and argues that books are needed that are concerned with emotions and the joys of life as well as its complexities.

KNOWLES, JOHN (1926-   )

A1395   ALLEY, DOUGLAS. "Teaching Emerson through *A Separate Peace.*" *English Journal* 70 (January 1981):19-21.
Shows that "Throughout the novel there are statements closely akin to concepts in Emerson's essays, poetry, and journals," especially Emerson's concept of friendship.

A1396   ELLIS, JAMES. "*A Separate Peace*: The Fall from Innocence." *English Journal* 53 (May 1964):313-18.
Discusses three sets of symbols as providing the basic structure of the novel: (1) summer and winter; (2) the Devon River and the Naguamsett River, and (3) peace and war.

A1397   GREILING, FRANZISKA L. "The Theme of Freedom in *A Separate Peace.*" *English Journal* 56 (December 1967):1269-72.
Traces themes of freedom, harmony, and unity as "fragments from the Greek themes in the book."

A1398   PIEHL, KATHY. "Gene Forrester and Tom Brown: *A Separate Peace* as School Story." *CLE*, n.s. 14, no. 2 (Summer 1983):67-74.
Explores Knowles's use of the school story tradition.

A1399   WITHERINGTON, PAUL. "*A Separate Peace*: A Study in Structural Ambiguity." *English Journal* 54 (December 1965):795-800.
Sees the ambiguity in tensions portrayed in the novel as the key to its interpretation.

KNOX, THOMAS WALLACE (1835-96)

A1400   SCHMIDT, NANCY. *Children's Fiction about Africa*, pp. 108-10.
Analyzes his depiction of Africa and Africans.

KONIGSBURG, E.L. (1930-   )

A1401   KONIGSBURG, E.L. "The Double Image: Language as the Perimeter
of Culture." *SLJ* 16 (February 1970):31-34. (Reprinted in Gerhardt,
Issues In Children's Book Selection, pp. 24-30.)
Discusses the ways in which language reflects and shapes a culture, and relates this to her efforts to capture the language of her
culture and expand its limits for children.

A1402   -----. "Newbery Award Acceptance." *Horn Book* 44 (August
1968):391-95.
Reports on her background and goals in writing. Biographical
sketch by her husband David follows, pp. 396-98.

A1403   -----. "Of Ariel, Caliban, and Certain Beasts of Mine Own." *Proceedings of the Children's Literature Association* 7 (1980):1-16.
Offers a statement of her purpose in writing for the "middle-
aged" child. "The purpose of my Beast is to help them know theirs."

A1404   -----. "Ruthie Britten and Because I Can." In Hearne, *Celebrating
Children Books*, pp. 62-72.
Tells some of the reasons why she writes children's books.

A1405   -----. "Spezzatura: A Kind of Excellence." *Horn Book* 52 (June
1976):253-61.
"I would like to tell you why I write for children by tracing
very specifically the roots of my last book, *The Second Mrs. Giac-
onda*."

A1406   REES, DAVID. "Your Arcane Novelist--E.L. Konigsburg." In *Marble
in the Water*, pp. 14-24. (Also in *Horn Book* 54 [February
1978]:79-84.)
Offers an English perspective on an American writer. Discusses
her work to date, praising her variety, style, wit, and originality.

A1407   TOWNSEND, JOHN ROWE. *Sounding*, pp. 111-24.
Comments that her books "differ remarkably from each other,"
"display impressively different forms of expertise," and "are decidedly
uneven." Includes a detailed discussion of *The Mixed-Up Files of
Mrs. Basil E. Frankweiler*.

KORCZAK, JANUSZ (1848-1942)

A1408   KIRCHNER, HANNA. "The Meaning of Janusz Korczak's Work for
World Literature." *Bookbird* 16, no. 2 (1978):12-21.
A biocritical overview of the Polish author, teacher, and doctor.

A1409   LYPP, MARIA. "The King Incognito or the Portrayal of the Child in
J. Korczak's *Matthew, the Young King*." In Escarpit, *Portrayal of
the Child*, pp. 365-77.
Examines the way Korczak handles the problem any writer of
children's literature faces: the incongruity between the horizon of

the author and that of the reader.

A1410   SCHWARCZ, JOSEPH. "Between Dream and Social Utopia." In *Ways of the Illustrator*, pp. 120-30.
Examines the ways in which five illustrators have approached Korczak's popular *King Mathew I* (*Mathew the Young King*), first published in 1923. Studies the illustrated versions of Irene Lorentowicz, S. Cohen, Jerzy Srokowski, Veronica Leo, and Waldemar Andrezejewski. In addition, unpublished sets of illustrations by Brakha Alhassid and Esther Katz are examined.

KRAUSS, RUTH (1911-   )

A1411   BADER, BARBARA. "Ruth Krauss; Ruth Krauss and Maurice Sendak." In *American Picturebooks*, pp. 416-33.
Discusses Ruth Krauss's contribution as the author of picturebook texts and her collaboration with a number of artists, especially Maurice Sendak.

A1412   COONEY, BARBARA. "Artist's Choice." *Horn Book* 32 (August 1956):278.
Discusses *Charlotte and the White Horse*, illustrated by Maurice Sendak, commenting that "Miss Krauss's words are linked inseparably to the misty moonlit pictures."

A1413   MARTIN, ANNE. "Ruth Krauss: A Very Special Author." *EE* 32 (November 1955):427-34. (Reprinted in Hoffman, *Authors and Illustrators*, pp. 247-55.)
Views Krauss as an experimenter with new forms and contents for the picture book. Discusses most of her books to date.

KREIDOLF, ERNST (1863-1956)

A1414   HÜRLIMANN, BETTINA. "The Picture-Books of Ernst Kreidolf." In *Three Centuries*, pp. 203-7.
Describes Kreidolf's books and his methods of working.

KRUMGOLD, JOSEPH (1908-80)

A1415   KRUMGOLD, JOSEPH. "Archetypes of the Twentieth Century: Mythic Roots of An Initiation Trilogy." *Library Journal* 93 (15 October 1968):3926-29. (Reprint of speech given at Catholic Library Association Convention in 1968.)
Provides a detailed discussion of the writing of *Henry 3* and its archetypal background.

A1416   -----. "Newbery Award Acceptance." *Horn Book* 30 (August 1954):221-32.
Contrasts the community of Los Cordovas, New Mexico, the setting for *And Now Miguel*, with Los Alamos, New Mexico, and its very different values.

KULLMAN, HARRY (1919-82)

A1417   MÄHLQVIST, STEFAN. "Harry Kullman." *Bookbird* 2 (1980):7-10.
Summarizes several books and points out Kullman's significance.

KURELEK, WILLIAM (1927-77)

A1418   LANGTON, JANE. "William Kurelek: North American Brueghel." *NYTBR*, 30 April 1978, Children's Book sec., pp. 26, 39.
Points out that Kurelek's children's books represent only a small part of his prodigious output of paintings, many of them Bosch-like nightmares.

A1419   MORLEY, PATRICIA. "The Good Life, Prairie Style: The Art and Artistry of William Kurelek." *Children's Literature* 6 (1977):141-49.
Analyzes the pictures, texts, and biographical influences of Kurelek's books, especially *A Prairie Boy's Winter* and *A Prairie Boy's Summer*, placing the works in the context of "prairie literature" and Canadian literature.

A1420   STOTT, JON C. "Kurelek's Vision." *ChLAQ* 2, no. 3 (Autumn 1977):1-2, 9-10.
Discusses Kurelek's first four children's books, their similarities, and their differences.

KUSKIN, KARLA (1932-   )

A1421   BURROWS, ALVINA T. "Profile: Karla Kuskin." *LA* 56 (December 1979):934-40.
An interview in which Kuskin talks about her life and work, poetry and children. Includes a bibliography of her works.

A1422   HELBIG, ALETHEA K. "Feelings and Language: The Poetry of Karla Kuskin." *ChLAQ* 5, no. 2 (Summer 1980):27-30.
An overview.

A1423   KUSKIN, KARLA. "Introducing Poetry and Children to Each Other." *Proceedings of the Children's Literature Association* 8 (1981):21-36.
Uses her own poetry as an example and in the process reveals much about her own methods of creating poetry and her aims in writing.

LA FONTAINE, JEAN De (1621-95)

A1424   CAULEY, JOSEPH C. "*Contes* of La Fontaine: A Study in Narrative Mode." Ph.D. dissertation, University of Wisconsin, 1972, 336 pp., DA 33:4402A.
Examines the *Contes* in terms of La Fontaine's experiments with narrative style.

A1425   TAILLEUX, DOMINIQUE. "The Sage of La Fontaine or a Certain Art of Living." *Children's Literature* 1 (1972):37-41.
Examines the image of the wise man in La Fontaine's *Fables*.

LADA, JOSEPH

A1426   AMOR, STUART. "Joseph Lada, Illustrator." *Signal* 21 (September 1976):108-14.
An appreciative evaluation.

LAGERLÖF, SELMA (1858-1940)

A1427   BERENDSOHN, WALTER. *Selma Lagerlöf: Her Life and Work.*
Translated and adapted by George F. Timpson. 1931. Reprint.
Port Washington, N.Y.: Kennikat Press, 1968, 136 pp.
Discusses *The Wonderful Adventures of Nils*, pp. 62-67, consider-
ing it to be in many ways the most successful of her longer books.

A1428   EDSTRÖM, VIVI B. *Selma Lagerlöf.* Twayne's English Author Series.
Boston: Twayne, 1984, 151 pp.
Chapter 4 concentrates on *The Wonderful Adventures of Nils*, pp.
58-59. Includes references.

A1429   LAGERROTH, ERLAND. "Selma Lagerlöf Research 1900-1964: A
Survey and An Orientation." *Scandinavian Studies* 37, no. 1 (Febru-
ary 1965):1-30.
Includes summaries of Scandinavian research pertaining to *Nils
Holgersson.*

A1430   SALE, ROGER. *Fairy Tales*, pp. 90-97.
Analyzes *The Wonderful Adventures of Nils* in terms of Lagerlöf's use of a combination of fantasy and realistic portrayal of
animals to make points about strength and power.

LAMORISSE, ALBERT (1922-70)

A1431   KINGSTON, CAROLYN T. *Tragic Mode*, pp. 155-57.
Analyzes the themes of loss and death in *White Mane.*

LANG, ANDREW (1844-1912)

A1432   GREEN, ROGER L. *Andrew Lang.* New York: Henry Z. Walck;
London: Bodley Head, 1962, 77 pp.
A biocritical overview.

A1433   -----. "Andrew Lang in Fairyland." *Junior Bookshelf* 26 (October
1962):171-80. (Reprinted in Egoff, *Only Connect*, 1st ed., pp.
270-78.)
A brief biocritical overview.

LANGTON, JANE (1922-   )

A1434   REES, DAVID. "Real and Transcendental--Jane Langton." In *Painted
Desert*, pp. 75-88.
Examines Langton as a writer of realistic stories and fantasy
rooted in history.

LANSING, ELIZABETH HUBBARD (1911-   )

A1435   KINGSTON, CAROLYN T. *Tragic Mode*, pp. 55-56.
Analyzes the theme of rejection in *Lulu's Window.*

LATHAM, JEAN LEE (1902-   )

A1436   LATHAM, JEAN L. "Newbery Acceptance Speech." *Horn Book* 32
(August 1956):283-92.
Describes her working methods as a writer and the background

of some of her books, especially *Carry On, Mr. Bowditch.* Biographical sketch by Ellen Fulton follows, pp. 293-99.

LAURENCE, MARGARET (1926-   )

A1437   LETSON, D.R. "Mother of Manawaka: Margaret Laurence as Author of Children's Stories." *CCL* 21 (1981):17-24.
A critical overview of Laurence's work for children.

LAURITZEN, JONREED (1902-   )

A1438   KINGSTON, CAROLYN T. *Tragic Mode*, pp. 67-69.
Analyzes *The Ordeal of the Young Hunter* in terms of its theme of entrapment.

LAWRENCE, ANN (1942-   )

A1439   RAY, SHEILA. "Children's Writers 9: Ann Lawrence." *School Librarian* 30 (September 1982):196-99.
Finds Lawrence's books "readable" and "original." Discusses briefly her books for young readers, her fantasy, and her historical fiction.

LAWSON, ROBERT (1892-1957)

A1440   BADER, BARBARA. *American Picturebooks*, pp. 143-47.
Analyzes Lawson's work from the *Hurdy Gurdy Man* and *Ferdinand* (its techniques "unthinkable before motion pictures"), to *Ben and Me* and *They Were Strong and Good.* Feels that over the years Lawson's "drawings lost all semblance of spontaneity," except for the animals.

A1441   BURNS, MARY MEHLMAN. "There is Enough for All: Robert Lawson's America." *Horn Book* 48 (February 1972):24-32; (April):120-28; (June):295-305.
"The theme of America-the-Bountiful, the fabulous nature of American storytelling, the modes of American speech, the use of comic narrators—are motifs which recur in many of his books." This major survey of Lawson's work includes an extensive bibliography.

A1442   CORNELL, ROBERT W. "Robert Lawson: For All Children." *EE* 50 (May 1973):718-25, 738.
Reviews Lawson's life and work and "comments on his writing and illustrating techniques as he used them to present his views on life." Includes an extensive bibliography of research sources.

A1443   FISH, HELEN DEAN. "Robert Lawson: Illustrator in the Great Tradition." *Horn Book* 16 (January-February 1940):16-26.
Praises Lawson's versatility and variety, and traces his development as an artist. Concludes with a discussion of his illustrations for Mary Godolphin's adaptation of *Pilgrim's Progress.*

A1444   JONES, HELEN L. *Robert Lawson Illustrator: A Selection of His Characteristic Illustrations.* Boston: Little, Brown, 1972, 121 pp.
Examines Lawson's work and his development as an illustrator, and provides numerous reproductions and a bibliography of his books.

A1445   LAWSON, ROBERT. "Lo, The Poor Illustrator." *Publishers Weekly* 128

(17 December 1935):2091.
Discusses the many difficulties facing an illustrator, using examples from his own experience to illuminate the process of illustration.

A1446   MADSEN, VALDEN. "Classic Americana: Themes and Values in the Tales of Robert Lawson." *L&U* 3, no. 1 (Spring 1979):89-106.
Discusses traditional values and their skillful presentation in *Mr. Revere and I*, *The Great Wheel*, and *Rabbit Hill*.

A1447   SALWAY, LANCE, and CHAMBERS, NANCY. "Book Post." *Signal* 26 (May 1978):99-107, passim.
Comments on *Rabbit Hill* and contrasts it with Penelope Lively's *The Voyage of QV66*.

A1448   Weston, Annette H. "Robert Lawson: Author and Illustrator." *EE* 47 (January 1970):74-84. (Reprinted in Hoffman, *Authors and Illustrators*, pp. 256-67.)
Primarily a history of the man and his books, providing much background although little in-depth criticism. Includes references.

LEAF, MUNRO (1905-76)

A1449   BELL, A. "About Ferdinand; Concerning the Book, *The Story of Ferdinand*." *Publishers Weekly* 190 (22 August 1966):54-55.
Describes the publishing history of *Ferdinand*'s first thirty years, from Munro Leaf's first draft to 1966.

A1450   GROTJAHN, MARTIN. "Ferdinand the Bull: Psychoanalytical Remarks About a Modern Totem Animal." *American Imago* 1, no. 3 (June 1940):33-41. (Reprinted in White, *Children's Literature*, pp. 30-36.)
Examines two aspects of Ferdinand from a psychoanalytical point of view: "1. What the artist expressed by the creation of a bull who refused to fight; 2. Why this creation struck a response in the unconscious of so large a portion of the public, hitting apparently upon deep emotional needs."

LEAR, EDWARD (1812-88)

A1451   BARKER, WAR REN J. "The Nonsense of Edward Lear." *Psychoanalytic Quarterly* 25, no. 4 (October 1966):568-86. (Reprinted in White, *Children's Literature*, pp. 12-19.)
Attempts to show connections between Lear's experiences and his nonsense creations, exploring the ways in which Lear was able to express his highly personal needs in acceptable ways.

A1452   BROCKWAY, J.T. "Edward Lear, Poet." *Fortnightly*, n.s. 1001 (May 1950):334-39.
Explores the nature of Lear's poetic gift, finding a key in the underlying sense of tragedy that pervades the nonsense verses.

A1453   BYROM, THOMAS. *Nonsense and Wonder: The Poems and Cartoons of Edward Lear*. New York: E.P. Dutton, Brandywine Press, 1977, 244 pp.
Contains a brief biography and an extended discussion of Lear's limericks and long poems. Includes a section analyzing "picture and poem discrepancy" and a bibliography of primary and secondary

sources.

A1454　COOLIDGE, BERTHA. "How Pleasant to Know Mister Lear." *Colophon* 3, no. 9 (February 1932):57-68.
　　　　Compares Lear and Lewis Carroll psychologically and in terms of their work.

A1455　FISHER, CRISPIN. "A Load of Old Nonsense: Edward Lear Resurrected by Four Publishers." *Growing Point* 8 (November 1969):1418-20. (Reprinted in Haviland, *Children and Literature*, pp. 198-201.)
　　　　Reviews five new illustrated versions of works by Lear.

A1456　HARK, INA RAE. *Edward Lear.* Twayne's English Author Series, no. 336. Boston: Twayne, 1982, 161 pp.
　　　　Surveys all of Lear, showing "how strongly connected each work is with all the others." Includes a brief biography and a bibliography of primary and secondary sources.

A1457　-----. "Edward Lear: Eccentricity and Victorian Angst." *Victorian Poetry* 16, nos. 1-2 (Spring-Summer 1978):112-22.
　　　　Argues that Lear's poetry can best be understood in relation to the nature of Victorian society and Lear's relationship to it.

A1458　HARMON, EDWARD. "Lear, Limericks, and Some Other Verse Forms." *Children's Literature* 10 (1982):70-76.
　　　　Examines Lear's nonsense verses, pointing out that few of them are actually limericks.

A1459　HOFER, PHILIP. "The Yonghy Bonghy Bo." *Harvard Library Bulletin* 15, no. 3 (July 1967):229-37.
　　　　Reports on finding a manuscript version, with Lear's own drawings, in a London bookshop. Describes and reproduces the manuscript and drawings and also the musical setting, with extensive analysis and commentary.

A1460　JACKSON, HOLBROOK. "Edward Lear: Laureate of Nonsense." *Dolphin* 4 (Fall 1940):10-18.
　　　　Provides a sensitive analysis of Lear's life and work.

A1461　LEHMAN, JOHN. *Edward Lear and His World.* New York: Scribner, 1977, 128 pp.
　　　　An extensively illustrated account of Lear's various careers: as nonsense poet, illustrator, painter and draughtsman, and travel-book writer.

A1462　MILLER, EDMUND. "Two Approaches to Edward Lear's Nonsense Songs." *Victorian Newsletter* 44 (Fall 1973):5-8.
　　　　Argues that serious attention to Lear's sexual obsessions is helpful in understanding all of his poetry and "necessary for understanding why some of his poems are failures or partial failures, why some of his poems are ridiculous, rather than sublime, nonsense."

A1463　ORWELL, GEORGE. "Nonsense Poetry." In *Shooting An Elephant and Other Essays.* New York: Harcourt, Brace, 1950, pp. 187-92.
　　　　Reviews *The Lear Omnibus*, edited by R.L. Mégroz. Finds Lear funniest "when a touch of burlesque or perverted logic makes its

appearance."

A1464   SMITH, WILLIAM JAY. "'So They Smashed That Old Man . . .': A Note on Edward Lear." *Horn Book* 35 (August 1959):323-26.
Argues that sound precedes sense in Lear and with children.

A1465   WHITE, ALISON. "With Birds in His Beard." *Saturday Review* (15 January 1966). (Reprinted in Egoff, *Only Connect*, 1st. ed., pp. 279-85.)
A brief biocritical overview.

LEE, DENNIS (1939-   )

A1466   *Canadian Children's Literature* 33 (1984):6-31.
Contains three articles on Lee: "Re-realizing Mother Goose: An Interview with Dennis Lee On *Jelly Belly*," by Cory Bieman Davies and Catherine Ross; a highly critical "Jelly Belly in the Perilous Forest," by M.A. Thompson; and "Cadence and Nonsense: Dennis Lee's Poems for Children and Adults," by Perry Nodelman.

A1467   DEMERS, PATRICIA. "Dennis Lee's Poetry for Children." *ChLAQ* 9, no. 3 (Fall 1984):129-30.
Analyzes Lee's techniques and his appeal.

A1468   LEE, DENNIS. "Roots and Play: Writing as a 35-Year-Old Children." *CCL* 4 (1979):28-58.
The Canadian poet attempts to explain why and how he writes, with many examples from his poems. In addition to explaining that he writes not for children but "as a 35-year-old children," he discusses the importance of roots and play in his writing.

A1469   NODELMAN, PERRY. "The Silverhonkabeest: Children and the Meaning of Childhood." *CCL* 12 (1978):26-34.
Argues that children enjoy Lee's poems because they "share [his] sadness and are themselves conscious of what they are giving up as they turn into grownups." Compares Lee's understanding of this sadness to A.A. Milne's. See also James S. Reaney's review of *Garbage Delight* in this same issue, pp. 72-74.

A1470   ------. "Who's Speaking? The Voices of Dennis Lee's Poems for Children." *CCL* 25 (1982):4-17.
Depicts Lee as capturing the voice of childhood anarchy. An exchange of letters between Nodelman and Roderick McGillis, based on this article, appears in *CLE*, n.s. 15, no. 1 (Spring 1984):58-60.

LEE, STAN (1922-   )

A1471   MONDELLO, SALVATORE. "Spider-Man: Superhero in the Liberal Tradition." *Journal of Popular Culture* 10, no. 1 (Summer 1976):232-38. (Reprinted in Lenz, *Young Adult Literature*, pp. 314-20.)
Examines the character and political beliefs of Spider-Man and his role in American life in the 1960s and 1970s.

LE GUIN, URSULA K. (1929-   )

A1472   ATTEBERY, BRIAN. *"The Beginning Place*: Le Guin's Metafantasy."

Children's Literature 10 (1982):113-23.
Finds the work a better commentary on fantasy than a fantasy tale.

A1473   BITTNER, JAMES WARREN. "Approaches to the Fiction of Ursula K. Le Guin." Ph.D. dissertation, University of Wisconsin, Madison, 1979, 511 pp., DA 40:3286A.
Chapter 3 of this "first full length exploration of Le Guin's fiction" explores the complimentarity of myth and science in Le Guin's juvenile fantasy and her science fiction.

A1474   -----. *Approaches to the Fiction of Ursula K. Le Guin.* Ann Arbor, Mich.: UMI Research Press, 1984, 161 pp.
This revision of Bittner's doctoral thesis (University of Wisconsin, 1979) attempts to show the relationships within and among Le Guin's novels and short stories. "My goal is to see some of the connections between parts and between part and whole, not to identify those qualities that divide and separate." Sees relationships and connections as a key theme in all of Le Guin's work.

A1475   BRADBURY, MARGARET. "What's in a Name?: Ursula K. Le Guin's Earthsea Trilogy." *School Librarian* 31, no. 3 (September 1983):205-10.
A concise critical introduction to Le Guin's trilogy.

A1476   CAMERON, ELEANOR. "High Fantasy: *A Wizard of Earthsea.*" *Horn Book* 47 (April 1971):129-38. (Reprinted in Heins, *Crosscurrents*, pp. 333-41.)
Calls the *Wizard of Earthesea* "a book of magic and learning" influenced by anthropology. Offers a detailed analysis of the book and praises it highly as "a work, which though it is fantasy, continually returns us to the world about us, its forces and powers; returns us to ourselves, to our struggles and aspirations, to the very core of human responsibility."

A1477   COGELL, ELIZABETH CUMMINS. *Ursula K. Le Guin: A Primary and Secondary Bibliography.* Boston: G.K. Hall, 1983, 244 pp.
Includes an annotated listing of 761 critical studies, including book reviews and brief notices.

A1478   CUNNEEN, SHEILA. "Earthseans and Earthteens." *English Journal* 74 (February 1985):68-69.
A college student reflects on the meaning of the rites of passage theme for adolescent readers of *A Wizard of Earthsea.*

A1479   DE BOLT, JOE. *Ursula K. Le Guin: Voyage to Inner Lands and to Outer Space.* New York: Kennikat Press, 1971, 221 pp.
A collection of essays on Le Guin, including "Circumstance as Policy: The Decade of Ursula K. Le Guin," by Barry N. Malzburg, "A Le Guin Biography," by Joe De Bolt, "A Survey of Le Guin Criticism," by James W. Bittner, "Solitary Being: The Hero as Anthropologist," by Karen Sinclair, "Science and Rhetoric in the Fiction of Ursula Le Guin," by Peter T. Koper, analysis of the Earthsea trilogy by Rollin A. Lasseter, John R. Pfeiffer, and Francis J. Molson, and additional essays by Elizabeth Cogell, Larry L. Tift, and Dennis C. Sullivan.

A1480   DOOLEY, PATRICIA. "Earthsea Patterns." *ChLAQ* 4 (Summer 1979):1-4. (Reprinted in Dooley, *First Steps*, pp. 14-15.)

Discusses Le Guin's use of patterning in the sentence-forms, plot, imagery, and thematic organization of the *Earthsea* trilogy. Argues that Le Guin's patterning "works toward the integration of the three independent books into one whole, in which each retains its separate character while it becomes part of a large work."

A1481   -----. "Magic and Art in Ursula Le Guin's *Earthsea Trilogy*." *Children's Literature* 8 (1980):103-10.

Sees the central function of magic in the novels as a metaphor for art. Identifies three types of magic: "use-magic," "illusion," and most important, "art-magic"; these reflect Le Guin's belief in the importance of language.

A1482   DUNN, MARGARET M. "In Defense of Dragons: Imagination as Experience in the *Earthsea Trilogy*." *Proceedings of the Children's Literature Association* 9 (1982):54-60.

Le Guin offers a "symbolic rendering of the journey from childhood to adulthood" which may be more relevant to the lives of young readers than factual and matter-of-fact accounts.

A1483   ESMONDE, MARGARET P. "The Good Witch of The West." *Children's Literature* 9 (1981):185-90.

Reviews four books of Le Guin criticism published in the late 1970s (by De Bolt, Olander, Scholes, and Slusser) and Le Guin's own essays *The Language of the Night*. Also summarizes earlier criticism.

A1484   *Extrapolation* 21 (Fall 1980):195-304.

Special issue. Includes an overview by Carl Yoke, "Precious Metal in White Clay," pp. 197-208; Dena C. Bain's "*The Tao Te Ching* as background to the novels of Ursula K. Le Guin; Rosemarie Arbur's "Le Guin's 'Song' of Inmost Feminism," pp. 223-61; Barbara Brown's "The Left Hand of Darkness: Androgyny, Future, Present, and Past," pp. 227-35. Tom Moylan's "Beyond Negation: The Critical Utopias of Ursula K. Le Guin and Samuel R. Delany," pp. 236-53; Edgar C. Bailey's "Shadows in Earthsea: Le Guin's Use of a Jungian Archetype," pp. 254-61; Roger Galbreath's "Taoist Magic in the Earthsea Trilogy," pp. 262-68; Brian Attebery's "On the Far Shore: The Myth of Earth Sea," pp. 269-77; Thomas J. Remington's "A Time to Live and a Time to Die: Cyclical Renewal in the Earthsea Trilogy," pp. 278-87; and C.N. Manlove's "Conservatism in the Fantasy of Le Guin," pp. 287-98. Also includes a review of *The Beginning Place*, pp. 299-301.

A1485   FOX, GEOFF, ed. "Notes on 'Teaching' *A Wizard of Earthsea*." *CLE*, o.s., no. 2 (May 1973):58-67.

Describes various classroom approaches to the book.

A1486   HOXMIER, KELLY. "A Positive Alternative: The Novels of Ursula K. Le Guin." *ALAN Review* 10, no. 1 (Fall 1982):3-7.

Explores positive aspects of several types of love relationships portrayed by Le Guin.

A1487   INGLIS, FRED. *Promise of Happiness*, pp. 245-47.

"Her books are spare and stark, consciously wrought and shaped . . . they smell . . . of the study and the library stack . . . ," but the best events "are set pieces of grand storytelling."

A1488 JAGO, WENDY. "A *Wizard of Earthsea* and the Charge of Escapism."
CLE, o.s., no. 8 (July 1972):21-29.
Concludes that children's books, such as Le Guin's *Wizard of
Earthsea* encourage "honest experience" and cannot be said to be an
escape from reality.

A1489 JENKINS, SUE. "Growing Up in Earthsea." *CLE*, n.s. 16, no. 1
(Spring 1985):21-31.
Discusses Le Guin's insights into coming of age.

A1490 LE GUIN, URSULA K. "The Child and the Shadow." In Haviland,
The Openhearted Audience, pp. 101-13.
Discusses the ways in which she believes fantasy tells the truth
and can be "the language of inner truth." Begins with Hans Christian Andersen's story of the man and his shadow and closes with a
brief discussion of Tolkien, along the way pointing out Jungian
insights into fairy tales and myths, and shedding light on the thinking behind her own work.

A1491 OLANDER, JOSEPH D., and GREENBERG, MARTIN HARRY, eds.
Ursula K. Le Guin. Writers of the 21st century. New York:
Taplinger Publishing Co., 1979, 258 pp.
This collection of essays includes two articles on the *Earthsea*
trilogy, "The Master Pattern: The Psychological Journey in the
Earthsea Trilogy," by Margaret P. Esmonde and "Words of Binding:
Patterns of Integration in the Earthsea Trilogy," by John H. Crow
and Richard D. Erlich. Includes a bibliography of works by and
about Le Guin.

A1492 REES, DAVID. "*Earthsea* Revisited: Ursula K. Le Guin." In *Marble
in the Water*, pp. 78-89.
Claims that "the three *Earthsea* books are almost as rich in
suggestion and association as the poetry of T.S. Eliot," and maintains
they sustain the belief in literature as a kind of magic.

A1493 SCHOLES, ROBERT. "The Good Witch of the West." *Hollins Critic* 11
(April 1974):2-12. (Reprinted in *Structural Fabulation: An Essay on
Fiction of the Future* [Notre Dame: University of Notre Dame Press,
1975], pp. 77-97.)
Provides a detailed exploration of the *Wizard of Earthsea*.

A1494 SHIPPEY, T.A. "The Magic Art and the Evolution of Words: Ursula Le
Guin's *Earthsea* Trilogy." *Mosaic* 10, no. 2 (Winter 1977):147-63.
Sees Le Guin's *Earthsea* trilogy as a "parable for our times," and
calls Le Guin as much "myth-breaker" as "myth-maker."

A1495 SLUSSER, GEORGE EDGAR. *The Farthest Shores of Ursula K. Le
Guin*. Milford Series: Popular Writers of Today, vol. 3. San Bernar-
dino, Calif.: R. Reginald Borgo Press, 1976, 60 pp.
Analyzes Le Guin's development as a novelist, seeing in her fiction a merger of genres--"the literature of speculation, science
fiction, and fantasy, with that of personal relationships and manners,
the so-called 'mainstream' novel."

A1496 WALKER, JEANNE MURRAY. "Rites of Passage Today: The Cultural

Significance of *The Wizard of Earthsea*." *Mosaic* 13 (Spring-Summer 1980):179-91.

Examines Le Guin's presentation of God's "symbolic transformation from childhood to adolescence" and explores the significance of fictional rites of passage for the adolescent reader.

LEMKUL, FEDOR (1914-   )

A1497   KOPYLOVA, N.   "Fedor Lemkul--An Illustrator from the Soviet Union." *Bookbird* 3 (1980):34-35. (Reprinted from *Books & Art in the USSR* 4, no. 23 [1979].)

A brief biocritical overview.

L'ENGLE, MADELEINE (1918-   )

A1498   JONES, K.   "A Pentaperceptual Analysis of Social and Philosophical Commentary in *A Wrinkle in Time* by Madeleine L'Engle." Ph.D. dissertation, University of Mississippi, 1977, 177 pp., DA 38:7325A.

Examines the literary techniques used by L'Engle to communicate her values and philosophy. These include the use of allegory, elements of fairy tales, quotations and maxims, allusions to *Alice in Wonderland*, and role modeling.

A1499   L'ENGLE, MADELEINE.   "Before Babel." *Horn Book* 42 (December 1966):661-70.

Maintains the writer's necessity is to communicate truth. Provides a framework by which to view her fiction.

A1500   -----.   "A Sense of Wonder." *Advocate* 2, no. 2 (Winter 1983):69-80.

Explores the meaning of a sense of wonder to her as a storyteller.

A1501   PATTERSON, NANCY-LOU.   "Angel and Psycho-pomp in Madeleine L'Engle's *Wind* Trilogy." *CLE*, n.s. 14, no. 4 (Winter 1983):195-203.

Examines Christian, mythological, and Jungian elements in *A Wrinkle in Time*, *The Wind in the Door*, and *A Swiftly Tilting Planet*.

A1502   PERRY, BARBARA.   "Profile: Madeleine L'Engle: A Real Person." *LA* 54 (October 1977):812-16.

Briefly discusses L'Engle's background, her significant themes, and her development as a writer.

A1503   TOWNSEND, JOHN ROWE. *Sense of Story*, pp. 120-29.

Identifies L'Engle's main themes as centering around the clash of good and evil. Calls her books "good bad books," maintaining they are full of contradictions: they are exciting, stylishly written, and difficult to assess.

A1504   WINTLE, JUSTIN, and FISHER, EMMA. *Pied Pipers*, pp. 249-62.

L'Engle discusses her life and work in an interview.

LENSKI, LOIS (1893-1974)

A1505   BADER, BARBARA. *American Picturebooks*, pp. 76-79.

Analyzes the Small books for young children.

A1506 -----. "A Second Look: The Little Family." *Horn Book* 61 (March 1985):168-71.
  Explores reasons for the survival of *The Little Family* and *Papa Small*.

A1507 HUCK, CHARLOTTE S. "Lois Lenski: Children's Interpreter." *Catholic Library World* 40 (1969):346-50. (Reprinted in Hoffman, *Authors and Illustrators*, pp. 268-74.)
  Praises her as author and illustrator for her "understanding of children of all ages" and for her authenticity and realism. "No author has interpreted American children more accurately or perceptively; no author has given more abundantly to children. . . ."

A1508 JACOBS, LELAND B. "Lois Lenski's Regional Literature." *EE* 30 (May 1953):261-66.
  Maintains that Lenski's work meets the criteria she established for good regional fiction.

A1509 KINGSTON, CAROLYN T. *Tragic Mode*, pp. 42-44.
  Analyzes the theme of rejections in *Judy's Journey*.

A1510 KUZNETS, LOIS R. "Fiction, Faction, and Formula in the Regional Novels of Lois Lenski." *Proceedings of the Children's Literature Association* 9 (1982):96-106.
  "An examination of Lenski's theory about her regional novels, of the life experience and literary practice that went into the theory, and of some of the works that were influenced by, or perhaps influenced that theory."

A1511 LENSKI, LOIS. *Adventure in Understanding: Talks to Parents, Teachers and Librarians, 1944-1966.* Tallahassee, Fla.: Friends of the Florida State University Library, 1968, 242 pp.
  Contains Lenski's views on children, children's literature, and her goals as a writer. Includes her Newbery Award acceptance speech and her definition of regional children's literature.

A1512 -----. "Creating Books." *Library Journal* 88 (15 October 1963):3987-90, 4004.
  Explores her aims in writing, her philosophy and methods. "Even in the picture book for the preschool child, I must somehow catch up the essence of the small child's world, forget my adult world and way of thinking, become a child at heart, live with him his simple doings and activity, listen to his every word with respect and try to interpret as he does."

A1513 -----. "Regional Children's Literature." *WLB* 21 (December 1946):289-92. (Reprinted in Robinson, *Readings About Children's Literature*, pp. 328-34.)
  Sets forth her views on regional literature.

A1514 -----. "The Story of *Phebe Fairchild and Her Book*." *Horn Book* 13 (December 1937):394-400. (Reprinted in Fryatt, *Horn Book Sampler*, pp. 19-22.)
  Tells about researching and writing the book.

A1515 RAM, MARIE L. "The Sociological Aspects of the Lois Lenski Literature--An Exploratory Study." Ed.D. dissertation, University of Buffalo, 1958, 644 pp., DA 19:3307A.

"Attempts to point out and to evaluate the contributions of the Lois Lenski literature to American elementary school children's understanding of the diverse cultural climates in America." Focuses on twenty picture books, six Roundabout America series, and twelve American regional stories.

A1516   TITZELL, JOSIAH. "Lois Lenski: A Serious Artist with a Sense of Humor." *Publishers Weekly* 118 (25 October 1930):1966-69.

A brief biocritical overview of Lenski as illustrator. Includes a bibliography of books she wrote and illustrated.

A1517   WILSON, GEORGE P. "Lois Lenski's Use of Regional Dialect." *North Carolina Folklore* 9 (December 1961):1-3.

Defends the use of dialect in children's literature, especially Lenski's use of it.

LENT, BLAIR (1930-   )

A1518   BADER, BARBARA. "The Japanese Advent and Blair Lent." In *American Picturebooks*, pp. 443-58.

Discusses Japanese influence on the American picture book after World War II, particularly in the work of Blair Lent.

A1519   LENT, BLAIR. "Artist at Work: Cardboard Cuts." *Horn Book* 41 (August 1965):408-12.

Describes the technique and ways in which he uses it.

A1520   SLEATOR, WILLIAM. "An Illustrator Talks." *Publishers Weekly* 195 (17 February 1969):126-28.

Lent discusses his art, his techniques, and his ideas on illustration in this article based on a series of conversations.

LESTER, JULIUS (1939-   )

A1521   GELLER, EVELYN. "Aesthetics, Morality, and the Two Cultures." *SLJ* 17 (October 1970):97-100. (Reprinted in MacCann, *Black Americans*, pp. 36-38.)

Discusses the differing responses of black and white critics to William Armstrong's *Sounder* and Julius Lester's *Black Folktales*.

A1522   -----. "Julius Lester: Newbery Runner-Up." *Library Journal* 94 (15 May 1969):2070-71. (Reprinted in Hoffman, *Authors and Illustrators*, pp. 275-79.)

Interviews Lester following his selection as Newbery runner-up for *To Be a Slave*, exploring his motives, approach, and background.

A1523   LESTER, JULIUS, and WOODS, GEORGE. "Black and White: An Exchange." In MacCann, *Black American*, pp. 28-35. (Reprinted from the *NYTBR*, 24 May 1970.)

An exchange of letters between Lester and George Woods, the *New York Times* children's book editor, concerning Lester's *To Be a Slave* and *Black Folktales*, and differing critical responses of blacks and whites to these books and others.

LEWIS, C[LIVE] S[TAPLES] (1898-1963)

A1524 AYMARD, ELIANE. "On C.S. Lewis and the Narnian Chronicles." *Caliban* 5 (1968):129-45.
Reports on an interview with Walter Hooper, Lewis's secretary and close friend. Concentrates on Lewis's use of Christian allegory.

A1525 BAKKE, JEANNETTE A. "The Lion, the Lamb and the Children: Christian Childhood Education through the *Chronicles of Narnia*." Ph.D. dissertation, University of Minnesota, 1975, 366 pp., DA 76:4021A.
Explores the use of myth in the *Chronicles of Narnia* as a basis for children's Christian education.

A1526 BECKER, JOAN QUALL. "Patterns of Guilt and Grace in the Development and Function of Character in C.S. Lewis's Romances." Ph.D. dissertation, University of Washington, 1981, 289 pp., DA 42:2361A.
Examines "the achievements and failures of Lewis in his development and use of characterization found in his imaginative fiction by considering his methods as well as his apparent aims." Discusses *Narnia* as well as Lewis's fiction for adults.

A1527 BLOUNT, MARGARET. "Fallen and Redeemed: Animals in the Novels of C.S. Lewis." In *Animal Land*, pp. 284-306.
Characterizes *Narnia* as the most memorable of Edens shared equally by humans and animals.

A1528 CHRISTOPHER, JOE R., and OSTLING, JOAN K., comps. *C.S. Lewis: An Annotated Checklist of Writings About Him and His Works.* Kent, Ohio: Kent State University Press, 1974, 389 pp.
Includes sections on *Narnia*, on pp. 99-116, and a very brief section entitled "Children's Literature," pp. 218-19. Annotated listings of reviews of individual volumes of *Narnia* are listed separately.

A1529 COMO, JAMES. "Mediating Illusions: Three Studies of Narnia." *Children's Literature* 10 (1982):163-68.
Reviews several recent books of Lewis scholarship.

A1530 GOUGH, JOHN. "C.S. Lewis and the Problem of David Holbrook." *CLE*, n.s. 8, no. 2 (Summer 1977):51-62.
A rebuttal of Holbrook's attack on the Narnia chronicles in *CLE*, o.s., no. 10. Claims "Holbrook's article is not merely idiosyncratic, it is bad scholarship, false information, and so internally contradictory as to verge now and then on incoherence."

A1531 GREEN, ROGER LANCELYN. *C.S. Lewis.* London: Bodley Head, 1963, 49 pp.
Defends Lewis's children's books against critics' attacks, maintaining that they "will live to take their permanent place among the great works of children's literature" because of "the whole cast of the author's mind, which has gone into their making."

A1532 HIGGINS, JAMES E. "A Letter from C.S. Lewis." *Horn Book* 42 (October 1966):533-39.
Higgins comments upon a letter from Lewis in which Lewis comments upon various questions relating to the Narnia books.

A1533   HOLBROOK, DAVID.   "The Problem of C.S. Lewis."   *CLE*, o.s., no. 10 (March 1973):3-25.   (Extract in Fox, *Writers, Critics, and Children*, pp. 116-24.)

"Under cover of his apparent religious intentions and his mask of benignity, C.S. Lewis conveys to his readers a powerful unconscious message that the world is full of malignancy; that one must be continually alert, that aggression is glorious, exciting and fully justified; that tenderness, cowardice and reticence are weak; that one may easily be assured as to one's righteousness; that magic works--and these messages are sometimes conveyed with undertones of a sadistic-sexual kind, or with powerful phantasies rooted in hate." See article in rebuttal by Gough, above, and Holbrook's reply in *CLE*, n.s. 9, no. 1 (Spring 1978):50-51.   Holbrook's interpretation was also criticized by Betty Levin in a letter in *CLE*, o.s., no. 17 (Summer 1975):99-101.

A1534   HOLLINDALE, P.   "The Image of the Beast: C.S. Lewis's *Chronicles of Narnia.*"   *Use of English* 28 (Spring 1977):16-21.

Attempts to explain the sense of unease that many adults feel about the series.   Concludes that "The Narnia books reveal a startlingly immature and vindictive sensibility."

A1535   HOOPER, Fr. WALTER.   "*Narnia*:   The Author, The Critics, and the Tale."   *Children's Literature* 3 (1974):12-22.   (Reprinted in *The Longing for a Form: Essays on the Fiction of C.S. Lewis*, edited by Peter Schakel [Kent, Ohio: Kent State University Press, 1977].)

Describes the background of the *Narnia* tales and discussions with Lewis about the books.   Answers objections critics such as Holbrook have made to the books and maintains that the key to their power and success is in their "meaning."

A1536   -----.   *Past Watchful Dragons: The Narnian Chronicles of C.S. Lewis.* New York: Collier-Macmillan, 1979, 140 pp.

A detailed account of the Narnia books by Lewis's biographer and former secretary.   Includes Lewis's own "Outline of Narnian History, So Far As It Is Known," reminiscences by Lewis's illustrator, Pauline Baynes, and Hooper's own interpretations of the books. Earlier versions of the essays in this book include "Past Watchful Dragons: The Fairy Tales of C.S. Lewis" and Hooper's article in *Children's Literature* 3 (1974).

A1537   HUTTON, M.   "Writers for Children 3:   C.S. Lewis."   *School Librarian and School Library Review* 12 (July 1964):124-32.

Summarizes a number of critical points of view concerning Lewis and includes a brief bibliography.

A1538   KARKAINEN, PAUL.   *Narnia Explored.*   Old Tappan, N.J.:   F.H. Revell, 1979, 192 pp.

"The purpose of *Narnia Explored* is to ferret out of the Narnia tales the principal themes, particularly those which reflect Lewis's Christian viewpoint . . . [and] to encourage the reader to look at the world as Lewis did; as a place that is rich with meaning and filled with the rumor of God's presence."   Provides a book by book analysis.

A1539   KEEFE, CAROLYN.   "*Narnia Tales*:   A Refracting of Pictures."   ERIC Educational Document Reproduction Service, 1978, 18 pp., ED 176

347.

Argues that the principles that Lewis felt made the fairy tale a suitable medium in which to express himself, also make the Narnia tales suitable for oral interpretation.

A1540 LEWIS, C.S. "Sometimes Fairy Stories May Say Best What's to Be Said." *NYTBR*, 18 November 1956, Children's Book sec., 3 p.

Lewis says he wrote fairy tales because "the Fairy Tale seemed the ideal form for the stuff I had to say."

A1541 LIVELY, PENELOPE. "The Wrath of God: An Opinion of the Narnia Books." *Use of English* 20, no. 2 (Winter 1968):126-29.

Accuses Lewis of writing at rather than for children and argues that the moral and message of the books, "and hence much of the content, is distasteful and alarming."

A1542 MONTGOMERY, JOHN W. "*The Chronicles of Narnia* and the Adolescent Reader." In *Religious Education* 54 (September 1959):418-28. (Reprinted in Hoffman, *Authors and Illustrators*, pp. 280-96.)

Analyzes the principles as literature in terms of the Aristotelian categories of plot and character, then analyzes their allegory, their appeal to adolescents, and their value. Includes extensive references.

A1543 MOORMAN, CHARLES. "'Now Entertain Conjecture of a Time'--The Fictive Worlds of C.S. Lewis and J.R.R. Tolkien." In Hillegras, Mark R., ed., *Shadows of the Imagination.* Carbondale: University of Southern Illinois, 1969, 170 pp.

Compares and contrasts Lewis's world of Narnia with J.R.R. Tolkien's Middle Earth.

A1544 POSKANZER, SUSAN C. "Thoughts on C.S. Lewis and the *Chronicles of Narnia*." *LA* 53 (May 1976):523-26.

Suggests that Lewis's ability to weave childhood thoughts and rituals into his plots is one key to his success. The children characters are very real; the adults one-dimensional. The language is surprisingly contemporary, and he makes skillful use of several literary devices.

A1545 QUINN, DENNIS B. "The Narnia Books of C.S. Lewis: Fantastic or Wonderful?" *Children's Literature* 12 (1984):105-21.

Traces the history of definitions of fantasy and then attempts to distinguish between "the wonderful" and "the fantastic" in the *Chronicles of Narnia*. Points out Lewis's Neoplatonism and his lack of skill as a storyteller (contrasting him with Edgar Rice Burroughs), and also points out the weakness in Lewis's characterization. Concludes that fantasy such as Lewis's is "harmful to the imagination" in its avoidance of reality. Instead of learning to see enchantment in an actual wood, the child is taught that "there are no wonders in the wood," but only in the mind.

A1546 RIGSBEE, SALLY. "Fantasy Places and Imaginative Belief: *The Lion, the Witch, and the Wardrobe* and *The Princess and the Goblin.*" *ChLAQ* 8, no. 1 (Spring 1983):10-11.

Compares the role of imaginative belief and fantasy places in C.S. Lewis's *The Lion, the Witch, and the Wardrobe* and George MacDonald's *The Princess and the Goblin.*

A1547   SAMMONS, MARTHA C. *A Guide through Narnia.* Wheaton, Ill.: H. Shaw, 1979, 164 pp.
"The purpose of this books is to tell you something about the creator of the seven Narnia books, how he came to write them, to summarize the history of Narnia, and then to talk about what the Pevensie children learn during their adventures, and their meaning to the readers of these chronicles." Includes an index of names and places.

A1548   SCHAKEL, PETER J. *Reading with the Heart: The Way Into Narnia.* Grand Rapids, Mich.: Wm. B. Eerdmans, 1979, 154 pp.
Provides a close reading of the Narnia chronicles, paying special attention to Christian motifs.

A1549   SMITH, LILLIAN H. "News from Narnia." *Canadian Library Association Bulletin* 15 (July 1958):36-37. (Reprinted in Egoff, *Only Connect*, pp. 170-75, and *Horn Book* 39 [October 1963]:470-73.)
Provides insights into Lewis's work, although the article contains much synopsis: "The fresh and vigorous winds of his imagination carry his readers exuberantly through strange and wild adventures that, half consciously, they come to recognize are those of a spiritual journey toward the heart of reality."

A1550   WATSON, JAMES DARRELL. "A Reader's Guide to C.S. Lewis: His Fiction." Ed.D. dissertation, East Texas State University, 1981, 135 pp., DA 42:2692A.
Examines the controlling religious imagery of Lewis's fiction: salvation from supernatural evil.

A1551   WALKER, JEANNE MURRAY. *"The Lion, The Witch, and The Wardrobe* as Rite of Passage." *CLE,* n.s. 16, no. 3 (Autumn 1985):177-88.
Analyzes the novel as a written rite of passage constructed specifically for Lewis's goddaughter.

LIGGETT, THOMAS (1918-   )

A1552   KINGSTON, CAROLYN T. *Tragic Mode,* pp. 34-36.
Analyzes *Pigeon Fly Home* in terms of its themes of rejection and physical disability.

LINDGREN, ASTRID (1907-   )

A1553   BAMBERGER, RICHARD. "Astrid Lindgren and a New Kind of Books for Children." *Bookbird* 5, no. 3 (1967):3-12.
Provides an extensive analysis of key elements of Lindgren's work: her juxtaposition of imagination and reality, her humor, and her creative originality.

A1554   -----. "Astrid Lindgren on the Occasion of Her 70th Birthday." *Bookbird* 15, no. 2 (1977):17-21.
Summarizes the outstanding characteristics of Lindgren's work including her juxtaposition of reality and fantasy.

A1555   COTT, JONATHAN. "Profiles: The Astonishment of Being." *New Yorker,* 28 February 1983, pp. 46-63. (Also in *Pipers,* pp. 137-58.)
Views Pippi Longstocking as, among other things, related to

legendary and mythological heroes, a female Emile, and a Reichian "child of the future." Includes an interview with Lindgren, biographical background, and discussions of *The Children of the Noisy Village* and *The Brothers Lionheart*.

A1556 HAGLIDEN, STEN. "Astrid Lindgren, the Swedish Writer of Children's Books." *Junior Bookshelf* 23 (July 1959):113-21. (Reprinted in Hoffman, *Authors and Illustrators*, pp. 297-301.)
A brief summary and slender analysis of Lindgren's early works.

A1557 HOFFELD, LAURA. "*Pippi Longstocking*: The Comedy of the Natural Girl." *L&U* 1, no. 1 (1977):47-55.
Suggests that Pippi's appetite for enjoyment of life is the key to the reader's pleasure and shock.

A1558 HÜRLIMANN, BETTINA. *Three Centuries*, pp. 81-83.
Describes Pippi as "a figure to strike terror to grown-ups." Unlike Peter Pan, who is a "child eternal," Pippi is a kind of "super-child."

A1559 LINDGREN, ASTRID. "Pippi Can Lift a Horse: The Importance of Children's Books." *Quarterly Journal of the Library of Congress* 40 (Summer 1983):188-201.
Reflects upon the importance of children's books, discusses her goals in writing, and shares the responses of children and critics to her books.

A1560 LINDGREN, ASTRID, and VON ZWEIGBERGK, EVA. "The Road to Sunnanang." *Bookbird* 9, no. 1 (1971):37-55.
Discusses *Pippi*, the fairy tales, *Mio My Son*, and Lindgren's portrayal of lonely children. Bibliography on pp. 42-55.

A1561 SLAYTON, RALPH. "The Love Story of Astrid Lindgren." *Scandinavian Review* 63, no. 4 (December 1975):44-53.
Analyzes Lindgren's warm and loving portrayals of lonely children. Concludes with an extensive discussion of *The Brothers Lionheart* and the controversies surrounding its handling of evil.

A1562 UDAL, JOHN. "Richard Kennedy and Pippi Longstocking." *Junior Bookshelf* 42, no. 2 (April 1978):75-77.
Reports on the interpretation of Pippi offered by illustrator Richard Kennedy.

LINDQUIST, WILLIS (1908-   )

A1563 KINGSTON, CAROLYN T. *Tragic Mode*, pp. 157-60.
Analyzes themes of death and loss in *Burma Boy*.

LINDSAY, NORMAN (1879-1969)

A1564 ROE, MARJORIE. "A Magic Pudding from Australia." *Bookbird* 6, no. 3 (1968):28-33.
Praises *The Magic Pudding* for its humor and its use of animals to satirize the "typical Australian."

LINDSAY, VACHEL (1879-1931)

A1565   *Elementary English Review* 9 (May 1932):115-31.
Special issue. Includes the following critical articles among other brief accounts and reminiscences: Edwin Arlington Robinson's "Vachel Lindsay," pp. 115, describes Lindsay as a "triumphant combination of the troubadour and the evangelist." Frederic G. Melcher's "Vachel Lindsay in the Schools," pp. 117-19, tells of Lindsay's interactions with high-school audiences. Hazelton Spencer's, "Lindsay and the Child's Approach to Art," pp. 120-21, 127, 131, maintains that Lindsay believed that poetry should be heard, not seen, and should be perpetuated through audiences of children. Argues that Lindsay's poems depict American history and geography and help children see beauty in daily surroundings.
Finally, on pp. 129, 131, Witter Bynner is critical of Lindsay's attempts to separate himself into one part for children and another for adults. "He thereby left behind him the whole Lindsay who should have remained a heaven-sent child through all vicissitudes."

A1566   WHITNEY, BLAIR. "'Shoes of Song and Wings of Rhyme': Vachel Lindsay's Poetry for Children." *Children's Literature* 2 (1973):142-47.
Calls him "one of the best children's poets of this century." Although his poetry may lack a coherent philosophy" it abounds in musicality.

LINEVSKI, A.

A1567   "*An Old Tale Carved Out of Stone*: The 1975 Batchelder Award." *TON* 31 (June 1975):384-90.
Includes an article by Maria Polushkin, translator of Linevski's book, about the book's background and plot.

LINGARD, JOAN (1932-   )

A1568   JAMES, DAVID. "Joan Lingard: Values in the Marketplace." *CLE*, o.s, no. 2 (Summer 1976):86-95.
Discusses Lingard's children's stories about the strife in Northern Ireland. "Her novels reveal, in a way that children can grasp, the very roots of bigotry and prejudice and their ensuing violence."

A1569   MARRIOTT, STUART. "'Me Mum She Says It's Bigotry': Children's Responses to *The Twelfth Day of July*." *CLE*, n.s. 16, no. 1 (Spring 1985):53-61.
Reports on responses of children in Northern Ireland to Joan Lingard's novel.

LIONNI, LEO (1910-   )

A1570   AGREE, ROSE. "Lionni's Artichokes: An Interview." *WLB* 44 (May 1970):947-50. (Reprinted in White, *Children's Literature*, pp. 25-30.)
Lionni discusses his life and work in this interview, relates various books to various stages in his life, describes children's reactions to *Little Blue and Little Yellow*, and discusses his views on art and children's book illustration.

A1571   ARNOLD, LINDA. "Leo Lionni: Modern Fabulist." *LA* 53 (September 1976):704-8.

Analyzes Lionni's tales as fables.

A1572   BADER, BARBARA. "Leo Lionni." In *American Picturebooks*, pp. 525-30.

Analyzes the ways in which Lionni uses the devices, techniques, and insights of design to tell a story.

A1573   COHN, ANNABELLE SIMON. "Leo Lionni, Artist and Philosopher." *Children's Literature* 2 (1973):123-29.

Lionni's "stories are didactic both in word and image, and the cumulative corpus makes a significant statement about Lionni's thought." Discusses influences and the development of his art and thought.

A1574   KUSKIN, KARLA. "Three By Lionni." *NYTBR*, 2 May 1976, Children's Book sec., pp. 28-30.

Reviews *A Color of His Own*, *In the Rabbit Garden*, and *Pezzettino*. See also "A Room of His Own," by Lionni in the same issue, pp. 30-32.

A1575   LIONNI, LEO. "Before Images." *Horn Book* 60 (November-December 1984):727-34.

Reflects upon his own creative processes and what he feels is the child's approach to words and images.

A1576   -----. "Mrs. Sanborn, I Love You." *Publishers Weekly* 189 (11 July 1966):134-35.

Reflects upon his attitudes toward his books, particularly his first, *Little Blue and Little Yellow*.

A1577   -----. "My Books for Children." *WLB* 39 (October 1964):142-45. (Reprinted in Hoffman, *Authors and Illustrators*, pp. 302-7.)

Discusses the aims and techniques of his children's books. "The protagonist of my books is often an individual who is, because of special circumstances, an outcast, a rebel, a victim, or a hero. His story ends happily because of his intelligence (the inchworm), his vitality and resourcefulness (Swimmy), his goodness (Tico), or simply because his will and patience turn the law of averages to his advantage."

LIPSYTE, ROBERT (1938-   )

A1578   DONELSON, KENNETH. "*One Fat Summer* as Adventure-Romance." In *Literature for Today's Young Adults*, pp. 207-9.

A1579   FELDMAN, SARI. "Up the Stairs Alone: Robert Lipsyte on Writing for Young Adults." *TON* 39 (Winter 1983):198-202.

An overview of Lipsyte's background and his books, with in-depth discussion of several titles. Includes a bibliography of his books.

A1580   SIMMONS, JOHN S. "Lipsyte's *Contender*: Another Look at the Junior Novel." *EE* 49 (January 1972):116-19.

Feels the novel deserves the attention of the teacher of literature to early adolescents because it follows several significant traditions in the junior novel and also incorporates more recent techniques and themes.

LITTLE, JEAN (1932-   )

A1581   KINGSTON, CAROLYN T. *Tragic Mode*, 132-34.
Analyzes the theme of loss through death in *Home from Far*.

A1582   ROSS, CATHERINE. "An Interview with Jean Little." *CCL* 34
(1984):6-22.
Little discusses her work and literary influences. Her own
account of her friendship with Rosemary Sutcliff, "A Long Distance
Friendship," follows, pp. 23-30.

A1583   ZOLA, MEGUIDO. "Profile: Jean Little." *LA* 58 (January
1981):86-92.
Little discusses her life and work; includes an annotated bibliography of Little's novels.

"Little Red Riding Hood"

A1584   BURNS, LEE. "Red Riding Hood." *Children's Literature* 1
(1972):30-36.
Analyzes the symbolism of numerous versions of "Little Red Riding Hood," dwelling on its darkness, violence and eroticism.

A1585   GRANT, AGNES. "A Canadian Fairy Tale: What Is It?" *CCL* 22
(1981):27-35.
Provides a Native American perspective on "Little Red Riding
Hood" in response to Nodelman's "Little Red Riding Hood as a Canadian Fairy Tale," *CCL* 20 (1980).

A1586   HANKS, CAROLE, and HANKS, T.D., Jr. "Perrault's "Little Red Riding Hood":   Victims of Revision." *Children's Literature* 7
(1978):68-77.
Outlines changes in the story between the Perrault version and
the Grimm version from which most American retellings have come,
arguing that the American and Grimm versions have revised away the
sex and death, metaphors for the maturing process.

A1587   HANNABUSS, C. STUART. "The Moral of the Story." *Times Educational Supplement*, 7 June 1974, p. 51.
Examines various versions of "Little Red Riding Hood" and
reflects upon the moral messages they convey.

A1588   MAVROGENES, NANCY A., and CUMMINS, JOAN S. "What Ever
Happened to Little Red Riding Hood?   A Study of a Nursery Tale
and Its Language." ERIC Educational Document Reproduction Service, 17 pp., ED 132 576. (Shorter version in *Horn Book* 55 [June
1979]:344-49, and reprinted in Barron, *Jump Over the Moon*, pp.
305-9.)
Explores the origins of the Perrault and Grimm versions of the
tale and examines some of its more recent variants. The ERIC article
contains supplemental information on readability and language characteristics.

A1589   NODELMAN, PERRY. "'Little Red Riding Hood' as a Canadian Fairy
Tale." *CCL* 20 (1980):17-27.
Reports on his experiment to have a group of students write the

tale as they remembered it. Concludes that "Little Red Riding Hood" "still maintains the qualities of the oral tradition it sprang from."

A1590 -----. "Little Red Riding Hood Rides Again--and Again and Again and Again." *Proceedings of the Children's Literature Association* 5 (1978):70-77.

Traces versions (and changes in attitudes they reflect), of Little Red Riding Hood over the centuries from Perrault's "Le Petit Chaperon Rouge" in *Histoires ou Contes du Temps Passe* of 1697, and the Grimms' "Rotkappchen" from *Kinder und Hausmarchen* in 1812, through contemporary versions found in popular editions. Includes a bibliography.

A1591 TUCKER, NICHOLAS. *The Child and the Book*, pp. 88-92.

Summarizes some of the many psychoanalytic interpretations of the tale, then analyzes it in terms of the psychological process of "splitting between good and the bad."

A1592 ZOHAR, SHAVIT. "The Notion of Childhood and the Child as Implied Reader (Test Case: 'Little Red Riding Hood')." *Journal of Research and Development in Education* 16, no. 3 (Spring 1983):60-67.

Examines how versions of "Little Red Riding Hood" written in different centuries illustrate "how the character of texts for children have changed as society's views of children and of education have evolved."

LIVELY, PENELOPE (1933-   )

A1593 ABBS, PETER. "Penelope Lively, Children's Fiction and the Failure of Adult Culture." *CLE*, o.s., no. 18 (Fall 1975):118-24.

Argues that children's literature, alone, in modern times "seems capable of forging the imagery of integration and transformation." Discusses Lively's work in these terms.

A1594 ARMSTRONG, JUDITH. "Ghosts as Rhetorical Devices in Children's Fiction: The Literary Use of the Ghost as in *The Ghost of Thomas Kempe* by Penelope Lively." *CLE*, n.s. 9, no. 2 (Summer 1978):59-66.

Considers the use of the ghost as a literary device to allow the exploration of "what is," "what has been," and "what might have been," particularly in *The Ghost of Thomas Kempe*.

A1595 INGLIS, FRED. *Promise of Happiness*, pp. 226-29.

Links Lively with Gillian Avery and William Mayne as writers of a kind of historical fiction "off the main road." Briefly discusses *The House in Norham Gardens*, *The Driftway*, and *Going Back*.

A1596 LIVELY, PENELOPE. "Bones in the Sand." *Horn Book* 57 (December 1981):641-51.

Discusses time, past experience, and history, and their part in her writing.

A1597 -----. "Children and the Art of Memory." *Horn Book* 54 (February 1978):17-23; (April 1978):197-203.

Explores her goals in writing for children, her attempt "to introduce to children the art of memory so that they can observe its possibilities and effects and wonder about them, as I do myself."

A1598   -----. *"The Ghost of Thomas Kempe."* *Junior Bookshelf* 38, no. 3 (June 1974):143-45.
Describes the origins of Thomas Kempe's ghost and how she created the story.

A1599   REES, DAVID. "Time Present and Time Past: Penelope Lively." In *Marble in the Water*, pp. 185-98. (Another version in *Horn Book* 51 [February 1975]:17-25. Reprinted in Heins, *Crosscurrents*, pp. 342-48.)
Analyzes Lively's juxtaposition of time present and time past, traces her development as a writer, and describes her as one of the most interesting authors of children's books to have emerged in the 1970s.

A1600   SMITH, LOUISA A. "Layers of Language in Lively's *The Ghost of Thomas Kempe.*" *ChLAQ* 10 (Fall 1985):114-16.
Points out how Lively "evokes historical periods by means of the linguistic trappings of various times."

A1601   TOWNSEND, JOHN ROWE. *A Sounding*, pp. 125-38.
Analyzes her ability to manipulate time scales and her deep feeling for the people and landscapes of England. Books discussed include *The Ghost of Thomas Kempe*, *The House in Norham Gardens*, and *A Stitch in Time*.

LOBATO, JOSÉ BENTO MONTEIRO (1882-1952)

A1602   BARROS, MARIA DIRCE DO VAL. "Monteiro Lobato and the Renewal of Children's Literature in Brazil." Ph.D. dissertation, Tulane University, 1982, 142 pp., DA 43:704A.
Establishes a set of criteria for evaluating children's books and applies these criteria to Lobato's books for children. Concludes that Lobato's works were "a direct response to a need to lead the development and writing of children's literature in Brazil down new diverse and relevant paths."

A1603   HAYDEN, ROSE LEE. "The Children's Literature of Jose Bento Monteiro Lobato of Brazil: A Pedagogy for Progress." Michigan State University, 1974, 333 pp., DA 35:3297A.
Examines Lobato's thirty-nine works and seven adaptations for the children of Brazil.

LOBEL, ARNOLD (1933-   )

A1604   LOBEL, ARNOLD. "Caldecott Medal Acceptance." *Horn Book* 57 (August 1981):400-404.
Tells how he came to write *Fables*. Biographical sketch by wife Anita follows, pp. 405-10.

A1605   -----. "A Good Picture Book Should. . . ." In Hearne, *Celebrating Children's Books*, pp. 73-80.
Explains why he creates picture books and what makes some better than others--the "subjective involvement" of the author. Uses his *Uncle Elephant* as his example.

A1606   NATOV, RONI, and DE LUCA, GERALDINE. "An Interview with

Arnold Lobel." *L&U* 1, no. 1 (1977):72-97.
Lobel discusses his work, especially the Frog and Toad stories.

A1607 ROLLIN, LUCY. "The Astonished Witness Disclosed: An Interview
with Arnold Lobel." *CLE*, n.s. 15, no. 4 (Winter 1984):191-97.
Lobel discusses his work in an interview.

LOFTING, HUGH (1886-1947)

A1608 BLISHEN, EDWARD. *Hugh Lofting*. London: Bodley Head, 1968, 61
pp. (Bound with *Geoffrey Trease* by Margaret Meek and *J.M. Barrie*
by Roger Lancelyn Green.)
Provides biographical background and an extensive analysis of the
Doctor Dolittle books, with briefer comments on Lofting's other
children's books and his illustrations.

A1609 CHAMBERS, DEWEY W. "How Now, Dr. Dolittle?" *EE* 45 (April
1968):437-39, 445.
Explores ways to approach the racist incidents in *The Story of
Dr. Dolittle* in a classroom setting.

A1610 FISH, HELEN DEAN. "Doctor Dolittle: His Life and Work." *Horn
Book* 24 (September 1948):339-46.
A brief account of Dr. Dolittle's life and work and also of Hugh
Lofting's. "Doctor Dolittle lives, as truly as any man whose portrait
has been painted, and his 'work' is, in its way, as important as that
of any prelate or potentate."

A1611 "John Dolittle, M.D." *TLS*, 23 November 1951, p. vii.
Singles out the key ingredients of the Dr. Dolittle books' appeal:
an engaging central character, storytelling ability, and imaginative and
truthful interpretation of animals.

A1612 SCHLEGELMILCH, WOLFGANG. "From Fairy Tale to Children's
Novel." *Bookbird* 8, no. 4 (1970):14-21. (Reprinted in Meek, *Cool
Web*, pp. 265-71.)
Maintains that Lofting found the final style of the Dolittle books
with the second book, *The Voyages of Doctor Dolittle*. The first,
The Story of Doctor Dolittle, was written in fairy-tale style, while
the later books were truly children's novels. Close analysis reveals
the stylistic differences in the first and later books.

A1613 SCHMIDT, NANCY. *Children's Fiction About Africa*, pp. 175-78.
Argues that Lofting not only perpetrates the standard stereotypes,
he also makes "Africans appear foolish and simpleminded in a way
that differs from that of other authors." His stories "have never been
right or inevitable to Africans. Nor are they to Euroamericans who
share in the changed intellectual climate of postindependence Africa."

A1614 SHENK, DOROTHY C. "Hugh Lofting: Creator of Dr. Dolittle." *EE*
32 (April 1955):201-8.
Cites nine reasons for the popularity of the Dolittle books.

A1615 SUHL, ISABELLE. "The 'Real' Doctor Dolittle." *IRBC* 2, nos. 1-2
(1969). (Reprinted in MacCann, *Black American*, pp. 78-88.)
Points out many examples of racial stereotypes and prejudices in
the Doctor Dolittle books.

LONDON, CAROLYN (1918-   )

A1616   SCHMIDT, NANCY. *Children's Fiction About Africa*, pp. 82-83.
Discusses London's treatment of Africa and Africans.

LONDON, JACK (1876-1916)

A1617   LACHTMAN, HOWARD. "Criticism of Jack London: A Selected
Checklist." *Modern Fiction Studies* 22, no. 1 (1976):107-25.
Includes general studies on London, articles on selected individual
works, and a bibliography.   A review article by Sam Baskett, pp.
101-5, examines two recent studies.

A1618   OWENBY, RAY WILSON. *Jack London: Essays in Criticism.*   Santa
Barbara, Calif.:   Peregrine Smith, 1978, 126 pp.

A1619   SHERMAN, JOAN. *Jack London: A Reference Guide.*   Boston: G.K.
Hall, 1977, 323 pp.
An annotated bibliography of works by and about London. The
introduction includes a survey of London's critical reputation,
1900-1976.

A1620   TAVERNIER-COURBIN, JACQUELINE, ed.   *Critical Essays on Jack
London.*   Boston: G.K. Hall, 1983, 298 pp.
Reprints a number of important critical essays on London and
publishes several for the first time.   Includes an update of Sherman's
1977 bibliography.

A1621   WARD, SUSAN. "Jack London as a Children's Writer." *Children's Literature* 5 (1976):92-103.
Examines London's numerous stories written for children's magazines between 1899 and 1907.

A1622   WILCOX, EARL J., comp. *The Call of the Wild: A Casebook with
Text, Background Sources, Reviews, Critical Essays and Bibliography.*
Chicago: Nelson-Hall, 1980, 254 pp.
Critical essays include "Jack London" by Earle Labor, and several
articles from the *Jack London Newsletter.*

LOVELACE, MAUD H. (1892-1960)

A1623   BEARDWOOD, VALERIE. "Betsy-Tacy Stories--Books to Grow On."
EE 36 (November 1959):465-70.
Examines the appeal of the Betsy-Tacy books.

LOW, JOSEPH (1911-   )

A1624   BADER, BARBARA. *American Picturebooks*, pp. 346-50.
Traces Low's contributions to the art of the picture book.

LOWREY, JANETTE SEBRING (1892-   )

A1625   JOHNSTON, LEAH CARTER. "A Texas Author." *Horn Book* 23 (Jan-
uary 1947):56-61.
A brief biographical and literary survey, with special praise for
The Lavender Cat. Includes a bibliography of Lowrey's works.

LUNN, JANET (1928-   )

A1626   JONES, RAYMOND E. "Border Crossing: Janet Lunn's *The Root Cellar*." *ChLAQ* 10, no. 1 (Spring 1985):43-44.
Points out that the book handles themes of national and adolescent identity and "sets up deliberate parallels to *The Secret Garden*."

LYNCH, PATRICIA (1898-1972)

A1627   CROUCH, MARCUS. *The Nesbit Tradition*, pp. 182-84.
Writes "the richest and most heart-warming of family stories." "She has never bettered *The Grey Goose of Kilnevin* in fantasy and *Fiddler's Quest* in homely adventure."

A1628   DEEVY, TERESA. "Patricia Lynch--A Study." *Junior Bookshelf* 17 (March 1949):17-27.
Finds the outstanding quality of Lynch's work lies in her "power of enjoyment. She leads her readers into a wider space."

A1629   GRAHAM, ELEANOR. "Patricia Lynch--An Appreciation." *Junior Bookshelf* 7 (March 1943):2-6.
Includes a brief statement by Lynch about her background and the origins of her stories.

"Mabinogion"

A1630   EVANS, W.D. EMRYS. "The Welsh Mabinogion: Tellings and Retellings." *CLE* n.s. 9, no. 1 (Spring 1978):17-33.
Compares a number of interpretations, including Evangeline Walton's *Prince of Annwn*, *The Children of Llyr*, *The Song of Rhiannon*, and *The Island of the Mighty*, Lloyd Alexander's Prydain Chronicles, and Alan Garner's *Owl Service*.

A1631   HERMAN, JOHN. "Recommended: Evangeline Walton." *English Journal* 74 (April 1985):75-76.
Praises Walton's retellings of the four branches of the Welsh epic, Mabinogion: *Prince of Annwn*, *The Children of Llyr*, *The Song of Rhiannon*, and *The Virgin and the Swine* (also published as *The Island of the Mighty*).

A1632   ZAHORSKI, KENNETH J., and BOYER, ROBERT H. *Lloyd Alexander, Evangeline Walton Ensley, and Kenneth Morris: A Primary and Secondary Bibliography*. Boston: G.K. Hall, 1981, 291 pp.
For each of these three authors, linked by their use of the Mabinogion in their fantasy writings, there is a biocritical introduction and annotated listings of primary and secondary sources.

MACAULAY, DAVID (1946-   )

A1633   AMMON, RICHARD. "Profile: David Macaulay." *LA* 59 (April 1982):374-78.
Reports on a visit to Macaulay and carefully traces his development as an artist. Includes a bibliography of Macaulay's books.

A1634   HOARE, GEOFFREY. "The Work of David Macaulay." *CLE*, n.s. 8, no. 1 (Spring 1977):12-20.
A critical assessment of Macaulay's drawings and texts, suggesting

areas that might have been improved.

A1635 STOTT, JON C. "Architectural Structures and Social Values in the Non-fiction of David Macaulay." *ChLAQ* 8, no. 1 (Spring 1983):15-17.
Explores the ways in which Macaulay, in each of six books, communicates his "own interpretation of the nature and value of the interrelationship between the various constructions and the socio-cultural beliefs of their builders."

McCLOSKEY, ROBERT (1914-   )

A1636 ARCHER, MARGUERITE P. "Robert McCloskey, Student of Human Nature." *EE* 35 (May 1958):287-96.
Analyzes the success of McCloskey's stories, especially those involving Homer Price.

A1637 BADER, BARBARA. *American Picturebooks*, pp. 154-57.
Discusses *Lentil* as the "All-American small-town boy," not very different from McCloskey himself. Also discusses *Make Way for Ducklings* and *Blueberries for Sal*. Feels *One Morning in Maine* and *Time of Wonder* express more adults' feelings than children's.

A1638 DUFF, ANNIS. "Robert McCloskey: Man, Author, Artist, All-of-a-Piece." *Catholic Library World* 45 (March 1974):382-83.
Sees McCloskey's integrity as a person, an author, and an artist as the key to his success with children.

A1639 GUGLER, ERIC, and DAUGHERTY, JAMES. "Comment." *Horn Book* 19 (November-December 1943):424-26.
"What a universal and delightful brat, this Homer Price!" writes Gugler. Daugherty praises the drawings: "The way these boys fit into their pants, wear their shirts, and the way the folds of their clothes pull with every movement is all there to intensify vivid humor and real character."

A1640 HARBAGE, MARY. "Robert McCloskey: He Doesn't Forget." *EE* 31 (May 1954):251-59.
Describes McCloskey's work and the sources of his writings.

A1641 LARRICK, NANCY. "Robert McCloskey's *Make Way for Ducklings*." *EE* 37 (March 1960):143-48.
Describes the work that went into the writing and design of the book. Explores McCloskey's protest against the overwhelming mechanization of society.

A1642 McCLOSKEY, ROBERT. "The Caldecott Medal Acceptance." *Horn Book* 4 (July-August 1942):277-82.
Tells how the idea for *Make Way for Ducklings* originated and how he did the drawings.

A1643 MAY, JILL P. "How to Sell Doughnuts: Media & Children's Literature." *LA* 56 (April 1979):375-79.
Reviews *Homer Price* and two films based on it.

A1644 PAINTER, HELEN. "Robert McCloskey: Master of Humorous Realism." *EE* 45 (February 1968):145-58. (Reprinted in Hoffman,

Authors and Illustrators, pp. 308-26.)
A biographical and critical survey, discussing works beginning with *Lentil* through *Burt Dow*. Extensive references.

A1645 SAWYER, RUTH. "Robert McCloskey: Good Craftsman and Fine Artist." *Publishers Weekly* 141 (27 June 1942):2348-50.
A brief biocritical overview.

McCORD, DAVID (1897-   )

A1646 LARSON, MARILYN HEERS. "David McCord: Poetry for the Young." *ChLAQ* 5, no. 2 (Summer 1980):22-24.
Provides an overview of McCord's poetry for the young.

A1647 LIVINGSTON, MYRA COHN. "David McCord: The Singer, the Song, and the Sung." *Horn Book* 55 (February 1979):25-39.
High praise for McCord with many of his poems and snatches of them included as evidence of his ability to assimilate the past, to give it a unique voice, and to capture his own childhood experience in a way that today's children understand.

McDERMOTT, GERALD (1940-   )

A1648 DOOLEY, PATRICIA. "Gerald McDermott." *ChLAQ* 3, no. 4 (Winter 1979):1-4.
McDermott's work "remains controversial for the best of reasons: it is original, thoughtful, and makes few concessions to common children's book conventions."

A1649 McDERMOTT, GERALD. "On the Rainbow Trail." *Horn Book* 51 (April 1975):123-31.
Tells of his background and of the making of *Arrow to the Sun*. This same issue includes his Caldecott Award acceptance speech for the book, pp. 349-54, and a biographical sketch by Priscilla Moulton, pp. 355-58.

A1650 STEVENS, CAROL. "Gerald McDermott: Animating Myth and Legend." *Print* 27 (November 1973):36-41.
A biocritical overview.

A1651 WHITE, DAVID E. "Profile: Gerald McDermott." *LA* 59 (March 1982):273-79.
In an interview McDermott discusses his background, the course of his career, and major influences--including that of the unconscious--on his work.

MacDONALD, GEORGE (1824-1905)

A1652 AUDEN, W.H. "Afterword." *Horn Book* 43 (April 1967):176-77. (Also in Meek, *The Cool Web*, pp. 103-5, in Auden's *Forewords and Afterwords* [New York: Random House, 1973], pp. 268-73.)
Analyzes MacDonald as a master of "Dream Literature."

A1653 CARPENTER, HUMPHREY. "George MacDonald and the Tender Grandmother." In *Secret Gardens*, pp. 70-85.
Examines MacDonald's work in relationship to that of Kingsley and Carroll, finding religious questioning and disillusionment, and

unusual sexual preoccupations.

A1654   DOUGLASS, JANE. "Dealings with the Fairies." *Horn Book* 37 (August 1961):327-35.

An appreciative introduction to MacDonald, summarizing the appraisals of past critics.

A1655   FABEN, ALINE SIDNEY. "Folklore in the Fantasies and Romances of George MacDonald." Ph.D. dissertation, State University of New York at Buffalo, 1978, 200 pp., DA 39:294A.

Finds that the "mythopoeic" strength of MacDonald's work comes from his use of the folklore of his native Scotland and the "imagery and structure borrowed from folklore by literary tradition," as represented by the Bible, Dante, Spenser, Bunyan, Wordsworth, and E.T.A. Hoffman.

A1656   HEIN, ROLLAND. *The Harmony Within: The Spiritual vision of George MacDonald.* Grand Rapids, Mich.: Eerdman's Christian University Press, 1962, 163 pp.

Provides a highly religious interpretation of MacDonald's fantasies for children, pp. 29-53.

A1657   HUTTON, M. "Writers for Children: 4. George MacDonald." *School Librarian* 12, no. 3 (December 1964):244-54.

Summarizes a number of critical points of view on MacDonald's work for children. Includes bibliographies.

A1658   JENKINS, SUE. "Love, Loss, and Seeking: Maternal Deprivaiton and the Quest." *CLE*, n.s. 15, no. 2 (Summer 1984):73-84.

Examines the influence of early loss of their mothers on the overall tone, attitudes, and assumptions in the fantasies of George MacDonald, C.S. Lewis, and J.R.R. Tolkien.

A1659   LOCHHEAD, MARION. *The Renaissance of Wonder in Children's Literature.* Edinburgh: Canongate, 1977, 169 pp.

Traces MacDonald's use and interpretation of traditional fairy lore, particularly that of Scotland, and his influence on later writers of fantasy and their use of fairy lore, including E. Nesbit, Rudyard Kipling, John Masefield and Walter De la Mare, James Stephens and Patricia Lynch in Ireland, and especially C.S. Lewis and J.R.R. Tolkien. Chapter 3, "Magic Journeys," pp. 18-35, concentrates on the fairy tales for children: *At The Back of the North Wind*, *The Golden Key*, *The Princess and the Goblin*, and *The Princess and Curdie.* Chapter 5, "George MacDonald and Hans Christian Andersen," points out similarities between the two in their handling of materials borrowed from the past. Chapter 7, "An Edwardian Successor," is devoted to E. Nesbit's fantasies, chapters 10-11, pp. 82-100, to C.S. Lewis's Narnia series, and chapters 12-14, pp. 101-25, to Tolkien. The final chapters briefly discuss a number of recent writers of fantasy including Susan Cooper, Alan Garner, and Ursula K. Le Guin.

A1660   MacDONALD, GEORGE. "*Signal* Reprints: The Fantastic Imagination." *Signal* 16 (January 1975):26-32.

MacDonald reveals his attitudes toward fairy tales and to his own "broken music."

A1661   McGILLIS, RODERICK. "Language and Secret Knowledge in *At the Back of the North Wind.*" *Proceedings of the Children's Literature Association* 7 (1980):120-27.

Explores the meaning of poetry and the nature of fantasy, reality, and truth in MacDonald's work.

A1662   PIERSON, CLAYTON JOY. "Toward Spiritual Fulfillment: A Study of the Fantasy World of George MacDonald." Ph.D. dissertation, University of Maryland, 1978, 287 pp., DA 39:6148A.

Sees MacDonald's work as unified by "the journey which leads to spiritual fulfillment." Analyzes the themes and symbols that he utilizes to communicate his "emphatic Christian world-view."

A1663   REIS, RICHARD H. *George MacDonald.* Twayne's English Authors Series, no. 119. New York: Twayne, 1972, 161 pp.

Attempts to understand MacDonald's place in literature by examining his life, his philosophical ideas, his attempts to teach through his writings, and his "ventures into the the unpopular symbolism for which he will be remembered."

A1664   SADLER, GLENN EDWARD. "An Unpublished Children's Story by George MacDonald." *Children's Literature* 2 (1973):18-34.

Includes a three-page introduction to the story "The Little Girl that Had No Tongue," which is also printed.

A1665   WILLARD, NANCY. "Goddess in the Belfry." *Parabola* 6, no. 3 (Summer 1981):90-94.

Explores MacDonald's mixture of pagan and Christian mysteries in a single figure of a "goddess," called different names in his various books.

A1666   -----. "The Nonsense of Angels: George MacDonald *At the Back of the North Wind.*" *Proceedings of the Children's Literature Association* 5 (1978):106-12. (Reprinted in May, *Children and Their Literature*, pp. 34-40.)

Claims that MacDonald hides truth under a veil of nonsense in his riddles, nursery rhymes, fairy tales, and dreams.

A1667   WILSON, ANITA C. Review of Rolland Hein's *The Harmony Within: The Spiritual Vision of George MacDonald. ChLAQ* 9, no. 1 (Spring 1984):40.

Concentrates on Hein's handling of MacDonald's works for children. "Hein's study provides both a good introduction to MacDonald and insights of interest to those well acquainted with MacDonald's work."

McFARLANE, LESLIE (1902-77)
[Wrote the first twenty-six Hardy Boys books and three of the Dana Girls series under the pseudonym Franklin W. Dixon]

A1668   McFARLANE, LESLIE. *Ghost of the Hardy Boys.* Agincourt, Ontario: Methuen, 1976, 211 pp.

McFarlane's autobiography provides insights into the workings of the Stratemeyer Syndicate.

A1669   PALMER, DAVID. "A Last Talk with Leslie McFarlane." *CCL* 11 (1978):5-17.

In an interview McFarlane discusses his literary career, especially his writing of the first Hardy Boys as Franklin W. Dixon. "A Selected McFarlane Bibliography" follows, pp. 18-19. See also "Robin Hood in the Arctic," by David Palmer, pp. 59-62, which primarily discusses Methuen's publication of adaptations of McFarlane's magazine stories from the 1920s and 1930s.

McGINLEY, PHYLLIS (1905-   )

A1670   WAGNER, LINDA W. *Phyllis McGinley.* Twayne's United States Authors Series, no. 170. New York: Twayne, 1971, 128 pp.
         This biocritical study discusses McGinley's poems and stories for children on pages 68-74, 82-87, and 109-10. Includes bibliographies of primary and secondary sources.

MACKEN, WALTER (1915-67)

A1671   ENGLAND, A.W. "Writers for Children: Walter Macken." *Use of English* 26 (Autumn 1974):44-49.
         Discusses the themes, style, and techniques in *God Made Sunday, The Island of the Great Yellow Ox,* and *The Flight of the Doves.*

McKINLEY, ROBIN (1952-   )

A1672   MEEK, MARGARET. "Happily Ever After." *TLS*, 25 November 1983, p. 1212.
         Reviews *Beauty,* a modern derivative of Madame de Beaumont's *Beauty and the Beast.*

McLEAN, ALLAN CAMPBELL (1922-   )

A1673   JONES, CORNELIA, and WAY, OLIVIA R. *British Children's Authors,* pp. 114-20.
         In an interview McLean discusses his background, philosophy, and method of working. Includes an annotated bibliography of his works.

MacPHERSON, MARGARET (1908-   )

A1674   JONES, CORNELIA, and WAY, OLIVIA R. *British Children's Authors,* pp. 121-26.
         In an interview MacPherson discusses her background, philosophy, and method of working. Includes an annotated bibliography of her works.

McNEILL, JANET (1907-   )

A1675   MOSS, ELAINE. "'Go On! Go On!': Janet McNeill and *The Battle of St. George Without.*" *Signal* 6 (September 1971):96-101.
         A biocritical overview.

Mad Magazine

A1676   CASKEY, JEFFERSON. "*Mad* Deserves Attention." *LA* 52 (November-December 1975):1157-58.
         Argues that *Mad* is "a highly sophisticated satiric commentary on virtually all phases of American culture," and deserves more serious

attention.

A1677 SPENCER, THOMAS E. "Alfred E. Neuman: Who Is He?" *Reading Improvement* 13 (Summer 1976):103-4.
Analyzes the character and role of *Mad*'s Alfred E. Neuman.

MAJOR, KEVIN (1949-   )

A1678 JONES, RAYMOND E. "Local Color, Universal Problems: The Novels of Kevin Major." *ChLAQ* 10 (Fall 1985):140-41.
Praises Major's novels of adolescent life in "the outports of Newfoundland."

MALKUS, ALIDA SIMS (1899-   )

A1679 DAVIS, MARY M. *"Caravans to Santa Fe, Raquel of the Ranch Country* and *The Dragon Fly of Zuni." Horn Book* 5 (May 1929):47-51.
Reviews the three books, concluding that *Caravans* "lacks life," *Raquel* does not make one "feel the tingle of the free life of the saddle," and the *Dragon Fly* lags and is bogged down in detail. More swift action and less description is urged.

A1680 MALKUS, ALIDA SIMS. "Two Thousand Miles of Background." *Horn Book* 5 (February 1929):38-46.
Describes her experiences in the Southwest, mainly in New Mexico, which provide the background for her books.

A1681 -----. "Who Can Tell It Best?" *Horn Book* 5 (August 1929):41-46.
In part a response to Mary Davis's review of her books in the previous issue; defends her techniques as accurately representing the cultures she describes.

MANNING, ROSEMARY (1911-   )

A1682 MOSS, ELAINE. "Rosemary Manning's *Arripay*: Variation on a Theme." *Signal* 2 (May 1970):31-35.
Praises Manning's combination of readability and quality.

MANNING, RUSS (1929-   )

A1683 HOLTSMARK, ERLING B. *"Magnus, Robot-Fighter*: The Future Looks at the Past." *Journal of Popular Culture* 12, no. 4 (Spring 1979):691-701.
Explores classical undercurrents (going back to the Greeks) of the comic strip *Magnus, Robot Fighter*.

MARK, JAN (1943-   )

A1684 HUNT, PETER. "Whatever Happened to Jan Mark?" *Signal* 31 (January 1980):11-19.
Traces changes in Mark's style from *Thunder and Lightnings* (1976) through *Divide and Rule* (1979).

A1685 MARCH-PENNY, ROBBIE. "I Don't Want to Learn Things, I'd Just Rather Find Out." *CLE*, n.s. 10, no. 1 (Spring 1979):18-24.
Analyzes *Thunder and Lightnings* and suggests critical approaches suitable for classroom use.

A1686 REES, DAVID. "No Such Thing as Fairness--Jan Mark." In *Painted Desert*, pp. 62-74. (Originally published in *School Librarian*, September 1981, in slightly different form.)

Analyzes *Thunder and Lightnings* and traces Mark's development as a writer, pointing out strengths and weaknesses in subsequent books. Disagrees with Peter Hunt's assessment in "Whatever Happened to Jan Mark?" (see above) that Mark has gone steadily downhill.

A1687 WHITEHEAD, WINIFRED. "Jan Mark." *Use of English* 33 (Spring 1982):32-39.

Provides detailed discussions of Mark's books to date. Sees the first four as concerned with "the problem of the isolated individual, stubbornly battling his own way against odds and in some measure bringing down upon himself his own consequent pain and retribution."

MARSHAK, SAMUEL (1887-1964)

A1688 BERMAN, DINA. "Samuel Marshak's Verses for Children: A Computer Aided Analysis." Ph.D. dissertation, University of Pennsylvania, 1966, 276 pp., DA 28:0222A.

Analyzes and describes the characteristics of Marshak's children's poetry, especially vocabulary and grammatical structure.

A1689 MORTON, MIRIAM. "'A Great Literature for Little Folk': Samuel Marshak, 1887-1964." *Horn Book* 42 (June 1966):335-44.

An overview of Marshak's contribution to Soviet children's literature.

MARTIN, BILL, Jr. (1916-   )

A1690 LARRICK, NANCY. "Profile: Bill Martin, Jr." *LA* 59 (May 1982):490-94.

Although there is little criticism here, Larrick presents a lively portrait of Martin and the mind and motivation behind his many books.

MARTIN, DAVID (1915-   )

A1691 FACTOR, JUNE. "David Martin's Writing for Children." *Overland* 79 (April 1980):47-54.

Follows Martin's development as a children's writer, noting the cultural and social values that underlie his work, and tracing the increasing skill and complexity of his writing.

A1692 McVITTY, WALTER. "David Martin: Alienation and Belonging." In *Innocence and Experience*, pp. 163-95.

Provides an extensive analysis of David Martin's works for children, which are seen as "essentially preoccupied with love, struggle, and a sorrowful awareness of man's unfortunate capacity for inhumanity towards man." Includes a biographical sketch, comments by Martin, and a bibliography of his books.

A1693 MARTIN, DAVID. "Books for and About Louts." *Overland* 65 (1976):63-67.

Reflects on the difficulty or impossibility of writing for children truly honest books which take into account difficult social and moral issues.

MARUKI, TOSHI (1912-   )

A1694   STUDIER-CHANG, CATHERINE. "Point of View: *Hiroshima No Pika*--for Mature Audiences." *Advocate* 3, no. 3 (Spring 1984):158, 166-70.
Studier-Chang argues that the book is not suitable for children; but Hiroko Sasaki, representing a Japanese perspective, disagrees, pp. 159-64. Children's comments follow, pp. 172-76.

Marvel Comics

A1695   MacDONALD, ANDREW, and MacDONALD, VIRGINIA. "Solid American: The Metamorphosis of Captain America." *Journal of Popular Culture* 10, no. 1 (Summer 1976):249-55.
"Captain America, the star-spangled superhero from the hallowed halls of Marveldom, has undergone a metamorphosis that parallels America's movement from the super-patriotic Forties to the disillusioned present."

A1696   PALUMBO, DONALD. "The Marvel Comics Group's Spider-Man is an Existentialist Super-Hero; or 'Life Has No Meaning without My Latest Marvel!'" *Journal of Popular Culture* 17, no. 2 (Fall 1983):67-81.
Analyzes Spider-Man as an existentialist hero.

MASEFIELD, JOHN (1878-1967)

A1697   FISHER, MARGERY. *John Masefield.* London: Bodley Head, 1963, 66 pp.
A biocritical overview, emphasizing Masefield's books for children. Includes a bibliography of books by Masefield that are of interest to children and young people.

A1698   HOLLINDALE, PETER. "John Masefield." *CLE*, o.s., no. 23 (Winter 1976):187-95.
Reevaluates Masefield as a children's writer and storyteller and discusses the influence of some of his works on more recent children's writers. Highly praises *The Midnight Folk* and *Box of Delights*.

MAVRINA, TATYANA (1902-   )

A1699   TURKOV, ANDREI. "Tatyana Mavrina--Fairy Tale, Native Country, Beauty." *Bookbird* 13, no. 2 (1976):7-9.
Reflects upon the art of the Soviet winner of the 1976 Hans Christian Andersen Award for illustration.

MAYER-SKUMANZ, LENE (1939-   )

A1700   MERGILI, TRUDI. "Lene Mayer-Skumanz--A Profile of An Award-Winning Austrian Author." *Bookbird* 3 (1981):24-28.
A brief biocritical overview of this winner of the two major Austrian prizes for juvenile literature in 1981 and 1982.

MAYNE, WILLIAM (1928-   )

A1701   ALDERSON, BRIAN. "On the Littoral: William Mayne's *The Jersey Shore*." *Children's Literature Review* 3, no. 5 (October 1973):133-35.
Feels that with this book Mayne has crossed the edge and written a book "where the complexity of experience requires more than childish resources for its appreciation."

A1702   BLISHEN, EDWARD. "Writers for Children 2: William Mayne." *Use of English* 20 (Winter 1968):99-103. (Reprinted in Butts, *Good Writers*, pp. 79-85.)
Praises Mayne's understanding and portrayal of children and his recognition of their use of language, their awareness of the senses, and their interest in his themes of bold constructions and disasters.

A1703   HEINS, PAUL. "Off the Beaten Path." *Horn Book* 49 (December 1973):580-81.
The Jersey Shore tells "a mere wisp of a story," straying like Alan Garner, but in another direction, from the "beaten path of children's fiction."

A1704   -----. Review. *Horn Book* 47 (February 1971):40.
Examines *Ravensgill*, and praises Mayne's style.

A1705   HUNT, PETER. "The Mayne Game: An Experiment." *Signal* 28 (January 1979):9-25.
Reports on an attempt to shed light on conflicting opinions on Mayne's work by giving his books to a group of postgraduate students in English to evaluate. Raises important questions about the definitions and criticism of children's literature. Hunt also illuminates Mayne's distinguishing characteristics and the disagreements about his work.

A1706   INGLIS, FRED. *Promise of Happiness*, pp. 12-15, 228-31, 253-57.
Groups Mayne with Gillian Avery and Penelope Lively as a writer of "historical fiction off the main road." Sees Mayne as addressing himself "to the point at which past and present, individual biography and historical movement may be caught in intersection." Discusses *No More School*, pp. 12-15, *Jersey Shore*, pp. 230-31, and *Earthfasts*, pp. 253-57. Judges *Earthfasts* to be classic and praises Mayne's plain, vivid prose.

A1707   MAYNE, WILLIAM. "A Discussion with William Mayne." *CLE*, o.s., no. 2 (July 1970):48-55.
A tense and enigmatic interview, perhaps revealing in that Mayne reflects so little about himself and his work. "My public expression is what I write, and I don't see that 'I' am relevant."

A1708   MOON, KENNETH. "Don't Tell It: Show It: The Force of Metaphor in *A Game of Dark*." *School Librarian* 31, no. 46 (December 1983):319-27.
Examines the powerful use of metaphor in the book, which he compares with Penelope Lively's *The Driftway* and Philippa Pearce's *A Dog So Small*.

A1709   SARLAND, CHARLES. "Chorister Quartet." *Signal* 18 (September 1975):107-13. (Reprinted in *Signal Approach*, pp. 217-24.)

Examines the style of the four Cathedral Choir School books: *A Swarm In May*, *Cathedral Wednesday*, *Words and Music*, and *Choristers' Cake*.

A1710 TOWNSEND, JOHN ROWE. *Sense of Story*, pp. 130-42.
Defends Mayne against charges that he's a children's writer only for adults. "If a book opens windows in the imagination of only one child, it justifies its existence." Feels that his tendency to shy away from the passions is the cause of his failure; nevertheless, admires his style and skill.

A1711 -----. *A Sounding*, pp. 139-52.
Updates and revises the earlier essay in *Sense of Story*. Feels Mayne grows closer to dealing with emotion and deep feeling in *Ravensgill*, *A Game of Dark* (which he is not sure is for children), and *The Jersey Shore*.

A1712 WALKER, ALISTAIR. "Landscape as Metaphor in the Novels of William Mayne." *CLE*, n.s. 11, no. 1 (Spring 1980):31-42.
Centers on "the way in which Mayne uses landscape as part of the rhetoric of his fiction."

MEANS, FLORENCE CRANNELL (1891-1980)

A1713 ANDREWS, SIRI. "Florence Crannell Means." *Horn Book* 22 (January-February):15-30.
Although there is little real criticism here, the article is a thorough summary of Means's work to date, linking her books to her background and methods of working.

A1714 CROSSON, WILHELMINA M. "Florence Crannell Means." *EER* 17 (December 1940):321-24, 26.
Summarizes several of Means's books from the perspective of cross-cultural understanding.

A1715 KINGSTON, CAROLYN T. *Tragic Mode*, pp. 48-52.
Analyzes *Shuttered Windows* in terms of its them of rejection.

A1716 MEANS, FLORENCE CRANNELL. "Mosaic." *Horn Book* 16 (January-February 1940):35-40.
Describes the background of several of her regional and ethnic books: her experiences among the Navajo, the Chinese, and the Gullahs on the South Carolina coast.

A1717 PEASE, HOWARD. "Without Evasion: Some Reflections After Reading Mrs. Means' *The Moved Outers*." *Horn 2.4HBook* 21 (January-February 1945):9-17.
Classes Means with Doris Gates and John R. Tunis as an author who is not afraid to take up a modern problem and think it through without evasion. Reflects on the relocation of Japanese-Americans to concentration camps during World War II.

MEGGENDORFER, LOTHAR (1847-1925)

A1718 *The Publishing Archive of Lothar Meggendorfer: Original Drawings, Hand-Colored Lithographs and Production Files for His Children's Book Illustrations.* Appreciation by Maurice Sendak. New York:

Justin G. Schiller, 1975, 32 pp.
Includes an introduction by Justin G. Schiller and Sendak's "Appreciation," which argues that Meggendorfer turned the toy book into a work of art.

MEIGS, CORNELIA (1884-1973)

A1719 MURDOCH, CLARISSA. "Cornelia Meigs: Chronicler of the Sea." *EER* 5 (May 1928):148-49, 153.
This early appraisal points out that Meigs makes history come alive, writes truthfully and entertainingly, demonstrates her love of her country, and establishes atmosphere and appeals to her readers' imaginations.

A1720 SAUER, JULIA L. "The Books of Cornelia Meigs." *Horn Book* 20 (September-October 1944):347-55.
An appreciative summary of Meig's work to date that praises her craftsmanship and broad conceptions. A biographical account by Doris Patee follows, pp. 356-62.

MELTZER, MILTON (1915-   )

A1721 DE LUCA, GERALDINE, AND NATOV, RONI. "An Interview with Milton Meltzer." *L&U* 4, no. 1 (Summer 1980):95-107.
This prolific author of biographies and histories for children and adults tells how he became interested in this type of writing. Also discusses his goals and techniques in the *Women of America* series, which he edited, and several other works.

A1722 MELTZER, MILTON. "Who's Neutral?" *CLE*, o.s., no. 14 (1974):24-36.
Shares experiences from his own background that led to the writing of his many books on minorities. Describes the research and writing of several of his books, and defends his "biased" approach to history.

A1723 TCHEN, JOHN. Review. *IRBC* 12, no. 1 (1981):17.
Although Tchen's response to *The Chinese Americans* was largely favorable he objected to some oversimplifications.

A1724 WEEDMON, JUDITH. "A Step Aside from Self: The Work of Milton Meltzer." *ChLAQ* 10, no. 1 (Spring 1985):41-42.
Provides an overview of Meltzer's career as an author of books of history, biography, and sociology for young people.

MERRIAM, EVE (1916-   )

A1725 SLOAN, GLENNA. "Profile: Eve Merriam." *LA* 58 (November-December 1981):957-64.
In an interview Merriam discusses her life, her opinions on poetry for children, and her own work.

MIKOLAYCAK, CHARLES (1937-   )

A1726 MIKOLAYCAK, CHARLES. "The Artist at Work: The Challenge of the Picture Book." *Horn Book* 62 (March 1986):167-73.
Discusses his approach to illustration.

A1727 WHITE, DAVID E. "Profile: Charles Mikolaycak." *LA* 58 (October 1981):850-57.
A biocritical overview.

MIERS, EARL SCHENK (1910-72)

A1728 "The Old South Rises Again." *IRBC* 10, no. 8 (1980):10-14.
A highly critical review of *The How and Why History of the Civil War*.

MILHOUS, KATHERINE (1894-1977)

A1729 FIELD, CAROLYN. "A Second Look: *Through These Arches: The Story of Independence Hall*." *Horn Book* 52 (June 1976):310-11.
Comments on Milhous's purpose in writing the book.

A1730 MILHOUS, KATHERINE. "*The Egg Tree* and How It Grew." *Horn Book* 27 (July-August 1951):219-28.
Tells the story behind *The Egg Tree* and describes the controversy that followed its publication.

A1731 TEMPLIN, ELAINE. "Enjoying Festivals with Katherine Milhous." *EE* 34 (November 1957):435-43. (Reprinted in Hoffman, *Authors and Illustrators*, pp. 327-39.)
Discusses biographical influences on Milhous's work, her love of festivals, her desire to create with her hands, and her standard that good art must have an intangible, undefinable force that is felt rather than seen. Includes a bibliography of Milhous's books and of articles about her.

MILLAR, H.R. (1869-1939)

A1732 SMITH, LOUISA A. "The Magician's Conjuror: E. Nesbit's Illustrator, H.R. Millar." *Proceedings of the Children's Literature Association* 9 (1982):130-36.
Explores the contributions of Nesbit and Millar to each other's art.

MILLENDER, DHARATHULA H. (1920-   )

A1733 GRAMBS, JEAN DRESDEN. "*Crispus Attucks, Boy of Valor*: A Book Review." *Harvard Educational Review* 38 (Summer 1968):605-11. (Reprinted in MacCann, *Black American*, pp. 124-34.)
Criticizes Millender's treatment of Attucks on historical grounds.

MILNE, A.A. (1882-1956)

A1734 CARPENTER, HUMPHREY. "A.A. Milne and *Winnie-the-Pooh*: Farewell to the Enchanted Places." In *Secret Gardens*, pp. 188-209.
Paraphrases Milne's theme as "children may be Arcadians in their physical appearance, but the Arcadia they inhabit is not an ideal world of fine feelings, not a dream-come-true land at all. It is distinguished by the naked selfishness of its inhabitants."

A1735 COCK, GEOFFREY. "A.A. Milne: Sources of His Creativity." *American Imago* 34 (1977):313-26.

Provides a psychoanalytic interpretation of elements in Milne's life and work, particularly in his children's books.

A1736   CREWS, FREDERICK C. *The Pooh Perplex*. New York: E.P. Dutton, 1963, 150 pp.
Uses *Winnie the Pooh*, "one of the greatest books ever written," as the basis for a spoof on literary criticism. Contains articles written by such familiar academics as Harvey C. Window, Duns C. Penwiper, and Simon Lacerous. Provides insights into Pooh and techniques of literary criticism.

A1737   CROUCH, MARCUS. "Pooh Lives--O.K.?" *Junior Bookshelf* (October 1976). (Reprinted in *Bookbird* 15, no. 2 [1977]:14-16.)
Analyzes Milne's craftsmanship. "Each chapter can be taken entirely seriously--in critical terms--as a short story."

A1738   FARJEON, ELEANOR. "A.A. Milne." *Junior Bookshelf* 20, no. 2 (March 1956):51-59.
Praises Milne's ability to find the right word and capture the personalities of the nursery toys.

A1739   GUNDERSON, ETHEL A., and GUNDERSON, AGNES G. "A.A. Milne and Today's Seven-Year-Olds." *EE* 39 (May 1962):408-11.
Explains why Milne's poems appeal to children.

A1740   HARING-SMITH, TORI. *A.A. Milne: A Critical Bibliography*. New York: Garland, 1982, 344 pp.
Includes an introductory essay, "Milne's Reception by the Critics," pp. xvii-xxv, and lists of Milne's writings, including his work for children and their reviews, writings about Milne and his work, articles on Pooh, and a section on the writings of members of Milne's family.

A1741   HOLMSTRUM, JOHN. "Whisper Who Dares." *New Statesman* 12 (November 1965):752.
Reviews the collected Pooh books upon their republication.

A1742   LURIE, ALISON. "Back to Pooh Corner." *Children's Literature* 2 (1973):11-17.
Mentions the difficulties of attempting serious criticism of Pooh since Crews's *The Pooh Perplex*, nevertheless discusses biographical links, themes, and the hidden messages that seemed to have a particular appeal to the young adult of the 1970s.

A1743   -----. "Now We Are Fifty." *NYTBR*, 14 November 1976, Children's Book sec., pp. 27.
Finds that Milne's work has "universal appeal to any child anywhere who finds himself, like most children, at a social disadvantage in the adult world."

A1744   NOVAK, BARBARA. "Milne's Poems: Form and Content." *EE* 34 (October 1957):355-61.
Suggests that Milne's lyrical, whimsical, and intimate poetry relies on content and formal structure.

A1745   PHIFER, KENNETH W. "A Bear of Very Little Brain: A Commentary on the Pooh Saga." *Religious Humanism* 13 (Winter 1979):32-38.

Analyzes Pooh as embodying the "four characteristics of a religious person: worship, acceptance, love, and quest."

A1746 SALE, ROGER. *Fairy Tales*, pp. 15-18.
Finds he no longer enjoys Milne as he once did, and is offended by Milne's snobbery.

A1747 SINGER, DOROTHY G. "Piglet; Pooh and Piaget." *Psychology Today* 6 (June 1972):70-74, 96.
Shows how Milne has unconsciously depicted the world exactly as Jean Piaget says a preoperational child would see it.

A1748 STERCK, KENNETH. "The Real Christopher Robin: An Appreciation of A.A. Milne's Children's Verse." *CLE* 37, n.s. 11, no. 2 (Summer 1980):52-61.
Uses knowledge of the Milne family to interpret Milne's verse.

A1749 SWANN, THOMAS B. *A.A. Milne.* Twayne's English Author Series, no. 113. New York: Twayne, 1971, 153 pp.
Devotes four chapters of the book, which mainly concentrates on Milne's writings for adults, to his juveniles. These, Swann agrees, are his best work. Includes a bibliography.

A1750 TREMPER, ELLEN. "Istigorating *Winnie the Pooh.*" *L&U* 1, no. 1 (1977):33-46.
Argues that Milne's "exquisitely side-splitting humor is available almost exclusively to the grown-ups reading to the children."

A1751 VON SCHWEINITZ, ELEANOR. "Pooh without Milne." *Children's Book News* 2, no. 1 (January-February 1967):5-8.
Analyzes recent adaptations of the Pooh books.

A1752 WOODS, GEORGE A. "Winnie Was Not Pooh-Poohed." *NYTBR*, 2 June 1968, pp. 7, 28.
Reports on responses of his children, ranging in age from nineteen to three, to *Winnie the Pooh.*

MITCHELL, LUCY SPRAGUE (1878-1967)

A1753 BLOS, JOAN W. "Form and Content in Children's Books: A Critical Tribute to Lucy Sprague Mitchell." *CLE*, n.s. 8, no. 1 (Spring 1977):39-46.
Proposes that "Mrs. Mitchell's foremost contribution to children's literature was not her stories themselves but rather the naming and identification of a new and legitimate genre: realistic fiction for the pre-school child." Further discusses the relationship between form and content, fantasy and art.

A1754 MAHONY, BERTHA E. Review of *Another Here and Now Story Book. Horn Book* 13 (May 1937):164-66.
"These experimental stories have rhythm, pattern, and form. While in content they deal with familiar things, they treat of them significantly and, as the age advances, they lead away to wider horizons." Preceding article, pp. 158-63, by Mary Phelps and Margaret Wise Brown, provides a portrait of Mitchell and a bibliography of her books.

A1755 MITCHELL, LUCY SPRAGUE. Introduction to *Here and Now Story Book*, pp. 1-72. New York: Dutton, 1921, 360 pp.

Mitchell expresses her "here and now" philosophy, telling how the content of the stories originated and describing the kinds of stories suitable for different age groups of young children. She argues against giving folk and fairy tales to young children, on pp. 32-42. Beginning on p. 46 she pays special attention to the forms suitable for young children.

MITCHELL, W.O. (1914-   )

A1756 RICOU, LAURENCE. "Notes on Language and Learning in *Who Has Seen the Wind?*" *CCL* 10 (1977-78):3-17.

Provides a detailed analysis of Mitchell's 1947 novel, focusing on his portrayal of the child's point of view.

MIZUMURA, KAZUE

A1757 BENEDUCE, ANN, and MIZUMURA, KAZUE. "Bridges of Sights and Sounds from Other Cultures." In *Children's Books International 1: Proceedings and Book Catalog*. Boston: Boston Public Library, 1976, pp. 1-6.

Beneduce and Mizumura discuss the work of Mizumura, a Japanese artist-poet and illustrator.

MONJO, F[ERDINAND] N[ICHOLAS] III (1924-   )

A1758 MONJO, FERDINAND. "Great Men, Melodies, Experiments, Plots, Predictability, and Surprises." *Horn Book* 51 (October 1975):433-41.

Discusses his own books in this exploration of the nature of biography for children.

A1759 -----. "Human Saints." *CLE*, o.s., no. 22 (Autumn 1976):121-24.

This "iconoclastic biographer" explains his approach, his attempt "to give us back our heroes and heroines, divested of their spurious Calvinistic sainthood, but reinvested in warm flesh tints of their indisputable humanity."

MONTGOMERY, LUCY MAUD (1874-1942)

A1760 BOLGER, FRANCIS W.P. *The Years Before "Anne": The Early Career of Lucy Maud Montgomery*. Charlottestown, P.E.I: Prince Edward Island Heritage Foundation, 1975, 229 pp.

Based on Montgomery's letters, scrapbooks, and her autobiographical "The Alpine Path" (from *Everywoman's World* (June through November 1917), this biography of Montgomery's early life illuminates her work.

A1761 *Canadian Children's Literature* 1, no. 3 (Autumn 1975).

Special issue. Articles include Elizabeth Waterston's "Lucy Maud Montgomery 1874-1942," pp. 9-26, a survey of her life and work; Mary Rubio's "Satire, Realism, and Imagination in *Anne of Green Gables*," pp. 27-36, which compares the book to *Tom Sawyer* and *Huckleberry Finn*; and Gillian Thomas's "The Decline of Anne: Matron vs. Child," pp. 37-41. In "Canadian Writers: Lucy Maud and Emily Byrd," pp. 42-49, Ann S. Cowan looks at the Emily books. In "'Queer Children': L.M. Montgomery's Heroines," pp.

50-59, Muriel Whitaker examines the question of what makes Montgomery's heroines so memorable. In "The Land of Lost Content: The Use of Fantasy in L.M. Montgomery's Novels," pp. 60-70, Jane Cowan Fredeman examines the tension between fantasy and reality in the books. And finally, Jean Little, in "But What About Jane?," pp. 71-81, divides Montgomery's children into four types: Stock children, Non-Children, Exaggerated Children, and Real Children.

A1762 FRAZER, F.M. "Scarcely an End." *Canadian Literature* 63 (Winter 1975):89-92.
        Reviews Montgomery's posthumously published collection of short stories, *The Road to Yesterday*.

A1763 FRYATT, NORMA R. "A Second Look: *Emily of the New Moon.*" *Horn Book* 62 (March 1986):174-75.
        Concludes that, despite its weaknesses, "*Emily of the New Moon* is in many ways still an ideal story for girls."

A1764 GILLEN, MOLLIE. *The Wheel of Things: A Biography of L.M. Montgomery.* Don Mills, Ontario: Fitzhenry & Whiteside, 1975, 200 pp.
        Primarily biographical, but provides background for her books and tells of the writing and critical reception of *Anne of Green Gables*.

A1765 KATSURA, YUKO. "Red-haired Anne in Japan." *CCL* 34 (1984):57-60.
        Discusses the popular success and appeal of *Anne of Green Gables* in Japan since its first translation into Japanese in 1952.

A1766 SOLT, MARILYN. "The Uses of Setting in *Anne of Green Gables.*" *ChLAQ* 9, no. 4 (Winter 1984-85):179-80, 198.
        Suggests that one reason for the longstanding popularity of the book is "Montgomery's superb use of setting."

A1767 TAUSKEY, THOMAS E. "L.M. Montgomery and 'The Alpine Path, so hard, so steep.'" *CCL* 30 (1983):5-20.
        Re-examines the Emily books and evaluates the way the author has transmuted her remembered past "into powerful and puzzling forms."

A1768 WILLIS, LESLEY. "The Bogus Ugly Duckling: Anne Shirley Unmasked." *Dalhousie Review* 56, no. 2 (Summer 1976):247-51.
        Argues that much of the appeal of *Anne of Green Gables* "consists in its catering to a desire for wish-fulfillment and, on the part of the older reader, nostalgia for a sentimentally-envisioned past; and these desires are catered to largely through the use, or misuse, of myth and fairy tale, which are so distorted that only their pleasant associations remain."

A1769 WILMSHURST, REA. "L.M. Montgomery's Short Stories: A Preliminary Bibliography." *CCL* 29 (1983):25-34.
        Lists in chronological order the titles of 560 stories by Montgomery, and their place of publication, if known. One of Montgomery's stories, "Anna's Love Letters," is reprinted on pages 35-41.

MONTRESOR, BENI (1926-   )

A1770   MONTRESOR, BENI. "Caldecott Award Acceptance." *Horn Book* 41 (August 1965):368-74.
Tells of his background and influences on his work. Biographical sketch by Velma V. Varner follows, pp. 374-79.

MOORE, CLEMENT C.   (1779-1863)

A1771   MacDONALD, Ruth K. "Santa Claus in America: The Influence of *The Night Before Christmas.*" *ChLAQ* 8, no. 3 (Fall 1983):4-6.
Explores the origins of the famous poem and its influences on Christmas traditions and the image of Santa Claus.

MORDVINOFF, NICHOLAS (1911-   )

A1772   BADER, BARBARA. *American Picturebooks*, pp. 333-38.
Traces Mordvinoff's contributions to the art of the picture book.

MOWAT, FARLEY (1921-   )

A1773   CARVER, JOSEPH E. "Farley Mowat, An Author for All Ages." *British Columbia Library Quarterly* 32, no. 4 (April 1969):10-18.
Defends Mowat's work against criticisms and analyzes his appeal for both children and adults.

A1774   LUCAS, ALEC. "Farley Mowat: Writer for Young People." *CCL* 5&6 (1976):40-51.
A thoughtful analysis of Mowat's children's books; concludes that his success depends not only on his prowess as a storyteller, but also on his seriousness of purpose and his views "that contribute much of the intensity that makes his children's books far superior to the general run in our literature."

MUKERJI, DHAN GOPAL (1890-1936)

A1775   MUKERJI, DHAN GOPAL. "Fruits from the Living Tree: Introduction to *Bunny, Hound and Clown.*" *Horn Book* 13 (July-August 1936):206-10.
Describes his aims and goals in writing Hindu tales for American children.

A1776   SEEGER, ELIZABETH. "Dhan Mukerji and His Books." *Horn Book* 13 (July-August 1937):199-205.
A tribute to and brief summary of Mukerji's life and children's books. Includes a bibliography.

MUNARI, BRUNO (1907-   )

A1777   CIMIMO, MARIA. "The Picture Books of Bruno Munari." *New York Public Library Bulletin* 60 (November-December 1956):585-88.
Analyzes the unity and diversity in Munari's picture books.

NAGIBIN, JURIJ (1920-   )

A1778   COCHRUM, E. "Jurij Nagibin's Short Stories: Themes and Literary Criticism." Ph.D. dissertation, Michigan State University, 1977, 235 pp., DA 39:313A.

Chapter 3 of this study of the Soviet writer concentrates on his children's stories, especially those written during his most mature period, 1965-74.

NAKATANI, CHIYOKO (1930-   )

A1779   MOSS, ELAINE. "Chiyoko Nakatani." *Signal* 12 (September 1973):135-39.

In an interview Nakatani discusses her life and work.

NEEDHAM, VIOLET (1876-1965)

A1780   SALWAY, LANCE E. "Survival of the Fittest." *Children's Book News* 4, no. 1 (January-February 1969):5-7.

Examines reasons for the enduring popularity of Needham's books.

A1781   WRIGHT, HILARY. "Violet Needham: The Last of the Victorians." *Junior Bookshelf* 47, no. 5 (October 1983):191-95.

Calls for a reassessment of the work of this forgotten twentieth-century children's author. Includes a bibliography of Needham's full-length works.

NESBIT, E. [Edith Nesbit Bland] (1858-1924)

A1782   ALEXANDER, LLOYD. "A Second Look: *Five Children and It.*" *Horn Book* 61 (May 1985):354-55.

Praises Nesbit's wit and wisdom and calls the book "one of the most gloriously funny stories written for any age."

A1783   ARMSTRONG, DENNIS LEE. "E. Nesbit: An Entrance to *The Magic City.*" Ph.D. dissertation, Johns Hopkins University, 1974, 300 pp., DA 35:7897A.

Considers Nesbit's work in terms of "first the narrative form which presents and holds it together, and second the interplay and testing of social and literary fictions within that world as well as the interplay between her created world and the 'real' world inhabited by Nesbit and her reader."

A1784   BELL, ANTHEA. *E. Nesbit.* New York: Walck; London: Bodley Head, 1964, 83 pp.

Provides biographical background and traces Nesbit's career as a writer, concentrating on her Bastable stories and fantasies. Includes brief plot summaries of her children's books and a bibliography of their British and American editions.

A1785   BUCKLEY, MARY F. "Words of Power: Language and Reality in the Fantasy Novels of E. Nesbit and P.L. Travers." Ed.D. dissertation, East Texas State University, 1977, 143 pp., DA 38:6686A.

Examines the relationship of reality and language as perceived by children and by E. Nesbit and P.L. Travers. Concentrates on a selection of Nesbit's magic books and the four major *Mary Poppins* books by Travers.

A1786   CARPENTER, HUMPHREY. "E. Nesbit: A Victorian in Disguise." In *Secret Gardens*, pp. 126-37.

Questions Nesbit's reputation as a great children's writer, suggesting she was, rather, an expert copier and a writer easy to copy. Sees her as popularizing and adapting Kenneth Grahame's view of childhood.

A1787 CROUCH, MARCUS. "E. Nesbit in Kent." *Junior Bookshelf* 19 (January 1955):11-12.

Traces the geographical influences in Nesbit's work.

A1788 -----. *The Nesbit Tradition*, p. 16.

Maintains, "No writer for children today is free of debt to this remarkable woman . . . she managed to create prototypes of many of the basic patterns in modern children's fiction." Explains why he has chosen her as the starting point for his book on recent British children's literature.

A1789 CROXSON, MARY. "The Emancipated Child in the Novels of E. Nesbit." *Signal* 14 (May 1974):51-64.

Sees Nesbit as one of the more powerful agents for change in children's lot at the beginning of the twentieth century. Examines the freedom of the children in her novels.

A1790 ELLIS, ALEC. "E. Nesbit and the Poor." *Junior Bookshelf* 38, no. 2 (April 1974):73-79.

Examines Nesbit's portrayal of poverty and her related political beliefs.

A1791 FROMM, GLORIA G. "E. Nesbit and the Happy Moralist." *Journal of Modern Literature* 11 (March 1984):45-65.

Relates Nesbit's art to her life and describes her strange mix of fiction and reality in "The Book of Beasts" (a story in *The Book of Dragons*) and *The Enchanted Castle*.

A1792 HAND, NIGEL. "The Other E. Nesbit." *Use of English* 26 (Winter 1974):108-16.

Argues that Nesbit's best books are *House of Arden* and *Harding's Luck*, which are little known and unavailable in paperback, but reflect her Fabian socialist views.

A1793 INGLIS, FRED. *Promise of Happiness*, pp. 113-17.

Sees *The Railway Children* in terms of altruism and "the best of liberal values" of Victorian society and praises the "light, bright, and brisk" tone.

A1794 *Junior Bookshelf* 22, no. 4 (October 1958).

Special issue. Includes Noel Streatfeild's "The Nesbit Influence," Roger Lancelyn Green's "E. Nesbit: Treasure-Seeker," and Marcus Crouch's "The Nesbit Tradition." Also includes a note on Nesbit's illustrators, pp. 199-201. Vol. 6 (December 1958):321-22, contains "A Further Note on Illustrators of E. Nesbit," by Roger L. Green.

A1795 KRENSKY, STEPHEN. "A Second Look: *The Story of the Treasure Seekers*." *Horn Book* 54 (June 1978):310-12.

Argues that Nesbit's characters may be the key to the survival of her books.

A1796 LANSNER, HELEN. "The Genius of E. Nesbit." *EE* 43 (January

1966):53-55.
An appreciative introduction to Nesbit's work.

A1797　"Magic and the Magician." *Horn Book* 34 (October 1958):347-73.
A special section on Nesbit on the 100th anniversary of her birth. Includes articles by Edward Eager, a personal recollection by Mavis Strange, a description by Eleanor Graham, of two of Nesbit's childhood homes, and a selection from Noel Streatfeild's biography.

A1798　MANLOVE, COLIN. "Fantasy As Witty Conceit: E. Nesbit." *Mosaic* 10, no. 2 (Winter 1977):109-30.
Sees Nesbit's work as fanciful rather than imaginative, as lacking "deeply felt spiritual meaning," but nevertheless reaching "a high point of wit and ingenuity," displaying "zest for life," and combining opposites with a "variety, skill and comic potential unequalled before her or since."

A1799　SMITH, BARBARA. "The Expression of Social Values in the Writing of E. Nesbit." *Children's Literature* 3 (1974):153-64.
Discusses the ways in which Nesbit's Fabian-Socialist views are expressed in her children's books. This issue also contains Joan Evans de Alonso's personal reminiscence, "E. Nesbit's Well Hall, 1915-1921: A Memoir."

A1800　STREATFEILD, NOEL. *Magic and the Magician: E. Nesbit and Her Children's Books.* London: Abelard-Schuman, 1958, 160 pp.
Explores Nesbit's childhood for the roots of her books, and examines ten of her books in depth.

NEVILLE, EMILY (1919-   )

A1801　KINGSTON, CAROLYN T. *Tragic Mode*, pp. 152-55.
Analyzes the themes of loss and death in *It's Like This, Cat.*

A1802　NEVILLE, EMILY CHENEY, "Optimism: Is It Possible in This World?" In Robinson, M., *Readings in Children's Literature*, pp. 271-93.
Expresses her views on children's literature in this speech given at an Australian seminar. Compares Australian and American children's books and values, and discusses the origins of her *Garden of Broken Glass.*

NEWBERRY, CLARE TURLAY (1903-70)

A1803　BADER, BARBARA. *American Picturebooks*, pp. 241-46.
Discusses *Herbert and the Lion* in its various incarnations, and Newberry's cat books.

NEWFELD, FRANK (1928-   )

A1804　GHAN, LINDA. "Interview with Frank Newfeld." *CCL* 17 (1980):3-19.
The Canadian illustrator discusses his work in this lengthy interview.

NICHOLS, RUTH (1948-   )

A1805　"Ruth Nichols: An Interview." *ChLAQ* 2, no. 2 (Summer 1977):2-4.

Discusses her approach to writing.

A1806 STORE, R.E. "Ruth Nichols: An Outstanding Canadian Author."
Orana 14 (November 1978):134-36.

A1807 STOTT, JON. "An Interview with Ruth Nichols." *CCL* 12 (1978):5-19.
Nichols discusses her life and her work in an interview. See also
Robert MacDonald's review of her *Song of the Pearl* in this same
issue, pp. 47-49.

NICHOLSON, NORMAN (1914-   )

A1808 HAY, PHILLIP, and WYANN-JONES, ANGHARAD. "An Interview
with Norman Nicholson." *Signal* 43 (January 1984):19-32.
The poet discusses poetry, his own and that of others, with two
children.

NICHOLSON, WILLIAM (1872-1949)

A1809 LANES, SELMA G. "A Second Look: *Clever Bill.*" *Horn Book* 53
(December 1977):694-96.
Analyzes the enduring, simple charm of the book.

NORDHOFF, CHARLES (1877-1947), and HALL, JAMES N. (1887-1951)

A1810 CORYELL, HUBERT, and CORYELL, HUBERT, Jr. Reviews of *Fal-
cons of France. Horn Book* 6 (February 1930):63-71.
Highly favorable pair of detailed reviews by father and son.

NORTON, ANDRE [Alice Mary Norton] (1912-   )

A1811 CROUCH, MARCUS. *The Nesbit Tradition*, pp. 54-55.
High praise for Norton, for her ability to create atmosphere, and
for her skill as a teller of tales.

A1812 FISHER, MARGERY. "Writers for Children: 8. Andre Norton." *School
Librarian* 15 (July 1967):146-50.
A critical survey of Norton's "space-operas." Schlobin calls this
article "The best of the critical discussions of Norton's fiction."

A1813 HENSLEY, CHARLOTTA. "Andre Norton's Science Fiction and Fantasy, 1950-1979: An Introduction to the Topics of Philosophical
Reflection, Imaginary Voyages and Future Prediction in Selected
Books for Young Readers." Ph.D. dissertation, University of Colorado at Boulder, 1980, 240 pp., DA 41:3580A.
Provides an introductory, chronological overview of three major
topics appearing in Norton's science fiction and fantasy for younger
readers since 1950.

A1814 McGHAN, BARRY. "Andre Norton: Why Has She Been Neglected?"
Riverside Quarterly 4 (January 1970):128-31.
Explores major elements of Norton's writing as well as the ques-
tion of why she has been neglected. Letters in response from Sam
Moskowitz and Sandra Miesel in June 1970, pp. 221-22.

A1815 SCHLOBIN, ROGER C. *Andre Norton: A Primary and Secondary
Bibliography.* Boston: G.K. Hall, 1980, 68 pp.

The introduction to this bibliography provides a biographical and critical overview. The bibliography includes all of Norton's writings and an extensively annotated listing of "Criticism, Biography and Selected Reviews," pp. 35-51.

A1816 SMITH, KAREN PATRICIA. "Claiming a Place in the Universe: The Portrayal of Minorities in Seven Works by Andre Norton." *TON* 42 (Winter 1986):165-72.
Explores Norton's use of realistic minority characters in "unusual and out-of-the-ordinary circumstances."

A1817 TOWNSEND, JOHN ROWE. *Sense of Story*, pp. 143-53.
Describes Norton's science fiction as "space opera." Discusses the "Star" books and her "hard, dry, somewhat impersonal style," praising her ability to tell "strong, fast-moving stories."

A1818 WOLF, VIRGINIA L. "Andre Norton: Feminist Pied Piper in SF." *ChLAQ* 10, no. 2 (Summer 1985):66-70.
Suggests that in Norton's novels since 1970, she has lured her readers to a feminist point of view.

NORTON, MARY (1903-   )

A1819 DAVENPORT, JULIA. "The Narrative Framework of *The Borrowers*: Mary Norton and Emily Brontë." *CLE*, n.s. 14, no. 2 (Summer 1983):75-79.
Finds parallels in the story-within-a-story technique used by Brontë in *Wuthering Heights* and by Norton in *The Borrowers*.

A1820 HAND, NIGEL. "Mary Norton and *The Borrowers*." *CLE*, o.s., no. 7 (March 1972):38-55.
Contends that Norton is one of the two or three most satisfying and rewarding writers for children of the last twenty years.

A1821 -----. "Mary Norton, Fred Inglis, and the World We Have Lost." In Butts, *Good Writers*, pp. 86-93.
Argues that "the creative imagination" is a central preoccupation of Mary Norton. Feels Inglis's analysis of Norton's theme as one of retreat from the world is inaccurate because she uses "reaching into the past" as "a creative process wherein grow values with which the present and the future can be met."

A1822 HARBAGE, MARY. "*The Borrowers* at Home and Afield." *EE* 33 (February 1956):67-75.
Reviews *The Borrowers* and *The Borrowers Afield*.

A1823 OLSON, BARBARA V. "Mary Norton and *The Borrowers*." *EE* 47 (February 1970):185-89.
A biocritical overview.

A1824 STOTT, JON C. "Anatomy of a Masterpiece: *The Borrowers*." *LA* 53 (May 1976):538-44.
Selects "seeing" as a unifying element in *The Borrowers* and analyzes the way in which it gives the novel its central meaning.

O'BRIEN, ROBERT [Robert Leslie Conly] (1918-73)

A1825 BOULANGER, SUSAN. "A Second Look: *The Silver Crown.*" *Horn Book* 61 (January 1985):95-99.
Provides a careful examination of the book's themes and structure.

A1826 HENKE, JAMES T. "Growing Up as Epic Adventure: The Biblical Collage in *Z for Zachariah.*" *CLE*, n.s. 13, no. 2 (Summer 1982):87-94.
Analyzes the heroine's struggle for growth and survival in a mythic setting as enhanced by biblical allusions. "O'Brien's heroine is an emblem of man's epic quest for growth, freedom, and renewal."

A1827 MORSE, BRIAN. "The Novels of Robert C. O'Brien." *Signal* 40 (January 1983):30-35.
Analyzes O'Brien's books, all written in his mature years: *The Silver Crown* (1968), *Mrs. Frisby and the Rats of NIMH* (1971), *Z for Zachariah* (1974), and an adult book, *A Report from Group 17* (1972).

O'DELL, SCOTT (1903-   )

A1828 JOHNSON, WALTER H. "A Stepping Stone to Melville." *English Journal* 73 (April 1984):69-70.
Finds parallels between Melville's *The Encantados* and O'Dell's *Island of the Blue Dolphins*; also finds other Melville influences in O'Dell's work.

A1829 KINGSTON, CAROLYN T. *Tragic Mode*, pp. 146-48.
Analyzes *The Island of the Blue Dolphins* in terms of its theme of loss and death.

A1830 McCORMICK, EDITH. "Scott O'Dell: Immortal Writer." *American Libraries* 4 (June 1973):356-57.
In an interview O'Dell discusses his development as a writer and his responses to the many writers who have influenced him--from Willa Cather to Dante. Also talks about his beliefs and his goals in writing.

A1831 NODELMAN, PERRY. "A Second Look: *Sing Down the Moon.*" *Horn Book* 60 (February 1984):94-98.
Considers the book "a small masterpiece of dogmatic understatement that never confuses painful conflict with good, clear fun." It is "very strange and very familiar --both at the same time."

A1832 O'DELL, SCOTT. "Acceptance Speech: Hans Christian Andersen Award." *Horn Book* 48 (October 1972):441-43. (Reprinted in White, *Children's Literature*, pp. 110-12.)
Gives background of *The Dark Canoe*, derived from his reading of *Moby-Dick*.

A1833 -----. "David: An Adventure with Memory and Words." *Psychology Today* 18 (January 1968):40-43, 70.
Reflects upon his writing and children's literature. Describes the origins of *Island of the Blue Dolphins*.

A1834   -----. "Newbery Award Acceptance." *Horn Book* 37 (August 1961):311-16.
Ｏ'Dell describes experiences in his own life which he was able to incorporate in *The Island of the Blue Dolphins*. A biographical note by Maud Hart Lovelace follows, pp. 316-19.

A1835   -----. "The Tribulations of a Trilogy." *Horn Book* 58 (April 1982):137-44.
Tells of writing *The Captive* and *The Feathered Serpent*.

A1836   PALOMARES, UVALDO. Review. *IRBC* 5, nos. 7-8 (1974):17.
Faults *Child of Fire* for misrepresenting "crucial elements of Chicano existence" and projecting "inaccurate images of La Raza."

A1837   STEWIG, JOHN. "A Literary and Linguistic Analysis of Scott O'Dell's *The Captive*." Paper presented at the Annual Meeting of the National Conference on Language Arts in the Elementary School, April 1981. ERIC Educational Document Reproduction Service, 19 pp., ED 200 993.
Examines O'Dell's literary style and characterization in terms of his ability to engage even the reluctant reader.

A1838   STOTT, JON C. "Narrative Technique and Meaning in *Island of the Blue Dolphins*." *EE* 52 (April 1975):442-46.
Provides a detailed analysis of O'Dell's narrative techniques.

A1839   TOWNSEND, JOHN ROWE. *Sense of Story*, pp. 154-62.
Discusses *Island of the Blue Dolphins* as a Robinsonade. "Among all the Newbery winners there are few better books." Also discusses *King's Fifth*, *Black Pearl*, and *Dark Canoe*. Calls O'Dell "a natural heavyweight."

A1840   WALD, RHOADA. "Realism in Children's Literature." *LA* 52 (October 1975):938-41, 949.
Describes the nature of realistic writing for children, using *Island of the Blue Dolphins* as her example.

A1841   WINTLE, JUSTIN, and FISHER, EMMA. *Pied Pipers*, pp. 171-81.
Ｏ'Dell discusses his life and work in an interview.

OLSEN, IB SPANG (1935-   )

A1842   JENSEN, VIRGINIA ALLEN. "Ib Spang Olsen." *Bookbird* 10, no. 2 (1972):5-10.
A profile of the Andersen Award-winning Danish author-illustrator.

A1843   OLSEN, IB SPANG. "A Meeting with Ib Spang Olsen." In Koefoed, *Children's Literature and the Child*, pp. 58-61.
Discusses issues in creating children's books from his own perspective. "I have been carefully trying to say what children want to hear me to say."

OTIS, JAMES (1848-1912)

A1844   JULEUS, NELS. "A Second Look: *Toby Tyler: or Ten Weeks with a Circus*." *Horn Book* 57 (February 1981):83-87.

Emphasizes the illustrations of various editions of the book.

O'NEAL, ZIBBY [ELIZABETH] (1934-   )

A1845   O'NEAL, ZIBBY. "Writing for Adolescents: Pleasures and Problems." *ALAN Review* 11, no. 2 (Winter 1984):1-2.
Discusses why she writes for young adults.

OUIDA [Marie Louise de la Ramée] (1839-1908)

A1846   CHANG, CHARITY. "'The Nürnberg Stove' as an Artistic Fairy Tale." *Children's Literature* 5 (1976):148-56.
Provides a detailed critical analysis of this story from *Bimbi*, a collection of nine of Ouida's stories first published in 1882.

OXENBURY, HELEN (1938-   )

A1847   OXENBURY, HELEN. "Drawing for Children." *Junior Bookshelf* 34, no. 4 (August 1970):199-201.
Brief comments upon her working habits and beliefs about children's books.

OXENHAM, ELSIE [E.J. Dunkerley] (d. 1960)

A1848   CADOGAN, MARY, and CRAIG, PATRICIA. "Camp Fire and Country Dance." In *You're A Brick*, pp. 159-77.
Discusses the Camp Fire and Abbey Girls series of Oxenham and others.

PARRISH, ANNE (1888-1957)

A1849   DAVIS, LAVINIA R. "Anne Parrish as a Writer of Children's Books." *Horn Book* 36 (January 1960):62-67.
Primarily a personal reminiscence containing some critical insights.

A1850   MAHONY, BERTHA E. "The Honey Heart of Earth: In The Books of Anne and Dillwyn Parrish." *Horn Book* 7 (February 1931):61-67. (Reprinted in Fryatt, *Horn Book Sampler*, pp. 4-7.)
Discusses and praises *Knee-High to a Grasshopper*, *Dream Coach*, and *Floating Island*.

A1851   MILLER, BERTHA MAHONY. "Anne Parrish's Memorable Nonsense Story." *Horn Book* 27 (1951):20-22.
Highly praises the *Story of Appleby Capple* with its nonsense and alphabet fun.

PATERSON, BANJO [Andrew Barton Paterson] (1864-1941)

A1852   ANDERSON, BARBARA POSTON. "Banjo Paterson's Poetry: A Picture Book Perspective." *Orana* 17 (May 1981):53-56.
Surveys picture books based on Banjo Paterson's poetry, including "Waltzing Matilda."

PATERSON, KATHERINE (1932-   )

A1853   BAGNALL, NORMA. "Terabithia: Bridge to a Better World." *LA* 56 (April 1979):429-31.

Analyzes Paterson's use of language and dialect, especially Jesse's changing speech patterns.

A1854   BELL, ANTHEA. "A Case of Commitment." *Signal* 38 (May 1982):73-81.
Examines Paterson's books in terms of her Christian commitment.

A1855   GOFORTH, CAROLINE R. "The Role of the Island in *Jacob Have I Loved.*" *ChLAQ* 9, no. 4 (Winter 1984-85):176-78.
Explores the influence of place on character and theme "by examining Rass Island in light of Jung's associations--as refuge, as limitation, and as region of danger."

A1856   HEINS, PAUL. Review of *Jacob Have I Loved*. *Horn Book* 56 (December 1980):622-23.
Calls it "a story that courageously sounds emotional depths."

A1857   HUSE, NANCY. "Katherine Paterson's Ultimate Realism." *ChLAQ* 9, no. 3 (Fall 1984):99-101.
Explores Paterson's difficult-to-categorize combination of realism and ethical and religious meaning and power.

A1858   JONES, LINDA T. "Profile: Katherine Paterson." *LA* 58 (February 1981):189-96.
In an interview, Paterson answers questions about her life and work. Includes a bibliography of her books.

A1859   McGAVRAN, JAMES HOLT, Jr. "Bathrobes and Bibles, Waves and Words in Katherine Paterson's *Jacob Have I Loved.*" *CLE*, n.s. 17, no. 1 (Spring 1986):3-15.
Questions the necessity of Paterson's ending with her heroine's acceptance of "quietistic and blatantly antifeminist womanhood."

A1860   MICHAELS, WENDY. "Service, Sublimation and Sacrifice in Three Novels by Katherine Paterson." *Orana* 20 (May 1984):91-92.
Questions Paterson's traditional, subservient, sacrificing female role models.

A1861   PATERSON, KATHERINE. *The Gates of Excellence: On Reading and Writing Books for Children.* New York: Elsevier/Nelson, 1981, 127 pp.
A collection of Paterson's essays, speeches, and book reviews from the *Washington Post Book World*. They are revealing of Paterson's attitudes and approach to writing and literature. Significant reviews include those of Beverly Cleary's *Ramona and Her Father*, Sue Ellen Bridgers's *All Together Now*, Rosa Guy's *The Disappearance*, Jill Paton Walsh's *Children of the Fox*, and Helen Cresswell's *Absolute Zero*

A1862   -----. "Newbery Award Acceptance." *Horn Book* 54 (August 1978):361-67.
Recounts the origins of *Bridge to Terabithia*. A biographical sketch by Virginia Buckley follows, pp. 368-71.

A1863   -----. "Newbery Medal Acceptance." *Horn Book* 57 (August 1981):385-93.
Tells of the background, origins and writing of *Jacob Have I*

Loved. Biographical sketch by Gene Inyart Namovicz follows, pp. 394-99.

A1864   -----. "Where Is Terabithia?" *ChLAQ* 9, no. 4 (Winter 1984-85):153-57.
Reflects on the importance of place in literature and describes the origins of Terabithia.

A1865   POWERS, DOUGLAS. "Of Time, and Place, and Person: *The Great Gilly Hopkins* and Problems of Story for Adopted Children." *CLE*, n.s. 15, no. 4 (Winter 1984):211-19.
Compares Gilly, and Paterson's telling of her story, to real foster children and their stories.

A1866   REES, DAVID. "Medals and Awards--Katherine Paterson." In *Painted Desert*, pp. 89-101.
Considers *Jacob Have I Loved* by far her best book, "in background detail, imagery, characterization, [and] above all in the sureness of tone of voice and sheer writing ability." Traces her development as a writer.

A1867   SMEDMAN, M. SARAH. "'A Good Oyster': Story and Meaning in *Jacob Have I Loved*." *CLE*, n.s. 14, no. 3 (Autumn 1983):180-87.
Discusses Paterson's use of biblical motifs to depict Louise Bradshaw's character development.

PATTEN, GILBERT [Burt L. Standish] (1866-1945)

A1868   CUTLER, JOHN LEVI. *Gilbert Patten and his Frank Merriwell Saga: A Study in Sub-Literary Fiction, 1896-1913*. Orono, Maine: University of Maine Studies, 2d ser., no. 31, 1934, 123 pp.
The first chapter traces the history of the dime novel in America, chapters 2-4 are devoted to Patten's biography, and chapter 5, pp. 84-110, concentrates on the Frank Merriwell books.

A1869   HOLBROOK, STEWART H. "Frank Merriwell At Yale Again--And Again and Again." *American Heritage* 12 (June 1961):24-27, 78-81.
Provides personal recollections of Patten and an overview and history of the Merriwell series.

A1870   LEFFERTS, BARNEY. "The Return of Frank Merriwell." *New York Times Magazine*, 19 August 1956, pp. 23, 34.
Explores reasons for the continuing popularity of the Merriwell stories.

PEAKE, MERVYN (1911-68)

A1871   CROUCH, MARCUS. "Mervyn Peake 1911-1968: An Appreciation." *Junior Bookshelf* 32 (December 1968):346-49.
An appreciative evaluation. Crouch believes Peake will be remembered not only for "The Gothic imagination, but also the fun, the uncloying tenderness and the wisdom of a great artist."

A1872   PEAKE, MERVYN. "Introduction from *The Drawings of Mervyn Peake*." *Signal* 1 (January 1970):16-19.
Expresses his personal views of creation, style, and the nature of criticism.

PEARCE, PHILIPPA (1920-   )

A1873   BILLMAN, CAROL. "Young and Old Alike: The Place of Old Women in Two Recent Novels for Children." *ChLAQ* 8, no. 1 (Spring 1983):6-8, 31.

Examines Mrs. Basil E. Frankweiler in E.L. Konigsburg's *From the Mixed-up Files of Mrs. Basil E. Frankweiler* and Mrs. Harriet Bartholomew in Philippa Pearce's *Tom's Midnight Garden* as "noteworthy extension of the fictional convention of the elderly storyteller used by a number of nineteenth-century writers for children."

A1874   CHAMBERS, AIDAN. "Letter from England: Reaching through a Window." *Horn Book* 57 (April 1981):229-33.

Sees *Battle of Bubble and Squeak* as "primarily about living together." A close analysis.

A1875   CROUCH, MARCUS. *The Nesbit Tradition*, pp. 198-200.

Analyzes Pearce's books in terms of the theme of self-discovery.

A1876   EVANS, DAVID. "The Making of *The Children of the House*." In Hunt, *Further Approaches*, pp. 51-60.

Compares the original Brian Fairfax-Lucy manuscript upon which Pearce based the book, and Pearce's version.

A1877   INGLIS, FRED. *Promise of Happiness*, pp. 257-67.

Concentrates on *Tom's Midnight Garden*, which he sees as a classic, and *Children of the House*. Compares Pearce's experiments with time to William Mayne's. He feels "there is fudging at the very heart" of *Tom's Midnight Garden* in the handling of time. Asks how was it that Hatty knew Tom when she was a girl and left him her skates? Feels *Children of the House* expresses the solidarity of children with each other against the world.

A1878   JACKSON, BRIAN. "Philippa Pearce in the Golden Age of Children's Literature." *Use of English* 21 (Spring 1970):195-203, 207. (Reprinted in Meek, *Cool Web*, pp. 314-24, and in Butts, *Good Writers*, pp. 94-103.)

Analyzes Pearce's themes, style, and technique and places her work in the context of the new Golden Age of children's literature.

A1879   PEARCE, PHILIPPA. "Writing a Book." *Horn Book* 43 (June 1967):317-22. (Reprinted in Meek, *Cool Web*, pp. 182-87, and in Blishen, *Thorny Paradise*, pp. 140-45.)

Describes how *A Dog So Small* grew on its own, and how she shaped it.

A1880   PHILIP, NEIL. "Tom's Midnight Garden and the Vision of Eden." *Signal* 37 (January 1982):21-25.

Examines the themes of Eden, innocence, and time in *Tom's Midnight Garden*. "The mystery at the heart of the text is that the relationship between Hattie and Tom is the same as that between author and reader."

A1881   REES, DAVID. "Achieving One's Heart's Desires." In *Marble in the Water*, pp. 36-55. (Also in *CLE*, o.s., no. 4 [March 1971]:40-53, entitled "The Novels of Philippa Pearce.")

Discusses *Tom's Midnight Garden*, which he admits is "the best of a certain kind of children's book," and *Children of the House*, which he sees as "a deliberate corrective to the view of the past suggested in *Tom's Midnight Garden*." Also discusses *Minnow on the Say* (U.S. version, *Minnow Leads to Treasure*) and *A Dog So Small*.

A1882   TOWNSEND, JOHN ROWE. *Sense of Story*, pp. 163-71.
Calls *Tom's Midnight Garden* the best children's book in twenty-five years. Also discusses *Minnow on the Say*, *Dog So Small*, and *Children of the House*. Praises Pearce's "profundity of thought and feeling" and her "joy that is just this side of sadness."

A1883   WOLF, VIRGINIA L. "Belief in *Tom's Midnight Garden*." *Proceedings of the Children's Literature Association* 9 (1982):142-46.
Explores the contribution of the novel's narrative technique to its credibility. The protagonist's point of view, the plot structure, and an evocative style assure the readers' participation in mysteries that are never explained.

PEASE, HOWARD (1894-1974)

A1884   JENNINGS, SHIRLEY MAY. "A Study of the Creative Genesis of the Twenty-Two Published Children's Novels by Howard Pease." Ed.D. dissertation, University of the Pacific, 1969, 437 pp., DA 30:1528A.
Analyzes the extent to which Pease's past experiences were incorporated into his novels and the extent to which he was influenced by external forces.

A1885   JENNINGS, Mrs. SHIRLEY, and CHAMBERS, DEWEY. "The Real Tod Moran." *EE* 46 (April 1969):488-91. (Reprinted in White, *Children's Literature*, pp. 19-25.)
Argues that Moran, hero of sixteen of Pease's books, is not only representative of the American junior literary hero, but is also very much a part of the life and personality of his creator.

PECK, RICHARD (1934-   )

A1886   BLACKBURN, WILLIAM. "The Quest for Values in Contemporary Adolescent Fiction." ERIC Educational Document Reproduction Service, 1982, 14 pp., ED 219 802.
Compares Richard Peck's *Are You in the House Alone?* with J.M. Barrie's *Peter Pan*, and concludes that Barrie handles "the same tensions of maturity in more subtle and complex ways."

A1887   HENKE, JAMES T. "The Death of the Mother: The Rebirth of the Son: *Millie's Boy* [by Robert Newton Peck] and *Father Figure* [by Richard Peck]." *CLE*, n.s. 14, no. 1 (Spring 1983):21-34.
Points out that these apparently dissimilar works both treat the theme of the passage from adolescence to adulthood in an unusual way: by using the death of the mother to occasion the rebirth of the son.

A1888   PECK, RICHARD. "Rape and the Teenage Victim." *TON* 34 (Winter 1978):173-77.
Discusses reactions of the public to his book *Are You in the House Alone?*, in which a high-school junior is raped by one of her classmates. Peck also considers the decisions that were made in the

process of writing.

PECK, ROBERT NEWTON (1928-   )

A1889   DONELSON, KENNETH. *Literature for Today's Young Adults*, p. 294.
Analyzes Papa in *A Day No Pigs Would Die* as a "quiet hero."

A1890   HARTVIGSEN, M. KIP, and HARTVIGSEN, CHRISTEN BROG.
"Haven Peck's Legacy in *A Day No Pigs Would Die*." *English Journal* 74 (April 1985):41-45.
Analyzes the book's structure and theme, pointing out the "careful framing of incidents underscoring the cycle of life."

A1891   HIPPS, G. MELVIN. "Male Initiation Rites in *A Day No Pigs Would Die*." *Arizona English Bulletin* 18, no. 3 (April 1976):161-63.
Explores the ways in which Rob is initiated into manhood by "doing what's got to be done."

PEET, BILL (1915-   )

A1892   BADER, BARBARA. *American Picturebooks*, pp. 209-10.
Sees Peet as the most humane of cartoonists.

PERRAULT, CHARLES (1628-1703)

A1893   HUBERT, RENÉE RIESE. "Mother Goose in Rags and Riches." *Journal of Popular Culture* 5 (Summer 1971):148-61.
Traces various illustrated versions of Perrault's tales by Sève, Chasselat, Staal, Grandville, and Doré to demonstrate the "incredible range of figurative interpretations in the eighteenth and nineteenth centuries."

A1894   LARUCCIA, VICTOR ANTHONY. "Progress, Perrault and Fairy Tales: Ideology and Semantics." Ph.D. dissertation, University of California, San Diego, 1975, 208 pp., DA 36:3655A.
Sees the relation of text to behavior "through the notion of double-bind," and applies "this notion to a reading of Perrault's "Little Red Riding Hood," where a paradox in the text, found through a structural analysis of the text, is put into the double context of the relation of tale to moral, and tale to illustration."

PETERSHAM, MAUD (1889-1971), and PETERSHAM, MISKA (1888-1960)

A1895   BADER, BARBARA. "Maud and Miska Petersham." In *American Picturebooks*, pp. 38-42.
A brief overview of the Petershams' career and an analysis of their work.

PETERSON, LEN (1917-   )

A1896   GHAN, LINDA. "Interview with Len Peterson." *CCL* 14 (1979):24-40.
The Canadian playwright discusses his work including *Almighty Voice*, a children's play, and ideas about children's theater.

PEYTON, KATHLEEN [Kathleen Heald; K.M. Peyton] (1929-   )

A1897   BUTTS, DENNIS. "Writers for Children: K.M. Peyton." *Use of*

English *23 (Spring 1972):195-202. (Reprinted in Butts,* Good Writers, *pp. 104-10, with an updating postscript, pp. 111-12.)*

Pays special attention to the *Flambards* trilogy, to Peyton's ability to provide "a serious and sustained view of both adolescence and historical movement."

A1898   CROUCH, MARCUS. *The Nesbit Tradition*, pp. 152-53, 177-79.

Discusses *Fly-By-Night* on pages 152-53, calling it one of the best pony stories, and *Flambards* on pages 177-79, in the context of the family saga. Sees the latter as coming "perilously near" to popular romance, but saved by the author's "historical integrity." Also discusses Peyton in his chapter "School Stories."

A1899   -----. "Streets Ahead In Experience." *Junior Bookshelf* 33 (June 1969):153-59.

A brief critical overview that traces Peyton's developing skill and artistry.

A1900   HIBBERD, DOMINIC. "The Flambards Trilogy: Objections to a Winner." *CLE*, o.s., no. 8 (July 1972):5-15. (Reprinted in Fox, *Writers, Critics and Children*, pp. 125-37.)

Attacks Peyton's plot, style, characterization, and themes. The books are enjoyable "interesting, readable, and decent," but not worthy of the praises heaped upon them. A reply from Colin Ray (see below) is also reprinted in Fox.

A1901   INGLIS, FRED. *Promise of Happiness*, pp. 221-24.

Praises the *Flambards* trilogy's plot and style, yet feels that in terms of interpreting the past its "scheme can seem at times ingenuous, at times even offensive."

A1902   JONES, CORNELIA, and WAY, OLIVIA R. *British Children's Authors*, pp. 127-36.

In an interview Kathleen Peyton discusses her background, philosophy, and method of working. Includes an annotated bibliography of her works.

A1903   LOOKER, ANN. "Children's Writers: 1. K.M. Peyton." *School Librarian* 25 (Summer 1977):223-28.

A critical overview and introduction to Peyton's work, stressing her social and moral awareness, and her sensitivity and compassion.

A1904   PEYTON, K.M. "On Not Writing a Proper Book." In Blishen *Thorny Paradise*, pp. 123-27.

Peyton comments on her approach to writing.

A1905   RAY, COLIN. "The Edge of the Cloud--A Reply to Dominic Hibberd." *CLE*, o.s., no. 9 (November 1972):5-6.

Argues that "literary quality" is only one aspect to be considered in granting the Carnegie Medal: that "Its potential impact on the young reader, its ideas, its chance of being read, its individual aspects which make it stand out from all the rest are all relevant." For further comment see Nigel Hand's article "Criticism and the Children's Fiction Industry" (*CLE*, o.s., no. 12 [September 1973]:3-9.)

A1906   TOWNSEND, JOHN ROWE. "A Second Look: *A Pattern of Roses*." *Horn Book* 60 (June 1984):361-64.

"The slender thread of fantasy is vital to the book and a source of much of its strength." Analyzes the book in terms of inner and outer story, calling it her best so far.

A1907 -----. *Sense of Story*, pp. 172-81.
Calls *Flambards* complete and rounded out and praises Peyton's "splendid heroines."

A1908 -----. *A Sounding*, pp. 166-78.
Revises and updates the essay published in *Sense of Story*. Discusses the Pennington and Ruth books. "She has extended her territory book by book. . . . And there is one vital moment that occurs sooner or later in the best of her novels and accounts for much of their depth and strengh: the moment of rejoicing at simply being here, to love and suffer and take what comes."

A1909 WINTLE, JUSTIN, and FISHER, EMMA. *Pied Pipers*, pp. 263-76.
Peyton discusses her life and work in an interview.

PHIPSON, JOAN (1912-)

A1910 McVITTY, WALTER. "Joan Phipson: Archetypal Australian Children's Books." In *Innocence and Experience*, pp. 37-65.
Sees Phipson's work as epitomizing the growth and development of Australian children's literature from the 1950s through the 1970s, from "innocence" to "experience." Includes a brief biography of Phipson and a bibliography of her books.

PICARD, BARBARA LEONIE (1917-)

A1911 CROUCH, MARCUS. *The Nesbit Tradition*, pp. 74-75.
Considers *Ransom for a Knight* a "tour-de-force," admires her masterly portrait of Alys, and feels the book has worn well.

A1912 JONES, CORNELIA, and WAY, OLIVIA R. *British Children's Authors*, pp. 137-45.
In an interview, Barbara Picard discusses her background, philosophy, and method of working. Includes an annotated bibliography of her works.

PIPER, WATTY [Mabel Caroline Bragg] (1870-1945)

A1913 LINGEMAN, RICHARD. "The Little Engine That Could." *NYTBR*, 2 May 1974, Children's Book sec., p.49.
Comments on the fiftieth anniversary of *The Little Engine That Could*. Finds it "more attuned to the folklore of childhood than the folklore of capitalism."

A1914 ORD, PRISCILLA. "Watty Piper." In Cech, *Dictionary of Literary Biography*, pp. 276-81.
Reveals that Watty Piper is a house name, and explores the long-standing popularity of *The Little Engine that Could*.

PINCUS, HARRIET (1938-)

A1915 BADER, BARBARA. *American Picturebooks*, pp. 559-63.
Discusses Pincus's illustrations for Sandburg's *The Wedding*

Procession of the Rag Doll and the Broom Handle and Who Was In It *and for Lore Segal's* Tell Me a Mitzi.

POLITI, LEO (1908-   )

A1916   LIVSEY, ROSEMARY.   "Leo Politi, Friend of All."   *Horn Book* 25 (March 1949):97-108.
Primarily biographical, with some critical insights.

A1917   POLITI, LEO.   "Acceptance of the Caldecott Medal."   *Horn Book* 26 (1950):269-71.
Traces the backgrounds of his books and tells how he composes them.   A brief biocritical portrait by Gladys English follows, pp. 272-75.

A1918   TEMPLIN, ELAINE.   "Leo Politi: Children's Historian."   *EE* 33 (October 1956):323-31.
Praises Politi's combining of old and new in his stories of early California history.   Traces the development of his career.

POPE, ELIZABETH MARIE (1917-   )

A1919   HEINS, ETHEL.   "A Second Look: *The Sherwood Ring*."   *Horn Book* 51 (December 1975):613.
Praises Pope's imaginative linking of fantasy and history.

PORTER, GENE STRATTON (1863-1924)

A1920   HAMBLEN, ABIGAIL ANN.   "*Laddie*: Journal of an Indiana Thoreau." *Journal of Popular Culture* 4 (Summer 1970):85-89.
Links Stratton-Porter's portrayals of nature with Henry David Thoreau's.

A1921   IFKOVIC, EDWARD.   "The Garden of the Lord: Gene Stratton-Porter and the Death of Evil in Eden."   *Journal of Popular Culture* 8 (Spring 1975):757-66.
Analyzes the ideal, escapist, Eden-like image of American life centered in the home and nature as presented by Stratton-Porter in *Girl of the Limberlost*, *The Harvester*, and *Laddie*.

A1922   RICHARDS, BERTRAND F.   *Gene Stratton Porter*.   Boston: Twayne, 1980, 165 pp.
Attempts to understand why Porter's books have such a broad appeal.   Discusses both her fiction and her nature books, and predicts that eventually Porter "will be elevated to a secure place amoung the minor American authors."   Includes an extensive bibliography of primary and secondary sources.

POSTMA, LIDIA (1952-   )

A1923   THIEL-SCHOONEBEEK, JOKE.   "Lidia Postma--Fantasy is Atmosphere."   *Bookbird* 1 (1980):62-64.
Discusses the balance between text and illustration.

POTTER, BEATRIX (1866-1943)

A1924   ALDERSON, BRIAN.   "*The Tailor of Gloucester*."   *Children's Book*

News *4, no. 6 (November-December 1969):309-12.*
Provides extensive comments on the publication of a facsimile of *The Tailor of Gloucester* and a trade version of the same book.

A1925   ANDERSON, CELIA CATLETT. "The Ancient Lineage of Beatrix Potter's *Mr. Tod.*" *Proceedings of the Children's Literature Association* 7 (1980):84-90. (Reprinted in Nodelman and May, *Festschrift*, pp. 45-47.)
Traces the origins of *Mr. Tod* in traditional literature, ranging from Aesop to La Fontaine to Uncle Remus, and analyzes the ways in which Potter has adapted these traditions in *Jemima Puddleduck* and *Mr. Tod.* See also Linnea Hendrickson's comments, "Literary Criticism as a Source of Teaching Ideas," in *ChLAQ* 9, no 4 (Winter 1984-85):202.

A1926   Beatrix Potter Society. Founded in 1980. It publishes a regular *Newsletter.*

A1927   CAMPBELL, A.K.D. "The Stories of Beatrix Potter: A Suggested Order for Reading." *CLE*, o.s., no. 5 (July 1971):12-19.
Classifies Potter's tales into three groups: suspense stories, comedies, and chronicles; and into age groups: for absolute beginners, for those with some experience, and for accomplished readers. Includes annotations on each tale.

A1928   CARPENTER, HUMPHREY. "Beatrix Potter: The Ironist in Arcadia." In *Secret Gardens*, pp. 138-50.
Argues that "when her books are looked at in the light of [her] journal they emerge as a linked, coherent body of writing, in which specific themes are developed and examined." Also suggests her "themes are close to the preoccupations" of other writers of her time, singling out especially escape to "Arcadia."

A1929   *Children's Literature Association Newsletter* 2, no. 4 (Winter 1978):16pp.
Special issue. Includes a review of *The Art of Beatrix Potter*, an annotated bibliography of Potter criticism, and a history of her writings.

A1930   COTT, JONATHAN. "Peter Rabbit and Friends." *NYTBR*, 1 May 1977, Children's Book sec., pp. 25, 38.
Reflects upon Potter's verbal precision and her use of drama and irony. Interspersed with the article are quotations from a number of famous writers on what Potter has meant to them.

A1931   CROUCH, MARCUS. *Beatrix Potter.* London: Bodley Head, 1960, 62 pp.
Surveys briefly Potter's life, the publishing history of her books, and their critical reception, pointing out numerous previous studies.

A1932   GILPATRICK, NAOMI. "The Secret Life of Beatrix Potter." *Natural History* 81 (October 1972):38.
Reproduces some of Potter's scientific drawings and tells how, after her rejection by the male scientific establishment, she turned to creating books for children.

A1933   GODDEN, RUMER. "Beatrix Potter." *Horn Book* 42 (August 1966):390-98.

An appreciative reflection on Potter's art and originality, and on her ability to endure and be loved by children.

A1934 -----. "An Imaginary Correspondence." *Horn Book* 39 (August 1963):369-75. (Reprinted in Haviland, *Children and Literature*, pp. 133-39, and in Egoff, *Only Connect*, 1st ed., pp. 62-69.)
 An imaginary correspondence between Potter and a Mr. V. Andal of De Base Publishing Company who wishes to publish a revised edition of her books for beginning readers.

A1935 -----. *The Tale of the Tales: The Beatrix Potter Ballet.* London: Frederick Warne, 1971, 208 pp.
 A richly illustrated book outlining the making of the ballet and film *The Tales of Beatrix Potter.*

A1936 GRAHAM, ELEANOR. "Beatrix Potter." *Junior Bookshelf* 3 (1939):171-75.
 Praises Potter's "sure contact" with the child, her warmhearted, even-tempered mothers, and her realism about the crueler aspects of life.

A1937 GREENE, GRAHAM. "Beatrix Potter." In *The Lost Childhood and Other Essays.* New York: Viking Press, 1952. (Reprinted in Egoff, *Only Connect*, 1st ed., pp. 291-98, 2d ed., pp. 258-65.)
 A close analysis of Potter's style and development as a writer. Potter later attacked Greene's view that a tragedy at some point in her life had deepened her writing and "deprecated sharply 'the Freudian school' of criticism."

A1938 HEARN, MICHAEL PATRICK. "A Second Look: Peter Rabbit Redux." *Horn Book* 52 (October 1977):563-66.
 Comments on Potter's style and grasp of detail and the relationship between picture and text.

A1939 HODGES, MARGARET. "A Second Look: *The Tailor of Gloucester.*" *Horn Book* 54 (December 1978):659-64.
 Background on creation and development of the tale that Potter considered her best work.

A1940 HOUGH, RICHARD. "The Tailors of Gloucester." *Signal* 42 (September 1983):150-54.
 A comparison of three texts of *The Tailor of Gloucester*, the original holograph, the privately printed edition, and the trade edition, revealing the superiority of the lengthier privately printed edition.

A1941 HURWITZ, JOHANNA. "Will the Real Peter Rabbit Please Stand Up?" *Library Journal* 94 (15 April 1969):1687-88.
 Compares the original Peter Rabbit with six mass-market imitations.

A1942 INGLIS, FRED. *Promise of Happiness*, pp. 109-11.
 "The imagery of Beatrix Potter's world balances a colonized, accomplished horticulture and agriculture, and the stable but mysterious Nature which lies untamed beyond the garden wall. Everybody's daydream of a perfect holiday for children occurs in such a scene." Places Potter in the "great tradition" with Lewis Carrol, Francis

Hodgson Burnett, Edith Nesbit, and Kenneth Grahame.

A1943 *Junior Bookshelf* 30, no. 4 (August 1966).
Special Issue. Contains two articles on Potter: Marcus Crouch's "A Long Apprenticeship," pp. 227-31, and Janice Dohm's "My Beatrix Potter," pp. 233-40, both of which reflect on the insights her journals provide.

A1944 LANE, MARGARET. "The Art of Beatrix Potter." *New Statesman and Nation*, 8 January 1944, pp. 23-24.
Calls Potter the great artist of the nursery, distinguished by her creative imagination. "She made and peopled a world, and brought it perfectly to life--which is what Dickens and Trollope did, on a different scale."

A1945 -----. *The Magic Years of Beatrix Potter*. London: Frederick Warne, 1978, 216 pp.
Lane here relies on Potter's drawings, paintings, books, journals, and "scattered fragments" to piece together a path of "happy self-discovery" of Potter's life and work. Includes many reproductions of Potter's art and manuscripts, and offers some critical analysis as well as many insights into the origins of the tales and their animal characters.

A1946 -----. *The Tale of Beatrix Potter: A Biography*. London: Frederick Warne, 1968, 173 pp.
A revised version of the biography originally published in 1946. Provides good coverage of Potter's life and her development as an artist and writer.

A1947 LINDNER, LESLIE. "The Beatrix Potter Centenary Exhibition, 1866-1966." *TON* 22 (June 1966):367-75.
Describes the exhibition held at the National Book League in London in 1966, including details about many of the paintings, drawings, and manuscripts displayed.

A1948 LINDNER, LESLIE, and LINDNER, ENID. *The Art of Beatrix Potter*. London: Frederick Warne, 1955, 406 pp.
This richly illustrated survey of Potter's art is divided into two parts, the first concentrating on her work as an artist, the second on her art in relation to her books. The second part includes reproductions of illustrations, sketches, and original drawings, published and unpublished, divided into the following categories: imagined happenings in the animal world; early ideas for illustrated books; her books--preliminary sketches and finished work; miscellany; and a section of photographs of Hill Top and Sawry associated with Potter and her work. All of the illustrations are commented on by the Lindners. There is also an introductory appreciation by Anne Carroll Moore and an appendix listing various editions and translations of her books.

A1949 MacDONALD, RUTH K. "Why This is Still 1893: *The Tale of Peter Rabbit* and Beatrix Potter's Manipulations of Timelessness." *ChLAQ* 10, no. 4 (Winter 1986):185-87.
Examines how Potter's revisions of *Peter Rabbit* "slow the narrative down and contribute to a greater sense of locating the narrative in a flow of time," and "how the changes contribute to the longevity

of Peter's popularity."

A1950   MESSER, PERSIS B. "Beatrix Potter: Classic Novelist of the Nursery: A Bibliographic Essay." *EE* 45 (March 1968):325-33.

Summarizes years of critical response to Potter's works and concludes that "They are indeed classic novels in miniature." Includes extensive references.

A1951   MILLER, BERTHA MAHONY. "Beatrix Potter and Her Nursery Classics." *Horn Book* 17 (May 1941):230-38. (Reprinted in Fryatt, *Horn Book Sampler*, pp. 228-33.)

Discusses the exactness of Potter's illustrations, relating them to their setting and children's responses. Also discusses *The Fairy Caravan*.

A1952   NAUMANN, NANCY. "Beatrix Potter: Childhood Magic for Now and September." *Learning* 11, no. 1 (August 1982):32-34.

A refreshing appraisal by a teacher newly discovering Potter.

A1953   POTTER, BEATRIX. *The History of the Tale of Peter Rabbit.* London: Frederick Warne, 1977, 63 pp.

Includes a facsimile of Potter's first version of the tale in her letter to Noel Moore, and recounts the publishing history of the book. Includes reprints of correspondence between Potter and Frederick Warne & Co., a reproduction of Potter's private printed edition, and postscript comments.

A1954   -----. "'Roots' of the Peter Rabbit Tales." *Horn Book* 5 (May 1929):69-72. (Reprinted in Meek, *Cool Web*, pp. 188-91.)

Tells of early influences and how she came to write the Peter Rabbit stories.

A1955   -----. "The Strength that Comes from the Hills." *Horn Book* 20 (March-April 1944):77. (Reprinted in Fryatt, *Horn Book Sampler*, pp. 28-29.)

Briefly tells about the origins of Peter Rabbit, Mr. McGregor, Squirrel Nutkin, and others.

A1956   QUINBY, JANE. *Beatrix Potter: A Bibliographical Check List.* London: Charles J. Sawyer, 1954, 121 pp.

A descriptive bibliography of Potter's books.

A1957   RAHN, SUZANNE. "Tailpiece: *Tale of Two Bad Mice.*" *Children's Literature* 12 (1984):78-91.

Suggests an interpretation of the tale based on political events of the time, Potter's known political convictions, and significant events in her private life during the time the tale was written.

A1958   RICHARDSON, PATRICK. "Miss Potter and the Little Rubbish." *New Society*, 7 July 1966. (Reprinted in Tucker, *Suitable for Children?*, pp. 173-78.)

Admits that the Potter books succeed as children's books, but dismisses "higher claims . . . for them as literature," such as those made by Grahame Green.

A1959   SALE, ROGER. "Beatrix Potter." In *Fairy Tales*, pp. 82-83, 126-63.

A detailed and admiring analysis of Potter's works. *Peter Rabbit* is discussed on pages 82-83, 139-41, *Roly-Poly Pudding*, pp. 150-52, *Jemima Puddleduck*, pp. 152-55, and *Mr. Tod*, "her last great book," pp. 155-63.

A1960 SENDAK, MAURICE. "The Aliveness of Peter Rabbit." *WLB* 40 (December 1965):345-48.

A spirited defense of *Peter Rabbit*, which, Sendak claims, "in its perfect tinyness transcends all arbitrary categories." Its vivid sense of life "is achieved through an imaginative synthesis of factual and fantastical components." Sendak analyzes several details in support of his thesis.

A1961 SICROFF, SETH. "Prickles under the Frock." *Children's Literature* 2 (1973):105-9.

A detailed analysis of Potter's prose style, her understated humor and word games, aphoristic sentence structure, and the ways in which her prose and pictures work together to "maintain a consistent literary world which exists between reality and fantasy, denying neither."

A1962 STEVENS, ELIZABETH H. "A Visit to Mrs. Tiggywinkle." *Horn Book* 34 (April 1958):131-36.

This first-person account of a visit to Potter perfectly captures her background and personality. One will never view Mrs. Tiggywinkle in quite the same way after reading this account.

A1963 "The Tailor of Gloucester." *TLS*, 8 January 1944, p. 15.

Explores key elements in Potter's success, noting especially the unself-consciousness of her books, their "plain honesty," and the fact that "they have a story to tell."

A1964 TUCKER, NICHOLAS. *The Child and the Book*, pp. 57-66.

Discusses Potter's attention to style, the genesis of her stories in her contacts with children, her basic plot of pursuit and prey, and her realistic treatment of animals and the harsher realities of life.

A1965 YOSHIDA, SHIN-ICHI. "The World of Beatrix Potter As Seen Through the Eyes of a Japanese Visitor." *International Library Review* 5 (April 1973):225-28.

Contends that "we cannot separate the climate and the scenery from the very essence of her books." Sees in them an appeal "to return to nature strongly but quietly." Describes Potter's settings as seen in her books and as they appear today.

PREUSSLER, OTFRIED (1923-   )

A1966 PREUSSLER, OTFRIED. "My Partner and I." *Bookbird* 10, no. 4 (1972):22-23. Biographical note and bibliography, pp. 24-27.

Andersen Award winner tells how he writes with his partner, "the little boy I once was myself."

PROVENSEN, ALICE (1918-   ), and PROVENSEN, MARTIN (1916-   )

A1967 "The Provensens: Book Artists for Children." *Publishers Weekly* 186 (13 July 1964):111-12.

A brief account of the Provensen's background and techniques they have employed.

"Puss'n Boots"

A1968   ARBUTHNOT, MAY HILL. "Puss, the Perraults and a Lost Manuscript." *EE* 46 (October 1969):715-21.

In Arbuthnot's words, "A light-hearted tribute to one of my favorite fairy tales, its author or authors and to that charming long-lost manuscript of five of the Perrault Fairy Tales. . . ."

PYLE, HOWARD (1853-1911

A1969   ABBOTT, CHARLES D. *Howard Pyle: A Chronicle.* New York: Harper & Brothers, 1925, 249 pp.

A basic source of information on Pyle. Includes chapters on his fairy tales and stories of the Middle Ages.

A1970   MAY, JILL P., ed. "Howard Pyle Commemorative." *ChLAQ* 8, no. 2 (Summer 1983):9-34

Contents: "Introduction," by Jill P. May; "Howard Pyle's Manuscripts: The Delaware Art Museum," by Rowland Elzea; "Pyle's *Robin Hood*: Still Merry After All These Years," by John Cech; Howard Pyle's Book Illustrations for Children," by Patricia Dooley; "Pyle's Fairy Tales: Folklore Remade," by Jill P. May; "Pyle's Sweet, Thin, Clear Tune: *The Garden Behind the Moon*", by Perry Nodelman; "A Milestone of Historical Fiction for Children: *Otto of the Silver Hand*," by Malcolm Usrey; "The Purposiveness of Evil: A Note on *Otto of the Silver Hand*," by Jon Stott; "Winsome Period Pieces: The Poetry of Howard Pyle," by Alethea Helbig; and "The Man with the Golden Touch: The Pyle of the Biographers," by Sarah Smedman.

A1971   NESBITT, ELIZABETH. *Howard Pyle.* New York: Henry Z. Walck, 1966, 72 pp.

Includes a biographical sketch and discussion of his work as illustrator and writer. Includes a bibliography of his writings and illustrations and lists secondary sources.

A1972   PITZ, HENRY C. *Howard Pyle: Writer, Illustrator, Founder of the Brandywine School.* New York: Clarkson N. Potter, 1975, 248 pp.

Chapter 6 concentrates on Pyle's children's books. Includes primary and secondary bibliographies, and numerous illustrations.

RACKHAM, ARTHUR (1867-1939)

A1973   CROUCH, MARCUS S. "Arthur Rackham, 1867-1939." *Junior Bookshelf* 31 (October 1967):297-302.

Reflects upon Rackham's steady appeal and popularity.

A1974   GETTINGS, FRED. *Arthur Rackham.* London: Studio Vista; New York: Macmillan, 1975, 192 pp.

A critical and technical examination of Rackham's art. Includes discussions of early artistic influences, matters of technique and style, and comments on Rackham's imagination and some of his best illustrations.

A1975   KAMENETSKY, CHRISTA. "Arthur Rackham and the Romantic Tradition: The Question of Polarity and Ambiguity." *Children's Literature* 6 (1977):115-29.

Explores Rackham's relationship to European romanticism and its influence on his subject choices and the ambiguities of his style.

A1976 LANES, SELMA. "Rackham and Sendak: Childhood through Opposite Ends of the Telescope." In *Down The Rabbit Hole*, pp. 67-78.
Contrasts the approaches of Rackham and Sendak to illustration.

A1977 LARKIN, DAVID. *Arthur Rackham 1867-1939.* London: Pan Books, 1975, 9 pp. (40 leaves of plates).
Examines Rackham as artist and illustrator.

A1978 LAWSON, ROBERT. "The Genius of Arthur Rackham." *Horn Book* 16 (May 1940):147-54. (Reprinted in Fryatt, *Horn Book Sampler*, pp. 55-59.)
Praise for Rackham, written at the time of his death.

A1979 McWHORTER, GEORGE. "Arthur Rackham: The Search Goes On." *Horn Book* 48 (February 1972):82-87.
Increasing interest in collecting Rackham's work spurred this brief appreciation of his talent.

A1980 MACY, GEORGE. "Arthur Rackham and *The Wind in the Willows.*" *Horn Book* 16 (May 1940):153-58. (Reprinted in Fryatt, *Horn Book Sampler*, pp. 50-54.)
Tells the story of how Rackham finally got to illustrate *Wind in the Willows.*

RAND, PAUL (1914-   )

A1981 BADER, BARBARA. *American Picturebooks*, pp. 338-42.
Traces Rand's contributions to the art of the picture book.

RANSOME, ARTHUR (1884-1967)

A1982 "Arthur Ransome: Charting the Course." *TLS*, 28 November 1963. (Reprinted in Egoff, *Only Connect*, 1st ed., pp. 310-15.)
Praises Ransome's ability to hold interest through his narrative skill and his ability to depict characters, technicalities, settings, and reality.

A1983 BROGAN, HUGH. *The Life of Arthur Ransome.* London: Jonathan Cape, 1984, 456 pp.
Primarily biographical in emphasis, with some background on the writing of *Swallows and Amazons* and Ransome's other children's books.

A1984 HUNT, PETER. "Ransome Revisited: A Structural and Developmental Approach." *CLE*, n.s. 12, no. 1 (Spring 1981):24-33.
Argues that "critics and reviewers have been right about Ransome for the wrong reasons . . . he is a classic example of a 'good' writer for children." Explores why this is so.

A1985 INGLIS, FRED. "Class and Classic--The Greatness of Arthur Ransome." In *Promise of Happiness*, pp. 124-45.
Chooses Ransome as an example of how "a gifted novelist, though starting inevitably from his or her class, criticizes the narrow

limits of its horizon by showing in the creation of a narrative what it would be like truly to live up to the terms of its best values." Provides detailed analysis of *We Didn't Mean to Go to Sea*, pp. 136-45.

A1986   *Junior Bookshelf* 28, no. 1 (January 1964).
Special issue devoted to Arthur Ransome. Includes "A Little Lower than the Angels: A Tribute to Arthur Ransome," by G. Bott; "'Those Ransome Kids': A Canadian View," by C. Duff Stewart; "Arthur Ransome--A Birthday Appreciation," by D. Lomas; "Arthur Ransome and a Treasure Chest for the Whole World," by R. Bamberger; and "Dr. Ransome in Sweden," by L.C. Persson.

A1987   PEARSON, KIT. "A Second Look: *Swallows and Amazons.*" *Horn Book* 59 (October 1983):601-5.
Considers the theme of freedom and independence, and sees Titty as the real heroine or heart of the book. Analyzes its continuing appeal.

A1988   READE, JUDY. "What Fun! What Fun! Characteristics of the Holiday Adventure Story!" *School Librarian* 32 (March 1984):5-12.
Discusses the holiday adventure story as written by Arthur Ransome and William Mayne and compares them to lesser imitators.

A1989   SHELLEY, HUGH. *Arthur Ransome.* New York: Walck, 1964, 72 pp.
Provides an in-depth evaluation of Ransome's twelve children's books, which "are really twelve volumes of one major work."

A1990   SMITH, LILLIAN. *Unreluctant Years*, pp. 138-41.
Praises the well-constructed plot of *Great Northern* and analyzes "three distinct styles of writing": detailed description, dialogue, and creation of atmosphere.

A1991   WOODROW, W.A. "Ransome in Retrospect." *Junior Bookshelf* 43 (June 1979):149-51.
Discusses the defects critics have pointed out in Ransome's work and argues that they have their virtues.

"Rapunzel"

A1992   CRAGO, HUGH, and CRAGO, MAUREEN. "The Untrained Eye? A Preschool Child Explores Felix Hoffman's *Rapunzel.*" *CLE*, o.s., no. 22 (Autumn 1976):135-51.
A detailed account of a preschool child's responses to repeated readings of the book. Concludes that "child and adult may not be as far apart in literary response as we have sometimes thought."

RASKIN, ELLEN (1928-84)

A1993   BACH, ALICE. "Ellen Raskin: Some Clues about Her Life." *Horn Book* 61 (March 1985):162-67.
Relates some elements in Raskin's life to her work.

A1994   BADER, BARBARA. *American Picturebooks*, pp. 538-39.
Briefly discusses the distinguishing characteristics of Raskin's picture books.

A1995   HIEATT, CONSTANCE B. "The Mystery of *Figgs and Phantoms.*" *Children's Literature* 13 (1983):128-38.

Argues that *Figgs and Phantoms*, although it has received less praise and attention than *The Westing Game*, is "a work of considerably greater depth and resonance."

RASMUSSEN, HALFDAN (1915-   )

A1996   WANIEK, MARILYN NELSON, and ESPELAND, PAMELA LEE. "The Poetry of Halfdan Rasmussen." *Children's Literature* 10 (1982):77-82.

A brief examination of Rasmussen's nonsense verses, with some translations for English-speaking children.

RAWLINGS, MARJORIE KINNAN (1896-1953)

A1997   BELLMAN, SAMUEL I. *Marjorie Kinnan Rawlings.* New York: Twayne, 1974, 164 pp.

Chapter 4 of this study concentrates on *The Yearling.* Sees Rawlings's portrayal of Jody as the key to the book's strong hold on the reader. "Because the author is so attached to him emotionally he is virtually an *animus* figure in the Jungian sense: a projection of the masculine configuration of a woman's interior personality." Includes bibliographies and indexes.

A1998   -----. "Marjorie K. Rawlings' Existentialist Nightmare, *The Yearling.*" *Costerus* 9 (1973):9-18.

"Far from being a negligible 'boy's book' as tradition holds, *The Yearling* is an existentialist nightmare. Embodying many of Mrs. Rawlings' experiences idealized in recollection, various of her attitudes and miseries, and her stoic Platonism, the story tells more than we can possibly take in--on a first reading. . . ."

A1999   -----. "Writing Literature for Young People: Marjorie Kinnan Rawlings' 'Secret River' of the Imagination." *Costerus* 9 (1973):19-27.

Examines the way in which Rawlings worked to build a story.

A2000   CECH, JOHN. "Marjorie Kinnan Rawlings's *The Secret River:* A Fairy Tale, A Place, A Life." *Southern Studies* 19 (1977):29-38.

Provides a detailed analysis of this neglected story, finding in it keys to Rawlings's personality and art.

A2001   GALBRAITH, LACHLAN N. "'Marjorie Kinnan Rawlings' *The Secret River.*" *EE* 52 (April 1975):455-59.

Analyzes this portrayal of an "innocent child in a world not yet corrupted by man" in hope that teachers will see in it an alternative to "relevance" and contemporary realism.

A2002   KINGSTON, CAROLYN T. *Tragic Mode,* pp. 148-52.

Examines the themes of loss and death in *The Yearling.*

A2003   McDONNELL, CHRISTINE. "A Second Look: *The Yearling.*" *Horn Book* 53 (June 1977):344-45.

Surprised to discover, as an adult, "a view so strong, bleak, but reassuring" in a book that has deeply affected so many children.

A2004   SAFFY, EDNA L. "Marjorie Kinnan Rawlings' *The Yearling:* A Study in the Rhetorical Effectiveness of the Novel." Ph.D. dissertation, University of Florida, 1976, 177 pp., DA 37:3985A.

Compares Rawlings's theory of composition "as evinced by her personal papers, lecture notes, scrap books, newspaper articles, and correspondence" with the results achieved in *The Yearling*.

A2005   YORK, LAMAR. "Marjorie Kinnan Rawlings's Rivers." *Southern Literary Journal* 9 (Spring 1977):91-107.

Explores Rawlings's use of the river to establish sense of place and as an instrument of rite of passage in *The Yearling* and her other books.

REANEY, JAMES (1926-   )

A2006   CAMERON, RON. "Quintessential Reaney: Myth, Magic, and Local Color." *CCL* 8-9 (1977):98-104.

A description and analysis of the four one-act plays in this Canadian writer's *Apple Butter and Other Plays for Children*.

REED, TALBOT BAINES (1852-93)

A2007   BLISHEN, EDWARD. "*The Fifth Form at St. Dominic's*: A Rereading." *CLE*, n.s. 12, no. 2 (Summer 1981):103-12.

A reassessment of *The Fifth Form at St. Dominic's*, a classic school story that influenced the genre.

A2008   PAXFORD, SANDRA. "The Happiest Days of Your Life." *Junior Bookshelf* 35, no. 3 (June 1971):153-56.

Considers the characters "brilliantly drawn," the moral standards high, and the dialogue full of "genuine humour."

REES, DAVID (1936 -   )

A2009   REES, DAVID. "On Katherine Paterson, Alexander Pope, Myself, and Some Others." *CLE*, n.s. 14, no. 3 (Autumn 1983):160-70.

Uses Katherine Paterson's *Gates of Excellence* as a springboard for discussing his own sense of direction as a writer of children's books.

REEVES, JAMES (1909-   )

A2010   BUTTS, DENNIS. "James Reeves: The Truthful Poet." *Junior Bookshelf* 30 (December 1966):358-63.

A brief critical overview of Reeves's poetry for children. Compares him with Robert Louis Stevenson.

A2011   ROBBINS, SIDNEY. "Interpreting in Sharing--James Reeves: *The Cold Flame*." *CLE*, o.s., no. 2 (July 1970):7-14.

A close analysis of the themes of love and lust that intermingle in *The Cold Flame*, an adaptation of the Grimm tale "The Blue Flame".

REISS, JOHANNA (1932-   )

A2012   POOLE, MARY F. "*The Upstairs Room*: Room for Controversy?" *Library Journal* 98 (15 December 1974):3725-26 and *SLJ* 20 (December 1974):67-68.

Objects to the award-winning book's "objectionable language." Numerous letters in response to Poole's position, pro and con, appear in the 15 September issue.

RETTICH, MARGRET

A2013   SCHWARCZ, JOSEPH H. "Explicit Artistry in Children's Books." In *Ways of the Illustrator*, pp. 188-91.
Examines Rettich's *The Voyage of the Jolly Boat* as an example of "illustrators who create pictures that are consciously presented as art, and still within the children's grasp."

REY, H.A. (1898-1977)

A2014   BADER, BARBARA. *American Picturebooks*, pp. 204-5, 247-50.
Discusses the Curious George books on pages 204-5, and Rey's illustrations for Zolotow's *The Park Book*, and for *Spotty* and other books by Margaret Rey, on pages 247-50.

RICE, EDWARD

A2015   ZIPES, JACK. "Marx and Engels without the Frills." *L&U* 4, no. 1 (Summer 1980):83-90.
An in-depth discussion of *Marx, Engels, and the Workers of the World*, concluding that "this antidote to orthodox mythopoeic biography is unfortunately in need of an antidote itself."

RICHARDS, LAURA E. (1850-1943)

A2016   ALEXANDER, ANNE STOKES. "Laura E. Richards, 1850-1943: A Critical Biography." Ph.D. dissertation, Columbia University, 1979, 407 pp., DA 40:2673A.
An in-depth study of Richards's life and work. An introduction summarizes the main influences in her life and the themes of her work, parts 1 and 3 tell her life story, and part 2 considers her work by genre.

A2017   McCORD, DAVID. "A Second Look: *Tirra Lirra*." *Horn Book* 55 (December 1979):690-94.
A thoughtful reconsideration, pointing out the influences, strengths, and weaknesses of *Tirra Lirra: Rhymes Old and New*.

RICHARDSON, HENRY HANDEL
[Ethel Florence (Lindesay) Richardson] (1870-1946.

A2018   KUZNETS, LOIS. "The Story Hour: Some Thoughts About Fiction for Children and Young Adults." *ChLAQ* 8, no. 3 (Fall 1983):44-45.
Compares the literary and film versions of the recently revived Australian classic *The Getting of Wisdom*, originally published in 1910.

RICHLER, MORDECAI (1931-   )

A2019   NODELMAN, PERRY. "*Jacob Two-Two* and the Satisfactions of Paranoia." *CCL* 15-16 (1980):31-37.
Provides a detailed critical analysis of the book.

A2020   PARR, JOHN. "Richler Rejuvenated." *CCL* 1, no. 3 (Autumn 1975):96-102.
> An in-depth review of *Jacob Two-Two Meets the Hooded Fang* that expresses some reservations but concludes with praise. "For this is a compellingly presented tale, replete with comic detail and story-line inventiveness."

A2021   RICHLER, MORDECAI. "Writing *Jacob Two-Two*." *Canadian Literature* 78 (Autumn 1978):6-8.
> Describes writing the book.

RICHTER, CONRAD (1890-1968)

A2022   LA HOOD, MARVIN J. "*The Light in the Forest*: History as Fiction." *English Journal* 55 (March 1966):298-304.
> Argues that careful research, a nearly perfect story, and Richter's style contribute to the outstanding quality of this novel.

RILEY, JAMES WHITCOMB (1849-1916)

A2023   REVELL, PETER. "The Child-World." In *James Whitcomb Riley*. Twayne's United States Author Series. New York: Twayne Publishers, 1970, pp. 74-86.
> Analyzes Riley's three volumes of children's verse--*The Book of Joyous Children*, *Rhymes of Childhood*, and *A Child World*--and the separately printed and often-anthologized "Little Orphan Annie."

RINGWOOD, GWEN PHARIS (1910-   )

A2024   ANTHONY, GERALDINE. "The Magic Carpets of Gwen Pharis Ringwood." *CCL* 8-9 (1977):74-83.
> Discusses the merits of the prize-winning *The Magic Carpets of Antonio Angelini*. Includes a bibliography of other Ringwood plays.

ROBERTS, CHARLES G.D., Sir (1860-1943)

A2025   GOLD, JOSEPH. "The Precious Speck of Life." *Canadian Literature* 26 (Autumn 1965):22-32.
> Argues that Roberts's stories are an important body of Canadian literature and deserve more critical attention.

A2026   HORNYANSKY, MICHAEL. "Roberts for Children." *CCL* 30 (1983):33-41.
> Reexamines three of Robert's books for children--*Children of the Wild*, *The Heart of the Ancient Wood*, and *In the Morning of Time*--to see how much archness afflicts him, and how he overcomes it.

A2027   McCORD, DAVID. "Introduction to a New Edition." *Horn Book* 48 (June 1972):255-58.
> Writes of *Red Fox*: "Just to read this book will make you ask yourself: Is man the true creature of dignity, courage, grace, and individual resourcefulness, or is it the better part of the wild populace which he is hastening, one by one, to its extinction?"

A2028   MAGEE, WILLIAM H. "The Animal Story: A Challenge in Technique." In Egoff, *Only Connect*, pp. 221-32.
> Detailed discussion of Roberts's realistic animal stories in his

books *Earth's Enigmas* and *Kindred of the Wild* as well as his precedents and influences.

A2029   MURRAY, TIM. "Charles Roberts' Animal Stories." *CCL* 1, no. 2 (Summer 1975):23-37.

Briefly reviews the history of criticism of Roberts's work, mainly centering on debates over his "realism." Then attempts to reveal the motive behind Roberts's stories and show that criticism directed at the level of realism is "critical nit-picking" and a waste of time. Separates the stories into three basic thematic types: stories of animals in the wild with almost no human intrusion, stories of "domestic" animals, and stories that focus on man in which he tries to analyze what makes man different from animals.

ROBERTS, ELIZABETH MADOX (1881-1941)

A2030   SMITH, WILLIAM JAY. "A Tent of Green." *Horn Book* 38 (April 1962):137-40.

An appreciative reflection on Roberts's poetry.

ROBERTS, THEODORE GOODRIDGE (1877-1953)

A2031   THOMPSON, RAYMOND. "The Pattern of Romance in T.G. Roberts' *The Red Feathers*." *CCL* 12 (1978):20-25.

Feels that modern critics have undervalued Roberts because they have failed to recognize his use of the elements of romance.

ROBINSON, JOAN (1910-   )

A2032   CROUCH, MARCUS. *The Nesbit Tradition*, pp. 208-10.

Describes *When Marnie Was There* as "a most beautiful and sensitive examination of a little girl and of the landscape which works too powerfully upon her."

ROBINSON, W[ILLIAM] HEATH (1872-1944)

A2033   CROUCH, MARCUS. "The Practical Fantasist." *Junior Bookshelf* 36 (April 1972):81-86.

A brief biocritical overview of the British illustrator.

ROCKWOOD, ROY [Stratemeyer Syndicate pseudonym]

A2034   PRAGER, ARTHUR. *Rascals at Large*, pp. 309-22.

Prager discusses Rockwood's Bomba series at length.

RODARI, GIANNI (1920-   )

A2035   BINDER, LUCIA. "Gianni Rodari--In Memory of the Renowned Italian Writer and Andersen Award Winner." *Bookbird* 3 (1980):28-30.

A brief biocritical overview.

A2036   POESIO, CARLA. "Gianni Rodari." *Bookbird* 6, no. 3 (1968):19-23.

Views Rodari's use of the fantastic and wonderful "inserted into the frame of current reality." Includes a bibliography of Rodari's books and a listing of reviews.

RODCHENKO, ALEXANDER (1891-1956)

A2037   SUMMER, SUSAN C., and ROMAN, GAIL H. "Cinematic Whimsey: Rodchenko's Photo-Illustrations For Autoanimals." *Art Journal* 41, no. 3 (Fall 1981):242-47.
Includes a translation and analysis of Rodchenko and Sergei Mikhailovich Tretiakov's (1892-1939) *Autoanimals* (*Samo z veri*).

ROHMER, SAX [Arthur Sarsfield Ward] (1883-1959)

A2038   PRAGER, ARTHUR. "The Mark of Kali." In *Rascals at Large*, pp. 47-69.
Vivid recollections and discussion of the appeal of the *Fu Manchu* stories.

ROJANKOVSKY, FEODOR (1891-1970)

A2039   AVERILL, ESTHER. "Feodor Rojankovsky and 'Les Peaux-Rouges.'" *Horn Book* 8 (February 1932):1.
Reviews Rojankovsky's *Daniel Boone*, a portfolio of lithographs with text in both French and English editions.

A2040   BADER, BARBARA. "Imported from France: The Domino Press, The Artists and Writers Guild, The First of Rojankovsky" and "Rojankovsky Concluded." In *American Picturebooks*, pp. 118-27, 295-301.
Traces Rojankovsky's significance as an illustrator from his breakthrough with *Daniel Boone* through other French publications to the publications of the Artists and Writers Guild. In "Rojankovsky Concluded," comments on *The Tall Book of Mother Goose*, *The Three Bears*, *I Play at the Beach*, and other books.

ROOSE-EVANS, JAMES (1927-   )

A2041   WRIGHT, JEAN. "The People and the Toys Behind the Odd and Elsewhere Stories." *Junior Bookshelf* 41, no. 2 (April 1977):67-72.
Examines the real-life origins of Roose-Evans's stories.

ROSSETTI, CHRISTINA (1830-1894)

A2042   BELLAS, RALPH A. *Christina Rossetti*. Twayne's English Author Series, no. 201. Boston: G.K. Hall, 1977, 139 pp.
Includes chapters on *Goblin Market* and *Sing-Song*.

A2043   EVANS, B. IFOR. "The Sources of Christina Rossetti's *Goblin Market*." *Modern Language Review* 28, no. 2 (April 1933):156-65.
Finds influences of *Arabian Nights* and Thomas Keightley's *Fairy Mythology* (1828) in *Goblin Market*.

A2044   GARLITZ, BARBARA. "Christina Rossetti's *Sing-Song* and Nineteenth-Century Children's Poetry." *PMLA* 70, no. 3 (June 1955):539-43.
Points out that critics have failed to note *Sing-Song*'s kinship with the moral and sentimental children's literature of the time.

A2045   MARY JOAN, Sister. "Christina Rossetti: Victorian Child's Poet." *EE* 44 (January 1967):24-28, 31.
An appreciative evaluation of Rossetti's poems. Includes a bibli-

ography.

A2046 WATSON, JEANIE. "'Men Sell Not Such in Any Town': Christina Rossetti's Goblin Fruit of Fairy Tale." *Children's Literature* 12 (1984):61-77.

Contends that *Goblin Market* has been examined primarily in terms of its allegorical framework, and that only by viewing it "as a tale for children," based on an interweaving of the fairy tale and the moral tale, can the poem's true moral be understood.

ROUNDS, GLEN (1906-   )

A2047 BADER, BARBARA. *American Picturebooks*, pp. 147-51.

Traces Rounds's career as an author and illustrator, emphasizing his style of illustration.

A2048 KINGSTON, CAROLYN T. *Tragic Mode*, pp. 36-38.

Examines the theme of rejection in *The Blind Colt*.

"Rumpelstiltskin"

A2049 CLODD, EDWARD. "The Philosophy of Rumpelstiltskin." *Folklore Journal* 8 (1889):135-68.

Provides a wide-ranging international comparison and exploration of the meanings of folktales of the "Rumpelstiltskin" pattern.

A2050 NATOV, RONI. "The Dwarf Inside Us: A Reading of Rumpelstiltskin." *L&U* 1, no. 2 (Fall 1977):71-76.

Interprets the tale as being about "the power of creative energy, what happens when it is not recognized, and why people fear it."

A2051 PARRY, IDRIS. "Kafka, Rilke, and Rumpelstiltskin." In *Animals of Silence*. London: Oxford University Press, 1972, pp. 1-9.

Links an interpretation of the tale to Rilke, and to Kafka's theories of the role of the artist in resolving contradictions. "The name is there, to be found and uttered."

A2052 ROHEIM, GÉZA. "Tom, Tit, Tot." *Psychoanalytic Review* 36, no. 4 (October 1949):365-69.

Provides a psychoanalytic interpretation of the folktale variants "Tom, Tit, Tot" and "Rumpelstiltskin."

RUSKIN, JOHN (1819-1900)

A2053 FILSTRUP, JANE MERRILL. "Thirst for Enchanted Views in Ruskin's *The King of the Golden River*." *Children's Literature* 8 (1980):68-79.

Compares Ruskin's tale with the original Grimm version, relating the differences to influences in Ruskin's life.

RUTGERS VAN DER LOEFF, AN (1910-   )

A2054 KINGSTON, CAROLYN T. *Tragic Mode*, pp. 78-80.

Analyzes *Avalanche* in terms of its theme of entrapment.

A2055 RUTGERS VAN DER LOEFF, AN. "A Sense of Audience-1." *CLE*, o.s., no. 5 (July 1971):5-11. (Reprinted in Fox, *Writers, Critics, and Children*, pp. 27-30.)

Discusses the motivation for her writing: she wants to pass certain material on to children. Comments by Gillian Avery, Alec Lea, Joan G. Robinson, and Roy Brown follow in *CLE*, o.s., no. 6 (November 1971), on their own views of themselves as writers for children.

S., SVEND OTTO [Svend Otto Sorenson] (1916-   )

A2056   GORMSEN, J. "Interview with Svend Otto S. the Famous Danish Illustrator." *Bookbird* 17, no. 1 (1979):6-12.
        Svend Otto S. discusses his life and work in an interview.

SAINT-EXUPÉRY, ANTOINE de (1900-1944)

A2057   DODD, ANNE W. "*The Little Prince*: A Study for Seventh Grade in Interpretation of Literature." *EE* 46 (October 1969):772-76.
        Suggests techniques for interpreting the story.

A2058   GAGNON, LAURENCE. "Webs of Concern: *The Little Prince* and *Charlotte's Web*." *Children's Literature* 2 (1973):61-66. (Reprinted in Butler, *Sharing*, pp. 442-46.)
        Applies aspects of Heidegger's philosophy to the interpretation of these two works. Both are seen as "about various personal struggles to live authentically."

A2059   HIGGINS, JAMES E. "*The Little Prince*: A Legacy." *EE* 37 (December 1960):514-15, 572.
        Argues that the book is unique, that it poses problems for readers of any age, that it respects the intelligence of even the youngest reader, and that it satirizes the belief that adults have a monopoly on wisdom.

A2060   HÜRLIMANN, BETTINA. "The Little Prince from Outer Space: An Attempt to Describe Antoine de Saint-Exupery's *Le Petit Prince*." In *Three Centuries*, pp. 93-98.
        Discusses factors that "in spite of everything" make *Le Petit Prince* a children's book, and relates it to Saint-Exupery's personal experiences.

A2061   MOONEY, PHILIP. "*The Little Prince*, A Story for Our Time." *America* 121 (20 December 1969):610-11, 614.
        Sees Christ extending love and peace in the Little Prince.

St. Nicholas

A2062   ERISMAN, FRED. "'There Was A Child Went Forth': A Study of *St. Nicholas* Magazine and Selected Children's Authors, 1890-1915." Ph.D. dissertation, University of Minnesota, 1966, 347 pp., DA 27:1818.
        Analyzes contrasting pictures of the world, the real and the ideal, as presented in *St. Nicholas* Magazine (where both views coexist), and in the novels of Ralph Henry Barbour, Kate Douglas Wiggin, and L. Frank Baum (who makes a conscious, and futile, attempt to "reconcile the conflict of the real and the ideal").

A2063   -----. "The Utopia of *St. Nicholas*: The Present as Prologue." *Children's Literature* 5 (1976):66-73.

Focuses on the middle-class values emphasized by *St. Nicholas*, its presentation of the "ideas of the past in the context of the present."

A2064 FULLER, LAWRENCE B. "Mary Mapes Dodge and *St. Nicholas*: The Development of a Philosophy and Practice of Publishing for Young People." ERIC Educational Document Reproduction Service, November 1984, 39 pp., ED 251 847.
Focuses on Dodge's development as a writer, the evolution of her philosophy of writing for children, her work as the editor of *St. Nicholas*, and her efforts to develop social and professional contacts with writers.

A2065 HOGARTH, W.D. "A Window to America." *Horn Book* 25 (January 1949):59-62.
An Englishman remembers the effect *St. Nicholas* had on him as a child during the years 1905-7, and how much it revealed to him about American life.

A2066 KENNEDY, REGINA DOLAN. "*St. Nicholas*: A Literary Heritage." *Catholic Library World* 37 (1965):239-41.
A concise history and overview of the magazine.

A2067 LANES SELMA. "Who Killed *St. Nicholas*?" In *Down the Rabbit Hole*, pp. 17-29.
Describes the way *St. Nicholas* reflected changes in American society.

A2068 ROGGENBUCK, MARY JUNE. "*St. Nicholas* Magazine: A Study of the Impact and Historical Influence of the Editorship of Mary Mapes Dodge." Ph.D. dissertation, University of Michigan, 1976, 434 pp., DA 37:6122A.
Provides a critical overview of *St. Nicholas* during the Dodge years, 1873-1905, concentrating on the literary aspects and the impact of Dodge's editorship.

A2069 SALER, ELIZABETH C., and CADY, EDWIN H. "The *St. Nicholas* and the Serious Artist." In *Essays Mostly on Periodical Publishing in America*. Edited by James Woodress. Durham, N.C.: Duke University Press, 1973, pp. 162-70.
Examines the battle over realism among the writers and editors of *St. Nicholas*.

A2070 STURGES, FLORENCE M. "The *St. Nicholas* Bequest." *Horn Book* 36 (October 1960):365-75. (Full version entitled "The Saint Nicholas Years," in Andrews, *The Hewins Lectures, 1947-1962*, pp. 267-95.)
A brief history and critical overview, highlighting some of *St. Nicholas's* most famous writers. See also "The Challenge of Quality," by Eulalie Steinmetz Ross, p. 363, in this same issue.

A2071 WRIGHT, CATHERINE M. "How *St. Nicholas* Got Rudyard Kipling and What Happened Then." *Princeton University Library Chronicle* 35 (Spring 1974):259-89.
Based on an extensive correspondence between Kipling and Mary Mapes Dodge.

SALINGER, J.D. (1919-   )

A2072   EDWARDS, JUNE. "Censorship in The Schools: What's Moral about *The Catcher in the Rye?*" *English Journal* 72 (April 1983):39-42.
Points out the book's morality on the basis of "the teachings of Jesus, the documents of our democracy, [and] Kohlberg's levels of moral reasoning."

A2073   McNAMARA, EUGENE. "Holden as Novelist." *English Journal* 54 (March 1965):166-70.
Examines *Catcher in the Rye* in terms of Holden's views of life, tradition, and art.

A2074   MOORE, ROBERT P. "The World of Holden." *English Journal* 54 (March 1965):159-65.
Analyzes Holden's character.

A2075   NASH, MILDRED J. "Holden and Alice: Adolescent Travellers." *English Journal* 72 (March 1983):30-31.
Finds similarities between Salinger's Holden Caulfield and Lewis Carroll's Alice.

A2076   PICKERING, JOHN KENNETH. "J.D. Salinger: Portraits of Alienation." Ph.D. dissertation, Case Western Reserve University, 1968, 347 pp., DA 30:3954A.
Analyzes loneliness and alienation in Salinger's works.

A2077   ROSEN, GERALD. "A Retrospective Look at *Catcher in the Rye.*" *American Quarterly* 29 (Winter 1977):547-62. (Reprinted in Lenz, *Young Adult Literature*, pp. 86-100.)
Analyzes the importance of Eastern thought and religion to Salinger. Includes a bibliography on Salinger.

SALTEN, FELIX (1869-1945)

A2078   FISHER, CLYDE. "*Bambi*: A Life in the Woods." *Horn Book* 3 (August 1928):58-59.
This early review highly praises the book and its illustrations by Kurt Wiese. "*Bambi* will do much to turn men and boys from the shotgun to the camera and the notebook."

SANCHEZ-SILVA, JOSÉ MARIA (1911-   )

A2079   HÜRLIMANN, BETTINA. *Three Centuries*, pp. 86-87.
Provides a brief analysis of *Marcelino*.

SANDBERG, INGER (1930-   ), and SANDBERG, LASSE (1924-   )

A2080   SANDBERG, INGER. "A Meeting with Inger Sandberg." In Koefoed, *Children's Literature*, pp. 62-66.
Discusses why she and Lasse have created the kinds of books they have and the way this Swedish husband-wife, author-illustrator team works.

SANDBURG, CARL (1878-1967)

A2081   LYNN, JOANNE L. "Hyacinths and Biscuits in the Village of Liver and Onions: Sandburg's *Rootabaga Stories.*" *Children's Literature* 8 (1980):118-32.

In the *Rootabaga Stories* Sandburg overcomes the flaws of much of his writing for adults and "speaks truth clearly." The article touches on many of the elements of the stories, their folkloric and incantatory qualities, their Midwesterness, their incongruity, and the poet-child relationship.

A2082 MASSEE, MAY. "Carl Sandburg as a Writer for Children." *EER* 5 (February 1928):40-42.

Pleads for adult acceptance of Sandburg's children's stories for children, with their ridiculous exaggeration, their understanding of human nature, and their lack of moralizing. Praises Sandburg's wordplays and his feeling for language.

SAUER, JULIA L. (1891-1983)

A2083 ELLEMAN, BARBARA. "A Second Look: *Fog Magic.*" *Horn Book* 56 (October 1980):548-51.

Provides a close examination of *Fog Magic.*

A2084 KINGSTON, CAROLYN T. *Tragic Mode*, pp. 72-73.

Analyzes the theme of entrapment in *The Light at Tern Rock.*

SAUNDERS, MARGARET MARSHALL (1861-1947)

A2085 McMULLEN, LORRAINE. "Marshall Saunders' Mid-Victorian Cinderella; or, the Mating Game in Victorian Scotland." *CCL* 34 (1984):31-39.

Traces the background and historical setting of one of Saunders's "rare ventures" away from animal protagonists: *Esther de Warren: The Story of a Mid-Victorian Maiden.*

SAVILLE, MALCOLM (1901-82)

A2086 MANNING, ROSEMARY. "A Book is a Book is a Book." *Signal* 3 (September 1970):81-90.

An appreciative overview.

SAWYER, RUTH (1880-1970)

A2087 HAVILAND, VIRGINIA. *Ruth Sawyer.* New York: Walck, 1965, 78 pp.

Provides biographical background and discusses *Roller Skates*, the Christmas stories, and Sawyer's storytelling.

A2088 KINGSTON, CAROLYN T. *Tragic Mode*, pp. 142-45.

Analyzes death and loss in *Roller Skates.*

A2089 OVERTON, JACQUELINE. "This Way to Christmas with Ruth Sawyer." *Horn Book* 20 (November-December 1944):447-60.

Describes the background for the Christmas scenes in *Roller Skates*, *The Year of Jubilo*, *This Way to Christmas* (especially "The Voyage of the Wee Red Cap"), *Tono Antonio*, *The Long Christmas*, and *The Christmas Anna Angel.* Sawyer's story "This Is the Christmas" is printed on pages 501-9 of this issue.

A2090   SAWYER, RUTH. "Newbery Medal Award Acceptance Speech." *Horn Book* 13 (July-August 1937):251-56.
Provides background and description of *Roller Skates*, particularly of the character Lucinda.

A2091   SEGEL, ELIZABETH. "A Second Look: *Roller Skates*." *Horn Book* 55 (August 1979):454-58.
The treatment of death in *Roller Skates* was shocking at the time but now seems surprisingly contemporary. Despite some mannerisms that tell its age, the story is still readable and engaging.

A2092   SULLIVAN, SHEILA R. "Fairy Gold in a Storyteller's Yarn." *EE* 35 (December 1958):502-7.
An enthusiastic introduction to Sawyer's books.

SCARRY, RICHARD M. (1919-   )

A2093   KENNEDY, MOPSY STRANGE. Review. *NYTBR*, 14 November 1976, p. 44.
Reviews *Busiest People Ever* and to a lesser extent Gyo Fujikawa's *Oh! What a Busy Day!* Suggests that Mr. Frumble be sent to Fujikawa's world for "a restorative 24 hours."

A2094   MOSS, ELAINE. "Richard Scarry." *Signal* 13 (January 1974):42-46.
Sees similarities between Scarry and the traditional English comics with their combination of entertainment and instruction. Scarry's banner, "Books are Fun!," summarizes his approach.

A2095   WINTLE, JUSTIN, and FISHER, EMMA. *Pied Piper*, pp. 64-76.
Richard Scarry discusses his life and work in an interview.

SCHMIDT, ANNIE

A2096   HARMSEL, HENRIETTA TEN. "Annie M.G. Schmidt: Dutch Children's Poet." *Children's Literature* 11 (1983):135-44.
This introduction to Schmidt's poems by their translator compares them to the tales of Hans Christian Andersen.

SCHULZ, CHARLES (1922-   )

A2097   BERGER, ARTHUR A. "*Peanuts*: An American Pastoral." *Journal of Popular Culture* 3, no. 1 (Summer 1969):1-8.
Describes his meeting with Schulz, links the man to the comic strip and justifies regarding it as an especially American form of pastoral.

A2098   HARRINGTON, MARY. "A Conversation with Charles Schulz." *Psychology Today* 18 (January 1968):18-21, 66-69.
In an interview discusses his life and work.

A2099   SCHULZ, CHARLES M. *Charlie Brown, Snoopy and Me and All the Other Peanuts Characters*. Garden City, N.Y.: Doubleday, 1980, 126 pp.
Schulz tells about his life, describes the origins of the Peanuts comic strips, and discusses his methods of working. Pictures show how the characters have changed over the years.

SEABROOK, KATIE

A2100   SCHMIDT, NANCY. *Children's Fiction about Africa*, pp. 78-80.
Analyzes treatment of Africa and Africans in *Gao of the Ivory Coast* and *Colette and Baba at Timbuctoo*.

SEBESTYEN, OUIDA (1924-   )

A2101   HALEY, BEVERLY. "Words by Ouida Sebestyen." *ALAN Review* 10, no. 3 (Winter 1983):2-6, 13.
Provides an overview of Sebestyen's work for young adults.

A2102   *Interracial Books for Children* 11, no. 7 (1980):12-18.
Includes Rudine Sims's "*Words by Heart*: A Black Perspective," pp. 12-15, 17; Fay Wilson-Beach and Glyger G. Beach's "*Words by Heart*: An Analysis of Its Theology," pp. 16-17; and Kathy Bixler's "*Words by Heart*: A White Perspective," p. 18.

SEED, JENNY (1930-   )

A2103   SCHMIDT, NANCY. *Children's Fiction About Africa*, pp. 161-64.
Argues that Seed's *The Broken Spear* contains stereotypes and lacks a Zulu perspective, even though it is based on historical research.

SEGAL, EDITH

A2104   SCHWARTZ, ALBERT V. "Edith Segal: Friend and Poet." *EE* 50 (November-December 1973):1223-27.
An appreciative biocritical overview.

SENDAK, MAURICE B. (1928-   )

A2105   ALDERSON, BRIAN. "Bodley-Headed Wild Things on the Horizon." *Children's Book News* 2, no. 2 (March-April 1967):53-56.
Analyzes Sendak's appeal on the eve of *Where the Wild Things Are*'s publication in Britain.

A2106   -----, comp. *Catalogue for an Exhibition of Pictures by Maurice Sendak at the Ashmolean Museum, Oxford, December 16 to February 29, 1975-76*. London: Bodley Head, 1975, 48 pp.
Alderson's introduction places Sendak's work as an illustrator in the context of pictures as accompaniment or collaboration with a text. Commentary on individual illustrations is divided into those before and after *The Wild Things*. Includes a brief bibliography of books and articles by Sendak.

A2107   ARAKELIAN, PAUL G. "Text and Illustration: A Stylistic Analysis of Books by Sendak and Mayer." *ChLAQ* 10 (Fall 1985):122-27.
Analyzes the arrangement of text and illustrations on the page, the structure of the text, the structure of the illustrations, and the relationship between the text and illustrations in Sendak's *Where the Wild Things Are* and Mercer Mayer's *There's a Nightmare in My Closet*.

A2108   BADER, BARBARA. "Maurice Sendak." In *American Picturebooks*, pp. 495-524.

Traces Sendak's evolution as an illustrator and picture-book author from the collaborations with Ruth Krauss and others, through *The Little Bear* books, *Kenny's Window*, *Very Far Away*, *The Sign on Rosie's Door*, *The Nutshell Library*, and finally *Where the Wild Things Are*, *Hector Protector*, and *In the Night Kitchen* (which she feels works "as a creation" but falters "as a story").

A2109 BELL, ARTHUR. "An Affectionate Analysis of *Higglety Pigglety Pop!*" *Horn Book* 44 (April 1968):151-54.
Explores some of the book's complexities and techniques.

A2110 BETTELHEIM, BRUNO. "The Care and Feeding of Monsters." *Ladies Home Journal* 86 (March 1969):48.
Discusses *Where the Wild Things Are* with a group of concerned mothers. At the time Bettelheim had not read the book.

A2111 BRAUN, SAUL. "Sendak Raises the Shade on Childhood." *New York Times Magazine*, 7 June 1970, pp. 34-37, 40-54.
Provides a thorough overview of Sendak's work and records an interview. Comments on Sendak's lack of didacticism and his opening of freedom to the child. "Sendak shouts a resounding 'No!' to the idea that there is something good about a tidy, obedient child."

A2112 COCHRAN-SMITH, MARILYN. "Directions in Research: Looking for the Roots of the Reading Process: Some Directions for Study (Part I)." *ChLAQ* 7, no. 1 (Spring 1982):42-48.
Reports on a study of the response of a group of three-to-five-year-old children to a recording and the illustrations of *In The Night Kitchen*.

A2113 CONRAD, BARNABY III. "Maurice Sendak." *Horizon* 24, no. 5 (May 1981):24-33.
The publication of *Outside Over There* is the occasion for this lavishly illustrated overview of Sendak's career. Provides a concise summary of critical responses to his work.

A2114 COTT, JONATHAN. "Maurice Sendak: King of All the Wild Things." In *Forever Young*, pp. 189-219. (Revised version of an interview first published in *Rolling Stone*, no. 229 [30 December 1976]:55, 59. Also in *Pipers*, pp. 41-84.)
Includes a brief biographical sketch, an interview, an exploration of the role of fantasy and fairy tale, Sendak's themes of incorporation (eating-up), nakedness, dreams, and music. Cott sees Sendak's works as falling into either a major or minor key. Also discusses influences of other writers and illustrators. *Pierre* is named for the novel of the same name by Melville. Concludes with a detailed discussion of *Outside Over There* and its literary and pictorial origins and sources.

A2115 DAHLIN, R. "Story Behind the Book: *Some Swell Pup: Or Are You Sure You Want a Dog?*" *Publishers Weekly* 209 (28 June 1976):78.
Describes the origins of *Some Swell Pup* by Matthew Margolis and Sendak and the considerations in designing it. "The dog in the book can be a metaphor for children," says Sendak.

A2116 DAVIS, DAVID C. "Wrong Recipe Used *In the Night Kitchen*." *EE* 48 (November 1971):856-64.

Davis provides a detailed analysis of *In the Night Kitchen* which he also compares with Sendak's other books, but his statements are so outrageous that it is difficult to know whether he is serious or satirical. He calls the book "a denial of civilized man" destined for the diaper pail.

A2117 DE LUCA, GERALDINE. "Exploring Levels of Childhood: The Allegorical Sensibility of Maurice Sendak." *Children's Literature* 12 (1984):3-24.

Analyzes Sendak's books, particularly *Outside Over There*, in terms of his use of allegory. Feels that at the end of *Outside Over There* we are left "with too much pain."

A2118 DOHM, J.H. "Twentieth Century Illustrators: Maurice Sendak." *Junior Bookshelf* 30, no. 2 (April 1966):103-11.

This early evaluation of Sendak as illustrator calls him irritating and disappointing and finds his illustration of others' works much better than his own books, especially *Where the Wild Things Are*.

A2119 DOOLEY, PATRICIA. "'Fantasy Is The Core . . . ?'--Sendak." *ChLAQ Newsletter* 1, no. 3 (Autumn 1976):1-4.

Summarizes Sendak's career and points out the value of the Sendak materials in the Rosenbach Foundation Museum in Philadelphia.

A2120 FORD, ROGER H. "Let the Wild Rumpus Start!" *LA* 56 (April 1979):386-93.

Analyzes the archetype of the trickster in Sendak's works, seeing Max, Hector, Jennie, Rosie, Pierre, and others in this role.

A2121 GARDNER, JOHN. "Fun and Games and Dark Imaginings." *NYTBR*, 26 April 1981, Children's Book sec., pp. 49, 64-65.

Review of *Outside Over There*. Provides insights into the dark mysteries of the book, which he calls "a profound work of art for children."

A2122 HARRIS, MURIEL. "Impressions of Sendak." *EE* 48 (November 1971):825-32.

Based partly on an interview with Sendak in his home, the article considers Sendak's portrayals of children, his own reflections upon children and childhood, and children's reactions to his books. Concludes with an analysis of *In the Night Kitchen*.

A2123 HAVILAND, VIRGINIA, and SENDAK, MAURICE. "Questions to An Artist Who Is Also an Author." *Quarterly Journal of the Library of Congress* 28 (October 1971):262-80. (Reprinted in Meek, *Cool Web*, pp. 241-56; in Hoffman, *Authors and Illustrators*, pp. 364-77; and in Haviland, *Openhearted Audience*, pp. 25-45.)

Sendak discusses his background and the origins of several of his books. Also comments on authors and artists who influenced him.

A2124 HEINS, ETHEL. Review. *Horn Book* 56 (June 1981):288-89.

Calls *Outside Over There* evocative and masterly and finds the story more fully realized in the illustrations than in the text.

A2125 HEINS, PAUL. Review. *Horn Book* 50 (April 1974):136-38.

Analyzes Sendak's techniques and interpretations in *The Juniper Tree and Other Tales from Grimm*.

A2126   HENTOFF, NAT. "Among the Wild Things." *New Yorker*, 22 January 1966. (Reprinted in Egoff, *Only Connect*, 1st ed., pp. 323-46.)
Personal observations on Sendak and his work, largely based on a series of interviews.

A2127   HOFFMAN, DARLENE HAFFNER. "Ten Days with Inga and *In the Night Kitchen*: An Episode in Language Development." *Communication Education* 25 (January 1976):1-15.
Describes the impact of the book on a three-year-old girl.

A2128   LANES, SELMA. *The Art of Maurice Sendak*. New York: Harry N. Abrams, 1980, 278 pp.
A major study of Sendak's work, lavishly illustrated, containing much biographical background and many of Sendak's own comments upon his work. Includes detailed discussions of *The Nutshell Library*, pp. 69-75, *Where the Wild Things Are*, pp. 77-107, *Hector Protector*, pp. 111-20, and *In the Night Kitchen*, pp. 173-90.

A2129   -----. "The Art of Maurice Sendak: A Diversity of Influences Inform an Art for Children." *Artforum* 9 (May 1971):70-73.
Argues that what is original about Sendak's work in a number of styles is "his uncanny ability to make palpable the emotional reality of any tale." Surveys his work to date.

A2130   -----. "Rackham and Sendak: Opposite Ends of the Telescope." In *Down the Rabbit Hole*, pp. 67-78.
Contrasts the approaches of Rackham and Sendak.

A2131   -----. "Sendak at Fifty." *NYTBR*, 29 April 1979, Children's Book sec., pp. 23, 48-49.
An overview of Sendak's career on his fiftieth birthday.

A2132   McALPINE, JULIE CARLSON. "Sendak Confronts the 'Now' Generation." *Children's Literature* 1 (1972):138-42.
Reports on a question-answer session between Sendak and a group of University of Connecticut students in December 1970.

A2133   MacCANN, DONNARAE, and RICHARD, OLGA. "Picture Books for Children." *WLB* 56 (September 1981):49-50.
This negative review of *Outside Over There* argues that its structure lacks coherence and its images are disjointed and irrelevantly symbolic. Includes a report on children's responses to the book.

A2134   MARTIN, C.M. "Wild Things." *Junior Bookshelf* 31 (December 1967):359-63.
Explores the duality of human nature, the appeal of horrible and wild things, the appeal of Sendak's *Where The Wild Things Are*, and its broader implications.

A2135   MAY, JILL P. "Sendak's American Hero." *Journal of Popular Culture* 12 (Summer 1978):30-35.
Argues that Sendak has created "a picture book prototype of the American preschooler," appealing to and easily identified with by both boys and girls, a hero "uninhibited by the adult moral code."

A2136   MIKKELSEN, NINA. "Talking and Telling: The Child as Storymaker." *LA* 61 (March 1984):229-39.

Reports on children's retellings and responses to *Outside Over There*.

A2137   NORDSTROM, URSULA. "Maurice Sendak." *Library Journal* 89 (15 March 1964):92-94.

Records Sendak's comments on his work with several authors, and their comments about him as an illustrator. Includes Ruth Krauss, Else Minarik, Charlotte Zolotow, and Meindert De Jong.

A2138   ROOT, SHELTON L. Review. *EE* 48 (February 1971):262-63.

A thoroughly disapproving review attacking the sexuality and sensuality of *In the Night Kitchen*. "It may be that America's children have been waiting with bated breath for this opportunity to vicariously wallow nude in cake dough and skinny-dip in milk--not to mention the thrill of kneading, punching, pounding, and pulling. Somehow, I doubt it." In a later issue (*EE* 48 [May 1971]:537), Root reaffirms his opinions of the book.

A2139   SENDAK, MAURICE. "Acceptance Speech Andersen Award, 1970." *Bookbird* 8, no. 2 (1970):6-7. (Also in *TLS*, 2 July 1970, p. 709.)

Mentions influences on his work: his Jewish childhood in Brooklyn, Mickey Mouse, "uptown" New York, and several illustrators and books. Presents his vision of what he wants his picture books to be: "something resembling the lush, immediate beauty of music and all its deep, unanalyzable mystery."

A2140   -----. "Caldecott Award Acceptance." *Horn Book* 40 (August 1964):345-51.

Discusses the origins of *Wild Things*, important influences on his work, and his views of childhood. A biographical sketch by Leo Wolfe follows, pp. 351-54.

A2141   -----. "Laura Ingalls Wilder Award Acceptance." *Horn Book* 59 (August 1983):474-77.

Very brief, but Sendak says that since reading the Little House Books while recovering from his coronary he realizes that "little houses" have appeared in his work: in *In the Night Kitchen*, in *The Juniper Tree*, in *Some Swell Pup*, and in *Outside Over There*.

A2142   -----. "Picture Book Genesis: A Conversation with Maurice Sendak." *Proceedings of the Children's Literature Association* 5 (1978):29-40.

Sendak expands upon the genesis of the then yet-to-be published *Outside Over There*, discusses his other works, collaborations, influence of music and television, and his themes and preoccupations. Provides insight into the man and his work. Talks about the original Rosie.

A2143   -----. "The Shape of Music." *New York Herald Tribune*, 1 November 1964, Book Week Fall Children's issue, pp. 1, 4-5. (Reprinted in Robinson, E., *Readings About Children's Literature*, pp. 201-5.)

Contemplates the relationship between music and illustration, in his own work and that of others, and the way illustrations "quicken" a work.

A2144   SEXTON, LYNDA. "Too Many Sides to Count." *Parabola* 6, no. 4

(Fall 1981):88-91.

Provides an in-depth analysis of *Outside Over There* and argues that Sendak shows the reader how "to move beyond dualism into the complexity of imagination."

A2145 STEIG, MICHAEL. "Reading *Outside Over There.*" *Children's Literature* 13 (1985):139-53.

Makes connections between *Outside Over There* and the work of George MacDonald, particularly *The Princess and the Goblin*, and Arthur Hughes's illustrations for that book and *At the Back of the North Wind*.

A2146 SWANTON, AVERILL. "Maurice Sendak's Picture Books." *CLE*, o.s., no. 6 (1971):38-48.

Provides detailed analysis of Sendak's handling of the theme of the child's anger against his mother in text and illustrations for *Where the Wild Things Are*, and his skill in illustrating *Mr. Rabbit and the Lovely Present*, which is interpreted as concerned with the child's "feelings of bewilderment in growing relationships with the opposite sex."

A2147 TAYLOR, MARY AGNES. "In Defense of the Wild Things." *Horn Book* 46 (December 1970):642-6.

Refutes Bettelheim's views as expressed in the *Ladies Home Journal* (March 1969). Argues that the pictures must be taken into account as well as the text, that there is a difference between traditional fairy tales and a modern original tale, and that Sendak's *Where the Wild Things Are* is "juvenile escape literature on an exceptionally high artistic level."

A2148 WALLER, JENNIFER. "Maurice Sendak and the Blakean Vision of Childhood." *Children's Literature* 6 (1977):130-40.

Compares Sendak's insights into childhood with Blake's, and compares Blake's and Sendak's responses to the challenges of "combining artistic vision and entertainment in a composite medium."

A2149 WATANABE, SHIGEO. "One of the Dozens: May Hill Arbuthnot Honor Lecture." *TON* 33 (Spring 1977):235-56.

Discusses his reactions to Dr. Hans A. Halbey's lecture "Analysis and Research on Children's Reception of the Picture Book *In The Night Kitchen*, by Maurice Sendak," presented at the Fifteenth Congress of the International Board on Books for Young People in 1976 in Athens, pp. 251-53.

A2150 WATERS, FIONA. "'How Much Does It Cost to Get to Where the Wild Things Are?'" *Book Window*, Spring 1976. (Reprinted in Culpan, *Variety is King*, pp. 123-25.)

Quotes Sendak at length on his development as an artist and on children's responses to *Where the Wild Things Are*.

A2151 WHITE, DAVID E. "A Conversation with Maurice Sendak." *Horn Book* 56 (April 1980):145-55.

Sendak discusses his "trilogy," as well as opera, theater, musical versions of his work, and his views on the children's book scene.

A2152 WINTLE, JUSTIN, and FISHER, EMMA. *Pied Piper*, pp. 20-34.

Maurice Sendak discusses his life and work in an interview.

SEREDY, KATE (1899-1975)

A2153   HIGGINS, JAMES E. "Kate Seredy: Storyteller." *Horn Book* 44 (April 1968):162-68.
Examines a number of aspects of Seredy's style and concludes that "each vividly reflects the person who is the author."

A2154   KASSEN, AILEEN M. "Kate Seredy: A Person Worth Knowing." *EE* 45 (March 1968):303-15. (Reprinted in Hoffman, *Authors and Illustrators*, pp. 378-93.)
A biographical and critical overview, concentrating on *The Good Master* and *The White Stag*. Includes references and a bibliography.

A2155   KINGSTON, CAROLYN T. *Tragic Mode*, pp. 29-32.
Analyzes the concepts of rejection and physical disability in *A Tree for Peter*.

A2156   MARKEY, LOIS R. "Kate Seredy's World." *EE* 29 (December 1952):451-57.
Analyzes Seredy's literary and artistic styles and relates them to her life.

A2157   SEREDY, KATE. "The Country of *The Good Master*." *EER* 13 (May 1936):167-68.
Describes the setting and childhood experiences that form the basis of this book.

SERRAILLIER, IAN (1912-   )

A2158   ALDERSON, BRIAN W. "Ian Serraillier and the Golden World." *Children's Book News*, January-February 1968. (Reprinted with slight changes in *Horn Book* 44 [June 1968]:281-88; and in Norton, *Folk Literature*, pp. 57-65.)
Compares Serraillier's approach to the Robin Hood legends in *Robin in the Greenwood: Ballads of Robin Hood* with others.

A2159   BULLEN, GILL. "Teachers at Work: Two Novels in the Classroom." *CLE*, n.s. 11, no. 2 (Summer 1980):85-88.
Comments on the classroom success of *The Silver Sword*.

A2160   CROUCH, MARCUS. *The Nesbit Tradition*, pp. 28-30.
Describes *The Silver Sword* as an open-ended adventure story, not shying away from cruelty and pain. He "pushes the bounds of tradition out as far as they will go."

A2161   -----. "The Poetry of Ian Serraillier." *Junior Bookshelf* 22 (December 1958):309-14.
Examines Serraillier's poetry.

A2162   KINGSTON, CAROLYN T. *Tragic Mode*, pp. 102-5.
Examines *The Silver Sword* in terms of its theme of war.

A2163   SCHECTER, ELLEN. Review. *Children's Literature* 3 (1974):211-13.
Reviews Serraillier's poetry and Ed Emberley's illustrations for *Suppose You Met a Witch*. "An excellent marriage of verbal and visual arts for children."

Sesame Street Library

A2164   CHARNES, RUTH; HOFFMAN, KAY E.; HOFFMAN, LYLA; and MEYERS, RUTH S. "The Sesame Street Library--Bad Books Bring Big Bucks." *IRBC* 10, no. 5 (1979):3-7.

        Finds fault with the Sesame Street Library on the grounds of sexism, racism, pedagogy, and commercialism. An article by Carole E. Gregory, "Parents Speak Out on Sesame Street Library Series," follows pp. 8-9.

SETON, ERNEST THOMPSON (1860-1946)

A2165   MacDONALD, ROBERT H. "The Revolt Against Instinct: The Animal Stories of Seton and Roberts." *Canadian Literature* 84 (Spring 1980):18-29.

        Examines Seton's and Sir Charles G.D. Roberts's animal stories in terms of Seton's distinction between instinct and reason, showing that the stories are part of a "popular revolt against Darwinian determinism" and "an affirmation of man's need for moral and spiritual values."

SEUSS, Dr. [Theodor Seuss Geisel] (1904-   )

A2166   BADER, BARBARA. "Dr. Seuss." In *American Picturebooks*, pp. 302-12.

        Traces Seuss's career and explores key elements of his appeal.

A2167   BAILEY, JOHN P. "Three Decades of Dr. Seuss." *EE* 42 (January 1965):7-12.

        Categorizes Seuss's works by time period: before World War II, 1947-57, and 1957 to the mid-1960s, showing changes in poetic style, illustration, and character depiction.

A2168   BURNS, THOMAS A. "Dr. Seuss' *How the Grinch Stole Christmas*: Its Recent Acceptance into the American Popular Christmas Tradition." *New York Folklore* 2, nos. 3-4 (Winter 1976):191-204.

        Suggests a number of reasons for the acceptance of the Seuss animated cartoon into American Christmas tradition.

A2169   COTT, JONATHAN. "The Good Dr. Seuss." In *Pipers*, pp. 1-37.

        "Just as *Pretty Little Pocketbook* (Newbery) opened up new possibilities for children's literature in its time, so did *Mulberry Street* in ours." Discusses Seuss's momentum and expansiveness, his theme of inventing or discovering something new, his "most extraordinary variety of ingeniously named, fantastical-looking animals," the use of anapestic tetrameter verse, and of fantasy emphasizing flexibility and possibility.

A2170   DOHM, JANICE H. "The Curious Case of Dr. Seuss: A Minority Report from America." *Junior Bookshelf* 27 (December 1963):323-29. (Reprinted in *TON* 21 [January 1965]:151-55.)

        Provides a British perspective on Dr. Seuss. Finds him a bit vulgar and difficult to assess, yet admits there "is something alive and kicking here that the others lack." Asks if he is another Carroll or an "all-American Lear?"

A2171 FADIMAN, CLIFTON. "Professionals and Confessionals: Dr. Seuss and Kenneth Grahame." In Egoff, *Only Connect*, 1st ed., pp. 316-22; 2d ed., pp. 277-83. (Reprinted from *Enter, Conversing* [New York: World, 1962].)

While Grahame put "his deepest sense of the meaning of his own adult life" into his book, Dr. Seuss writes not as "self-revelation, but to please and entertain himself and his young readers."

A2172 FREEMAN, DONALD. "Who Thunk You Up, Dr. Seuss?" *San Jose Mercury*, 15 June 1969, Parade Magazine sec., pp. 12-13. (Reprinted in Hoffman, *Authors and Illustrators*, pp. 165-71.)

Lighthearted insight into the man and his work.

A2173 GOODMAN, ELLEN. "This Time Doctor Seuss Left a Bad Feeling." *Albuquerque Journal*, 24 April 1984, p. A4.

Attacks Seuss's *The Butter Battle Book* on ideological grounds, specifically the lack of dissenters and the bleak "anxiety-ridden non-conclusion."

A2174 JENNINGS, C.R. "Doctor Seuss: What Am I Doing Here?" *Saturday Evening Post* 238 (23 October 1965):105-9.

Profiles Seuss's life and work.

A2175 KAHN, E.J., Jr. "Profiles: Children's Friend." *New Yorker* 36 (17 December 1960):47-93.

Describes Seuss's personality and life-style and comments upon the origins and development of many of his books, relating them to events in his life.

A2176 KUSKIN, KARLA. "Seuss at Seventy-Five." *NYTBR*, 29 April 1979, Children's Book sec., pp. 23, 41-42.

Points out Seuss's lasting appeal.

A2177 LANES, SELMA. "Seuss for the Goose Is Seuss for the Gander." In *Down the Rabbit Hole*, pp. 79-89.

Sees Seuss as providing an outlet for anxiety through laughter.

A2178 NILSEN, DON L.F. "Dr. Seuss as Grammar Consultant." *LA* 54 (May 1977):567-72.

Analyzes the grammatical deviations in thirty-four Dr. Seuss books written between 1937 and 1973.

A2179 ORT, LORRENE LOVE. "Theodore Seuss Geisel--The Children's Dr. Seuss." *EE* 32 (March 1955):135-42.

Tells why Dr. Seuss's books are well-liked. Discusses illustrations, satirical touches, wordplay, suspense, and continuity from book to book.

A2180 SALE, ROGER. *Fairy Tales*, pp. 8-12.

A close analysis that is full of praise for the power and technique of *The 500 Hats of Bartholomew Cubbins*.

A2181 SCHROTH, EVELYN. "Dr. Seuss and Language Use." *Reading Teacher* 31 (April 1978):748-50.

Examines the distinguishing characteristics of Dr. Seuss's use of language.

A2182   SEE, CAROLYN. "Dr. Seuss and the Naked Ladies." *Esquire* 81, no. 6 (June 1974):118-19, 176.

         Primarily of interest for its biographical and anecdotal material.

A2183   STEIG, MICHAEL. "Dr. Seuss's attack on Imagination: *I Wish that I Had Duck Feet* and the Cautionary Tale." *Proceedings of the Children's Literature Association* 9 (1982):137-41.

         Maintains that "the didactic content of *I Wish that I Had Duck Feet* is more oppressive than the vocalized parental edict or the traditional cautionary tale," and "although the bright funny pictures conveying sexual and aggressive images" appeal to children the message is that the child should accept his place in the family and community by consigning his dreams to the garbage can.

A2184   STONG, EMILY. "Juvenile Literary Rape in America: A Post-Coital Study of the Writings of Dr. Seuss." *Studies in Contemporary Satire* 4 (1977):34-40.

         Provides a satirical analysis of Dr. Seuss as the pinnacle, the "phallic tower" of "Kiddie Porn."

A2185   VANDERGRIFT, KAY E. *Child and Story*, pp. 189-93.

         Five-and six-year-olds demonstrate growing critical abilities in examining the structure of *And to Think that I Saw It on Mulberry Street*, which they compare with Sendak's *Where the Wild Things Are* in the relation of "believe" to "make believe."

A2186   WINTLE, JUSTIN, and FISHER, EMMA. *Pied Pipers*, pp. 113-23.

         Dr. Seuss discusses his life and work in an interview.

SEWELL, ANNA (1820-1878)

A2187   BLOUNT, MARGARET. *Animal Land*, pp. 249-54.

         Analyzes Sewell's techniques and the place of *Black Beauty* in the context of the development of the humanized nature story.

A2188   CHAMBERS, AIDAN. "Letter from England: A Hope for Benefit." *Horn Book* 53 (June 1977):356-60.

         Summarizes events, as outlined by Susan Chitty, leading up to and following the publication of *Black Beauty*.

A2189   CHITTY, SUSAN. *The Lady Who Wrote Black Beauty*. London: Hodder and Stoughton, 1971, 256 pp.

         Part three of this biography, pp. 183-246, is primarily devoted to *Black Beauty*. Includes reflections on the the social order portrayed and comments on the information on horses and horsemanship conveyed. Discusses later editions, film versions and influences of the book.

A2190   STIBBS, ANDREW. "*Black Beauty*: Tales My Mother Told Me." *CLE*, o.s., no. 22 (Autumn 1976):128-34.

         Argues that *Black Beauty*, although one of the most popular books of all time, is not a quality work, that its language is limp and furthermore that the soft attitudes expressed in it are misleading and even dangerous, encouraging "unquestioning acceptance" of the precepts of one's mentors and of one's role and lot.

SEWELL, HELEN (1896-1957)

A2191   BADER, BARBARA. "Helen Sewell." *American Picturebooks*, pp. 81-87.
A survey and analysis of Sewell's ever-changing style of illustration.

A2192   BECHTEL, LOUISE SEAMAN. "Helen Sewell, 1896-1956, the Development of a Great Illustrator." *Horn Book* 33 (October 1957):369-88.
A biocritical summary with a complete list of books illustrated by Sewell on pp. 427-31.

A2193   PITZ, HENRY C. "The Book Illustrations of Helen Sewell." *American Artist* 22 (January 1958):34-39.
A well-illustrated bio-critical overview.

A2194   SEWELL, HELEN. "Illustrator Meets the Comics." *Horn Book* 24 (March 1948):137-40.
Tells how the comics have influenced her work.

SHANNON, MONICA (d. 1965)

A2195   MILLER, ELIZABETH CLEVELAND. "Monica Shannon." *Horn Book* 11 (March-April 1935):73-81.
Praises *California Fairy Tales*, *Eyes for the Dark*, and *Dobry*, which receives a detailed analysis.

SHARP, MARGERY (1905-   )

A2196   BLOUNT, MARGARET. *Animal Land*, pp. 163-69.
Discusses Sharp's tales about Miss Bianca, the mouse.

SHEPARD, E[RNEST] H[OWARD] (1879-1976)

A2197   KNOX, RAWLE, ed. *The Work of E.H. Shepard*. London: Methuen, 1979, 256 pp.
A biocritical overview containing numerous reproductions of Shepard's illustrations, many in color. Includes a critical essay, "A Master of Line," by Bevis Hillier, pp. 246-51.

A2198   SLOBODKIN, LOUIS. "Artist's Choice." *Horn Book* 26 (1950):293-95.
Analyzes Shepard's style of illustration in *Bertie's Escapade*.

SHULEVITZ, URI (1935-   )

A2199   SHULEVITZ, URI. "*Rain, Rain Rivers*." *Horn Book* (June 1971): 311-12.
Tells how he developed the images for this book.

A2200   -----. "Within the Margins of a Picture Book." *Horn Book* 47 (June 1971):309-11.
Using his *Fool of the World and the Flying Ship: A Russian Tale* as his example, Shulevitz argues that a picture book must have a "life-affirming attitude." Says children can identify with the fool.

A2201   -----. "Writing with Pictures." *Horn Book* 58 (1982):17-22. (Based on

the introduction to *Writing with Pictures* [New York: Watson-Guptill, 1982].)
Discusses his approach to the picture book.

SHULMAN, ALIX (1932-   )

A2202   NATOV, RONI. "Portrait of a Revolutionary: Emma Goldman for Young Readers." *L&U* 4, no. 1 (Summer 1980):41-53.
An in-depth analysis, within the context of feminist biography, of *To the Barricades: The Anarchist Life of Emma Goldman.*

SIDNEY, MARGARET [Also known as Harriet Lothrop] (1844-1924)

A2203   JOHNSON, ELIZABETH. "Margaret Sidney v.s. Harriet Lothrop." *Horn Book* 47 (June 1971):313-19.
This conclusion to a two-part article concentrates on Sidney's writing.

A2204   LEVIN, BETTY. "Peppers' Progress: One Hundred Years of the Five Little Peppers." *Horn Book* 57 (April 1981):161-73.
Places *Five Little Peppers and How They Grew* in a historical context, showing their connection with children from the seventeenth century through the twentieth.

SIGSGAARD, JENS

A2205   HOYLE, KAREN NELSON. "*Palle* in New Clothes: The Translation of a Danish Picture Book." *Proceedings of the Children's Literature Association* 6 (1979):122-27.
Examines the changes and variations in the translated versions of *Palle Alene I Verden* (*Nils All Alone*, *Paul is Alone*, and *Paul Alone in the World*).

SILVERSTEIN, SHEL (1932-   )

A2206   HEMPHILL, JAMES. "Sharing Poetry with Children: Stevenson to Silverstein." *Advocate* 4 (Fall 1984):38-45.
Explores the appeal of Silverstein's poetry to children.

A2207   JACKSON, JACQUELINE, and DELL, CAROL. "The Other Giving Tree." *LA* 56 (April 1979):427-29.
Presents an alternative to *The Giving Tree* that raises questions about values and interpretations of the original.

A2208   KENNEDY, F.X.J. "Rhyme is a Chime." Review of *A Light in the Attic*. *NYTBR*, 15 November 1981, pp. 51, 60.

A2209   SCHRAM, BARBARA. "Misgivings about *The Giving Tree*: Book Reaching Cult Status Glorifies Sexist Values." *IRBC* 5, no. 5 (1974):1, 8.
Attacks the book as perpetuating myths of the "happy slave" and an all-giving, selfless earth-mother.

A2210   STRANDBURG, WALTER L., and LIVO, NORMA J. "*The Giving Tree* or There is a Sucker Born Every Minute." *CLE*, n.s. 17, no. 1 (Spring 1986):17-24.
Surveys the responses of teachers, children, and social scientists to

The Giving Tree, and suggests that it is actually a satirical piece for adults "that has taken an incredible twist" and "has passed as children's literature."

SINGER, ISAAC BASHEVIS (1904-   )

A2211   BERKELEY, MIRIAM. "Isaac Bashevis Singer." *Publishers Weekly* 223 (18 February 1983):65-66.
Ĺ In an interview, Singer discusses his writing for children.

A2212   BERNHEIM, MARK A. "The Five Hundred Reasons of Isaac Singer." *Bookbird* 1-2 (1982):31-36.
Ĺ Extensive quotes from Singer on his reasons for writing for children, plus some analysis of his stories.

A2213   KIMMEL, ERIC. "I.B. Singer's *Alone in the Wild Forest*: A Kabbalistic Parable." *CLE*, o.s., no. 18 (Fall 1975):147-58.
Ĺ Argues that to truly understand Singer's work it is necessary to have some understanding of "the soul" of the "murdered world of traditional Polish Jewry." *Alone in the Wild Forest*, especially, requires knowledge of this background to be appreciated and understood. Kimmel provides detailed explication of the tale.

A2214   LEVENTHAL, NAOMI SUSAN. "Storytelling in The Works of Isaac Bashevis Singer." Ph.D. dissertation, Ohio State University, 1978, 193 pp., DA 39:4938A.
Ĺ Applies techniques of folklore study to an analysis of two aspects of Singer's fiction: fictional representations of storytelling in his work and the actual reading performance of the text itself.

A2215   MORSE, NAOMI S. "Values for Children in the Stories of Isaac Bashevis Singer." In MacLeod, *Children's Literature*, pp. 13-16.
Ĺ Compares and contrasts the children's stories of Isaac Bashevis Singer and Hans Christian Andersen.

A2216   PATTERSON, SYLVIA W. "Isaac Singer: Writer for Children." *Proceedings of the Children's Literature Association* 8 (1981):69-76.
Ĺ Examines Singer's works for children, emphasizing his respect for his audience and his ability to cross cultural lines.

A2217   SINGER, ISAAC. "Are Children the Ultimate Literary Critics?" *TON* 29 (1972):32-36.
Ĺ Sets forth his own aims in writing for children and laments "slice of life" and chaos in children's literature. Maintains that children like good plots, logic, and clarity, and that they have a concern for "so-called eternal questions."

A2218   -----. "Isaac Bashevis Singer: Interview." In Butler, *Sharing*, pp. 155-60.
Ĺ Discusses his writing and his views on children's literature in an interview with a class of students at the University of Connecticut.

A2219   WOLF, H.R. "Singer's Children's Stories and *In My Father's Court*: Universalism and the Rankian Hero." In *The Achievement of Isaac Bashevis Singer*. Edited by Marcia Allentuck. Carbondale: Southern Illinois University Press; London: Feffer & Simons, 1969, pp. 145-58.

Discusses *Mazel and Schlimazel* and *Zlateh the Goat* in psychoanalytic and Rankian terms.

A2220 WOLKSTEIN, DIANE. "The Stories Behind the Stories: An Interview with Isaac Bashevis Singer." *CLE*, o.s., no. 18 (Fall 1975):136-45.
Singer discusses the Jewish folk origins of his tales, his background, and the influences on his work. Preceded by "A Note on Isaac Bashevis Singer," pp. 134-35, which provides biographical background and a bibliography of his books for children and adults.

"Sleeping Beauty"

A2221 ANDERSON, WILLIAM. "Fairy Tales and the Elementary Curriculum or 'The Sleeping Beauty' Reawakened." *EE* 46 (May 1969):563-69.
Shows how the tale could be used to introduce children "to the themes, archetypes, convention, and symbols of the corpus of Western literature," and to show "how plots can make statements about Justice, Fate, the Order, and the Hero."

A2222 CARY, JOSEPH. "Six Beauties Sleeping." *Children's Literature* 6 (1977):224-34.
Analyzes the common elements of the five versions of "Sleeping Beauty" collected by P.L. Travers in *About the Sleeping Beauty*, and comments on Travers's own version, which he sees as flawed but "light-giving."

A2223 SMITH, LILLIAN. *Unreluctant Years*, pp. 46-51.
Analyzes the conventions, plot, repetition, diction, and rhythm of the "Sleeping Beauty."

SLEIGH, BARBARA (1906-82)

A2224 MOSS, ELAINE. "Barbara Sleigh: The Voice of Magic." *Signal* 8 (May 1972):43-48.
Relates Sleigh's autobiography, *A Smell of Privet*, to her fantasies for children.

SLOBODKIN, LOUIS (1903-75)

A2225 SLOBODKIN, LOUIS. "The Caldecott Medal Acceptance." *Horn Book* 20 (July-August 1944):307-17.
Describes in detail the process of illustrating *The Middle Moffat* by Estes and *Many Moons* by Thurber. See also the preceding article by Eleanor Estes, "Louis Slobodkin: A Sculptor Enters the Book World," pp. 299-306, a biographical account laced with appreciation for the illustrator's work.

SMARIDGE, NORAH (1903-   )

A2226 GILPATRICK, NAOMI. "Power of Picture Book to Change Child's Self-Image." *EE* 46 (May 1969):570-74. (Reprinted in White, *Children's Literature*, pp. 79-85.)
An application of new criticism to the text and pictures of *Peter's Tent* (illustrated by Brinton Turkle), "tracing the structure of meanings through the counterplay of symbols and images."

SMITH, DORIS BUCHANAN (1934-   )

A2227   SMITH, DORIS B. "Honey in the Heart." *Advocate* 1, no. 1 (Fall 1981):10-18.
Smith describes her background and her approach to writing.

A2228   VANDERGRIFT, KAY. *Child and Story*, pp. 164-66.
Analyzes *A Taste of Blackberries* in terms of character, mood, and symbol.

SMITH, E. BOYD (1860-1943)

A2229   BADER, BARBARA. "E. Boyd Smith." In *American Picturebooks*, pp. 13-22.
An overview of Smith's career, analysis of individual works, and discussion of his influence on and place in the development of the American picture book for children. Includes references.

A2230   HEARN, MICHAEL PATRICK. "A Second Look: *The Farm Book*." *Horn Book* 58 (December 1982):670-73.
Traces the influence of Swedish illustrator Carl Larsson and others on Smith. Praises Smith's "clear, stately prose."

SMITH, JESSIE WILLCOX (1863-1935)

A2231   FREEMAN, RUTH S. *Jessie Willcox Smith: Childhood's Great Illustrator: Resume of Her Work (1863-1935).* Watkins Glen, N.Y.: Century House, 1977, 24 pp.
Provides a brief overview of Smith's life and work.

A2232   ISON, MARY M. "Things Nobody Ever Heard of: Jessie Willcox Smith Draws the Water-Babies." *Quarterly Journal of the Library of Congress* 39 (Spring 1982):90-101.
Examines Smith's illustrations of Charles Kingsley's *The Water-Babies*. Includes reproductions, several in color.

A2233   MITCHELL, GENE. *The Subject Was Children: The Art of Jessie Willcox Smith*. New York: Dutton, 1979, 66 pp.
Includes a brief introduction, an autobiographical sketch, and numerous color plates.

A2234   SCHNESSEL, S. MICHAEL. *Jessie Willcox Smith*. New York: Crowell, 1977, 224 pp.
Chapter 3, "A Child's Garden," concentrates on her children's book illustrations.

SMUCKER, BARBARA (1915-   )

A2235   DAVIES, CORY BIEMAN. "Remembrance and Celebration: Barbara Smucker's *Days of Terror*." *CCL* 25 (1982):18-25.
A detailed analysis of this historical novel about the mass migration of Russian Mennonites to Canada in the early 1920s.

"Snow White"

A2236   CRAGO, HUGH. "Who Does Snow-White Look At?" *Signal* 45 (September 1984):129-45.

Compares, at length, four picture-book versions of "Snow-White," including Nancy Ekholm Burkert's, Trina Schart Hyman's, and two mass-market volumes--a Japanese puppet storybook published by Grosset & Dunlap and a Walt Disney Golden Press book.

A2237   CRAGO, MAUREEN. "'Snow White': One Child's Response in a Natural Setting." *Signal* 31 (January 1980):42-56.
Discusses her child's responses to two versions of "Snow-White."

A2238   FARRELL, DIANE. Review of the Hyman-Heins version of *Snow White*. *Horn Book* 51 (February 1975):36-37.
Praises Hyman's detailed illustrations.

A2239   GIRARDOT, N.J. "Initiation and Meaning in the Tale of Snow White and the Seven Dwarfs." *Journal of American Folklore* 90 (July 1977):274-300.
Provides a detailed analysis of "Snow White" in terms of a pattern of initiation comprised of phases of separation, liminality, and reincorporation and rebirth. Reply with rejoinder by S. Jones in 92 (January 1979):69-76.

A2240   JONES, STEVEN SWANN. "The Construction of the Folktale: 'Snow White.'" Ph.D. dissertation, University of California, Davis, 1979, 231 pp., DA 40:5538A.
Argues that the structural construction of folktales explains certain folktales' "longevity and consistency, despite variation in style and motif."

A2241   SALE, ROGER. *Fairy Tales*, pp. 38-43.
Criticizes Bettleheim's interpretation of "Snow White" as the story of a parent's maintaining dominance by arresting a child's development, and analyzes the tale in terms of the "central" relationship of the older to the younger woman.

A2242   "Snow White and the Seven Dwarfs." *Junior Bookshelf* 3, no. 1 (October 1938):19-20.
Compares the Wanda Gág and Walt Disney Versions of "Snow White."

SNYDER, ZILPHA KEATLEY (1928-   )

A2243   KARL, JEAN. "Zilpha Keatley Snyder." *EE* 51 (September 1974):785-89.
Snyder's editor provides insights into her writing processes.

SOBOL, DONALD J. (1924-   )

A2244   CRICHTON, JEAN. "Encyclopedia Brown, After Twenty Years Is Still Sleuthing--and Selling." *Publishers Weekly* 224 (11 November 1983):35-36.
Emphasizes sales and popularity, but also provides insights into the appeal of the series.

SOMMERFELT, AIMÉE (1892-1975)

A2245   KINGSTON, CAROLYN T. *Tragic Mode*, pp. 60-63.
Analyzes the theme of entrapment in *The Road to Agra*.

SORENSON, VIRGINIA (1912-   )

A2246   KINGSTON, CAROLYN T. *Tragic Mode*, pp. 139-42.
Analyzes the theme of death and loss in *Miracles of Maple Hill*.

SOUTHALL, IVAN (1921-   )

A2247   BAYFIELD, JULIANA. "From *Simon Black* to *Ash Road* and Beyond."
Bookbird 6, no. 4 (1968):33-35. (Condensed from *Reading Time*,
March 1968, pp. 3-6.)
Analyzes changes in Southall's style and level of seriousness from
Simon Black to *Ash Road* and *The Fox Hole*.

A2248   BUNBURY, RHONDA M. "The Forces of the Australian Continent
Forge the Children's Identity: Through the Eyes of Patricia Wrightson and Ivan Southall." In Escarpit, *Portrayal of the Child*, pp.
87-94.
Discusses Wrightson and Southall's exploration of "the identity of
their child characters within the context of the demands made on
them by the land amidst the powerful and conflicting forces of fire,
water and air, the People and the spirits."

A2249   FOX, GEOFFREY. "Growth and Masquerade: A Theme in the Novels
of Ivan Southall." *CLE*, o.s., no. 6 (1971):49-64.
Suggests that Southall "offers his readers a criticism of life which
is often excruciating (perhaps indulgently so) in its insistence upon
the pain, disillusionment and embarrassed failures which are integral
to adolescence." Provides a detailed analysis of Southall's work,
defending him against charges of excessive harshness.

A2250   HUGHES, FELICITY. "Literary Criticism of Two Australian Novels."
In *Children's Literature: The Whole Story*. Deakin University School
of Education.   Waurn Ponds, Victoria, Australia, 1980, pp. 43-88.
Examines Ethel Turner's *Seven Little Australians* (1894) and Ivan
Southall's *Josh* within the context of Australian literary and critical
history.

A2251   LANGLEY-KEMP, JENNIFER. "Initiation: Ivan Southall Style."
Orana 13 (November 1977):95-99.

A2252   McVITTY, WALTER. "Ivan Southall: Wounding and Regeneration." In
Innocence and Experience, pp. 233-75.
Provides an in-depth critique and analysis of Southall's major
themes and his style.   Includes a brief biographical note preceding
the essay, with comments by Southall.   A bibliography of his works
follows.

A2253   MORRISON, ALLAN. "Letting the Characters Go: Ivan Southall."
Children's Literature Review 1, no. 6 (December 1971):184-86.
Sees Southall as a "man's man" whose writing is both "characteris-
tically masculine" and "femininely sensitive."

A2254   NILSSON, ELEANOR. "Bully Beef and Honey." *CLE*, n.s. 10, no. 2
(Summer 1979):103-10.
Calls *Bread and Honey* "Southall's greatest achievement so far"
and suggests that the celebration of the coming of age of a nation on

Anzac Day is of central importance to the book's theme of the coming of age of a boy.

A2255   PIRANI, ALEX. "Writers for Children." *Use of English* 22 (Spring 1971):233-37. (Reprinted in Meek, *Cool Web*, pp. 294-98, and in Butts, *Good Writers*, pp. 129-37.)
Defends Southall's treatment of realistic themes against David Holbrook's attack in *Books for Your Children*, arguing that although Southall's control of his material sometimes falters he shows a "respect for and trust in children."

A2256   SOUTHALL, IVAN. "Call It A Wheel." *Horn Book* 50 (October 1974):43-49.
Tells how *Josh* started.

A2257   -----. "Depth and Direction." *Horn Book* 44 (June 1968):343-46. (Reprinted in Heins, *Crosscurrents*, pp. 60-64.)
Describes his development as a writer from *Meet Simon Black* (1950) to *Ash Road* (1965).

A2258   -----. *A Journey of Discovery: On Writing for Children.* London: Kestrel, 1975; New York: Macmillan, 1976, 102 pp.
A collection of Southall's lectures on the subject of writing for children. These lectures "go on developing, thought by thought, out of my search for literary and self-understanding and are very much a personal statement."

A2259   -----. "One Man's Australia." In Egoff, *One Ocean*, pp. 18-37.
Discusses his childhood and his Australian background and relates them to his writing.

A2260   -----. "Real Adventure Belongs to Us." *Arbuthnot Lectures*, pp. 83-101. (Also in *TON* 30 [June 1974]:373-93.)
Describes his experiences growing up in Australia and how these experiences and his search for heroes found their way into his books.

A2261   -----. "Sources and Responses." *Quarterly Journal of the Library of Congress* 31 (April 1974):81-91. (Reprinted in Haviland, *The Open-hearted Audience*, pp. 83-99.)
Explores his thoughts on children and children's literature. "Adult scaling-down of the intensity of the child is a crashing injustice, an outrageous distortion of what childhood is all about." Suggests what "a good children's books is not" and describes his approach to writing.

A2262   TOWNSEND, JOHN ROWE. *Sense of Story*, pp. 182-92.
Praises Southall's "cinematic technique." Maintains that while "the force and intensity of his imagination have been fully demonstrated; its depth remains yet to be proved." Discusses *Let the Balloon Go, Finn's Folly, Hills End, To the Wild Sky,* and *Chinaman's Reef Is Ours.*

A2263   -----. *A Sounding*, pp. 179-93.
A revision and updating of the essay in *Sense of Story*. "A group of later books--most notably *Bread and Honey, Josh,* and *What About Tomorrow*--have concentrated on the joys and agonies of a single central character and have gone deeply down inside of that

person, using a technique increasingly close to stream-of-consciousness."

SPEARE, ELIZABETH GEORGE (1908-   )

A2264   COHEN, PHYLLIS. "A New Look at Old Books: *The Bronze Bow.*" *Young Readers' Review* 3 (October 1966):12. (Reprinted in White, *Children's Literature*, pp. 78-80.)
Criticizes the book's "omission of admirable characters on the side fighting for justice and freedom."

A2265   HUTTON, MURIEL. "Writers for Children: 13. Elizabeth George Speare." *School Librarian* 18 (September 1970):275-79.
Provides an introduction to Speare's historical fiction from a British point of view.

A2266   SPEARE, ELIZABETH GEORGE. "Newbery Award Acceptance." *Horn Book* 35 (August 1959):265-70.
Describes the process of the creation of *The Witch of Blackbird Pond*. A biographical account by Helen Reeder Cross follows, pp. 271-74.

A2267   -----. "Report of a Journey: Newbery Award Acceptance." *Horn Book* 38 (August 1962):337-41.
Tells the background of *The Bronze Bow*.

SPENCE, ELEANOR (1928-   )

A2268   BISNETTE, PAUL J. "A Conversation with Eleanor Spence." *Orana* 17 (February 1981):3-11.
Spence discusses her life and work in an interview. An annotated bibliography of works by and about her follows, pages 12-18.

A2269   GRGURICH, RUTH. "Eleanor Spence: A Critical Appreciation." *Orana* 18 (February 1982):31-36.
Analyzes Spence's fiction for teenagers.

A2270   McVITTY, WALTER. "Eleanor Spence: Observer of Family Life." In *Innocence and Experience*, pp 67-98.
Provides an overview and analysis of Spence's work. Includes a brief biographical sketch and a bibliography of her books. "Eleanor Spence is a writer with whose work increased familiarity breeds content--beyond the apparent blandness a richly rewarding experience awaits the reader who is prepared to give it the close attention it deserves."

SPERRY, ARMSTRONG (1897-1976)

A2271   KINGSTON, CAROLYN T. *Tragic Mode*, pp. 17-20.
Analyzes the theme of rejection in *Call It Courage*.

A2272   SPERRY, ARMSTRONG. "Newbery Medal Acceptance." *Horn Book* 17 (July 1941):258-68.
Tells of his experiences in Bora Bora that provided the foundation for *Call It Courage*.

SPIER, PETER (1927-   )

A2273   MOORE, ROBERT. Review. *IRBC* 12, no. 1 (1981):14.
Argues that although there are grotesquely drawn faces of all
colors in *People*, the "people of color seem most hideous." Feels the
book perpetuates white and male chauvinism.

A2274   SPIER, PETER. "Caldecott Award Acceptance." *Horn Book* 54 (August
1978):372-78.
Tells about the background of *Noah's Ark*, including his research
on various versions of the Noah story. A biographical sketch by
Janet D. Chenery follows on pp. 379-81.

SPYKMAN, E.C. (1896-1965)

A2275   ENRIGHT, ELIZABETH. "The Long Life of Jane Cares." *Book Week*,
8 May 1966, Spring Children's issue, p. 22. (Reprinted in Haviland,
Children and Literature, pp. 274-76.)
Praises Spykman's ability to create real, live children.

SPYRI, JOHANNA (1827-1901)

A2276   ENRIGHT, ELIZABETH. "At 75, Heidi Still Skips Along." *NYTBR*
59 (13 November 1955):42. (Reprinted in Haviland, *Children and
Literature* pp. 78-80.)
Maintains that Heidi's character continues to ring true.

A2277   "*Heidi*--Or the Story of a Juvenile Best Seller." *Publishers Weekly* 164
(25 July 1953):318-21.
Provides an overview of *Heidi*'s publishing history and a bit of
background about Spyri.

A2278   KOPPES, PHYLLIS BIXLER. "Spyri's Mountain Miracles: Exemplum
and Romance in *Heidi*." *L&U* 3, no. 1 (Spring 1979):62-73.
Argues that *Heidi* successfully combines the form of the pastoral
romance and the exemplum ("a literary form devoted to the portrayal
of ideals . . . especially in the evangelical tradition"), which may
explain its survival as a classic despite its didacticism and sentimentality.

STARBIRD, KAYE (1916-   )

A2279   HELBIG, ALETHEA. "Abigail, Elaine, and the Pheasant on Route
Seven: Kaye Starbird's Poems for Children." *ChLAQ* 8, no. 3 (Fall
1983):39-40.
An overview of Starbird's poetry.

A2280   USREY, MALCOLM. "Social Awareness in the Persona of Kaye Starbird's Poetry." *Proceedings of the Children's Literature Association* 5
(1978):93-99.
Examines the persona of the child in Starbird's poems and the
developing social awareness "revealed in her sympathy for insects,
animals, and people; her recognition of the relative value of things;
and her growing realization of the differences in people."

STEEDMAN, CAROLYN

A2281   CHAMBERS, AIDAN. "Letter from England." *Horn Book* 59 (December 1983):747-51.
Detects the influence of television as a "literary model" in the child-written book *The Tidy House*, which he praises highly.

STEELE, WILLIAM O. (1917-79)

A2282   BURNS, PAUL C. "Tennessee's Teller of Tall Tales--William O. Steele." *EE* 38 (December 1961):545-48.
Concentrates on Steele's tall tales rather than on his historical fiction.

A2283   STEELE, WILLIAM O. "The Last Buffalo Killed in Tennessee." *Horn Book* 45 (April 1969):196-99.
Describes the background and process of writing *The Lone Hunt*.

STEIG, WILLIAM (1907-   )

A2284   ABRAHAMSON, RICHARD F. "Classroom Uses for the Books of William Steig." *Reading Teacher* 32 (December 1978):307-11.
Suggests numerous approaches to Steig in the elementary school classroom.

A2285   BADER, BARBARA. *American Picturebooks*, pp. 563-64.
Concentrates on *Sylvester and the Magic Pebble*, which she considers a classic.

A2286   BOTTNER, BARBARA. "William Steig: The Two Legacies." *L&U* 2, no. 1 (Spring 1978):4-16.
Maintains that as a cartoonist accustomed to an adult audience, Steig brings an added dimension to his books for children, which are "tales full of magic, searching, death, and love of life; so that thematically his work is classic in scope, yet absolutely accessible in nature." Analyzes several of Steig's themes.

A2287   COTT, JONATHAN. "William Steig and His Path." In *Pipers*, pp. 87-133.
Traces the influence of Wilhelm Reich on Steig. In his children's books Steig "created and tested the possibilities of an unarmoured life." Discusses *Dominic* in depth, relating it to Reich's theories. Provides biographical background and discusses *The Bad Island*, *Sylvester and the Magic Pebble* (including the police-pig controversy), *Amos and Boris*, *The Real Thief*, *Abel's Island*, *Caleb and Kate*, and, briefly, several other titles.

A2288   HEARN, MICHAEL PATRICK. "Drawing Out William Steig." *Washington Post*, 11 May 1980. (Reprinted in *Bookbird* 3-4 [1982]:61-65.)
Interviews Steig about his work. Includes a bibliography of his children's books.

A2289   HIGGINS, JAMES. "William Steig: Champion for Romance." *CLE*, n.s. 9, no. 1 (Spring 1978):3-16.
An insightful appreciation of Steig's work, including an interview with the author.

A2290   KUSKIN, KARLA. ". . . and William Steig." *NYTBR*, 14 November 1976, Children's Book sec., pp. 24, 34.
Reviews the *Amazing Bone* and comments on others. "The uninhibited ego of childhood sings out of these books."

A2291   LANES, SELMA G. "Books: A Reformed Masochist Writes a Sunlit Children's Classic." *Harper's* 245 (October 1972):122-26.
A favorable review of *Dominic*.

A2292   MOSS, ANITA. "The Spear and the Piccolo: Heroic and Pastoral Dimensions of William Steig's *Dominic* and *Abel's Island*." *Children's Literature* 10 (1982):124-40.
Places these works in the tradition of the quest romance accented by pastoral interludes.

STEIN, GERTRUDE (1874-1946)

A2293   BECHTEL, LOUISE SEAMAN. "Gertrude Stein for Children." *Horn Book* 15 (October 1939):287-91. (Reprinted in Fryatt, *Horn Book Sampler*, pp. 128-32.)
Examines *The World Is Round*: "to those who honestly enjoy it, let me say it should be used, none too solemnly, with the most varied sorts of children. We don't want them all to write like Miss Stein! We do want to jog them out of the horribly ordinary prose that engulfs them."

A2294   HOFFELD, LAURA. "Gertrude Stein's Unmentionables." *L&U* 2, no. 1 (Spring 1978):48-55.
Analyzes *The World is Round* in terms of the way a child comes to grips with the complexities and ambiguities of the world.

A2295   O'HARA, J.D. "Gertrude Stein's *The World Is Round*." In Butler, *Sharing*, pp. 446-49.
Explores the meaning of Stein's children's story.

STEINBECK, JOHN (1902-68)

A2296   BARTEL, RONALD. "Proportioning in Fiction: *The Pearl* and *Silas Marner*." *English Journal* 56 (April 1967):542-46.
Examines the amount of space allocated to various episodes, characters, and themes as a means of interpreting novels.

A2297   KARSTEN, ERNEST E. "Thematic Structure in *The Pearl*." *English Journal* 54 (January 1965):1-7.
Provides a detailed analysis.

A2298   SHUMAN, R. BAIRD. "Initiation Rites in Steinbeck's *The Red Pony*." *English Journal* 59 (December 1970):1252-55.
Points out that the four interrelated short stories show Jody changing from a self-centered boy into a feeling young man.

STEINER, JÖRG (1930-)

A2299   VANDERGRIFT, KAY. *Child and Story*, pp. 166-71.
Pays close attention to illustrations, point-of-view, and perspective of *Rabbit Island*, as they "complement and extend the written

word." Calls the book "a powerful aesthetic composition that may be read on many levels."

STEPTOE, JOHN (1950-   )

A2300   STEPTOE, JOHN. "Stevie: Realism in a Book About Black Children." *Life* 67 (29 August 1969):54-59.
Reprints *Stevie* and includes a brief profile of Steptoe.

STERLING, DOROTHY (1913-   )

A2301   BANFIELD, BERYLE. Review of *Black Foremothers: Three Lives.* *IRBC* 11, nos. 1-2 (1980):26.
Praises Sterling's careful research and skillful storytelling.

A2302   KINGSTON, CAROLYN T. *Tragic Mode*, pp. 44-46.
Analyzes the them of rejection in *Mary Jane.*

STERNE, EMMA GELDERS (1894-1971)

A2303   SHERWIN, ANNE. "Emma Gelders Sterne as Playwright." *Horn Book* 12 (May 1936):150-52.
Briefly discusses five of Sterne's plays.

STEVENSON, ROBERT LOUIS (1850-94)

A2304   BEER, PATRICIA. *"Kidnapped."* *CLE*, n.s. 14, no. 1 (Spring 1983):54-62.
A rather rambling, personal response to *Kidnapped*, touching on moral dilemmas, good story, and style.

A2305   BLAKE, KATHLEEN. "The Sea-Dreams: *Peter Pan* and *Treasure Island*." *Children's Literature* 6 (1977):165-81.
Compares handling of the "sea-dream" or Robinson theme by Stevenson and Barrie. Concludes that *Treasure Island* is "the sea-dream pure and fine, its apotheosis, while *Peter Pan* is the dream's deathblow, elegy, and obsessive half-life, artfully rendered in the medium of bad form."

A2306   BROWN, DOUGLAS. "R.L.S.: Inspiration and Industry." In Ford, *Young Writers, Young Readers*, pp. 123-29.
Considers Stevenson a gifted but minor writer, "an important novelist for boys, but for adults only a novelist interesting in certain ways." Points out what Stevenson has to offer the young, and how *Treasure Island* and *Kidnapped* can prepare the young reader for adult reading of great literature.

A2307   BUTTS, DENNIS. "The Child's Voice." *Junior Bookshelf* 29 (December 1965):331-37.
Discusses the origins of the poems in *A Child's Garden of Verses* and offers critical insights.

A2308   -----. *R.L. Stevenson*. New York: Walck, 1966, 72 pp.
Provides a critical overview of Stevenson's works for children.

A2309   CAPEY, A.C. *Treasure Island* and the Young Reader." *Use of English* 25 (Spring 1974):228-38.

Discusses Stevenson's appeal to young boys and argues that the book is much more finely constructed than a typical adventure story and that perhaps some of that fine technique "rubs off on to the young reader."

A2310   DAICHES, DAVID. "Adventure." In *Robert Louis Stevenson: The Makers of Modern Literature*. Norfolk, Conn.: New Directions Books, 1947, pp. 32-73.
The second chapter of Daiches's biography is devoted to detailed analysis of *Treasure Island*, pp. 32-51, and *Kidnapped*, pp. 51-73.

A2311   HARDESTY, WILLIAM H., III, and MANN, DAVID D. "Historical Reality and Fictional Daydream in *Treasure Island*." *Journal of Narrative Technique* 7, no. 2 (Spring 1977):94-103.
Praises Stevenson's craftsmanship in anchoring the reader firmly in reality before launching into the world of daydream and imagination.

A2312   HEINS, PAUL. "A Centenary Look: *Treasure Island*." *Horn Book* 59 (April 1983):197-200.
Sketchily summarizes changing critical opinions of the book and comments briefly on characterization and narrative style.

A2313   JACKSON, DAVID HAROLD. "Robert Louis Stevenson and the Romance of Boyhood." Ph.D. dissertation, Columbia University, 1981, 196 pp., DA 42:2685A.
Views Stevenson's children's adventure tales: *Treasure Island*, *The Black Arrow*, *Kidnapped*, and *Catriona* as a "four-part romance in which an immature hero quests, literally and metaphorically, towards a goal of bourgeois adult identity."

A2314   LUKENS, REBECCA. "Stevenson's *Garden*: Verse Is Verse." *L&U* 4, no. 2 (Winter 1980-81):49-55.
Argues that Stevenson's verses lack intensity, make disappointing use of rhythm and sound patterns, are full of sentimentality, didacticism, condescension, "thoughts of a grown man remembering in a rosy haze what it was like to be a child." Contrasts Stevenson with vivid examples from modern poets.

A2315   NODELMAN, PERRY. "Editorial: A Hundred Years of Treasure, or Grime Does Not Pay." *ChLAQ* 8, no. 3 (Fall 1983):2-3, 6.
Finds similarities between *Treasure Island* and the *Dukes of Hazzard* television series.

A2316   SMITH, LILLIAN. *Unreluctant Years*, pp. 136-37.
Argues that *Treasure Island's* first-person narrative provides unity, that the plot is a masterpiece, and the story is eloquently told.

A2317   WARD, HAYDEN W. "'The Pleasure of Your Heart': *Treasure Island* and the Appeal of Boys' Adventure Fiction." *Studies in the Novel* 6, no. 3 (Fall 1974):304-17.
Explores reasons why *Treasure Island* appeals as much to adult readers as to boys.

A2318   YATES, JESSICA. "*Treasure Island* and Its Sequels." In Hunt, *Further Approaches*, pp. 113-14.
Briefly reports on her research comparing five sequels to *Treasure*

Island written in the twentieth century.

STOCKTON, FRANK (1834-1902)

A2319   GRIFFEN, MARTIN I.J. *Frank R. Stockton, A Critical Biography.*
1939. Reprint. Port Washington, N.Y.: Kennikat Press, 1965, 178
pp.
Includes a primary and secondary bibliography.

STOLZ, MARY (1920-   )

A2320   KASER, BILLIE F. "The Literary Value and Adolescent Appeal of
Mary Stolz's Novels." *Arizona English Bulletin* 14, no. 3 (April
1972):14-19.
Discusses Stolz's use of epiphany as a literary technique.

STOREY, MARGARET (1926-   )

A2321   CROUCH, MARCUS. *The Nesbit Tradition*, pp. 210-12.
Discusses two of Storey's books, *Kate and the Family Tree*, pp.
210-11, and *Pauline*, pp. 211-12.

STRATEMEYER, EDWARD (1862-1930)

A2322   DONELSON, KEN. "Nancy, Tom and Assorted Friends in the Stratemeyer Syndicate Then and Now." *Children's Literature* 7
(1978):17-44.
Chronicles the history of the Stratemeyer Syndicate, concentrating
on the efforts of Franklin K. Mathiews, chief librarian for the Boy
Scouts, to destroy the Syndicate. Includes references.

A2323   "For Indeed It Was He." *Fortune* 9 (April 1934):86. (Reprinted in
Egoff, *Only Connect*, 1st ed., pp. 41-61.)
A highly influential, unfavorable view of the Stratemeyer Syndi-
cate, which admits admiration for Stratemeyer's business acumen.

A2324   JOHNSON, DEIRDRE. *Stratemeyer Pseudonyms and Series Books: An
Annotated Checklist of Stratemeyer and Stratemeyer Syndicate Publications.* Westport, Conn.: Greenwood Press, 1982, 343 pp.
An indispensable source of information on the Stratemeyer Syndicate. The main part of the book consists of an annotated listing, by
pseudonym, of the Syndicate's publications. An introduction, pp.
xiii-xxxvi, provides a history of the Syndicate and its contributors,
with extensive references. Appendix E is a secondary bibliography
of articles and books containing information about Edward Stratemeyer and the Syndicate. There are also appendixes containing
information on illustrators, publishers, and library collections with
Stratemeyer holdings.

A2325   KUSKIN, KARLA. "Nancy Drew and Friends." *NYTBR*, 4 May 1975,
Children's Book sec., pp. 20-21.
Explores "The Secret of Their Smashing Success" in the Nancy
Drew and Hardy Boys books.

A2326   SODERBERGH, PETER A. "Edward Stratemeyer and the Juvenile
Ethic." *International Review of History and Political Science*
(Meerut, India) 11 (February 1974):61-71.

Examines the values expressed by Stratemeyer in the prefaces to a number of his books.

A2327   -----. "The Stratemeyer Strain: Educators and the Juvenile Series Book, 1900-1973." *Journal of Popular Culture* 7, no. 4 (Spring 1974):864-72. (Reprinted in *Only Connect*, 2d ed., pp. 63-73.)
Surveys the history of conflicts, censorship, and attitudes toward the Stratemeyer series books throughout the twentieth century. Includes references.

A2328   ZUCKERMAN, ED. "The Great Hardy Boys' Whodunit." *Rolling Stone*, 9 September 1976, pp. 36-40.
Traces changes in the Stratemeyer Syndicate's series, especially the Hardy boys, in response to social changes of the time. "Mrs. Adams and her colleagues, like Soviet historians, have been systematically re-writing the past."

STREATFEILD, NOEL (1895-   )

A2329   CADOGAN, NANCY, and CRAIG, PATRICIA. *You're a Brick*, pp. 286-96.
Points out that Streatfeild's *Ballet Shoes* was the first and best of the family stories with a theatrical basis. Traces Streatfeild's development through *The Painted Garden*, after which "there is a slight but perceptible falling off."

A2330   KUZNETS, LOIS R. "Family as Formula: Cawelti's Formulaic Theory and Streatfeild's 'Shoe' Books." *ChLAQ* 9, no. 4 (Winter 1984-85):147-49, 201.
Applies Cawelti's formulaic theories to an analysis of the family story type, specifically Noel Streatfeild's "shoe" stories.

A2331   McDONNELL, CHRISTINE. "A Second Look: *Ballet Shoes*." *Horn Book* 54 (April 1978):191-93.
Finds Streatfeild's strong female characters surprisingly up-to-date after forty years.

A2332   PAXFORD, SANDRA. "Children Who Have Far to Go." *Junior Bookshelf* 35 (1971):290-92.
Analyzes the determined nature of Streatfeild's child characters.

A2333   STREATFEILD, NOEL. "Myself and My Books." *Junior Bookshelf* 3 (May 1939):121-24.
Describes her background and the writing of her books.

A2334   WILSON, BARBARA KER. *Noel Streatfeild*. London: Bodley Head, 1961; New York: Henry Z. Walck, 1964, 64 pp.
Includes a biographical sketch, and comments upon Streatfeild's storytelling style, her family-based content, and her characterization, especially of grown-ups.

STRETTON, HESBA (1832-1911)

A2335   SALWAY, LANCE. "Pathetic Simplicity: An Introduction to Hesba Stretton and Her Books for Children." *Signal* 1 (January 1970):20-28.
An overview and reevaluation.

STRUMILLO, ANDRZEI (1928-   )

A2336   WRÓBLEWSKÁ, DANUTA. "Andrzei Strumillo." *Bookbird* 10, no. 3 (1972):73-80.
A profile and critical analysis of the Polish illustrator. Includes a bibliography.

STUART, JESSE (1907-84)

A2337   LE MASTER, J.R., and CLARKE, MARY WASHINGTON, eds. *Jesse Stuart: Essays on His Work.* Lexington: University Press of Kentucky, 1977, pp. 149-61.
Points out the strengths and weaknesses of Stuart's books for children. Concludes that "the field of children's literature is richer because he walked the hills of Eastern Kentucky, knew them and the children and animals of the area, and was able to present them with a warm human touch."

SUDBERY, RODIE (1943-   )

A2338   REES, DAVID. "Middle of the Way: Rodie Sudbery and Beverly Cleary." In *Marble in the Water*, pp. 90-103.
Argues that although she is ignored by critics, Sudbery's books are read by children and her craftsmanship is excellent. Examines *Pigsleg* and *A Curious Place* in detail.

SUTCLIFF, ROSEMARY (1920-   )

A2339   ADAMSON, LYNDA GOSSETT. "A Content Analysis of Values in Rosemary Sutcliff's Historical Fiction for Children." Ph.D. dissertation, University of Maryland, 1981, 176 pp., DA 42:3475A.
Concludes that Sutcliff's characters demonstrate values important to Western contemporary society and that the complexity of the values underscores the complexity of character development achieved by Sutcliff.

A2340   COLWELL, EILEEN H. "Rosemary Sutcliff--Lantern Bearer." *Horn Book* 36 (June 1960):200-205.
Praises Sutcliff for her ability as a storyteller and for her meticulous research, memorable characters, and sense of place. Her ability to "bring history to life" makes her a "lantern bearer."

A2341   CROUCH, MARCUS. *The Nesbit Tradition*, pp. 63-66.
Admires Sutcliff's ability to make the reader feel and see the past. Considers *The Mark of the Horse Lord* her "grimmest" and "potentially her finest" book.

A2342   DUFF-STEWART, CHRISTINA. "More Songs Tomorrow." *Junior Bookshelf* 28 (November 1964):279-84.
"In Rosemary Sutcliff's trilogy *The Lantern Bearers*, *Sword at Sunset*, and *Dawn Wind* we have a superb example of that best of all historical fiction in which the past illumines the present."

A2343   -----. "Scarlet On The Loom." *Junior Bookshelf* 23 (November 1959):253-62.
Summarizes the plots of Sutcliff's books, but also offers insights into her development as a writer and her techniques of writing his-

torical fiction.

A2344   GARD, ROGER. "Rosemary Sutcliff's *Dawn Wind.*" *Use of English* 21 (Summer 1970):317-21.
Analyzes Sutcliff's ability to create an "internal sense of the past" and to "get inside the minds of her remote heroes." Points out her complex and consciously shaped patterns.

A2345   INGLIS, FRED. *Promise of Happiness*, pp. 217-21.
Although he does not discuss Sutcliff's works in detail here, Inglis comments on her love of the English landscape and her romancing, her "lamenting the age of chivalry and its demise." She seems to say "that the individual spirit will survive the loss of nation, family, tribe, or regiment."

A2346   -----. "Reading Children's Novels: Private Culture and the Politics of Literature." *Ideology and the Imagination*, pp. 122-39. (Also in *CLE*, o.s., no. 5 [July 1971]:60-75 and in Fox, *Writers, Critics, and Children*, pp. 157-73.)
Examines Sutcliff's novels as a means to demonstrate how she exemplifies "the ideology and system of myths scattered less intelligently and less boldly through the works of her contemporaries." Examines her prose, characters, structures, images, values, and politics.

A2347   JONES, CORNELIA, and WAY, OLIVIA R. *British Children's Authors*, pp. 146-54.
In an interview Sutcliff discusses her background, philosophy, and method of working. Includes an annotated bibliography of her works.

A2348   MARDER, JOAN V. "The Historical Novels of Rosemary Sutcliff." *Use of English* 20 (Autumn 1968):10-13. (Reprinted in Butts, *Good Writers*, pp. 138-40.)
Provides a brief introduction to Sutcliff's historical fiction and her development as a writer. Includes a bibliography of her books.

A2349   MEEK, MARGARET. *Rosemary Sutcliff.* New York: Henry Z. Walck; London: Bodley Head, 1962, 72 pp.
Provides biographical background, discusses Sutcliff's methods of working and her development as a writer, and finally concentrates on her central themes and their interest to today's young people. Includes Sutcliff's bibliography for *The Lantern Bearers*, and a list of her books.

A2350   POTTER, ELIZABETH. "Eternal Relic: A Study of Setting in Rosemary Sutcliff's *Dragon Slayer.*" *ChLAQ* 10 (Fall 1985):108-10.
Praises Sutcliff's use of setting as a source of symbolism in her retelling of *Beowulf.*

A2351   RYAN, J.S. "Romance Blighted but Pain Vanquished: Or, the Making of Rosemary Sutcliff." *Orana* 19 (August 1983):61-67.
Responds to Sutcliff's memoir *Blue Hills Remembered.*

A2352   "Search for Selfhood: The Historical Novels of Rosemary Sutcliff." *TLS*, 17 June 1965, p. 498. (Reprinted in Egoff, *Only Connect*, 1st ed., pp. 249-55.)

Traces Sutcliff's development as a writer and concludes: "*The Mark of the Horse Lord* shows the coming-of-age of Miss Sutcliff's hero and the total assurance of the writing indicate an author fully in command of her power."

A2353 SUTCLIFF, ROSEMARY. "Combined Ops." *Junior Bookshelf* 24 (July 1960):121-27. (Reprinted in Egoff, *Only Connect*, 1st ed., pp. 244-48; 2d ed., pp. 284-88.)

Describes the process of writing *Eagle of the Ninth* and *The Lantern Bearers*.

A2354 -----. "Thank-You Address to the Children's Literature Association in Ann Arbor, Michigan, 19th May 1985 upon Receipt of the Phoenix Award." *ChLAQ* 10 (Winter 1986):176.

Sutcliff's response to the awarding of the first Phoenix Award to *The Mark of the Horse Lord*. Discusses the book.

A2355 TOWNSEND, JOHN ROWE. *Sense of Story*, pp. 193-203.

Discusses the entire body of Sutcliff's work, its themes and characteristics, without discussing any particular book at length. Sees her work as rooted in myth, legend, and saga. Her great themes are "death and rebirth as a condition of continuance of life." Maintains that "the past comes out of her pages alive and breathing and now."

A2356 WEBER, ROSEMARY. "A Second Look: *Dawn Wind*." *Horn Book* 55 (June 1979):335-36.

Maintains that in *Dawn Wind* Sutcliff has created memorable characters not overshadowed by the themes and scenes.

A2357 WINTLE, JUSTIN, and FISHER, EMMA. *Pied Pipers*, pp. 182-91.

Sutcliff discusses her life and work in an interview.

A2358 WRIGHT, HILARY. "Shadows on the Downs: Some Influences of Rudyard Kipling on Rosemary Sutcliff." *CLE*, n.s. 12, no. 2 (Summer 1981):90-102.

Sees in both Sutcliff and Kipling a common theme: the "conflict of duty and inclination," but where "Kipling is detached and objective, she is involved and subjective."

A2359 YOUNG, CAROL C. "Good-bye to Camelot." *English Journal* 74 (February 1985):54-58.

Examines Rosemary Sutcliff's "jarringly different version of the Arthurian adventures," as presented in *The Sword and the Circle*, in the context of American traditions and beliefs regarding Camelot.

SUTTON, MARGARET (1903-   )

A2360 MASON, BOBBIE ANN. "The Secret of the Phantom Friends." In *The Girl Sleuth*, pp. 76-91.

Feels that the Judy Bolton series comes closer to realism and is less escapist and less damaging than most other series books. It struggles "to be something more."

SWERDLOW, ROBERT (1941-   )

A2361 RUBIO, GERALD J. "Rejuvenating Out of Date Plays." *CCL* 8-9

(1977):144-51.
Discusses the problems of producing and staging the play *Copper Mountain* if one has a cast less talented than a major opera company.

SWIFT, HILDEGARDE H. (1890-1977)

A2362   "Power of a Child's Book." *Saturday Review* 46 (11 May 1963):43.
Discusses *The Little Red Lighthouse.*

SWIFT, JONATHAN (1667-1745)

A2363   HAZARD, PAUL. *Books, Children and Men*, pp. 61-69.
Analyzes the appeal to children of those aspects of *Gulliver's Travels* they have appropriated.

TAYLOR, MILDRED D.

A2364   DUSSEL, SHARON L. "Profile: Mildred D. Taylor." *LA* 58 (May 1981):599-604.
A biocritical overview.

A2365   JORDAN, JUNE. "Mississippi in the Thirties." Review of *Let the Circle Be Unbroken. NYTBR*, 15 November 1981, pp. 55, 58.

A2366   REES, DAVID. "The Color of Skin: Mildred Taylor." In *Marble in the Water*, pp. 104-13.
Compares approaches of American and British writers to racial and cultural differences.   Praises Taylor's *Roll of Thunder, Hear My Cry* for her portrayal of the effects of racial prejudice.

A2367   TAYLOR, MILDRED D. "Newbery Award Acceptance." *Horn Book* (August 1977):401-9.
Tells of the experiences behind *Roll of Thunder, Hear My Cry.* A biographical sketch by Phyllis J. Fogelman follows, pp. 410-14.

TAYLOR, SIDNEY (1904-   )

A2368   "Profile of an Author--Sydney Taylor." *Judaica Book News* (Fall-Winter 1972-73).   (Reprinted in *TON* 20 [April 1973]:218-25.)
In an interview Taylor discusses the origins of her books in her Jewish childhood in New York's Lower East Side.

TAYLOR, THEODORE (1921-   )

A2369   BAGNALL, NORMA. "Profile: Theodore Taylor: His Models of Self-Reliance." *LA* 57 (January 1980):86-91.
Taylor discusses his philosophy of writing and the background for his Cape Hatteras trilogy and *The Cay.* Includes an annotated bibliography of Taylor's works.

A2370   SCHWARTZ, ALBERT V. *"The Cay:* Racism Still Rewarded." *IRBC* 3, no. 4 (Autumn 1971):7-8.   (Reprinted in MacCann, *Black American*, pp. 108-11.)
"Rather than praise for literary achievement on behalf of 'brotherhood,' *The Cay* . . . should be castigated as an adventure story for white colonialists to add to their racist mythology."

TERHUNE, ALBERT PAYSON (1872-1942)

A2371   LAWSON, SARAH. "Albert Payson Terhune." *Junior Bookshelf* 42 (December 1978):287-90.

An appreciative reevaluation. "The dog stories of Albert Payson Terhune may seem slightly old-fashioned today, but only the details are out of date. The dogs are timeless."

THEROUX, PAUL (1941-   )

A2372   WRIGHT, ANN. "Paul Theroux's Christmas Tales." *CLE*, n.s. 15, no. 3 (Autumn 1984):141-46.

Discusses Theroux's theme of "truthful discoveries about human behavior and values" in his two Christmas stories, *A Christmas Card* and *London Snow.*

THIELE, COLIN (1920-   )

A2373   HUME, HAZEL. "Thiele Is Tops: Or a Critical Analysis of Colin Thiele's Writings for Children." *Children's Libraries Newsletter* 8 (May 1972):51-55.

Preceded by Thiele's own essay "The Quality of Experience," pp. 48-50.

A2374   McKEMMISH, SUSAN. "Teacher or Writer? Didacticism in the Children's Novels of Colin Thiele." *Orana* 18 (November 1982):152-56.

Argues that any writer, including Thiele, succeeds best when the message is fully integrated into the structure of the work.

A2375   McVITTY, WALTER. "Colin Thiele: Universality in the Heart of Man." In *Innocence and Experience*, pp. 197-232.

Provides critical analysis of this "most beloved of contemporary Australian children's writers." Includes a brief biographical sketch, Thiele's own comments, and a bibliography of Thiele's books.

THOMSEN, EDWARD WILLIAM (1849-1924)

A2376   McMULLEN, LORRAINE. "E.W. Thomsen and the *Youth's Companion*." *CCL* 13 (1979):7-20.

Examines the writings and career of E.W. Thomsen, especially his numerous stories for *The Youth's Companion.*

Thorndike Library

A2377   BISHOP, CLAIRE HUCHET. "An Obstacle Race." *Horn Book* 11 (July-August 1935):203-9.

Attacks Thorndike's rewriting of the classics: Andersen's *Fairy Tales*, *Black Beauty*, *Pinocchio*, *Heidi*, and others, with ample examples and critiques comparing the original words with Thorndike's "mutilation."

THORNDYKE, HELEN LOUISE

A2378   MASON, BOBBIE ANN. "The Land of Milk and Honey." In *The Girl Sleuth*, pp. 19-28.

Examines the the bland, sweet, central character of the Honey Bunch series.

"The Three Bears"

A2379   ELMS, ALAN C. "'The Three Bears': Four Interpretations." *Journal of American Folklore* 90 (July 1977):257-73.
Summarizes studies of the origins of "The Three Bears" and numerous interpretations of the tale, and suggests further directions for research.

A2380   LEXAU, JOAN M. "The Story of the Three Bears and the Man Who Didn't Write It." *Horn Book* 40 (February 1964):88-94.
Traces various retellings of "The Three Bears" since Robert Southey's in 1837 in *The Doctor*.

A2381   MURE, ELEANOR. *The Story of the Three Bears.* New York: Henry Z. Walck, 1967, unpaginated.
This facsimile of Mure's hand-written and illustrated story, written in 1831, includes a note "About Eleanor Mure's Story of the Three Bears" by Judith St. John.

A2382   OBER, WARREN U., ed. *The Story of the Three Bears: The Evolution of an International Classic.* New York: Scholars' Facsimiles & Reprints, 1981, 308 pp.
Explores the origins of various versions of "The Three Bears" and discusses the differences among them, as well as provides facsimile reproductions of fifteen texts.

A2383   "The Three Bears." *TLS*, 23 November 1951, p. xiii.
Reports on the discovery of Eleanor Mure's manuscript of "The Three Bears" and the interest it has aroused; and attempts to discover the origins of the tale.

"Three Billy Goats Gruff"

A2384   SMITH, LILLIAN. *Unreluctant Years*, pp. 52-55.
Maintains that "All the essentials of a good short story may be found in this Norse folk tale."

"Three Little Pigs"

A2385   ROBINSON, ROBERT D. "The Three Little Pigs: From Six Directions." *EE* 45 (March 1968):356-59, 366.
Applies six critical approaches to the tale: ethical, historical, psychological, sociological, formal, and archetypal.

THURBER, JAMES (1894-1961)

A2386   HILDEBRAND, ANN M. "A New Phase of James Thurber's *Many Moons*." *CLE*, n.s. 15, no. 3 (Autumn 1984):147-56.
Analyzes elements of *Many Moons* in terms of key events in Thurber's life.

TOLKIEN, J.R.R. (1892-1973)

A2387   CHANT, JOY. "Niggle and Numenor." *CLE*, o.s., no. 19 (Winter 1975):161-71.
Attempts to pierce through the controversy surrounding Tolkien's

books and "to understand what in them has evoked such a response."

A2388   CROUCH, MARCUS S. "Another Don in Oxford." *Junior Bookshelf* 14, no. 2 (March 1950):50-53.
Calls *The Hobbit* a great book that makes Tolkien's position in the world of children's literature secure. Compares his position to Carroll's.

A2389   CURTIS, JARED. "On Re-Reading *The Hobbit*, Fifteen Years Later." *CLE*, n.s. 15, no. 2 (Summer 1984):113-20.
Based on an examination of the changes in his own responses to *The Hobbit* after fifteen years, Curtis suggests ways in which "child readers evolve into adult readers, re-forming the fiction in response to inner claims and emotions."

A2390   EVANS, W.D. EMRYS. "Illusion, Tale and Epic." *School Librarian* 21 (March 1973):5-11.
Applies Suzanne Langer's theories of literature as expressed in *Feeling and Form* to four books for children: J.R.R. Tolkien's *The Hobbit*, C.S. Lewis's *The Voyage of the Dawn Treader*, Ursula K. Le Guin's *A Wizard of Earthsea*, and Alan Garner's *Elidor*.

A2391   GLOVER, WILLIS B. "The Christian Character of Tolkien's Invented World." *Criticism* 13, no. 1 (Winter 1971):39-53.
Explores the significance of the Christian intellectual tradition in *Lord of the Rings*.

A2392   GREEN, WILLIAM HOWARD. "The Four-Part Structure of Bilbo's Education." *Children's Literature* 8 (1980):133-40.
Maintains that "patterns of opposition and return" unite the four separate tales about Bilbo's education: "the departure from the Shire," "the adventures in the Misty Mountains," "the adventures in Mirkwood," "and the adventures at the "Lonely Mountain."

A2393   -----. "*The Hobbit* and Other Fiction by J.R.R. Tolkien: Their Roots in Medieval Heroic Literature and Language." Ph.D. dissertation, Louisiana State University at Baton Rouge, 1969, 195 pp., DA 30:4944A.
Discusses medieval antecedents and influences in *The Hobbit*. Concludes that "its deepest roots are in Northern Europe; its world is essentially the world of Norse heroic fiction and of *Beowulf*."

A2394   HANNABUSS, C. STUART. "Deep Down: Thematic and Bibliographical Excursion." *Signal* 6 (September 1971):87-95.
Explores the origins of Tolkien's symbolism. "I believe Tolkien was working out a quasi Christian morality in pagan terms, using a former culture and literary tradition to furnish the scenario to a quest which incorporated the major issues of Life."

A2395   INGLIS, FRED. *Promise of Happiness*, pp. 197-200.
Describes *The Hobbit* as "a rattling good yarn for children. . . . Its pace and fullness, its good temper, the scale of its protagonists, its manageable horrors and disasters, its simple triumphs and morals, all fit it to the child's eye view."

A2396   NODELMAN, PERRY. "A Tolkien Bibliography." *ChLAQ* 4, no. 1 (Summer 1979):17-18.

A brief annotated list of some recommended critical resources.

A2397   RYAN, J.S.   "Frothi, Frodo--and Dodo and Odo." *Orana* 16 (May 1980):35-38.
Explores the origins of Tolkien's names.

A2398   -----.   "Gollum and the Golem: A Neglected Tolkien Association with Jewish Thought." *Orana* 18 (August 1982):100-103.
Connects the Jewish Golem with Tolkien's Gollum and explores the significance of this connection.

A2399   SKLAR, ROBERT.   "Tolkien & Hesse: Top of the Pops." *Nation* 204 (8 May 1967):598-601.   (Reprinted in Lenz, *Young Adult Literature*, pp. 422-24.)
"Tolkien and Hesse's visions of life accord with the contemporary visions of youth."   Analyzes their works in these terms.

A2400   WALKER, STEVEN C.   "Super Natural Supernatural: Tolkien as Realist." *Proceedings of the Children's Literature Association* 5 (1978): 100-105.
Argues that Tolkien's "Middle-Earth" is grounded in reality, that he is a highly realistic fantasist.

A2401   WEST, RICHARD C.   *Tolkien Criticism: An Annotated Checklist.* Rev. ed.   Kent, Ohio: Kent State University Press, 1981, 177 pp.
Contains annotated listings of Tolkien's writings, popular and scholarly Tolkien criticism, and an unannotated list of book reviews.

A2402   WOOD, MICHAEL.   "Tolkien's Fictions." *New Society*, 27 March 1969. (Reprinted in Tucker, *Suitable for Children?*, pp. 165-72.)
Analyzes Tolkien's appeal in terms of its "power and coherence" as romance in a time of "rising darkness."

TOLSTOY, LEO (1828-1910)

A2403   COHEN, A.   "Children's Literature in the Work of Leo Tolstoy." *Journal of Reading* 22 (January 1979):296-311.
"Many of the principles presented by Tolstoy in *What Is Art?* found expression in his writing for children."   Examines Tolstoy's legends, fairy tales, fables, and folktale adaptations for children in terms of his aesthetic theory.   Includes references.

A2404   HANSON, EARL.   "Leo Tolstoy: Pedagogue and Storyteller of Old Russia." *LA* 56, no. 4 (April 1979):434-36.
A brief introduction to Tolstoy stressing his stories for children. Includes a bibliography of titles available in English and references to secondary sources.

A2405   McKILLOP, IAN.   "Tales by Tolstoy." *CLE*, o.s., no. 11 (May 1973): 49-57.
Argues that Tolstoy's tales for children still deserve a place "on classroom shelves and in children's bedrooms."

TOPELIUS, ZACHARIAS (1818-98)

A2406   LAUKKA, MARIA.   "Topelius's 'Lasning for barn' and Its Illustrators." *Phaedrus* 9 (1982):41-44.

Examines a number of illustrated versions of fairy tales by the Finnish writer Topelius who wrote in Swedish during the time when Finland was a part of the Russian empire.

TOURNIER, MICHEL (1924-   )

A2407   McMAHON, JOSEPH H. "Michel Tournier's Texts for Children." *Children's Literature* 13 (1985):154-68.
Discusses the differences between Tournier's works for children and his works for adults. A translation of Tournier's story "Pierrot, or the Secrets of the Night" follows on pp. 169-79, with Tournier's own account of his encounters with children, "Writer Devoured by Children," on pp. 180-87.

TOWNSEND, JOHN ROWE (1922-   )

A2408   BARNES, RON. "John Rowe Townsend's Novels of Adolescence." *CLE*, o.s., no. 19 (Winter 1975):178-90.
An exploration of Townsend's handling of "crisis of identity, class relationships, parent-child relations and the awakening of adolescent love" in four novels for young adults: *The Intruder*, *Good-Night, Prof, Love*, *The Summer People*, and *The Forest of the Night*.

A2409   CROUCH, MARCUS. *The Nesbit Tradition*, pp. 206-8.
"In its setting, characterization, and narrative power, *The Intruder* is one of the outstanding books of its decade." However, Crouch finds it has "a coldness in it which is repellant."

A2410   HANSEN, CAROL A. "Recommended: John Rowe Townsend." *English Journal* 73 (March 1984):89-90.
Provides an overview of Townsend's fiction.

A2411   HEINS, PAUL. Review of *Forest of the Night*. *Horn Book* 51 (April 1975):133.

A2412   REES, DAVID. "A Sense of Story--John Rowe Townsend." In *Painted Desert*, pp. 102-14. (Originally published in *School Librarian*, September 1981, in slightly different form.)
Argues that Townsend's early novels, like his criticism, exemplify the virtues of "decency, humanity, good sense," and the failings of "lack of imagination, of genuine originality." Concludes that *The Islanders* is his best, but that in over twenty years of writing Townsend has not created an outstanding novel.

A2413   TOWNSEND, JOHN ROWE. "Under Two Hats." *Quarterly Journal of Library of Congress* 34 (April 1977). (Reprinted in Haviland, *The Openhearted Audience*, pp. 133-51.)
Explores his dual roles as creative writer and critic of children's literature.

A2414   -----. "Writing a Book: *Goodnight, Prof, Love*." In Blishen, ed., *Thorny Paradise*, pp. 146-57.
Describes how he wrote *Goodnight, Prof, Love*.

A2415   WINTLE, JUSTIN, and FISHER, EMMA. *Pied Pipers*, pp. 236-48.
In an interview Townsend discusses his life.

TRAILL, CATHERINE PARR (1802-99)

A2416   ELLIS, SARAH. "Tales of Crusoes." *CCL* 23-24 (1981):74-80.
Examines *Canadian Crusoes* in the context of the Robinsonade tradition.

TRAVERS, P[AMELA] L. (1906-   )

A2417   "Authors and Editors." *Publishers Weekly* 200 (13 December 1971):7-9.
Reports on the background of *Friend Monkey* and on Travers's response to the movie version of *Mary Poppins*. Quotes her at length on children and children's books.

A2418   BART, PETER, and BART, DOROTHY. "As Told and Sold by Disney." *NYTBR*, 9 May 1965, Children's Book sec., pp. 2,32-34.
Compares the Disney book version of Mary Poppins with the original.

A2419   BERGSTEN, STAFFAN. *Mary Poppins and Myth*. Stockholm, Sweden: Almquist & Wiksell International, 1978, 79 pp.
Bergsten describes his method as "a comparative and analytical study." Examines the influence and undercurrents of fairy tales and myths that permeate Travers's work.

A2420   COTT, JONATHAN. "The Wisdom of Mary Poppins: Afternoon Tea with P.L. Travers." In *Pipers*, pp. 195-238.
Interviews Travers, discussing the Poppins books, *Friend Monkey*, and her basic themes, beliefs and motifs ranging widely through literature and mysticism.

A2421   "Elusive Author Expansive with Children." *Library Journal* 91 (15 March 1966):1640 and *SLJ* 13 (March 1966):174.
Reports on Travers's responses to children's questions at Philadelphia's Logan Square Library.

A2422   HEARN, MICHAEL PATRICK. "P.L. Travers in Fantasy Land." *Children's Literature* 6 (1977):221-24.
Hearn finds fault with Travers's retelling of "Sleeping Beauty" and with Charles Keepings's illustrations and the entire design of the book.

A2423   LINGEMAN, RICHARD R. "Visit with Mary Poppins and P.L. Travers." *New York Times Magazine*, 25 December 1966, pp. 12-13, 27-29.
A biocritical overview based on an interview and comments from students and faculty at Smith College where she was writer-in-residence.

A2424   MOORE, ANNE CARROLL. "Mary Poppins." *Horn Book* 11 (January-February 1935):6-7.
A first highly favorable review in *Horn Book*. Views the book in the context of the depression.

A2425   RODDY, JOSEPH. "A Visit with the Real Mary Poppins." *Look* 30 (13 December 1966):84-86.
Reports on a visit to Travers at Smith College. Travers reiterates

her well-known "I don't write for children at all," and shares some of her insights and interests.

A2426 SCHWARTZ, ALBERT V. "*Mary Poppins* Revised: An Interview with P.L. Travers." *IRBC* 5, no. 3 (1974). (Reprinted in MacCann *Cultural Conformity*, pp. 134-40, and in White, *Children's Literature*, pp. 75-77.)

Concerns charges of racism in *Mary Poppins* and Travers's responses to those charges.

A2427 STONE, KAY F. "Re-Awakening the Sleeping Beauty: P.L. Travers' Literary Folktale." *Proceedings of the Children's Literature Association* 8 (1981):84-90.

Critiques Travers's retelling of the classic tale, pointing out places in which she fails and succeeds.

A2428 TRAVERS, P.L. *About the Sleeping Beauty.* New York: McGraw-Hill, 1975; London: Thames, 1977, 111 pp.

Five versions of the "Sleeping Beauty" tale are accompanied by Travers's own version and an essay on the meaning of fairy tales, the "Sleeping Beauty" in particular. Illustrations by Charles Keeping.

A2429 -----. "The Heroes of Childhood: A Note on Nannies." *Horn Book* 11 (May-June 1935):147-55.

Travers talks about nannies she has known. No reference is made to her writing, but the nannies she describes appear to have provided the foundation for Mary Poppins.

A2430 -----. "I Never Wrote for Children." *New York Times Magazine*, 2 July 1978, pp. 16-18, 30.

Shares recollections of her childhood and her views on writing and fairy tales.

A2431 -----. "A Letter from the Author." *Children's Literature* 10 (1982):214-17.

Travers defends herself against charges of racism and explains why she has revised *Mary Poppins*.

A2432 -----. "On Not Writing for Children." *Bookbird* 6, no. 4 (1968):3-7.

Argues that children's literature is for everybody, not just for children, and reminds the reader that all adults once were children.

A2433 -----. "Only Connect." *Quarterly Journal of the Library of Congress*, 24 October 1967, pp. 238-48. (Reprinted in Haviland, *The Openhearted Audience*, pp. 3-23.)

Discusses early influences on her work, particularly classic myths and fairy tales and "the Celtic Twilight."

A2434 -----. "Where Do Ideas Come From?" *Bookbird* 5, no. 4 (1967):7-8.

"A book itself is a writer's explanation, it is as far as he can go. We do not know what happens in fairy tales after Happy Ever After."

A2435 -----. "Who is Mary Poppins?" *Junior Bookshelf* 18 (March 1954):45-50.

Says she does not know where Mary Poppins came from, she "just happened."

A2436   ZINER, FEENIE. "Mary Poppins as a Zen Monk." *NYTBR*, 7 May 1972, pp. 2, 22.

        Reports on a meeting with Travers at the New York Public Library and Travers's response to the suggestion that Mary Poppins is a Zen monk.

TREASE, GEOFFREY (1909-   )

A2437   CROUCH, MARCUS. *The Nesbit Tradition*, pp. 59-60.

        Calls Trease "one of the best theorists among modern writers for the young. His principles are unexceptionable." Adds that "Trease's recent work is purged of the crudities of style and thought which mark his earlier writing, but he has bought this technical competence at a high price. The adventuring spirit has faded, and he no longer sparkles with a fresh vision."

A2438   MEEK, MARGARET. *Geoffrey Trease*. London: Bodley Head, 1960, 64 pp.

        Critically examines Trease's career as a writer of historical fiction, of formula fiction, of criticism, and travel fiction. Does not deal with his novels for adults.

A2439   -----. "Writers for Children 5: Geoffrey Trease." *School Librarian* 13 (July 1965):132-37.

        Evaluates Trease's place in the development of modern children's literature in *Tales Out of School*, first published in 1949. Includes a bibliography.

A2440   TREASE, GEOFFREY. "Fifty Years On: A Writer Looks Back." *CLE*, n.s. 14, no. 3 (Autumn 1983):149-59.

        Reflects on changes in his writing of historical fiction in over fifty years and on changes in the larger field of children's books as well.

A2441   -----. "The Historical Novelist at Work." *CLE*, o.s., no. 7 (March 1972):5-16.

        Describes his approach to writing historical fiction.

A2442   -----. "Old Writers and Young Readers." In *Essays and Studies*. Edited by John Lawlor. London: John Murray for the English Association, 1973, pp. 99-112. (Reprinted in Meek, *Cool Web*, pp. 145-56, and in *Bookbird* 12, nos. 1-2 [1974]:3-8, 13-19.)

        Looks over his past fifty years as a children's book writer and discusses the backgrounds of many of his books.

A2443   -----. "Problems of the Historical Storyteller." *Junior Bookshelf* 15, no. 6 (December 1951):259-64.

        Comments and correspondence follow in 16, nos. 1-2.

A2444   -----. *A Whiff of Burnt Boats*. London: Macmillan, 1971, 191 pp.

        An early autobiography.

A2445   -----. "Why Write for Children?" *School Librarian* 2 (1960). (Reprinted in *Bookbird* 5, no. 4 [1967]:3-6.)

        Explores reasons why he writes: "to communicate information and enthusiasm, re-create the past, interpret the present," and to tell a story.

TREECE, HENRY (1911-66)

A2446   CROUCH, MARCUS. *The Nesbit Tradition*, pp. 66-69.
Feels Treece's death at age fifty-five came "as he seemed to be discovering his full strength." Finds his work difficult to evaluate, especially *The Dream-Time*.

A2447   FISHER, MARGERY. *Henry Treece*. London: Bodley Head, 1969, 104 pp.
Provides a brief biographical sketch and a detailed analysis of Treece's children's books.

A2448   "Henry Treece: Lament for a Maker." *TLS 5, Essays and Reviews from the Times Literary Supplement*, 1966. (Reprinted in Egoff, *Only Connect*, 1st ed., pp. 256-64.)
Devotes particular attention to Treece's Viking stories, and briefly summarizes other books set in ancient and contemporary Britain.

TREFFINGER, CAROLYN (1891-   )

A2449   KINGSTON, CAROLYN T. *Tragic Mode*, pp. 12-14.
Analyzes the theme of rejection in *Li Lun, Lad of Courage*.

TRESSELT, ALVIN (1916-   )

A2450   TRESSELT, ALVIN. "Books and Beyond." *Childhood Education* 51 (March 1975):261-66.
Shares his background, his approach to children's books and his feelings about a number of his contemporary authors and illustrators.

TUDOR, TASHA (1915-   )

A2451   HONTZ, HSE L. "Tasha Tudor." *Catholic Library World* 42 (February 1971):351-54.
"Tasha Tudor radiates a deep appreciation of family life, animals, nature. She brings another world of peacefulness into our consciousness." Despite its extravagantly appreciative tone, this article provides some insights into Tudor's work.

TUNIS, JOHN R. (1889-1975)

A2452   CLARKE, LORETTA. "*His Enemy, His Friend*: A Novel of Global Conscience." *English Journal* 62 (May 1973):730-36.
This close analysis considers the way Tunis shapes the three parts of his book in view of his statement that "This is a book about the conscience of man."

A2453   HAMMER, ADAM. "Kidsport: The Works of John R. Tunis." *Journal of Popular Culture* 17, no. 3 (Winter 1983):146-49.
Analyzes the messages of three of Tunis's books: *Iron Duke, World Series*, and *All-American*. Concludes that "Buried deep inside these books, underneath the same old line about good sportsmanship and good citizenship, was that one intriguing message: You kid, you're all right. The old folks? Washed up."

A2454   JACOBS, WILLIAM JAY. "John R. Tunis: A Commitment to Values." *Horn Book* 43 (February 1967):48-54. (Reprinted in Hoffman, *Authors and Illustrators*, pp. 394-402.)
"Superbly realistic and well-written stories" that portray values of "persistence, courage, a sense of proportion."

A2455   SHEREIKIS, RICHARD. "How You Play the Game: The Novels of John R. Tunis." *Horn Book* 53 (December 1977):642-48.
Argues that while Tunis captured the excitement and beauty of sports, he also pointed out its commercialism, racism, and hypocrisy.

TURNER, ETHEL (1872-1958)

A2456   COUPE, SHEENA. "All the World Ought to be Respectably Comfortable: Aspects of the Social Philosophy of Ethel Turner." *Orana* 15 (February 1979):15-19.

A2457   RYAN, J.S. "The Ongoing Significance of Ethel Turner." *Orana* 16 (November 1980):141-48.
Explores Turner's importance to art, life, and literature.

TURNER, PHILIP (1925-   )

A2458   BOARD, M.J. "Children's Writers: 5. Philip Turner." *School Librarian* 27, no. 3 (September 1979):209-14.
Discusses Turner's nostalgic, escapist fiction for children.

TWAIN, MARK [Samuel L. Clemens] (1835-1910)

A2459   ALLEN, MARGOT. "*Huck Finn*: Two Generations of Pain." *IRBC* 15, no. 5 (1984):9-12.
Tells of her experiences and her son's with the reading of *Huck Finn* in the classroom and chronicles the State College, Pennsylvania, controversy over the book. See also the article below by Bradford Chambers.

A2460   CHAMBERS, AIDAN. "Letter from England: A Tale of Two Toms." *Horn Book* 52 (April 1976):187-90. (Reprinted in Heins, *Crosscurrents*, pp. 326-29.)
Compares *Tom Sawyer* and *Tom Brown*.

A2461   CHAMBERS, BRADFORD. "Scholars and *Huck Finn*: A New Look." *IRBC* 15, no. 4 (1984):12-13.
Reports on a panel discussion on "Teaching of Huck in the Public Schools" held at Pennsylvania State University in April 1984 as part of a conference on American Comedy attended by leading Twain scholars. See also article by Margot Allen, above.

A2462   CLOONAN, MICHELE V. "The Censorship of *Huckleberry Finn*: An Investigation." *TON* 40 (Winter 1984):189-96.
Explores reasons for the almost continuous censorship of *Huckleberry Finn* from 1885 to the present.

A2463   ELIOT, T.S. "*Huckleberry Finn*: A Critical Essay." In Egoff *Only Connect*, 1st ed., pp. 299-309; 2d ed., pp. 266-76.
Argues that this book is "the only one in which his [Twain's] genius is completely realized. Eliot does not consider the book

juvenile fiction. "We look at Tom [in *Tom Sawyer*] as the smiling adult does: Huck we do not look at--we see the world through his eyes."

A2464 FADIMAN, CLIFTON. "A Second Look: A Centennial for Tom." *Horn Book* 52 (April 1976):139-44. (Reprinted in Heins, *Crosscurrents*, pp. 139-44.)
Concludes that at one hundred years of age, *Tom Sawyer* is of more than historical interest to today's children; not only is Twain a great teller of tales, he also still speaks to the child's inner self.

A2465 GELLER, EVELYN. "Tom Sawyer, Tom Bailey, and Bad-Boy Genre." *WLB* 51 (November 1976):245-50.
Explores *Tom Sawyer* as an example of the "Bad-Boy" genre.

A2466 GIBSON, DONALD B. "Mark Twain's Jim in the Classroom." *English Journal* 57 (February 1968):196-99, 202. (Reprinted in MacCann, *Black American*, pp. 136-42.)
Discusses ways to approach the novel critically to interpret Twain's treatment of Jim.

A2467 HEARN, MICHAEL PATRICK, ed. *The Annotated Huckleberry Finn.* New York: Clarkson N. Potter, 1981, 378 pp.
Contains a fifty-page introduction to the book and extensive notes on each page of text. A bibliography lists works by Twain, notable editions of *Huckleberry Finn*, and work about Twain, about *Huckleberry Finn*, and about Edward W. Kemble (1861-1933), the book's original illustrator.

A2468 PECK, RICHARD. "A Second Look: *The Prince and the Pauper.*" *Horn Book* 61 (September 1985):541-43.
Examines the appeal of *The Prince and the Pauper* and connects it with Twain's life and with *Huckleberry Finn.*

A2469 RANTA, TAIMI. "*Huck Finn* and Censorship." *ChLAQ* 8, no. 4 (Winter 1983):35.
Argues that the novel is neither racist nor immoral and should not be denied to young people.

A2470 WALTERS, T.N. "Twain's Finn and Alger's Gilman: Picaresque Counterdirections." *Markham Review* 3 (May 1972):53-58.
Views Huck Finn and Jed Gilman as illustrating the "latitude and complexity of the picaresque tradition in American literature."

A2471 WOLFF, C.G. "Adventures of Tom Sawyer: A Nightmare Vision of American Boyhood." *Massachusetts Review* 21 (Winter 1980):637-52.
Provides a detailed analysis of *Tom Sawyer*, claiming, as Huck says in his own book, that to understand him we need to know where he has been before.

A2472 WOODARD, FREDERICK, and MacCANN, DONNARAE. "*Huckleberry Finn* and the Traditions of Blackface Minstrelsy." *IRBC* 15, nos. 1-2 (1984):4-13.
A close analysis of Twain's classic in terms of aspects of its messages about race and sex roles. Includes extensive notes and quotations about the book, as well as guidelines for classroom discussion.

UCHIDA, YOSHIKO (1921-   )

A2473   CHANG, CATHERINE E. STUDIER. "Profile: Yoshiko Uchida." *LA* 61 (February 1984):189-93.
A brief biocritical overview. Includes a bibliography of Uchida's books.

UDRY, JANICE (1928-   )

A2474   BADER, BARBARA. *American Picturebooks*, pp. 470-72.
Discusses Udry's works, especially *A Tree Is Nice*.

UNGERER, TOMI (1931-   )

A2475   BADER, BARBARA. *American Picturebooks*, pp. 544-52.
Maintains that the expression "devilishly clever" could have been coined for Ungerer. Discusses the variety, movement, and satire evident in his work.

A2476   MICHEL, JOAN HESS. "A Visit with Tomi Ungerer." *American Artist* 33 (May 1969):40-45, 78-79.
A biocritical overview.

A2477   SIEGEL, R.A. "The Little Boy Who Drops His Pants in a Crowd: . . ." *L&U* 1, no. 1 (1977):26-32.
Maintains that Ungerer's humor is communicated "through the traditional structure of comic grotesque imagery" which is universal in appeal and relevant to the child's sense of humor.

UPTON, FLORENCE (1873-1922)

A2478   OSBORNE, EDGAR. "The Birth of Golliwog." *Junior Bookshelf* 12 (December 1948):159-65.
Tells of the origins of the Golliwog character in Upton's *The Adventures of Two Dutch Dolls*.

UTTLEY, ALISON (1884-1976)

A2479   GRAHAM, ELEANOR. "Alison Uttley: An Appreciation." *Junior Bookshelf* 5 (December 1941):115-20.
Discusses the influences of country life in all of Uttley's work. Praises her versatility.

A2480   SAINTSBURY, ELIZABETH. *The World of Alison Uttley: A Biography*. London: Baker, 1980, 177 pp.
Emphasizes the settings and incidents in Uttley's life that found their way into her books. Pages 132-47 concentrate on the Little Grey Rabbit books.

VAN ALLSBURG, CHRIS (1949-   )

A2481   GARDNER, JOHN. "Fun and Games and Dark Imaginings." *NYTBR*, 26 April 1981, Children's Book sec., pp. 49, 64.
Review of *Jumanji*. Finds the pictures of higher quality than the text.

A2482   MacCANN, DONNARAE, and RICHARD, OLGA. "Picture Books for Children." *WLB* 56 (November 1981):212-13.

A thoughtful review of *Jumanji*, analyzing elements of plot and style of illustration.

VAN DOREN, MARK (1894-1972)

A2483   HILL, HELEN. "A Secret Harmony: Some Poems of Mark Van Doren for Children." *ChLAQ* 5, no. 2 (Summer 1980):30-35.

Provides a detailed analysis of Van Doren's poetry for children.

VAN KERKWIJK, HENK

A2484   "Portrait of a Dutch Author: Henk Van Kerkwijk." *Bookbird* 10, no. 1 (1972):27-28.

Praises the author's skill and versatility in several genres and his uniformly critical attitude toward social issues.

VAN LOON, HENDRICK (1882-1944)

A2485   "A Critical Review of Van Loon's *America*." *Horn Book* 4 (1928):42-43.

Denounces the book's "flippant style" and verbosity, its lack of "coherence and unity."

VAN STOCKUM, HILDA (1908-)

A2486   KINGSTON, CAROLYN T. *Tragic Mode*, pp. 98-101.

Analyzes the theme of war in *The Winged Watchman*.

VERNE, JULES (1828-1905)

A2487   GALLAGHER, EDWARD J. *Jules Verne: A Primary and Secondary Bibliography*. Boston: G.K. Hall, 1980, 387 pp.

Provides listings of Verne's fiction and nonfiction writings and annotated lists of critical studies in English and in French, arranged by date of publication.

A2488   LOWNDES, MARIE BELLOC. "*Signal* Reprints: Jules Verne at Home." *Signal* 10 (January 1973):3-13.

Reprinted from *Strand Magazine*, Fall 1895. Describes Verne's working methods.

VIPONT, ELFRIDA (1902-)

A2489   WOODFIELD, E.R. "Way Will Open." *Junior Bookshelf* 15, no. 3 (July 1951):104-11.

Analyzes key qualities of Vipont's work. An account by Vipont precedes, pp. 98-103.

VOIGHT, CYNTHIA (1942-)

A2490   DRESANG, ELIZA T. "A Newbery Song for Gifted Readers." *SLJ* 30 (November 1983):33-37.

Examines the qualitative details of *Dicey's Song* that make it particularly suitable for gifted readers.

A2491   HENKE, JAMES T. "Dicey, Odysseus, and Hansel and Gretel: The Lost Children in Voight's *Homecoming*." *CLE*, n.s. 16, no. 1 (Spring 1985):45-52.
Explores mythic and fairy tale parallels in *Homecoming*.

VON BODECKER, ALBRECHT

A2492   KUHN, HANNELORE. "The Illustrator Albrecht von Bodecker." *Bookbird* 2 (1984):61-63.
Provides an overview and stylistic analysis of von Bodecker's work, including a bibliography and list of his awards.

VOSNETSOV, YOURI

A2493   "The Life and Work of the Soviet Illustrator Youri Vosnetsov." *Bookbird* 12, no. 2 (1974):42-45.
A biocritical overview. Includes a bibliography of Vosnetsov's work and excerpts from reviews of his books.

WABER, BERNARD (1924-   )

A2494   BADER, BARBARA. *American Picturebooks*, pp. 480-83.
"A host of interesting and enlivening picturebook developments rebound in Waber's work, and while he is too good to be called typical, he is broadly representative." Discusses especially his ability to portray feelings.

A2495   HARMON, MARY K. "Bernard Waber." *EE* 51 (September 1974):773-76.
Waber's editor discusses his books.

WAGNER, JENNY, and BROOKS, RON (1948-   )

A2496   SCHWARCZ, JOSEPH H. "Adult Experience in Children's Books." In *Ways of the Illustrator*, pp. 191-95.
Examines Wagner and Brooks's *The Bunyip of Berkeley's Creek* and *John Brown, Rose and The Midnight Cat* as examples of recent picture books that introduce themes of "adult experience and art expression" to children.

A2497   SCOTT, PATRICIA. "John Brown, Max & Mr. Gumpy's Outing." *Orana* 14 (May 1978):39-41.
Discusses Jenny Wagner and Ron Brooks's *John Brown, Rose and the Midnight Cat*, Maurice Sendak's *Where the Wild Things Are*, and John Burningham's *Mr. Gumpy's Outing*.

WALSH, JILL PATON (1939-   )

A2498   REES, DAVID. "Types of Ambiguity: Jill Paton Walsh." In *Marble in the Water*, pp. 141-54.
Feels the criticism Walsh has so far received has masked her faults and failed to determine what her virtues are. Rees feels she sets out the old-fashioned virtues in black and white, with no gray areas, and she shows ineptitude in handling working-class characters. Compares the pointillist style of *Goldengrove* to Virginia Woolf's *To the Lighthouse* and considers it Walsh's best book.

A2499   TOWNSEND, JOHN ROWE. *A Sounding*, pp. 153-65.
Traces Walsh's development as a writer from her first book to more recent books. Praises *Unleaving* (1976) and points out the elements of fantasy, historical fiction, and contemporary realism in *A Chance Child* (1978).

A2500   WALSH, JILL PATON. "The Lords of Time." *Quarterly Journal of the Library of Congress* 36 (Spring 1979):96-113.
Expresses her views on the differences between writing for children and for adults. Feels writing for children is important, since they are "The Lords of Time," and nothing is more certain than that they will survive us.

WARD, LYND (1905-   )

A2501   PAINTER, HELEN W. "Lynd Ward: Artist, Writer, and Scholar." *EE* 39 (November 1962):663-71.
A biocritical overview.

A2502   WARD, LYND. "Caldecott Award Acceptance." *Horn Book* 29 (August 1953):297-304.
Tells of his background and some of the influences on his work. A biographical sketch by his wife May McNeer precedes.

WARNLÖF, ANNA LISA (1911-   )

A2503   BOLIN, GRETA. "A Meditative Girl: A Study in the Authorship of Claque (Anna Lisa Warnlöf)." *Bookbird* 7, no. 2 (1969):22-29. (Originally published in Swedish in *Perspektiv* 14, no. 9 [November 1963]:406-9. Translated by Roger G. Tanner.)
Discusses the Pella books and Frederika books, relating them to Warnlöf's childhood. Includes a bibliography of Warnlöf's works, including translations.

WEIK, MARY HAYS (1898-1979)

A2504   KINGSTON, CAROLYN T. *Tragic Mode*, pp. 73-75.
Analyzes the theme of entrapment in *The Jazz Man*.

WEISGARD, LEONARD (1916-   )

A2505   BROWN, MARGARET WISE. "Leonard Weisgard Wins The Caldecott Medal." *Publishers Weekly* 152 (5 July 1947):40-42.
A fascinating account of Weisgard as person and illustrator, as only Margaret Wise Brown could write it.

A2506   FLOETHE, RICHARD. "Artist's Choice." *Horn Book* 38 (April 1962):190-91.
Highly praises Weisgard's illustrations in *Nibble, Nibble* which "flow as simply and as naturally as the poems."

A2507   PAINTER, HELEN W. "Leonard Weisgard: Exponent of Beauty." *EE* 47 (November 1970):922-35.
An overview and appraisal of Weisgard's career as an illustrator, with discussion of many individual works, influences, and techniques. Includes references and a bibliography of books illustrated by Weisgard.

A2508   WEISGARD, LEONARD. "The Artist at Work." *Horn Book* 40 (August 1964):409-14.

Explores the role of the picture book illustrator, using many examples from his own work and reasons for employing certain techniques.

WELCH, RONALD [Robert Oliver Felton] (1909-   )

A2509   CROUCH, MARCUS. *The Nesbit Tradition*, pp. 72-74.

Traces Welch's development as a writer. "As in later books he learnt more about the craft of novel-writing, Welch lost the keen edge of his enthusiasm and declined into a writer of scholarly, honestly prepared books from which the sparkle of a creative impulse had faded."

A2510   WELCH, RONALD. "Attention to Detail: The Workbooks of Ronald Welch." *CLE*, o.s., no. 8 (Summer 1972):30-38.

Welch explains his methods for incorporating small, background details in his historical fiction.

WELLS, HELEN (1910-   )

A2511   MASON, BOBBIE ANN. In *The Girl Sleuth*, pp. 107-15.

Mason analyzes the appeal of the *Cherry Ames Nurse* stories and *Vicki Barr Flight Stewardess* series, some volumes of which were written by Julie Tatham (who also wrote the Trixie Belden Books as Julie Campbell). Both books involve career girls who solve mysteries on the job.

WELLS, ROSEMARY (1943-   )

A2512   MERCIER, JEAN F. "Rosemary Wells." *Publishers Weekly* 217 (29 February 1980):72-73.

Wells discusses her background and her work in this brief interview, particularly the origins of her board books for very young children.

WERNSTRÖM, SVEN

A2513   GRAVES, PETER. "Sven Wernström: Traditionalist and Reformer." *Signal* 26 (May 1978):73-80.

Response by Norwegian librarian Kari Schei follows, pp. 81-83, with rebuttal by Graves, pp. 83-84. Graves and Schei agree that Wernström is the "most discussed writer for young people in Sweden over the last decade," but Schei feels his Marxism deserves more attention. According to Graves, none of Wernström's books has so far been translated into English.

WESTALL, ROBERT (1929-   )

A2514   CHAMBERS, AIDAN. "Letter from England: Children at War." *Horn Book* 52 (August 1976):438-42.

Feels *The Machine-Gunners* has two qualities that make it exceptional compared to other children's books about the war: (1) the sharpness of his re-creation of the time, and (2) its sense of also being about the present.

A2515   REES, DAVID. "Macho Man, British Style--Robert Westall." In *Painted Desert*, pp. 115-25.

      Maintains that "the seeds of later decline were sown" in *The Machine-Gunners*, Westall's first novel, with its increasingly improbable plot, macho characteristics, and emphasis on "guts" and unpleasant violence.

WESTON, JOHN (1932-)

A2516   BLAKELY, W. PAUL. "Growing Pains in Arizona: Youth in the Fiction of John Weston." *Arizona English Bulletin* 14, no. 3 (April 1972):44-50.

      Analyzes Weston's portrayals of coming of age against an Arizona background in *Jolly* and *Hail, Hero!*

WHITAKER, MURIEL

A2517   EVANS, MURRAY J. "Bright Parable of Pernilla." *CCC* 18, no. 19 (1980):117-20.

      An in-depth review of *Pernilla in the Perilous Forest* praising both the text and the illustrations by Jetske Ironside.

WHITE, ELIZA ORNE (1856-1947)

A2518   MILLER, BERTHA MAHONY. "Eliza Orne White and Her Books for Children." *Horn Book* 31 (April 1955):89-105. (Reprinted in Andrews, *The Hewins Lectures, 1947-1962*, pp. 151-62.)

      A biocritical essay.

WHITE, E.B. (1899-1985)

A2519   ALBERGHENE, JANICE M. "Writing in *Charlotte's Web*." *CLE*, n.s. 16, no. 1 (Spring 1985):32-44.

      Discusses the ways in which White explores what it means to be a "good writer." ("It is not often that someone comes along who is a true friend and a good writer.")

A2520   ANDERSON, ARTHUR JAMES. *E.B. White: A Biography.* Scarecrow Author Bibliographies, no. 37. Metuchen, N.J.: Scarecrow Press, 1978, 199 pp.

      Primarily an unannotated checklist of White's writings, a brief section of "Writings About E.B. White" contains a few entries pertaining to his children's books, and lists reviews of *Charlotte's Web*, pp. 157-58, *Stuart Little*, p. 155, and *The Trumpet of the Swan*, pp. 160-62.

A2521   "Anne Carroll Moore Urged Withdrawal of *Stuart Little*." *Library Journal* 91 (15 April 1966):2187-88 and *SLJ* 13 (April 1966):71-72.

      A brief note of historical and literary interest, citing reactions of Miss Moore, Harold Ross, and Edmund Wilson, among others, to the character of Stuart.

A2522   CAMERON, ELEANOR. "McLuhan, Youth, and Literature." *Horn Book* 48 (October 1972):572-79.

      Contrasts *Charlotte's Web* with *Charlie and the Chocolate Factory*, which she has found wanting, and shows how *Charlotte's Web* meets "standards set by some of the finest critics and writers of adult literature."

A2523   ELLEDGE, SCOTT. *E.B. White: A Biography*. New York: W.W. Norton, 1984, 400 pp.
Stuart Little*'s creation and critical reception are treated in chapter 13, pp. 250-66, *Charlotte's Web*'s in chapter 15, pp. 289-305, and *Trumpet of the Swan*'s, pp. 345-49.

A2524   GLASTONBURY, MARION. "E.B. White's Unexpected Items of Enchantment." *CLE*, o.s., no. 11 (May 1973):3-12. (Reprinted in Fox, *Writers, Critics, and Children*, pp. 104-15.)
Examines White's three books for children in terms of their themes and the relationships of those themes to White's life and personal characteristics and preoccupations.

A2525   GRIFFITH, JOHN. "*Charlotte's Web*: A Lonely Fantasy of Love." *Children's Literature* 8 (1980):111-17.
"In this story of Wilbur, a good-hearted but lonely and vulnerable pig, White creates a consoling fantasy in which a small Everyman survives and triumphs over the pathos of being alone." Relates the story to a child's growing insight and changing perspective as she grows up.

A2526   GUTH, DOROTHY LOBRANO, ed. *Letters of E.B. White*. New York: Harper & Row, 1976, 686 pp.
Scattered throughout this collection of letters are references, many providing valuable background information, to White's three children's books. They are easily accessed through the book's index.

A2527   INGLIS, FRED. *Promise of Happiness*, pp. 178-80.
Compares the book and film versions of *Charlotte's Web*.

A2528   MASON, BOBBIE ANN. "Profile: The Elements of E.B. White's Style." *LA* 56 (September 1979):692-96.
Analyzes White's style in writing for children. "White's vision-- trained by Thoreau's economy of effort and Strunk's economy of words . . . clear the way for a direct look at essential issues."

A2529   NEUMEYER, PETER F. "The Creation of *Charlotte's Web*: From Drafts to Book." *Horn Book* 58 (October 1982):489-97; (December 1982):617-25.
Describes White's creative processes.

A2530   -----. "The Creation of E.B. White's *The Trumpet of the Swan*: The Manuscripts." *Horn Book* 61 (January 1985):17-28.
An examination of White's manuscript drafts for *Trumpet of the Swan* at the Pierpont Morgan Library reveals a creative process similar to that revealed by the manuscript drafts for *Charlotte's Web*, and also gives "a hint of why *The Trumpet of the Swan* is not as highly regarded a novel as *Charlotte's Web*."

A2531   -----. "What Makes a Good Children's Book? The Texture of *Charlotte's Web*." *South Atlantic Bulletin* 44, no. 2, 1979, pp. 66-75.
Examines the "denseness of texture" and the "mythopoeic dimension" that make *Charlotte's Web* a great book.

A2532   NODELMAN, PERRY. "Text as Teacher: The Beginning of *Charlotte's Web*." *Children's Literature* 13 (1985):109-27.
       Explores the ways in which the structure of *Charlotte's Web* allows "young readers who know only simple fictions to comprehend their [the more complex novels'] greater complexity."

A2533   NULTON, LUCY. "Eight-Year-Olds in *Charlotte's Web*." *EE* 31 (January 1954):11-16.
       Describes children's analyses of situation and character that emerged during class reading.

A2534   SALE, ROGER. *Fairy Tales and After*, pp. 258-67.
       Sees *Charlottes Web* as a "hymn" of celebration and praise, and a "gem."

A2535   SAMPSON, EDWARD C. *E.B. White*. Twayne's U.S. Authors Series, no. 232. New York: Twayne Publishers, 1974, 190 pp.
       Chapter 6, "Stories for Children," pp. 94-105, analyzes *Stuart Little*, *Charlotte's Web*, and *The Trumpet of The Swan*.

A2536   SINGER, DOROTHY G. "*Charlotte's Web*: Erikson's Life Cycle." *SLJ* 22 (November 1975):17-19.
       Analyzes *Charlotte's Web* in terms of the eight developmental stages proposed by Erik Erikson in *Identity, Youth and Crisis*.

A2537   SOLHEIM, HELENE. "Magic in The Web: Time, Pigs, and E.B. White." *South Atlantic Quarterly* 80 (Autumn 1981):391-405.
       Argues that "In White, and particularly in *Charlotte's Web*, there is nothing in his children's stories inconsistent with or unlike the substance of his articles, or essays or poems."

A2538   WEALES, GERALD. "Designs of E.B. White." *NYTBR*, 24 May 1970, Children's Book sec., pp. 2, 40. (Reprinted in Hoffman, *Authors and Illustrators*, pp. 407-11.)
       Analyzes *Stuart Little* and *Charlotte's Web* in terms of White's own rule 8 from his *Elements of Style*: "Choose a suitable design and hold to it."

A2539   WHITE, E.B. "Death of a Pig." *Atlantic Monthly* 181 (January 1948):30-33.
       White provides intimations of Wilbur in this account of the death of his pig.

A2540   -----. "On Writing for Children." *Paris Review* 48 (Fall 1969). (In Haviland, *Children and Literature*, p. 140.)
       Describes his views on writing for children: "You have to write up, not down."

A2541   WINTLE, JUSTIN, and FISHER, EMMA. *Pied Pipers*, pp. 124-31.
       White discusses his life and work in an interview.

WHITE, T[ERENCE] H[ANBURY] (1906-64)

A2542   CRANE, JOHN K. *T.H. White*. New York: Twayne, 1974, 202 pp.
       Chapter 4, pp. 75-122, is devoted to *Once and Future King*, and pp. 123-34 of chapter 5 concentrate on *Mistress Masham's Repose*.

A2543   IRWIN, W.R. "Swift and the Novelists." *Philological Quarterly* 45 (1966):102-13.
        Discusses *Mistress Masham's Repose* and Walter De la Mare's *Memoirs of a Midget*, and their basis in *Gulliver's Travels*.

A2544   LANGTON, JANE. "A Second Look: *Mistress Masham's Repose.*" *Horn Book* 57 (October 1981):565-70.
        Explores the pleasure provided to both grown-ups and children in this witty, humorous book.

A2545   WARNER, SYLVIA TOWNSEND. *T.H. White: A Biography.* London: Cape--Chatto & Windus, 1967, 352 pp.
        Concentrates on White's life rather than his writings.

WIESE, KURT (1887-1974)

A2546   BADER, BARBARA. *American Picturebooks*, pp. 65-68.
        Analyzes *Liang and Lo, Ping*, and the *Five Chinese Brothers*.

A2547   BERTRAM, JEAN DE SALES. "Kurt Wiese--Prolific Artist, Author." *EE* 33 (April 1956):195-200.
        Discusses the influence of Wiese's past on his work.

WIGGIN, KATE DOUGLAS (1856-1923)

A2548   ERISMAN, FRED. "Transcendentalism for American Youth." *New England Quarterly* 41 (1968):238-47.
        Explores the influences of transcendentalism in Wiggin's children's books.

A2549   KINGSTON, CAROLYN T. *Tragic Mode*, pp. 127-30.
        Analyzes themes of loss and death in *The Birds' Christmas Carol*.

WILBUR, RICHARD (1921-   )

A2550   NADEL, ALAN. "Roethke, Wilbur, and the Vision of the Child: Romantic and Augustan in Modern Verse." *L&U* 2, no. 1 (Spring 1975):94-113.
        Compares the two poets, placing Roethke in the romantic tradition with its pure and free projection of childhood, and Wilbur in the neoclassical tradition of the rational, social poet. Analyzes several poems in these terms.

A2551   SCULLEY, JAMES. Review. *Children's Literature* 2 (1973):241-42.
        A scathing review of *Opposites*.

WILDE, OSCAR (1856-1900)

A2552   GRISWOLD, JEROME. "Sacrifice and Mercy in Wilde's *The Happy Prince*." *Children's Literature* 3 (1974):103-6.
        Identifies the Wilde's theme as advocating mercy rather than sacrifice.

A2553   KOTZIN, MICHAEL C. "'The Selfish Giant' As Literary Tale." *Studies in Short Fiction* 16 (Fall 1979):301-9.

In-depth examination of "The Selfish Giant" as an example of the nineteenth-century literary fairy tale.

A2554 MARTIN, ROBERT K. "Oscar Wilde and the Fairy Tale: *The Happy Prince* as Self-Dramatization." *Studies in Short Fiction* 16 (Winter 1979):74-77.

Argues that "Wilde used the fairy tale to express some of his deepest concerns and to record his own growing commitments, including one to homosexual love, in a way which would have been impossible without the protection offered by the conventions of fantasy."

A2555 MONAGHAN, DAVID M. "The Literary Fairy-Tale: A Study of Oscar Wilde's *The Happy Prince* and *The Star-Child.*" *Canadian Review of Comparative Literature* 1, no. 2 (Spring 1974):156-66.

A2556 QUINTUS, JOHN ALLEN. "The Moral Prerogative in Oscar Wilde: A Look at the Fairy Tales." *Virginia Quarterly Review* 53, no. 4 (Autumn 1977):708-17.

Claims that "the moral direction so obvious in them is analogous to the morality Wilde espouses throughout his art."

A2557 SHEWAN, RODNEY. "*The Happy Prince and Other Tales.*" In *Oscar Wilde: Art and Egotism*, pp. 40-57.

Discusses "The Happy Prince," "The Selfish Giant," and other tales from *The Happy Prince and Other Tales* in terms of egotism and pastoral themes.

A2558 SPELMAN, MARILYN KELLY. "The Self-Realization Theme in *The Happy Prince* and *A House of Pomegranates.*" Ph.D. dissertation, University of Colorado at Boulder, 1978, 107 pp., DA 39:2959A.

Analyzes Wilde's fairy tales in terms of the unifying theme of self-realization and comments on their "moralism" through Christian metaphor.

A2559 TREMPER, ELLEN. "Commitment and Escape: The Fairy Tales of Thackeray, Dickens and Wilde." *L&U* 2, no. 1 (Spring 1978):38-47.

Examines Thackeray's *The Rose and the Ring*, Dickens's *The Magic Fishbone*, and Wilde's *The Happy Prince* to determine whether "The attitudes usually present in these writers' adult fiction are, for some reason, overturned in their juvenile stories." Argues that while Thackeray and Dickens wrote realistic novels for adults, their fairy tales are escapist whereas Wilde, whose adult works were escapist, reflects the "bitter waters of worldly experience" in his children's stories.

WILDER, LAURA INGALLS (1867-1957)

A2560 ANDERSON, WILLIAM T. "The Laura Ingalls Wilder Classics." *AB Bookman's Weekly* 68 (16 November 1981):3408, 3410, 3412.

Chronicles the prepublication history of the Little House books.

A2561 BOSMAJIAN, HAMIDA. "Vastness and Contraction of Space in *Little House on the Prairie.*" *Children's Literature* 11 (1983):49-63.

Compares the intimacy of the inner space represented by the house with the vastness of the prairie and all it represents of the larger world.

A2562   BUTTENSCHØN, ELLEN. "A Danish Book about Laura Ingalls Wilder." *Bookbird* 12, no. 2 (1974):20-28.

Reports on her research for her book: *Laura Ingalls Wilder, Bondekonen der Blev Digter* (Copenhagen: Gyldendal, 1971), 123 pp.

A2563   CAPEY, A.C. "Laura Ingalls and Mrs. Wilder: The Writer as Recreator." *Use of English* 29 (Summer 1978):25-31.

Praises Wilder's ability to re-create the experiences of daily life, and the skill and style of her prose, for which he suggests a possible origin.

A2564   COLWELL, EILEEN H. "Laura Ingalls Wilder." *Junior Bookshelf* 26 (November 1962):237-43.

An English view of Wilder, primarily plot summary.

A2565   COOPER, BERNICE. "The Authenticity of the Historical Background of the *Little House* Books." *EE* 40 (November 1963):696-702.

Verifies the historical authenticity and accuracy of the books.

A2566   DALPHIN, MARCIA. "Christmas in the Little House Books." *Horn Book* 29 (December 1953):431-35.

Examines the portrayal of Christmas in the Little House books.

A2567   DYKSTRA, RALPH RICHARD. "The Autobiographical Aspects of Laura Ingalls Wilder's "Little House" Books." Ed.D. dissertation, State University of New York at Buffalo, 1980, 271 pp., DA 41:1003A.

Identifies and analyzes autobiographical elements in Wilder's work, especially those events that may have influenced her writing and the ways in which she interpreted her life.

A2568   ERISMAN, FRED. "The Regional Vision of Laura Ingalls Wilder." In *Studies in Medieval, Renaissance, American Literature: A Festschrift.* Edited by Betsy F. Colquitt. Fort Worth: Texas Christian University Press, 1971, pp. 165-71.

Sees Wilder's works as providing "a statement of literary regionalism that is unsurpassed by many better-known 'serious' works." Praises her sense of time and place and her awareness of being part of a larger American culture.

A2569   FLANAGAN, FRANCES. "A Tribute to Laura Ingalls Wilder." *EE* 34 (April 1937):203-13.

Argues that not only the material but its combination with a command of style, and a gift for storytelling, perhaps inherited from her father, make Laura Ingalls Wilder's books among the best.

A2570   INGLIS, FRED. *Promise of Happiness*, pp. 165-71.

Sees *Long Winter* as portraying "an ideal social order" in "a real past. . . . The pacing of the book is unimprovable. Each chapter is quite short, nicely adjusted to a young reader's stamina, but each shifts the story a little way on in to the long, rhythmless tedium of the winter."

A2571   JACOBS, WILLIAM JAY. "Frontier Faith Revisited: The Little House Books of Laura Ingalls Wilder." *Horn Book* 41 (October 1965):465-73.

Explores the significance of frontier faith and pioneer values, as presented by Wilder, for the modern reader.

A2572 KINGSTON, CAROLYN, T. *Tragic Mode*, pp. 164-67.
Analyzes *By the Shores of Silver Lake* in terms of its theme of loss.

A2573 *Laura Ingalls Wilder Lore.* Six-page newsletter issued twice a year since 1974 by the Laura Ingalls Wilder Memorial Society. De Smet, South Dakota 57231.

A2574 LEE, ANNE THOMPSON. "'It is better farther on': Laura Ingalls Wilder and the Pioneer Spirit." *L&U* 3, no. 1 (Spring 1979):74-88.
Concentrates on the portraits of Ma and Pa in the Little House books. Although Pa is adored, "Laura's slow progress toward a sympathetic understanding of her mother parallels her own growth toward acceptance of her identity as a woman."

A2575 MOONEY-GETOFF, MARY J. *Laura Ingalls Wilder: A Bibliography.* Southold, N.Y.: Wise Owl Press, 1980, 40 pp.
Lists books and articles by and about Laura Ingalls Wilder, including literary criticism. Contains a section entitled "Research Still Needed on Laura Ingalls Wilder's Other Writings." Also includes listings of audiovisual materials and addresses of historical societies and museums concerned with Wilder.

A2576 MOORE, ROSA ANN. "Laura Ingalls Wilder and Rose Wilder Lane: The Chemistry of Collaboration." *CLE*, n.s., 11, no. 3 (Autumn 1980):101-9.
An examination of unpublished correspondence between Laura Ingalls Wilder and her daughter Rose reveals how the Little House books reflect collaboration.

A2577 -----. "Laura Ingalls Wilder's Orange Notebooks and the Art of the Little House Books." *Children's Literature* 4 (1975):105-19.
A comparison of the posthumously published *The First Four Years* and available notebooks with *These Happy Golden Years* and other books reveals the restyling and restructuring that turned the unretouched autobiography into a finished work "both less literal and more true and beautiful."

A2578 -----. "The Little House Books: Rose Colored Classics." *Children's Literature* 7 (1978):7-16.
A study of Laura Ingalls Wilder's papers reveals how much her daughter Rose had to do with her books as editor and mentor.

A2579 MOWREY, JANET B. "Portrait of a Pioneer." *LA* (January 1976):51-55.
Examines Laura's portrayal of Pa as a pioneer.

A2580 ROSENBLUM, DOLORES. "'Intimate Immensity': Mythic Space in the Works of Laura Ingalls Wilder." In *Where the West Begins: Essays on Middle Border and Sioux-land Writing, in Honor of Herbert Krause.* Edited by Arthur R. Huseboe and William Geyer. Sioux Falls, S.D.: Center for Western Studies Press, 1978, pp. 72-79.
Sees Wilder as making sense of "child Laura Ingalls's prairie world by organizing empty space around actual structures--a variety of 'little houses.'" Applies Gaston Bachelard's theories of the paradox

of "intimate immensity" to Laura's handling and eventual synthesis of a number of opposites.

A2581   SEGEL, ELIZABETH.   "Laura Ingalls Wilder's America: An Unflinching Assessment." *CLE*, n.s. 8, no. 2 (Summer 1977):63-70.
Argues that the Little House books convey the ethics and values of American pioneers and portray also a "child's courageous questioning" of the "pernicious doctrines of repressive gentility and racial superiority."

A2582   SMITH, IRENE.   "Laura Ingalls Wilder and the Little House Books." *Horn Book* 19 (September-October 1943):293-306.
Explores the relationship between Wilder's life and her writings.

A2583   SPAETH, JANET L.   "Over the Horizon of the Years: Laura Ingalls Wilder and the Little House Books." Ph.D. dissertation, University of North Dakota, 1982, 161 pp., DA 43:1148A.
Consists of five essays, each one devoted to an aspect of Wilder's writing heretofore ignored in critical analysis. The essays examine (1) the family traditions and folklore and their relationship to the general structure of *Little House in The Big Woods*, (2) the effect of the Homestead Act as portrayed in the series, (3) female social training as revealed in the series, (4) Laura's growth to adulthood as revealed in changing ordering of environment and use of language, and (5) particulars of Wilder's technique (point of view, plot, theme, tone, imagery, personification, and character) and their contributions to the enduring success of her stories.

A2584   WALKER, BARBARA.   *The Little House Cookbook: Frontier Foods from Laura Ingalls Wilder's Classic Stories.* New York: Harper & Row, 1979, 240 pp.
The introductory chapters in this cookbook provide insights about the significance of food in the Little House books and factual background related to the books. Even the remaining chapters, which are mainly recipes, contain strong links to the books themselves.

A2585   WARD, NANCY.   "Laura Ingalls Wilder--An Appreciation." *EE* 50 (October 1973):1025-27, 1038.
Wonders how Wilder, with few books in her childhood and little time to read in her adult life, became such a masterful writer. Praises her ability to make us "see and feel everything with her own delight," her depiction of life's small pleasures, of the joys of food, especially in *Farmer Boy*, and her picture of family life. Also comments upon the many lessons the books teach about details of pioneer life and work, and about self-control and unselfishness.

A2586   WENZEL, EVELYN.   "'Little House' Books of Laura Ingalls Wilder." *EE* 29 (February 1952):65-74.
Discusses qualities of the Little House books that give children insight into their own problems and needs.

A2587   WILLIAMS, GARTH.   "Illustrating the Little House Books." *Horn Book* 29 (December 1953):413-22.
Describes how he retraced the Ingalls's steps in the process of illustrating the Little House books.

A2588   WILNER, ISABEL.   "Laura Ingalls Wilder." *Bookbird* 5, no. 3

(1967):34-36.
Briefly summarizes the outstanding qualities and the impact of the Little House books.

A2589 WOLF, VIRGINIA. "Plenary Paper: The Magic Circle of Laura Ingalls Wilder." *ChLAQ* 9, no. 4 (Winter 1984-85):168-70.
Argues that in contrast to *Little House in The Big Woods* where the little house in the center of the circle of woods is the focus, in *Little House on the Prairie* the focus is on the circle and "The center, paradoxically becomes a moving house, a covered wagon, or a skeleton house open to the light, air, and danger of the wild, endless prairie."

A2590 -----. "The Symbolic Center: *Little House in the Big Woods*." *CLE*, n.s. 13, no. 3 (Autumn 1982):107-14. (Reprinted in May, *Children and Their Literature*, pp. 65-70.)
Categorizes the work as more romance than fiction, and analyzes it in terms of harmony and antithetical balance: the contrast between the domesticity and warmth of family life in the little house and the wilderness and immensity of the big woods, and the pioneer family's life in harmony with nature and the cycle of seasons.

A2591 ZOCHERT, DANIEL. *Laura: The Life of Laura Ingalls Wilder.* Chicago: Henry Regnery, 1976, 260 pp.
This primarily biographical account provides insights into the origins of Laura's writing.

WILDSMITH, BRIAN (1930-   )

A2592 JONES, CORNELIA, and WAY, OLIVIA R. *British Children's Authors*, pp. 155-66.
In an interview Wildsmith discusses his background, philosophy, and method of working. Includes an annotated bibliography of his works.

A2593 WILDSMITH, BRIAN. "Antic Disposition: A Young Illustrator Interviews Himself." *Library Journal* 90 (15 November 1965):5035-38 and *SLJ* 12 (November 1965):21-24.
Wildsmith sheds light on his background and his approach to illustrating.

WILKINS, VAUGHAN (1890-1959)

A2594 CROUCH, MARCUS. "*After Bath*--Fourteen Years After." *Junior Bookshelf* 23 (December 1959):324-27.
Regards *After Bath* as the most interesting children's book to come out of World War II.

WILLARD, BARBARA (1909-   )

A2595 CROUCH, MARCUS. "Foresty Folk." *Junior Bookshelf* 46 (April 1982):55-59.
Examines Willard's theme of the forest.

A2596 -----. "Women of Iron." *TLS*, 20 September 1974, p. 1004.
Reviews the last of the Mantlemass novels, *Harrow and Harvest*.

A2597   FISHER, MARGERY. "Barbara Willard." *School Librarian* 17 (December 1969):343-48.

Calls Barbara Willard the "Louisa Alcott of our time." Provides a fine introduction to her work and a bibliography of her books.

A2598   JONES, CORNELIA, and WAY, OLIVIA R. *British Children's Authors*, pp. 167-76.

In an interview Willard discusses her background, philosophy, and method of working. Includes an annotated bibliography of her works.

A2599   MEEK, MARGARET. "The Fortunes of Mantlemass." *TLS*, 18 July 1980, p. 805.

Provides a brief critical overview of the Mantlemass series.

WILLARD, NANCY (1936-   )

A2600   HALL, DONALD. "Clouds for Breakfast." *NYTBR*, 15 November 1981, pp. 51, 60.

Reviews *A Visit to William Blake's Inn*.

A2601   PERKINS, AGNES. "Scribe of Dreams." *ChLAQ* 10, no. 1 (Spring 1985):38-40.

Finds a common theme of dreams and free-association throughout all of Willard's prose, poetry, and fiction, for both children and adults.

A2602   WANIEK, MARILYN NELSON. "A Trio of Poetry Books for Children." *Children's Literature* 11 (1983):182-90.

Critical of Willard's *A Visit to William Blake's Inn*, Waniek also discusses Michael Patrick Hearn's anthology *A Day in Verse: Breakfast, Books, and Dreams* and Annie Schmidt's *Pink Lemonade*.

WILLIAMS, GARTH (1912-   )

A2603   FAVA, RITA. "Artist's Choice." *Horn Book* 37 (June 1961):244-45.

Praises the pictures, design, and total unity of *Bedtime for Frances* (written by Russell Hoban).

WILLIAMS, URSULA MORAY (1911-   )

A2604   MOSS, ELAINE. "Ursula Moray Williams and *Adventures of the Little Wooden Horse*." *Signal* 5 (May 1971):56-61.

A biocritical overview. Regards *Adventures of the Little Wooden Horse* "one of the outstanding books" of the 1930s.

WILLIAMS, VERA B. (1927-   )

A2605   WILLIAMS, VERA. "Boston Globe-Horn Book Award Acceptance." *Horn Book* 60 (February 1984):34-38.

Tells how she came to write *A Chair for My Mother*.

WILLIAMSON, HENRY (1897-1977)

A2606   DAVIS, MARNI AYRES. Review. *Horn Book* 5 (February 1929):24-26.

An early review of *Tarka The Otter*, praising it as "so piercingly true that it makes you remember things not consciously noticed when you watched woods and water grow."

WINFIELD, ARTHUR M. [Stratemeyer Syndicate pseudonym]

A2607 PRAGER, ARTHUR. *Rascal at Large*, pp. 220-51.
Prager mingles personal recollection, standard plot outlines, and analysis in his discussion of the Stratemeyer Syndicate's Rover Boys series.

WOJCIECHOWSKA, MAIA (1927-   )

A2608 HANSEN, IAN V. "The Spanish Setting: A Re-Appraisal of Maia Wojciechowska." *CLE*, n.s. 12, no. 4 (1981):186-91.
This reevaluation of Wojciechowska's *Shadow of a Bull* and *A Single Light* suggests that their didactic moralizing is more bothersome to adult readers than to children, that "These novels breathe a myth-quality that makes some sense of a violent world of pain, uncertainty, and rejection."

A2609 KINGSTON, CAROLYN T. *Tragic Mode*, pp. 14-16.
Analyzes the theme of rejection in *Shadow of a Bull*.

A2610 WINTLE, JUSTIN, and FISHER, EMMA. *Pied Pipers*, pp. 295-307.
Wojciechowska discusses her life in an interview.

A2611 WOJCIECHOWSKA, MAIA. "Shadow of a Kid." *Horn Book* 41 (August 1965):349-52.
Enlarges upon the origins and background of *Shadow of a Bull*. A biographical sketch by Selden Rodman follows, pp. 353-57.

WRIGHTSON, PATRICIA (1921-   )

A2612 FISHER, MARGERY. "Writers for Children: 10. Patricia Wrightson." *School Librarian* 17 (March 1969):22-26.
Provides a fine introduction to Wrightson's work.

A2613 GILDERDALE, BETTY. "The Novels of Patricia Wrightson." *CLE*, n.s. 9, no. 1 (Spring 1978):43-49.
Examines Wrightson's themes and techniques in books up to *The Nargun and the Stars* (1973).

A2614 McDONNELL, CHRISTINE. "A Second Look." *Horn Book* 56 (April 1980):196-99.
Praises Wrightson's refreshing, sensitive handling of Andy's specialness in *A Racecourse for Andy*: "Wrightson shows us that innocence is a gift."

A2615 McVITTY, WALTER. "Patricia Wrightson: At the Edge of Australian Vision." In *Innocence and Experience*, pp. 99-132.
Feels Wrightson's later work "is stretching the bounds of children's literature beyond reasonable reach of audience." Provides a brief biography, extensive critical analysis, comments by Wrightson, and a bibliogaphy of her books.

A2616 TOWNSEND, JOHN ROWE. *Sense of Story*, pp. 204-14.
Discusses *I Own the Racecourse* which he considers a turning

point and big success, and several earlier works.

A2617   -----. *A Sounding*, pp. 194-206.
A revision and update of the essay in *Sense of Story*. In the newer books "important parts are played . . . by those indigenous spirits of Australia which Patricia Wrightson has adopted and adapted." Discusses *An Older Kind of Magic, Nargun and the Stars*, and *The Ice Is Coming*.

A2618   WRIGHTSON, PATRICIA. "The Fellowship of Man and Beast." *Horn Book* 61 (January 1985):38-41.
Comments on writing *A Little Fear* and excessive fear of anthropomorphism.

A2619   -----. "Stones Into Pools." *TON* 41 (Spring 1985):283-92.
Shares her views on writing, storytelling, and fantasy.

A2620   YOUNG, DONALD. "Patricia Wrightson, O.B.E." *Junior Bookshelf* 45 (December 1981):235-41.
A critical evaluation of Wrightson's development as a writer.

WYETH, N.C. (1882-1945)

A2621   MEYER, S. "N.C. Wyeth." *American Artist* 39 (February 1975):38-45, 94-100.
Provides an overview of Wyeth's career as part of a special issue devoted to three generations of the Wyeth family.

WYSS, JOHANN (1743-1818)

A2622   HÜRLIMANN, BETTINA. "Fortunate Moments in Children's Books." *TON* 29 (June 1973):331-50.
Selects fortunate moments from a number of classic children's books, concentrating on Wyss's *Swiss Family Robinson*, the Grimms' tales, Hoffmann's *Struwwelpeter*, Spyri's *Heidi*, and De Brunhoff's *Babar*.

YASHIMA, TARO [Jun Atsushi Iwanmatsu] (1908-   )

A2623   MORDVINOFF, NICHOLAS. "Artist's Choice." *Horn Book* 32 (December 1956):429-30.
Examines the illustrations of *Crow Boy*.

YATES, ELIZABETH (1905-   )

A2624   MacCAMPBELL, JAMES C. "The Work of Elizabeth Yates." *EE* (November 1952):381-89.
Analyzes Yates's literary style.

A2625   PAINTER, HELEN W. "Elizabeth Yates: Artist with Words." *EE* 42 (October 1965):617-28, 650. (Reprinted in Hoffman, *Authors and Illustrators*, pp. 421-35.)
Includes biographical background, plus discussion of *Carolina's Courage* and the background of *Mountain Born, A Place for Peter, Patterns on the Wall, Pebble in a Pool, Amos Fortune, Free Man*, and *Someday You'll Write*.

A2626   MacCANN, DONNARAE. "Racism in Prize-Winning Biographical Works." In *Black American*, pp. 94-101.
Analyzes racial stereotypes in the Newbery Award winning *Amos Fortune, Free Man*.

A2627   YATES, ELIZABETH. "Climbing Some Mountain in the Mind." *Horn Book* 27 (July 1951):268-78.
Tells of the research and writing of *Amos Fortune, Free Man*.

A2628   -----. "Enys Tregarthen 1851-1923." *Horn Book* 25 (May 1949):231-238.
Tells the story of Nellie Slogett, also known as Nellie Cornwall, and Enys Tregarthen, whose Cornish legends Yates edited in 1940. Includes bibliography.

A2629   -----. "How Enys Tregarthen's Cornish Legends Came to Light." *Horn Book* 16 (September 1940):334-37. (Reprinted in Fryatt, *Horn Book Sampler*, pp. 23-27.)
The story behind *Piskey Folk: A Book of Cornish Legends*.

YEP, LAURENCE (1948-   )

A2630   DINCHAK, MARLA. "Recommended: Laurence Yep." *English Journal* 71 (March 1982):81-82.
Argues that Yep deserves more attention in the junior high school classroom.

A2631   YEP, LAURENCE. "Writing *Dragonwings*." *Reading Teacher* 30 (January 1977):359-63.
The story behind the book.

YOLEN, JANE (1939-   )

A2632   WHITE, DAVID E. "Profile: Jane Yolen." *LA* 60 (May 1983):652-60.
Highlights the influence of Yolen's experience and philosophy on her work. Includes bibliography of her work.

A2633   YOLEN, JANE. "The Girl--from Where?--Who Loved the Wind." *WLB* 48, no. 2 (October 1973):159-61.
Describes the process of establishing the setting for *The Girl Who Loved the Wind* and ruminates on the influences on modern literature of the availability of the folklore of a wide range of cultures.

YOUNG, ELLA (1865-1956)

A2634   EATON, ANNE T. "Ella Young's Unicorns and Kyelins." *Horn Book* 9 (August 1933):115-20. (Reprinted in Fryatt, *Horn Book Sampler*, pp. 237-42.)
This overview of Young's work pays special attention to *The Unicorn with Silver Shoes*.

A2635   SAYERS, FRANCES CLARKE. "The Flowering Dusk of Ella Young." *Horn Book* 21 (May-June 1945):214-20. (Reprinted in Sayers, *Summoned by Books*, pp. 133-39.)
Praises Young's use of language, her freshness and conviction. Describes *The Flowering Dusk* as an "autobiography of mind and spirit" which "illumines all the books preceding it."

ZEI, ALKI

A2636   *"Petros' War*: The 1974 Batchelder Award." *TON* 30 (June 1974): 363-68.
Includes editor Ann Durrell's "A Little Background on *Petros' War*" and translator Edward Fenton's "A View from a Foreign Window."

ZEMACH, MARGOT (1931-   )

A2637   BADER, BARBARA. *American Picturebooks*, pp. 565-72.
Traces Zemach's career as an illustrator of folklore.

A2638   BANFIELD, BERYLE. Review. *IRBC* 14, nos. 1-2 (1983):32-33.
Sees *Jake and Honeybunch Go to Heaven* as an example of the dangers inherent in adapting the folklore of another culture without a firm understanding of the people who developed it.

A2639   "Black Folklore Controversy Erupts: Farrar Questions Selection Policies." *SLJ* 29 (March 1983):1968.
Reports on the emergence of criticism and the debate over Margot Zemach's *Jake and Honeybunch Go to Heaven*.

A2640   *"Jake and Honeybunch Go to Heaven*: Children's Book Fans Smoldering Debate." *American Libraries* 14 (March 1983):130-32.
Includes statements of a number of points of view on the controversy surrounding Margot Zemach's books. Stephen Roxburgh, publisher, responds in 14 (May 1983):315.

A2641   ZEMACH, MARGOT, and ZEMACH, HARVEY. "Profile of an Author and an Illustrator." *TON* 27 (April 1971):248-55.
The Zemachs answer questions about their life and work.

ZIMNIK, REINER (1930-   )

A2642   DANISCHEWSKY, NINA. "Re-Viewing Reiner Zimnik or 'Don't Mind Me! I'm Happy!'" *Signal* 6 (September 1971):115-25.
Reexamines *Drummers of Dreams* and *The Crane*.

ZINDEL, PAUL (1936-   )

A2643   ABRAHAMSON, RICHARD F., and PERRY, MERRIAN. "Visual Literacy and Adolescent Novels--The Reading Connection." ERIC Educational Reproduction Service, 1979, 11 pp., ED 172 248.
Shows how teachers can mesh the teaching of "visual literacy" and literary analysis by analyzing the novels of Paul Zindel in terms of film technique and camera shots.

A2644   CLARKE, LORETTA. *"The Pigman*: A Novel of Adolescence." *English Journal* 61 (November 1972):1163-69, 1175.
A detailed close analysis.

A2645   DAVIS, JOHN. "Welcome Back, Zindel." *ALAN Review* 9, no. 1 (1981):2-4, 10. (Also in ERIC Educational Document Reproduction Service, ED 208 419.)
Feels Zindel's newer books, *The Pigman's Legacy* (1980) and *A*

Star for the Latecomer *(1980), are a welcome return to the style and content of the vintage Zindel of* The Pigman, My Darling, My Hamburger, *and* I Never Loved Your Mind, *in contrast to the "blackness" of* Confessions of a Teenage Baboon *and* Pardon Me, You're Stepping on My Eyeball.

A2646   EAGLEN, AUDREY. "Of Life, Love, Death, Kids, and Inhalation Therapy: An Interview with Paul Zindel." *TON* 34 (Winter 1978):178-85.
Zindel discusses his life and work in an interview.

A2647   FISHER, MAXINE. Review. *IRBC* 10, no. 5 (1979):15-16.
Finds *The Undertaker's Gone Bananas* sexist and full of stereotypes.

A2648   HALEY, BEVERLY A. "*The Pigman*--Use It!" *Arizona English Bulletin* 14, no. 3 (April 1972):89-92.
Sees *The Pigman* as a popular novel that can exemplify an author's use of language, metaphor, and structure.

A2649   HALEY, BEVERLY A., and DONELSON, KENNETH L. "Pigs and Hamburgers, Cadavers and Gamma Rays: Paul Zindel's Adolescents." *EE* 51 (October 1974):941-45.
Analyzes Zindel's ability to speak to adolescents by looking at the world through their eyes, utilizing humor, a keen ear for language, and appropriate themes.

A2650   HENKE, JAMES T. "Six Characters in Search of the Family: The Novels of Paul Zindel." *Children's Literature* 5 (1976):130-40. (Reprinted in Lenz, *Young Adult Literature*, pp. 132-41.)
Identifies adolescent aspirations to parenthood as Zindel's major theme, and traces its development in *The Pigman, My Darling, My Hamburger,* and *I Never Loved Your Mind.*

A2651   HOFFMAN, STANLEY. "Winning, Losing, But Above All Taking Risks: A Look at the Novels of Paul Zindel." *L&U* 2, no. 2 (Fall 1978):78-88.
Reflects on the erratic quality of Zindel's novels, the good and bad; and concludes that even though Zindel may at times be disappointing he can never be accused of mediocrity.

A2652   JAKIEL, S. JAMES. "Paul Zindel: An Author for Today's Adolescents." *Arizona English Bulletin* 18, no. 3 (April 1976):220-24.
Raises a number of questions concerning Zindel's highly unfavorable portraits of adults, especially teachers, librarians, guidance counselors, and parents.

A2653   MOEGLING, LARRY. "Paul Zindel's Lost Children: The Near Misbegotten." *Focus: Teaching English Language Arts* 3, no. 2 (Winter 1977):42-48. (Also ERIC Educational Document Reproduction Service, ED 157 082.)
Views Zindel's protagonists as "lost children" alienated from the real world in the "so-called time-tunnel of growing up."

A2654   REES, DAVID. "Viewed from a Squashed Eyeball: Paul Zindel." In *Marble in the Water,* pp. 25-35.
Finds Zindel's hyperbole and immature voice tedious. Traces his

style to Salinger. Feels *The Undertaker's Gone Bananas* shows more control and richness than previous works and may indicate Zindel is taking a new direction.

A2655   TOWNSEND, JOHN ROWE. "It Takes More Than Pot and the Pill." *NYTBR*, 9 November 1969, Children's Book sec., p. 2.
Reflects on a number of examples of recent young adult realistic fiction, and singles out *My Darling, My Hamburger* as having special merit.

A2656   WADDEY, LUCY E. "Cinderella and the Pigman: Why Kids Read Blume and Zindel Novels." *ALAN Review* 10, no. 2 (Winter 1983):6-9.
Explores reasons for the appeal of Blume and Zindel.

A2657   ZINDEL, PAUL. "Magic of Special People." *School Media* 2, no. 8 (Fall 1979):29-32.
Describes the real life origins of many of the "special people" in his won books.

ZION, GENE (1913-75)

A2658   BADER, BARBARA. *American Picturebooks*, pp. 466-70.
Discusses the contributions of author Gene Zion and his wife, illustrator Margaret Bloy Graham, to the picture book. "All the books revolve upon child ideas." Zion has a "knack of spinning a realistic tale from an imagined situation, usually one that has no adult antecedent or equivalent." Discusses *The Park Book* at length, pp. 246-48, and *One Step, Two, The Storm Book*, and others on pp. 464-66.

ZOLOTOW, CHARLOTTE (1915-   )

A2659   CHAPMAN, KAREN LENZ. "Themes of Charlotte Zolotow's Books and her Adult Development." M.A. thesis, Claremont Graduate School, 1981. ERIC Educational Document Reproduction Service, 1981, 82 pp., ED 204 797.
Pages 37-42 describe and discuss the books, pp. 15-36 are purely biographical, and the remainder of the thesis centers on theories of adult development and their relationship to Charlotte Zolotow's life. Includes bibliographies of writings by and about Zolotow.

A2660   WINTLE, JUSTIN, and FISHER, EMMA. *Pied Pipers*, pp. 87-100.
Zolotow discusses her life in an interview.

A2661   ZOLOTOW, CHARLOTTE. "Writing for the Very Young." *Horn Book* 61 (September 1985):536-40.
Explores the ways she tries to capture the emotions of the very young child.

Part B: Subjects, Themes, and Genres
An Annotated Listing of Criticism

ADAPTATIONS

B1   GEISLER, ROLF. "Adapting Works of World Literature--Sacrilege or Necessity?" *Bookbird* 8, no. 1 (1970):3-9.
     Argues in favor of adaptations, but with careful limits that take into account the meaning, structure, and intention of the original work.

B2   HAINES, MICHAEL. "Emasculated Classics." *Use of English* 32, no. 1 (Autumn 1980):66-69.
     Reviews a number of recent British adaptations of classics and other works designed for the foreign speaker of English and finds them "substitutes which cancel out the vital and meaningful confrontation between author and reader which we call reading."

B3   LOFTIS, ANNE, and MARSHALL, RACHELLE. "Gresham's Law of Literature." *Saturday Review* 46 (21 September 1963):64-65.
     Argues against adaptations of classic literature for children, for "most great writing . . . requires a period of apprenticeship in the art of creative reading."

B4   STEIN, RUTH. "The ABC's of Counterfeit Classics: Adapted, Bowdlerized, and Condensed." *English Journal* 55 (December 1966):1160-63.
     An indictment of revised classics.

ADULTS

B5   ELY, AMANDA, Sister. "The Adult Image in Three Novels of Adolescent Life." *English Journal* 56 (November 1967):1127-31.
     Examines Golding's *Lord of the Flies*, Knowles's *A Separate Peace*, and Salinger's *Catcher in the Rye* in terms of their portrayal of adults.

B6   STORCK, PATRICIA A., and CUTLER, MARION B. "Pictorial Representations of Adults as Observed in Children's Literature." *Educational Gerontology* 2 (July-September 1977):293-300.
     Concludes from a survey of Caldecott-winning and runner-up books that adults are not portrayed realistically in children's books.

B7   WATSON, JERRY J. "The Less-than-Perfect Adult Image in Children's Books. Why." ERIC Educational Document Reproduction Service, 1977, 10 pp., ED 150 605.

       Defends the increasing appearance of negative portrayals of well-known adults--parents, teachers, and librarians--in children's books. Lists and annotates twenty-five books presenting these negative images, and discusses children's and adults' reactions to them.

B8   WEICK, PAULA M. "Adult Portrayal in Novels for Teen-Age Girls." ERIC Educational Document Reproduction Service, 1977, 55 pp., ED 172 220.

       Analyzes the portrayal of adults in seven novels written for teenaged girls in the 1950s and late 1960s on the basis of four criteria: consistency, evident motivation, plausibility, and scope of activity. Concludes that stereotyping persists.

ADVENTURE STORIES

B9   BLACKBURN, WILLIAM, ed. *ChLAQ* 8, no. 3 (Fall 1983):7-33.

       Special Issue. Contents: "Mirror in the Sea: *Treasure Island* and the Internalization of Juvenile Romance," pp. 7-12, by William Blackburn, compares and contrasts *Treasure Island*, *Robinson Crusoe*, and *Peter Pan*; "Captain Marryat and Sea Adventure," pp. 13-15, 30, by Anita Moss, traces the influence of Captain Frederick Marryat (1792-1848) on the nautical adventure story; "Youngsters 'in the Great Lone Land': Early Canadian Adventure Stories," pp. 16-18, by Patricia Demers, discusses Catherine Parr Traill's *Canadian Crusoes*, James De Mille's *The "B.O.W.C."*, G.A. Henty's *With Wolfe in Canada*, Egerton Ryerson Young's *Three Boys* stories, and Ernest Thompson Seton's *Two Little Savages*; "Fantasy as Adventure: Nineteenth Century Children's Fiction," pp. 18-22, by Roderick McGillis, discusses works of L.M. Montgomery, Lewis Carroll, George MacDonald, and others; "Authority, Autonomy, and Adventure in Juvenile Science Fiction," pp. 22-26, by Janis Svilpis, traces the influences of Jules Verne and adult science-fiction magazines on juvenile science-fiction writers, including Eleanor Cameron and Robert A. Heinlein; "The Adventurer and/or Hero: Paul Zweig's *The Adventurer*," pp. 26-29, by Glenn S. Burne; "Combining the Stereotypical and Archetypal: John Cawelti's *Adventure, Mystery, and Romance*," pp. 29-30, by Lois Kuznets; "Women as Heroes," p. 31, by Susan R. Gannon, reviews Carol Pearson's and Katherine Pope's *The Female Hero in American and British Literature*; "Some Help Along the Way," p. 32, by Linda Carroll, reviews Jean Craighead George's *Journey Inward*; and "The Expectations of Genre," pp. 32-33, by Robert Di Yanni, reviews Dennis Porter's *The Pursuit of Crime*."

B10   CROUCH, MARCUS. "High Adventure." In *The Nesbit Tradition*, pp. 26-47.

       Examines the "adventure stories" of Ian Serrallier, Leon Garfield, Joan Aiken, René Guillot, Paul Berna, Nina Bawden, and others.

B11   DONELSON, KENNETH. "Adventure Stories." In *Literature for Today's Young Adults*, pp. 229-34.

       Contains a checklist for evaluating adventure stories and discusses key elements of the genre with examples from contemporary young adult literature.

B12 FISHER, MARGERY. "The Child in Adventure Stories." In Escarpit, *Portrayal of the Child*, pp. 273-81.
Examines the degree of responsibility allowed young people in two branches of the adventure story, the crime thriller and the castaway tale or Robinsonade.

B13 JAN, ISABELLE. "Adventure." In *On Children's Literature*, pp. 122-40.
Sees adventure stories as stemming from one of three interpretations of the journey: "that of Ulysses, of Sinbad, or of Robinson Crusoe," and traces their permutations in children's literature.

AFGHANISTAN--FOLKLORE

B14 NILSEN, ALLEEN PACE. "Afghanistan: The 'Tales' Behind the News." *TON* 37, no. 2 (Winter 1981):168-73.
An overview of Afghan folktales.

AFRICA

B15 COUGHLAN, MARGARET N., comp. *Folklore from Africa to the United States: An Annotated Bibliography*. Washington, D.C.: Library of Congress, 1976, 161 pp.
Provides critical evaluations of African folklore collections, divided into those for children and those for adults, from all areas of Sub-Saharan Africa, as well as those from cultures of African origin or influence in the West Indies and the United States.

B16 HALL, SUSAN J. "Tarzan Lives!: A Study of the New Children's Books about Africa." *IRBC* 9, no. 1 (1978):3-7.
Points out ten common stereotypes in children's books on Africa published since 1977.

B17 HERMAN, GERTRUDE B. "Africana: Folklore Collections for Children." *SLJ* 18 (May 1972):35-39.
Outlines general criteria for evaluating folklore for children, particularly African folklore. Includes a bibliography of recommended sources of African folklore for children.

B18 OSA, OSAYIMWENSE. "The Rise of African Children's Literature." *Reading Teacher* 38 (April 1985):750-54.
Reports on the recent growth of African children's literature and the increasing scholarly attention it is receiving. Includes references.

B19 OSAZEE, FAYOSE. "Picture Books for African Children." *Orana* 16 (February 1980):12-18.
Argues that more and better books and more serious criticism are needed.

B20 SCHMIDT, NANCY J. "African Folklore for African Children." *Research in African Literature* 8 (1977):304-26.
An introductory essay and annotated bibliography of African folklore written in English for children.

B21 -----. "African Women Writers of Literature for Children." *World Literature Written in English* 17 (April 1978):7-21.
A brief critical survey.

B22   -----. "Books By African Authors for Non-African Children." *Africana Library Journal* 2, no. 4 (Winter 1971):11-13.
Reviews the differences between children's books by African authors published in America and Britain in hard-cover editions, and those published in paperback editions for African children in Africa. A previous article in 2, no. 3 (Autumn 1971):5-6, examines titles in the African Readers Library, one of many series which are intended for use by African school children.

B23   -----. "Children's Books by Well-Known African Authors." *World Literature Written in English* 18 (April 1979):114-23.
A brief critical survey. Includes bibliography.

B24   -----. *Children's Fiction About Africa in English.* New York and Owerri: Conch Magazine Limited, 1981, 248pp.
Covers, in terms of their African context, books written for African children and 542 volumes of children's fiction written for Europeans. Individual authors discussed at length have been indexed separately in this bibliography.

B25   -----. "Children's Literature About Africa." *African Studies Bulletin* 8 (December 1965):61-70.
Provides a brief introduction and a bibliography of children's books about Africa.

B26   -----. "The Development of Written Literature for Children in Subsaharan Africa." *Zeitschrift fur Kulturaustausch* 29 (1979):267-70.
Reports on oral literature background, mission-produced literature, literature published in Europe, and literature published in Africa.

B27   -----. "The Politics of African Independence in American Children's Books." *Africa Today* 27, no. 3 (1980):29-37.

B28   -----. "The Writer as Teacher: A Comparison of the African Adventure Stories of G.A. Henty, René Guillot and Barbara Kimenye." *African Studies Review* 19 (September 1976):69-80.
Finds none of the books teaches youthful readers about more than a "very limited, segment of African life." All, including Kimenye's, are grounded in European rather than African tradition.

AGED

B29   ABRAHAMSON, RICHARD F. "The Elderly Person as a Significant Adult in Adolescent Literature." *Arizona English Bulletin* 18, no. 3 (April 1976):183-89.
Explores the roles of elderly characters in four recent adolescent novels: Norma Fox Mazer's *A Figure of Speech*, Barbara Wersba's *The Dream Watcher*, Theodore Taylor's *The Cay*, and John Donovan's *Remove Protective Coating a Little at a Time.*

B30   ANSELLO, EDWARD F. "Age and Ageism in Children's First Literature." *Educational Gerontology* 2 (July-September 1977):255-74.
Examines the portrayal of the aged in juvenile picture books and easy readers. Concludes that the image of old age which emerges is "noncreative and boring."

B31   -----. "Ageism in Picture Books, Part I: How Older People are Stereotyped. Part II: The Rocking Chair Syndrome in Action. Part III: Old Age as a Concept." *IRBC* 7, nos. 6-8 (1976):4-6, 7-10, 6-8.
        Part 1 presents statistics on age stereotypes in children's literature; part 2, examples and illustrations of age stereotypes; and part 3, summary and conclusions.

B32   -----. "Ageism: The Subtle Stereotype." *Childhood Education* 54 (January 1978):118-22.
        Reports on research on negative stereotypes of the elderly in children's books.

B33   ASHLEY-BROWN, ELIZABETH. "Grandparents in Children's Literature." *Orana* 18 (November 1982):129-37.
        Examines the role of grandparents in past and present children's literature and in today's society.

B34   BAGGETT, CAROLYN. "Ageism in Contemporary Young Adult Fiction." *TON* 37 (Spring 1981):259-63.
        Reports on a study of the portrayal of the elderly in books for young adults. Finds the overall image "less positive in the seventies than it had been in the sixties."

B35   -----. "Positive Portraits of the Elderly in Realistic Fiction for Young Adults." *Catholic Library World* 54 (September 1982):60-63.
        Surveys research on negative portrayals of the elderly in children's books and discusses a number of titles offering positive portrayals. Includes extensive references.

B36   BAGGETT, MARY. "A Study of the Image of the Senior Adult in Selected Recommended American Fiction Intended for Adolescents, 1960-1978." Ed.D. dissertation, Mississippi State University, 1980, 243 pp., DA 41:3306A.
        Analyzes the depiction of the aged by using a forty-category checklist based on Butler's six myths of aging. Finds a difference in depiction of the aged between the 1960s and 1970s in most categories, four showing improvement and fifteen deterioration.

B37   BARNUM, PHYLLIS WINET. "The Aged in Young Children's Literature." *LA* 54 (January 1977):29-32. (Reprinted in Barron, *Jump Over the Moon*, pp. 245-49.)
        Examines the treatment of the elderly in books for children of preschool through third grade. Concludes that the many negative stereotypes are reinforced.

B38   -----. "Discrimination Against the Aged in Young Children's Literature." *Elementary School Journal* 77 (March 1977):301-7.
        Concludes that "old people appear infrequently in children's literature, and when they do appear they are depicted as "more passive, more sickly, and less self-reliant than other adults."

B39   BENNE, MAE. "Leavening for the Youth Culture." *PNLAQ* [*Pacific Northwest Library Association Quarterly*] 41 (October 1976):4-8.
        Explores the portrayals of the aged and grandparents in a number of children's books.

B40   BLUE, GLADYS F. "The Aging as Portrayed in Realistic Fiction for

Children 1945-1975." *Gerontologist* 18 (April 1978):187-92.
Concludes that portrayals of the aged were "neither negative nor stereotypic but were varied in presentation."

B41 -----. "The Aging as Portrayed in Realistic Fiction for Children 1945-1975." Ph.D. dissertation, University of Akron, 1977, 296 pp., DA 38:2711A.
Concludes there is "great diversity of characterization" and a "lack of negative or stereotyped portrayals."

B42 CONSTANT, HELEN. "The Image of Grandparents in Children's Literature." *LA* 54 (January 1977):33-40.
Points out that although a wide variety of grandparents are presented in children's books, most of them seem to have warm feelings toward their grandchildren. Asks if this is a stereotpye.

B43 HORNER, CATHERINE T. *The Aging Adult in Children's Books and Non-Print Media: An Annotated Bibliography.* Metuchen, N.J.: Scarecrow, 1982, 242 pp.
The introduction to this bibliography, pp. vii-xxiii, provides a fine overview of the topic.

B44 KATZ, CAROL. "Outcasts and Renegades: Elderly People in Current Children's Fiction." *Horn Book* 54 (June 1978):316-21.
Disagrees with studies which find that children's fiction stereotypes the aged, and cites examples of recent works offering insights into old age and evidence of special bonds between young and old.

B45 MAVROGENES, NANCY A. "Positive Images of Grandparents in Children's Picture Books." *Reading Teacher* 35 (May 1982):896-901.
Surveys the role of grandparents in children's books published between 1960 and 1980. Includes a list of books with positive images for young children, grades kindergarten through three.

B46 PETERSON, DAVID A., and EDEN, DONNA Z. "Teenagers and Aging: Adolescent Literature As An Attitude Source." *Educational Gerontology* 2, no. 3 (July-September 1977):311-25.
Concludes from an analysis of fifty-three Newbery Medal books that older people are "underdeveloped and consistently given peripheral roles within the plot."

B47 PETERSON, DAVID A., and KARNES, ELIZABETH L. "Older People in Adolescent Literature." *Gerontologist* 16 (June 1976):225-30.
Found that although older people were not underrepresented in adolescent fiction they were underdeveloped and peripheral to the action.

B48 ROSE, KAREL. "The Young Learn About the Old: Aging and Children's Literature." *L&U* 3, no. 2 (Winter 1979-80):64-75.
Argues that many aged characters in children's literature are stereotypes. Exceptions may be found in Charlotte Zolotow's *William's Doll*, Barbara Williams's *Kevin's Grandma*, Mildred Kantrowitz's *Maxie*, Marjorie Weinman Sharmat's *Edgement*, Rose Blue's *Grandma Didn't Wave Back*, Norma Fox Mazer's *A Figure of Speech*, Gil Kaben's *Changes*, and Hadley Irwin's *The Lilith Summer*.

B49 RUTHERFORD, WILMA. "An Exploratory Study of Ageism in Children's Literature." Ed.D. dissertation, University of The Pacific, 1981, 168 pp., DA 42:1938A.

Finds little stereotyping of the aged in eighty fictional books for children aged five to fifteen.

B50　SEEFELDT, CAROLYN, et al. "The Coming of Age in Children's Literature." *Childhood Education* 54 (January 1978):123-27.

Discusses portrayals of the elderly in a number of books, and includes a bibliography of additional articles and books on the topic as well as a selected bibliography of children's books.

B51　SELTZER, MILDRED M. "Changing Concepts of and Attitudes Toward the Old As Found in Children's Literature, 1870-1960." Ph.D. dissertation, Miami University, 1969, 191 pp., DA 31:4268A.

Found little consistency and uniformity in attitudes toward, and stereotypes about, the old.

B52　SELTZER, MILDRED, and ATCHLEY, ROBERT C. "Concept of Old: Changing Attitudes and Stereotypes." *Gerontologist* 11 (Autumn 1971):226-30.

Found decreasingly positive attitudes toward the elderly and the aging process in a content analysis of children's books published between 1870 and 1960.

B53　SHACKFORD, JANE. "Images of the Elderly in 19th Century Children's Literature: The Legacy of Author and Artist." *Proceedings of the Children's Literature Association* 5 (1978):87-92.

Concludes that many older books provide valuable and meaningful images of the aged and cautions against sugar-coated, one-dimensional images that can follow sociological demands.

B54　STOREY, DENISE C. "Fifth Graders Meet Elderly Book Characters." *LA* 56 (April 1979):408-12.

Reports on a study of children's responses to the treatment of the elderly in children's books.

B55　-----. "Gray Power: An Endangered Species? Ageism as Portrayed in Children's Book." *Social Education* 41 (October 1977):528-33.

Finds that stereotyped and negative images of the elderly in children's books misinform and prejudice young readers. Includes an annotated bibliography of books portraying the elderly.

B56　VRANEY, MARY W., and BARRETT, CAROL J. "Marital Status: Its Effects on the Portrayal of Older Characters in Children's Literature." *Journal of Reading* 24 (March 1981):487-93.

Summarizes research on the aged in children's literature and reports on a study to determine how marital status of the aged affects the way they are portrayed. Includes references.

B57　WATSON, JERRY J. "A Positive Image of the Elderly in Literature for Children." *Reading Teacher* 34 (April 1981):792-98.

Discusses a number of children's books that present positive portrayals of the elderly.

ALCOHOL

B58　SALESI, ROSEMARY. "Alcohol Consumption in Literature for Children and Adolescents: A Content Analysis of Contemporary Realistic Fiction." Ed.D. dissertation, University of Georgia, 1977, 186 pp., DA 38:4572A.

Identifies and classifies images of alcohol consumption that appear in contemporary realistic fiction for children and adolescents.

ALIENATION

B59 GOODRICH, CATHERINE. "The Many Faces of Aloneness." *EE* 40 (February 1963):135-41.

Examines children's books with aloneness as a theme.

B60 LENZ, MILLICENT. "Varieties of Loneliness: Alienation in Contemporary Young People's Fiction." *Journal of Popular Culture* 13 (Spring 1980):672-88.

Classifies loners according to the factors that precipitate their alienation and points out identifiable patterns. Also notes key images of loneliness and positive and negative results of loneliness. Examines treatment of this theme in a number of recent novels for young adults.

B61 MORGAN, ARGIRO L. "The Child Alone: Children's Stories Reminiscent of *E.T.: The Extraterrestrial.*" *CLE*, n.s. 16, no. 3 (Autumn 1985):131-42.

Points out that "the isolation of the protagonist from his home" is one of the fundamental story patterns of folklore and children's literature. Identifies four structural variations of isolation: the abandoned child, self-imposed isolation, isolation due to imprudence, and isolation due to catastrophe.

ALPHABET BOOKS

B62 PRESSLER, C. "Old ABC Books--Learning Through Pictures." *Novum Gebrauchsgraphik* 50 (March 1979):44-52.

Discusses antique ABC books and reproduces pictures.

B63 STEINFIRST, SUSAN. "The Origins and Development of the ABC Book in English from the Middle Ages through the Nineteenth Century." Ph.D. dissertation, University of Pittsburgh, 1976, 385 pp., DA 37:3973A.

Attempts to show "how the ABC book has reflected the historical, educational, cultural, social, religious, and literary trends throughout this period."

B64 STEWIG, JOHN WARREN. "Alphabet Books: A Neglected Genre." *LA* 55 (January 1978):6-11. (Reprinted in Barron, *Jump Over the Moon*, pp. 115-21.)

Explores ways alphabet books can be used to develop children's visual and verbal skills.

B65 TAYLOR, MARY AGNES. "From Apple to Abstraction in Alphabet Books." *CLE*, n.s. 9, no. 4 (Winter 1978):173-80.

A careful critical overview of the alphabet book, which is categorized as falling into one or several combinations of four basic patterns: (1) word-picture format, (2) simple narrative, (3) a collection of nonsense verse, or (4) a subject-oriented content.

B66   THOMAS, DELLA. "From Aardvark to Zymurgy." *Library Journal* 93 (15 December 1967):4582-86.

Primarily a bibliographic essay on alphabet books but also categorizes the books and discusses their ingenuity, variety, and literary imagination. Includes an extensive bibliography.

ANIMALS

B67   BIRKS, JOHN. "Horses in Books." *Junior Bookshelf* 10, no. 4 (December 1946):166-72.

Discusses Will James's *Smoky*, Mary O'Hara's *My Friend Flicka*, Anna Sewell's *Black Beauty*, and Primrose Cumming's *Ben*, as well as, briefly, a number of "pony" stories.

B68   BLOUNT, MARGARET. *Animal Land: The Creatures of Children's Fiction.* London: Hutchinson, 1974, 336 pp.

Explores the role of animals--real, toy, and imaginary--in children's literature. Also indexed separately in this bibliography under individual authors and topics treated at length.

B69   BURNFORD, SHEILA. "Animals All The Way." *Canadian Library* 19 (July 1962):30-32.

Explores the role of animals in children's books from those for the very youngest up to the adult level.

B70   BUSH, MARGARET. "In Search of the Perfect Shark Book." *SLJ* 25 (March 1979):108-9.

Reviews a number of recent nonfiction books on sharks.

B71   BYRNE, BARBARA. "Cats in Literature." *EE* 51 (October 1974):955-58.

A brief bibliography of six fictional works and one informational book about cats. Each annotation includes "not only a summary of the work, but a statement of basic concepts within the work, a critique of literary value, read-aloud possibilities and illustrations within the work."

B72   CAMPBELL, A. "Stories About Dogs: A Critical Survey." *School Librarian* 20, no. 2 (June 1972):107-12.

A critical international bibliography of dog stories.

B73   *Canadian Children's Literature* "The Canadian Animal Story." 1, no. 2 (Summer 1975).

Special issue. Includes articles on Roderick Haig-Brown, Charles G.D. Roberts, and a general survey, "Tales of the Wilderness: The Canadian Animal Story," by Muriel Whitaker (pp. 38-46).

B74   COLWELL, EILEEN. "Of Mice and Men: Some Light-Hearted Thoughts on Mice in Children's Books." *Junior Bookshelf* 21, no. 4 (1957):180-86.

After examining a number of stories about mice, concludes, "But *why* do children enjoy reading about mice in stories? Let a six-year-old boy answer: 'Because they are small--and because they have whiskers.'"

B75   CROUCH, MARCUS. "Open Air." In *The Nesbit Tradition*, pp. 142-60.

Analyzes several stories about outdoor adventure and animals, many by British and Australian authors. Includes Ransome's *Great Northern*, Kathleen Peyton's *Fly-By-Night*, and others.

B76 ELLEMAN, BARBARA. "The Animal Fact." *Booklist* 73 (1977):664-65.
Sets forth criteria for evaluating various categories of children's informational books about animals.

B77 ELLIS, ALEC. "Man and Beast." *Junior Bookshelf* 32, no. 5 (October 1968):279-83.
Considers briefly the theme of kindness to animals.

B78 FARMER, LILLAH. "Rabbits in Children's Books." *LA* 53 (May 1976):527-30.
An overview of many favorite rabbit books for children. Includes a bibliography.

B79 FORD, MARY. "The Wolf as Victim." *CCL* 7 (1977):5-15.
Traces the history of the wolf in literature, emphasizing children's literature, showing the falseness of the stereotypes, and concluding with the more accurate portrayals of wolves in the works of Charles G.D. Roberts, and the favorable views in *Julie of the Wolves* and works by Farley Mowat and Claude Aubrey.

B80 JAN, ISABELLE. "Animal Land." In *On Children's Literature*, pp. 79-89.
Explores the role of animals in children's literature, particularly in Kipling's books. Sees the animal world as the child's earthly paradise, as represented in such works as Kenneth Grahame's *Wind in the Willows* and Randall Jarrell's *Animal Family*.

B81 JORDAN, ALICE M. "Animals in Fairyland." *Horn Book* 17 (November 1941):439-43. (Reprinted in Fryatt, *Horn Book Sampler*, pp. 146-49.)
Discusses "real animals in an unreal world" in a number of books from the 1930s.

B82 LAWRENCE, JOSEPH. "Animals and 'Dressed Animals.'" *Junior Bookshelf* 21 (December 1967):289-94.
Provides a brief overview of various categories of animal books.

B83 MAGEE, WILLIAM H. "The Animal Story: A Canadian Specialty." *CCL* 14 (1979):67-69.
Reviews Muriel Whitaker's anthology, *Great Canadian Animal Stories*, commenting on the nature of the Canadian contribution to the genre.

B84 -----. "The Animal Story: A Challenge in Technique." *Dalhousie Review*, Summer 1964. (Reprinted in Egoff, *Only Connect*, pp. 221-32.)
Discusses the development of the realistic animal story beginning with Anna Sewell's *Black Beauty* and Margaret Marshall Saunders' *Beautiful Joe*, but emphasizing the work of Canadian writer Sir Charles G.D. Roberts.

B85 O'DONNELL, HOLLY. "Animals in Literature." *LA* 57 (April 1980):451-54.

A bibliographic essay mentioning critical articles on animals in children's literature available in documents from the Educational Document Reproduction Service.

B86 OSBORNE, EDGAR. "Animals In Books." *Junior Bookshelf* 9, no. 1 (March 1945):1-9;no. 2 (July 1945):47-56.
Part 1 discusses the realistic animal story, up to Kipling; part 2 the fanciful and nonsense animal story.

B87 PITTS, DEIRDRE DWEN. "Discerning the Animal of a Thousand Faces." *Children's Literature* 3 (1974):169-72.
Discusses the animal as hero in myth, folklore, and children's literature.

B88 POLL, BERNARD. "Why Children Like Horse Stories." *EE* 38 (November 1961):473-75.
Discusses the psychological reasons for children's love of horse stories.

B89 PROCTER, GERALDINE. ". . . Masses of Bears. . . ." *Junior Bookshelf* 25 (March 1961):63-70.
Surveys bears in children's books. Additional comments by Roger L. Green, "Sing Ho! The Life of a Bear," follow in October 1961, pp. 202-4.

B90 RAYNER, MARY. "Some Thoughts on Animals in Children's Books." *Signal* 29 (May 1979):81-87.
Discusses the ways in which predatory aggression is handled in children's fiction and nonfiction about animals.

B91 SALE, ROGER. *Fairy Tales*, pp. 77-99.
Sees the animal story as the strongest link between fairy tales and modern children's literature. Discusses the conventions of "talking animals."

B92 "Sense and Sensibility: The Course of Animal Fiction." *TLS*, 2 July 1971, pp. 763-4.
Comments on the history of animal stories with an animal point of view and reviews several recent titles.

B93 SIMON, MINA LEWITON. "Crickets, Raccoons, and Writers." *Library Journal* 90 (15 May 1965):2336-37 and *SLJ* 12 (May 1965):32-33.
Urges awareness of stereotyped and prejudiced portrayals of animals in children's books and argues animals should be presented fairly and accurately.

B94 TULLY, DEBORAH SHIELDS. "Nature Stories--Unrealistic Fiction." *EE* 51 (March 1974):348-52.
Discusses danger in animal stories that are too realistic to be fantasy but are full of half-truths about animals.

B95 VINSON, ESTHER. "The Newer Animal Story." *EER* 6 (October 1929):197-200.
Sees a trend toward simple realism and away from sentimentalism and pseudorealism. Comments upon several books illustrating this trend.

B96 WIDDICOMBE, JOAN T. "Children's Science Books About Animals--Criteria and Evaluation." In MacLeod, *Children's Literature*, pp. 36-54.

Provides criteria for evaluating informational books about animals and evaluates a number of titles based upon these criteria. Includes a bibliography on children's science book evaluation.

ANTHROPOMORPHISM

B97 DERBY, JAMES. "Anthropomorphism in Children's Literature or 'Mom, My Doll's Talking Again.'" *EE* 47 (February 1970):190-92.

A brief introduction to the topic of anthropomorphism in children's literature.

B98 MARKOWSKY, JULIET KELLOGG. "Why Anthropomorphism in Children's Literature?" *EE* 52 (April 1975):460-62, 466.

Examines the role of talking animals in children's books by Robert Lawson, L. Leslie Brooke, Beatrix Potter, and E.B. White. Suggests that writers use anthropomorphic animals to help children identify with the characters, to engage in a needed flight of fancy, for variety, and for humor. Suggests a few outstanding anthropomorphic animal fantasy stories and discusses them briefly.

B99 SCHWARCZ, JOSEPH. "The Benign Image of Dehumanization." In *Ways of the Illustrator*, pp. 150-68. (Reprinted in part from "Machine Animism in Modern Children's Literature," in Fenwick, *Critical Approaches*, pp. 78-95.)

Provides a fairly extensive discussion of a number of books featuring anthropomorphized machines.

B100 VON ZWEIGBERGK, EVA. "What Are They Saying, Those Flowers and Animals?" *Bookbird* 10, no. 3 (1972):23-28.

Traces the development of the anthropomorphic animals and flowers so common to children's literature back to J.J. Grandville (pseudonym of Jean-Ignace-Isidore Gerard, 1803-1847).

APPALACHIA

B101 HATHAWAY, JOYCE A. "The Uses of Appalachian Culture and Oral Tradition in the Teaching of Literature to Adolescents." Ph.D. dissertation, Ohio State University, 1979, 182 pp., DA 40:3933A.

Emphasizes the Jack Tales and compares their use in the oral tradition and their use in written literature.

B102 HINSON, CAROLYN M. "Appalachian Literature and the Adolescent Reader." *ALAN Review* 11, no. 1 (Fall 1983):4-10.

Discusses the portrayal of Appalachian mountain life in five young adult novels.

B103 TROY, ANNE. "Appalachia in Children's and Adolescents' Fiction." *LA* 54 (January 1977):55-58.

A bibliographic essay focusing on the characteristics of children's literature of the Appalachian region. Includes a bibliography.

ARCHAEOLOGY

B104 LUBELSKI, AMY. "Archaeology: A Young Science for Young Readers." *L&U* 6 (1982):77-83.

An overview of children's literature in the field, which concludes that "mixing of fact and conjecture is a major problem in archaeology books for children."

ARGENTINA

B105   COLAVITA, FEDERICA DOMINGUEZ. "The Current State of Children's Literature in Argentina." *Children's Literature* 7 (1978):169-80.

Summarizes information about research trends, professional organizations, children's writers, publishers, and information sources.

ARMENIA

B106   FRASER, JAMES H. "Armenian Language Maintenance in the United States and Literature for Children." *Phaedrus* 6, no. 1 (Spring 1979):79-81.

Discusses the programs of the Armenian General Benevolent Union and cooperating organization to develop literature and programs for teaching the language to American-born Armenian children.

ART

B107   GAINER, RUTH STRAUS. "Beyond Illustration: Information about Art in Children's Picture Books." *Art Education*, March 1982, pp. 16-19. (Reprinted in Barron, *Jump Over the Moon*, pp. 487-91.)

Suggests using picture books to help teach children about art. Includes a short list of picture books "which have been rich sources of information in our art studio."

B108   WILTON, SHIRLEY M. "The Pleasure Principle: Where Is It in Kids' Art Books?" *SLJ* 23 (February 1977):44-45.

Criticizes the concentration in children's art books on art history, on art as an intellectual activity, and on the development of creativity. Recommends what good children's art books should do, and offers examples. Comment and corroboration by Phyllis J. Yuill in a letter in *SLJ* 23 (May 1977):6.

ARTISTS

B109   ALBERGHENE, JANICE MARIE. "From Alcott to *Abel's Island*: The Image of the Artist in American Children's Literature." Ph.D. dissertation, Brown University, 1980, 206 pp., DA 41:5100A.

This study of image of the artist in American children's literature concludes that "Despite the widely-held belief that modern children's literature encourages creativity and expressiveness . . . most images of the artist provide very little encouragement for choosing to become an artist."

B110   HOFFMAN, B. "Studies in the Quest of the Artist-Hero in Children's Literature of the Past Century." Ph.D. dissertation, Case Western Reserve University, 1979, 186 pp., DA 40:2645A.

Explores the portrayal of the developing artist-hero in six juvenile books: Louise de la Ramée's (Ouida) *A Dog of Flanders*, Louisa May Alcott's *Little Women*, Kenneth Grahame's *Wind in the Willows*, and E.B. White's *Stuart Little*, *Charlotte's Web*, and *The Trumpet of the Swan*.

ARTHURIAN LEGENDS

B111   WHITAKER, MURIEL. "Swords at Sunset and Bog-Puddings: Arthur in
Modern Fiction."   *CLE*, n.s. 8, no. 4 (Winter 1977):143-53.
Examines the treatment of Arthurian legends in modern children's
fiction, including William Mayne's *Earthfasts*, Mary Stewart's *The
Hollow Hills*, Rosemary Sutcliff's *Sword at Sunset*, Henry Treece's
The Eagles Have Flown, and T.H. White's *The Sword in the Stone*.

ASIA AND ASIAN AMERICANS

B112   AOKI, ELAINE M. "'Are You Chinese? Are You Japanese? Or Are
You Just a Mixed-Up Kid?': Using Asian American Children's Lit-
erature." *Reading Teacher* 34 (January 1981):382-85.
Suggests guidelines for evaluating and using books portraying
Asians and Asian-Americans.

B113   *Bridge* 4 (July 1976):5-29.
Special issue on Asian American images in children's books.
Presents criteria for evaluating children's books and reports on
widespread stereotyping and misrepresentation.

B114   COUNCIL ON INTERRACIAL BOOKS FOR CHILDREN.   "Asian
Americans in Children's Books." *IRBC* 7, nos. 2-3 (1976):40 pp.
(Excerpt in MacCann, *Cultural Conformity*, pp. 83-96.)
Special Double issue.   Includes an article pointing out common
stereotypes of Asian-Americans in children's literature, a statement of
criteria for analyzing books on Asian Americans, and sections of
reviews of books relating to Chinese Americans, Japanese Americans,
Korean Americans, and Vietnamese Americans.   Also includes an
article by Frank Chin stating that "Only in the works of Taro Yashima and Laurence Yep are the literary sensibility, language and vision
of the universe Asian and Asian American."

B115   HARADA, VIOLET. "Ginger Root and Ginseng Tea: The World of The
Asian Novel." *TON* 31 (January 1975):167-71.
Discusses four books recommended to dispel some of the mystery
of the Orient for the young reader: Rama Mehta's *The Life of
Keshar*, Yukio Mishima's *The Sound of Waves*, Mary Lois Dunn's
The Men in The Box: A Story from Vietnam, and Elizabeth Fore-
man Lewis's *To Beat a Tiger*.

B116   -----. "The Treatment of Chinese and Japanese Characters in American
Settings in Selected Works of Fiction for Children." Ed.D. dissertation,
University of Hawaii, 1982, 248 pp., DA 43:1027A.
Notes certain stereotypic tendencies, particularly in books written
by non-Asians prior to 1970.

B117   KAMM, ANTONY. "Children's Literature: The South Asian Picture."
International Library Review 1 (April 1969):183-96.
Surveys the nature of children's literature in each of the follow-

ing countries as of 1966: Burma, Ceylon, India (Hindi speaking),
India (Southern Region), Iran, Nepal, Pakistan (East and West), and
Thailand.

ASTRONOMY

B118   GREENLEAF, SARAH A. "Astronomy Through the Centuries." *Appraisal* 15, no. 2 (Spring-Summer 1982):4-14.

    Surveys astronomy books for children, including several twentieth-century books, and discusses approaches to science writing for children.

AUNTS

B119   QUIGLEY, MARJORY C. "Aunts in Literature: Or Farewell to Orphans." *Horn Book* 8 (February 1932):20-25.

    A humorous survey of aunts in children's books from the latter half of the nineteenth century to 1930. Includes a bibliography and quotations by and about "a few particular aunts."

AUSTRALIA

B120   ANDERSON, HUGH. *The Singing Roads: A Guide to Australian Children's Authors and Illustrators.* 4th ed. 2 vols. Surrey Hills, N.S.W: Wentworth Press, 1970, 76 pp.; 1972, 117 pp..

    Includes brief biographies, personal statements, and bibliographies of primary works of a number of Australian authors and illustrators.

B121   BARLOW, ALEX. "Holding the Country: Carrying the Law." *Orana* 19 (May 1983):98-108.

    Reflections on the Aborigines in Australian children's literature.

B122   BUICK, BARBARA. "An Indigenous Children's Literature." *SLJ* 14 (November 1967):35-37. (Reprinted in Haviland, *Children and Literature*, pp. 340-44.)

    Provides a concise overview of the development of Australian children's literature from 1841 to the 1960s.

B123   BUICK, BARBARA, and WALKER, MAXINE. "Books for Children." In *The Literature of Western Australia.* Edited by Bruce Bennett. Nedlands: University of Western Australia Press, 1979, pp. 215-49.

    Surveys Western Australian children's literature according to a number of recurrent themes: Aborigines and race relations, sense of place, treasure-seeking, convicts, and bushrangers. Also examines the use of humor and satire, conventions, and illustrations. Includes bibliographies of primary and secondary sources.

B124   CRAGO, HUGH. "Australian Children's Periodicals: Scope for Research." *Phaedrus* 4, no. 2 (Fall 1977):17-18.

    Discusses Australian children's periodicals and the fact that no research has been done on them.

B125   CRAGO, HUGH, and CRAGO, MAUREEN. "Children's Literature Research: A Bibliographic Essay." *Phaedrus* 3, no. 1 (Spring 1976):26-27.

    States that the level of scholarship on children's literature in Australia is low compared to that in Germany and Scandinavia, and that it lacks institutional support. Discusses several recent studies of Australian children's literature.

B126   DONKIN, NANCE; FATCHEN, MAX; INGRAM, ANNE; GREEN-
       WOOD, TED; WRIGHTSON, PATRICIA; and PHIPSON, JOAN.   "Is
       There a Distinct Australian Identity in Children's Literature?"   In
       Robinson, M., *Readings in Children's Literature*, pp. 148-72.
           The panelists discuss the extent and the nature of a distinct
       Australian identity in children's literature.

B127   DUGAN, MICHAEL, comp.   *Early Dreaming: Australian Children's
       Authors and Childhood.*   Queensland, Australia: Jacaranda Press,
       1980, 114 pp.
           Australian authors of books for children recollect their own
       childhoods and influences on their writing.   Authors are Hesba Brins-
       mead, Mavis Thorpe Clarke, Max Fatchen, Christobel Mattingley, Lil-
       ith Norman, Joan Phipson, Noreen Shelley, Ivan Southall, Eleanor
       Spence, and Colin Thiele.   Includes biographical sketches, portraits,
       and bibliographies.

B128   DUNKLE, MARGARET.   "Changing Attitudes in Australian Children's
       Literature: An Historical View."   *Orana* 17 (February 1981):30-31.
           A brief summary of changes.

B129   FRASER, GAEL.   "Small Press Children's Books: An Alternative View
       of the World."   *Australian Library Journal* 26 (1 April 1977):68-79.
           Surveys the social aspects of Australian small-press children's
       books.   Includes a bibliography.

B130   FURNISS, ELAINE R.   "Australian Adventuring Through Children's
       Books."   *LA* 54 (January 1977):59-62.
           A concise overview of Australian children's literature.   Includes
       bibliography.

B131   HILL, MARJI.   "Of the Lives and Deeds of the Immortal Beings,
       Aboriginal Stories: A Cultural Perspective."   *Orana* 19 (May
       1983):109-12.
           Suggests guidelines for the responsible handling of traditional
       Aboriginal literature.

B132   LEVERSON, DOROTHY.   "We looked in the library but. . . ."   *IRBC* 9,
       no. 2 (1978):13-14.
           Discusses portrayals of Australian native people (Aborigines) in
       Australian children's fiction and nonfiction.

B133   LIPPMANN, LORNA, ed.   "Children's Literature and the Aborigines."
       In *Generations of Resistance: The Aboriginal Struggle for Justice.*
       Melbourne: Longman Chesire, 1981, pp. 212-26.
           Includes criteria for evaluating racism in textbooks.   Comments on
       writings by white authors about Aborigines and on the writings of
       Aborigine writers.   Includes references.

B134   MacKENZIE, MAVIS.   "Children's Literature in the '80s."   *Orana* 17
       (November 1981):141-45.
           Compares the children's literature of the 1980s with that of the
       fifties, sixties, and seventies.

B135   McVITTY, WALTER.   "Australian Children's Literature: Some Thoughts
       on Two Decades of Change."   *Orana* 18 (May 1982):39-42.
           Questions whether children's literature is becoming more "about"

rather than for children.

B136   -----. *Innocence and Experience: Essays on Contemporary Australian Children's Writers.* Melbourne, Australia: 1981, 277 pp., bibl.
Sees Australian children's literature as becoming increasingly sophisticated and proposes reasons for this development. Discusses Mavis Thorpe Clark, Joan Phipson, Eleanor Spence, Patricia Wrightson, H.F. Brinsmead, David Martin, Colin Thiele, and Ivan Southall in separate chapters.

B137   MUSGRAVE, P.W. "From 'Chummy Innocence' to Concerned Individuality: A Case Study in the Sociology of Literature." *Australian and New Zealand Journal of Sociology* 18, no. 2 (June 1982):162-71.
Responds to McVitty's *Innocence and Experience*, arguing that the nature and causes of change in Australian children's and young adult literature is "different and more complex" than he suggests.

B138   ORME, NEDRA. "The Image of the Migrant in Australian Children's Fiction." *Orana* 15 (February 1979):20-23.
Surveys the portrayal of migrants in Australian children's literature.

B139   RYAN, J.S. "Australian Fantasy and Folklore." *Orana* 17 (May 1981):63-79; (August 1981):112-33; (November 1981):164-77.
This three-part article provides an extensive overview and analysis of Australian fantasy and folklore traditions.

B140   SAXBY, H.M. *A History of Australian Children's Literature 1941-1970.* Sidney: Wentworth Books, 1971, 316 pp.
Provides a comprehensive overview of Australian children's literature, but contains little in-depth discussion of individual authors.

B141   SIMPSON, ANNE. "Australian Fiction for Adolescents." *Orana* 15 (May 1979):45-52.
An overview.

B142   SINGH, MICHAEL J. "Aboriginal Children's Literature: Continuing Resistance to Colonization." *Reading Time* 86 (January 1983):9-18.
Emphasizes the importance of mythology to traditional Aboriginal communities and the problems associated with its exploitation by non-Aboriginal authors. Suggests guidelines for its use.

AUSTRIA

B143   BAMBERGER, RICHARD. "Children's Literature in Austria." In *Reading and Children's Books*, pp. 56-76.
Provides an overview of the history and current trends in Austrian children's literature, briefly discussing significant authors.

B144   BINDER, LUCIA. "Theoretical work in Children's Literature and Research in Reading in Austria: An Overview." *Phaedrus* 2, no. 2 (Fall 1975):12-15.
Discusses research centering on such organizations as the Austrian Children's Book Club, the Institute for Children's Literature and Reading Research, and the pedagogical academies.

B145   HELLER, FRIEDRICH C. "Stilkunst and Viennese Children's Book Illus-

tration 1895-1925." *Phaedrus* 9 (1982):1-6.
A scholarly account of children's book illustration in turn-of-the-century Vienna.

B146   LEDERER, EVA M. "Children's Literature in Austria." *Children's Literature* 3 (1974):43-47.
Discusses the status of research in children's literature in Austria.

BATCHELDER AWARD BOOKS

B147   HELBIG, ALETHEA K. "Innocence and Experience in Batchelder Books." *Proceedings of the Children's Literature Association* 6 (1979):112-21.
Examines the world visualized by European Batchelder award-winners, as compared to that generally envisioned in British and American books for young people, and finds the Batchelder books far more didactic and polarized "in their attitudes toward life and in the treatment of their subjects."

B148   HOYLE, KAREN NELSON, and SCAPPLE, SHARON M. "Panel: The Mildred L. Batchelder Award." *Proceedings of the Children's Literature Association* 6 (1979):31-39.
Discusses the award committee and its selection criteria. Includes a bibliography of articles relating to the awards and to translation and internationalism in children's books.

B149   NIST, JOAN STIDHAM. "Cultural Constellations in Translated Children's Literature: Evidence from the Mildred L. Batchelder Award." *Bookbird* 17, no. 2 (1979):3-8.
Discusses the difficulties of translating books from one culture to another and comments on characteristics of Batchelder books to date.

B150   -----. "The Mildred L. Batchelder Award Books, 1968-1977: A Decade of Honored Children's Literature in Translation." Ph.D. dissertation, Auburn University, 1977, 156 pp., DA 38:4633A.
Examines the characteristics of Batchelder Award and nominee books for the first ten years. Finds that (1) many publishers are included, (2) many translators are involved, (3) Germanic language books dominate, (4) European settings predominate, (5) contemporary or recent past settings are preferred, (6) modern and historical fiction are the main genres, and (7) progressive narrative is the main structural form.

B151   -----. "Patterns of Cultural Interchange in Children's Literature." *Proceedings of the Children's Literature Association* 6 (1979):136-45. (A version entitled "The Mildred L. Batchelder Award: Around the World with Forty-Two Books" appears in *LA* 56 [April 1979]:368-74.)
Reports on a study to identify patterns in original languages, settings, genres, and structures in Batchelder Award-Winning books and nominees. Includes a bibliography.

BIBLE STORIES

B152   HARMS, JEANNE M., AND LETTOW, LUCILLE J. "A Flood of Noah Stories: A Concern About the Re-Telling of Old Stories." *TON* 40 (Fall 1983):56-61.
Examines a number of picture-book retellings, adaptations, and

imaginative and modern versions of the story of Noah's ark. Suggests criteria for evaluating the retelling of traditional tales.

B153   MAY, JILL P. "Looking at the Twentieth Century: Three Picture Book Adaptations of Noah's Ark." *Catholic Library World* 51 (September 1979):54-57.
Examines three versions of the Noah story: Maud and Miska Petersham's *The Ark of Father Noah and Mother Noah* (1930), Peter Spier's *Noah's Ark* (1977), and Gail E. Haley's *Noah's Ark* (1971).

B154   PIEHL, KATHY. "Noah As Survivor: A Study of Picture Books." *CLE*, n.s. 13, no. 2 (Summer 1982):80-86.
Examines a number of picture-book versions of the story of Noah.

B155   SCHWARCZ, JOSEPH. "Jonah: Seven Images of a Prophet." In *Ways of the Illustrator*, pp. 131-49.
Examines seven recent picture-book versions for children of the story of Jonah and the whale, including two English-language editions: Beverly Brodsky's *Jonah: An Old Testament Story* and Clyde Robert Bulla's *Jonah and the Great Fish* illustrated by Helga Aichinger.

BIOGRAPHY

B156   BILLMAN, CAROL. "Once Upon a Time . . . Telling Children Biographical History." *Proceedings of the Children's Literature Association* 7 (1980):91-97.
Argues that biography and history for children are often more fantastic than realistic. Discusses William Armstrong's *Education of Abraham Lincoln* as an example of a realistic biography.

B157   CARR, JO, ed. "Biography: Facts Warmed By Imagination." In *Beyond Fact*, pp. 118-53.
Contains Carr's introductory essay, "What Do We Do About Bad Biographies?"; Margery Fisher's "Biography," adapted from chapter 4, pp. 300-308 of *Matters of Fact*; Denise Wilms's "An Evaluation of Biography," reprinted from *WLB* 49 (October 1974):146-50; and Elizabeth Segel's "In Biography for Readers, Nothing is Impossible," reprinted from *L&U* 4, no. 1 (Summer 1980):4-14.

B158   -----. "What Do We Do About Bad Biographies?" *SLJ* 27 (May 1981):19-22. (Reprinted in Barron, *Jump Over The Moon*, pp. 226-35.)
Examines the dismal state of biography for children and suggests alternatives: use of autobiography, use of books focusing on a short segment of someone's life, and use of biographical material in non-fiction and historical fiction. Concludes with criteria for evaluating biographies.

B159   COOLIDGE, OLIVIA. "My Struggle with Facts." *WLB* 49 (October 1974):146-51. (Reprinted in Varlejs, *Young Adult Literature*, pp. 374-80, and in Carr, *Beyond Fact*, pp. 141-48.)
Describes the difficulties a biographer, particularly one writing for children and young adults, has in ascertaining and selecting facts, reconciling contradictions, making judgments, limiting research, determining how much background information is necessary, and

handling one's own opinions.

B160   DONELSON, KENNETH. "Current Trends in Biographies." In *Litera-
        ture for Today's Young Adults*, pp. 287-93.
        Includes a checklist for evaluating biographies.

B161   FISHER, MARGERY. "Life Course or Screaming Force?" *CLE*, o.s.,
        no. 22 (Autumn 1976):108-15.
        Points out the need for better biographies for young people.
        Discusses different approaches and argues for better writing, more
        enterprising use of material, a greater respect for readers' intelligence,
        and more personal writing. "It is the task of the biographer to
        select, from material more or less limited, those facts that will best
        enable him to reveal to his readers a particular person as he sees
        him."

B162   GROFF, PATRICK. "Biography: The Bad or the Bountiful?" *TON* 29
        (April 1973):210-17.
        Attempts to show that biography does not have the moral and
        psychological influences credited to it; and questions whether "true
        biography can be written for children" and whether children can
        understand or identify with the adult lives depicted. Concludes that
        common assumptions about biography for children are wrong.

B163   -----. "How Do Children Read Biography About Adults?" *Reading
        Teacher* 24 (April 1971):609-15, 629.
        Questions standard assumptions about the responses of children to
        biographies.

B164   HERMAN, GERTRUDE B. "Footprints on the Sands of Time: Biogra-
        phy for Children." *CLE*, n.s. 9, no. 2 (Summer 1978):85-93.
        Examines biography and autobiography for children in terms of
        its relationship to personality integration and suggests criteria for
        selection. Contains a section on pitfalls for both the authors and
        critics of biographies.

B165   JURICH, MARILYN. "What's Left Out of Biography for Children?"
        Children's Literature 1 (1972):143-51.
        Surveys the field of juvenile biography and concludes there is a
        need for biographies of great human beings who are not famous, and
        a need for fuller treatment of the subjects, written without conde-
        scension.

B166   KOCH, SHIRLEY LOIS. "Portrayal of Life Form in Selected Biogra-
        phies for Children Eight to Twelve Years of Age." ERIC Educa-
        tional Document Reproduction Service, ED 089 311.
        Examines the literary devices and symbolism used by writers of
        biography for children to communicate the biographees' religious and
        social commitment.

B167   *Lion & Unicorn* 4, no. 1 (Summer 1980).
        Special issue on biography. Includes an article on Dorothy Aldis's
        biography of Beatrix Potter, articles on picture-book and sports
        biographies, and on biographies of Emma Goldman, George Sand,
        Mary Shelley, Billy Holiday, Bessie Smith, Mahalia Jackson, Marx and
        Engels, and others.

B168   McCONNELL, GAITHER. "Achievement Factors in Juvenile Biographies." *EE* 32 (April 1955):240-44.
        A content analysis of twenty-four biographies for children.

B169   -----. "Criteria for Juvenile Biographies." *EE* 33 (April 1956):231-35.
        Argues that individuality and truth are the two most important criteria for juvenile biography and that identification with heroes is important in forming character.

B170   -----. "Modern Biographies for Children." *EE* 30 (May 1953):286-89.
        A survey of children's biographies indicates (1) there are still heroes to be written about, (2) better writing is needed, (3) more biographies for younger children are needed, (4) more biographies about women are needed, and (5) new biographies of old subjects are needed.

B171   MARCUS, LEONARD S. "Life Drawings: Some Notes on Children's Picture Book Biographies." *L&U* 4, no. 1 (Summer 1980):15-31.
        Discusses the work of Ingri and Edgar Parin D'Aulaire, Anne Rockwell, Jean Fritz, Margot Tomes, and others. "The biographer's task is life drawing in which the comic sense, fantasy, and common sense have a part."

B172   MARTIN, FRAN. "Stop Watering Down Biographies." *Library Journal* 84 (15 December 1959):3887-88.
        Castigates the convention, common in popular children's biography series, that "great men and women invariably started out as normal and likeable youngsters, good mixers, and good sports." Compares popular treatments of Nancy Hanks and Mary Todd Lincoln with Carl Sandburg's. Calls for accuracy and realism in biography for children.

B173   MELTZER, MILTON. "Notes on Biography." *ChLAQ* 10, no. 4 (Winter 1986):172-75.
        Offers insights into the art of biography and comments upon its criticism.

B174   MORGAN, C.J. "Biography for Children." *Orana* 14 (February 1978):5-9; (May 1978):58-64.

B175   SAYERS, FRANCES CLARKE. "Biography for Children." *EER* 9 (1932):197-99, 216.
        Stresses that well-written biographies are not merely collections of facts. Biography should be a tale of "mystic and symbolic combats."

B176   SCULLEY, JAMES DAVID. "An Analysis of Five United States Military Officers As They Are Portrayed by Authors and Illustrators in Biographical Literature for Intermediate Grade Children Published during the World War II Years of 1941-1946 and Viet Nam Years of 1970-1975." Ed.D. dissertation, Temple University, 1981, 102 pp., DA 42:5022A.
        Analyzes biographies of Dwight D. Eisenhower, George Washington, Ulysses S. Grant, Robert E. Lee, and John Paul Jones.

B177   STOTT, JON C. "Biographies of Sports Heroes and the American Dream." *CLE*, n.s. 10, no. 4 (Winter 1979):74-85.
        "This article examines relationships between four areas: children's

fairy tales, the North American dream of going from rags to riches, the role of sports in North American society, and the uses and misuses of biographies written for younger readers."

B178 -----. "Biography for Children." *Children's Literature* 3 (1974):245-48.
   Stott makes some general comments about biography for children and reviews seven books.

B179 SUTHERLAND, ZENA. "Biography in the United States." *CLE*, o.s., no. 22 (Autumn 1976):116-20.
   Sets forth, briefly, criteria for judging juvenile biography and then compares recent trends with past standards. Among recent trends she mentions, with examples, "more books about minorities, minor figures, more varied approaches, more books for young children, more candor in presentation, and more documentation." Concludes that on the whole biographical writing is better than it used to be.

B180 TAYLOR, M. IONA. "A Study of Biography as a Literary Form for Children." Ed.D. dissertation, Indiana University, 1970, 119 pp., DA31:5679A.
   Identifies distinctive qualities of biography for children as compared to that intended for adults. Traces the development of the genre away from didacticism and toward imaginative appeal, realism, and humor.

B181 VIPOND, Mary. "Biography for Children: The Case of Dr. Frederick Banting." *CCL* 30 (1983):21-32.
   Comments on the problems confronting biographers; uses as an example four juvenile biographies of Dr. Frederick Banting.

B182 WILMS, DENISE M. "An Evaluation of Biography." *Booklist* 75 (15 September 1978):218-20. (Reprinted in Barron, *Jump Over the Moon*, pp. 220-25.)
   Sets forth criteria for evaluating biographies for children and criticizes a frequent disregard for quality, questionable notions of suitability, and excessive fictionalization.

B183 WITUCKE, VIRGINIA. "Trends in Juvenile Biography." *TON* 37 (Winter 1981):158-67.
   Surveys and comments upon the characteristics of juvenile biographies published in 1978. Finds an emphasis on young, contemporary Americancs, often entertainers or athletes.

B184 -----. "Trends in Juvenile Biography: Five Years Later." *TON* 42 (Fall 1985):45-53.
   This follow-up to the above study examines juvenile biographies published in 1983. Finds an improved balance between living and deceased biographies, but fewer books published.

B185 ZANDERER, LEO. "Evaluating Contemporary Children's Biography: Imaginative Reconstruction and Its Discontents." *L&U* 5 (1981):33-51.
   Places biography for children in the context of recent theories of biography for adults. An examination of three examples finds them falling short of standards set forth by Michael Holroyd and Jean Paul Sartre.

BLACKS

B186 AGREE, ROSE HYLA. "Black American in Children's Books: A Critical Analysis of the Portrayal of the Afro-American as Delineated in the Contents of a Select Group of Children's Trade Books Published in America from 1950-1970." Ed.D. dissertation, New York University, 1973, 245 pp., DA 34:3442A.

Concludes that the portrayal of the black American in children's books during this period is unenlightening, lacks honesty and integrity, and for the most part lacks distinction.

B187 ANDERSON, ORA S. "Fiction for the Young Black Reader: A Critique of Selected Books." *Journal of Negro Education* 50 (Winter 1981):75-82.

Concludes that very few unbiased books of fiction for black juvenile readers exist.

B188 BACHNER, SAUL. "Three Junior Novels on the Black Experience." *Journal of Reading* 24 (May 1981):692-95.

Discusses Robert Lipsyte's *The Contender*, Dorothy Sterling's *Mary Jane*, and Mary Elizabeth Vroman's *Harlem Summer*.

B189 BADER, BARBARA. "Negro Identification, Black Identity." In *American Picturebooks*, pp. 373-82.

Discusses the evolution in the portrayal of blacks in picture books through the 1960s.

B190 BAKER, AUGUSTA. "The Black Experience in Children's Books: An Introductory Essay." *Bulletin of the New York Public Library* 75 (March 1971):143-46.

Originally published as the introduction to *The Black Experience in Children's Books*, a 109-page bibliography compiled by Baker and published by the New York Public Library in 1971, this article sets forth criteria for evaluating children's books portraying blacks.

B191 -----. "The Changing Image of the Black in Children's Literature." *Horn Book* 51 (February 1975):79-88.

Traces the changes in depictions of blacks in children's literature from the 1920s and 1930s to the 1970s, and raises new concerns.

B192 -----. "Guidelines for Black Books: An Open Letter to Juvenile Editors." *Publishers Weekly* 196 (14 July 1969):131-33. (Reprinted in MacCann, *Black American*, pp. 50-56, and in Haviland, *Children and Literature*, pp. 110-15.)

Discusses criteria for illustrations, language, themes, and attitudes. Also discusses guidelines for selecting imported books and reprints and reissues. Concludes that the final criterion is that "The books must be worth reading."

B193 BANFIELD, BERYLE, and WILSON, GERALDINE L. "The Black Experience through White Eyes--The Same Old Story Once Again." *IRBC* 14, no. 5 (1983):4-13.

Argues that two award-winning picture books, Margot Zemach's *Jake and Honeybunch Go to Heaven* and Marcia Brown's *Shadow*, raise serious questions about the presentation of the black experience in children's books. Provides charts analyzing the uses of cultural symbols in the two books, statements from well-known writers, illustrators, and critics on the two books and related issues, and discussions of evaluation versus censorship.

B194   BAXTER, KATHERINE B. "Combating the Influence of Black Stereotypes in Children's Books." *Reading Teacher* 27 (May 1974):540-44. (Excerpt in MacCann, *Cultural Conformity*, pp. 155-61.)
        Concentrates on ways of evaluating stereotypes, using several popular titles as examples.

B195   BECKER, JÖRG. "Racism in Children's and Young People's Literature in the Western World." *Journal of Peace Research* 10, no. 3 (1973):295-303.
        Makes an international and historical examination of the portrayals of blacks in Western children's literature. Includes a lengthy international bibliography of books and journal articles.

B196   BINGHAM, JANE MARIE. "A Content Analysis of the Treatment of Negro Characters in Children's Picture Books 1930-1968." Ph.D. dissertation, Michigan State University, 1970, 218 pp. DA 31:2411A.
        "The purpose of the study was to ascertain how the American Negro had been depicted in the illustrations of children's picture books published between 1930 and 1968."

B197   -----. "The Pictorial Treatment of Afro-Americans in Books for Young Children 1930-68." *EE* 48 (November 1971):880-85.
        Based on the author's doctoral dissertation, the article discusses the pictorial treatment of Afro-Americans in children's books from 1930 to 1968 and makes several recommendations for improvements. Includes a list of the forty-one books studied.

B198   BIRTHA, JESSIE M. "Portrayal of the Black in Children's Literature." *Philadelphia Library Association Bulletin* 24 (July 1969):187-97. (Also in *TON* 26 [June 1970]:395-408 and MacCann, *Black Americans*, pp. 63-71.)
        Offers criteria for evaluating children's books relating to black Americans. Includes book lists and selection aids.

B199   BOOTH, MARTHA F. "Black Ghetto Life Portrayed in Novels for the Adolescent." Ph.D. dissertation, University of Iowa, 1971, 172 pp., DA 32:1503A.
        Examines and evaluates "selected aspects of adolescent novels published since 1950, treating the Black adolescent, aged 10-19, living in an inner-city ghetto."

B200   BRODERICK, DOROTHY M. *Image of the Black in Children's Fiction.* New York: Bowker, 1973, 219 pp.
        Examines the portrayal of blacks in children's fiction between 1827 and 1967. Considers such topics as slavery, religion and superstition, music, segregation, and black-white relationships. "The major problem with the books in the study and most of the Black books published and accepted since its cutoff date, is that they personalize the race issue instead of recognizing it as the social-economic-political problem it is." Based on the author's doctoral dissertation, Columbia University, 1971.

B201   -----. "Lessons in Leadership." *SLJ* 18 (February 1971):31-33.

Reports on reactions of librarians and reviewers to the depictions of blacks, particularly in illustrations, in children's books over a number of years. Comments especially on the work of Ellis Credle and Marguerite de Angeli. Feels *Tobe* by Stella Sharpe, with photographs by Charles Farrell, should have been a landmark book but was overlooked.

B202   BROWN, ESTELLE. "Emerging Concepts of Social-Developmental Tasks of the Young Black Adolescent in Ten Selected Black Junior Novels." Ed.D. dissertation, Temple University, 1974, 192 pp., DA 36:3380A.

Identifies the handling of the following themes in ten "Black junior novels" published from 1902 to 1972: achievement of individuality, the social milieu, social values and ethnic understanding, group-peer relationships, family relationships, and world view and social change.

B203   CARLSON, JULIE ANN. "A Comparison of the Treatment of the Negro in Children's Literature in the Periods 1929-38 and 1959-68." Ph.D. dissertation, University of Connecticut, 1969, 165 pp., DA 30:3452A.

Concludes that stereotyping of the Negro in children's literature decreased in the period from 1929-38 to 1959-68.

B204   CHALL, JEANNE S., et al. "Blacks in the World of Children's Books." *Reading Teacher* 32 (February 1979):527-33.

This replication of Nancy Larrick's 1965 study finds definite improvements in the portrayal of blacks in children's books, but concludes that much remains to be done "with regard to both quantity and quality."

B205   COOLIDGE, ANN ELIZABETH. "Origins of Our Negro Folk Story." *EER* 9 (June 1932):161-62.

Describes some of the origins of Negro folklore, including African, American regional, and American Indian influences. Includes a bibliography.

B206   CROSSON, WILHELMINA. "The Negro in Children's Literature." *EER* 10 (December 1933):249-55.

Suggests children need to become more familiar with literature by and about Negroes. Provides extensive discussion of several works and appends a bibliography. Useful primarily for its historical perspective.

B207   DAVIS, MAVIS WORMLEY. "Black Images in Children's Literature: Revised Editions Needed." *Library Journal* 97 (15 January 1972):261-63 and *SLJ* 19 (January 1972):37-39. (Reprinted in Gerhardt, *Issues in Children's Book Selection*, pp. 75-80.)

Argues that the classics should be edited to remove offensive racial and social stereotypes.

B208   DEANE, PAUL C. "The Persistence of Uncle Tom: An Examination of the Image of the Negro in Children's Fiction Series." *Journal of Negro Education* 37, no. 2 (Spring 1968):140-45.

Examines the stereotypes of blacks in children's fiction series, concluding that although dialects have been removed, the traditional images remain.

B209   DUFF, OGLE. "Treatment of Blacks in Selected Literature Anthologies for Grades Nine through Twelve Published Since 1968." Ph.D. dissertation, University of Pittsburgh, 1974, pp. 155, DA 35:2219A.
Concludes that "although the image of blacks in high school literature anthologies is improving, there are still critical omissions."

B210   DYBEK, CAREN. "Black Literature for Adolescents." *English Journal* 63 (January 1974):64-67. (Reprinted in Varlejs, *Young Adult Literature*, pp. 245-50.)
Surveys recent trends in adolescent literature by black writers. Includes bibliography.

B211   EVANS, EVA KNOX. "The Negro in Children's Fiction." *Publishers Weekly* 140 (30 August 1941):650-53.
Argues that books portraying real people in real situations are needed, and discusses the reactions of black and white children to dialect and illustrations in books portraying blacks. Letters in response to Evans's comments on dialect follow, in "Negro Dialect in Children's Books," *Publishers Weekly* 140 (18 October 1941):1555-58, and in "A Further Statement on Negro Dialect in Children's Books," *Publishers Weekly* 141 (10 January 1942):104-5.

B212   FISHER, WINIFRED MAXINE. "Images of Black American Children in Contemporary Realistic Fiction for Children." Ed.D. dissertation, Columbia University, 1971, 174 pp., DA 32:2302A.
Describes the images of the everyday lives of black American children in contemporary realistic fiction, based on a sample of forty books.

B213   FRANK, ZELMA ANN LLOYD. "The Portrayal of Black Americans in Pictures and Content in the Caldecott Award Books and Honor Books from 1938-1978." Ed.D. dissertation, University of Missouri-Columbia, 1979, 193 pp., DA 40:4398A.
Investigates the "qualitative and quantitative portrayal of black Americans in illustrations and content in Caldecott Award and Honor books from 1938 to 1978."

B214   GANT, LIZ. "That One's Me." *Redbook*, August 1972. (Reprinted in Meek, *Cool Web*, pp. 348-54.)
A positive view of new directions in children's books having a black perspective and utilizing black English. Authors cited and quoted include Walter Myers, Sonia Sanchez, Sharon Bell Mathis, and Lorenz Graham.

B215   GODDARD, ROSALIND K. "Humanizing the Black Hero in Fiction for Children." *California Librarian* 34 (October 1973):50-54.
Argues that "quality fiction which depicts the experience of black people must embody all of the standards of character development, plot development and setting, but at the same time be consciously committed to realism and above all authenticity."

B216   GRAHAM, BERYL. "Multi-Ethnic Literature: Where Are We Now?" *Bulletin of the Children's Literature Assembly* 6, no. 2 (Spring-Summer 1981).
Delineates common stereotypes in literature about black children and provides a brief overview of ten positive and realistic books published between 1978 and 1980.

B217 HAMILTON, VIRGINIA. "High John Is Risen Again." *Horn Book* 51 (April 1975):113-21. (Reprinted in Heins, *Crosscurrents*, pp. 59-67.)
Discusses the role of black folklore and slave tradition in children's and adult's literature.

B218 HOPKINS, LEE BENNETT. "Negro Life in Current American Children's Literature." *Bookbird* 6, no. 1 (1968):12-16.
Surveys picture books, juvenile fiction, biography, nonfiction, and books about Africa.

B219 JORDAN, JUNE. "Black English: The Politics of Translation." In *Issues in Children's Book Selection*, New York: Bowker, 1973, pp. 85-89. (Also in *Library Journal* 98 [15 May 1973]:1631-34 and *SLJ* 19 [May 1973]:21-24.)
Argues in favor of children's books written in black English.

B220 KIAH, ROSALIE BLACK. "The Black Teenager in Young Adult Novels By Award-Winning Authors." Paper presented at the Southeast National Council of Teachers of English Affiliate Conference (Atlanta, Georgia, 25-27 September, 1980). ERIC Educational Document Reproduction Service, 1980, 14 pp., ED 193 636.
Examines over eighty young adult novels for blacks "to determine how they revealed the shared experience of black people in the family setting and the social world (including the world of work)." Concludes that more authenticity and development of social problems are needed.

B221 -----. "Content Analysis of Children's Contemporary Realistic Fiction About Black People in the United States to Determine If and How a Sample of These Stories Portray Selected Salient Experiences of Black People." Ph.D. dissertation, Michigan State University, 1976, 274 pp., DA 37:3781A.
Concludes that writers are focusing on "salient shared experiences of black people" and are focusing on social issues but "are not developing the stories to the extent that the child will be able to gain from the experience."

B222 KRAUS, K. "From Steppin Stebbins to Soul Brothers: Racial Strife in Adolescent Fiction." *Arizona English Bulletin* 18, no. 3 (April 1976):154-60. (Reprinted in Varlejs, *Young Adult Literature*, pp. 235-44.)
Traces the changing portrayals of black-white relations in adolescent fiction. Among works examined are Hope Newell's *A Cap for Mary Ellis*, Jesse Jackson's *Call Me Charley*, Gilbert Douglas's *Hard to Tackle*, Gretchen Sprague's *A Question of Harmony*, and Kristin Hunter's *The Soul Brothers and Sister Lou*.

B223 LANES, SELMA. "Black Is Bountiful." In *Down the Rabbit Hole*, pp. 158-77.
Begins by summarizing the publishing history and controversies surrounding Helen Bannerman's *Little Black Sambo*, then discusses several aspects of the portrayal of blacks in children's books. Concludes with a brief discussion of John Steptoe's *Stevie*.

B224 LARRICK, NANCY. "The All-White World of Children's Books." *Saturday Review* 48 (11 September 1965):63-65, 84-85. (Also in Mac-

Cann, *Black American*, pp. 156-74.)
This highly influential article was one of the first to raise the public's awareness of the extent of racism in children's books. Letters in response in 48 (16 October 1965):78-79.

B225　LASS, BONNIE. "Trade Books for Black English Speakers." *LA* 57 (April 1980):413-19.
An annotated bibliography of twenty-two books containing black English, with synopsis and language sample for each.

B226　LATIMER, BETTYE I. "Children's Books and Racism." *Black Scholar* 4 (May-June 1973):21-27.
Classifies flaws in the portrayal of blacks in children's literature as the romantic syndrome, the avoidance syndrome, the bootstrap syndrome, the oasis syndrome, and the ostrich-in-the-sand syndrome.

B227　MacCANN, DONNARAE, and RICHARD, OLGA. "Picture Books for Children." *WLB* 57 (December 1982):332-33, 365.
Reviews Margot Zemach's *Jake and Honeybunch Go to Heaven* and Marcia Brown's *Shadow*, and concludes that in both "The problems with portrayal of black life and culture seem to be caused by unconscious ethnocentrism and historical stereotyping."

B228　MacCANN, DONNARAE, and WOODARD, GLORIA, eds. *Black American in Books for Children: Readings in Racism.* Metuchen, N.J.: Scarecrow, 1972, 223 pp.
This anthology is divided into sections on criteria for judging the treatment of blacks in literature, racism in Newbery prize books, examples of racism in recent and older books, and racism in the publishing world. Also indexed separately under authors and topics covered in depth.

B229　McGUIRE, ALICE. "The Minority Image in Books for Youth: Evolution and Evaluation." ERIC Educational Document Reproduction Service, 1971, 13 pp., ED 052 907.
Traces changes in the portrayals of blacks in children's literature from the forties and fifties to the present.

B230　MADISON, JOHN. "School Integration in Children's Literature." *Integrated Education* 16 (May-June 1978):10-11.
Looks at "interesting and disconcerting results" in the way school integration is handled in May Justus's *New Boy In School*, Natalie Savage Carlson's *The Empty Schoolhouse*, and *Dead End School* by Robert Coles.

B231　MIKKELSEN, NINA. "Censorship and The Black Child: Can the Real Story Ever Be Told?" *Proceedings of the Children's Literature Association* 9 (1982):117-27.
Censorship of the black child in American children's literature has meant misrepresentation and neglect and also rejection, banning, and revision of books. A historical approach may help disseminate the "real story" that children greatly need.

B232　MILLENDER, DHARATHULA H. "Through a Glass Darkly: Representation of the Negro in Books for Children." *Library Journal* 92 (15 December 1967):4571-76. (Excerpted in MacCann, *Black American*, pp. 143-52.)

Describes the evolution of the representation of blacks in children's books and the long history of distorted reality and stereotypes. Includes detailed listings of books discussed.

B233   MULLER, AL. "Some Thoughts on the Black Young Adult Novel." *SLJ* 24 (April 1978):1963. (Reprinted from *ALAN Review*, Winter 1978.)
Explores reasons for the decline of interest in the black young adult novel.

B234   MUSE, DAPHNE. "Black Children's Literature: Rebirth of a Neglected Genre." *Black Scholar* 7 (December 1975):11-15.
Praises the renaissance of a new black children's literature.

B235   NOLEN, ELEANOR W. "The Colored Child in Contemporary Literature." *Horn Book* 18 (September 1942):348-55.
Interesting in part for its historical perspective, this article discusses the problems and controversies surrounding dialect as well as several other issues. Includes a short reading list entitled "Some Well-Written, Sincere Stories of Negro Child Life."

B236   OTEY, RHETA WASHINGTON. "An Inquiry into the Themes of Isolation in Adolescent Literature about Black Youth: An Examination of Its Treatment by Selected Writers." Ph.D. dissertation, Ohio State University, 1978, 248 pp., DA 29:4699A.
Focuses mainly on Virginia Hamilton, but includes a survey of blacks in children's literature from 1936 through 1975. Concludes that most works for children inadequately portray black life.

B237   PARKS, CAROLE A. "Good-bye Black Sambo." *Ebony*, November 1972, pp. 60-70.
Provides an overview of recent literature by black children's writers.

B238   PREER, BETTE BANNER. "Guidance in Democratic Living through Juvenile Fiction." *WLB* 22 (May 1948):679-81, 708.
Summarizes the history of the portrayals of blacks in children's books up to the 1940s, offers a set of guidelines for judging the portrayal of any minority group, and concludes with a rated list of books about blacks.

B239   RICHARDSON, JUDY. "Black Children's Books: An Overview." *Journal of Negro Education* 43 (Summer 1974):380-400.
Chronicles changes in black children's literature before and after 1954 and 1966.

B240   ROLLINS, CHARLEMAE. "The Role of the Book in Combating Prejudice." *WLB* 42 (October 1967):176-79.
Summarizes briefly the history of the portrayals, distortions, and omissions of blacks in children's books and the efforts of herself and others to effect change.

B241   ROSNER, SOPHIE P. "A Descriptive Study to Identify Manifestations of Racist Ideology of Whites toward Blacks in Picture Books Published in the United States: 1959, 1964, 1969." Ph.D. dissertation, New York University, 1975, 358 pp., DA 36:8063A.
"The purpose of this study was to determine how the text and/or

illustration of children's picture books convey to young children the values of society concerning black and White people."

B242 SHEPARD, RAY ANTHONY. "Adventures in Blackland with Keats and Steptoe." *IRBC* 3, no. 4 (Autumn 1971):3.
Compares Ezra Jack Keats's books about Peter (an outsider's view) of the black world) with John Steptoe's *Stevie* (an insider's view).

B243 SIMS, RUDINE. "A Question of Perspective." *Advocate* 3, no. 3 (Spring 1984):145-56.
Discusses the complexities of whites writing about the black experience.

B244 -----. *Shadow and Substance: Afro-American Experience in Contemporary Children's Fiction.* Urbana, Ill.: National Council of Teachers of English, 1982, 111 pp.
Chapter 1 places "contemporary realistic fiction about Afro-Americans in a sociocultural and historical context." Chapter 2 discusses "'social conscience' books . . . written to help whites know the condition of their fellow humans." Chapter 3 discusses the "'melting pot' books" Chapter 4 discusses "'culturally conscious' books . . . written primarily for Afro-American readers." Chapter 5 provides "brief overviews of the work of five Afro-American writers who have made major contributions to Afro-American children's fiction since 1965." These are Lucille Clifton, pp. 80-82, Eloise Greenfield, pp. 83-86; Virginia Hamilton, pp. 86-90; Sharon Bell Mathis, pp. 90-92, and Walter Dean Myers, pp. 92-96. A final chapter "summarizes the current status of children's fiction about Afro-Americans and suggests some frontiers yet to be explored."

B245 -----. "What Has Happened to the 'All-White' World of Children's Books?" *Phi Delta Kappan* 64 (May 1983):650-53.
Argues that despite a growing group of prolific black writers, the characters, authors, and audience of children's books remain largely white.

B246 SIMS, RUDINE, and HURMENCE, BELINDA. "Point of View: A Question of Perspective II and III." *Advocate* 4 (Fall 1984):20-23.
Sims and Hurmence debate the issue of whether whites can write about blacks from a black perspective.

B247 SMALL, ROBERT C. "An Analysis and Evaluation of Widely Read Junior Novels with Major Negro Characters." Ed.D. dissertation, University of Virginia, 1970, 395 pp., DA 31:4634A.
Explores the question: To what extent do junior novels with major Negro characters possess recognized literary qualities? Found six books that received consistently high ratings for literary quality, listed in order: Lipsyte's *The Contender*, Means's *Shuttered Windows*, Bonham's *Durango Street*, Hentoff's *Jazz Country*, Vroman's *Harlem Summer*, and Fox's *How Many Miles to Babylon?*.

B248 -----. "The Junior Novel and Race Relations." *Negro American Literature Forum* 8, no. 1 (Spring 1974):184-89.
Argues that "although motivated by good intentions, the authors of a large number of recent junior novels on the theme of race relations have, to a great extent, been unable to break away from the narrow conventions and overt moralizing which have spoiled many

junior novels with other themes." Discusses a number of well-known titles.

B249   SODERBERGH, P.A. "Bibliographical Essay: The Negro in Juvenile Series Books, 1899-1930." *Journal of Negro History* 58 (April 1973):179-86.
    Examines series books as reinforcers of Negro stereotypes.

B250   TATE, BINNIE. "In House and Out House: Authenticity and the Black Experience in Children's Books." *Library Journal* 95 (15 October 1970):3595-98. (Reprinted in MacCann, *Black American*, pp. 39-49.)
    Compares the responses of black and white librarians to several books by black and white authors about the black experience.

B251   THOMPSON, JUDITH, and WOODARD, GLORIA. "Black Perspective in Books for Children." *WLB* 44 (December 1969):416-24. (Reprinted in MacCann, *Black American*, pp. 14-27.)
    Points out examples of stereotyping in a number of children's books and argues for more awareness of unconscious prejudices and stereotypes and for the validity of racial attitude as a criteria for judging literature.

B252   TREMPER, ELLEN. "Black English in Children's Literature." *L&U* 3, no. 2 (Winter 1979-80):105-24.
    Discusses the role of black English in John Steptoe's *Stevie* and *Trainride*, in Lucille Clifton's *My Brother Fine with Me*, and in June Jordan's *His Own Where*.

B253   WHARTON, LINDA R. "Black American Children's Singing Games: A Structural Analysis." Ph.D. dissertation, University of Pittsburgh, 1979, 513 pp., DA 40:2356A.
    Collects and investigates American black children's singing games and analyzes their roles and functions.

B254   WILLIAMS, LILLIANN B. "Black Traditions in Children's Literature: A Content Analysis of the Text and Illustrations of Picture Story Books about Black People in the United States to Determine How Selected Black Traditions Have Been Portrayed and to Determine What Impact These Portrayals Have on the Self-Concept of Children Who Are Exposed to These Books." Ph.D. dissertation, Michigan State University, 1979, 267 pp., DA 40:4888A.
    Studies the impact on third graders of selected picture books portraying blacks.

B255   WUNDERLICH, ELAINE. "Black Americans in Children's Books." *Reading Teacher* 28 (December 1974):282-85.
    Attempts to show an improvement in the portrayal of blacks in children's books since 1972.

B256   YOUNG, JACQUELINE. "Criteria in Selection of Black Literature for Children." *Freedomways* 13 (1973):107-16.
    "Black literature must completely nullify the deceptive influences that prevent Black children from finding self esteem; Black literature must convey realism; and Black literature must be authentic."

BOOK DESIGN

B257   BEILENSON, EDNA. "Children's Books in 'The Fifty Books of the Year.'" *Horn Book* 26 (May 1950):161-70.
Examines the design qualities of the six children's books included in the fifty best selected by the American Institute of Graphic Arts and four which were not selected among the fifty that she felt had special merit.

B258   DALGLIESH, ALICE, and EVANS, MARGARET B. "Designing Children's Books." *Bulletin of the New York Public Library* 60 (November 1956):573-78.
Comments on considerations in the design of books for children.

B259   HOGROGIAN, NONNY. "The Story Sets The Pace: An Illustrator's View of Design." *Publishers Weekly* 189 (21 February 1966):100-103.
Discusses various considerations in book design, with examples from her own work. Emphasizes the priority of the text, the significance of typeface, and the use of another designer's format.

BOONE, DANIEL

B260   SMITH, CAROLYN. "Literary Image of Daniel Boone: A Changing Ideal in Nineteenth- and Twentieth-Century Popular Literature." Ph.D. dissertation, University of Utah, 1974, 184 pp., DA 35:1635A.
Examines the image of Daniel Boone in juvenile as well as in adult popular literature.

BOYS' FICTION

B261   SPARAPANI, HENRY R. "American Boy-Book: 1865-1915." Ph.D. dissertation, Indiana University, 1971, 181 pp., DA 32:7006A.
Examines the "bad boy" in American literature, beginning with Thomas Bailey Aldrich's *The Story of A Bad Boy* (1870) and ending with Booth Tarkington's Penrod series (1914-16).

B262   TURNER, E.S. *Boys Will Be Boys: The Story of Sweeney Todd, Deadwood Dick, Sexton Blake, Billy Bunter, Dick Barton, et al.* London: Michael Joseph, 1948, 269 pp.
A history of popular British periodicals for boys since the early nineteenth century. Includes sections on the *Boy's Own Paper* (pp. 93-98), *Gem* and *Magnet* (pp. 198-220), and a detailed index.

B263   UNSWORTH, ROBERT. "Holden Caulfield, Where Are You?" *SLJ* 23 (January 1977):40-41.
Argues that more books are needed that portray "rites-of-passage" for adolescent boys, that "relates to and possibly relieves their anxieties," especially about sex, and "convinces them they do not agonize alone."

BRAZIL

B264   WERNECK, REGINA YOLANDA MATTOSO. "Illustration of Children's Books in Brazil." *Bookbird* 11, no. 2 (1973):64-69.
A summary of the history and current state of children's book illustration in Brazil.

BRITAIN

B265   DONOVAN, JOHN. "American Dispatch." *Signal* 28 (January 1979):3-8.
Includes comments of prominent American reviewers and critics
concerning differences between American and British juvenile fiction.

B266   EYRE, FRANK. "British Children's Books in the Twentieth Century."
In Haviland, *Children and Literature*, pp. 335-39. (Excerpts from
Frank Eyre, *British Children's Books in the Twentieth Century*, pp.
26-30, 35, 77-79.)
An overview of trends in children's books since World War II
and the recent growth in criticism of children's literature.

B267   HANNABUSS, STUART. "What We Used to Read: A Survey of Children's Reading in Britain, 1910-1950." *CLE*, n.s. 8, no. 3
(1977):127-34.
Compares what was actually read during these years with what
experts advised teachers, librarians, and children to read.

B268   LEESON, ROBERT. *Children's Books and Class Society: Past and Present*. Edited by the Children's Rights Workshop Papers on Children's
Literature, no. 3. London: Writers & Readers Publishing Coopera-
tive, 1977, 62 pp.
Examines issues of social class in British children's books over
two centuries.

B269   MOSS, ELAINE. "The Seventies in British Children's Books." In
Chambers, *Signal Approach*, pp. 48-80.
Surveys sociological concerns of the seventies, publishing economics, fiction, picture books, verse, information books, and book
reviewing and promotion.

B270   TOWNSEND, JOHN ROWE. "The Present State of English Children's
Literature." *WLB* 43 (October 1968):126-33.
An overview.

B271   TREASE, GEOFFREY. "The Revolution in English Children's Literature." *Bookbird* 9, no. 4 (1971):6-13.
Discusses changes in the scope and subject matter of English
children's books since the 1930s. Warns against future dangers from
pressure groups, and expresses fears that in the desire to raise critical
standards and achieve academic respectability "we shall produce books
to please teachers and librarians more than the children themselves."
A similar article, entitled "The Revolution in Children's Literature,"
appears in Blishen's *Thorny Paradise*, pp. 13-24.

BULGARIA

B272   BOSSER, ASSEN. "Children's Literature in Bulgaria." *Bookbird* 10, no.
3 (1972):14-18.
A survey of Bulgarian authors, illustrators, and periodicals.

CANADA

B273   BLAIR, HEATHER. "Canadian Native Peoples in Adolescent Literature." *Journal of Reading* 26 (December 1982):217-21.

Examines the content and readability of young adult fiction about Canadian native peoples by both native and nonnative authors. Includes an annotated chart of books discussed.

B274   *Canadian Literature* 78 (Autumn 1978):135 pp.
Special issue. Includes articles indexed separately in this bibliography by and about Mordecai Richler, Christie Harris, and Catherine A. Clark.

B275   CARPENTER, CAROLE HENDERSON. "Native Folklore for Canadian Children." *Proceedings of the Children's Literature Association* 5 (1978):57-63.
Discusses problems and difficulties of using folklore with children and urges that more care be taken in presenting "other cultures" to children. Includes examples from Canadian native American folklore.

B276   CLEMENT, BEATRICE. "Children's National Literature in French Canada." *TON* 17 (December 1960):27-31.
Provides an overview of the history and development of French-Canadian children's literature. See also in the same issue Guy Sylvester's "The Young Adult and French-Canadian Writing," pp. 9-12.

B277   EGOFF, SHEILA. "Children's Literature." In *Literary History of Canada*. Edited by Carl Frederick Klinck. 2d ed. Toronto: University of Toronto Press, 1976, 3:204-11.
Provides a brief overview of Canadian children's literature.

B278   -----. "Reflections and Distortions: Canadian Folklore as Portrayed in Children's Literature." *International Library Review* 4 (July 1972):265-79.
Discusses the use of Eskimo, Indian, French, and English-Canadian folklore in Canadian children's literature.

B279   -----. *The Republic of Childhood: A Critical Guide to Canadian Children's Literature in English*. 2d ed. Toronto: Oxford University Press, 1975, 335 pp.
Includes discussions of Indian and Eskimo legends, folktales, fantasy, historical fiction, the realistic animal story, realistic fiction, history and biography, poetry and drama, illustration and design, picture books, and early Canadian children's books.

B280   ELLIS, SARAH. "News from the North." *Horn Book* 60 (February 1984):99-103.
Discusses three recent Canadian books for young adults, Brian Doyle's *Up to Low*, Kevin Major's *Hold Fast*, and Jan Truss's *Jasmin*, seeing each as firmly rooted in time and place.

B281   -----. "News from the North." *Horn Book* 60 (June 1984):375-79.
Discusses four Canadian picture books written from the perspective of an adult looking back: William Kurelek's *A Prairie Boy's Summer* (1975) and *A Prairie Boy's Winter* (1973), Sing Lim's *West Coast Chinese Boy* (1979), and Shizuyo Takashima's *A Child in Prison Camp* (1971).

B282   FEE, MARGERY. "Romantic Nationalism and the Child in Canadian Writing." *CCL* 18-19 (1980):46-61.

Explores the connection between the romantic invention of the modern child, the romantic concept of nationalism, and the relationship between the two in Canadian literature.

B283   GAGNON, ANDRE. "French Canadian Literature for Children." *Proceedings of the Children's Literature Association* 6 (1979):106-11.
An overview of recent French Canadian children's literature.

B284   MENDELSOHN, LEONARD R. "The Current State of Children's Literature in Canada." *Children's Literature* 4 (1975):138-52.
Maintains that the overshadowing by English and American publishers has led to a relatively small number of books of excellent quality by Canadian authors. Discusses several recent examples. Includes a bibliography of Canadian children's books published from 1970 to 1974.

B285   ORD, PRISCILLA, ed. "Canadian Children's Literature." *ChLAQ* 2, no. 3 (Autumn 1977):16pp. (Reprinted in part in Dooley, *First Steps*, pp. 6-10.)
Includes articles on Canadian children's literature as a mirror of culture, by Carole Henderson Carpenter, on Canadian children's poetry, by William Blackburn, and on the realistic animal story, by Margaret Wilson. Also includes articles, indexed separately, on William Kurelek and Ruth Nichols, and a lengthy review by Patricia Dooley of Lillian Smith's *Unreluctant Years* and Sheila Egoff's *Republic of Childhood*.

B286   SORFLEET, JOHN R. "Children's Books in Canada, or, the Twittering of the Penguins." In *Children's Books International 2. Proceedings and Book Catalog*. Boston: Boston Public Library, 1977, pp. 41-48.
Provides an overview of Canadian children's literature, pointing out some of its distinguishing regional characteristics.

B287   -----. "Children's Periodicals in Canada." *Phaedrus* 4, no. 2 (Fall 1977):19-20.
Provides an introduction to the field, designed "to spur additional research."

B288   ZOLA, MEGUIDO. "Children's Magazines: High-Flyers of Canadian Publishing." *Bookbird* 3 (1981):33-38.
An overview.

CARNEGIE MEDAL BOOKS

B289   CROUCH, MARCUS, and ELLIS, ALEC, eds. *Chosen for Children: An Account of Books Which Have Been Awarded the Library Association Carnegie Medal, 1936-1975*. 3d ed. London: Library Association, 1977, 180 pp.
Each section contains a short introduction to an award-winning book, an account of the circumstances of the award, an excerpt from a chapter of the winning book, and a comment by the author on the origins of the book.

CENSORSHIP

B290   BRODERICK, DOROTHY. "Censorship--Reevaluated." *Library Journal* 96 (15 November 1971):3816-18 and *SLJ* (November 1971):30-32.

(Reprinted in Gerhardt, *Issues in Children's Book Selection*, pp. 61-66.)

Argues that intellectual freedom should not be an issue in cases of pornography and racism. "The whole concept of social responsibility implies value judgments--some things are right and some things are wrong and it is that simple." Argues that bigotry is not just another point of view. Against Broderick's point of view, James A. Harvey's "Acting for the Children?" follows, in Gerhardt, pp. 67-72, and in *SLJ* (February 1973), arguing that some individuals may find valuable and useful those works Broderick detests.

B291 -----. "A Different Look at *The Diviners.*" *Emergency Librarian* 4, no. 2 (November-December 1976):14-15. (Reprinted in Varlejs, *Young Adult Literature*, pp. 208-10.)

Examines the real issues in the censorship of Margaret Laurence's book and comments on censorship.

B292 DARLING, RICHARD L. "Censorship--An Old Story." *EE* 51 (May 1974):691-96.

A historical overview of the censorship of children's books. Includes references.

B293 HEARNE, BETSY. "Sex, Violence, Obscenity, Tragedy, Scariness and Other Facts of Life in Children's Literature." *Learning* 10, no. 7 (February 1982):104-7.

Attempts to strike a balance between freedom and protection.

B294 HENTOFF, NAT. "Any Writer Who Follows Anyone Else's Guidelines Ought to Be in Advertising." *SLJ* 24 (November 1977):27-29. (Reprinted in Lenz, *Young Adult Literature*, pp. 454-60, and in Carr, *Beyond Fact*, pp. 176-80.)

Attacks the checklists and activities of the Council on Interracial Books for Children as censorship. The "CIBC not only distrusts individualism . . . but it also distrusts children."

B295 KLEIN, NORMA. "Some Thoughts on Censorship: An Author Symposium." *TON* 39 (Winter 1983):137-53.

A number of authors comment on the way censorship by editors and libraries has affected their literary careers. Writers are Robin Brancato, Judy Blume, Sandra Scoppettone, David Rees, and Betty Miles. In the second part of the symposium Klein discusses her own experiences with editors and her own books.

B296 KOSINSKI, JERZY. "Against Book Censorship." *Media and Methods* 12 (January 1976):21-24. (Reprinted in Lenz, *Young Adult Literature*, pp. 460-64.)

Censorship "undermines one of the basic reasons for teaching contemporary literature: to present the students with hypothetical situations--emotional, moral, political, religious, sexual--which they are likely to face once they leave the protective structure of school, family, or community, or which they may be struggling to face already."

B297 LEHMANN-HAUPT, HELMUT. "What the Nazis Did to Children's Books." *Horn Book* 25 (May 1949):220-30.

Describes how Nazi propaganda was "cunningly grafted onto existing concepts," resulting in subtle changes that were in many ways more effective and lasting than overt indoctrination.

B298   LETTIS, RICHARD. "The Book Is Not for Burning." *Journal of Reading* 21 (November 1977):106-8. (Reprinted in Lenz, *Young Adult Literature*, pp. 452-54.)

Compares censorship as "protection" with Holden Caulfield's role as a "catcher" in Salinger's *Catcher in the Rye*, suggesting that Holden learns, in the course of the novel, the dangers and impossibilities of the role of "catcher," while the censors have not.

B299   McCLURE, AMY. "Censorship." *ChLAQ* 8, no. 1 (Spring 1983):22-25.

Provides a brief historical overview of the history of censorship of children's literature. Includes references.

B300   -----. "Intellectual Freedom and the Young Child." *ChLAQ* 8, no. 3 (Fall 1983):41-43.

Surveys the reasons for censorship in various categories of issues and explores ways of balancing intellectual freedom with the need to protect.

B301   MacLEOD, ANNE SCOTT. "Censorship and Children's Literature." *Library Quarterly* 53 (January 1983):26-38.

Attempts to place current arguments over censorship of children's books into a historical context. Suggests that the consensus and homogeneity among people involved in the production of children's books broke up in the 1960s, and "enormous changes in the content of children's literature followed. . . . The 1980s promises to be a period of conflict, as conservative reaction against the liberal trends of the 1970s tries to reverse an accomplished transformation in the literature."

B302   MAZER, NORMA FOX. "Comics, Cokes, and Censorship." *TON* 32 (January 1976):167-70. (Reprinted in Varlejs, *Young Adult Literature*, pp. 211-14.)

Comes out strongly against the censorship of children's reading matter yet leaves the reader with the questions "What is censorship?" and "If we are censoring, however discreetly, whether as parents, readers, teachers, librarians, or writers, what are we risking?"

B303   MOOD, ROBERT G. "Let' em Read Trash." *EE* 34 (November 1957):444-50.

Censorship to protect children from corrupting their taste and intelligence does not keep children from reading trash. Defends comics and maintains that the four elements people most often want to eliminate in them are also found in the classics. These are: (1) violence and terror, (2) incitement to misconduct and crime, (3) banality, and (4) sex.

B304   MOORE, ROBERT B., and BURRESS, LEE. "Bait/Rebait: Criticism vs. Censorship." *English Journal* 70 (September 1981):14-19.

Issue: "The criticizing of racism and sexism by the Council on Interracial Books for Children is not censorship."

B305   MUSSER, LOUISE A. "Censoring Sexist and Racist Books: Unjustified and Unjust." *ChLAQ* 9, no. 1 (Spring 1984):36-37.

Summarizes briefly a number of recent censorship issues and cases. Concludes that "arguments against censorship in general must also apply to censorship of those books that may be sexist or racist."

B306 NODELMAN, PERRY. "The Case of the Disappearing Jew." *CLE*, n.s. 10, no. 1 (Spring 1979):44-48.
Examines the disappearance of the anti-Semitic tale "The Jew in the Bush" from a Puffin "reprint," raising questions of values, censorship, and literary criticism.

B307 SULLIVAN, PEGGY, ed. "Freedom and Constraint in Children's Literature." *WLB* 51 (October 1976):144-76.
Special issue. Contains "What shall They Read? A History Perspective," by W. Boyd Rayward, pp. 146-53; "Children's Books in a Pluralistic Society," by Donnarae MacCann, pp. 154-62; "The Intellectual Rights of Children," by Pamela Ellen Procuniar, pp. 163-67; "The Students Right to Free Expression," by Eileen S. Sullivan, pp. 168-76; and "Somewhat Free: Post-Civil War Writing for Children," by Evelyn Geller, pp. 172-76.

B308 WARD, NANCY. "Feminism and Censorship." *LA* 53 (May 1976):536-37.
Argues not to take away or change older, sexist materials, but to add new.

B309 WEST, MARK I. "Not to Be Circulated: The Response of Children's Librarians to Dime Novels and Series Books." *ChLAQ* 10 (Fall 1985):137-39.
Reviews the history of librarians' attempts to censor dime novels and series books, and shows that librarians have not always defended freedom to read.

B310 WHITE, MARY LOU. "Censorship--Threat Over Children's Books." *Elementary School Journal* 75 (October 1974):2-10.
Points out the wide range of opinions on many censored children's books.

B311 YATES, JESSICA. "Censorship in Children's Paperbacks." *CLE*, n.s. 11, no. 4 (Winter 1980):180-91.
Discusses the prevalence of moral and political censorship in children's books, particularly the changes frequently made in paperback editions, with examples from many well-known books. Letters in response and Yates's reply follow in *CLE*, n.s. 12, no. 1 (Spring 1981):56-58.

CHILD ABUSE

B312 FIEDLER, LESLIE. "Child Abuse and the Literature of Childhood." *Children's Literature* 8 (1980):147-53.
Discusses approaches to child abuse in children's literature.

B313 HEARNE, BETSY. "The American Connection." *Signal* 31 (January 1980):36-41.
Discusses two recent children's books centering on child abuse.

B314 SHANNON, GEORGE. "The Survival of the Child: Abuse in Folktales." *CLE*, n.s. 12, no. 1 (Spring 1981):34-38.
Examines the treatment of child abuse in the folktales of several cultures.

B315 WOOLRIDGE, CONNIE N. "Masquerading as Realism: Child Abuse in Juvenile Novels." *SLJ* 24 (March 1978):102-3.

Examines the treatment of child abuse in five juvenile novels: Irene Hunt's *The Lottery Rose*, Willo D. Roberts's *Don't Hurt Laurie*, Jacklyn O'Hanlon's *Fair Game*, Betsy Byars's *Pinballs*, and Marion D. Bauer's *Foster Child*.

CHILDREN

B316 BARRICK, JEAN ANNE. "The Authority of Childhood: Three Components of the Childlike Spirit in Poems by Robert Louis Stevenson, Kate Greenaway, and Christina Rossetti." Ed.D. dissertation, Columbia University, 1971, 249 pp., DA 32:3146A.

Discusses wonder, play, and construction/reconstruction as means by which young children "author and authenticate their life-experiences, values, and commitments" in literature written for adults about children and in literature written for children.

B317 BILDMAN, JOAN. "Study of Child-Adult Relationships as Revealed in Selected Contemporary Picture-Storybooks for Children in the Primary Grades." Ed.D. dissertation, Columbia University, 1972, 510 pp., DA 33:950A.

Explores the depiction of child-adult relationships in one hundred picture books published between 1950 and 1970.

B318 CAMERON, ELEANOR. "The Characterization of the Child in Translated Books." *Ripples* 5, no. 3 (Fall-Winter 1980):4-10.

Analyzes the characters and weighs the relative importance of character and place in several translated books, including Jörg Steiner's *Rabbit Island*, Maria Gripe's *The Night Daddy*, Tove Jansson's *Tales from Moominvalley*, and Van Iterson's *Pulga*.

B319 ESCARPIT, DENISE, ed. *The Portrayal of the Child in Children's Literature: Proceedings of the Sixth Conference of the International Research Society for Children's Literature.* Bordeaux, France: University of Gascony, September 1983. Munich: K.G. Saur, 1985, 392 pp.

Includes 36 papers in French and in English, with summaries in the alternate language. Papers are grouped under the following topics: the child in national literature, the child in illustration, the child in minority groups, the child in the literary genres, and individual visions of the child. Selected papers have been indexed under individual topics in this bibliography.

B320 GLASSER, WILLIAM. "Creative Children: Characterized and Criticized." *L&U* 1, no. 2 (Fall 1977):40-46.

Examines two picture books which "foster the idea that the child's creative capacities should be selectively restrained," Edward Fenton's *Fierce John* and Else Minarik's *Little Bear*.

B321 HAYDEN, GRETCHEN PURTELL. "A Descriptive Study of the Treatment of Personal Development in Selected Children's Fiction Books Awarded the Newbery Medal." Ed.D. dissertation, Wayne State University, 1969, 303 pp., DA 31:1663A.

Examines four Newbery award-winning books in terms of their depiction of the personal development of the main character: Irene

Hunt's *Up a Road Slowly*, Joseph Krumgold's *And Now Miguel*, Emily Neville's *It's Like This Cat*, and Esther Forbes's *Johnny Tremain*.

B322   HOMZE, ALMA CROSS. "Interpersonal Relations in Children's Literature, 1920 to 1960." Ed.D. dissertation, Pennsylvania State University, 1963, 222 pp., DA 24:5079A.

Found adult characters becoming decreasingly authoritarian and decreasingly critical in their relationships with child characters, child characters increasingly outspoken and critical in interactions with adult characters, child characters increasingly independent, and increasing competition and less affection among adults and children.

B323   KELLY, R. GORDON. "Changing Lifestyles in Children's Books." *Catholic Library World* 53 (Summer 1981):65-69.

Reflects on the changing nature of childhood and the child's preparation for the adult world in Louisa May Alcott's *Little Women*, in Horatio Alger's *Ragged Dick*, in Richard Hughes's *Tom Brown's School Days*, in Mark Twain's *The Adventures of Tom Sawyer*, in Kate Douglas Wiggin's *Rebecca of Sunnybrook Farm*, and in Mary Stolz's *Look Before You Leap*.

B324   KORTH, VIRGINIA. "The Gifted Child in Children's Fiction." *Gifted Child Quarterly* 21 (Summer 1977):246-60.

Describes research to identify children's fiction about gifted children. Finds mostly positive portrayals.

B325   NYE, MARILYN L. "Children's Literature to Educate Adults." *LA* 54 (January 1977):51-54.

Discusses several books that provide insights into children's feelings and actions in terms of child-child and child-adult relationships.

B326   PEARCE, PHILIPPA. "The Writer's View of Childhood." *Horn Book* 38 (February 1962):74-78.

Reflects on attitudes toward childhood expressed by various well-known and classic writers.

B327   TODD, ROBERT. "The Treatment of Childhood Stress in Children's Literature." *CLE*, o.s., no. 5 (1971):26-45. (Originally published in *Child in Care*, the magazine of the Residential Childcare Association, in a slightly different form.)

Examines depictions of stress in books ranging from "Snow White" to a number of modern problem novels. Comments by David Evans follow, pp. 46-50.

B328   TWAY, EILEEN. "The Gifted Child in Literature." *LA* 57 (January 1980):14-20.

Surveys the gifted child in more than two dozen contemporary children's books.

CHILDREN AS AUTHORS

B329   MOLSON, FRANCIS. "Portrait of the Young Writer in Children's Fiction." *L&U* 1, no. 2 (Fall 1977):77-90.

Discusses Louise Fitzhugh's *Harriet the Spy*, Irene Hunt's *Up the Road Slowly*, Jean Little's *Look Through My Window*, Eleanor Cameron's *A Room Made of Windows*, and Mollie Hunter's *A Sound of Chariots*.

B330 SMITH, LOUISA A. "Child Writers in Children's Literature." *LA* 57 (May 1980):519-23.

Discusses the portrayal of the child as a writer in Louisa May Alcott's *Little Women*, Carol Ryrie Brink's *Louly*, Eleanor Cameron's *Julia and the Hand of God*, and Maud H. Lovelace's *Betsy and Tacy Go Downtown*.

CHILE

B331 BRAVO-VILLASANTE, CARMEN. "The History of Juvenile Literature in Chile." *Bookbird* 5, no. 3 (1967):28-34.

Concentrates on Chilean folktale collections.

CHINA

B332 BLUMENTHAL, EILEEN P. "Models in Chinese Moral Education: Perspectives from Children's Books." Ph.D. dissertation, University of Michigan, 1976, 250 pp., DA 37:6357A.

Investigates Chinese children's books that are produced as part of a broad program of moral education in China, paying particular attention to the Chinese theory of model emulation.

B333 CHANG, PARRIS H. "Children's Literature and Political Socialization." In *Moving a Mountain: Cultural Change in China*. Edited by Godwin C. Chu and Francis L.K. Hsu. Honolulu: University Press of Hawaii for East-West Center, 1979, 446 pp.

Discusses Chinese picture story books, identifying major themes, and explores the implications of early political socialization.

B334 CHU, LEONARD L. "Sabers and Swords for the Chinese Children: Revolutionary Children's Folk Songs." In *Popular Media in China: Shaping New Cultural Patterns*. Edited by Godwin C. Chu. Honolulu: University Press of Hawaii, 1978, pp. 16-50.

Provides an extensive account, with examples, of Chinese children's folk songs, contrasting the traditional songs of the past, which were communicated by parents and grandparents, to the modern revolutionary songs, which are mass circulated. Includes extensive references.

B335 COLE, DAVID, and COLE, DOROTHEA. "Two Cultures, Two Kinds of Children's Books." *IRBC* 8, no. 7 (1977):9-11.

Identifies major themes and values expressed in Chinese literature for children and contrasts them with American themes and values.

B336 DOOLEY, PATRICIA. "Porcelain, Pigtails, Pagodas: Images of China in Nineteenth and Twentieth Century Illustrated Editions of the Nightingale." *Proceedings of the Children's Literature Association* 6 (1979):94-105.

Examines European ideas of China as revealed in nineteenth- and twentieth-century illustrations and translations of "The Nightingale," and provides extensive background information on the various versions.

B337 ECO, UMBERTO. "Little Red Comic Books." *Atlas* 20 (November

1971):36-38.
Finds Mao's new way of reaching the people through comics to be humane, educational, and revolutionary. "With few exceptions, there is no distinction between strips for children and for adults."

B338   HANNABUSS, STUART. "Muscular Ideology: A Look at Chinese Children's Books." *Signal* 20 (May 1976):68-77.
Discusses what he sees as the almost overwhelming emphasis on ideology in Chinese children's books.

B339   HWANG, JOHN C. "Lien Huan Hua: Revolutionary Serial Pictures." In *Popular Media in China: Shaping New Cultural Patterns.* Edited by Godwin C. Chu. Honolulu: University Press of Hawaii, 1978, pp. 51-72.
Discusses the Chinese equivalents of Western comic books, placing them in their historical centers and showing how they are used to communicate political messages.

B340   KRASILOVSKY, PHYLLIS. "What Chinese Children Read: A Morality Tale." *Publishers Weekly* 203 (26 February 1973):100-101. (Reprinted in White, *Children's Literature*, pp. 64-68.)
Examines the messages communicated in a sampling of Chinese children's books.

B341   MITCHELL, EDNA. "Children's Books from the People's Republic of China." *LA* 57 (January 1980):30-37.
Surveys recent Chinese children's literature discussing trends, artistic qualities, and values portrayed.

B342   "'Monkey': A Chinese Children's Classic." In *Childhood in Contemporary Cultures.* Edited by Margaret Mead and Martha Wolfenstein. Chicago: University of Chicago Press, 1955, pp. 246-52.
Provides a detailed analysis of the traditional tale "Monkey," a favorite of Chinese children between the ages of six and ten, and attempts to explain the reasons for its appeal to this age group.

B343   "People's Republic of China: Educating the Masses with Picture-Story Books." *Interracial Books for Children* 5, nos. 1-2 (1974):7-10.
A lengthy report on children's books in China that includes the following categories: (1) stories written as object lessons, (2) stories about the "Bitter Years," 1920s-1940s, (3) stories about revolutionary movements in other countries, (4) adaptations of works by foreign authors, (5) reading texts, and (6) folklore.

B344   SCOTT, DOROTHEA H. *Chinese Popular Literature and the Child.* Chicago: American Library Association, 1980, 181 pp.
Surveys China's popular literature, oral and written, over several centuries and shows its influences on Chinese children's literature. Includes a bibliography and index.

B345   -----. "Chinese Stories: A Plea for Authenticity." *Library Journal* 99 (15 April 1974):1183-87 and *SLJ* 20 (April 1974):21-25. (Comments in *Library Journal* 99 [15 September 1974]:2189 and *SLJ* 21 [September 1974]:3.)
Discusses numerous books about China and the Chinese, pointing out problems, inaccuracies, and difficulties, as well as citing what is excellent.

B346   -----. "Lu Hsun and Chinese Literature for Children." *International Library Review* 7 (January 1975):29-37.
Traces the influences of Lu Hsun (pseudonym of Chou Shu-jen) on Chinese children's literature in the twentieth century.

B347   SMITH, LYNN COZETTE. "China: A New Perspective for Adolescent Readers." *TON* 37 (Summer 1981):344-48.
Discusses changes in young adult literature about China since United States recognition of Communist China; includes the availability of Chinese works in translation.

B348   STONES, ROSEMARY. "An Introduction to Children's Books in the People's Republic of China." *Bookbird* 15, no. 1 (1977):8-18.
A brief history of children's literature in China and a summary of its current status. Concludes that "there now exists a substantial body of literature for children in China that is very worthy of our attention." Includes a bibliography of Chinese children's books.

B349   ZANIELLO, THOMAS A. "Flowers in Full Bloom: The Variety of Chinese Children's Literature." *Children's Literature* 7 (1978):181-90.
A follow up to Zaniello's article in *Children's Literature* (1974) (below), reevaluating the influences of the Cultural Revolution. Concludes that "The 'liberalism' of the Hundred Flowers movement of the 1950s may be blossoming once more in Chinese children's literature."

B350   -----. "Heroic Quintuplets: A Look at Some Chinese Children's Literature." *Children's Literature* 3 (1974):36-42.
Examines Claire Huchet Bishop's *Five Chinese Brothers* and compares it with the anonymous Chinese *Five Little Liu Brothers* (1960) with illustrations by Wang Yu-Chuan (available in English translation from the Foreign Languages Press in Peking). Sees the significant difference between the tales in the source of the brothers' difficulty and its resolution. The Chinese version reflects recent Chinese history and stages in the development of a communist society. Discusses briefly the ways in which other Chinese tales also reflect changes wrought by the Cultural Revolution.

CHINESE AMERICANS

B351   WONG, JEAN H. "Chinese-American Identity and Children's Picture Books." ERIC Educational Document Reproduction Service, 1973, 17 pp., ED 067 663.
Surveys the portrayal of Chinese and Chinese Americans in books for young children. Concludes that (1) tales and legends of ancient China have been well-executed, (2) stories of pre-World War II China are old-fashioned and in some cases outdated, and (3) stories with American China-town settings tend to contain occupational stereotypes and overgeneralizations of the culture and show little interaction with the dominant American culture.

CHRISTMAS

B352   EATON, ANNE T. "Christmas in Books." *Horn Book* 12 (November-December 1936):339-43.
A brief overview of treatment of Christmas, in text and illustra-

tion, in children's books from around the world.

CITIES

B353 DELLA ROCCA ORIENTE, LOUISA. "Images of City Life as Depicted in Contemporary Realistic Fiction for Children, Ages Eight to Twelve." Ed.D. dissertation, Columbia University, 1976, 420 pp., DA 37:6236A.

Describes and analyzes the portrayal of city life in contemporary, realistic literature for children ages eight to twelve.

B354 LLOYD, BONNIE. "The Changing City Landscape in Children's Books." *Journal of Outdoor Education* 13, no. 2 (1979):15-20.

Explores changes in portrayals of urban and rural life in children's books and suggests they reveal "how much the political and social climate of the country influences our landscape imagery."

B355 STEIN, RUTH M. "Of Skies and Skyscrapers: Rural-Urban Imagery in Children's Literature." *EE* 46 (November 1969):940-49.

Although urban living has been upgraded in recent children's books, the Jeffersonian ethos remains.

B356 THOMAS, JANE R. "The Infernal City: The Arcadian Lament in Children's Picture Books." *Horn Book* 54 (February 1975):24-31.

"While many authors have discovered in city life the rewards and discomforts of community, some however, have found in it the root of all evil." Examines "the myth of pastoral bliss" in a number of children's books, including Helen Oxenbury's *Pig's Tale*, Virginia Burton's *The Little House*, Nicholas Brennan's *Olaf's Incredible Machine*, and others. Also recommends books with positive portrayals of urban life.

CLASSICS

B357 AKE, MARY, moderator. "Panel Discussion: Developing a Canon of Children's Literature." *Proceedings of the Children's Literature Association* 7 (1980):45-67.

Panel members Jane Bingham, Alethea Helbig, Marcia Shafer, and Jon Stott discuss why a canon of children's literature is desirable, propose various criteria for selection, and present proposed lists for the canon.

B358 ALDERSON, BRIAN. "What Makes a Book Survive? or, 'Wild Tales Which Made the Child a Man.'" *WLB* 47 (October 1972):172-77.

Concludes that the children's classics that seem destined to survive share "a certain imaginative density and a certain narrative vigor."

B359 DODERER, KLAUS. "German Children's Classics: Heirs and Pretenders to an Eclectic Heritage." *WLB* 48, no. 2 (October 1973):146-52.

Attempts to define a classic by examining four "classic" German children's books: Grimms' *Fairy Tales*; Johanna Spyri's *Heidi* (which he recommends consigning to history), Wilhelm Busch's *Max and Moritz*, and Erich Kästner's *Emil und die Detektive*.

B360 FADIMAN, CLIFTON. "Children's Reading." In *Party of One: The Selected Writings of Clifton Fadiman*. Cleveland: World Publishing

Co., 1955, pp. 369-420.
Includes "Portrait of The Author as a Young Reader"; "Books for Children," which ranges widely over classics and recent works of children's literature; "Mother Goose"; "The Maze in the Snow," which concerns *Alice*; and "How Pleasant to Know Mr. Lear!" which sees nonsense as "the comic spirit's organized defiance of experience."

B361   -----. "Three Perspectives on: Children's Classics in a Non-Classical Age." *WLB* 47, no. 2 (October 1972):158-61.
Introduces a special issue on classics from French, English, and American children's literature. Includes articles by Isabelle Jan, Brian Alderson, and Sara Innis Fenwick.

B362   FENWICK, SARA INNIS. "American Children's Classics: Which Will Fade, Which Endure." *WLB* 47, no. 2 (October 1972):178-85.
Examines the characteristics of classic works of American children's literature that seem destined to survive, and extends the study to certain additional titles from the 1930s and 1940s. Also discusses the influence of the Newbery award.

B363   LAWRENCE, ANN. "Children's Classics." In Hunt, *Further Approaches*, pp. 109-10.
Briefly summarizes her research into various groupings of "classics" of children's literature.

B364   NODELMAN, PERRY. "Grand Canon Suite." *ChLAQ* 5, no. 1 (Summer 1980):1, 3-8. (Reprinted in Dooley, *First Steps*, pp. 38-41.)
Discusses the Children's Literature Association's process of developing its list of important children's books and offers his own "Tentative List of Books Everyone Interested in Children's Literature Should Know." Responses to this article are reported in *ChLAQ* 5, no. 4 (Winter 1981):28-30, and also reprinted in Dooley, *First Steps*, pp. 68-69.

B365   RAWSON, CLAUDE. "Elements of a Children's Classic." *TLS*, 25 November 1983, pp. 1309-10.
Reviews the new Puffin classics series and ponders the significance of the ubiquitous orphan in so many children's classics, which, nevertheless, reaffirm family values. In this same issue, p. 1311, twelve writers and critics select and comment on books which they think will become classics.

B366   SAYERS, FRANCES CLARKE. "Books That Enchant: What Makes a Classic?" *NEA Journal*, January 1957, pp. 9-11. (Reprinted in Sayers, *Summoned By Books*, pp. 152-61.)
Looks for common elements in children's classics and finds breathtaking events, the development of character, vivid personalities, originality, atmosphere, and genuine emotion. "Even the youngest children, in the period of their first reading experience, are capable of responding to the great elements of art: to drama and originality, to conflict and resolution, to feeling of place and atmosphere, to the emotions of fear and love and hate, to the inevitability of character and the mystery of personality, to humor and nonsense, to truth, and to the Wizardry of words in the hands of the masters."

B367   TOWNSEND, JOHN ROWE. "A Working List of Children's Fiction." *CLE*, o.s., no. 9 (November 1972):57-63.

Provides his own list of the best recent children's fiction.

COMICS

B368   ARBUTHNOT, MAY HILL. "Children and the Comics." *EE* (March 1947):171-83.
Identifies seven types of comics and argues that they will not harm children if they are used wisely and supplemented by good books.

B369   ARMSTRONG, DAVID T. "How Good Are the Comic Books?" *EER* 21 (December 1944):283-85.
Upon close examination of an early Superman comic, a teacher formerly opposed to comics concedes that (1) the vocabulary is on a high level, (2) reading and reading speed are encouraged, (3) the values are wholesome, (4) the comics are reaching a large audience often unreached by the schools.

B370   BAILEY, BRUCE. "An Inquiry into Love Comic Books: The Token Evolution of the Genre." *Journal of Popular Culture* 10, no. 1 (Summer 1976):245-48.
Sees little change and development in the love comic since its inception in 1949 to the present.

B371   BALL, HOWARD G. "Who Is Snoopy?" *LA* 53 (October 1976):798-802.
Summarizes objections to comic strips, briefly describes the history and development of the medium, and provides criteria for determining the "instructional appropriateness" of any particular comic.

B372   BECCHETTI, MARIO DI FRANCESCO; FACE, ANDREA; and OTTAVIANI, GIOIA. "From 'Mickey Mouse' to 'Diabolik.'" *Bookbird* 8, no. 3 (1970):20-24.
This Italian study examines comic book themes ranging from violence, racism, and the Wild West, to war and horror, finds comics lacking in "positive" and "educative" figures.

B373   BECHTEL, LOUISE SEAMAN. "The Comics and Children's Books." *Horn Book* 17 (July-August 1941):296-303.
Expresses dismay at the popularity of comics, particularly the magazine versions, and suggests tactics for turning children away from them to books.

B374   BERGER, ARTHUR. "Comics and Culture." *Journal of Popular Culture* 5, no. 1 (Summer 1971):164-77.
Explores the role of comics in American life and the reflection of American culture in the comics.

B375   *Comic Books and Juvenile Delinquency: Interim Report of the Committee on the Judiciary.* Washington, D.C.: Government Printing Office, 1955, 50 pp.
Includes a brief history of comic books. Discusses the nature of crime and horror comics, the methods used to portray violence, and the contribution of comics to juvenile delinquency. Includes an appendix listing comic book publishers.

B376   CUTRIGHT, FRANK, Jr. "Shall Our Children Read the Comics? Yes!"

EER 19 (May 1942):165-67.

A spirited defense of comics, maintaining that the three aspects that are most decried may be found in any kind of literature: (1) unhealthy excitement and presentation of horror, (2) sex or pornography, and (3) lack of artistry. Includes a list of beneficial aspects of comics with the statement that they usually "exhibit a high integrity quotient" by showing good triumphing over evil.

B377   DOHM, J.H.   "Comic Books: An American View." *Junior Bookshelf* 39 (June 1975):159-67.
A rgues that research is needed on the mental and physical processes used in reading comics and on the ways in which they are used by children.

B378   FAUST, WOLFGANG M. "Comics and How to Read Them." *Journal of Popular Culture* 5 (Summer 1971):194-202.
Suggests new ways to read and analyze comics that link verbal and pictorial fields.

B379   FEIFFER, JULES. *The Great Comic Book Heroes.* New York: Dial Press, 1965, 189 pp.
This compilation of excerpts from comics includes Feiffer's personal critical and historical introduction, pp. 11-53, and afterword, pp. 185-89.

B380   FIEDLER, LESLIE A. "Up, Up and Away: The Rise and Fall of Comic Books." *NYTBR*, 5 September 1976, pp. 1, 9-11. (Reprinted in Varlejs, *Young Adult Literature*, pp. 339-44.)
Traces the history and development of twentieth-century comics from the 1920s through the 1960s.

B381   FOSTER, DAVID WILLIAM. "*Mafalda*: An Argentine Comic Strip." *Journal of Popular Culture* 14 (Winter 1980):497-508.
Applies some general semiological principles to highlight the complex ironies of *Mafalda*.

B382   FRANCIS, MADELEINE. "Girls Only." *New Society*, 28 September 1972, pp. 627-28.
Examines popular British girls' comics.

B383   HANNA, WILLARD A. *Indonesian Komik.* AUFS Report, no. 16. Hanover, N.H.: American Universities Field Service, 1979, 11 pp.
Provides an overview of the phenomenon of the Indonesian comics and their principle themes.

B384   HARVEY, ROBERT C. "The Aesthetics of the Comic Strip." *Journal of Popular Culture* 12, no. 4 (Spring 1979):640-52.
Proposes an aesthetic theory of comics.

B385   HORN, MAURICE. *Comics of the American West.* New York: Winchester Press, 1977, 224 pp.
Includes a history of the western comic strip and comic book, and chapters on the portrayal of the west, the western comic around the world, and major themes and inspirations. Includes a bibliography and index.

B386   HÜRLIMANN, BETTINA. "Wham! Sok! Thinks!: The Development of

Comic Strips from Wilhelm Busch to Walt Disney." In *Three Centuries*, pp. 160-72.
Traces the evolution of comics.

B387   INGE, M. THOMAS. "The Comics as Culture." *Journal of Popular Culture* 12, no. 4 (Spring 1979):631-39.
An introductory overview of the serious study of comics.

B388   KASEN, JILL HELENE. "Portraits from the Dream: The Myth of Success in the Comic Strip, 1925-1975." Ph.D. dissertation, Rutgers University, 1978, 441 pp., DA 39:6341A.
Analyzes some of the myths of the American class system as unfolded through the comic strip from 1925 to 1975.

B389   LUPOFF, RICHARD A., and THOMPSON, DON, eds. *All in Color for a Dime.* New Rochelle, N.Y.: Ace Books, 1970, 255 pp.
An anthology of articles on two dozen heroes, by a number of professional writers and editors.

B390   MIRA, EDUARD J. "Notes on a Comparative Analysis of American and Spanish Comic Books." *Journal of Popular Culture* 5, no. 1 (Summer 1971):203-20.
Compares and contrasts the evolution of comics in the United States and in Spain.

B391   NEFF, WILLIAM A. "The Pictorial and Linguistic Features of Comic Book Formulas." Ph.D. dissertation, University of Denver, 1977, 239 pp., DA 38:3786A.
Applies John Cawelti's definitions and formulas of adventure, romance, mystery, and alien beings or states, to the study of comic books.

B392   PEREBINOSSOFF, PHILIPPE. "'What Does a Kiss Mean?' The Love Comic Formula and Creation of the Ideal Teen-Age Girl." *Journal of Popular Culture* 8 (Spring 1975):825-35.
"Love comics reflect in condensed or capsule form the values popular culture requires of the ideal teen-age girl." Discusses the conservative, traditional values that "love comic heroines must learn to accept if they are going to be successful wives and mothers."

B393   RICHLER, MORDECAI. "The Great Comic Book Heroes." *Encounter* 28, no. 5 (May 1967):46-53. (Reprinted in Meek, *Cool Web*, pp. 299-308.)
A favorable and nostalgic view of the often maligned comic book heroes of the 1940s, 1950s, and 1960s. Reviews Feiffer's *The Great Comic Book Heroes.*

B394   "Roughage: Comics." In Culpan, *Variety is King*, pp. 49-70.
Includes Bob Dixon's "Cartoon Comics," pp. 50-53 (from *Catching Them Young 2: Political Ideas in Children's Fiction*), an analysis of social issues; Margaret Marshall's "Have You Read Your Child's Comic Recently?," pp. 54-56, a presentation of some positive aspects of comics; and Nicholas Tucker's "A New Look at the British Comic," reprinted from *Where.*

B395   SHADOIAN, JACK. "Yuh Got Pecos! Doggone, Belle, Yuh're as Good As Two Men." *Journal of Popular Culture* 12 (Spring 1979):721-36.

Analyzes strong female cowgirl characters in some short-lived comics of the late 1940s and early 1950s.

B396 SKIDMORE, MAX J., and SKIDMORE, JOEY. "More than Mere Fantasy: Political Themes in Contemporary Comic Books." *Journal of Popular Culture* 17 (Summer 1983):83-92.

Analyzes the shift in political themes between the comics of the Golden Age (the 1940s and 1950s) to those of the present. Includes extensive references.

B397 SKINNER, KENNETH A. "Salaryman Comics in Japan: Images of Self-Perception." *Journal of Popular Culture* 13 (Summer 1979):141-51.

Analyzes common characteristics and concerns of Japan's salaryman ("sarariman manga") comic strips between 1974 and 1976.

B398 SMITH, COLIN. "Himmel! The Englanders Won't Stop Fighting." *Observer Colour Supplement*, 16 July 1972. (Reprinted in Meek, *Cool Web*, pp. 338-43.)

A journalist's report on war comics produced by the British-based International Publishing Corporation, with comments by their writers.

B399 SMITH, RODNEY DALE. "A Study of the International Political Events and Commentary in Selected American Comic Strips from 1940-1970." Ed.D. dissertation, Ball State University, 1979, 248 pp.

Traces the ways in which five comic strips commented on international political events over a thirty-year period. The strips are Al Capp's *Li'l Abner*, Harold Gray's *Little Orphan Annie*, Zack Mosley's *Smilin Jack*, Milton Caniff's and George Wunder's *Terry and the Pirates*, and Walt Kelly's *Pogo*.

B400 STEVENS, JOHN D. "Reflections in a Dark Mirror: Comic Strips in Black Newspapers." *Journal of Popular Culture* 10 (Summer 1976):239-44.

Examines comics in black newspapers for their insights into black aspirations and frustrations.

B401 STOTT, JON C. "Pseudo-Sublimity and Inarticulate Mumblings in Violent Juxtaposition: The World of Comic Books." *ChLAQ* 7, no. 1 (Spring 1982):10-12.

Surveys currently popular comic books and notes their similarity to television format, their purple prose, and their similarities to Northern mythology.

B402 SWARTZ, J. "The Anatomy of the Comic Strip and the Value World of Kids." 2 vols. Ph.D. dissertation, Ohio State University, 1978, 558 pp., DA 37:5780A.

Analyzes the contribution of Richard F. Outcault, creator of *Buster Brown*, to the development of American comic strip history.

B403 TUCKER, NICHOLAS. "A New Look at the British Comic." *Where* 122 (November 1976):291-93, 326-29.

Provides an overview of current British children's comics.

B404 -----, ed. "Part Two: Comics." In *Suitable for Children?*, pp. 77-112.

Includes reprints of articles by Tucker, Nicholas Johnson, J.B.

Priestley, and Angela Carter.

B405   -----. "What Was All the Fuss About?" *TES* 3349 (22 August 1980):15.
Examines the battle to ban comics, spearheaded by Frederick Wertham in the 1950s.

B406   VIGUS, ROBERT. "The Art of the Comic Magazine." *EER* 19 (May 1942):168-70.
Explores the influences of comic book art and summarizes arguments for and against. Urges that comics be given more careful criticism. Includes references for the arguments.

B407   VOLPER, R. "Feminist Goals As Depicted in the Behavior of the Husband Versus the Wife in Selected American Family Comic Strips 1960-1974--A Content Analysis." Ph.D. dissertation, New York University, 1975, 242 pp., DA 36:7717A.
Examines *Blondie, Moon Mullins*, and *Gasoline Alley* from their beginnings through 1974. Finds the feminist movement has not had a significant impact upon comic-strip husbands and wives.

B408   WALP, RUSSELL LEE. "Comics as Seen By the Illustrators of Children's Books." *WLB* 26 (October 1951):153-56, 159.
Surveys twenty-five well-known illustrators to gather opinions on comics. Opinions range from those who believe "comics are a menace to welfare and reading habits" to those who believe there are some "good" and some "bad" comics.

B409   WERTHAM, FREDERICK. *Seduction of the Innocent.* New York: Holt, Rinehart & Winston, 1954, 400 pp.
"This book, thoroughly documented by facts and cases, gives the substance of Dr. Wertham's expert opinion on the effects that comic books have on the minds and behavior of children who come in contact with them." Wertham concentrates especially on crime comics, but examines the entire field, detailing its detrimental influences on children and society.

B410   WIDZER, MARTIN E. "Comic-book Superhero: A Study of the Family Romance Fantasy." *Psychoanalytic Study of the Child* 32 (1977):565-603.
"Viewing the comic book as contemporary mythology, I shall focus specifically on the comic-book superheroes and consider them in relation to the myth of the birth of the hero of classical mythology. The manner in which the superheroes acquire their powers will be related to the phases of the family romance fantasy." Widzer also relates this fantasy to stages of psychological development. Includes extensive references.

B411   YOUNG, WILLIAM H., Jr. "The Serious Funnies: Adventure Comics during the Depression, 1929-1938." *Journal of Popular Culture* 3 (Winter 1969):404-27.
Examines the way adventure comic strips responded to the depression of the 1930s. Comics discussed include *Tarzan, Dick Tracy, Radio Patrol, Terry and the Pirates*, and *Buck Rogers.*

CONFLICT

B412 BLACKBURN, WILLIAM. "'Daddy, Daddy, You Bastard, I'm Through':
Rebellion in Children's Literature." ERIC Educational Document
Reproduction Service, 1977, 12 pp., ED 147 825
Examines the way in which children's rebellion against adults is
handled in three works in which adults meet their deaths at the
hands of children: "Hansel and Gretel," *Treasure Island*, and *Peter
Pan*.

B413 -----. "Terrible Thoughts: The Instinct of Revolt in Children's Literature." ERIC Educational Document Reproduction Service, 1983, 14
pp., ED 240 616.
Examines the portrayal of children's rebellion against their parents
in three classic works of children's literature: the Grimms' "Hansel
and Gretel," R.L. Stevenson's *Treasure Island*, and J.M. Barrie's *Peter
Pan*.

B414 BOND, NANCY. "Conflict in Children's Literature." *Horn Book* 60
(June 1984):297-306.
Identifies three kinds of conflict in children's books (global,
personal, and internal) and discusses them, chiefly in terms of her
own books.

CONSUMER EDUCATION

B415 HEYLMAN, KATHERINE M. "No Bargains for Francis: Children's
Trade Books and Consumer Education." *SLJ* 18 (October 1971):77-92.
(Reprinted in Gerhardt, *Issues in Children's Book Selection*, pp.
125-35.)
This critical bibliographic essay examines approaches to consumer
education in children's fictional and informational books.

COOKBOOKS

B416 JENKS, CAROLYN. "The Basic Ingredients: Cookbooks for Children."
SLJ 23 (March 1977):120-21.
Provides criteria for evaluating children's cookbooks and a briefly
annotated bibliography.

CRITICAL THEORY

B417 ABRAHAMSON, RICHARD F. "Children's Literature Scholarship:
Implications of Favat's *Child and Tale*." *LA* 55 (April 1978):502-4.
Suggests directions the scholarship of children's literature might
take if guided by Favat's suggestions.

B418 AIKEN, JOAN. "Purely for Love." *Books: Journal of the National
Book League*, Winter 1970, pp. 9-21. (Reprinted in Haviland, *Children and Literature*, pp. 141-54.)
In a roundabout way, sets forth criteria for writers of children's
books and their critics. "Really good writing for children should
come out with the force of Niagara, it ought to be concentrated; it
needs to have everything that is in adult writing squeezed into a
smaller compass."

B419   ALDERSON, BRIAN W. "Bibliography and Children's Books: The Present Position." *Library* 32 (1977):203-13.
        Argues that children's books need a firmer bibliographical base--especially in the area of illustration.

B420   -----. "Literary Criticism and Children's Books; or, 'Could Be Worse.'" In Fox, *Responses to Children's Literature*, pp. 59-75.
        Explores the ways in which various varieties of "literary critics" might approach Edward Lear's poem "Daddy Long-Legs and the Fly": The Educationist, The Utilitarian, The Authoritarian, The Child Minder. Argues that the critic should be concerned with the "integrity--the wholeness and truth" of the secondary world created within a work and that the means to this is textual analysis.

B421   -----. "Opinions are Free: Facts are Expensive." In Hunt, *Further Approaches*, pp. 77-82.
        Argues that bibliographical and historical research to establish accurate textual and bibliographic information about works of children's literature is essential to critical understanding of both historical and modern children's literature.

B422   BAMBERGER, RICHARD. "Principles for the Evaluation of Children's Books." In *Reading and Children's Books*, pp. 77-89.
        Examines aesthetic, psychological, and pedagogical principles as means of evaluating children's books.

B423   BATOR, ROBERT, ed. *Signposts to Criticism of Children's Literature.* Chicago: American Library Association, 1983, 346 pp.
        Selects critical articles on children's literature that "exemplify much of the serious treatment that has emerged so far." Individual topics and authors have been indexed separately in this bibliography.

B424   BEKKEDAL, TEKLA K. "Content Analysis of Children's Books." *Library Trends* 22 (October 1973):109-26.
        A literature review of content analysis studies on children's books, examining content analysis as a tool, studies of human relationships, studies on values and cultural content, studies on racial and ethnic groups, and other studies. Concludes with suggestions for further research. Includes extensive references and numerous doctoral dissertations.

B425   BENTON, MICHAEL, ed. *Approaches to Research in Children's Literature.* Southampton, England: University of Southampton, Department of Education, February 1980, 41 pp.
        This report, from a two-day research seminar on children's literature held at Southampton University in September 1979, includes Nicholas Tucker's "Can We Ever Know the Reader's Response?," Peter Hunt's "Children's Books, Children's Literature, Criticism and Research," and Margaret Meek's "Prologomena for a Study of Children's Literature." Tucker explores the applications of developmental psychology for criticism of children's literature. Hunt attempts to define children's literature and distinguish between "literature" and "non-literature" and "quality" and "value." Meek questions the assumptions that are made about children and their response to literature and explores the role of criticism of children's literature and its present stage of development. "It seems that we have reached the point where we must look at the prospects for research into a liter-

ary theory that can encompass literature written with children as part of the acknowledged audience, so that developmental considerations can be included, so that judgements relevant to 'adult' literature need not be excluded, and the historical progression can be enlightening."

B426   BLOS, JOAN. "Of Children's Literature and Child Psychology." *CLE*, n.s. 9, no. 2 (Summer 1978):101-5.
        Explores the different, yet complementary, approaches of psychology and literature to childhood.

B427   BRETT, BETTY. "A Study of the Criticism of Children's Literature 1969-1979." Ph.D dissertation, Ohio State University, 1981, 501 pp., DA 42:1947A.
        See annotation for the following item.

B428   BRETT, BETTY M., and HUCK, CHARLOTTE S. "Research Update: Children's Literature--The Search for Excellence." *LA* 59 (November-December 1982):877-82. (Also available from ERIC Educational Document Reproduction Service, 41 pp., ED 220 846.)
        Summarizes the nature of children's literature criticism in the years 1969-79. Based on Brett's doctoral dissertation, criticism is classified into three categories: work-centered, child-centered, and issue-centered. Each category is defined and discussed. Concludes that "There *is* a valid criticism of children's literature, a criticism which appears to be moving away from a narrow preoccupation with text to a more comprehensive criticism which embraces the author, the work, the social environment in which the work develops, and the audience to whom the work is addressed."

B429   -----. "What Makes a Good Story?" *LA* 55 (April 1978):460-66.
        Analyzes the qualities that make a story good in relationship to children's understanding. Identifies characteristics such as identifiable structures, the difficulty of recognizing and using these structures, reliance on the reader's prior beliefs and expectations, and the complexity of the story.

B430   CAMERON, ELEANOR. "For Whom Does the Critic Write--and Why?" *ChLAQ* 9, no. 4 (Winter 1984-85):181-83, 198.
        The critic, after satisfying him or herself, is, or should be, writing, indirectly, for children. The critic of children's literature should have, as Lawrence Clark Powell notes Frances Clarke Sayers had, a "gift of celebration."

B431   -----. "Why *Not* for Children?" *Horn Book* 42 (February 1966):21-33. (Revised and published as "The Sense of Audience," in *Green and Burning*, pp. 203-8.)
        A spirited defense of children's literature and those who admit they write for children as well as to please themselves.

B432   -----. "With Wrinkled Brow and Cool Fresh Eye." *Horn Book* 61 (May-June 1985):280-88; (July-August 1985):426-31.
        Explores the role of the literary critic.

B433   CHAMBERS, AIDAN. "Letter from England: Three Fallacies About Children's Books." *Horn Book* 54 (June 1978):322-26. (Reprinted in Bator, *Signposts*, pp. 54-59.)
        The three fallacies are that (1) only good stories today are in

children's books, (2) didacticism is an old-fashioned literary weakness, and (3) I write for myself.

B434   CIANCIOLO, PATRICIA J. "Responding to Literature as a Work of Art--An Aesthetic Literary Experience." *LA* 59 (March 1982):259-64.
Explores approaches to the aesthetic aspects of literature, emphasizing "an intense internal happening, an awareness of literary structure, and the identification of multiple meanings." For another approach to literature as art see the article preceding Cianciolo's in this same issue: Diane Monson's "The Literature Program and the Arts," pp. 254-58.

B435   -----. "To Each His Own!" *TON* 27 (June 1971):406-15.
Categorizes children's literature according to the desires of the readers who cry, "Comfort me. Amuse me. Touch me. Make me shudder. Make me weep. Make me think," and the few who say, "Give me something fine in any form which may suit you best, according to your own temperament." Mentions books that might satisfy the reader in each category.

B436   COOPER, SUSAN. "In Defense of the Artist." In *Proceedings of the Children's Literature Association* 5 (1978):20-28. (Reprinted in Bator, *Signposts*, 98-108.)
An attack on "pseudo-scientific" criticism and the issues approach and a plea to treat literature as art, to "Be careful how you treat the magic of books . . . if you peer at it too hard . . . it will vanish." (See reply by Lois Kuznets, below.)

B437   COUPLAND, JUSTIN. "What's in a Story: Narrative Structure and Realisation in Children's Fiction." In Hunt, *Further Approaches*, pp. 85-91.
Explores ways of analyzing and comparing narrative structure in children's books. Includes extensive references.

B438   CRAGO, HUGH. "Children's Literature: On the Cultural Periphery." *Children's Book Review* 4, no. 4 (Winter 1974-75):137-38. (Reprinted in Bator, *Signposts*, pp. 61-65.)
Applies the tenet "tradition survives longest on the periphery" to children's literature, explores parallels between children's literature and rock music, and ponders the political effects of decompartmentalizing children's literature.

B439   -----. "Cultural Categories and the Criticism of Children's Literature." *Signal* 30 (September 1979):140-50.
Attempts to address these large questions: "What is being a critic about? What assumptions do critics of children's literature work on? Are they valid? Are there real differences between child and adult responses to literature?"

B440   DALE, RUTH ELLEN. "A Critical Inquiry into the Nature of Wholeness and Fragmentation in Selected Prose Fiction for Young Children." Ed.D. dissertation, Columbia University, 1965, 594 pp., DA 26:2544A.
"This study probes the nature of wholeness and fragmentation and their relationship to prose fiction for young children, with a view toward a theory of literature for children." Finds that today's children's literature tends to express fragmentation.

B441   DAVIS, DAVID C. "It's This Way, Kid!" *Horn Book* 40 (October 1964):523-27.
       In a humorous, colloquial style, Davis sets forth criteria for a "good" book.

B442   DE ANGELO, RACHAEL, ed. "Book Selection for Children." *Drexel Library Quarterly* 2 (January 1966):5-26.
       Includes an overview, "Children's Literature Today--Its Background and Problems," by William A. Jenkins; "Criteria for Children's Books," by Anne Izard; and summaries of small group discussions centered on criteria for evaluating various categories of books: picture and easy books, factual and fictional series, and retellings, adaptations, and abridgements.

B443   EBERT, GUNTER. "Critics and Criticism." *Bookbird* 10, no. 4 (1972):3-7.
       Discusses differences in the ways in which children and adults approach books. Stresses that the successful authors of children's books are those who "reach the dialectic of worldliness and naiveté," and discusses the role and definition of "adventure" and "excitement" in children's books.

B444   ELLEMAN, BARBARA. "The Real Book and the Real Child." *Booklist* 75 (1979):40-42.
       Book-reviewer Elleman persuasively argues that those working with children and books should not lose sight of the child.

B445   FADIMAN, CLIFTON. "The Case for Children's Literature." *Children's Literature* 5 (1976):9-21. (Reprinted in Bator, *Signposts*, pp. 7-18.)
       Summarizes arguments against children's literature as an art form and worthwhile entity, then argues in favor of children's literature on the basis of tradition, recognized masterpieces, the suitability of genres such as nonsense and fantasy, and themes central to the form. Finally, Fadiman points out the growing critical apparatus and numbers of institutions in support of the field.

B446   FAVAT, ANDRE F. "Achieving a State of Grace." *English Education* 2 (Spring 1971):136-41.
       Suggests a plan to help critics and teachers of children's literature "achieve a state of grace." It must be decided whether children's literature is "apart from or a part of literature in general," a "semantically viable" vocabulary of criticism must be found, criticism and reviewing must be joined, and focus on the author's life must not be substituted for focus on the author's work. Calls for a moratorium on textbooks and booklists, and argues that as well as training in literature, the critic of children's literature needs training in psychoanalytic and developmental psychology. "Those of us who practice or use criticism of children's literature must decide just what the relationship is between children's literature and conventional literature. We must employ or insist upon a precise critical vocabulary in the reviews we write to take on the functions of criticism, and must eschew appreciations in favor of in-depth, topical studies. And we must bring to bear upon our writing and teaching, knowledge of literature and psychology and not pedagogy or bibliography alone."

B447   FIELD, CAROLYN W. "Criteria and the Individual." *Horn Book* 40 (October 1964):527-29.
Suggests that the criteria for excellence are generally agreed upon and may even seem self-evident, but because judges differ in personality, experience, and background, disagreements over selection of distinguished books occur.

B448   FISHER, MARGERY. "Coming to Books." *Signal* 33 (September 1980):127-29.
Fisher shares her approach to appreciating and evaluating books.

B449   -----. "Rights and Wrongs." In *Arbuthnot Lectures*, pp. 3-20. (Also in *TON* 26 [June 1970]:373-91.)
Urges we approach books as lovers first, critics second. Comments on various trends in children's literature, including somewhat extended discussions of the following books: Zindel's *My Darling, My Hamburger*, Ivan Southall's *Finn's Folly*, Jill Walsh's *Fireweed*, Lucy Boston's *Stranger at Green Knowe*, and Peter Dickinson's *Heartsease*.

B450   FRANK, JOSETTE. "What Makes a Book for Children Good." *Library Journal* 84 (15 March 1959):978-80.
Provides criteria for both fiction and nonfiction, starting with the statement that a book must have "integrity."

B451   FRASER, JAMES. "Children's Literature as a Scholarly Resource: The Need for a National Plan." *Library Journal* 94 (15 December 1969):4490-91. (Reprinted in Gerhardt, *Issues in Children's Book Selection*, pp. 198-201.)
Discusses the need for systematic collection of children's books for the use of research scholars; not only "quality" children's literature but all kinds are needed to meet the needs of researchers in the social sciences.

B452   GEORGIOU, CONSTANTINE. "A Compilation and Analysis of Elements of Literary Quality Expressed in Fictional Works Found in Children's Classics and the John Newbery Medal Books." Ed.D. dissertation, New York University, 1963, 231 pp., DA 26:1020A.
Explores the dimensions of quality found in standard children's classics and in Newbery award-winning fiction. Attempts to produce a guide for analyzing juvenile fiction.

B453   GIBLIN, JAMES CROSS. "Does It Have to Be Fantasy to Be Imaginative?" *CLE*, n.s. 9, no. 3 (Autumn 1978):151-55. (Letters follow in *CLE*, n.s. 10, no. 1 [Spring 1979]:49-51.)
Imaginative quality in literature does not depend upon whether the work is labeled "fantasy" or "realism," but depends upon the quality of execution of character, plot, setting, sense perceptions, language, and illustrations.

B454   GODDEN, RUMER. "Have the Courage to Tell a Story." *Bookseller*, 31 July 1976. (Reprinted in Culpan, *Variety is King*, pp. 111-13.)
Questions whether the importance of "story" is being overlooked in today's emphasis on standards and quality in children's literature.

B455   GORDON, JESSE E. "The Wrong Rights in Children's Literature." *Michigan Quarterly Review* 6 (January 1967):54-56. (Reprinted in

TON 23 [June 1967]:376-78, along with a response and rebuttal, "Flashing Dr. Gordon," by Peggy Sullivan and others, pp. 379-85.)

Gordon argues that compared to traditional literature, recent children's literature lacks "significant themes." Peggy Sullivan's spirited reply begins, "The inhabitant of the ivory tower has opened his window and spit." Among books upon which Sullivan and Gordon disagree are Robert McCloskey's *Make Way for Ducklings* and Lynd Ward's *The Biggest Bear*.

B456 HAND, NIGEL. "Criticism and the Children's Fiction Industry." *CLE*, o.s., no. 12 (September 1973):3-9.

Points out weaknesses in much children's literature criticism, which he describes as neither searching nor generous.

B457 HANNABUSS, STUART. "Beyond the Formula: Ways of Extending the Obvious for Children and Young People." *Junior Bookshelf* 46, no. 4 (August 1982):123-27; no. 5 (October 1982):173-76.

Urges that writers for children avoid the obvious, the cliché, and points out ways that some writers have done this. Hannabuss expresses related ideas in his discussion of popular adult fiction, "A Bridge to Far," *Junior Bookshelf* 47, no. 3 (June 1983):101-5.

B458 HARDGRAVE, WILMA JEAN BAKER. "An Interpretation of Kenneth Burke's Order and the Narrative Applied to Selected Newbery Medal Novels for Children." Ed.D. dissertation, New Mexico State University, 1970, 131 pp., ERIC Educational Document Reproduction Service, ED 054 156.

Concludes that only six of the seventeen novels considered were judged to be "properly constructed narratives" according to Burke's concept of ultimate order, and that applying Burkean concepts to children's novels "gave more questions than answers."

B459 HEDGES, NED SAMUEL. "The Fable and the Fabulous: The Use of Traditional Forms in Children's Literature." Ph.D. dissertation, University of Nebraska, 1968, 255 pp., DA 29:2213A.

Examines the ways in which children's books are modeled on the traditional literary forms of fable, myth, epic, and romance. Sees Kipling's *Just So Stories* as combining the forms of beast fable and nature myth, Kenneth Grahame's *Wind in the Willows* as combining fable and epic, and Tolkien's *The Hobbit* as employing the devices of the medieval chivalric romance.

B460 HEINS, ETHEL L. "The Criticism and Reviewing of Children's Books." *Proceedings of the Children's Literature Association* 5 (1978):48-56.

Distinguishes between reviewing and criticism, and warns critics against going too far, echoing Susan Cooper's comments.

B461 HEINS, PAUL. "Coming to Terms with Criticism." *Horn Book* 46 (August 1970):370-75. (Reprinted in Heins, *Crosscurrents*, pp. 82-87, and in Haviland, *Children and Literature*, pp. 408-12.)

Lists topics worthy of consideration by critics of children's literature. These include seeing children's literature and its criticism as a part of the whole of literature, identifying the distinguishing characteristic of children's literature, and considering the trends of the age, the judgment of time, and the effect of stressing excellence.

B462 -----. "Literary Criticism and Children's Books." *Quarterly Journal of the Library of Congress* 38 (Fall 1981):255-63. (Reprinted in Bator, *Signposts*, pp. 85-90.)

Discusses the importance of literary criticism in casting "the introspective light," and differentiates this approach from others.

B463   -----. "Some Random Thoughts on the Present State of the Criticism of Children's Literature." *Horn Book* 46 (June 1970):264-73. (Reprinted in Heins, *Crosscurrents*, pp. 72-81, and as "Out on a Limb with the Critics," in Haviland, *Children and Literature*, pp. 400-407.)

Examines the relationship between reviewing and criticism. Concludes, "The prime function, then, of the reviewer and even of the critic of children's books is to recognize those books which appealing at present to children will seem even better when they are reread by those same children in adulthood."

B464   HELSON, RAVENNA. "Change, Tradition, and Critical Styles in the Contemporary World of Children's Books." *Children's Literature* 5 (1976):22-39.

Reports on a study of the personalities and psychology of critics of children's literature.

B465   HUGHES, FELICITY A. "Children's Literature: Theory and Practice." *ELH* [English Literary History] 45 (Fall 1978):542-61. (Reprinted in Bator, *Signposts*, pp. 26-36, 242-48.)

Maintains that as the novel became elevated to the status of serious literature in the 1880s, fantasy was "abandoned to the child." Failure to recognize that this is the case has led to confusion in the theory of criticism of children's literature.

B466   HUNT, PETER. "All Art is One Art: The Holistic Approach to Children's Literature." *Advocate* 2, no. 3 (Spring 1983):170-74.

Suggests that children's book studies "epitomize--and are a paradigm for--all the most advanced critical and educational and sociological and philosophical ways of dealing with text and reader."

B467   -----. "Childist Criticism: The Subculture of the Child, the Book and the Critic." *Signal* 43 (January 1984):42-60.

Questions whether books said to represent a child's point of view actually do that or whether they represent what adults think is a child's point of view and children go along with it to please adults. Suggests new viewpoints may start with studies of children's responses, such as the Cragos' work, and with the book itself and post structuralist critical theory. Finally suggests that we might begin by looking at a book written by a child.

B468   -----. "Critical Method for Children's Literature: A Booklist by Peter Hunt." *Signal* 19 (January 1976):12-21.

Recommends a basic list of works on criticism useful to children's literature scholars.

B469   -----. "Criticism and Children's Literature." *Signal* 15 (September 1974):117-30. (Reprinted in Bator, *Signposts*, pp. 114-25.)

Defines children's literature as books written for a particular child or children, and literature "in terms of the critical process applied to it." Divides criticism into factual, objective, and subjective phases, and further divides these phases into textual, contextual, generic, and moral approaches; formal, linguistic, stylistic, exponential, mythological, archetypal, psychological, and sociological criticism. Urges that "a firm foundation of academic disciplines would be valuable" in the study of children's literature and that "criticism can make a contribution."

B470   -----. "Criticism and Pseudocriticism." *Signal* 34 (January 1981):14-21.
        Responds to Rees's *Marble in the Water* which he labels a "poor book," exemplifying the pseudocriticism which has flourished among children's books for too long.

B471   -----. "A Fine Skepticism: Academics, Children, and Books." *Signal* 36 (September 1981):175-81.
        Reviews Neil Philip's study of Alan Garner, *A Fine Anger*. Devotes a final two pages to Nicholas Tucker's *The Child and the Book*, linking them with discussion on the nature and problems of criticism of children's literature.

B472   -----. "The Good, The Bad and the Indifferent: Quality and Value in Three Contemporary Children's Books." In Chambers, *Signal Approach*, pp. 225-46.
        In an attempt to provide a model for more rigorous critical thinking about children's books, Hunt examines Richard Adams's *Watership Down*, William Mayne's *It*, and Leon Garfield's *The Pleasure Garden*.

B473   -----. "Narrative Theory and Children's Literature." *ChLAQ* 9, no. 4 (Winter 1984-85):191-94.
        Explores the difficulties of applying narrative theory to children's literature, yet argues that theory and radical thinking are necessary or "it may well be that we will continue to get the books we seem to deserve." Suggests a "children's-literature-specific theory" must be developed that takes into account ways in which children's literature differs from that for adults.

B474   -----. "Questions of Method and Methods of Questioning: Childist Criticism in Action." *Signal* 45 (September 1984):180-200.
        Applies his theories of "childist criticism" in an interpretation of Betsy Byars's *The Eighteenth Emergency.*

B475   HUNTER, MOLLIE. "Talent Is Not Enough." *Arbuthnot Lecture* (1975):105-19. (Also in *TON* 31 [June 1975]:391-406.)
        Maintains that "There must be a person behind the book." The children's writer must be in touch with the deep, unblunted emotions of childhood, must be able to relate the significance of a theme to the reader, yet the story must remain paramount.

B476   HUUS, HELEN. "Common Denominators in Children's Books." *Reading Teacher* 34 (March 1981):633-39.
        Briefly surveys similarities in genres, themes, and topics of an international array of children's books.

B477   INGLIS, FRED. "The Awkward Ages, or What Shall We Tell the Children?" *CLE*, o.s., no. 13 (1974):13-34.
        Using some examples from great children's literature from the past as touchstones, Inglis proposes a theory for evaluating recent children's literature based on a liberal ideology and a search for

goodness.

B478   JACOBS, LELAND B. "Children and the Voices of Literature." May
        Hill Arbuthnot Honor Lecture. *TON* 40 (Fall 1983):95-104.
        Explores the various ways in which authors' voices appeal to "the
        authority of childhood," to "the children's needs, their sense of
        wonder, their playfulness, their perpetual constructions--
        reconstructions of ideas, of opinions and judgements and reactions, of
        meanings, of feelings."

B479   JAN, ISABELLE. *On Children's Literature.* New York: Schocken,
        1974, 189 pp.
        Examines the question "Is there such a thing as literature for
        children?" The various chapters discuss aspects of children's litera-
        ture, the final chapter, "Childhood Regained," asserting that "Chil-
        dren's literature has nothing whatsoever to lose by insisting on its
        own individuality."

B480   JENNERICH, EDWARD J. "Panel: A Symposium on the Teaching of
        Children's Literature." *Proceedings of the Children's Literature
        Association* 7 1980):68-83.
        Includes presentations on various approaches to children's litera-
        ture and its criticism at the college level by Jane Bingham (education
        department perspective), Mildred Laughlin (library science perspec-
        tive), and Joy Andersen (English department perspective).

B481   KARL, JEAN. "Excellence in Children's Books." *Bookbird* 5, no. 2
        (1967):17-20.
        Points out what children's trade books are not and suggests ways
        in which "the climate in which excellence can be created can be
        established."

B482   KAYE, MARILYN. "The Critical Front." *Booklist* 76 (February
        1980):769-70. (Reprinted in Bator, *Signposts*, pp. 142-46.)
        Summarizes and lists pros and cons of various methods of criti-
        cism: archetypal, sociocultural, and formalist. Concludes it is time
        to pick and choose from the many approaches to develop an
        approach suitable for children's literature. Urges less attention to
        content and more to form, better definition of audience, and a
        clearer distinction between popular and "high" literature.

B483   KERTZER, ADRIENNE. "Inventing the Child Reader: How We Read
        Children's Books." *CLE*, n.s. 15, no. 1 (Spring 1984):12-21.
        Examines John Newbery's *Little Goody Two Shoes* and Richard
        Hughes's *High Wind in Jamaica* to show how writers invent their
        readers, and points out the ways in which recognition of this fact
        "helps us make sense of children's literature."

B484   KIMMEL, ERIC A. "Children's Literature without Children." *Chil-
        dren's Literature* 13 (Spring 1982):38-43.
        Expresses concern over what he sees as a growing trend toward
        ignoring children's tastes and preferences by critics of children's
        literature as literature. Letter in Response (*CLE*, n.s. 13, no. 4
        [Winter 1982]:195-97) from Perry Nodelman argues against "narrow
        conceptions both of what children are capable of and of what chil-
        dren's books should be." Kimmel holds fast to his position, saying
        we should accept the wisdom of children's choices. "Newberys are

always in [in libraries]; Blumes are always out."

B485   -----. "Toward a Theory of Children's Literature." *LA* 56 (April 1979):357-62.

Discusses four basic trends in children's literature that reflect four possible ways of viewing childhood: (1) Mythic, (2) Didactic, (3) Rousseauvian, and (4) Nihilistic. In the end links the Nihilistic to the Mythic level where "we return, battered and disillusioned by the contemporary world, to draw renewed strength and inspiration through simple contemplation of the wonder of being."

B486   KINGSBURY, MARY. "Perspectives on Criticism." *Horn Book* 60 (February 1984):17-23. (Reprinted in *Bookbird* 3 [1984]:4-8.)

Examines the role of the critic, maintaining that new criticism's "Loyalty to the Text" should be the "first law of the critical jungle." Urges that the improvement of criticism of children's literature is important for "the very survival of the culture we live in."

B487   KUSKIN, KARLA. "The Language of Children's Literature." In *The State of the Language*. Edited by Leonard Michaels and Christopher Ricks. Berkeley: University of California Press, 1980, pp. 213-25.

Discusses the changing language of children's books, the influence of the fairy tales and the storyteller, the influence of illustration on language, the importance of the sounds of words to the very young, and the influence of the simplified language of the "read-alone" books. Among books used in extended examples are William Nicholson's *Clever Bill* and Margaret Wise Brown's *Good Night Moon*.

B488   KUTTY, K. NARAYAN. "Roger Sale Puts in a Word for Children's Literature." *Children's Literature* 7 (1978):208-14.

Praises Sale's *Fairy Tales and After*, but also feels "he undermines the role of the child in children's literature."

B489   KUZNETS, LOIS R. "Susan Cooper, A Reply." *Children's Literature Association Newsletter* 3 (Spring-Summer 1978):14-16. (Reprinted in Bator, *Signposts*, pp. 109-13.)

Refutes Susan Cooper's attack on criticism (above). Defends the right of the critic to ask "Why?" and apply his or her own experience, training, and interests to a work in the attempt to discover the author's answers.

B490   LANES, SELMA. "Once Upon the Timeless: The Enduring Power of A Child's First Books," and "When All the Sky Is Clear and Blue." In *Down The Rabbit Hole*, pp. 179-203, 204-11.

In these final chapters of her book, Lanes examines a number of factors that may make a young child's book particularly memorable, and reflects on the differences in the reactions of child and adult to particular scenes.

B491   LANGTON, JANE. "Down to the Quick: The Use of Daily Reality in Writing Fiction." *Horn Book* 59 (February 1973):24-30.

Defines three levels of truth-telling, with examples from children's books: "there is the telling of the truth as it appears on the surface; there is the telling of the truth a little farther in"; and, "finally, there is a telling of the truth even farther toward the center, and this third truth may deny the other two."

B492   LAWSON, ROBERT. "Make Me a Child Again." *Horn Book* 16 (November-December 1940):447-56.
Suggests that people connected with children's books should add to their prayers "make me a child again" so they can see books as children see them. Lawson criticizes the concern with "doing good" for children through books and attacks the "dreary" trends which result. Expresses similar sentiments in somewhat different terms in his Caldecott Medal acceptance speech in *Horn Book* 17 (July-August 1947):278-84.

B493   LEE, BRIAN. "Children's Books Grow Up." *Contemporary Review* 233 (1980):85-90.
Comments on the new adult-type of children's books, discussing briefly, Richard Adams's *Watership Down*, Russell Hoban's *Mouse and His Child*, Alan Garner's *Red Shift*, and Robert Westall's *Machine-Gunners*. Concludes, "If you want a good read it often pays to take a look around the children's section of the nearest library or book shop."

B494   LEESON, ROBERT. "To the Toyland Frontier." *Signal* 16 (January 1975):18-25. (Also in Chambers, *Signal Approach*, pp. 208-16.)
Disputes Townsend's (B540) "purist position in children's book criticism." We need "synthesis" not "rejection of non-literary criteria." ("These days turning to adult lit-crit is like asking to be rescued by the *Titanic*.") Rejects the idea of "consensus" on quality as a middle class assumption. "Rather than purge criticism of non-literary elements, let us renew and enrich literary standards with those elements, that literature may better reflect and in its turn enrich life."

B495   LEHTONEN, MAIJA. "Reflections on Children's Literature." *Bookbird* 11, no. 2 (1973):22-28.
Analyzes various critical approaches to children's literature ranging from new criticism to Göte Klingberg's theory of "adaptation," to biographical analysis and to historical, national, and sociological (including Marxist and structuralist) approaches. Especially helpful for its summary of the work of European critics not translated into English.

B496   LEWIS, C.S. "On Three Ways of Writing for Children." In *Proceedings of the Bournemouth Conference*. London: Library Association, 1952. (Reprinted in Egoff, *Only Connect*, 2d ed., pp. 207-20; in *Horn Book* 39 [October 1963]:231-40; in *Canadian Library Association Bulletin* 15 [June 1958]:28-35, and in Lewis's *Of Other Worlds: Essays and Stories* [New York: Harcourt Brace, 1966].)
Much quoted by critics and authors of children's literature, Lewis herein describes two good and one bad way of writing for children. The bad: give the children what they want. The good: tell a story to a particular child, and "writing a children's story because a children's story is the best art-form of something you have to say." Lewis also provides insights into the nature of fantasy and fairy tales.

B497   LUKENS, REBECCA. "The Child, the Critic, and a Good Book." *LA* 55 (April 1978):452-54, 546.
"Good literature is good literature; it satisfies both children and critics." Points out qualities that make a book good to both critic

and child.

B498   -----. *A Critical Handbook of Children's Literature.* 2d ed. Glenview, Ill.: Scott Foreman, 1982, 264 pp. (Introduction reprinted in May, *Children and Their Literature*, pp. 173-78.)

This introductory text takes a critical approach to children's literature, discusses many classic and contemporary books in passing, and contains many detailed references to E.B. White's *Charlotte's Web* which it uses as a touchstone. Includes chapters analyzing character, plot, setting, theme, point of view, style, and tone, as well as sections devoted to various genres.

B499   LURIE, ALISON. "On the Subversive Side." *TLS*, 28 March 1980, pp. 353-54.

Argues that many of the classic and most famous of children's books represent the child's point of view and are subversive of the status quo.

B500   -----. "Vulgar, Coarse, and Grotesque: Subversive Books for Kids." *Harper's* 259 (December 1979):66-68.

Points out that the classic great books of children's literature tend to be subversive and appeal to the real child many grown-ups would prefer not to acknowledge.

B501   MacCANN, DONNARAE. "A Valid Criticism for Children's Books." *WLB* 44, no. 4 (December 1969):369-96.

This introduction to a special issue devoted to criticism of children's books tells why this criticism is necessary and points out some of its elements and functions.

B502   McGILLIS, RODERICK. "Calling A Voice Out of Silence: Hearing What We Read." *CLE*, n.s. 15, no. 1 (Spring 1984):22-29.

Explores ways in which readers interact with texts. "The conversation with the text is the reader's subjective rendering of the objective voice that exists as a text, and at this level the reader objectifies his subjectivity." See also exchange of letters on this topic, between McGillis and Perry Nodelman, pp. 58-60 in this same issue.

B503   -----. "Utopian Hopes: Criticism Beyond Itself." *ChLAQ* 9, no. 4 (Winter 1984-85):184-86.

Argues that the goal of criticism should be "the experience of literature itself" and summarizes various approaches that might be applied to Kenneth Grahame's *Wind in the Willows*.

B504   MARCUS, LEONARD S. "Small Worlds: The Recovery of Children's Literature." *Michigan Quarterly Review* 18 (Fall 1979):661-67.

This review of Sale's *Fairy Tales and After*, the journals *Children's Literature* and *The Lion and the Unicorn*, and Robin Gottlieb's *Publishing Children's Books in America, 1919-1976* provides insights into the status of children's literature and its criticism.

B505   MEEK, MARGARET, et al. "Introduction: Approaches to Criticism." In *Cool Web*, pp. 262-64.

A brief overview of some of the major approaches to criticism of children's books.

B506 -----. "Questions of Response." *Signal* 31 (January 1980):29-35.
Proposes a sequence of rhetorical questions every adult reactor to children's books should answer before writing on the subject. Also offers a brief list of suggested readings.

B507 MOSS, ANITA, ed. "MLA Special Session: Structuralist Approaches to Children's Literature." *ChLAQ* 7, no. 3 (Fall 1982):33-58.
Includes Anita Moss's introductory overview of structuralist criticism, pp. 33-36; "Child Reader and the Saussurean Paradox," by Boyd H. Davis, pp. 36-38, which comments on the impact of Ferdinand de Saussure and the implications of his theories of criticism of children's literature, demonstrated through an examination of "language awareness" in Kipling's *Kim*, Le Guin's *The Tombs of Atuan*, and Virginia Hamilton's *Zeely*; "Makers of Meaning: A Structuralist Study of Twain's *Tom Sawyer* and Nesbit's *The Enchanted Castle*," by Anita Moss, pp. 39-45; "The Limits of Structures: A Shorter Version of a Comparison between Toni Morrison's *Song of Solomon* and Virginia Hamilton's *M.C. Higgins the Great*," by Perry Nodelman, pp. 45-48, which notes that most critics have commented on "the adult qualities of the children's novel and the childlike qualities of the adult one"; "*Anno's Counting Book*: A Semiological Analysis," by Stephen Roxburgh, pp. 48-52, which applies Roland Barthes's theories to the picture book; and finally "Appropriating the Theory: Structuralism and Children's Literature," by Elizabeth Frances, pp. 52-58, which comments on each of the preceding essays in relation to "structuralist activity," and suggests further directions for structuralist criticism of children's literature.

B508 MOSS, ELAINE. "What Is a Good Book?: The 'Peppermint' Lesson." In Meek, *Cool Web*, pp. 140-42.
Shows how one nondescript book was of utmost importance to a child and concludes that "a book by itself is nothing . . . one can only assess its value by the light it brings to a child's eye."

B509 NESBITT, ELIZABETH. "The Critic and Children's Literature." In Fenwick, *Critical Approach*, pp. 119-26.
Explores the nature of criticism and succinctly distinguishes between criticism and reviewing.

B510 NEUMEYER, PETER F. "A Structural Approach to the Study of Literature for Children." ERIC Educational Document Reproduction Service, 1966, 14 pp., ED 011 328. (Also in *EE* 44 [December 1967]:883-87 and reprinted in White, *Children's Literature*, pp. 185-90.)
Suggests that through a structural approach to children's literature certain functions basic to the stories, as outlined by Vladimir Propp, are identified. These functions are viewed as sequences of action and reaction and are common denominations within stories, no matter how the superstructure may vary.

B511 NILSEN, ALLEEN PACE. "Children's Literature and Mass Media." *SLJ* 23 (March 1977):106-9.
Finds ways references to well-known works of children's literature are used to convey messages by the mass media. Concludes that the traditional and classic works of children's literature "show, better than almost anything else, the foolishness combined with the hopes and fears that make us all human," and this accounts for their popu-

larity.

B512 NODELMAN, PERRY, ed. "Children's Literature and Literary Theory." *ChLAQ* 6, no. 1 (Spring 1981):9-40. (Introduction reprinted in Nodelman, *Festchrift*, p. 37; entire special section reprinted in Dooley, *First Steps*, pp. 73-92.)

"An introduction to the current state of critical theory, particularly as it might apply to children's literature." Glenys Stow and Lois Kuznets comment on books that offer an overview of criticism in general, and of the novel in particular. Susan Gannon and Phyllis Bixler describe some influential theories of fiction. Anita Moss discusses structuralism and its aftermath, and Perry Nodelman looks at the theory of genre and also at the relationship of linguistics to literature. Roderick McGillis examines "reader response" theory, Carol Billman discusses interpretation, and William Blackburn the "Yale critics."

B513 -----. "Defining Children's Literature." *Children's Literature* 8 (1980):184-90.

Reviews four recent books of criticism relevant to children's literature: *Once Upon a Time: On the Nature of Fairy Tales*, by Max Lüthi; *Fantastic in Literature*, by Eric S. Radkin; *Fairy Tales and After*, by Roger Sale, and *The Hills of Far Away*, by Diana Waggoner.

B514 -----. "Thirty Writers Talk About Writing." *Children's Literature* 12 (1984):200-205.

Reviews three recent collections of articles on children's literature in which thirty writers talk about writing. Discusses this common genre of writing about children's literature and explores ways in which, limited as it is, it may open the way for true criticism, for concern with the finished work, not the creative process.

B515 OHANIAN, VERA. "Cherished Books of Children: What Makes Them So?" *EE* 47 (November 1970):946-52.

Examines three "favorite" books: Armstrong Sperry's *Call it Courage*, Rumer Godden's *Impunity Jane*, and A.A. Milne's *Winnie-the-Pooh* in terms of apparent and hidden stories. Concludes that favorite books "explore problems common to childhood and permit their solution," but that these problems are hidden in the apparent story.

B516 OLSON, JOAN BLODGETT PETTERSON. "An Interpretive History of the *Horn Book Magazine*, 1924-1973." Ph.D. dissertation, Stanford University, 1976, 299 pp., DA 37:2875A.

Provides a history and interpretation of *Horn Book*'s first fifty years, characterizing the magazine as "a major source of literary criticism of children's books."

B517 OLSON, MARY S. "Regional-Psychological Story for Children, Ages Eight to Twelve: An Evolution of Some Critical Insights." Ed.D. dissertation, Columbia University, 1972, 400 pp., DA 33:4249A.

Explores the literary characteristics of the fusion of two genres, in this case regional and psychological fiction. Includes considerable attention to the work of Lois Lenski.

B518 PEASE, HOWARD. "An Author's View of Criticism." *Horn Book* 22

(May 1946):196-202. (Reprinted in Fryatt, *Horn Book Sampler*, pp. 96-103.)

Outlines a pattern for the critic, based on evaluation of form, story, characterization, content, craftsmanship, prose, and reaction.

B519 PELLER, LILI. "Daydreams and Children's Favorite Books." *Psychoanalytic Study of the Child* 14 (1959):414-33.

Discusses a number of "typical childhood fantasies" and some of the stories based on them. "At the core of every successful story there is a universal daydream." Explores the role of "story" in the young child's psychological development.

B520 PHILIP, NEIL. Review of Nicholas Tucker's *The Child and the Book*. *CLE*, n.s. 12, no. 3 (Autumn 1981):164-67.

Reviews Tucker's psychological, child-development approach to children's literature and illuminates various approaches to criticism of children's literature.

B521 -----. "This Way Confusion?" *Signal* 43 (January 1984):12-18.

Argues that "The critic must be a reader first." Responds to Bator's collection, *Signposts to Criticism of Children's Books*. Discusses the importance of reader response as proposed by Chambers in "The Reader in the Book" (*Signal* 23) and Myles McDowell in "Fiction for Children" (in Fox, *Writers, Critics, and Children*). "However criticism in children's literature develops, it cannot afford, as so much in Bator's book does, to keep one eye only glancing at the text, the other nervously fixed on university English departments."

B522 PICKERING, SAMUEL, Jr. "The Function of Criticism in Children's Literature." *Children's Literature in Education* 13, no. 1 (Spring 1982):13-18.

"Perhaps all that can be attempted is to make good literature accessible to more people." Argues "if criticism is ever to assume a significant role in society, it must provide insight into human experience and examine the problems which must concern society." Because children's literature reflects many of society's concerns rapidly, "good criticism of children's literature could in the future become the model for much literary study." Stresses the importance of historical research, and concludes "Why not demand that criticism influence the important affairs of life?"

B523 ROSE, JACQUELINE. *The Case of Peter Pan or the Impossibility of Children's Fiction*. London: Macmillan, 1984, 181 pp.

This complex work centers on J.M. Barrie's *Peter Pan* as a means of demonstrating a number of interpretations of the nature of children's literature. Rose asks "what adults, through literature, want or demand of the child," rather than "what children want, or need from literature." She hopes to contribute to the "dismantling" of "the ongoing sexual and political mystification of the child." Provides numerous detailed analyses of the complexities of Barrie's style, explores works by Alan Garner, and ranges over the history of children's literature interpretations of childhood, and theories of language, education, and Freudian analysis.

B524 SALE, ROGER. "Child Reading and Man Reading: Oz, Babar, and Pooh." *Children's Literature* 1 (1972):162-72. (See also introduction to *Fairy Tales and After*, pp. 1-20.)

Goes back to favorite books of his childhood in an attempt to discover the child reader who "defines not only the man reader, but the man," and to discover "what most matters to us, and why." Uses books by L. Frank Baum, Jean de Brunhoff, and A.A. Milne as his examples.

B525   SALMON, EDWARD. "*Signal* Reprints: Should Children Have a Special Literature?" *Signal* 11 (May 1973):94-101, 111.
Reprints an 1890 essay.

B526   SANDERS, JACQUELYN. "Psychological Significance of Children's Literature." *Library Quarterly* 37 (January 1967):15-22.
"The best authors are the best psychologists. They provide, through their writings, deep insight into human nature and, thereby, a powerful tool for better living." Suggests children's literature be examined in terms of (1) its interest and importance to the child, (2) in terms of providing manageable models of useful and desirable behavior, and (3) in terms of the feasibility and constructiveness of the solutions offered.

B527   SARLAND, CHARLES. "False Premises." *Signal* 37 (January 1982):11-20.
Critiques Fred Inglis's *Promise of Happiness*, maintaining that his approach is based on false premises.

B528   SAUL, E. WENDY. "Homage to Metaphor." *SLJ* 30 (March 1984):118-19.
Argues that the nature of a work is often most apparent in its metaphorical meaning, something that literary classification schemes seldom take into account.

B529   SEBESTA, SAM; CALDER, JAMES; and CLELAND, LYNNE N. "Story Structures in Children's Book Choices." ERIC Educational Document Reproduction Service, April 1981, 12 pp., ED 203 370.
Concludes, after applying Applebee's six basic categories of story structure to selected children's books, that "no single story structure can be designated as an exclusive favorite," and "variety and integrity in story structure rather than adherence to the critically approved true narrative might guide us in selecting literature."

B530   SEELYE, JOHN. "Notes on the Waist-High Culture." *Children's Literature* 9 (1981):178-82.
Examines literature children have "appropriated" and discusses its "subversive" appeal.

B531   SHAVIT, ZOHAR. "The Ambivalent Status of Texts: The Case of Children's Literature." *Poetics Today: Theory and Analysis of Literature and Communication* 1, no. 3 (1980):75-86.
Applies semiotic analysis to the problem of ambivalence in texts of children's literature, that is, texts which, though written for children, are primarily read and commented upon by adults. Uses three versions of Lewis Carroll's *Alice's Adventures in Wonderland* to demonstrate the difference between univalent (appealing only to children) and ambivalent (appealing to both children and adults) texts. Michael Steig comments upon Shavit's analysis in *Poetics Today* 2 (Winter 1980-81):193-97, criticizing her failure to take into account historical circumstances and definitions of childhood, and disagrees

with her evidence that Carroll wrote two of his versions primarily for adults and one for children. Shavit responds, and Steig further questions her handling of theory, pp. 199-201.

B532　SHOHET, RICHARD MATTHEW. "Functions of Voice in Children's Literature." Ed.D. dissertation, Harvard University, 1971, 184 pp., DA 32:3270A.

Focuses on "the presence--the role and function--of the voice of the implied author or narrator or storyteller" in children's literature.

B533　SILVER, LINDA. "From Baldwin to Singer: Authors for Kids and Adults." *SLJ* 25 (February 1979):27-29.

Discusses the works for children of a number of successful writers for adults. Includes Donald Barthelme's *The Slightly Irregular Fire Engine*, James Baldwin's *Little Man, Little Man*, Mordecai Richler's *Jacob Two-Two Meets the Hooded Fang*, and a number of books by John Gardner, Graham Greene, Paula Fox, and Isaac Bashevis Singer.

B534　SINGER, ISAAC BASHEVIS. "I See the Child As a Last Refuge." *NYTBR*, 9 November 1969, Children's Book sec., p. 1. (Reprinted in Bator, *Signposts*, pp. 50-54.)

Argues that children's literature is the only place where one can still tell a good story that does not have to be didactic, utilitarian, or subject to complex interpretation. "We are no longer allowed to enjoy a sunset without footnotes."

B535　SMITH, JAMES STEEL. "Children's Literature: Form or Formula?" *EE* 35 (February 1958):92-95.

Distinguishes between books that have strong structure or form, and those that follow a formula and in which the unity is mainly one of tone or feeling.

B536　STEELE, MARY Q. "As Far As You Can Bear to See: Excellence in Children's Literature." *Horn Book* 51 (April 1975):250-55.

Raises the question of how much our determination of excellence depends upon our own quixotic reactions.

B537　SUTTON, WENDY KATHLEEN. "A Study of Selected Alternate Literary Conventions in Fiction for Children and Young Adults and an Examination of the Responses of Professionals Influential in Juvenile Literature to the Presence of These Conventions." Ph.D. dissertation, Michigan State University, 1978, 425 pp., DA 40:513A.

Identifies twenty distinctive literary conventions and innovations in contemporary juvenile fiction but finds they are not adequately recognized by teachers, librarians, and reviewers.

B538　SWINGER, ALICE K. *Children's Books: A Legacy for the Young.* Fastback, no. 164. Bloomington, Ind.: Phi Delta Kappa Educational Foundation, 1981, 45 pp. ERIC Educational Document Reproduction Service, ED 208 406.

Discusses children's literature by genre, provides a history of children's literature in the United States in the twentieth century, and suggests references for further study.

B539　TOWNSEND, JOHN ROWE. "In Literary Terms." *Horn Book* 47 (August 1971):347-53. (From introduction to *Sense of Story*. Also in

Heins, *Crosscurrents*, pp. 65-71.)
Agrees with the commonly held view that children's literature is thriving while adult literature is ailing, and maintains the need for sound literary criticism of children's books.

B540   -----. "Standards of Criticism for Children's Literature." *TON* 27 (June 1971):374-87. (Reprinted in *Signal* 14 [May 1974]:91-105 and in Chambers, *Signal Approach*, pp. 193-207, and excerpted in *Arbuthnot Lectures*, pp. 23-36.)
Arbuthnot Lecture for 1971. Distinguishes between child-centered standards and standards of literary merit. Places criticism of children's literature in the context of criticism of adult literature, yet says it does matter whether or not the book actually speaks to the child. A book's popularity or lack of it may tell us something. Robert Leeson (see B494) disagrees with Townsend, and calls this statement "the most comprehensive and best" statement of "the purist position in children's book criticism."

B541   TREASE, GEOFFREY. *Tales Out of School*. London: Heinemann Educational Books, 1964, 181 pp.
Contains personal reflections on children's literature ranging from fairy tales to picture books, fantasy, popular periodicals, adventure stories, historical fiction, school and family stories, and career stories.

B542   WALSH, JILL PATTON, and TOWNSEND, JOHN ROWE. "Writers and Critics: A Dialogue Between Jill Paton Walsh and John Rowe Townsend." *Horn Book* 58 (October 1982):498-504; (December 1982):680-85.
The creative process is described as a partnership between "producer" and "shaper," between the purely creative and the critical parts of the writer. The role of the writer as critic is also explored by these two writers who are also critics. Part 2 concentrates on reviews and their effects on writers.

B543   WESTWATER, A. MARTHA. "Towards Understanding Coincidence in Children's Literature." *CCC* 5-6 (1976):16-22.
While the adult has learned to belittle coincidence, the child loves it. Relates "meaningful coincidence" in children's books to Jung's archetypal foundations and concludes that the child's-eye view of reality can be a corrective to the adult twofold worship of action and intellect.

B544   WHALEN-LEVITT, PEGGY. "The Critical Theory of Children's Literature: A Conceptual Analysis." Ph.D. dissertation, University of Pennsylvania, 1983, 251 pp., DA 44:3618A.
Identifies and analyzes essential concepts and assumptions underlying criticism of children's literature and offers suggestions regarding appropriate tasks for children's literature criticism and means of undertaking them.

B545   WHITE, MARY LOU. *Children's Literature: Criticism and Response*. Columbus, Ohio: Charles E. Merrill, 1972, 252 pp.
Divides criticism into four categories--psychological, sociological, archetypal, and structural--and gathers together a number of essays of each type. A final chapter discusses ways to use the four types of literary criticism with children. Articles are indexed separately under specific topics in this bibliography.

B546   -----. "Structural Analysis of Children's Literature: Picture Story-books." Ph.D. dissertation, Ohio State University, 1972, 227 pp., DA 33:3274A.

Analyzes one hundred picture storybooks in terms of plot and structural components.

B547   WIGHTON, ROSEMARY, and FINNIS, ERN. "Children's Books: Adult Pleasures." In Robinson, M., *Readings in Children's Literature* pp. 244-70.

Explores the rewards for adults of the "purely literary approach" to children's literature without consideration of "the schoolroom, the clinic, or even the child." Includes a "Freudian psychoanalytical approach" to Sendak's *In the Night Kitchen*, pp. 256-58, an analysis of the maturation theme and symbolic structure of Ivan Southall's *Josh*, pp. 258-62, and the use of animal imagery in William Armstrong's *Sounder*, pp. 262-64.

B548   WOLF, VIRGINIA LEORA. "The Children's Novel as Romance." Ph.D. dissertation, University of Kansas, 1980, 413 pp., DA 41:2107A.

Using the methods of structuralism and modern critical studies of the novel, Wolf determines that the formal characteristics of the children's novel are most closely akin to the adult novels identified as romance "and should be understood and evaluated accordingly."

CRITICAL THEORY--READER RESPONSE CRITICISM

B549   AGEE, HUGH, and GALDA, LEE, eds. "Reader Response Research." *Journal of Research and Development in Education* 16 (Spring 1983), 1-77.

Special issue. Includes Lee Galda's "Research in Response to Literature," pp. 1-7; Janet Hickman's "Everything Considered: Response to Literature in an Elementary School Setting," pp. 8-13; Barbara Kiefer's "The Responses of Children in a Combination First/Second Grade Classroom to Picture Books in a Variety of Artistic Styles," pp. 14-20; Rudine Sims's "Strong Black Girls: A Ten Year Old Responds to Fiction About Afro-Americans," pp. 21-28; Bernice E. Cullinan's "The Reader and the Story: Comprehension and Response," pp. 29-38; Richard Beach's "Attitudes, Social Conventions and Response to Literature," pp. 47-54; Hugh Agee's "Literary Allusion and Reader Response: Possibilities for Research," pp. 55-59; Zohar Shavit's "The Notion of Childhood and the Child as the Implied Reader (Test Case 'Little Red Riding Hood')," pp. 60-67; and Michael Benton's "Secondary Worlds," pp. 68-75, which explores the secondary worlds of writers and readers and their relationships.

B550   BEINLICH, ALEXANDER. "On the Literary Development of Children and Adolescents." *Bookbird* 6, no.1 (1968):17-22.

Explores the significance of child development to children's reading and summarizes a number of research studies.

B551   BENTON, MICHAEL. "Children's Responses to the Text." In Fox, *Responses to Children's Literature*, pp. 13-33.

Explores various approaches to the study of reader response and offers a conceptual model of his own.

B552   CARTER, BETTY, and HARRIS, KAREN. "The Children and the Critics: How Do Their Book Selections Compare?" *School Library*

Media Quarterly 10 (Fall 1981):54-58.
Studies children's reading choices and compares their evaluations with the critics.

B553　CHAMBERS, AIDAN. "The Reader in the Book: Notes from Work in Progress." *Signal* 23 (May 1977):64-87. (Also in *Proceedings of the Children's Literature Association* 5 [1978]:1-19. Reprinted in Chambers, *Signal Approach*, pp. 250-75, and excerpted in Bator, *Signposts*, pp. 127-35.)
　　　Argues that criticism of children's books must take into account the readers for whom they were intended. "The concept of the implied reader . . . offers a critical approach which concerns itself less with the subjects portrayed in a book than with the means of communication . . . It can help determine "whether a book is for children or not, what kind of book it is, and what kind of reader it demands." Applies the "implied reader" theory to several well-known modern works for children, and examines at length Lucy Boston's *The Children of Green Knowe*. (This last part is omitted in Bator's excerpt.)

B554　COCHRAN-SMITH, MARILYN. "Directions in Research: The Parent-Diary as a Research Tool." *ChLAQ* 5, no. 3 (Fall 1980):3-7. (Reprinted in Dooley, *First Steps*, pp. 51-52.)
　　　Considers the parent-diary as a means of literary research and summarizes two articles by Elinor Ochs, and one by Susan R. Braunwald and Richard W. Brislin, as important background reading for those interested in conducting such research. Diana Kelly-Byrne reponds in *ChLAQ* 5, no. 4 (Winter 1981):39-41, and in ibid., 6, no. 2 (1981):6-9. (Reprinted in Dooley, pp. 70-71, 109-11.)

B555　CRAGO, HUGH. "The Reader in the Reader: An Experiment in Personal Response and Literary Criticism." *Signal* 39 (September 1982):172-82.
　　　This follow-up to Crago's earlier *Signal* article attempts to apply his theories through an analysis of Jill Paton Walsh's *A Chance Child*.

B556　FRIEDLAENDER, KATE. "Children's Books and Their Function in Latency and Prepuberty." *American Imago* 3 (April 1942):129-50.
　　　Explores what children read in their latency period, and why. Advises that children of this age be given freedom to read what they choose.

B557　GREEN, GEORGIA M., and LAFF, MARGARET O. "Five-Year-Olds Recognition of Authorship By Literary Style." Technical Report, no. 181. ERIC Educational Document Reproduction Service, 1980, 44 pp., ED 193 615.
　　　Reports that "at least some five-year-old children have the ability to appreciate and discriminate among literary styles," and recommends that children beginning to read be given more challenging, interesting literature than the strictly measured and uniform basic readers.

B558　HICKMAN, JANET. "Research Currents: Researching Children's Response to Literature." *LA* 61 (March 1984):278-84.
　　　Outlines ways of utilizing and conducting reader-response research with children in a classroom situation.

B559　"Kids vs. Adults on Children's Books." *Publishers Weekly* 20 (4 November 1974):22-24.

Reports on the choices of three juries, of children, retailers, and designers, for best books. There is agreement only on four titles.

B560   McNAMARA, SHELLEY. "Focus: Dialogue on Response to Literature." *Ripples* 5, no. 2 (Summer 1979):2-4.

Reviews the literature on reader response as an aspect of literary criticism.

B561   MAXWELL, RHODA. "The Young Critic." *Ripples* 5, no. 2 (Summer 1979):9-11.

Describes the responses of a group of sixth graders to books they have read.

B562   MEARNS, HUGHES. "Bo Peep, Old Woman, and Slow Mandy." *New Republic*, 10 November 1926, pp. 344-46.

An early, influential study of children's reading interests.

B563   MIKKELSEN, NINA. "Literature and the Storymaking Powers of Children." *ChLAQ* 9, no. 1 (Spring 1984):9-14.

Categorizes children's storytelling responses to literature as retellings, borrowings, re-creations, blendings, and transformations. Finds more borrowings and retellings among younger children and more blendings and transformations among older children. Suggests further avenues of research into "the creative processing of literature."

B564   -----. "Sendak, *Snow White*, and the Child as Literary Critic." *LA* 62 (April 1985):362-73.

Reports on a four to five-year-old child's responses to *Outside Over There*, *Snow White* (Disney and Burkert versions) and *Peter Rabbit*.

B565   NILSEN, ALLEEN PACE; PETERSON, RALPH; and SEARFOSS, LYNDON W. "The Adult as Critic vs. The Child as Reader." *LA* 57 (May 1980):530-39.

Explores reasons for the discrepancy between books acclaimed by critics and those most popular with children. Includes lists of books published from 1951 to 1975, with indications of popularity and critical acclaim.

B566   POLICASTRO, MARGARET MARY. "The Concept of a Story: A Comparison Between Children and Teachers." Ph.D. dissertation, Northwestern University, 1981, 114 pp., DA 42:3931A.

Examines the differences in the way teachers and second-grade children classified stories.

6567   PROTHEROUGH, ROBERT. "How Children Judge Stories." *CLE*, n.s. 14, no. 1 (Spring 1983):3-13.

Applies E.A. Peel's theories, as expressed in *The Nature of Adolescent Judgement*, to three broad stages in the development of children's critical responses to literature.

B568   TABBERT, REINBERT. "The Impact of Children's Books: Cases and Concepts." *CLE*, n.s. 10, no. 2 (Summer 1979):92-102; no. 3 (Autumn 1979):144-50. (Reprinted in Fox, *Responses to Children's Literature*, pp. 34-58.)

Explores various critical theories based upon reader response and the implied reader.

B569   TUCKER, NICHOLAS. "How Children Respond to Fiction." *CLE*, o.s., no. 9 (November 1972):48-56.
        Explores elements of literature that seem to appeal to children and comments upon some earlier critics' observations.

B570   WHALEN-LEVITT, PEGGY. "Pursuing the Reader in the Book." *ChLAQ* 4 (Winter 1980):10-14. (Reprinted in Bator, *Signposts*, pp. 135-41, and in May, *Children and Literature*, pp. 154-59.)
        "We can respect the aesthetic function of the text and consider the reader as well." Considers the implications of the work of Wolfgang Iser and Louise Rosenblatt for criticism of children's literature.

B571   YOUNG, DORIS. "Evaluation of Children's Responses to Literature." *Library Quarterly* 37 (January 1967):100-109.
        Reviews much of the early literature on children's responses to literature.

CRITICAL THEORY--STUDY AND TEACHING

B572   AGEE, HUGH. "Responding to Response: An Application of Research in the Classroom." *Advocate* 1, no. 2 (Winter 1982):92-98.
        Discusses ways in which teachers might utilize research studies on reader response.

B573   AITKEN, JOHAN L. "The Tale's the Thing: Northrop Frye's Theory Applied to the Teaching of Tales in the Elementary School." *Interchange* 7, no. 2 (1977):63-72, 76-77.
        Proposes Northrop Frye's archetypal criticism as the basis of a method for teaching literature.

B574   ALLEN, ARTHUR T., and SEABERG, DOROTHY I. "Toward a Rationale for Teaching Literature to Children." *EE* 45 (December 1968):1043-47.
        A comparison of one aspect of the theories of Northrop Frye and Kornei Chukovsky as a basis for teaching literature to young children.

B575   BENNEE, FLORENCE E. "Selected Applications of Frye's Academic Criticism in the Senior High School Years." Ed.D. dissertation, Columbia University, 1971, 259 pp., DA 32:3131A.
        Explores ways in which Frye's theories can be applied to teaching criticism to high-school students.

B576   BROWN, MERRILL. "Reading Together: Eight-to-ten-year-olds as Critics." *CLE*, o.s., no. 21 (Summer 1976):74-80.
        Describes a technique used to elicit critical discussion of books by children, with examples of their comments on some current British books.

B577   BRUCE, BERTRAM. "Stories within Stories." *LA* 58 (November-December 1981):931-36.
        Examines the rhetorical devices by which stories are embedded within stories and discusses the implications for teaching reading to children.

B578   BUTLER, FRANCELIA; McWILLIAMS, J. BRUCE; and MINER, ROB-
ERT G., Jr. "Educational Survival Kit: Learning Basic Human
Interests, and the Teaching of Children's Literature." *Children's
Literature* 2 (1973):244-51.

       Relates various works of children's literature to basic physiologi-
cal categories of respiration, ingestion, digestion, excretion, and
reproduction.

B579   CAMPBELL, PATRICIA. "Helping Young Readers Become Book Critics: Here's How." *IRBC* 14, no. 5 (1983):22-23.

       Concentrates on teaching children an issues approach to criticism.

B580   COUGHLIN, WILLIAM F. Jr., and DESILETS, BRENDAN. "Frederick
the Field Mouse Meets Advanced Reading Skills as Children's Literature Goes to High School." *Journal of Reading* 24 (December
1980):207-11.

       Contends that principles of criticism can be taught best by using
relatively simple stories for children, rather than extremely complex
and difficult adult works. Lists twelve stories, including *Frederick*
by Lionni, along with "literary concepts which can appropriately be
stressed in each."

B581   CULLINAN, BERNICE E. *Its Discipline and Content.* Literature for
Children Series. Edited by Pose Lamb. Dubuque, Iowa: William C.
Brown, 1971, 108 pp.

       Outlines a program for teaching literature to elementary school
children, emphasizing the role of literary criticism and narrative
forms.

B582   KUTZER, M. DAPHNE. "Children's Literature in the College Classroom." *College English* 43 (November 1981):716-23.

       Suggests approaches to children's literature for the college English
classroom based on questions of audience, purpose, literary merit,
social and educational value, censorship, and dangers of nostalgia.

B583   NORTON, DONNA E. "Using a Webbing Process to Develop Children's
Literature Units." *LA* 59 (April 1982):348-56.

       Discusses the use of webbing as a practical means of organizing
children's literature teaching units; however, the technique may also
have applications for the literary critic.

B584   ROSENBLATT, LOUISE, M. "'What Facts Does This Poem Teach
You?'" *LA* 57 (April 1980):386-94.

       Explores some of the implications for teaching of her theories of
"evocation from the text" and her distinction between efferent and
aesthetic reading.

B585   SLOAN, GLENNA D. "Practice of Literary Criticism in the Elementary
School as Informed by the Literary and Educational Theory of Nor-
throp Frye." Ed.D. dissertation, Columbia University, 1972, 311 pp.,
DA 33:1084A.

       "Explores the proposition that literary criticism may have mean-
ingful beginnings in the elementary school, that it is at this level of
formal education a study of vital importance, and that its practice
maybe informed by significant literary theory, in this case that of
the critic, Northrop Frye." *Child as Critic: Teaching Literature in
the Elementary and Middle Schools* (New York: Teachers College

Press, 1984, 168 pp.) updates this research.

B586 STEINLEY, GARY. "Left Brain/Right Brain: More of the Same?" *LA*
60 (April 1983):459-62.
Suggests activities in literature teaching which emphasize "right
brain" aspects of the literary experience.

B587 STOTT, JON C. "Criticism and the Teaching of Stories to Children."
Signal 32 (May 1980):81-92.
Discusses the interrelationship among the areas of the study of
children's literature, the university teaching of the subject, and the
presentation of stories to children. Selects three works of children's
literature for his examples: Beatrix Potter's *The Tale of Peter
Rabbit*, Leslie Brooke's *Johnny Crow's Garden*, and Frances Hodgson
Burnett's *The Secret Garden*.

B588 -----. "'It's Not What You'd Expect': Teaching Irony to Third Graders." *CLE*, n.s. 13, no. 4 (Winter 1982):153-63.
Applies Wayne C. Booth's theories of irony to Lynd Ward's *The
Biggest Bear* and demonstrates how the technique can be used to
teach third graders about that book and other ironic stories. Includes
a list of ironic stories studied in third grade.

B589 -----. "A Structuralist Approach to Teaching Novels in the Elementary
Grades." *Reading Teacher* 36 (November 1982):136-43.
Uses Tolkien's *The Hobbit* to show how the details and patterns
of stories can help children understand literature, and "to see how
patterns in a novel contribute to its total meaning."

B590 -----, ed. "Teaching Literary Criticism in the Elementary Grades: A
Symposium." *CLE*, n.s. 12, no. 4 (Winter 1981):192-206. (Reprinted
in May, *Children and Their Literature*, pp. 160-72.)
Four professors of children's literature offer suggestions for
teaching critical attitudes and insights in grades 2-6. Sonia Landes
uses Potter's *The Tale of Peter Rabbit* as an example. Stott explains
how stories could be arranged into a sequential curriculum for second
graders, Anita Moss demonstrates use of narrative structure, and
Norma Bagnall the uses of language games.

B591 STUDIER, CATHERINE E. "Children's Responses to Literature." *LA* 58
(April 1981):425-30.
Describes the basis for an approach to teaching children "to
become discriminating life-time readers."

B592 USERY, MARY LOU. "Critical Thinking through Children's Literature." *EE* 43 (February 1966):115-18, 120.
Demonstrates how children's literature can be used to teach critical thinking. Uses Lynd Ward's *The Biggest Bear* and Armstrong
Sperry's *Call It Courage* as examples. Steps outlined are: perceiving,
analyzing, predicting, and judging.

B593 VANDERGRIFT, KAY E. "The Elements of Story," and "Compositional
Elements and Genres: A Matrix." In *Child and Story*, pp. 103-33
and pp. 134-79.
With an eye toward training the child as literary critic, the
elements are defined as character, point of view, structure,
plot/setting, tone/mood, language/symbol, style, with frequent

examples from well-known children's books. The following chapter places these into a matrix with genres.

B594   -----. "Teaching Children to Be Critics of a Story: A Handbook for Teachers in the Later Elementary Grades." Ed.D. dissertation, 1978, 185 pp., DA 39:5939A.

B595   WISER, NELL FUNDERBURK. "Teaching Strategies for Enabling Elementary Pupils to Develop Inductively the Literary Concepts of Plot, Theme, Characterization and Setting." Ed.D. dissertation, Memphis State University, 1975, 204 pp., DA 36:4247A.
Develops strategies for teaching students literary concepts of plot, theme, characterization, and setting by synthesizing research in areas of concept formation and levels of questioning, child development, behavioral objectives, and literary concepts.

CUBA

B596   ELIZAGARAY, ALGA MARINA. "Some Considerations on Cuban Revolutionary Poetry for Children." *Phaedrus* 8 (1981):49-51.
An overview.

B597   -----. "A Survey of Literature for Children and Adolescents in Socialist Cuba." *Phaedrus* 5 (Fall 1978):25-30.
Provides a historical overview of recent activities in the field and mentions several recent theoretical and critical studies.

B598   WALD, KAREN. "Cuba: Book Power as Revolutionary Power." *IRBC* 5, nos. 1-2 (1974):5-6.
Reports on children's book publishing in Cuba and the values of the revolution the new books portray.

B599   WALD, KAREN, and BACON, BETTY. "New Literacy for New People: Children and Books in Cuba." *Journal of Reading* 25 (December 1981):251-60. (Reprinted in *Bookbird* 1-2 (1982):10-18.)
Surveys the current state of children's literature in Cuba.

CZECHOSLOVAKIA

B600   HOLEŠOVSKÝ, FRANTIŠEK. "New Creative Trends in Czechoslovak Books for the Youngest." *Bookbird* 1 (1981):61-64.
Discusses work of Aloiz Klíma, Viera Bombová, Zdeněk Seydl, and Květa Pacovská.

B601   MACH, HELGA. "Children's Literature in Czechoslovakia." In Koefoed, *Children's Literature and the Child*, pp. 30-34.
Summarizes developments in Czechoslovakian children's literature since the "Spring of Prague" (1968).

B602   -----. "Czech and Slovak Children's Literature." *De Openbare Bibliotheek* 14, no. 9 (1971). (Reprinted in Haviland, *Children and Literature*, pp. 365-73.)
Provides an overview of trends and developments throughout the history of Czechoslovakian children's literature.

B603   ØRVIG, MARY. "Children's Books in Czechoslovakia." *International Library Review* 2 (1970):275-85.

An overview of publishing, literary, and organizational trends.

B604 "Publisher's Profile: The Mlade Leta Publishing House, Bratislava, Czechoslovakia." *Bookbird* 6, no. 1 (1968):50-58.
Provides a historical overview of the only publishing house in Czechoslovakia specializing in children's books.

DEAFNESS

B605 BATSON, TRENTON. "Deaf Person in Fiction--From Sainthood to Rorschach Blot." *IRBC* 11, nos. 1-2 (1980):16-18.
Examines the history of the treatment of the deaf in literature, especially in recent works.

B606 GROFF, PATRICK. "Children's Fiction and the Psychology of Deafness." *School Librarian* 24, no. 3 (September 1976):196-202.
Examines the depiction of deafness in children's books, concentrating on the way the psychological effects of the disability are portrayed and the way the fictional characters manage their problems. Suggests future ways for such novels to develop.

B607 -----. "The Child's World of the Fictional Deaf." *TON* 32 (April 1976):261-67.
Examines the portrayal of deaf children in five children's books, and raises questions about the ways in which they are portrayed.

B608 SCHWARTZ, ALBERT V. "Books Mirror Society: A Study of Children's Materials." *IRBC* 11, nos. 1-2 (1980):19-24.
In this accompaniment to Batson's article, Schwartz points out "stereotypic, inaccurate and handicappist portrayals of deafness and deaf "people in children's books.

DEATH

B609 APSELOFF, MARILYN. "Death in Current Children's Fiction: Sociology or Literature." ERIC Educational Document Reproduction Service, 1974, 17 pp., ED 101 371.
Analyzes four books for the sociological and psychological attitudes they take toward death. Also examines their style, plot, and characterization. The books are *Annie and the Old One*, by Miska Miles, *The Magic Moth*, by Virginia Lee, *A Taste of Blackberries*, by Doris Buchanan Smith, and *Grover*, by Vera and Bill Cleaver.

B610 BAILIS, LAWRENCE A. "The Concept of Death in Children's Literature on Death." Ph.D. dissertation, Case Western Reserve University, 1974, 207 pp., DA 35:6566A.
"The purpose of this study was to determine and classify the concepts of death that occur in children's literature on death for ages three through twelve." Includes a bibliography of children's books about death.

B611 -----. "Death in Children's Literature: A Conceptual Analysis." *Omega* 8, no. 4 (1977-78):295-303.
Examines and classifies concepts of death in a sample of forty children's books.

B612 BEASLEY, MARY. "The Effect of Death Awareness on the Protagonists of Selected Adolescent Novels." Ed.D. dissertation, University of Tennessee, 1981, 160 pp., DA 42:3851A.

Analyzes the effect of awareness of death on the maturation process of adolescent protagonists in Paul Annixter's *Swiftwater*, Paul Zindel's *Pardon Me, You're Stepping on My Eyeball*, James Lincoln Collier and Christopher Collier's *My Brother Sam Is Dead*, Richard E. Peck's *Something for Joey*, Lois Lowry's *A Summer to Die*, Judith Guest's *Ordinary People*, John Gunther's *Death Be Not Proud*, Doris Lund's *Eric*, Norma Klein's *Sunshine*, and Gunnel Beckman's *Admission to the Feast*.

B613   BERNSTEIN, JOANNE. "Suicide in Literature for Young People." *ALAN Review* 6 (Winter 1979):5-13. (Reprinted in Lenz, *Young Adult Literature*, pp. 161-67.)

Briefly summarizes twenty-nine books for young adults, both fiction and nonfiction, that concern suicide.

B614   BIRX, CHARLES. "Concepts of Death Presented in Contemporary Realistic Children's Literature: A Content Analysis." Ed.D. dissertation, Northern Arizona University, 1979, 189 pp., DA 40:1235A.

Examines the concepts of death in contemporary realistic children's literature and evaluates the appropriateness of these concepts to various age groups.

B615   BUTLER, FRANCELIA. "Death in Children's Literature." *Children's Literature* 1 (1972):104-24.

Traces the history of the handling of death in children's literature from earliest times through George MacDonald and C.S. Lewis.

B616   CARR, ROBIN L. "Death As Presented in Children's Books." *EE* 50 (May 1973):701-5.

Surveys the treatment of death in children's literature from the 1600s to the present, from death as "poetic justice" and a religious experience, to sentimentality, vagueness, realism, and sensationalism. Concludes with an annotated bibliography of recent children's fiction treating death.

B617   CORNELISON, GAYLE LYNN. "Death and Childhood: Attitudes and Approaches in Society, Children's Literature and Children's Theatre and Drama." Ph.D. dissertation, University of Kansas, 1975, 245 pp., DA 37:37A.

Investigates the question: "Can and should the topic of death be openly and honestly presented to children in their drama?" Chapter 4 reviews critical works on the subject of death in children's literature, and chapter 6 analyzes the topic in terms of typical children's plays, while chapter 7 "considers atypical approaches in children's drama."

B618   CRAIN, HENRIETTA. "Basic Concepts of Death in Children's Literature." *EE* 49 (January 1972):111-15.

An unusual arrangement of quotations and citations from various works of children's and adult's literature that expand on a number of statements about death.

B619   DELISLE, ROBERT G., and WOODS, ABIGAIL S. "Death and Dying in Children's Literature: An Analysis of Three Selected Works." *LA* 53 (September 1976):683-87.

The three books examined are *Charlotte's Web*, by E.B. White, *The Magic Moth*, by Virginia Lee, and *A Taste of Blackberries*, by Doris Smith. Elizabeth Kubler-Ross's five stages in the acceptance of death--denial, anger, bargaining, depression, and acceptance are--used as framework.

B620   DORR, RONALD FRED. "Death Education in McGuffey's Readers, 1836-1896." Ph.D. dissertation, University of Minnesota, 1979, 416 pp., DA 40:3377A.

Concludes that McGuffey's treatment of death was "soothing and bracing" and a "powerful agent of death education, adding to the fundamental mystery of, yet confidence in, life."

B621   DORVAL, JEFFREY. "A Comparison of Selected Authors' Intended Ideas and The Actual Understandings by Young Children of Selected Primary Books in which Death is the Main Theme." Ed.D. dissertation, Temple University, 1981, 114 pp., DA 42:522A.

Investigates why five authors of books for young children chose death as a theme and explores children's understanding of the theme. Concludes that the authors had personal reasons for writing about death and determines that in the case of two authors most children did not understand the presentations, while in the case of three they had either full or partial understanding.

B622   GREEN, MARY LOU JOHNSON. "The Image of Death as Portrayed in Fiction for Children." Ed.D. dissertation, Lehigh University, 1975, 126 pp., DA 36:2501A.

Examines death imagery, vocabulary, and themes in ninety children's books.

B623   KIMMEL, ERIC A. "Beyond Death: Children's Books and the Hereafter." *Horn Book* 56 (May-June 1980):265-73.

Explores recent children's literature about death. In contrast to nineteenth-century literature, which "presented the existence of heaven as a counterpoise to the inevitability of death," modern books leave the issue unresolved. Sees as an exception Astrid Lindgren's *The Brothers Lionhart* and Ruth Nichols's *Song of the Pearl*.

B624   MARSHALL, JOANNE G., and MARSHALL, VICTOR W. "The Treatment of Death in Children's Books." *Omega* 2 (February 1971):36-45.

Uses Eulalie Steinmetz Ross's work as a critical basis for "a documented study of the treatment of death in children's books . . . to determine to what extent children's books support the developmental needs of children as they work towards a mature concept and acceptance of death." Includes reference and a briefly annotated bibliography of children's books.

B625   MOORE, DAVID; MOORE, SHARON ARTHUR; and READENCE, JOHN E. "Understanding Characters' Reactions to Death." *Journal of Reading* 26 (March 1983):540-44.

Applies Elizabeth Kubler-Ross's five stages of confronting death to the interpretation of characters' responses to death in literature.

B626   MOSS, JUDITH P. "Death in Children's Literature." *EE* 49 (April 1972):530-32.

Recommends and briefly discusses six modern books for children, including two nonfiction works.

B627 MYERS, JEANETTE. "'Werewolves' in Literature for Children." *LA* 53 (May 1976):552-56.

An exploration and report on research of young children's attitudes toward death, with references to its treatment in children's literature.

B628 PERRY, PHYLLIS. "A Comparative Analysis of the Treatment of The Death Theme in Children's and Adolescent Literature Pre and Post 1970." Ed.D. dissertation, University of Colorado at Boulder, 1980, 308 pp., DA 41:1378A.

Finds "remarkable consistency" in the handling of themes of death in children's literature during the twentieth century. Identifies major characteristics of this literature, and notes trends and areas for further research.

B629 REES, DAVID. "Timor Mortis Conturbat Me: E.B. White and Doris Buchanan Smith." In *Marble in the Water*, pp. 68-77.

Call's *Charlotte's Web* "the one great modern classic about death," and compares it with Doris Buchanan Smith's *A Taste of Blackberries*, which he also praises for its handling of death in a way that helps children to cope and grow.

B630 ROMERO, CAROL E. "The Treatment of Death in Contemporary Children's Literature." ERIC Educational Document Reproduction Service, 1975, ED 101 664.

Reviews the treatment of death in American children's literature from colonial times to the present. Relates the child's concepts of death at various developmental stages to reactions a child might display and to cultural attitudes of present-day American society toward death.

B631 SWENSSON, EVELYN J. "The Treatment of Death in Children's Literature." *EE* 49 (March 1972):401-4.

Points out that although children's literature through the end of the nineteenth-century frequently dwelt upon death, twentieth-century children's literature has all but ignored the topic until recently. Several books from the 1960s are discussed briefly.

B632 WALKER, MAXINE. "Last Rites for Young Readers." *CLE*, n.s. 9, no. 4 (Winter 1978):188-97.

Traces changing attitudes toward death in children's books, in traditional folklore, and from Victorian times to the present. Among recent examples discussed are Letitia Parr's *Flowers for Samantha*, K.M. Peyton's *A Pattern of Roses*, and books by Vera and Bill Cleaver.

B633 WASS, HANNELORE, and SHAAK, JUDITH. "Helping Children Understand Death through Literature." *Childhood Education* 53 (November 1976):80-85.

Examines the topic of death in children's literature and provides a brief annotated bibliography of children's books.

B634 WILSON, LAURA W. "Helping Adolescents Understand Death and Dying through Literature." *English Journal* 73 (November 1984):78-82.

Discusses fiction and nonfiction relevant to the study of death and dying through literature.

DEFINITIONS OF CHILDREN'S LITERATURE

B635 ARTHUR, ANTHONY. "An Interview with Clifton Fadiman." *CLE*, o.s., no. 17 (Summer 1975):67-75. (Reprinted in Culpan, *Variety is King*, pp. 94-101.)

A wide-ranging examination of a number of children's books, the nature of children's literature itself, and the goals of the magazine *Cricket*.

B636 BABBITT, NATALIE. "Happy Endings? Of Course, and Also Joy." *NYTBR*, 75, pt. 2, (8 November 1970):1, 50. (Reprinted in Haviland, *Children and Literature*, pp. 155-59.)

Suggests ways in which children's literature differs from that for adults: children's literature contains more joy, continues to retain "Everyman" as hero, bars graphic sex, but most of all usually has a happy ending.

B637 BROOKS, PETER. "Toward Supreme Fictions." *Yale French Studies* 43 (1969):5-14.

Attempts to define children's literature and concludes that what it does, better than anything else, is teach the young the power of language "to express their imaginative reformation of reality."

B638 HOLLAND, ISABELLE. "The Walls of Childhood." *Horn Book* 50 (April 1974):113-20. (Reprinted in Heins, *Crosscurrents*, pp. 27-34.)

Examines the question of what is a children's book, looking at how the answer has changed over time.

B639 HUCK, CHARLOTTE S. "Children's Literature Defined." *EE* 41 (May 1964):467-70.

Maintains that children's literature has a social conscience, a commitment, and an integrity that seeks to present sound moral and ethical principles. Criteria for evaluating children's literature are (1) lively, well-constructed, and credible plots, (2) worthy content and themes, (3) convincing characterizations, (4) action-filled style without too much description, and (5) attractive format.

B640 McDOWELL, MYLES. "Fiction for Children and Adults: Some Essential Differences." *CLE*, o.s., no. 10 (March 1973):48-63. (Reprinted in Fox, *Writers, Critics, and Children*, pp. 140-56.)

"A good children's book makes complex experience available to its readers; a good adult book draws attention to the inescapable complexity of experience." Uses many examples from modern writers.

B641 TOWNSEND, JOHN ROWE. "An Elusive Border." *Horn Book* 50 (October 1974):33-42. (Reprinted in Heins, *Crosscurrents*, pp. 41-50.)

Discusses the problems in categorizing books as "children's," "young adult," and "adult."

B642 WALSH, JILL PATON. "The Rainbow Surface." *TLS*, 3 December 1971. (Reprinted in Meek, *Cool Web*, pp. 192-95, and in Tucker, *Suitable for Children?*, pp. 212-15.)

Discusses the nature of children's books and what distinguishes them from adult fiction. Examines the problem of conveying adult thought and emotion at a level comprehensible to the child.

DENMARK

B643 BUTTENSCHØN, ELLEN. "A Curious and Particular Bird." In Koefoed, *Children's Literature and the Child*, pp. 51-53.
Discusses censorship and issues debates on Danish children's books, lamenting that the authors and the readers are not consulted.

B644 NELSON, KAREN ANNE. "Contemporary Danish Children's Authors and Illustrators." *TON* 29 (January 1973):133-45.
An overview and bibliographic essay on recent Danish children's literature.

B645 -----. "The Fidelity of the Text and Illustrations of Selected Danish Children's Fiction Translated and Published in Great Britain and the United States, Excluding Works by Hans Christian Andersen." Ph.D. dissertation, University of Minnesota, 1975, 539 pp., DA 36:1880A.
Compares the fidelity of American and British translations of Danish children's books.

B646 ROSTRUP, SUS. "Danish Picture Books." In Koefoed, *Children's Literature and the Child*, pp. 5-13.
Discusses Danish picture books, particularly those of Ib Spang Olsen, Halfdan Rasmussen, Egon Mathiesen, and Louis Moe.

B647 SHINE, NORMAN. "Danish Youth Periodicals." *Phaedrus* 4, no. 2 (Fall 1977):21-25.
Surveys the history of Danish children's periodicals, beginning in the late eighteenth century, and briefly summarizes research in the field.

DIALECT

B648 AIKEN, JOAN. "'Bred and Bawn in a Briar-Patch'--Dialect and Colloquial Language in Children's Books." *CLE*, o.s., no. 9 (November 1972):7-23.
Defends the use of dialect as a means of accepting each other's differences.

DIVORCE

B649 BARTCH, MARIAN. "Divorce--Children's Literature Style." *LA* 53 (May 1976):574-76.
Surveys current children's books on the topic.

B650 GIFFORD, RICHARD W. "A Content Analysis of Selected Adolescent Novels Dealing with Divorce, Separation, and Desertion Published between January, 1970 and May, 1979." Ph.D. dissertation, University of Colorado, 1981, 151 pp., DA 42:117A.
Compares fictional portrayals of marital breakup in twenty-eight young adult novels published between 1970 and 1979, and actual statistics and real-life studies from that time.

B651 HALEY, BEVERLY. "Once Upon a Time--They Lived Happily Ever After." *LA* 52 (November-December 1975):1147-53.

Discusses the treatment of divorce and separation, parental death, and single parents in several recent children's books. Includes a bibliography "of books that present life realistically."

B652 JENKINSON, DAVID H. "Divorce as Portrayed in Selected Juvenile Fiction Published in America between 1947 and 1977." Ph.D. dissertation, 1983, 174 pp., DA 43:3448A.
Examines the picture of divorce presented in American juvenile fiction between 1947 and 1977.

DOLLS

B653 COLWELL, EILEEN H. "Stories about Dolls." *Junior Bookshelf* 7, no. 1 (March 1943):7-11.
Examines briefly a number of doll stories.

B654 GLOVER, JOYCE. "The Doll as Heroine." *Junior Bookshelf* 35, no. 6 (December 1971):353-57; 36, no. 1 (February 1972):13-18.
Provides a brief history of dolls as heroines of children's books.

DRAGONS

B655 BERMAN, RUTH. "Victorian Dragons: The Reluctant Brood." *CLE*, n.s. 15, no. 4 (Winter 1984):220-33.
Summarizes the history of dragons in folklore and literature and discusses the Victorian handling of dragons, especially Grahame's "The Reluctant Dragon," E. Nesbit's *The Book of Dragons*, L. Frank Baum's dragons, and Tolkien's Smaug.

B656 BLOUNT, MARGARET. "Dragons." In *Animal Land*, pp. 116-30.
Identifies Kenneth Grahame's Reluctant Dragon as the prototype of most modern dragons. Also discusses a number of more recent dragons, including Sendak's Wild Things.

B657 PETERSON, VERA O. "Dragons--in General." *EE* 39 (January 1962):3-6.
Discusses the place that dragons occupy in literature of many countries. Considers Kenneth Grahame's dragon in *Dream Days*, chapter 1, separately published as *The Reluctant Dragon*, to be the most memorable of them all.

B658 STEIN, RUTH M. "The Changing Styles in Dragons--from Fafnir to Smaug." *EE* 45 (February 1968):179-83.
A brief history of the dragon in Western literature, from those of Siegfried, Beowulf, and St. George, to the soft cuddly, shy dragons of more recent literature, to Tolkien's fierce Smaug, "the truest literary dragon since Beowulf's day."

B659 YOLEN, JANE. "Dealing with Dragons." *Horn Book* 60 (June 1984):380-88.
Discusses the dragon as a symbol in literature and the dragons in her own books.

DRAMA

B660 BALLET, ARTHUR. "An Analysis of Value Judgments in Selected Secondary School Plays." Ph.D. dissertation, University of Minnesota,

1953, 632 pp., DA 14:567A.

Explores the value judgments expressed by the nine plays most frequently produced during 1950-51 in secondary schools having National Thespian affiliation.

B661   BARNIEH, ZINA ROSSO. "Some Myths in Canadian Theatre for Young Audiences." *CCL* 8-9 (1977):7-12.

Identifies the following myths: (1) children are the most difficult audience to please, (2) one can tell immediately if children do not like a play, (3) a play for children should not be too frightening, (4) plays should have happy endings, (5) plays should be easily understood, (6) there is a correct genre of theater for young audiences, and (7) we are preparing the audience of tomorrow.

B662   CHAMBERS, AIDAN. "Letter from England: Curtain Call." *Horn Book* 55 (April 1979):224-28.

Feels that the outlook for children's drama is changing, at least in England. Cites authors he feels are developing excellent material, including Alan Garner with his *Holly from the Bongs*.

B663   -----. "Letter from England: Curtain Call." *Horn Book* 59 (February 1983):96-98.

Discusses trends in plays for children, urging that more plays are needed and more critical attention must be paid.

B664   DAVIS, DESMOND. "The Participation Play for Children--A New Genre." *CCL* 8-9 (1977):19-26.

Defines and describes the participation play, citing many examples from Canadian children's theater. Includes a bibliography.

B665   DEVERELL, REX. "Towards a Significant Children's Theatre." *CCL* 8-9 (1977):13-18.

Offers criteria for play selection: (1) Is the play true? (2) Is it about something that matters? (3) Is it interesting? (4) Does it do anything?

B666   GAY, CAROL. "The Play's the Thing: The Need for Some Critical Perspectives in Children's Drama." ERIC Educational Document Reproduction Service, 1974, 8 pp., ED 101 356.

Argues that there is a dearth of good drama of "literary worth" for children, that good drama belongs to children's literature as an accepted literary genre, that it needs to be examined critically and practically on all levels, and that it needs "an active and viable body of criticism to grow in stature".

B667   HARRIS, ALBERT JAMES. "Criteria for the Evaluation of Playscripts for Children's Theatre; *The Magic Glen*: An Original Children's Play." Ed.D. dissertation, University of Tennessee, 1965, 128pp., DA 27:602A.

Develops criteria for evaluating playscripts for children's theater, and writes an original play.

B668   KINGSLEY, WILLIAM HARMSTEAD. "Happy Endings, Poetic Justice and the Depth and Strength of Characterization in American Children's Drama: A Critical Analysis." Ph.D. dissertation, University of Pittsburgh, 1964, 348 pp., DA 26:3534A.

Found that happy endings, poetic justice, and simplified and softened characterizations "were evident to the exclusion of any variations" in the children's plays written at the time of the study.

B669 LORIMER, ROWLAND M. "Playing What for Whom Out in B.C." *CCL* 8-9 (1977):61-69.

A survey of Canadian plays for children that examines several specific plays and concludes that "the majority of the plays examined were undistinguished and overly didactic."

B670 MANNA, ANTHONY L. "Special Section: Children's Drama." *ChLAQ* 9, no. 3 (1984):102-28.

Contents: Introduction by Manna, p. 102; "Sara, Jack, Ellie: Three Generations of Characters," by Roger L. Bedard, pp. 103-4, discusses changes in children's drama over the past one hundred years through an examination of the major characters in F.H. Burnett's *A Little Princess*, Charlotte B. Chorpenning's *Jack and the Beanstalk*, and Susan Zeder's *Step on a Crack*; "Beyond Pinocchio: Stylistic Developments in Plays for Young Audiences," by Jed H. Davis, pp. 105-7, 128; "The Child Audience: Toward a Theory of Aesthetic Development," by Moses Goldberg, pp. 108-10; "Instruction and Delight in Moses Goldberg's Plays for the Maturing Child," by Anthony L. Manna, pp. 111-14; "Aurand Harris: Children's Playwright," by Nellie McCaslin, pp. 114-16; "Joan Aiken: Literary Dramatist," by Marilyn Apseloff, pp. 116-18, 128; "Strindberg's Legacy to Drama for Young People," by Lowell Swortzell, pp. 119-21; "In Search of Drama: A Study of James Reaney's Plays for Children," by Kay Unruh, pp. 122-25; and "I've Heard Some of Them Before," by Susan Zeder, pp. 125-28, in which she reflects upon the experience of writing plays for children.

B671 MASHIACH, SELLINA. "Allegory in Children's Theatre and Drama." Ph.D. dissertation, University of Kansas, 1975, 243 pp., DA 37:38A.

Provides an allegorical interpretation, a structural analysis of literary sources, and an analysis of the dramatic means and structural devices of five plays: *The Blue Bird*, *Punch and Judy*, *Androcles and the Lion*, *Little Red Riding Hood*, and *Hansel and Gretel*.

B672 PERLSTEIN, SUSAN, and LAURINO, FRANK. "Children's Theater as a Reflection of Contemporary Values." *L&U* 3, no. 2 (Winter 1979-80):96-104.

Reviews two collections of plays: *Political Plays for Children*, edited and translated by Jack Zipes (St. Louis: Telos Press, 1976), and *Contemporary Children's Theatre*, edited by Betty Jean Lifton (New York: Avon, 1974).

B673 POKORNY, AMY. "Théâtre pour Enfants." *CCL* 8-9 (1977):90-97.

Describes seven French language plays, six of them written for the Théâtre Rideau Vert in Montreal, by Luan Asllani, André Cailloux, Marie-Francine Hébert, and Pierre Morency.

B674 RADLIFF, SUZANNE P. "A Study of the Techniques of Adapting Children's Literature to the Stage." Ph.D. dissertation, Bowling Green State University, 1969, 271 pp., DA 30:4601A.

Provides a critical analysis of the techniques play-wrights use in adapting literary works for the stage. Concentrates on scripts based on three literary sources: Lewis Carroll's *Alice's Adventures in Wonderland* and *Through the Looking Glass*; *Hansel and Gretel*;

and Mark Twain's *The Adventures of Tom Sawyer.*

B675　SUCKE, GREER WOODWARD. "Participation Plays for Young Audiences: Problems in Theory, Writing, and Performance." Ph.D. dissertation, New York University, 1980, 963 pp., DA 41:853A.
　　Investigates some of the problems encountered in writing participation plays for young audiences.

B676　SWORTZELL, LOWELL S. "Five Plays: A Repertory of Children's Theatre to Be Performed by and for Children." 2 vols. Ph.D. dissertation, New York University, 1963, 680 pp., DA 26:2923.
　　Includes eighty rules essential to writing a good children's play. These extend the rules for evaluating children's plays set forth by Kenneth L. Graham in his "An Introductory Study of Evaluation of Plays for Children's Theater in the United States." (Ph.D. dissertation, University of Utah, 1952.)

B677　*Use of English.* Numerous issues.
　　Contains numerous reviews of play, television, and film scripts, as well as reviews of books on theater of interest to secondary-level teachers.

B678　ZEDER, SUZAN LUCILLE. "A Character Analysis of the Child Protagonist as Presented in Popular Plays for Child Audiences." Ph.D. dissertation, Florida State University, 1978, 400 pp., DA 39:3236A.
　　Concludes that the child protagonists in popular plays for children, with whom children are supposed to identify, reinforce dependent, stereotyped characteristics and do not provide "adequate role models for older children."

B679　ZIPES, JACK. "Children's Theater in East and West Germany: Theories, Practice, and Programs." *Children's Literature* 2 (1973):173-91.
　　An overview, concentrating on developments since 1945.

B680　ZOLA, MEGUIDO. "Potions, Pies, and Puns: Participation Plays for the Primaries." *CCL* 8-9 (1977):108-12.
　　Briefly discusses four Canadian participation plays.

EASTER

B681　BADER, BARBARA. "Expanding Possibilities: Easter, for Instance." In *American Picture Books*, pp. 323-31.
　　Discusses the trend of picture books for special occasions, using Easter as an example. Considers especially DuBose Heyward's *The Country Bunny and The Little Gold Shoes*, illustrated by Marjorie Flack; Priscilla and Otto Friedrich's *The Easter Bunny that Overslept*, illustrated by Adrienne Adams; and William Littlefield's *The Whiskers of Ho Ho*, illustrated by Vladimir Bobri.

EGYPT

B682　BESHAI, JAMES A. "Content Analysis of Egyptian Stories." *Journal of Social Psychology* 87 (August 1972):197-203.
　　"Content analysis of Egyptian stories selected from children's readers, short stories, and folktales representing three periods of social change showed a significant rise in achievement imagery of

current children's readers."

ELVES

B683   CALHOUN, MARY. "Tracking Down Elves in Folklore." *Horn Book* 45 (June 1969):278-82. (Reprinted in Norton, *Folk Literature of the British Isles*, 1978, pp. 28-32.)
Examines the varieties of European elves of folklore.

ENTRAPMENT

B684   KINGSTON, CAROLYN T. "The Tragic Moment: Entrapment." In *Tragic Mode*, pp. 57-80.
Discusses a number of books for children and young people in terms of the theme of "entrapment." Individual authors and titles have been indexed separately in this bibliography.

ENVIRONMENT

B685   HEYLMAN, KATHERINE M. "The Little House Syndrome vs. Mike Mulligan and Mary Anne." *SLJ* 16 (1970):44-50. (Reprinted in Gerhardt, *Issues in Children's Book Selection*, pp. 142-53.)
Evaluates a number of fictional and informational books touching on environment, ecology, conservation, and pollution. Includes a bibliography.

EPIC LITERATURE

B686   SMITH, LILLIAN. "Heroes of Epic and Saga." In *Unreluctant Years*, pp. 80-95.
Discusses various versions of Homer's *Iliad* and *Odyssey*, from Charles Lamb to Alfred J. Church and Padraic Colum, translations of Icelandic sagas by Sir George Dasent and William Morris, and retellings by Allen French and Dorothy Hosford.

EPIPHANIES IN LITERATURE

B687   BUYZE, JEAN. "The Use of Literary Epiphany in Children's Literature." *EE* 49 (November 1972):986-88.
Discusses the crucial moments of truth in six children's books: Eleanor Estes's *The Middle Moffat*, Emily Neville's *It's Like This Cat*, Mary Stolz's *A Wonderful Terrific Time*, Evaline Ness's *Sam, Bangs and Moonshine*, Kenneth Grahame's *Wind in the Willows*, and Mary Hays Weik's *The Jazz Man*.

ESKIMOS

B688   GEDALOF, ROBIN. "Publishing Eskimo Literature: Developments in the Circumpolar World." *Phaedrus* 8 (1981):45-48.
Examines the problems and progress in publishing literature in the native languages of Eskimo peoples of the various countries of the Arctic.

B689   McGRATH, ROBIN. "Genuine Eskimo Literature: Accept No Substitutes." *CCL* 31-32 (1983):23-39.
An overview of Eskimo literature, arguing for stricter authenticity. "It is ironic that monsters, sex, and violence are routinely being

expurgated from Inuit legend by modern publishers just at a time
when they are being restored to the tales of the Brothers Grimm and
lauded in the works of Maurice Sendak."

ETHNIC GROUPS

B690 BERNSTEIN, JOANNE E. "Minorities in Fiction for Young Children."
Integrated Education 11 (May-June 1973):34-37.
Analyzes ninety-eight stories with school settings in terms of
their portrayals of minority groups. Finds trends in recent multicultural portrayals hopeful. Includes a bibliography.

B691 -----. "Minority Group Representation in Contemporary Fiction for
American Children between the Ages of 3-7." *Urban Review* 5
(May 1972):42-44.
Reports on an analysis of the way in which the primary school
experiences of minority groups is reflected in contemporary fiction
for American children.

B692 BREED, CLARA E. "Books that Build Better Racial Attitudes." *Horn
Book* 21, no. 1 (January-February 1945):55-61.
Critically surveys contemporary books about various ethnic groups:
American Indians, Mexican Americans, blacks, Jews, Germans, Ital-
ians, Chinese, and Japanese.

B693 BRODERICK, DOROTHY. "Minority Groups in Children's Books." In
Frontiers of Library Service for Youth. New York: Columbia University School of Library Service, 1979, pp. 35-42.
Comments on the philosophical background of content analysis of
literature, surveys current research on portrayals of blacks, women,
and other minorities, and summarizes what she sees as long-range
issues. Includes references.

B694 DODSON, DIANA RODGERS. "A Critical Analysis of Ethnic Coexis-
tence and Minority Representation in Selected Contemporary Junior
Novels." Ph.D. dissertation, University of Mississippi, 1977, 157 pp.,
DA 38:1377A.
Analyzes the portrayal of minority cultures in recommended juve-
nile fiction.

B695 ELKINS, HILDA ARNOLD. "An Analysis of the Social and Ethnic
Attributes of the Characters in Children's Books Which Have Won
Awards." Ed.D. dissertation, Northern Texas State University, 1967,
106 pp., DA 28:3359A.
Examines the social and ethnic group distribution of early and
recent Newbery and Caldecott award-winning books.

B696 GAST, DAVID K. "Characteristics and Concepts of Minority Americans
in Contemporary Children's Fictional Literature." Ed.D. dissertation,
Arizona State University, 1965, 206 pp., DA 27:390A.
Investigates the depiction of present-day American Indians, Chinese, Japanese, Negroes, and Spanish-Americans in children's fiction,
identifying stereotypes and comparing the portrayals to those in adult
magazine fiction and school instructional materials.

B697 -----. "Minority Americans in Children's Literature." *EE* 44 (January
1967):12-23.

Surveys characterizations of minority groups in recent children's literature and concludes that (1) traditional, uncomplimentary stereotypes have largely disappeared, (2) occupational stereotypes of all groups except the Negro are still present, (3) Japanese and Negroes are more thoroughly assimilated than are American Indians, Chinese, and Spanish-Americans; and (4) social acceptance of Negroes is dominant in books about Negroes. Recommends fewer generalizations and suggests areas for further research.

B698   GRIESE, ARNOLD. "Multi-Ethnic Literature: Where Are We Today?" *Children's Literature Assembly Bulletin* 6, no. 2 (Spring-Summer 1981).
       Summarizes conflicts between two approaches to multi-ethnic literature: the approach that sees literature as having direct instructional responsibility, exemplified by the Council on Interracial Books for Children, and a less direct approach that emphasizes developing empathetic understanding of the human condition through use of the imagination.

B699   KIMMEL, ERIC A. "Multi-Ethnic Literature--Where Are We Now?" *Children's Literature Assembly Bulletin* 6, no. 2 (Spring-Summer 1981):1-4.
       Briefly summarizes the increases in ethnic group representation in children's books in the 1960s and 1970s (it was not as great as people seem to think), then looks at the various groups: blacks, Hispanics, Native Americans, Asian Americans, and Jewish Americans. Concludes that while we have come a long way in the past two decades, we still have a long way to go.

B700   MADISON, JOHN PAUL. "Analysis of Values and Social Action in Multi-Racial Children's Literature." Ed.D. dissertation, University of Illinois at Urbana-Champaign, 1972, 138 pp., DA 34:516A.
       Identifies and analyzes "the values content and the social actions in a sample of thirty-two children's books containing interracial and intercultural settings and situations."

B701   SHAW, SPENCER G. "Legacies for Youth: Ethnic and Cultural Diversity in Books." *SLJ* 30 (December 1983):17-21.
       Traces trends and problems in ethnic and multicultural literature for the young.

B702   SINGH, M.J. "Children's Literature for Our Multicultural Society." *Orana* 17 (August 1981):92-104.
       Suggests guidelines and considerations for literature meeting the needs of Australia's many ethnic groups.

B703   WHITE, MARY LOU. "Ethnic Literature for Children: A View from the Heartland." *Catholic Library World* 51 (March 1980):326-29.
       Reports on a decrease in the publication, promotion, and use of ethnic literature for children in the 1970s.

ESTONIA

B704   VIISE, RIINA M. "Estonian Children's Literature in the Diaspora." *Phaedrus* 6, no. 1 (Spring 1979):64-71.
       Relates the history of Estonian children's literature outside of Estonia since 1944-45.

FABLES

B705   BLOUNT, MARGARET. "Folklore and Fable." In *Animal Land*, pp. 23-41.
Explores the roles of animals in fables and traditional literature.

B706   REED, JANET GRAYCE. "Sixth Graders' Need for, Use and Acquisition of Background Knowledge in Comprehending Fables." Ed.D. dissertation, Temple University, 1981, 161 pp., DA 42:636A.
Concludes that background knowledge increases students' understanding of fables.

FAIRIES

B707   AVERY, GILLIAN. "The Quest for Fairyland." *Quarterly Journal of the Library of Congress* 38, no. 4 (Fall 1981):221-27.
Examines the fascination of a number of early twentieth-century children's writers for fairies.

B708   BRIGGS, KATHERINE. *An Encyclopedia of Fairies, Hobgoblins, Brownies, Bogies, and Other Supernatural Creatures.* New York: Pantheon, 1976, 481 pp.
A comprehensive guide to fairies and other creatures from myths, legends, folklore, and fairy tales. Includes pronunciation keys, illustrations, a bibliography, and a type and motif index.

B709   ELLIS, ALEC. "Little Folk and Young People." *Junior Bookshelf* 30, no. 2 (April 1966):97-102.
Surveys briefly the role of fairies and little folk in children's literature from traditional folktales to Mary Norton's *The Borrowers.*

B710   HUNTER, MOLLIE. "The Otherworld." In *Talent Is Not Enough*, pp. 78-102.
Delves into the origins of fairies in Celtic folklore and the importance of "the otherworld" to children's literature.

FAIRY TALES

B711   ADAMS, RICHARD. Review. *NYTBR*, 3 November 1974, Children's Book sec., pp. 23, 32-36.
Reviews the reissue of Padraic Colum's 1944 edition of *The Complete Grimm's Fairy Tales* and Iona and Peter Opie's *The Classic Fairy Tales.*

B712   ARTHUR, ANTHONY. "The Uses of Bettelheim's *The Uses of Enchantment.*" *LA* 55 (April 1978):455-59, 533. (Reprinted in Barron, *Jump Over the Moon*, pp. 310-16.)
Reflects on the usefulness of Bettelheim's book to the critic of fairy tales as children's literature.

B713   ASTBURY, E.A. "Other and Deeper Worlds." *Junior Bookshelf* 39 5 (October 1975):301-5.
Argues for the benefits of fairy tales and fantasy for children.

B714   AUDEN, W.H. "Grimm and Andersen." In *Forewords and Afterwords.* New York: Random House, 1973, pp. 198-207.

Defends the use of fairy tales with children and analyzes elements in tales by Andersen and the Grimms.

B715 BARCHILON, JACQUES, and PETIT, HENRY. *The Authentic Mother Goose Fairy Tales and Nursery Rhymes.* Denver: Alan Swallow, 1960, 287 pp.

The introduction to this facsimile reprint of the original 1729 translation of Perrault's *Mother Goose's Tales* and the early *Mother Goose's Melody* includes discussions of the origins of the tales and rhymes and analysis of them as literature. Includes a bibliography, pp. 41-43.

B716 BETTELHEIM, BRUNO. *The Uses of Enchantment: The Meaning and Importance of Fairy Tales.* New York: Alfred A. Knopf, 1977, 339 pp.

Examines the "psychological meaning and impact" of fairy tales, showing how they "represent in imaginative form . . . the process of healthy human development." The second half of the book analyzes a number of tales at length: "Hansel and Gretel," pp. 159-66, "Little Red Riding Hood," pp. 166-83, "Jack and the Beanstalk," pp. 183-93, "Snow White," pp. 199-215, "Goldilocks and the Three Bears," pp. 215-24, "The Sleeping Beauty," pp. 225-36, "Cinderella," pp. 236-77, and a number of tales Bettelheim classifies as "animal groom" stories, including "Snow White and Rose Red," "The Frog King," "Cupid and Psyche," "The Enchanted Pig," "Bluebeard," and "Beauty and the Beast."

B717 BLAMIRES, DAVID. "Challenge of Fairy Tales to Literary Studies." *Critical Quarterly* 21 (Autumn 1979):33-40.

Provides a concise overview of recent approaches to fairy tales and argues that they should not be neglected by literary scholars and the schools.

B718 BLOOM, HAROLD. "Driving Out Demons." *NYRB*, 15 July 1976, p. 10.

Reviews Bettelheim's *Uses of Enchantment.* Concludes that Bettelheim is right, "but for the wrong reasons." Fairy tales are good for us "not because they are paradigms or parables that teach us how to adjust to an adult reality" but "because their uncanny energies liberate our potential for the sublime."

B719 BOWEN, ELIZABETH. "The Comeback of Goldilocks, et al." *New York Times Magazine*, 26 August 1962, pp. 18-19, 74-75.

Reflects upon the increased popularity of fairy tales and their effects on the young. Comments on their moral and aesthetic qualities, and urges that they be told or read aloud.

B720 BUCHAN, JOHN. "The Novel and the Fairy Tale." *English Association Pamphlet*, no. 79 (July 1931):6-16. (Reprinted in Haviland, *Children and Literature*, pp. 221-29.)

Identifies and classifies plots, themes, and character types of literature, especially the great Victorian novels, all traceable to folk and fairy tales.

B721 CHANG, CHARITY. "The Psychological Implications of Fairy Tales." In Robinson, M., *Readings in Children's Literature*, pp. 207-19.

Summarizes the approaches of Von Franz and others to the psychological truths of fairy tales and argues for their suitability for children. Includes extensive references.

B722 CHESTERTON, G.K. "Fairy Tales." In *All Things Considered.* New York: Sheed & Ward, 1956, pp. 186-90.

Argues that fairy tales are, above all, moral, and that through them all runs the theme "that peace and happiness can exist only on some condition." The basis for the morality of fairy tales is not logical but mystical.

B723 -----. "The Red Angel." In *Tremendous Trifles.* New York: Sheed & Ward, 1955, pp. 85-89.

Argues that fairy tales are suitable for children, rebutting a number of common objections.

B724 CHUKOVSKY, KORNEI. "The Inevitability of Story Telling: There Is No Such Thing as a Shark." In *Two to Five,* pp. 118-20. (Reprinted in Meek, *Cool Web,* pp. 48-50, and in Haviland, *Children and Literature,* pp. 213-20, entitled "The Battle for the Fairy Tale: Three Stages.")

Argues that if fairy tales are denied to a child, he or she will make up similar tales.

B725 COOK, ELIZABETH. *The Ordinary and the Fabulous: An Introduction to Myths, Legends and Fairy Tales for Teachers and Storytellers.* Cambridge: Cambridge University Press, 1969, 152 pp.

Following introductory material on "myths, legends and fairy tales in the lives of children," and sections on choices of materials and suggestions for classroom presentations for various ages, Cook attempts to show the "language and temper of fabulous storytelling" through the examination of several versions of seven "crucial scenes" from traditional literature. The scenes are (1) Medea Bewitches the Serpent while Jason Snatches the Golden Fleece from the Grove of Ares, pp. 60-67, (2) Odysseus is Driven by Storm to the Coast of Phaeacia, pp. 68-77, (3) The Golden Touch of King Midas, pp. 78-85, (4) The Lair of Grendel's Mother, and Beowulf's Fight with Her Beneath the Waters of the Lake, pp. 86-93, (5) Gawain's Winter Journey and His First Sight of the Green Knight's Castle on Christmas Eve, pp. 94-101, (6) Cinderella's Sisters Get Ready for a Ball, pp. 102-12 and, (7) The Courtiers of the Emperor of China Look for the Real Nightingale, and the Artificial Nightingale Takes Her Place, pp. 113-20. Includes an annotated "Short List of Books" of versions for children, originals in translation, and background reading.

B726 COOPER, SUSAN. "A Review of *Womenfolk and Fairy Tales.*" *NYTBR,* 13 April 1975, p. 8. (Reprinted in Butler, *Sharing,* pp. 331-32.)

Feels that concern about sex roles in fairy tales is "an adult neurosis foisted upon children." Concludes that "ten television commercials can do more to damage your daughter's image of Woman than ten centuries of fairy tales."

B727 DARNTON, ROBERT. "The Meaning of Mother Goose." *NYRB* 31, no. 1 (2 February 1984):41-47.

Examines many versions and variants of well-known fairy tales collected in France in the seventeenth century and concludes that (1) although the tales contain touches of fantasy they are rooted in reality (the desire for food is paramount), (2) the tales reveal some particularly French characteristics (especially a reliance on wit and tricksterism), and (3) they also provide insights into the subsequent course of French history. See also Jack Zipes's letter in response in 31 (10 May 1984):4712.

B728 DUFF-STEWART, C. "The Dragon's Grandmother." *Junior Bookshelf* 22 (March 1958):47-54.
Argues for the benefits of fairy tales for children. Sees a key characteristic as "interesting plot." Lists tales in the categories of accumulative tales, droll stories, realistic tales, talking beast stories, and tales of magic. Also mentions some of the best-known collectors and collection of tales.

B729 FAVAT, ANDRE. *Child and Tale: The Origins of Interest.* Research Report no. 19. Urbana, Ill.: National Council of Teachers of English, 1977, 102 pp. (Based on Ed.D. dissertation, Harvard University, 1971, DA 32:2480A.)
Examines the question, "What is it about the reader and the book that causes interest?" Analyzes the child's psychological background as set forth by Piaget, but also looks at Bettelheim's and Jung's interpretations. Analyzes the fairy tales of Grimm and Andersen by using Propp's *Morphology of the Folktale.* By combining the approaches of Piaget and Propp, Favat determines that the tales "embody an accurate representation of the child's conception of the world," particularly in regard to "the child's egocentrism and conceptions of animism, causality, magic, and certain aspects of morality."

B730 FLAUMENHAFT, A.S. "Children's 'Sick' Stories." *Educational Forum* 33 (May 1969):473-77.
Argues that demoralizing and violent comic books and television programs are mild in comparison with the brutality, violence, and viciousness of such fare as "The Three Little Pigs," "Little Red Riding Hood," and other traditional tales for children.

B731 FRAIBERG, SELMA. "Tales of Discovery of the Secret Treasure." *Psychoanalytic Study of the Child* 9 (1954):218-41.
Provides a psychoanalytic interpretation of the meaning of myths and stories concerning buried treasure so popular with children. Among tales discusses at length are "Aladdin," Robert Louis Stevenson's *Treasure Island*, H.C. Andersen's "The Tinder Box," "Ali Baba and the Forty Thieves," and D.H. Lawrence's "The Rocking Horse Winner."

B732 GÁG, WANDA. "I Like Fairy Tales." *Horn Book* 15 (April-May 1939):75-80.
Defends the "goriness" of fairy tales and emphasizes their folk origins and deep roots.

B733 -----. Introduction to *Tales from Grimm.* New York: Coward, McCann, 1936, pp. vii-xiii.
Describes her approach to translating the tales and provides insights into their origins, meanings, and complexities.

B734 GARDNER, HOWARD. "Brief on Behalf of Fairy Tales." *Semiotica* 21, nos. 3-4 (1977). (Reprinted in *Phaedrus* 5, no. 2 [Fall

1978]:14-23.)

Comments on Bettelheim's theories as developed in *The Uses of Enchantment*. Generally favorable, although some of Bettelheim's premises are questioned and suggestions for further research that might prove or disprove Bettelheim's hypotheses are made.

B735   GREENE, ELLIN. "'A Peculiar Understanding': Recreating the Literary Fairy Tale." *Horn Book* 59 (June 1983):270-78.

Discusses the literary fairy tale--"a piece of imaginative writing that often uses the form and motifs of the traditional folk tale but has an identifiable author."

B736   HARTLAND, EDWIN S. "The Forbidden Chamber." *Folk-Lore Journal* III (1885):193-242.

Examines a number of folktales with the forbidden chamber motif.

B737   HARTMANN, WALTRAUT. "Identification and Projection in Folk Fairy-Tales and in Fantastic Stories for Children." *Bookbird* 7, no. 2 (1969):8-17.

Concerns the following three questions: (1) "What characteristics must literature, and in particular the hero figure, have to insure that the child will instinctively and necessarily identify with the hero?" (2) "What psychological processes occur within the child when he identifies with the hero of a story?" and (3) "What functions does this process of identification fulfill in the development of the child's personality?"

B738   HEISIG, JAMES. "Bruno Bettelheim and the Fairy Tale." *Children's Literature* 6 (1977):93-114.

Although Heisig feels Bettelheim's study of fairy tales is welcome and timely, and that he succeeds in opening the tales up, he disagrees with some of Bettelheim's basic premises and interpretations, specifically his interpretations of "Rapunzel," "Cinderella," and "Sleeping Beauty."

B739   HOFER, M. "A Study of the Favorite Childhood Fairy Tales of an Adult Psychiatric Population." Ph.D. dissertation, California School of Professional Psychology, San Francisco, 1976, 196 pp., DA 37:4683A.

Examines "the relationship between favorite childhood fairy tales and the psychodynamics of an adult psychiatric population."

B740   HOOKER, BRIAN. "Fairy Tales." *Forum* 40 (1908):375-84. (Reprinted in Bator, *Signposts*, pp. 168-76.)

Discusses modern and traditional fairy tales in terms of symbolism. Sees them as the purest form of romance in the broadest sense, and as, above all, disclosers of truth.

B741   HORNYANSKY, MICHAEL. "The Truth of Fables." In Egoff, *Only Connect*, pp. 121-32.

A modern father takes a psychological approach to the appeal of the classic fairy tales, emphasizing "Snow White," "Hansel and Gretel," "Jack and the Beanstalk," and "Rumpelstiltzkin."

B742   HORRELL, RUTH C. "Fairy Tales and Their Effect Upon Children." *Illinois Libraries* 38 (September 1956):235-39; (November 1956):278-82.

(Reprinted in Robinson, E. *Readings about Children's Literature*, pp. 263-76.)

Defines traditional and modern fairy tales, summarizes criticism for and against their effect on children, and concludes that they should be used with judgment and mixed with realistic stories. Includes references.

B743 HÜRLIMANN, BETTINA. "Once Upon a Time: Some Notes on Fairy Stories and How They Have Come Down to Us." In *Three Centuries*, pp. 21-44.

Identifies the distinguishing characteristics of fairy tales and examines the ways in which they have been transmitted.

B744 HUTCHINSON, EARL R. "These Modern Children's Tales." *EE* 35 (November 1958):456-68.

Questions the modern, softened and expurgated versions of some of the classic fairy tales.

B745 JACKSON, ANTHONY. "The Science of Fairy Tales?" *Folklore* 84 (Summer 1973):120-41.

Proposes a method of charting the misfortunes that occur in fairy tales and a means of studying "shifts in the meaning and beliefs about spirits in Britain."

B746 JACOBS, LELAND B. "Another Look at the Fairy Tales." *Reading Teacher* 14 (November 1960):108-11.

Suggests criteria for selecting fairy tales to be shared with individual children.

B747 LANES SELMA. "America as Fairy Tale." In *Down the Rabbit Hole*, pp. 91-111.

Traces America's own fairy tales, from Washington Irving's "Rip Van Winkle," through Baum, Thurber, Sendak, and others.

B748 LANGFELDT, J. "The Educational and Moral Values of Folk and Fairy Tales." *Junior Bookshelf* 25 (January 1961):7-15. (Reprinted in Tucker, *Suitable for Children?*, pp. 56-63.)

Summarizes past and present objections to fairy tales on moral and educational grounds, concurring with some of the objections but defending certain tales and their uses. Argues that children should be given tales that help them develop courage and security, and that tales such as "Hansel and Gretel" and "Cinderella" should not be given to them.

B749 LIEBERMAN, MARCIA. "Some Day My Prince Will Come: Female Acculturation through the Fairy Tale." *College English* 34 (December 1972):383-95. (Reprinted in Butler, *Sharing*, pp. 332-43.)

Analyzes the portrayal of women in Andrew Lang's selection of tales in *The Blue Fairy Book*. Points out that "There are only a few powerful good women in *The Blue Fairy Book* and they are nearly all fairies." Speculates on the impact that the traditional attributes of femininity as portrayed in popular children's literature may have on children.

B750 LURIE, ALISON. "Fairy Tales for a Liberated Age." *Horizon* 19, no. 4 (July 1977):80-85.

Selects three tales depicting women who "are not only beautiful and good, but also strong, brave, clever, and resourceful," and provides a brief introduction detailing why these tales have been neglected and remain largely unknown. The tales are "Clever Gretchen," "Molly Whuppie," and "Tomlin."

B751 -----. "Witches and Fairies: Fitzgerald to Updike." *NYRB* 17 (2 December 1971):6-11.

Explores four roles of women--(1) princess, (2) the poor girl who marries the prince, (3) the fairy godmother or wise woman, and (4) the wicked stepmother or witch--in traditional fairy tales and in modern literature. Sees the legacy of "Cap O'Rushes" in Fitzgerald's *Tender Is The Night*, Cinderella in *Jane Eyre* and Jean Stafford's *Boston Adventure*, the wicked stepmother in Philip Roth's Sophie Portnoy in *Portnoy's Complaint*, and the wise woman witch in John Updike's Mrs. Robinson in *Of the Farm*.

B752 LÜTHI, MAX. *Once Upon a Time: On the Nature of Fairy Tales*. New York: Frederick Ungar Publishing Co., 1970, 179 pp.

Applies techniques of literary analysis to the study of fairy tales. Among tales discussed at length are "Sleeping Beauty," "Cinderella," "Hansel and Gretel," the "White Snake," and "Rapunzel" (as a representation of a maturation process), as well as numerous other less familiar tales. Also includes discussions on saints' legends and local legends, style, symbolism, animal stories, riddle tales, the image of the hero, and the miracle in literature. Includes extensive references.

B753 MacDONALD, RUTH K. "The Tale Re-Told: Feminist Fairy Tales in Modern Collections." *Proceedings of the Children's Literature Association* 9 (1982):112-16. (Reprinted in *ChLAQ* 7, no. 2 [Summer 1982]:18-20.)

Discusses three options available to feminists who dislike the role models presented in traditional fairy tales: write new tales, retell old ones, or stay with the original versions. Concludes that, at least for the time being, the old tales are the best.

B754 MacVEAGH, CHARLES PETER, and SHANDS, FRANCES. "Fairy Stories: Fantasy, Fact, or Forecast?" *LA* 59 (April 1982):328-35.

Proposes that the giants, dwarfs and goblins, fairies, transformations, and talking animals of fairy tales may provide a glimpse of facts from a long-lost past or even "foretell of future discoveries of things once known by some high civilizations of the past." Includes references.

B755 MARKMAN, ROBERTA HOFFMAN. "The Fairy Tale: An Introduction to Literature and the Creative Process." *College English* 45 (January 1983):31-45.

Discusses teaching fairy tales to college students and relating the tales to more sophisticated forms of literature.

B756 MAY, JILL P. "American Literary Fairy Tale and Its Classroom Use." *Journal of Reading* 22 (November 1978):149-52.

Defines the literary fairy tale and discusses its appeal to young people, especially in the stories of Washington Irving, Frank Stockton, Carl Sandburg, Evaline Ness's *The Girl and the Goatherd*, and Patricia Coombs's *Mouse Cafe*. Includes a bibliography and references.

B757   MOORE, ROBERT. "From Rags to Witches: Stereotypes, Distortions and Anti-Humanism in Fairy Tales." *IRBC* 6, no. 7 (1975):1-3.
Argues that fairy tales reinforce many "unhealthy and destructive images" for the reader. Points out examples of overemphasis on beauty, the inferior role of women, materialism, magic and luck, elitism, and "whiteness."

B758   MOSS, ANITA. "Crime and Punishment, or Development in Fairy Tales." *Proceedings of the Children's Literature Association* 7 (1980):132-38.
Contrasts didactic fairy tales with fantasies in terms of techniques used to express "complex spiritual, ethical, or emotional truths." Modern works discussed include Roald Dahl's *Charlie and the Chocolate Factory*, Andrew Lang's *The Gold of Fairnilee*, and Natalie Babbitt's *Tuck Everlasting*.

B759   MOUSTAKIS, CHRISTINA, ed. "Special Section: Fairy Tales: Their Staying Power." *ChLAQ* 7, no. 2 (Summer 1982):2-37.
Articles include "Criticism in the Woods: Fairy Tales as Poetry," by Roderick McGillis, pp. 2-8; "Teaching a Unit of Fairy Tales," by Perry Nodelman pp. 9-11; "The Importance of Being Ernest: The Fairy Tale in 19th-century England," by Patricia Miller, pp. 11-14; "Varieties of Fairy Tale," by Anita Moss, pp. 15-17; "The Tale Retold: Feminist Fairy Tales," by Ruth MacDonald, pp. 18-20; "The Grimms' Housekeepers: Women in Transition Tales," by Janet Spaeth, pp. 20-22; "Towards a Social History of the Literary Fairy Tale for Children," by Jack Zipes, pp. 23-26; "A Pica for Heads: Illustrating Violence in Fairy Tales," by Christina Moustakis, pp. 26-30; "From Rags to Riches: Fairy Tales and the Family Romance," by Maria M. Tatar, pp. 31-34; and "Initiatory Scenarios: Von Franz's Archetypal Approach to Fairy Tales," by Joyce A. Thomas, pp. 35-37.

B760   NICHOLSON, DAVID B., III. "The Fairy Tale in Modern Drama." Ph.D. dissertation, City University of New York, 1982, 442 pp., DA 43:1349A.
Traces the influence of fairy tales and their motifs on modern drama.

B761   NODELMAN, PERRY. "And the Prince Turned into a Peasant and Lived Happily Ever After." *Children's Literature* 11 (1983):171-74.
Review of Jack Zipes's *Breaking the Magic Spell: Radical Theories of Folk and Fairy Tales*. Concludes that fairy tales allow us to devise our own meanings, and to "explore and discover ourselves and our own stories. Wise children respect and enjoy that gift; so should wise critics."

B762   -----. Review of Jack Zipes's *Fairy Tales and the Art of Subversion* and *The Trials and Tribulations of Little Red Riding Hood. ChLAQ* 9, no. 2 (Summer 1984):81-82.
Nodelman feels that Zipes misrepresents both history and the tales he is analyzing in order to make his case. Zipes responds in *ChLAQ* 9, no. 3 (Fall 1984):131-32. For a more favorable response to *The Trials and Tribulations of Little Red Riding Hood* see Roni Natov's review in *Children's Literature* 13 (1985):199-203.

B763   OPIE, IONA, and OPIE, PETER. *The Classic Fairy Tales.* Oxford: Oxford University Press, 1974, 255 pp.

"Introduction," pp. 11-28, provides an overview of the fairy tales, with discussions of Perrault, Madame d'Aulnoy, Madame de Beaumont, the Grimms, and Andersen. Each tale is also preceded by a scholarly essay. Tales included, in the versions in which they first appeared in English, are "Tom Thumb," "Jack the Giant Killer," "The Yellow Dwarf," "Sleeping Beauty," "Little Red Riding Hood," "Diamonds and Toads," "Bluebeard," "Puss in Boots," "Cinderella," "Hop o' my' Thumb," "Beauty and the Beast," "The Three Wishes," "The Three Heads in the Well," "Jack and the Beanstalk," "Snow White and the Seven Dwarfs," "The Frog Prince," "The Twelve Dancing Princesses," "Rumpelstiltskin," "Goldilocks and the Three Bears," "The Tinder Box," "The Princess and the Pea," "Thumbelina," "The Swineherd," and "Hansel and Gretel."

B764   PROPP, VLADIMIR. *The Morphology of Folktales.* Bloomington: Publications of the Indiana University Center in Anthropology, Folklore, and Linguistics, no. 10, 1958, 134 pp.
       This pioneering structural analysis of Russian fairy tales has been extremely influential.

B765   RAUSCH, HELEN MARTHA. "The Debate Over Fairy Tales." Ph.D. dissertation, Columbia University Teachers College, 1977, 266 pp., DA 38:3918A.
       Outlines the historical and psychological backgrounds of the twentieth-century debates over the "suitability" of fairy tales for children. Summarizes arguments for and against, concluding that "the weight of general opinion points to sustained support for fairy tales."

B766   RÓHEIM, GÉZA. "Fairy Tale and Dream." *Psychoanalytic Study of the Child* 8 (1953):394-403.
       Applies techniques of dream interpretation to two fairy tales: "Little Red Riding Hood" and "Fearless John."

B767   ROSCOE, WILLIAM CALDWELL. "*Signal* Reprints: Children's Fairy Tales and George Cruikshank." *Signal* 9 (September 1972):115-22.
       Castigates Cruikshank's rewriting of the tales, but praises his illustrations.

B768   ROWE, KAREN E. "Feminism and Fairy Tales." *Women's Studies* 6 (1979):237-57.
       Concludes that "fairy tales perpetuate the patriarchal status quo by making female subordination seem a romantically desirable, indeed an inescapable fate."

B769   RUSKIN, JOHN. "*Signal* Reprints: Fairy Stories." *Signal* 8 (May 1972):81-86.
       From the introduction to *German Popular Stories*, edited by Edward Taylor (1868). Ruskin expresses his admiration for the tales and for Cruikshank's illustrations.

B770   RYAN, CALVIN T. "Advocate for the Fairies." *EER* 11 (December 1934):268-71, 278.
       Summarizes arguments pro and con fairy tales and concludes that there are no rules, but fairy tales "represent the childhood of a race, hence are most suitable for children. They are no more bad, wicked, cruel, vulgar, or immoral than a child can be."

B771   SALE, ROGER. "Fairy Tales." *Hudson Review* 30 (Autumn 1977):372-394.
       Comments upon the insights and excesses of Bettelheim's approach to fairy tales and attempts to explain his own approach, which acknowledges them as "the great well of narrative possibility; when one is there the stories can go anywhere because life, crimped and fearful though it be, is wonderful and full and one must accept it all."

B772   -----. ""Fairy Tales" and "Written Tales: Perrault to Andersen." In *Fairy Tales*, pp. 23-47 and 49-75.
       The first chapter discusses folktales, especially "Snow White" and "The Juniper Tree." The second chapter emphasizes more highly embellished tales like "The Green Snake," "Beauty and the Beast," "The Little Mermaid," and "The Snow Queen."

B773   SCHERF, WALTER. "Family Conflicts and Emancipation in Fairy Tales." *Children's Literature* 3 (1974):77-93.
       Examines family conflicts as portrayed in folktales as a means of understanding the nature of the tales. Includes references.

B774   SEGAL, ELIZABETH. "Feminists and Fairy Tales." *SLJ* 29 (January 1983):30-31.
       Surveys 1970s feminist criticism of fairy tales and concludes that the criticism has resulted in recent collections of tales emphasizing strong heroines.

B775   SMITH, LILLIAN. "The Art of the Fairy Tale." *Unreluctant Years*, pp. 45-63.
       Analyzes "Sleeping Beauty," "Three Billy Goats Gruff," and "Puss n' Boots" to show national and universal characteristic of each. Points out the style and details that make them "great literature."

B776   STONE, KAY F. "Märchen to Fairy Tale: An Unmagical Transformation." *Western Folklore* 40 (July 1981):232-44.
       Explores the reasons fairy tales have become the domain of children.

B777   -----. "Romantic Heroines in Anglo-American Folk and Popular Literature." Ph.D. dissertation, Indiana University, 1975, 406 pp., DA 36:3016A.
       Analyzes the occurrence and roles of heroines in popular fairy tales and finds that the passive and pretty princesses, while most popular in North America, are not in fact the most prevalent type of heroines, but "retain their position in part because they coincide with the feminine ideal still maintained for North American women."

B778   STORR, CATHERINE. "Why Folk Tales and Fairy Stories Live Forever." *Where* 53 (January 1971):8-11. (Reprinted in Tucker, *Suitable for Children?*, pp. 64-73, and in Bator, *Signposts*, pp. 177-84.)
       Argues that fairy tales survive because they reflect man's "desire to impose a pattern on what mystifies and frightens him." They should be valued for "their beautiful form and for their message."

B779   SWINDELLS, MINNIE H. "Fairy Tales as Folklore." *EER* 11 (January 1934):5-8, 30; (February 1934):1-45; (March 1934):81-85.

Sees fairy tales as containing elements of primitive beliefs and practices of faraway ancestors and reflecting tribal rituals, customs, and organization as presented in *The Science of Fairy Tales*, by Edwin Sidney Hartland. Concludes with an analysis of Perrault's versions of "Little Red Riding Hood" and "The Three Billy Goats Gruff."

B780 TAYLOR, PAULINE BIRD. "Ethics in Fairy and Household Tales." *EER* 17 (May 1940):190-91, 198.
Contends that fairy tales do not offer a code of ethics for children. States four reasons for the twisted ethical conception found in fairy tales. Concludes they should simply be enjoyed as entertainment.

B781 TAYLOR, UNA ASHWORTH. "*Signal Reprints*: Fairy Tales as Literature." *Signal* 21 (September 1976):123-38; 22 (January 1977):48-56.
Reprinted from *Edinburgh Review*, July 1898. Presents a strong argument in favor of fairy tales for children.

B782 THOMAS, JOYCE AUGUSTA. "The Fairy Tale: An Analysis of Matter, Rhetoric, and Theme." Ph.D. dissertation, State University of New York, Albany, 1978, 411 pp., DA 39:6109A.
Analyzes fairy tales from a literary perspective in terms of the functions of physical things, the role of animals, analysis of character, form and structure, and language and theme. Concludes that the fairy tale is "a genuine work of art."

B783 TOLKIEN, J.R.R. "On Fairy Stories." Excerpt in *Horn Book* 39 (October 1963):457.
Provides an influential definition and defense of fairy tales.

B784 TRAVERS, P.L. "Grimm's Women." *NYTBR*, 16 November 1975, Children's Book sec., p. 59.
Finds the fairy tales provide endless prototypes for women.

B785 TUCKER, NICHOLAS. "Dr. Bettelheim and Enchantment." *Signal* 43 (January 1984):33-41.
Provides an extended critique of Bettelheim's interpretations.

B786 -----. "Fairy Stories, Myths and Legends." In *The Child and the Book*, pp. 67-96.
Explores the significance for children of fairy tales, myths, and legends.

B787 -----. "Part One: Fairy Stories." In *Suitable for Children?*, pp. 31-73.
Summarizes arguments and approaches to fairy tales and includes excerpts by Mrs. Trimmer, George Cruikshank, Charles Dickens, J. Langfeldt, and Catherine Storr.

B788 USPENSKY, LEV. "How Marvelous Are These Fairy Tales." *Anglo-Soviet Journal* 35 (May 1975):35-40. (Translated from *Literaturnaya Gazeta* 29, no. 1, [1975] by James Riordan.)
Defends the folktale as a rich source of moral education.

B789 VON FRANZ, MARIE-LOUISE. *An Introduction to the Psychology of Fairy Tales* [Title on cover: *Interpretation of Fairy Tales*] 2d ed. Zurich, Switzerland: Spring Publications, 1973, 155 pp.

Offers a Jungian interpretation of fairy tales and interprets the Grimm's "The Three Feathers" to demonstrate her methods.

B790   WILSON, ANNE. "The Civilizing Process in Fairy Tales." *Signal* 44 (May 1984):81-88.
Discusses Jack Zipes's *The Trials and Tribulations of Little Red Riding Hood* and his *Fairy Tales and the Art of Subversion*. Disagrees with Zipes's overreliance on Marxist and feminist interpretations of the tales, to the exclusion of the psychological, which she feels runs deeper. Wilson admits that Zipes offers new perspectives and valuable information.

B791   -----. "Magical Thought in Story." *Signal* 36 (September 1981):138-51.
Reports on her pursuit of the nonsense and absurdities in traditional literature that is also full of good sense. She tries to determine a level at which the absurdities make sense. Includes discussions of "Jack and the Beanstalk," "The Golden Bird," "The Goose Girl," and "The King of the Golden Mountain," and concludes with an extended discussion of Daphne du Maurier's *Rebecca*.

B792   -----. *Traditional Romance and Tale--How Stories Mean.* London: D.S. Brewer, 1976, 116 pp.
Examines medieval romances and traditional fairy tales as dreamlike forms in which the reader-listener's identification with the protagonist is paramount. Shows how this interpretation enables us to make sense of much that appears to be illogical and accounts for the tales' lasting popularity and deep appeal.

B793   WRIGHT, MAY M. "Terrible Tales for Tots." *EER* 18 (May 1941):190-91.
Summarizes some of the "terrible" incidents from traditional children's literature and is happy to report that now children are able to find up-to-date nonfiction and realistic and inspiring juvenile stories to replace the gloomy old tales.

B794   YOLEN, JANE. *Touch Magic: Fantasy, Faerie and Folklore in the Literature of Childhood.* New York: Philomel, 1981, 96 pp.
Includes "The Lively Fossil," pp. 21-28, which discusses the ways in which folk and fairy tales and their variants have been passed on; "Once Upon a Time," pp. 29-39, which examines transformations and values in "Little Red Riding Hood," "The Princess and the Frog," and "Cinderella"; "The Eye and the Ear" (reprinted in Dooley, *First Steps*, pp. 133-34), which discusses the role of illustrations in fairy tales, and compares the Burkert, Hyman, and Disney versions of "Snow White"; "Touch Magic," pp. 49-57, which explores the ways in which the fairy tales "catch a glimpse of the soul beneath the skin"; "The Mask on the Lapel," pp. 61-67, "Tough Magic," pp.69-74, and "Here There Be Dragons," pp. 75-79, which explore the role of fantasy. The final section, "Wild Child, Feral Child," pp. 83-91, explores wild children in folklore and in real life.

B795   ZIPES, JACK. *Breaking the Magic Spell: Radical Theories of Folk and Fairy Tales.* Austin: University of Texas Press, 1979, 201 pp. (Excerpt reprinted in May, *Children and Literature*, pp. 14-33.)
Places the fairy tales in their social and historical settings and then views them in terms of their values, separating good from bad, and suggesting ways in which the tales could be revised to be more

acceptable. He attacks Bettelheim's approach and interpretations. See Nodelman and Wilson (above) for in-depth reviews of Zipes's approach.

B796   -----. *Fairy Tales and the Art of Subversion: The Classical Genre for Children and the Process of Civilization*. London: Heinemann; New York: Wildman Press, 1983, 214 pp.
Concentrating on the fairy tales most often read by children in English-speaking countries, Zipes shows how the tales are used to repress and indoctrinate children.

B797   -----. "On the Use and Abuse of Folk and Fairy Tales with Children." *Proceedings of the Children's Literature Association* 5 (1978):113-22.
Critical of Bettelheim's views, Zipes presents his own theories on "the importance of the imaginative components in folk and fairy tales" and suggests "ways in which they can be used with children to heighten their awareness of the social forces acting upon them." Uses "Cinderella" as example.

B798   -----. "The Potential of Liberating Fairy Tales for Children." *New Literary History* 13 (Winter 1982):309-25.
Explores means of liberating fairy tales from repressive and regressive social and political values and points out hindrances to this.

FAMILY STORIES

B799   BERNARD, JOY. "The Image of The Family in Young Adult Literature." Ph.D. dissertation, Arizona State University, 1981, 257 pp., DA 42:4271A.
Examines the quality of family life as portrayed in "twenty-two outstanding contemporary young adult novels."

B800   BOOTHBY, PAULA. "Three Dimensions of the Parental Role in Selected Children's Literature, 1950-1974." Ed.D. dissertation, University of North Dakota, 1975, 220 pp., DA 37:702A.
Concludes that children's fiction has moved toward "the depiction of a parenting figure who appears less emotionally supportive and acceptive of the fictional child, while at the same time more concerned about the child's development intellectually, socially, and emotionally."

B801   CHAUDOIR, MARY HYDE. "The Single Parent Family in Contemporary Realistic Fiction for Young People." Ph.D. dissertation, Indiana University, 1979, 169 pp., DA 40:1731A.
Reports on a study of sixty-two contemporary realistic novels published in the United States from 1964 through 1974.

B802   CROUCH, MARCUS. *The Nesbit Tradition*, pp. 171-83.
Discusses the family stories of Antonia Forest, Gillian Avery, Kathleen Peyton, Meriol Trevor, and others. Points out American and Australian influences, and comments on Margot Benary's *The Ark* and the works of Irish writer Patricia Lynch.

B803   ELLIS, ALEC, and ELLIS, ANNE. "The Family Story as a Reflection of Reality." *Junior Bookshelf* 31 (October 1967):303-7.
Brief reflections on the origins of the family story and its ability to reflect life and incorporate social commentary.

B804 ELLIS, ANNE W. *The Family Story in the 1960s*. London: Clive Bingley, 1970, 105 pp.

Traces the evolution of the family story from its beginnings, concentrating on its evolution during the 1960s. "This is an attempt to capture a picture of family life in the 1960s as reflected in children's books of the period from three main angles: human relationships; everyday life; and problems facing the characters." Includes bibliographies of children's books and secondary sources.

B805 ELLISON, CAROLYN. "A Study to Determine the Credibility of Foster Home Situations Portrayed in Contemporary Realistic Fiction for Purposes of Reading Guidance." Ph.D. dissertation, Michigan State University, 1982, 253 pp., DA 43:1454A.

Found that there is room for improvement in the realistic portrayal of foster homes in realistic fiction for adolescents.

B806 FINCKE, KATE. "The Breakdown of the Family: Fictional Case Studies in Contemporary Novels for Young People." *L&U* 3, no. 2 (Winter 1979-80):86-95.

Discusses books portraying families in trouble, or lacking adult leadership: Isabelle Holland's *Man Without a Face*, Susan Terris's *The Downing Boy*, Louise Fitzhugh's *Nobody's Family Is Going to Change*, and Vera and Bill Cleaver's *Where the Lilies Bloom*.

B807 GILLIS, RUTH J. "An Exploratory Study of Divorce, Religion, and Discipline in Family Relationships as Found in the Texts and Illustrations of Picture Books." Ed.D. dissertation, Indiana University, 1977, 144 pp., DA 38:5234A.

Examines the treatment of the selected topics in picture books designed for children from ages five through eight.

B808 JAN, ISABELLE. "The Home." In *On Children's Literature*, pp. 90-121.

Explores the development of attitudes toward home and family life in children's literature, particularly in the nineteenth century.

B809 KAROLIDES, NICHOLAS J. "The Trouble with Parents." *Wisconsin English Journal* 20, no. 2 (January 1978):23-26. (ERIC Educational Document Reproduction Service, ED 149 373.)

Examines changes in the depictions of parents in the adolescent novel from the 1940s through the 1970s.

B810 LUKENBILL, W. BERNARD. "Fathers in Adolescent Novels: Some Implications for Sex Role Interpretations." *SLJ* 20 (February 1974):26-30. (Reprinted in Lenz, *Young Adult Literature*, pp. 245-54.)

Reports on a survey that examined the "father image in a body of fiction currently recommended for children and adolescents."

B811 LYSTAD, MARY. *At Home In America: As Seen Through Its Books for Children*. Cambridge, Mass.: Schenkman, 1984, 154 pp.

Traces the history of the family story in American children's books from colonial times to 1980.

B812 -----. "Family as Seen in American Books for Children." *Children Today* 8 (March-April 1979):2-5.

Traces changes from idealistic to realistic portrayals of family life from the eighteenth and nineteenth centuries to the present.

B813 McBRIDE, WILLIAM L. "Parent-Adolescent Relationships and Familial Environments in the Realistic Problem Novel: A Content Analysis." Ph.D. dissertation, University of North Carolina, Chapel Hill, 1982, 174 pp., DA 43:1493A.

Examines the characteristic familial environments and interpersonal relationships portrayed in 103 adolescent novels published between 1967 and 1980.

B814 POSTON, GAYLE TERESA. "Preadolescent Needs and Problems as Seen in Family Life Fiction Published between the Years 1965 and 1975: A Content Analysis." Ph.D. dissertation, Florida State University, 1977, 242 pp., DA 38:1717A. (Summarized in *TON* 34 [Summer 1978]:342-47.)

Reports on an examination of sixty books published from 1965 to 1975 in categories relating to family life to see the ways in which preadolescent needs and problems were portrayed.

FANTASY

B815 ALEXANDER, LLOYD. "Fantasy as Images: A Literary View." *LA* 55 (April 1978):440-46.

Sees the images of fantasy as its key, its tradition, its basic stuff, its DNA.

B816 -----. "High Fantasy and Heroic Romance." *Horn Book* 47 (December 1971):577-84. (Reprinted in Heins, *Crosscurrents*, pp. 170-77.)

Touches on the link between fantasy, heroic romance, and mythology. "Does the vitality of fantasy come from . . . its deliberate use of the archaic, the imagery of our most ancient modes of thought?"

B817 -----. "Substance and Fantasy." *Library Journal* 91 (15 December 1966):6157-59 and *SLJ* 13 (December 1966):19-21.

Examines the nature of fantasy; tells how it reflects reality. Also comments on his Prydain series and his attempts to give each book "its own particular tone and mood, in the same way that a single musical composition has its allegro and andante movements, its lyrical passages as well as its scherzos."

B818 -----. "The Truth About Fantasy." *TON* 24 (January 1968):168-74.

Discusses similarities between fantasy and fairy tales. They both reflect reality and truth. Fantasy is a "hopeful dream."

B819 -----. "Wishful Thinking--or Hopeful Dreaming?" *Horn Book* 44 (August 1968):383-90. (Reprinted in *Bookbird* 7, no. 3 [1969]:3-9.)

Explores fantasy as a means of dreaming and a catalyst of hope, rather than "wishful thinking." Comments that the "ability to accept fantasy joyously and wholeheartedly is one step, a giant step, into real adulthood."

B820 BABBITT, NATALIE. "The Purposes of Fantasy." *Proceedings of the Children's Literature Association* 9 (1982):22-29.

Sees fantasy as a means of interpreting life, as a universal language, a system of symbols that "enriches and simplifies our lives and makes them bearable."

B821 BILLMAN, CAROL. "Reading and Mapping: Directions in Children's Fantasy." *Proceedings of the Children's Literature Association* 9 (1982):40-46.
Explores mapping and visualizing places in fantastic realms. Concludes that "mapping provides, not simply a metaphor for what goes on in reading fantasy, but also a working description of the actual process by which young readers engage themselves in or 'play' the game of fantasy."

B822 BINGHAM, JANE M., and SCHOLT, GRAYCE. "Enchantment Revisited: Or, Why Teach Fantasy?" *CEA Critic* 39 (January 1978):11-15. (Reprinted in Bator, *Signposts*, pp. 261-64.)
Argues that although fantasy is particularly suited to children it has much to offer persons of all ages and is suitable for literary analysis.

B823 BODEM, MARQUERITE M. "The Role of Fantasy in Children's Reading." *EE* 52 (April 1975):470-71, 538.
Comments on Ravenna Helson's theories of fantasy and suggests ways in which teachers might apply them.

B824 CAMERON, ELEANOR. "The Eternal Moment." *ChLAQ* 9, no. 4 (Winter 1984-85):157-64.
Discusses style, sense of place, characterization, and unifying techniques that communicate "almost unanalyzable overtones" in a number of recent fantasies and time fantasies, especially K.M. Peyton's *Pattern of Roses*, Jill Paton Walsh's *A Chance Child*, Penelope Lively's *The House in Norham Gardens*, and Ruth Park's time fantasy *Playing Beatie Bow*.

B825 -----. *Green and Burning Tree*, pp. 3-47, 71-134, and 258-74.
The following essays are devoted to fantasy literature for children: "Unforgettable Glimpse," first published in October 1962 issue of *WLB*, and rewritten for *Green and Burning Tree*, attempts to define fantasy and outline the qualities of great fantasy, using examples from children's literature. "Green and Burning Tree: A Study of Time Fantasy," discusses at length E. Nesbit's *The Story of the Amulet*, the time tales of Edward Eager, Jane Louise Curry's *The Sleepers*, Elizabeth Marie Pope's *The Sherwood Ring*, Alison Uttley's *A Traveler In Time*, Lucy Boston's Green Knowe books, especially *The River at Green Knowe* (which she finds disappointing), Philippa Pearce's *Tom's Midnight Garden*, and William Mayne's *Earthfasts*. "The Dearest Freshness Deep Down Things," originally published in *Horn Book* 40 (October 1964):459-72, explores the relationship between imagination (or fantasy) and realism. Each needs to exist in the presence of the other.

B826 -----. "The Inmost Secret." *Horn Book* 59 (February 1983):17-24.
Examines the way several authors of modern fantasy have handled secrets in their books. Among authors considered are Lucy Boston, Philippa Pearce, Penelope Lively, E.B. White, William Mayne, Pauline Clarke, and Nancy Bond.

B827 *Canadian Children's Literature* 15-16 (1980), 143 pp.
Special issue on fantasy. Contains "Analyzing Enchantment:

Fantasy After Bettelheim," by Constance B. Hieatt, pp. 6-14; "'Nothing Odd Ever Happens Here': Landscape in Canadian Fantasy," by Gwyneth Evans, pp. 15-30; "Jacob Two-Two and the Satisfactions of Paranoia," by Perry Nodelman, pp. 31-37; "Gordon R. Dickson: Science Fiction for Young Canadians," by Raymond H. Thompson, pp. 38-46; "Stories and Stlalakums: Christie Harris and the Supernatural World," by Susan Wood, pp. 47-56; "Monsters from Native Canadian Mythologies," by Muriel A. Whitaker, pp. 57-66; and "Fantasy and Transformation in Shadow Puppetry," by Elizabeth Cleaver, pp. 67-79.

B828 CIANCIOLO, PATRICIA JEAN. "A Look at the Modern Fantasy Currently Available to Young Readers." ERIC Educational Document Reproduction Service, 1977, 14 pp., ED 144 109.

  Analyzes twenty-two children's books in terms of good storytelling and lively imagination. Examines recurring themes, satires and wordplay, original fairy tales, the divided self, the occult, and parapsychology.

B829 COHEN, JOHN ARTHUR. "An Examination of Four Key Motifs Found in High Fantasy for Children." Ph.D. dissertation, Ohio State University, 1975, 389 pp., DA 36:5016A.

  Analyzes four motifs in fantasy for children: created worlds, time displacement, quest, and combat between good and evil. Suggests that, although the roots of fantasy are in myth and folklore, "its concerns are very much those of the present." Fantasy provides a framework in which authors can deal with philosophical questions without moralizing while at the same time projecting the reader into marvelous new worlds and experiences.

B830 COLBATH, MARY LOU. "Worlds as They Should Be: Middle-Earth, Narnia and Prydain." *EE* 48 (December 1971):937-45.

  Discusses the fantasy worlds of J.R.R. Tolkien, C.S. Lewis, and Lloyd Alexander, concentrating on their qualities of adventure, enchantment, and heroism.

B831 COOPER, SUSAN. "Escaping Into Ourselves." In Hearne, *Celebrating Children's Books*, pp. 14-23.

  Reflections on the nature of fantasy by one of the foremost writers of the genre. "Fantasy goes on stage beyond realism; requiring complete intellectual surrender. . . . Fantasy is the metaphor through which we discover ourselves."

B832 CROUCH, MARCUS. "Magic Casements." In *The Nesbit Tradition*, pp. 112-41.

  Discusses briefly a great many, primarily British, writers of fantasy, including Russell Hoban, Alan Garner, William Mayne, David Severn, Margot Benary, Clive King, Tove Jansson, Lucy Boston, and Mary Norton.

B833 CURRY, JANE. "On the Elvish Craft." *Signal* 2 (May 1970):42-49. (Reprinted in Chambers, *Signal Approach*, pp. 83-93.)

  Distinguishes between "contemporary" and "traditional" fantasy. Discusses E. Nesbit's *Enchanted Castle* and works of other British fantasists for children.

B834   DE LUCA, GERALDINE, and NATOV, RONI. "The State of the Field in Contemporary Children's Fantasy: An Interview with George Woods." *L&U* 1, no. 2 (Fall 1977):4-16.

Personal reflections and comments on current children's fantasy.

B835   DONELSON, KENNETH. "Fantasy." In *Literature for Today's Young Adults*, pp. 265-72.

Discusses the appeal of "fantasy to young adults--especially Lloyd Alexander's Prydain books, Ursula K. Le Guin's *Earthsea* trilogy, Saint-Exupery's *Little Prince*, Peter Beagle's *Last Unicorn*, and Robin McKinley's *Beauty*.

B836   DRURY, ROGER W. "Realism Plus Fantasy Equals Magic." *Horn Book* 48 (April 1972):113-19. (Reprinted in Heins, *Crosscurrents*, pp. 178-84.)

Explores the connection between fantasy and reality.

B837   EGOFF, SHEILA. "The New Fantasy." In *Thursday's Child*, pp. 80-129.

Describes fantasy as "a literature of paradox" of "the real within the unreal, the credible within the incredible, the believable within the unbelievable." Discusses characteristics of the "new fantasy" in such categories as epic and heroic fantasy "with its cosmic battles and invaders from the mythic past" (e.g., works of Alan Garner and Susan Cooper); enchanted realism, which depends upon "distortion of time and space (e.g., Boston's *Green Knowe* stories and Pearce's *Tom's Midnight Garden*); beast tales and animal fantasy (e.g., Richard Adams); and light fantasy, which "wears the mask of comedy" (e.g., the works of Joan Aiken).

B838   FARMER, PENELOPE. "*Jorinda and Jorindel* and Other Stories." *CLE*, o.s., no. 7 (March 1972):23-37. (Reprinted in Fox, *Writers, Critics, and Children*, pp. 55-72.)

Distinguishes fantasy (based on personal, private experiences) from fairy tale (based in the mass subconscious). Divides fantasies into "introvert" and "extrovert" and gives examples of each type. Includes detailed discussions of Catherine Storr's *Marianne Dreams* and *Rufus*. Discusses the effect of fantasy as opposed to effects of fairy tales on the audience. Uses examples from Andersen and Hoban's *Mouse and His Child*.

B839   "Fiction for Children 1970-1980: Myth and Fantasy." *CLE*, n.s. 12, no. 3 (Autumn 1981):119-39.

A listing, with critical annotations, of books chosen as both worthwhile and popular in the categories of fantasy and myth. The "Special Mention" list, which includes works chosen by two or more compilers, contains fairly lengthy evaluations of the following works: John Christopher's *The Guardians*, Susan Cooper's *The Dark Is Rising*, Penelope Farmer's *Castle of Bone*, Florence Parry Heide's *The Shrinking of Treehorn*, Ursula K. Le Guin's *The Tombs of Atuan* and *The Farthest Shore*, Penelope Lively's *A Study in Time*, Robert C. O'Brien's *Mrs. Frisby and the Rats of NIMH*, and Philippa Pearce's *The Shadow Cage* and *Other Tales of the Supernatural*. Seventy-three other titles on the general list are annotated briefly. A critical review of trends by Ralph Lavender follows, pp. 140-50.

B840   GAGNON, LAURENCE. "Philosophy and Fantasy." *Children's Literature* 1 (1972):98-103.
       Rat and Mole (from *Wind in the Willows*) debate the relationship between philosophy and fantasy.

B841   HARE, DELMAS EDWIN. "In This Land There Be Dragons: Carl G. Jung, Ursula K. Le Guin, and Narrative Prose Fantasy." Ph.D. dissertation, Emory University, 1982, 231 pp., DA 43:165A.
       Argues that the structure of fantasy is similar to the Jungian complex and demonstrates its use in the analysis of Ursula K. Le Guin's *Wizard of Earthsea*.

B842   HELSON, RAVENNA. "Fantasy and Self-Discovery." *Horn Book* 46 (April 1970):121-34. (Reprinted in White, *Children's Literature*, pp. 117-26.)
       Proposes a type classification of modern fantasy based partially on Jungian personality theory. Divides fantasies into those by men and those by women, and under each defines three types: by men--(1) wish fulfillment and humor, (2) heroism, and (3) tender feeling; and by women--(1) independence and self expression, (2) transformation, and (3) inner mystery and love. Several titles are discussed and listed as examples in each category.

B843   -----. "The Imaginative Process in Children's Literature: A Quantitative Appraisal." *Poetics* 7 (June 1978):135-53.
       Examines children's fantasy literature as projections of the authors' personalities in terms of Jungian psychology and archetypal criticism.

B844   -----. "The Psychological Origins of Fantasy for Children in Mid-Victorian England." *Children's Literature* 3 (1974):66-76.
       "The thesis of this essay is that these works of fantasy for children [e.g., John Ruskin's *King of the Golden River*, George MacDonald's *At the Back of the North Wind*, and Lewis Carroll's *Alice in Wonderland*] reflect experiences of inner conflict, growth, and renewal of the sort Jung described as accompanying the individuation process and that the intensity of these experiences, and also their themes and characters, may be understood in relation to the particular social conditions of mid-Victorian England."

B845   -----. "Sex-Specific Patterns in Creative Literary Fantasy." *Journal of Personality* 38 (September 1970):344-63.
       Identifies three types of creative fantasy by male authors of children's books: the heroic, the tender, and the comic; and two types by women authors: "one emphasizing independence and the other contact with the irreal and tender emotion."

B846   -----. "Through the Pages of Children's Books." *Psychology Today* 7, no. 6 (November 1973):107-17.
       Examines children's fantasy as a mirror of culture, and shows how it reflects the social pressures, problems of sex role and personal identity, and the changing role of the artist of its time.

B847   HIGGINS, JAMES, EDWARD. *Beyond Words: Mystical Fancy in Children's Literature.* New York: Teachers College Press, 1970, 112 pp. (Based on doctoral dissertation, Columbia University, 1965, DA 26:4629.)

Examines a number of modern literary fairy tales which reach the "inner child," including J.R.R. Tolkien's *The Hobbit*, pp. 18-31, C.S. Lewis's *Narnia*, pp. 32-48, the stories of George MacDonald, pp. 58-69, W.H. Hudson's *A Little Boy Lost*, pp. 73-86, and Antoine de Saint-Exupery's *The Little Prince*, pp. 88-102.

B848   HOFFELD, LAURA. "Where Magic Begins." *L&U* 3, no. 1 (Spring 1979):4-13.
Discusses the special appeal of classic children's fantasies, which hover on the boundary between fantasy and reality.

B849   HUNTER, MOLLIE. "One World." *Horn Book* 51 (December 1975):557-63; 52 (February 1976):32-38. (Reprinted in *Talent Is Not Enough*, pp. 57-77.)
Examines the origins of all fantasy in folklore, arguing that "a solid base of fact or apparent fact is required for the reader to be able to identify," and concludes that the significance of fantasy for the child is its ability to integrate the real and imagined worlds that are part of his or her own developing personality.

B850   ISSAYEVA, ALEXANDRA. "The Contemporary Children's Tale: Images and Intent." *Bookbird* 3 (1984):18-32.
An extensive analysis of an international array of children's fantasy that has been made available in the Soviet Union within the past thirty years. Concentrates on a number of prominent themes and motifs.

B851   JAN, ISABELLE. "Through the Looking Glass." In *On Children's Literature*, pp. 56-78.
Discusses the "deliberately nonrealistic" literature that is especially characteristic of English children's literature, and although she does not label it "fantasy," she is in fact exploring the nature and distinguishing characteristics of that genre.

B852   JENKINS, SUE. "'I will take the ring': Responsibility and Maturity in Modern Fantasy Fiction for Young People." In Hunt, *Further Approaches*, pp. 61-62.
Briefly summarizes her research into two related aspects of fantasy: (1) the descent of fantasy from ancient sources on myth, folktale, and fairy tale; and (2) the reasons why this genre derived from these sources has such an appeal to the young.

B853   KLINGBERG, GÖTE. *The Fantastic Tale for Children: A Genre Study from the Viewpoints of Literary and Educational Research.* Gothenberg, Sweden: Gothenberg School of Education Department of Educational Research, 1970, 34 pp. (Also ERIC Educational Document Reproduction Service, 1970, 38 pp., ED 058 225.)
Defines the fantastic tale as one in which wonders, or magic, exist side by side with reality. Examines motifs and psychological aspects of the genre in authors ranging from E.T.A. Hoffmann to Philippa Pearce and Maria Gripe. Among motifs identified as characteristic of fantasy are living toy figures, strange children, modern witches, supernatural animals, mythical worlds, combat between good and evil, journeys through space and time, and the door.

B854   -----. "The Fantastic Tale for Children--Its Literary and Educational

Problems." *Bookbird* 5, no. 3 (1967):13-20.
Summarizes information in the above book.

B855   KUZNETS, LOIS R. "Games of Dark: Psychofantasy in Children's Literature." *L&U* 1, no. 2 (1977):17-24.
Discusses books that use "fantasy as a device within the realistic
problem novel," specifically, Georgess McHargue's *Stoneflight* and
William Mayne's *A Game of Dark*.

B856   LANGTON, JANE. "The Weak Place in the Cloth: A Study of Fantasy
for Children." *Horn Book* 49 (October 1973):433-41; (December
1973):570-78. (Reprinted in Culpan, *Variety is King*, pp. 32-42.)
"The three primary questions fantasy asks and answers are: What
If? Then What? So What?" Defines eight categories of "What If"
fantasy, with examples from well-known children's literature in part
1, and in part 2 examines the ways in which "Then What?" and "So
What?" are answered.

B857   LEWIS, NAOMI. "The Road to Fantasy." *Children's Literature* 11
(1983):201-10.
Explores the meanings, role, and development of fantasy in children's literature.

B858   *The Lion and the Unicorn* 1, no. 2 (Fall 1977).
Special issue on fantasy. Articles have been indexed separately
under individual topics and authors in this bibliography.

B859   LODER, REED ELIZABETH. "Personal Identity Concepts in the Context of Children's Fantasy Literature." Ph.D. dissertation, Boston
University, 1979, 254 pp., DA 40:2734A.
Explores ways in which "philosophical theories of identity apply
to depictions of unfamiliar beings" in selected children's fantasy
literature.

B860   LOURIE, HELEN. "Where is Fancy Bred?" In Egoff, *Only Connect*,
pp. 106-10.
"The wilder the fantasy, the younger the reader." Maintains the
great writers of fantasy have been and continue to be men.

B861   MacCANN, DONNARAE. "Wells of Fancy, 1865-1965." *WLB* 40
(December 1965):334-43. (Reprinted in Egoff, *Only Connect*, pp.
133-49.)
Summarizes the development of fantasy literature for children
from *Alice* to the present.

B862   MERLA, PATRICK. "'What is Real?' asked the Rabbit One Day." *Saturday Review of the Arts*, 4 November 1972, pp. 43-50. (Reprinted
in Egoff, *Only Connect*, 2d ed., pp. 337-55.)
Contrasts the increasing realism in children's books with the
increasing fantasy in adults'. Heralds the books of Evangeline
Walton, C.S. Lewis, and T.H. White as "the best fantasies of the
twentieth century" and "great works of fiction." Suggests adults may
be looking for fantasy in current literature; children for realism.

B863   MILNE, ROSEMARY. "Fantasy in Literature for Early Childhood." In
Robinson, M., *Readings in Children's Literature*, pp. 124-37.
Expresses reservations about the use of fantasy with children

under the age of seven on the basis of Piaget's theories of child development. Hypothesizes that the young child is unable to see "where and how fantasy goes beyond logical human experience," and urges that adults avoid violence and the imposition of "their own unresolved conflicts on young children."

B864   MOBLEY, JANE. "Toward a Definition of Fantasy Fiction." *Extrapolation* 15 (May 1974). (Reprinted in Bator, *Signposts*, pp. 249-60.)
       Distinguishes fantasy fiction from dream, horror, and science fiction by its key element of "magic," which she defines. Lists elements of fantasy as (1) poetic quality, (2) creation of secondary magical worlds, (3) multidimensionality, (4) essential extravagance, (5) spirit of carnival, and (6) mythic dimension.

B865   NODELMAN, PERRY. "Some Presumptuous Generalizations about Fantasy." *ChLAQ* 4, no. 1 (Summer 1979):5-6, 18. (Reprinted in Dooley, *First Steps*, pp. 15-16, and in Nodelman, *Festschrift*, pp. 26-27.)
       Explores connections between children's literature and fantasy: both "place readers in a position of innocence about the reality they describe."

B866   OWEN, LUCIA. "Dragons in the Classroom." *English Journal* 73 (November 1984):76-77.
       Argues that fantasy does three things better than other fiction: (1) it exercises the imagination, (2) it allows us to see ourselves more clearly "precisely because it takes place in the imagination," and (3) it "allows escape and generates hope."

B867   PFLEIGER, PAT. *A Reference Guide to Modern Fantasy for Children.* Westport, Conn.: Greenwood Press, 1984, 690 pp.
       Provides an introduction to the work of thirty-six nineteenth- and twentieth-century British and American writers of fantasy for children. Omits Lewis Carroll, A.A. Milne, and L. Frank Baum. Lists primary and secondary works for each writer, and discusses each writer's work as a whole, with separate discussions of individual titles, characters, places, objects, and events.

B868   PRICKETT, STEPHEN. *Victorian Fantasy.* Bloomington: Indiana University Press, 1979, 257 pp.
       Examines the evolution of fantasy among Victorian writers, with chapters devoted to the children's books of Lear and Carroll, pp. 114-47; Kingsley and MacDonald, pp. 150-97; and Kipling and Nesbit, pp. 198-239. Includes extensive notes and a bibliography.

B869   RICHARDSON, CARMEN C. "The Reality of Fantasy." *LA* 53 (May 1976):549-51, 563.
       Maintains that fantasy helps children accept the need for heroism in daily life, and allows them to experience human emotion without embarrassment and explore inner conflicts without fear. Cites examples from children's fantasy.

B870   RUPERT, PAMELA RAE. "An Analysis of the Need Fulfillment Imagery in Fantasy Literature for Children." Ph.D. dissertation, University of Akron, 1979, 295 pp., DA 40:664A.
       Concludes that recent children's fantasy fiction addresses and fulfills basic human needs, and suggests "resolutions to problems

which promote growth toward maturity and independence."

B871   SALESI, ROSEMARY A. "Fanciful Literature and Reading Comprehension." ERIC Educational Document Reproduction Service, 1978, 16 pp., ED 159 625.

Discusses those characteristics of fanciful novels that often pose difficulties for readers. Suggests teachers prepare children by reading works of fantasy aloud to provide a framework of experience.

B872   SINGH, MICHAEL J. "Law and Emotion in Fantasy." *Orana* 18 (May 1982):49-54.

"Fantasy must obey its own law to achieve artistic merit," and "the provision of a form of wish fulfillment corresponding the reader's stage of emotional development is essential." Examines Russell Hoban's *Mouse and His Child* as an example of a successful fantasy.

B873   SMITH, LILLIAN. "Fantasy." In *Unreluctant Years*, pp. 149-62.

"Fantasy demands something extra, perhaps a kind of sixth sense. All children have it, but most adults leave it behind with their cast-off childhood." Sees *Alice in Wonderland* as a prime example of fantasy. The quality of fantasy "lies in the creative imagination of the writer and in his own personal expression of that imagination."

B874   STIBBS, ANDREW. "For Realism in Children's Fiction." *Use of English* 32, no. 1 (Fall 1980):18-24.

Argues for more realism and less suspension of disbelief in children's fantasy. Feels the new generation of teachers has been unduly influenced by Tolkien. A response, "In Defense of Fantasy," by Jessica Yates, follows in 32, no. 3 (Summer 1981):70-73.

B875   STOTT, JON C. "Midsummer Night's Dreams: Fantasy and Self-Realization in Children's Fiction." *L&U* 1, no. 2 (Fall 1977):25-39.

Discusses fantasies involving a variant of the "circular journey" in which a child "moves into a new world, where, although apparently escaping reality, he is forced to confront his own problems and solve them, thus making possible his healthy return to his own world." Concentrates on Virginia Hamilton's *Zeely*, Mordecai Richler's *Jacob Two-Two Meets the Hooded Fang*, and Madeleine L'Engle's *A Wrinkle in Time*.

B876   THOMPSON, HILARY. "Doorways to Fantasy." *CCL* 21 (1981):8-15.

Examines where Canadian writers of fantasy Ruth Nichols and Catherine Anthony Clark have set their entrances into fantasy world, and compares them to the entrances of a number of other writers.

B877   WAGGONER, DIANA. *The Hills of Faraway: A Guide to Fantasy.* New York: Atheneum, 1978, 326 pp.

Presents a theory of fantasy, discusses trends in fantasy, and provides annotated listings of books in various subgenres of fantasy. Although the book is not limited to children's literature, many of the examples and discussions are based on important children's books.

B878   WEBER, ROSEMARY. "Folklore and Fantasy--Mix or Match." ERIC Educational Document Reproduction Service, 1978, 11 pp., ED 154 424.

Stresses the elements that folklore, fairy tales, and modern fantasy have in common, such as supernatural beings, strange locales, imaginative content, and moral lessons, often embodied in a struggle between good and evil, assisted by magical devices.

B879   WRIGHTSON, PATRICIA. "The Nature of Fantasy." In Robinson, M. *Readings in Children's Literature*, pp. 220-43.
Explores the origins and nature of fantasy, its different categories, its roots in reality and traditional lore, its limitations, and its failures and successes. Concludes with a brief mention of her attempts to create an Australian fantasy rooted in folk magic.

B880   YEP, LAURENCE. "Fantasy and Reality." *Horn Book* 54 (April 1978):137-43.
Discusses the interrelationship between fantasy and reality in a number of well-known recent and classic books.

B881   YOLEN, JANE. "Here There Be Dragons." *TON* 39 (Fall 1982):54-56.
Muses on what qualities comprise the essence of fantasy.

B882   -----. "The Voice of Fantasy." *Advocate* 3, no. 1 (Fall 1983):50-56.
Explores the voice of fantasy as the voice of truth in a metaphoric mode, as the voice of story itself.

B883   ZANGER, JULES. "Goblins, Warlocks, and Weasels: Classic Fantasy and the Industrial Revolution." *CLE*, n.s. 8, no. 4 (Winter 1977):154-62.
Examines three classic fantasies of the late nineteenth century to show how their writers revealed their predispositions toward tradition and the past and against the changes wrought by the industrial revolution: George MacDonald's *The Princess and the Goblin* (1871), H.G. Wells's *The Time Machine* (1898), and Kenneth Grahame's *The Wind in the Willows* (1908).

B884   ZIPES, JACK. "The Age of Commodified Fantasticism: Reflections of Children's Literature and the Fantastic." *ChLAQ* 9, no. 4 (Winter 1984-85):187-90.
Suggests that a framework is needed for serious critical examination of fantasy as a genre and proposes ways in which "a sociohistorical critique might enable us to grasp the significance of the commodified fantasticism which has become part and parcel of our lives."

FICTION

B885   AVERY, GILLIAN. "Fashions in Children's Fiction." *CLE*, o.s., no. 12 (September 1973):10-19. (Reprinted in Bator, *Signposts*, pp. 222-31.)
Argues that it is the child who ultimately decides what endures in fiction, not the critics and educators.

B886   FISHER, MARGERY. "Is Fiction Educational?" *CLE*, o.s., no. 1 (March 1970):11-21. (Reprinted in Bator, *Signposts*, pp. 232-39.)
Speech delivered at the conference on "Recent Children's Fiction and Its Role in Education," August 1969, Saint Luke's College, Exeter, England. Argues that fiction is primarily an experience and that its power is based on the author's style.

B887   HIGGINS, JAMES E. "Forum: The Primary Purpose of Fiction." *CLE*,

n.s. 12, no. 2 (Summer 1981):113-16.
Argues that the element of surprise is at the very heart of a story's existence, and *real* stories are often not welcome in the classroom.

B888   LEWIS, ROGER. "Fiction and the Imagination." *CLE*, o.s., no. 19 (Winter 1975):172-77.
Justifies the teaching of fiction in the schools as a means of developing the imagination.

FINLAND

B889   *Books from Finland* 13, no. 2 (1979).
Includes three articles on children's literature: Kristine Alapuro's "Exploring the Child's World with Anna Tauriala and Camilla Mickwitz," pp. 48-52, based on interviews with two author-illustrators of books for preschoolers; Pekka Suhonen's "The Illustrated Fairy Tale," pp. 53-55, which comments upon new illustrated versions of classic Finnish folktales; and Helakisa Kaarina's "Stories for the Young at Heart," pp. 56-63, which discusses modern Finnish "novel-length" fairy tales by Tove Jansson, Irmelin Sandman Lilius, Hannu Makela, Marja-Leena Mikkola, Pekka Suhonen, and Leena Krohn.

B890   LEHTONEN, MAIJA. "The Finnish Juvenile Book in the 1960s: A Summary." *Bookbird* 9, no. 1 (1971):11-12. (Reprinted in Haviland, *Children and Literature*, pp. 389-90.)
Summarizes trends in Finnish juvenile books in the 1960s, especially the development of the young adult novel.

B891   RAJALIN, MARITA. "Finland." *Phaedrus* 8 (1981):57-60.
Reports on recent Finnish scholarship, highlighting Ulla Lehtonen's *Lasten Kirjallisuus Suomessa, 1543-1850* (Children's Literature in Finland, 1543-1850) (Tampere: Suomen Nuorisokirjallisuuden Instituutin Julkaisuja I [Publications of the Finnish Institute for Children's Literature I], 1981), 216 pp.

FIRST BOOKS

B892   DALGLIESH, ALICE. "Small Children and Books." In Fryatt, *Horn Book Sampler*, pp. 219-23.
Observes what appeals to the youngest children in books and comments on some longstanding favorites.

B893   DOOLEY, PATRICIA. "'First Books': From Schlock to Sophistication." *ChLAQ* 7, no. 1 (Spring 1982):7-10. (Reprinted in May, *Children and Their Literature*, pp. 112-16.)
Examines board books for very young children and finds a few to praise--those of Rosemary Wells, "Keussen," and Peter Spier. Suggests areas for improvement.

B894   HALL, MARY ANNE, and MATANZO, JANE. "Children's Literature: A Source for Concept Enrichment." *EE* 52 (April 1975):487-94.
Provides a discussion of the nature of concept books and an annotated bibliography grouped according to concepts of some outstanding examples.

B895   HEARNE, BETSY. "The American Connection." *Signal* 35 (May

1981):91-95.

Hearne reflects on books for toddlers--board books and cloth books--and highly praises those by Rosemary Wells and Helen Oxenbury. Stresses the need for playfulness in children's books.

B896   JACOBS, LELAND B. "Literature Written for Young Children." *EE* 47 (October 1970):781-83.

Applies criteria of "lightness of touch" established by Hamilton Wright Mabie in his *My Study Fire, Second Series* (New York: Dodd, Mead, 1894), to picture books for the youngest child.

B897   JORDAN, ANNE DEVEREAUX, and MERCIER, JEAN. "Baby Lit." *Publishers Weekly* 225 (20 April 1984):29-31.

Reports on the boom in books for babies and points out distinguishing characteristics of the books.

B898   REEVES, KATHERINE. "Literature at the Linen Level." *Horn Book* 16 (January-February 1940):30-33.

Criticizes the "here and now" focus of much literature for the youngest, which is printed on "outsize linen pages" but "allows virtually no escape for imagination." Concludes that "Literature, for any age, should go beyond life, or it has very little reason for being."

B899   THISTLETHWAYTE, CHRISTINE. "Picture Books Before Picture Story Books." *Orana* 17 (May 1981):48-50.

Reports on the first books presented to her young son.

B900   WILLSHER, VALERIE. "Books for the Under-Twos." *Signal* 38 (May 1982):103-12.

Explores the world of books for the very youngest children and includes a critically annotated list of recommended titles.

B901   WOLCOTT, PATTY. "An Approach to Earliest Readers." *CLE*, n.s. 13, no. 3 (Autumn 1982):122-29.

Discusses books for beginning readers with limited numbers of words, including her own ten-word series. Tells why they work and what children like about them.

FOLKLORE

B902   ABRAHAMS, ROGER D., and RANKIN, LOIS, eds. *Counting-out Rhymes: A Dictionary.* Austin: Texas University Press, 1980, 243 pp.

B903   BETT, HENRY. *Nursery Rhymes and Tales: Their Origin and History.* London: Methuen & Co., 1924. Reprint. Detroit: Singing Tree Press, 1968, 130 pp.

Examines the mythological elements in nursery rhymes, counting rhymes, and cumulative tales.

B904   BROSE, DUNN. "Analysis of the Functioning of Gothic Themes in the Folklore and Writing of Children in the Second and Fifth Grades." Ph.D. dissertation, University of Nebraska-Lincoln, 1973, 172 pp., DA 34:2154A.

Analyzes children's use of gothic elements in their own stories and folklore.

B905   CECH, JOHN. "Notes on American Children's Folklore." *Children's Literature* 8 (1979):176-83.
    Review of Mary and Herbert Knapp's *One Potato, Two Potato.* Argues for more collections and analysis of this type of material.

B906   *Children's Books International 4. Folklore, Unique and Universal. Proceedings.* Boston: Boston Public Library, 1979, 76 pp.
    Includes Richard M. Dorson's "Folklore and Fakelore," pp. 8-16; Isabel Schon's "Legends and Folktales from Spanish-Speaking Countries," pp. 18-22; Nancy Schmidt's "All-Africa Folklore," pp. 46-55; and Einar Haugen's "The Shape of the Fabulous: Three Generations of Norwegian Folktale Illustrations," pp. 57-67.

B907   CRABBE, KATHARYN F. "Folk Over Fakelore--but Is It Art?" *SLJ* 26 (November 1979):42-43.
    Maintains that "most of the highly structured folktales for children are really fakelore."

B908   DUNDES, ALAN. "Folklore as a Mirror of Culture." *EE* 46 (April 1969):471-82.
    Explores the use of folklore as a means of teaching cross-cultural understanding.

B909   EGOFF, SHEILA. "Folklore, Myth, and Legend." In *Thursday's Child*, pp. 193-220.
    A critical overview of recent editions of traditional literature, with comments on scholarship, philosophy, audience, and styles of illustration. Includes not only European, but also American, Australian, Jewish, and Ancient Greek folklore (especially the Garfield, Blishen, and Keeping books, *The God Beneath the Sea* and *The Golden Shadow*).

B910   GARVEY, LEONE. "Children's Literature--Old." *EE* 41 (May 1964): 475-83.
    Part of symposium entitled "What Is Children's Literature?" and edited by Virginia M. Reid. Fables, myths, legends, and folktales are defined and discussed as part of the traditional literature of children.

B911   HALPERT, HERBERT. "Folktales in Children's Books: Some Notes and Reviews." *Midwest Folklore* 2, no. 1 (Spring 1952):59-71.
    Surveys children's folktale collections as items of interest to folklorists, pointing out their strengths and weaknesses and suggesting criteria for evaluation. Discusses the importance of authenticity and scholarship, pointing out the work of Richard Chase and Harold Courlander as outstanding examples.

B912   HAND, W.D. "European Fairy Lore in the New World." *Folklore* 92, no. 2 (1981):141-48.
    Points out the strength and diversity of European folklore that has found roots in American soil.

B913   JAN, ISABELLE. "Once Upon a Time." In *On Children's Literature*, pp. 30-44.
    Discusses the folktale as the foundation for children's literature.

B914   KARL, JEAN. "Bringing Chicken Licken to Life." *Publishers Weekly* 199 (22 February 1971):81-83.

Suggests that modern realistic fiction treats "old beasts in new disguises." Discusses the ways in which some of the traditional tales handle current human problems.

B915   KAY, HELEN. "In Quest of Ms. Mouse." *Children's Literature* 3 (1974):165-68.

Traces versions of a tale, told in many countries over many centuries, of the mouse in search of a husband.

B916   KIMMELMAN, LOIS. "Literary Ways Toward Enjoyable Thinking." *LA* 58 (April 1981):441-47.

Describes the use of "formula tales" from folklore, (those with rhythmic, predictable plot structures), to stimulate children's appreciation of literature. Includes a bibliography of seventy-five books listed by plot types identified as "Henny Penny," "King Midas," and "Old Woman and her Pig" stories.

B917   KNAPP, MARY, and KNAPP, HERBERT. *One Potato, Two Potato: The Secret Education of American Children*. New York: W.W. Norton, 1976, 274 pp.

Collects and analyzes numerous examples of children's folklore. For example, games, jeers, jokes, riddles, rhymes, rope-skipping rhymes, and songs, mainly from the 1960s and 1970s.

B918   LASSER, MICHAEL. "Weaving the Web of Story: Archetype and Image as Bearers of the Tale." *CLE*, n.s. 10, no. 1 (Spring 1979):4-10.

Examines the elements of three traditional tales that keep them alive. Jan Carew's *The Third Gift*, Grimms's *The White Snake*, and Gail E. Haley's Ananse tale, *A Story, A Story*.

B919   MacDONALD, MARGARET READ. "An Analysis of Children's Folktale Collections with an Accompanying Motif-Index of Juvenile Folktale Collections." 2 vols. Ph.D. dissertation, Indiana University, 1979, 1257 pp., DA 40:1000A.

Finds that the "folklore" given to children is frequently "fakelore." "Few collections were found to attain standards of folkloric authenticity." Includes a motif-index of children's folktale collections and picture books, based on Stith Thompson.

B920   MIDDLESWARTH, VICTORIA. "Folklore Books for Children: Guidelines for Selection." *TON* 34 (Summer 1978):348-52.

Suggests that a wide variety of genres, excellence of illustration, accurate documentation and annotation, and contextual information should all be considerations in selecting folklore books for children.

B921   NORTON, ELOISE S., ed. *Folk Literature of the British Isles: Readings for Librarians, Teachers, and Those Who Work with Children and Young Adults*. Metuchen, N.J.: Scarecrow, 1978, 263 pp.

Reprints a number of articles concerning folklore in children's literature, devoting separate sections to the folklore of England, Ireland, Scotland, and Wales. The final chapter discusses the handling of British folk material in the United States. Includes bibliographies.

B922   ORD, PRISCILLA, ed. "Special Section: Folklore." *ChLAQ* 6, no. 2 (Summer 1981):11-33.
        Includes both folklore for children and folklore of children. Kay Stone discusses oral tales, their use and abuse, Jill May compiles critics' opinions of adaptations, particularly Disney's, Brian Sutton-Smith discusses children's own folk stories, Edith Fowke and Linda Hughes discuss singing and verbal play and games, Mark West discusses folk toys, John McDowell discusses children's speech play, and Gary Alan Fine, discusses folk speech. Finally, Kate Rinzer discusses children's folklore collected at the annual folk festival on the Mall at the Smithsonian Institution, Washington, D.C.

B923   PHILIP, NEIL. "Children's Literature and the Oral Tradition." In Hunt, *Further Approaches*, pp. 5-22.
        Explores ways in which the formal devices and symbolic approaches of children's literature resemble those of oral storytellers in pre- or nonliterate communities.

B924   ROSS, ELINOR P. "Comparison of Folk Tale Variants." *LA* 56 (April 1979):422-26. (Reprinted in Barron, *Jump Over the Moon*, pp. 300-305.)
        Compares variants of "Cinderella," "Little Red Riding Hood," and "The Three Bears," with suggestions for classroom use. Includes a bibliography.

B925   SHANNON, GEORGE. *Folk Literature for Children: An Annotated Bibliography of Secondary Materials*. Westport, Conn.: Greenwood, 1981, 124 pp.
        Contains four hundred sixty-five entries arranged under categories of literature, education, and psychology, with additional access through detailed author, title, and subject indexes. Includes extensive coverage of censorship, children's lore, fables, fairy tales, nursery rhymes, tale selection, rewriting, and storytelling.

B926   SHEVIAK, MARGARET R., and ANDERSON, MERRILEE. "American 'Fake' Folk Heroes." *EE* 46 (March 1969):273-78.
        Explores the controversy surrounding American folk heroes such as Paul Bunyan, Pecos Bill, and Joe Magarac. Are they folklore or "fakelore"?

B927   SMITH, RICHARD E. "Study of the Correspondences Between the *Roman De Renard*, Jamaican Anansi stories, and West African Animal Tales Collected in Culture-Area V." Ph.D. dissertation, Ohio State University, 1971, 179 pp., DA 32:6394A.
        Concludes that the Jamaican folktales are of West African rather than European origin.

B928   TAYLOR, MARK. "Television Is Ruining Our Folktales." *Library Journal* 84 (15 December 1959):3882-84.
        Comments on and protests against the distortion and mutilation of folktales by the mass media and suggests ways the tales might be treated that would preserve their integrity.

B929   WADE, BARRIE. "That's Not a Book." *Children's Literature* 13, no. 1 (Spring 1982):32-37.
        Examines children's rhymes used in games and concludes they

have many characteristics useful in teaching reading.

B930   WEBER, EUGEN. "Fairies and Hard Facts: The Reality of Folktales." *Journal of the History of Ideas* 42, no. 1 (1981):93-113.
         Explores the realities of stepmothers and starvation in the historical European world in which the Grimm tales are based, and then suggests ways in which this information might influence our interpretations of the tales.

B931   WESTERN, LINDA E. "A Comparative Study of Literature through Folk Tale Variants." *LA* 57 (April 1980):395-402, 439.
         Offers a plan for studying folklore variants in the classroom. Includes references and a bibliography of variants of nine well-known tales, including several versions suitable for children.

B932   WINSLOW, DAVID J. "Children's Picture Books and the Popularization of Folklore." *Keystone Folklore Quarterly* 14 (Winter 1969):142-57.
         Provides an overview of children's picture-book versions of folklore, arguing that they are worthy of attention by folklorists.

FOOD

B933   KATZ, WENDY R. "Some Uses of Food in Children's Literature." *CLE*, n.s. 11, no. 4 (Winter 1980):192-99.
         Sees food in children's books as directly related to the essentially comic spirit: "eating and drinking are part of the form" and also appeal to children.

B934   KESSLER, LOUISE. "Banquets in Books." *Illinois Libraries* 25 (October 1943):3324-27. (Reprinted in *Ontario Library Review* 28 [February 1944]:14-17.)
         Surveys the gustatory delights in a number of classic children's books.

FOOL

B935   GRISWOLD, JEROME. "The Fool and the Child." In Butler, *Sharing*, pp. 153-54.
         Explores reasons for the fool's appeal to the child and his frequent appearance in children's literature.

FRANCE

B936   CORBETT, ANNE. "France: Good Books and BD's." *TLS*, 28 March 1980, p. 358.
         Reviews recent trends and developments in French children's literature.

B937   JAN, ISABELLE, and PATTE, GENEVIEVE. "Children's Literature in France." In Haviland, *Children and Literature*, pp. 355-64.
         Argues that there is a sameness in modern French literature for children. Two tendencies are identified: didacticism and literary nostalgia. Remoteness in time and/or space is common, but a realistic tradition also exists.

B938   JAN, ISABELLE. "French Children's Classics: Tradition in a Non-Traditional Age." *WLB* 47 (October 1972):162-71.

Provides an overview of the history of French children's literature and argues that, despite its many masterpieces, it lacks continuity and traditions.

B939 LOTTMAN, HERBERT. "No Time for Childhood." *Library Journal* 91 (15 November 1966):5709-12.
Surveys the status of children's literature in France. "The problem in France is that nothing worthwhile has been published for children in the past 50 years."

B940 PATTE, GENEVIEVE. "French Children's Literature and French Children's Libraries." In Koefoed, *Children's Literature and the Child*, pp. 21-29.
Looks at problems, developments, and trends in French children's literature as of the early 1970s.

B941 *Yale French Studies* 43 (1969):1-172.
Special issue entitled "The Child's Part," that is devoted to children's literature. Includes Philippe Aries's "At the Point of Origin," pp. 15-23, a discussion of the origins of children's literature in France; Marc Soriano's "From Tales of Warning to Formulettes," pp. 24-43, a discussion of the influence of the oral tradition; Isabelle Jan's "Children's Literature and Bourgeois Society in France Since 1860," pp. 57-72; Esther S. Kanipe's "Hetzel and the Bibliotheque d'Education et de Recreation," pp. 73-84, which documents the influence documents the influence of publisher Hetzel on children's literature; Marion Durand's "One Hundred Years of Illustrations in French Children's Books," pp. 85-96; Andre Winandy's "The Twilight Zone: Imagination and Reality in Jules Verne's *Strange Journeys*," pp. 97-110; Jean Chesneaux's "Jules Verne's Image of the United States," pp. 111-127; and Richard Howard's "Childhood Amnesia," pp. 165-69, which explores the French attitude toward "childhood," a state for which he points out the French language has no word.

FRIENDSHIP

B942 SHERMAN, CAROLYN. "Friendship as Portrayed in Children's Books." *LA* 52 (April 1975):449-54, 494.
Children may find answers to the question of how to make friends in the books discussed. Includes an annotated bibliography of fiction on the topic of friendship.

GERMANY

B943 BECKER, JÖRG. "Racism in West German Children's Books." *IRBC* 4, nos. 3-4 (Winter 1972-73):3.
Points out stereotyped portrayals of blacks in German children's literature.

B944 BELL, ANTHEA. "Germany: The Serious Matters of Life." *TLS*, 28 March 1980, p. 358.
Reviews recent trends and developments in children's literature in the German-speaking areas of Europe.

B945 DAHRENDORF, MATTI. "Contemporary Issues of Central Europe and the Literature for Children and Young People in the Federal Republic of Germany." *Bookbird* 4 (1981):7-11.

Discusses the depiction of industrialization and ecology, youth protest, drug addiction, violence, juvenile crime, neo-Nazism, and the division of Germany, in literature for children and young adults.

B946 *Dimension: Contemporary German Arts and Letters* 12, no. 1 (1979):219 pp.

This collection of translations of recent German children's literature includes an introductory essay on German children's poetry by Ruth Lorbe, pp. 7-13, and an overview of German children's literature and the featured selections, pp. 14-18.

B947 DODERER, KLAUS. "German Children's Classics." *Bookbird* 12, no. 1 (1974):8-16.

Explores the nature of four German classics of children's literature, the Grimms' fairy tales, *Heidi* (which he believes should be consigned to history), *Max und Moritz*, by Wilhelm Busch (1827-1901), and Erich Kästner's *Emil und die Detektive*.

B948 FRASER, SIBYLLE. "German Language Children's Youth Periodicals in North America: A Checklist." *Phaedrus* 6, no. 1 (Spring 1979):27-31.

A compilation based on *German-American Newspapers and Periodicals, 1732-1955: History and Bibliography* (Heidelberg: Quelle & Meyer, 1961), by Carl G. Arnat and May E. Olson, and its third edition *Die Deutschprachege Presse der Amerikas* (Munich: Verlag Dokumentation, 1976). Although the title indicates "North America," South American publications are also included.

B949 KAMENETSKY, CHRISTA. *Children's Literature in Hitler's Germany: The Cultural Policy of National Socialism.* Athens: Ohio University Press, 1984, 359 pp.

Discusses (1) literary theory and cultural policy, including pre-Nazi German children's literature, Nazi book-burning and censorship, and the Nazi Theory of "Volkish" literature; (2) Nazi interpretation of folktales, mythology, sagas, fiction, classics, and picturebooks; (3) primers, readers, theater and "Volkish Rituals," and (4) the system of censorship, curricular, and folklore reforms, the role of school libraries, and trends in publishing and children's reading interests.

B950 KÜNNEMANN, HORST. "Periodicals for Children and Young People-- The Forgotten Medium." *Phaedrus* 4, no. 2 (Fall 1977):30-31.

Surveys research in this area, concluding that much remains to be done.

B951 -----. "Twenty Years Later." *SLJ* 13 (15 November 1966):37-41.

Surveys the development of German children's literature in the twenty years since World War II.

B952 LANGFELDT, J. "Children's Books in Germany." *Junior Bookshelf* 12, no. 2 (July 1948):66-74.

A concise historical overview.

B953 MÉTRAUX, RHODA. "A Portrait of the Family in German Juvenile Fiction." In *Childhood in Contemporary Culture.* Edited by Margaret Mead and Martha Wolfenstein. Chicago: University of Chicago Press, 1955, pp. 253-75.

Discusses the depiction of German family life in popular German family stories written between 1880 and 1939. Includes extensive references.

B954   *Phaedrus* 2, no. 2 (Fall 1975).
Special issue on German children's literature. Includes Klaus Doderer's, "A Few Comments on German Children's Literature Research in the Federal Republic of Germany," pp. 5-7, which discusses the increasing research in children's literature since World War II; Heinz Wegehaupt's "Research on Children's and Youth Literature in the German Democratic Republic," pp. 8-11, which summarizes the status of children's literature and research; Horst Kunnemann's "Children's and Youth Literature and Language Minorities in the Federal Republic of Germany," pp. 16-19, which discusses the portrayal of the problems of foreign immigrants to Germany in recent children's books; Alfred Clemens Baumgartner's "Comics and Comic Research in the Federal Republic of Germany," pp. 19-20; Sheryl Smith's "A Guide to Research Collections of Children's Literature in the Federal Republic of Germany," pp. 23-27; and James Fraser's "German Language Books, Catalogs, Bibliographies," pp. 30-33, which surveys the publications of Germany's two leading publishers of children's literature research, Verlag Dokumentation and Beltz Verlag, and discusses the *Lexicon der Kinder and Jugendliteratur*, the "first scholarly encyclopedia for the field of children's literature in any language."

B955   PRIBIC, RADO. "Young People's Literature in the Federal Republic of Germany Today." *Journal of Reading* 24 (January 1981):304-7.
A brief overview of recent trends in West German children's and adolescent literature.

B956   SACHSENMEIR, PETER. "Sociological Aspects of Modern German Youth Literature." *Modern Languages* 56 (June 1975):89-93.
Examines modern German children's literature within historical and sociological frameworks.

B957   SCHERF, WALTER. "Across the Rhine: Juvenile Literature in German-Speaking Countries." *TON* 26 (January 1970):180-87, 205. (Reprinted in Haviland, *Children and Literature*, pp. 345-54.)
Surveys the children's literature in the German-speaking countries of Europe. Covers picture books, poetry, realistic fiction and fantasy, informational books, and young adult literature.

B958   SHEVIAK, MARGARET R. "West German Literature for German Youth: Cowboys and Indians." *TON* 30 (January 1974):176-87.
Examines the portrayals, fictional and factual, of America and Americans in literature published in West Germany in the years 1949-69.

B959   VON ENGELBRECHTAN, ERIKA. "Federal Republic of Germany." *Phaedrus* 8 (1981):52-56.
A bibliography of recent German publications relating to children's literature, covering an international array of authors and illustrators.

B960   WILLS, F. "Children's Books from East and West Germany." *Novum Gebrauchsgraphik* 46 (January 1975):10-23.
Provides a brief but well-illustrated overview of recent picture books from East and West Germany.

B961   ZIPES, JACK. "Down with Heidi, Down with Struwwelpeter, Three Cheers for the Revolution: Towards a New Socialist Children's Literature in West Germany." *Children's Literature* 5 (1976):162-79.

Provides a socialist critique of Heinrich Hoffmann's *Struwwelpeter* and Johanna Spyri's *Heidi*, discusses the production of new anti-authoritarian and socialist books, and discusses prospects for a new socialist children's literature in West Germany.

B962   -----. "Running Risks with Language: Contemporary Prose and Poetry for Children in West Germany." *Children's Literature* 11 (1983):191-94.

Review of *Dimension* 12, no. 1 (see above). An overview of some recent developments in German children's literature in West Germany as represented in this special issue of *Dimension*.

GHANA

B963   KOTEI, S.I.A. "Themes for Children's Literature in Ghana." *African Book Publishing Record* 4 (1978):233-39.

Suggests possibilities based on folktale and legend for the further development of Ghanaian children's literature.

GHOSTS AND GHOST STORIES

B964   ARMSTRONG, JUDITH. "Ghost Stories: Exploring the Conventions." *CLE*, n.s. 11, no. 3 (Autumn):111-23.

Examines and explores the conventions and possibilities of ghost stories.

B965   DAVIS, DAVID C. "Phantoms in Children's Literature." *EE* 39 (May 1962):403-7, 417.

Phantom and ghost stories are not usually recognized as quality literature by experts and critics. Describes seven outstanding phantom forms based on (1) the Penny Dreadful, (2) The New England Primer, (3) Grandmother Goose, (4) Little Orphan Annie, (5) Raggedy Ann, (6) Old Mother West Wind, and (7) Edward Everett Hale's *The Man Without a Country*.

B966   RABURN, JOSEPHINE. "Shuddering Shades! A Ghostly Book List." *TON* 41 (Spring 1985):275-81.

Primarily a reading list with some comments on categorizing various types of ghost stories.

B967   -----. "Who-o-o Reads Ghost Stories?" ERIC Educational Document Reproduction Service, 1982, 28 pp., ED 218 590.

Explores reasons for the great appeal of ghost stories to children aged eleven to fourteen, and discusses briefly a number of recent well-known examples of the genre.

GIRLS' FICTION

B968   ASHFORD, RICHARD K. "Tomboys and Saints: Girls' Stories of the Late Nineteenth Century." *SLJ* 26 (January 1980):23-28.

Finds two predominant patterns of heroines in late nineteenth-century girls' fiction: saints and tomboys; and finds those patterns persist today in more modern form. Discusses Martha Finley's Elsie

Dinsmore (a saint) and Susan Coolidge's Katy (a tomboy). Includes extensive references.

B969   CADOGAN, MARY, and CRAIG, PATRICIA. *You're a Brick, Angela: A New Look at Girls' Fiction from 1840 to 1976.* London: Gollancz, 1976, 397 pp.

        This survey is also indexed separately under individual topics and authors discussed at length. The chapter entitled "Stretchers, Stoves and Sphagnum Moss," pp. 140-58, discusses a number of books, stories, and periodicals concerned with Girl Guides. "Orphans and Golden Girls," pp. 89-110, compares five "catalytic small girls" in popular and influential books by American and Canadian women writing between 1902 and 1915: *Rebecca of Sunnybrook Farm*, by Kate Douglas Wiggin, *Anne of Green Gables*, by L.M. Montgomery, *Pollyanna*, by Eleanor H. Porter, *Girl of the Limberlost*, by Gene Stratton Porter, and *Daddy-Long-Legs*, by Jean Webster.

B970   NODELMAN, PERRY. "Progressive Utopia: Or, How to Grow Up without Growing-Up." *Proceedings of the Children's Literature Association* 6 (1979):146-54.

        Examines themes and values relating to the nature of home, childhood, and utopia in traditional novels for girls: Kate Douglas Wiggin's *Rebecca of Sunnybrook Farm*, Eleanor H. Porter's *Pollyanna*, L.M. Montgomery's *Anne of Green Gables*, Frances Hodgson Burnett's *The Secret Garden*, and Johanna Spyri's *Heidi*.

B971   RAY, SHEILA G. "Girls' Reading in the United Kingdom: A Personal View." *Bookbird* 13, no. 1 (1976):6-10.

        Reflects on books popular with British girls over the past one hundred years.

B972   ROBERTS, ALASDAIR. "What Bunty Does At School: School Stories in Girls' Weekly Papers." *TES* 3349 (22 August 1980):14-15.

        Examines "the new breed of school stories in girls' weekly papers" and the social attitudes they convey.

GOTHIC NOVELS

B973   LEDER, SHARON. "Contemporary Adolescent Gothic." *L&U* 2 (Fall 1977):111-15.

        A review of three recent novels for adolescents: Frances Eager's *Time Tangle*, Valerie Lutters's *The Haunting of Julie Unger*, and Phyllis Reynolds Naylor's *Witch Water*.

GREECE

B974   PETROVITS-ANDROUTSOPOULOU, LOTY. "Greece: A Brief Overview of Research in Children's Literature." *Phaedrus* 8 (1981):65-67.

        An overview with a bibliography of books and articles (in Greek with annotations in English) published since 1972.

B975   PLACOTARI, ALEXANDRA. "Literature for the Children of Greece." *Children's Literature* 3 (1974):56-60. (Also in *Bookbird* 12, no. 3 [1974]:37-43.)

        Discusses the development of children's literature in modern Greece.

GYPSIES

B976   RAY, SHEILA G. "The Changing Face of Gypsies in Children's Fiction." *Junior Bookshelf* 38 (October 1974):262-66.
        Examines the changing attitudes toward gypsies in children's books.

B977   STEVENS, CARLA. "Attitudes towards Gypsies in Children's Literature." *IRBC* 5, nos. 1-2 (1974):4.
        Examines three nonfiction books about gypsies: Bernice Kohn's *The Gypsies*, Katherine Esty's *Gypsies, Wanderers in Time*, and John Hornby's *Gypsies*, and also Kate Seredy's fictional *The Good Master*.

B978   TÓTH, BÉLA. "Portrayal of a Gipsy Child in a Contemporary Hungarian Juvenile Novel: Contribution to the Nature of Racial Prejudice." In Escarpit, *Portrayal of the Child*, pp. 239-46.
        Examines the way Maria Halasi's juvenile novel *The Last Bench* (Budapest: Mora, 1963) handles the problem of prejudice.

HANDICAPPED

B979   BASKIN, BARBARA. *Notes from a Different Drummer: A Guide to Juvenile Fiction Portraying the Handicapped.* New York: Bowker, 1977, 375 pp.
        Society and the handicapped, and the literary portrayal of disabilities are discussed in introductory chapters. Guidelines are given for the assessment and use of juvenile literature. The major portion of the book consists of an annotated guide to juvenile fiction, 1940-75. Each entry includes a two-part annotation consisting of plot summary and analysis, and indicates reading level and the disability portrayed.

B980   BIKLEN, DOUGLAS, and BOGDAN, ROBERT. "Media Portrayals of Disabled People: A Study in Stereotypes." *IRBC* 8, nos. 6-7 (1977):4-9.
        A survey of classic literature and contemporary media reveals ten common stereotypes about people with disabilities.

B981   HAMMOND, HELEN A. "A Review of the Changing Trends in the Portrayal of Handicapped Children in the Last 200 Years." In Hunt, *Further Approaches*, pp. 95-101.
        Reports on her research.

B982   HAYNES, JOHN. "No Child Is An Island: Three Books That Focus on Handicapped Children." *CLE*, o.s., no. 15 (1974):3-18.
        Discusses Ivan Southall's *Let the Balloon Go*, Alan Marshall's *I Can Jump Puddles*, and Patricia Wrightson's *I Own the Racecourse (A Racecourse for Andy)*.

B983   KINGSTON, CAROLYN T. "Rejection Due to Physical Disability." In *Tragic Mode*, pp. 27-38.
        Discusses a number of children's books in terms of their handling of the theme of rejection because of physical disability.

B984   LITTLE, GRETA D. "Handicapped Characters in Children's Literature: Yesterday and Today." *ChLAQ* 10, no. 4 (Winter 1986):181-84.
        Traces the changes in portrayal of the handicapped in children's

literature from the eighteenth and nineteenth centuries to the present.

B985   MAUER, RUTH A. "Young Children's Affective Responses to a Physically Disabled Story Book Hero." Ed.D. dissertation, Columbia University Teachers College, 1976, 155 pp., DA 37:918A.
"The purpose of this study was to determine whether identification with a story book hero is a function of physical status of hero and reader, and whether friendship preference is also a function of physical status."

B986   OAKLEY, MADELEINE COHEN. "Juvenile Fiction About the Orthopedically Handicapped." *TON* 30 (November 1973):57-68.
Surveys the good and the bad in children's books portraying the orthopedically handicapped, and provides insightful comments upon a number of well-known books. Includes a bibliography.

B987   ORJASAETER, TORDIS. "The Handicapped in Literature." *Bookbird* 1-2 (1980):3-6, 21-25.
Discusses the use of handicaps as symbols, usually unfortunate, in the works of a number of European and American writers. Concludes that "literature reflects the attitudes of society" and "literature perhaps also creates attitudes."

B988   PARKER, VIRGINIA. "Some Thought on Walls." *LA* 54 (January 1977):25-28.
Discusses several children's books using walls as a metaphor for problems that are overcome or accepted. Among the walls are those of handicaps, environment, and inner conflict.

B989   SAGE, MARY. "A Study of the Handicapped in Children's Literature." In MacLeod, *Children's Literature*, pp. 97-117.
Examines a number of stories about handicapped children, evaluating them as fiction and in terms of their understanding of the problems and feelings of the handicapped.

B990   SAPON-SHEVIN, MARA. "You Can't Judge Kids by Their Covers." *Advocate* 1, no. 2 (Winter 1982):80-90.
Suggests approaches to evaluating the portrayal of the handicapped in literature and examines a number of "excellent books."

B991   SCHWARTZ, ALBERT V. "Disability in Children's Books: Is Visibility Enough?" *IRBC* 8, nos. 6-7 (1977):10-15.
Examines images of the disabled in contemporary children's books.

B992   STROUD, JANET G. "The Handicapped in Adolescent Fiction." *Journal of Reading* 24 (March 1981):519-22.
Discusses the positive treatment of the handicapped in ten recent works of adolescent fiction.

B993   WATSON, EMILY STRAUSS. "Handicapism in Children's Books: A Five-Year Update." *IRBC* 13, nos. 4-5 (1982):3-7.
A survey and overview of more than seventy books for children published since 1977 that concerned various kinds of handicaps. Each book is briefly evaluated.

B994   ZIEGLER, CARLOS RAY. *The Image of the Physically Handicapped in Children's Literature.* New York: Arno Press, 1980, 156 pp. (Based on his Ed.D. dissertation, "The Image of the Physically Handicapped in Children's Literature," Temple University, 1971, 166 pp., DA 32:1842A.)

    Studies nine categories of interpersonal behavior in forty-seven selected children's fiction books with at least one physically handicapped character. Concentrates on enumeration and statistical analysis rather than literary criticism. Bibliographies include numerous unpublished masters theses.

HAWAII

B995   CANHAM, STEPHEN. "'DaKine': Writing for Children in Hawaii--and Elsewhere." *ChLAQ* 9, no. 4 (Winter 1984-85):174-76.

    Explores reasons why there has been no major children's writer in Hawaii.

HEROES AND HEROINES

B996   ASHLEY, L.F. "Curious Company: Some Juvenile Heroes, 1840-1940." *EE* 47 (March 1970):356-60.

    Argues that heroes of today's juvenile fiction are sadly lacking in the vitality and greatness common in Victorian times.

B997   DONELSON, KENNETH. "Types of Heroes." In *Literature for Today's Young Adults*, pp. 293-306.

    Divided into quiet heroes (Papa in Robert Newton Peck's *A Day No Pigs Would Die*), war heroes (Howard Fast's *April Morning* and Paula Fox's *How Many Miles to Babylon?*), and sports heroes (women in sports, and sports nonfiction).

B998   ENRIGHT, ELIZABETH. "The Hero's Changing Face." In *Contents of the Basket.* Edited by Frances Lander Spain. New York: New York Public Library, 1960, pp. 27-34.

    Traces the changing nature of the hero from the fairy tales through didactic and Victorian writers to the present.

B999   JONES, RAY. "Heroes in the Perilous Land: Pattern and Meaning in Arctic Fiction for Children." *CCL* 31-32 (1983):30-40.

    Examines "both the tales of Inuit culture and those of cultural comparison to show how they use the pattern of heroism and invest it with thematic significance." Concentrates on the work of James Houston.

B1000   NODELMAN, PERRY. "Some Heroes Have Freckles." In *Children's Books International Eight. Proceedings.* Boston: Boston Public Library, 1983. (Reprinted in May, *Children and Their Literature*, pp. 41-52.)

    Compares the traditional heroes and heroines of the fairy tales with the modern heroes and superheroes of television and finds them similarly lacking in character but excellent vehicles for "wish-fulfillment for powerless people." Contrasts them with another kind of hero, identified by Northrop Frye as the *Alazon* or tragic hero, and finds the heroes and heroines of some of the memorable classics of children's literature more closely resemble the *Alazon*, with his or her imperfection and freckles, than the perfect superhero.

B1001   OYLER, MARGARET MARY. "An Examination of the Heroine of the Junior Novel in America as Revealed in Selected Junior Novels, 1850-1960." Ed.D. dissertation, Columbia University, 1970, 362 pp., DA 31:3516A.

Focuses on "the heroine as an individual seen in relationship with her family and her community." Her social and economic status, the make-up of her family group, and her relationship to the opposite sex are examined. Concludes that the heroine generally "represents those values which the author wishes to impress on the mind of the reader . . . the 'minority' heroine with her aspirations and problems receives little attention. When she does appear, she differs only in the color of her skin."

B1002   SIEGE, SELMA R. "Heroines in Recent Children's Fiction--An Analysis." *EE* 50 (October 1973):1039-43.

Detects a new kind of heroine in children's literature in the 1960s "whose behavior is a form of psychological protest against an environment that hurts them." They are antiheroines in a limited sense. Based on an examination of fourteen books.

B1003   TICHÝ, JAROSLAV. "Robinson and Children's Literary Heroes." *Bookbird* 11, no. 3 (1973):9-16.

A historical survey that attempts to define the characteristics of the heroes of children's classics. Sees as central the Robinsonian attitude, "the passionate desire to turn one's idea into reality."

B1004   TÓTH, BÉLÁ. "The Meaning of the Hero and Heroic Traits for the Literary Experience of the School Child." *Bookbird* 11, no. 3 (1973):16-21.

Summarizes the results of a survey of literary heroes among Budapest school children.

B1005   *Wilson Library Bulletin.* "The Children's Hero: Rebel or Conformist." 38 (October 1963):154-64.

Symposium that includes Jason Epstein's "The Genteel Conspiracy," pp. 156-60, which argues that teachers, publishers, and librarians are conspiring to lead children into a pattern of middle-class conformity; "Tootle: A Modern Cautionary Tale," pp. 160-61 (text by Gertrude Crampton, pictures by Tibor Gergely), by David Riesman (an excerpt from *The Lonely Crowd*), which argues that the story directs children into an "other-directed mode of conformity"; and "In Quest of Value," by Elizabeth H. Gross, pp. 162-64 who agrees that the hero has been debased.

HIGH INTEREST/LOW READING

B1006   BATES, BARBARA S. "Identifying High Interest/Low Reading Level Books." *SLJ* 24 (November 1977):19-21.

Offers a set of criteria based on appearance, content, and style. Includes references.

HISPANICS

B1007   BLATT, GLORIA T. "The Mexican-American in Children's Literature." *EE* 45 (April 1968):446-51.

Concludes from a study of thirty-two books portraying Mexicans and Mexican-Americans that the quality of the books and their illustrations is high and that they do not convey stereotypes and prejudiced attitudes. Includes a list of books evaluated and additional references.

B1008 GARCIA, RICARDO. "Overview of Chicano Folklore." *English Journal* 65 (February 1976):83-87.
Includes a bibliography.

B1009 *Interracial Books for Children* 5, nos. 7-8 (1975):1-20. (Excerpts reprinted in MacCann, *Cultural Conformity*, pp. 55-64.)
Special double issue on Chicano culture in children's literature. Focuses on a Council survey of two hundred children's books on Chicano themes. Survey "reveals an overall pattern of cultural misrepresentation." Includes bibliographies.

B1010 MOYER, DOROTHY. "The Growth and Development of Children's Books About Mexico and Mexican Americans." Ed.D. dissertation, Lehigh University, 1974, 380 pp., DA 35:1878A.
Examines children's books about Mexico and Mexican Americans in terms of content, illustrations, and format to determine "whether there has been a change in the image."

B1011 SCHON, ISABEL. "Recent Detrimental and Distinguished Books about Hispanic People and Cultures." *TON* 38 (Fall 1981):79-85.
Discusses more than a dozen recent books portraying Hispanic people and culture, pointing out strengths and weaknesses. "The overwhelming majority of recent books incessantly repeat the same stereotypes, misconceptions and insensibilities that were prevalent in the books published in the 1960s and the early 1970s."

B1012 -----. "Recent Notorious and Noteworthy Books About Mexico, Mexicans, and Mexican Americans." *Journal of Reading* 24 (January 1981):293-99.
Examines acceptable and unacceptable treatment of Hispanic culture and people in recent books for children and young adults.

B1013 TAYLOR, JOSÉ. "The Chicano in Children's Literature." *California Librarian* 34 (January 1973):38-39. (Reprinted in MacCann, *Cultural Conformity*, pp. 65-67.)
Points out the lack of positive portrayals of Chicanos in children's literature, especially criticizing Ets's *Bad Boy, Good Boy* and Bonham's *Viva Chicano*.

B1014 TROUT, LAWANA. "Chicano Literature in Paperback." *English Journal* 65 (May 1976):78-80.
An overview, followed by an annotated bibliography, "Mexican-American Short Fiction for the High School Program," by Albert D. Trevino, pp. 81-85.

HISTORICAL FICTION

B1015 ATKINSON, DAVID W. "Canadian Historical Fiction: A Survey." *CCL* 23-24 (1981):28-29.
Identifies realism as a dominant trend in Canadian children's historical fiction since the 1950s.

B1016   BOSMAJIAN, HAMIDA. "Nightmares of History--The Outer Limits of Children's Literature." *ChLAQ* 8, no. 4 (Winter 1983):20-22.
Examines Paula Fox's *The Slave Dancer*, Hans Peter Richter's *Friedrich*, and Toshi Maruki's *Hiroshima No Pika*, and the ways in which the disasters of civilization are depicted in each.

B1017   BURTON, HESTER. "The Writing of Historical Novels." *Horn Book* 45 (June 1969):271-77. (Reprinted in Haviland, *Children and Literature*, pp. 299-304, and in Meek, *Cool Web*, pp. 159-65.)
Discusses some of the difficulties the writer of historical novels faces and outlines her own rules for writing.

B1018   CIANCIOLO, PATRICIA. "Yesterday Comes Alive for Readers of Historical Fiction." *LA* 58 (April 1981):452-62.
Discusses several examples of contemporary historical fiction in terms of the writers' diverse reactions to historical reality, in terms of readers' imaginative identification with historical characters, in terms of authenticity of the portrayals of the past, and in terms of making dehumanizing events accessible to the reader.

B1019   COBLENTZ, CATHERINE CATE. "Walking Into Yesterday." *Horn Book* 20 (July-August 1944):293-98.
Stresses that the author's knowledge of the time period and an ability to take the child along are essential. The child is looking for himself in the story, "and if the storyteller be wise enough, the child finds himself on the first page, perhaps in the first line." Includes examples from past and current authors.

B1020   COHEN, MARK. "What Shall We Tell the Children?" *History Today* 29 (December 1979):845-46. (Reprinted in Bator, *Signposts*, 273-76.)
Discusses approaches to problems in historical fiction for children: temporal location, language, realistic character, authenticity, and significance. Criticizes much historical fiction as smile-resistant--"the majority of tales are ones of daring-dour."

B1021   COLLIER, CHRISTOPHER. "Criteria for Historical Fiction." *SLJ* 28 (August 1982):32-33.
Offers four criteria for evaluating historical fiction: "Focus on an important historical theme, an understanding of which helps us to deal with the present, center on an episode in which the theme inheres in fact, attend to the historiographic elements, present accurate detail."

B1022   CROUCH, MARCUS. "The Abysm of Time." In *The Nesbit Tradition*, pp. 57-85.
Discusses works of Geoffrey Trease, Cynthia Harnett, Rosemary Sutcliff, Henry Treece, Ronald Welch, Walter Hodges, and Barbara Leonie Picard, among others, in this overview of historical fiction. Also indexed separately under authors' names in this bibliography.

B1023   -----. "The Art of Authenticity." *TLS*, 25 March 1977, p. 346.
Compares various approaches to writing historical fiction and conveying a sense of authenticity.

B1024   DONELSON, KENNETH. "Historical Fiction." In *Literature for Today's Young Adults*, pp. 244-48.

Contains a checklist for evaluating historical fiction. Mentions Leon Garfield and Rosemary Sutcliff as two outstanding writers of the genre for young adults.

B1025 EGOFF, SHEILA. "Historical Fiction." In *Thursday's Child*, pp. 159-92.

Provides a brief developmental overview of the genre. Sees recent trends away from the fast-paced plot toward emphasis on character and historical accuracy, realism rather than romance. Authors discussed include Hester Burton, Katherine Paterson, Rosemary Sutcliff, and Leon Garfield.

B1026 HILSON, JEFF F. "The Reflective Use of Novels to Focus on Controversial Issues in American History." Ph.D. dissertation, Ohio State University, 1980, 198 pp., ERIC Educational Document Reproduction Service, ED 196 050.

Explores the use of historical novels as a supplement in teaching American history in senior high school. "This study attempts to identify recognizable areas in American history, look at controversial issues that arose from the historical events of those eras, and match the controversial issues with representative sampling of quality novels that can illuminate those issues."

B1027 HOROWITZ, CAROLYN. "Dimensions in Time: A Critical View of Historical Fiction for Children." *Horn Book* 38 (June 1962):255-67.

"A great piece of historical fiction, written with absolute unity and depth of time, place, characters, and plot, is a unique achievement." Among historical novelists whom Horowitz names as top rank are Esther Forbes (for *Johnny Tremain*), Rosemary Sutcliff (for *The Eagle of the Ninth*), and Howard Pyle (for *Men of Iron*).

B1028 HUNTER, MOLLIE. "Shoulder the Sky: On the Writing of Historical Fiction for Children." Anne Carroll Moore Lecture. *Bulletin of the New York Public Library* 79, no. 2 (Winter 1976):124-38. (Also in *Talent Is Not Enough*, pp. 31-56.)

Reflects on the influence of her Scottish history and heritage on her early life and its relationship to the techniques and problems of writing historical fiction. Concludes that the writer must re-create "the feelings behind the pattern of that past time . . . feelings he [the reader] will then discover are essentially the same as his own," thus enabling the child to identify with those of all times who have sought, in the words of A.E. Housman, to "shoulder the sky."

B1029 JACOBS, LELAND B. "Historical Fiction for Children." *Reading Teacher* 14 (January 1961):191-94.

Defines the genre and explores its significance for children, pointing out pitfalls and suggesting criteria for evaluation.

B1030 -----. "Some Observations on Children's Historical Fiction." *EE* 29 (April 1952):185-86. (Reprinted in Bator, *Signposts*, pp. 267-69.)

Provides a brief definition of children's historical fiction.

B1031 JALONGO, MARY RENCK, and RENCK, MELISSA A. "Looking Homeward: Nostalgia in Children's Literature." *SLJ* 31 (Summer 1984):36-39.

Explores nostalgia in children's literature as a literary device.

B1032   JOHNSTON, PATRICIA E. "Atlantic Canadian Historical Fiction: Where Is the Drama?" *CCL* 23-24 (1981):51-58.
Characterizes Canadian historical fiction (quoting Sheila Egoff) as "a succession of failures." Examines several recent books to support the premise.

B1033   LEESON, ROBERT. "The Spirit of What Age?: The Interpretation of History from a Radical Standpoint." *CLE*, o.s., no. 23 (Winter 1976):172-82.
Describes a new approach to historical fiction since the 1950s which searches for roots of the present in the past, and attempts not to impose a twentieth-century view on the past, but to "throw light on that apparently distant age by seeking recognizable elements."

B1034   LOCHHEAD, MARION. "Clio Junior: Historical Novels for Children." *Quarterly Review* (January 1961). (Reprinted in Egoff, *Only Connect*, 1st ed., pp. 233-43.)
Surveys the historical novel for children from the mid-nineteenth century into the twentieth.

B1035   SMITH, LILLIAN. "Historical Fiction." In *Unreluctant Years*, pp. 164-76.
Maintains that adventure is the first requirement for historical fiction for children. The successful historical novel is written by a writer who is thoroughly "steeped in the life of a period."

B1036   TAXEL, JOEL ARTHUR. "The American Revolution in Children's Fiction." ERIC Educational Document Reproduction Service, 1980, 43 pp., ED 206 334. (An abridged version in *IRBC* 12, nos. 7-8 [1981]:3-9).
Reports on a study of thirty-two children's novels published between 1899 and 1976 to discover how the authors explained the American Revolution as a historical event.

B1037   -----. "The American Revolution in Children's Fiction: An Analysis of Historical Meaning and Narrative Structure." *Curriculum Inquiry* 14 (Spring 1984):7-55.
Provides a Marxist analysis of children's fiction set during the American Revolution, showing how the books were influenced by their socioeconomic and historical milieus.

B1038   -----. "The Depiction of the American Revolution in Children's Fiction: A Study in the Sociology of School Knowledge." Ph.D. dissertation, University of Wisconsin-Madison, 1980, 371 pp., DA 41:3868A.
Analyzes the meanings and ideologies of thirty-two recommended children's Revolutionary War novels published between 1899 and 1976. Finds most books conform to the "Whig" or conservative view of the Revolution, and progressive and revisionist interpretations are ignored.

B1039   -----. "Historical Fiction and Historical Interpretation." *ALAN Review* 10, no. 2 (Winter 1983):32-36.
Points out the educational value of several historical novels.

B1040   TREASE, GEOFFREY. "The Historical Novelist at Work." *CLE*, o.s., no. 7 (March 1972). (Reprinted in Fox, *Writers, Critics, and Chil-*

dren, pp. 39-51.)
  Discusses approaches to writing historical fiction for children, emphasizing the importance of plot and pointing out difficulties with dialogue, authenticity, and atmosphere, with examples from some of his own works.

B1041 -----. "The Historical Story--Is It Relevant Today?" *Horn Book* 53 (February 1977):21-28. (Reprinted in Bator, *Signposts*, pp. 277-82.)
  Argues that the historical novelist can bring the past to life. Discusses the background of many of his own works.

B1042 -----. "Problems of the Historical Storyteller." *Junior Bookshelf* 15 (December 1951):559-64. (Reprinted in Bator, *Signposts*, pp. 269-72.)
  Considers the problems of archaic language, accuracy, and realism in terms of character and social history.

B1043 WALSH, JILL PATON. "History Is Fiction." *Horn Book* 48 (February 1972):17-23. (Reprinted in Heins, *Crosscurrents*, pp. 219-25.)
  Answers objections to the historical novel from aesthetic purists and historians.

HISTORY

B1044 BARKMAN, DONNA, and GRIFFITH, SUSAN G. "The Woman's Suffrage Movement in Children's Books." *IRBC* 13, no. 1 (1982):3-7.
  Examines the treatment of the woman's suffrage movement in histories, biographies, and historical fiction for children.

B1045 CARR, JO, comp. "History: The Past Realized, Remembered, and Enjoyed." In *Beyond Fact*, pp. 90-116.
  Includes Carr's introductory essay, "History: Factual Fiction or Fictional Fact?"; Frances Clark Sayers's "History Books for Children" (adapted from *Anthology of Children's Literature*, 3d ed., by Edna Johnson, Evelyn R. Sickels, and Frances Clarke Sayers); F.N. Monjo's "The Ten Bad Things About History"; Milton Meltzer's "Who's Neutral?" (reprinted from *CLE*, o.s., no. 14 [1974]:24-35); and Carol Gay's "History Books: Making America's History Come Alive" (adapted from "Children's Literature and the Bicentennial," *LA* 53 [January 1976]:11-16.)

B1046 FRITZ, JEAN. "The Education of an American." In *Arbuthnot Lectures* pp. 123-38.
  Recalls her personal experiences of discovering what it is to be an American, her reading of the boys' stories and family classics of American literature, and finally her approach to history and the importance of that approach to history for the young.

B1047 -----. "Make Room for the Eighteenth Century." *Horn Book* 50 (October 1974):177-81.
  Argues for the importance of accurate history and biography for the young.

B1048 -----. "The Very Truth." In Hearne, *Celebrating Children's Books*, pp. 81-86.
  Examines the difficulties historians have in telling "the very truth," and explores the necessity for a sense of humor and specific anecdotal information about people, as well as scholarship.

B1049   HOBERMAN, JUDITH SLOAN. "Recycling the Red, White, and Blue:
         The Bicentennial and Books for Children." *Harvard Educational
         Review* 46 (August 1976):468-76.
             Discusses the flaws of many books related to American history,
         traces the place of these books in publishing cycles, and suggests
         ways in which educators "can use all the literature at their disposal to
         enhance children's historical sense."

B1050   MELTZER, MILTON. "Beyond the Span of a Single Life." In Hearne,
         Celebrating Children's Books, pp. 87-96.
             Examines the state of history-writing for young people--its pur-
         poses and problems.

B1051   -----. "The Fractured Image: Distortions in Children's History Books."
         Library Journal 93 (October 1968):3921-25.
             Discusses inaccuracies and inadequacies in children's history
         books, primarily textbooks, and points out some steps in new direc-
         tions.

B1052   MOYNIHAN, RUTH BARNES. "American History for Young People at
         Bicentennial." *Children's Literature* 5 (1976):261-69.
             Critically examines eleven recent histories and biographies.

B1053   ODLAND, NORINE. "American History in Fact and Fiction: Litera-
         ture for Young Readers." *Social Education* 44 (October 1980):474-81.
             Explores the varieties of literature available to teach children
         about the past: folktales and legends, fantasy, poetry, picture books,
         realistic fiction, historical fiction, biographies, and nonfiction.
         Includes a selected annotated bibliography of titles of children's books
         relating to American history.

HOLOCAUST

B1054   KIMMEL, ERIC A. "Confronting the Ovens: The Holocaust and Juve-
         nile Fiction." *Horn Book* 53 (February 1977):84-91.
             A fine critical overview of holocaust fiction for children and
         youth. Organizes the books "into a pattern similar to that of Dante's
         Inferno. The smoking chimneys of Birkenau are at the center with
         the lesser hells ringed around it in ascending order."

B1055   MITCHELL, JUDY. "Children of the Holocaust." *English Journal* 69
         (October 1980):14-18.
             Discusses a number of children's books relating to the holocaust,
         including books by Judy Blume, James Forman, Anne Frank, Bette
         Greene, Judith Kerr, Ilse Koerner, Myron Leroy, Michel Murray,
         Johanna Reiss, Hans Peter Richter, and Marilyn Sachs.

HOME

B1056   CLAUSEN, CHRISTOPHER. "Home and Away in Children's Fiction."
         Children's Literature 10 (1982):141-51.
             Suggests that attitude toward home may be one of the criteria for
         distinguishing children's books from adults'. For the adult, home
         may be a place from which to escape, as in *Huckleberry Finn*,
         whereas in the true children's book, Grahame's *Wind in the Willows*
         and Tolkien's *The Hobbit*, for example, home is the place to which

one always returns.

B1057 FREY, CHARLES. "The Siren Call of Child-Romance." *Southern Humanities Review* 12 (Winter 1978):1-6.

Comments on "the romance form of quest journey and ultimate return home" in "some of the very greatest works of children's literature": *The Snow Queen, Alice's Adventures, Treasure Island, Huckleberry Finn, The Jungle Books, Peter Pan,* and *The Little Prince.* However, he feels these child-romances are distinguished by "their general indifference, mistrust, and even antipathy toward worlds of home, civilization, parents, and grown-ups."

B1058 SADLER, DAVID F. "From *Where the Wild Things Are* to *Wild in the World.*" *CLE,* o.s., no. 13 (1974):53-67.

Examines the pattern, recurrent in children's literature, of "escape, adventure, and return, as it appears in four books of contemporary realistic fiction: Paula Fox's *Stone-Faced Boy,* Vera and Bill Cleaver's *Grover,* and John Donovan's *I'll Get There, It Better Be Worth the Trip* and *Wild in the World.*

B1059 STOTT, JON C. "Running Away to Home--A Story Pattern in Children's Literature." *LA* 55 (April 1978):473-77.

Points out that a version of the circular journey; escape from home to learn about self, society, and return home again with greater understanding is common in children's books. Analyzes five children's books in terms of this theme: *The Story About Ping,* by Marjorie Flack and Kurt Wiese, *Where The Wild Things Are,* by Maurice Sendak, *Jacob Two-Two Meets the Hooded Fang,* by Mordecai Richler, *Call It Courage,* by Armstrong Sperry, and *Julie of the Wolves,* by Jean Craighead George.

B1060 WADDEY, LUCY E. "Home in Children's Fiction: Three Patterns." *ChLAQ* 8, no. 1 (Spring 1983):13-15.

Categorizes three attitudes toward home in children's fiction: the Odyssean, the Oedipal, and the Promethean.

HOMOSEXUALITY

B1061 AMERICAN LIBRARY ASSOCIATION. Social Responsibilities Roundtable's Gay Task Force. "What to Do Until Utopia Arrives." *WLB* 50 (March 1976). (Reprinted in Varlejs, *Young Adult Literature,* pp. 441-43.)

A set of guidelines for evaluating "gay themes in children's and young adults' literature."

B1062 GOODMAN, JAN. "Out of the Closet, But Paying the Price: Lesbian and Gay Characters in Children's Literature." *IRBC* 14, nos. 3-4 (1983):13-15.

Finds offensive stereotypes and inaccuracies in recent books with lesbian and gay characters.

B1063 HANCHEL, FRANCES, and CUNNINGHAM, JOHN. "Can Young Gays Find Happiness in Young Adult Books?" *WLB* 50 (March 1976):528-34. (Reprinted in Lenz, *Young Adult Literature,* pp. 204-12, and in Varlejs, *Young Adult Literature,* pp. 302-9.)

Summarizes plots of four pioneering young-adult novels portraying homosexuality and finds them wanting.

B1064   HOLLAND, ISABELLE. "Tilting at Taboos." *Horn Book* 49 (June 1973):299-305. (Reprinted in Heins, *Crosscurrents*, pp. 137-43.)
Argues that without taboos there could be no storytelling. Examines changing mores and values in terms of her own *Man Without a Face* and other works.

B1065   JENKINS, C.A., and MORRIS, JULIE L. "Recommended Books on Gay/Lesbian Themes." *IRBC* 14, nos. 3-4 (1983):16-19.
An annotated bibliography of recent books, both fiction and non-fiction.

B1066   LUKENBILL, BERNARD. "Homosexual Conflicts and Their Resolutions in Five Adolescent Novels: A Psychosocial Inquiry." In Lenz, *Young Adult Literature*, pp. 212-24.
Partly in response to Hanchel and Cunningham, analyzes *I'll Get There, It Better Be Worth the Trip* by John Donovan, *Man Without a Face* by Isabelle Holland, *Sticks & Stones* by Lynn Hall, *Trying Hard to Hear You* by Sandra Scoppettone, and *Ruby* by Rosa Gay.

B1067   MITCHELL, JUDITH NAUGHTON. "Changes in Adolescent Literature with Homosexual Motifs, Themes, and Characters." Ph.D. dissertation, University of Connecticut, 1982, 121 pp., DA 43:133A.
Finds little change in portrayals of homosexuality in adolescent literature in recent books, despite increased attention to the topic. The one exception is that since 1973 more characters are homosexual by definition rather than as a temporary phase.

B1068   -----. "Loving Girls." *ALAN Review* 10, no. 1 (Fall 1982):32-35.
Discusses a number of books depicting love relationships between girls.

B1069   STENSON, LEAH DELAND. "Playing Favorites: The Trouble with Sex Education Guides." *SLJ* 23 (November 1976):34-35.
Points out problems with the handling of homosexuality in juvenile sex education books.

B1070   WHITE, DAVID. "The Young Adult Gay Novel." *SRRT Newsletter* 33:21-23. (Reprinted in Varlejs, *Young Adult Literature*, pp. 298-301.)
Reviews Isabelle Holland's *Man Without a Face* and Lynn Hall's *Sticks and Stones*.

B1071   WHITLOCK, KATHERINE, and DiLAPI, ELENA M. "'Friendly Fire': Homophobia in Sex Education Literature." *IRBC* 14, nos. 3-4 (1983):20-23.
Points out that sex education materials, although showing some improvement, still convey extremely negative attitudes toward homosexuality. Includes "Guidelines for Evaluating Sex Education Materials for Homophobia."

B1072   WOLF, VIRGINIA. "Same-Sex Relationships in the Contemporary Novel for Adolescents." *Wisconsin English Journal* 20, no. 2 (January 1978):27-32. (ERIC Educational Document Reproduction Service, ED 149 373.)
Examines same-sex relationships in six contemporary adolescent novels which attempt to raise and resolve a problem regarding homo-

sexuality. Points out that "There are no adolescent novels told from a lesbian's or a gay male's point of view. . . . There are no fully developed and complex characterizations of gay individuals in the contemporary adolescent novel."

HUMOR

B1073   BATEMAN, ROBIN. "Children and Humorous Literature." *School Librarian* 15 (July 1967):153-61.
Categorizes "six different sets of circumstances in literature which provoke mirth in the young": (1) the funny incident, (2) the comic pictorial image, (3) the pleasure in words, (4) the misuse of words which produces a sense of superiority in the child, (5) nonsense that is ludicrous, and (6) subtlety ("noticed only by the very intelligent").

B1074   BENNETT, JOHN E., and BENNETT, PRISCILLA. "What's So Funny? Action Research and Bibliography of Humorous Children's Books --1975-80." *Reading Teacher* 35 (May 1982):924-27.
Analyzes the characteristics of a group of children's books found humorous by children in grades four through six. Includes an annotated list of titles.

B1075   BERDING, MARY CORDELIA, Sister. "Humor as a Factor in Children's Literature." Ed.D. dissertation, University of Cincinnati, 1965, 245 pp., DA 26:3691A.
Identifies "what plot situations are humorous," how authors have "treated certain situations to make them humorous to the reader," the aspects of style that contribute to humor, and the contribution of characterization to humor. Concludes with a set of criteria for "a good humorous book for children."

B1076   BINDER, LUCIA. "Humour in Children's Books." *Bookbird* 8, no. 4 (1970):8-14; 9, no. 1 (1971):8-10; 9, no. 2 (1971):19-23.
Surveys trends in humorous children's books beginning with the classics and emphasizing the books of various European countries. Concludes that while there are similar trends, "humour takes on a slightly different colour in each country." Feels that in American and German literature all trends meet.

B1077   BLOS, JOAN W. "Getting It: The First Notch on the Funny Bone." *SLJ* 25 (May 1979):38-39.
Explores preschoolers' responses to humor in children's books.

B1078   CLEARY, BEVERLY. "The Laughter of Children." *Horn Book* 58 (October 1982):555-64.
Explores the nature of humor in children's books and what children find funny. Uses examples from her own and others' books.

B1079   "Comedy in Children's Literature." *L&U* 1, no. 1 (1977). Edited by Geraldine De Luca and Roni Natov.
Special issue. Includes "Comedy in Children's Literature: An Overview," by Natov and DeLuca, pp. 4-8; "Once Upon a Shtetl: Schlimazels, Schlemiels, Schnorrers, Shadchens, and Sages: Yiddish Humor in Children's Books," by Marilyn Jurich, pp. 9-25; "The Little Boy Who Drops His Pants in the Crowd: Tomi Ungerer's Art of the Comic Grotesque," by R.A. Siegel, pp. 26-32; "'Instigorating' *Winnie the Pooh*," by Ellen Tremper, pp. 33-46; "*Pippi Longstocking*: The

Comedy of the National Girl," by Laura Hoffeld, pp. 47-53; "The Seriocomic World of Tin-Tin," by Nicholas Pease, pp. 54-61; "From Huck to Holden to Dinky Hocker: Current Humor in the American Adolescent Novel," by Robert J. Lacampagne, pp. 62-71; and "An Interview with Arnold Lobel," by Roni Natov and Geraldine De Luca, pp. 72-97. Also indexed separately under individual topics and authors in this bibliography.

B1080   CROUCH, MARCUS. "Laughter." In *The Nesbit Tradition*, pp. 101-11.
Discusses briefly books that are primarily humorous, including Astrid Lindgren's Pippi books, Helen Cresswell, and several others.

B1081   FARDELL, JOYCE. "Humour in Children's Fiction." *Orana* 16 (August 1980):82-92.
Provides an extensive examination of various categories of humor.

B1082   FENNER, PHYLLIS. "Funny, Is It?" *Library Journal* 85 (15 October 1960):3822-24.
Explores what children find funny and comments on the characteristics of the humor of a number of popular children's books.

B1083   FLEISCHMAN, SID. "Laughter and Children's Literature." *Horn Book* 52 (October 1976):465-70 and *Claremont Reading Conference Yearbook* 40 (1976):88-92. (Reprinted in Heins, *Crosscurrents*, pp. 199-204.)
Explores reasons for the paucity of humor in children's books, especially for older readers, and points out that folklore is rich in comic possibilities.

B1084   GUARNIERI, ROSSANA. "Humor and Society." *Bookbird* 8, no. 1 (1970):10-13.
"Humor can make society accessible at the child's level." Cites examples from children's literature and the testimony of well-known psychologists.

B1085   HAWKINS, KARLA JEAN. "Elementary School Children's Preferences for Selected Elements of Humor in Children's Books as Determined by Sex and Grade Level." Ph.D. dissertation, Georgia University, 1977, 132 pp., DA 38:4569A.
Concludes that humor preference is an individual trait. Found few differences in grade level, sex, and appreciation of type of humor. One book was the overwhelming favorite of all groups, while other titles increased or decreased in popularity according to age groups.

B1086   KAPPAS, KATHERINE. "A Developmental Analysis of Children's Responses to Humor." *Library Quarterly* 37 (January 1967):67-77.
Applies a developmental analysis of children's responses to humor to the analysis of humorous children's literature.

B1087   LANDAU, ELLIOTT D. "Quibble, Quibble: Funny? Yes; Humorous, No!" *Horn Book* 38 (April 1962):154-64.
Distinguishes between what is humorous and what is merely funny in a number of classic children's books. Includes an exchange of letters with James Thurber on the topic of humor.

B1088   MONSON, DIANNE LYNN. "Children's Responses to Humorous Situations in Literature." Ph.D. dissertation, University of Minnesota, 1966, 238 pp., DA 27:2448A.

Compares two methods for eliciting children's responses to humor in literature, investigates children's judgments of humor in children's books, and investigates children's choices of specific types of humor.

B1089   -----. "A Look at Humor in Literature and Children's Responses to Humor." ERIC Educational Document Reproduction Service, 1979, 22 pp., ED 162 285.

Summarizes research relating to humor in literature and children's responses to humor, and suggests further avenues of exploration. Includes extensive references and a list of humorous children's books.

B1090   NELSON, ROBERT. "Responses of Sixth-Grade Students to Two Types of Humor Present in Fiction for Children, and an Investigation of the Types of Humor Found in Books for the Middle Grade Reader." Ph.D. dissertation, Michigan State University, 1974, 311 pp., DA 35:1534A.

Examines the reactions of sixth-grade children to humor based on a physical action of some sort and humor based upon words used by the characters in stories. Also analyzes a selection of humorous literature for children, classifying the humor as word humor or action humor. Found that humor is a very individual trait.

B1091   NILSEN, DON L.F., and NILSEN, ALLEEN PACE. "An Exploration and Defense of the Humor in Young Adult Literature." *Journal of Reading* 26 (October 1982):58-65.

Finds that teenagers choices in humor "are understandable when looked at in relation to teenagers' interests, levels of maturity and experience, and intellectual and psychological development." Includes a bibliography.

B1092   PETRY, ANNE KATHERINE. "Young Children's Response to Three Types of Humor." Ph.D. dissertation, University of Connecticut, 1978, 159 pp., DA 39:5525B.

Explores "to what extent and in what manner age, sex, verbal ability, and self-concept explain variations in five and seven year olds' comprehension and appreciation of three types of humor found in children's books: incongruity, exaggeration, and nonsense language." Age appeared to be the most influential variable, followed by verbal ability and self-concept.

B1093   PFORDRESHER, JOHN. "An Approach to Analyzing Jokes." *English Journal* 70 (October 1981):50-54.

Outlines an approach based on Freud's *Jokes and Their Relation to the Unconscious.*

B1094   SCHWARTZ, ALVIN. "Children, Humor and Folklore." *Horn Book* 53 (June 1977):281-87; (August 1977):471-476.

Tells, from a folklore perspective, what humor children like and how humor travels.

B1095   SMITH, JAMES S. "The Hoot of Little Voices: Humor in Children's Books." In *A Critical Approach to Children's Literature.* New York: McGraw-Hill, 1967, pp. 203-24.

Provides a good introduction to the topic and lists books according to the categories of humor they express.

B1096 STEINBERG, SYBIL S. "What Makes a Funny Children's Book: Five Writers Talk About Their Methods." *Publishers Weekly* 213 (27 February 1978):87-90.
Dr. Seuss, Sid Fleischman, Daniel Manus Pinkwater, Mark Alan Stamaty, and Susan Jeschke talk about what makes a funny book.

B1097 STEINFIRST, SUSAN. "More About the Funny Bone: A Response." *SLJ* 26 (January 1980):42-43.
Responds to Joan Blos's reflections about children and humor, and reports on additional research on the topic.

HUNGARY

B1098 ASZÓDI, EVA. "Lyric Poetry for Children in Hungary." *Bookbird* 8 (1970):14-17.
Surveys modern Hungarian children's poetry.

B1099 BALÁZS, VARGHA. "Current Trends in Children's Literature: Children's Literature in the Future: The Hungarian Experience." *International Library Review* 5 (1973):269-75.
Summarizes history and trends in Hungarian children's literature.

B1100 BRESTÝANSZKY, ILONA. "Contemporary Children's Book Illustration in Hungary." *Bookbird* 9, no. 2 (1971):68-75.
Surveys recent trends, singling out many outstanding illustrators and showing a few examples (in black and white) of their work.

B1101 ORTH, HELEN K. "Hungary: Stories of Heroic Struggle." *WLB* 48 (June 1974):826-31.
An overview of Hungary's rich tradition of classic children's literature.

B1102 TÓTH, BÉLÁ. "The History of Hungarian Children's and Youth Periodicals." *Phaedrus* 4, no. 2 (Fall 1977):26-30.
A survey with an extensive bibliography of articles, in Hungarian, on children's periodicals.

ICELAND

B1103 ADALSTEINSDOTTIR, SILJA. "Iceland." *Phaedrus* 4, no. 1 (Spring 1977):38-39.
Surveys current research on children's literature in Iceland. Includes a brief bibliography; all items in Icelandic except one in Danish.

B1104 -----. "Iceland." *Phaedrus* 8 (1981):68-69.
Summarizes her book *Islenskar Barnabaeker 1780-1979* (Icelandic Children's Literature, 1780-1979 (Reykjavik: Malognenning, 1981) 402 pp.

B1105 ASTGEIRSSON, GUNNLAUGUR. "Writing for Children in Iceland." *Bookbird* 3 (1981):3-6. Originally published in Swedish in *Bur Nytt* 3, no. 4 (1980).
A general survey.

B1106 KINGMAN, LEE. "A Search for Children's Books in Iceland." *Horn*

Book 47 (October 1971):462-69.
Tells mostly about imported books found in Icelandic bookstores.

IDENTITY

B1107   CROUCH, MARCUS. "Self and Society." In *The Nesbit Tradition*, pp. 196-229.
"Some of the most powerful of children's novels are about identity." Discusses Anne Holm's *I Am David*, Philippa Pearce, Sheena Porter, Ruth Arthur, Patricia Wrightson, John Rowe Townsend, and Joan Robinson. Concludes with a discussion of race and class and the works of H.F. Brinsmead, Mary Treadgold, Anne Barrett, and Eric Allen. Also indexed separately under authors' names in this bibliography.

B1108   PETITT, DOROTHY. "A Search for Self-Definition: The Picture of Life in the Novel for the Adolescent." *English Journal* 49 (December 1960):616-26.
A survey of "best-written" novels for adolescents, selected as describing the ways in which they depict the adolescent's search for self-definition. Includes booklist.

IMMIGRANTS

B1109   BARR, JANET LOUISE COOK. "The Immigrants in Children's Fictional Books Recommended for American Libraries, 1883-1938." Ph.D. dissertation, Indiana University, 1976, 185 pp., DA 37:1852A.
Compares the depiction of immigrants in American children's literature to reality.

INDIA

B1110   DEY, PROVASH RONJAN. *Children's Literature of Bengal.* Calcutta: Academy for Documentation and Research on Children's Literature, 1978, 32 pp.
Surveys Bengali children's literature from the beginning of the nineteenth century up to the middle of the twentieth.

B1111   -----. *Children's Literature of India.* Calcutta: Academy for Documentation and Research on Children's Literature, 1977, 56 pp.
A survey of Indian children's literature.

B1112   KUMAR, KRISHNA. "Rise of the Adult-Centered Child in Hindi Children's Literature (1930-1980)." In Escarpit, *Portrayal of the Child*, pp. 71-78.
Examines the effect of social changes in India between 1930 and 1980 on the portrayal of the child in Indian children's literature during that time.

B1113   ROWLAND, CLARISSA. "Bungalow and Bazaar: India in Victorian Children's Fiction." *Children's Literature* 2 (1973):192-96.
From Mrs. Sherwood through Kipling and *Little Black Sambo*.

B1114   ROY, KULDIP KUMAR. "Publishing for Children and Professional Work with Children's Literature in India." *Bookbird* 3 (1981):11-13.
Emphasizes journals for children, but also mentions research, reference books, and teaching.

B1115   -----. "The Refugee Child in the Children's Literature of the Indian Subcontinent." In Escarpit, *Portrayal of the Child*, pp. 195-206.
The refugee child "has become for all writers and poets an uncannily evocative symbol."

B1116   SHEORAN, KAMAL. "Contemporary Children's Literature in India." *Children's Literature* 4 (1975):127-37.
A survey encompassing the rich oral tradition of the multilingual folktales and written literature for children.

B1117   UMAPATHY, K.S. "Children's Literature in Kannada." *International Library Review* 13 (October 1981):435-43.
Reports on the children's literature published in Kannada, the spoken and written language of the people of Karnataka, India.

B1118   -----. "Children's Literature in Karnataka (India)." *Bookbird* 3 (1981):6-9.
A survey.

INDIANS OF NORTH AMERICA

B1119   ABEL, MIDGE B. "American Indian Life as Portrayed in Children's Literature." *EE* 50 (February 1973):202-8.
Traces the evolution in portraits of Native Americans in children's literature from Cooper's *Last of the Mohicans* to recent times, and concludes that more meaningful literature for young Indian children is needed.

B1120   BADER, BARBARA. "Of the American Indian." In *American Picturebooks*, pp. 158-66.
Discusses the portrayal of Native Americans in picture books, concentrating on works by Naomi Averill, Ann Nolan Clark and her illustrators, and E-Yeh-Shure's (Louise Abeita's) *I Am a Peublo Indian Girl*.

B1121   BARRON, PAMELA. "The Characterization of Native Americans in Children's and Young Adult's Fiction, with a Contemporary Setting by Native and Non-Native American Authors: A Content Analysis." Ph.D. dissertation, Florida State University, 1981, 191 pp., DA 42:2342A.
Concludes that many of the obvious stereotypes of Native Americans have given place to more subtle ones. Finds fewer stereotypes in books by non-Native Americans than in those by Native Americans. Finds a lack of humor in all the books analyzed. Recommends that more books be written by Native Americans and that more insight be shown into "the dynamics of Native American Culture."

B1122   BERKMAN, BRENDA. "The Vanishing Race: Conflicting Images of the American Indian in Children's Literature, 1880-1930." *North Dakota Quarterly* 44, no. 2 (1976):31-40.
Americans' conflicting attitudes toward Indians is revealed and passed on, unresolved, in their literature for children.

B1123   BROWN, RICHARD WILLIAM. "Characteristics and Concepts of American Indians in Children's Fictional Literature Published between 1963 and 1973." Ed.D. dissertation, Temple University, 1978, 144 pp., DA 37:738A.

Concludes that "American Indians in children's literature published between 1963 and 1973 are generally depicted very positively and in a dignified fashion. Although stereotypes remain the most predominant ones are complimentary in nature."

B1124 BYLER, MARY GLOYNE. Introduction to *American Indian Authors for Young Readers*. New York: Association on American Indian Affairs, 1973, pp. 5-11. (Reprinted and excerpted in MacCann, *Cultural Conformity*, pp. 27-38, and in *SLJ* 20 [February 1974]:36-69, and *Library Journal* 99 [February 1974]:546-49. Comments in *Library Journal* 99 [15 May 1974]:1420-21, 1454-55, and *SLJ* 20 [May 1974]:2-3, 36-39.)

Provides an overview of the portrayal of Native Americans in children's books. Concludes, "Only American Indians can tell non-Indians what it is to be Indian. There is no longer any need for non-Indian writers to "interpret American Indians for the American public."

B1125 *Canadian Children's Literature* 31-32 (1983):144 pp.

Entire issue is devoted to the children's literature and mythology of the Native peoples of Canada. Articles include Gwyneth Evans's "The Mouse Woman and Mrs. Harris," about Christie Harris; Agnes Grant's "Bridging the Cultural Gap"; Perry Nodelman's "Non-Native Primitive Art"; Elizabeth Cleaver's "Indian Legends"; and Gordon Johnston's "Obiquadj: Instruction and Delight for Children in White Versions of Indian Stories." The issue also contains numerous review articles.

B1126 CATA, JUANITA O. "The Portrait of American Indians in Children's Fictional Literature." Ph.D. dissertation, University of New Mexico, 1977, 220 pp., DA 38:3266A.

This survey and analysis of the portrayal of the American Indian in children's fiction between 1900 and 1972 concludes that "most writers of children's fictional literature need to provide a more accurate portrayal of their American Indian characters. There is also a need for more children's books to be authored by Indian people."

B1127 FISHER, LAURA. "All Chiefs, No Indians: What Children's Books Say About American Indians." *EE* 51 (February 1974):185-89.

Surveys children's fiction, about Native Americans and points out some of the well-constructed, accurate books among the hackneyed and stereotyped majority. Includes a bibliography of recommended books.

B1128 HELBIG, ALETHEA K. "Manabozho of the North Central Woodlands: Hero of Folktale or of Myth?" *Children's Literature* 4 (1975):30-35.

Examines the Manabozho tales as literature and argues that they are suitable for children.

B1129 -----. "Teaching American Literature from Its Real Beginnings: Native American Stories." *ALAN Review* 6 (Fall 1978):3-4, 8-9. (Reprinted in Lenz, *Young Adult Literature*, pp. 259-66.)

Argues that traditional Native American tales and legends should be included in the study of American literature.

B1130   HERBST, LAURA. "That's One Good Indian: Unacceptable Images in Children's Novels." *TON* 31 (January 1975):192-98. (Reprinted in MacCann, *Cultural Conformity*, pp. 39-47.)
Points out objectionable treatment of Indians and Indian culture in many well-known and acclaimed children's books.

B1131   HILL, ELBERT. "Tales and Trials: Children's Stories and Cultural Alienation Among the Winnebago." Ph.D. dissertation, University of Nebraska-Lincoln, 1973, 608 pp., DA 34:7706A.
Finds "great differences" in the value systems of the dominant American white culture and Winnebago culture by analyzing and comparing thirty dominant-culture folktales and three Winnebago cycles of traditional tales.

B1132   HIRSCHFELDER, ARLENE B. *American Indian Stereotypes in the World of Children: A Reader and a Bibliography.* Scarecrow, 1982, 296 pp.
Includes Mary Gloyne Byler's Introduction to *American Indian Authors for Young Readers: A Selected Bibliography*, pp. 34-45, and Robert B. Moore and Arlene B. Hirschfelder's "Feather's, Tomahawks and Tipis: A Study of Stereotyped 'Indian' Imagery in Children's Picture Books" (reprinted from *Unlearning "Indian" Stereotypes*, by the Council on Interracial Books for Children, 1977, pp. 46-79). Chapter 4 contains four articles on the stereotyping of Native Americans in school textbooks. Extensive bibliographies, including a listing of articles and books on the image of Native Americans in American and European literature, and a listing of "'correctives,' a variety of materials that can be employed in trying to undo the incorrect, offending images of Native Americans."

B1133   HOILMAN, GRACE DONA GUBLER. "Voices and Images of the American Indian in Literature for Young People." Ph.D. dissertation, Ball State University, 1981, DA 41:3566A.
Analyzes informational books, biographies, fiction, folklore, and poetry, finding much stereotyping and misinformation still in existence. Finds the most positive and distinctive images in poetry by Native Americans.

B1134   HÜURLIMANN, BETTINA. "From Deerslayer to Old Shatterhand: Some Thoughts on the Attractiveness of Red Indians and on the Literary Sources Which Have Given Children Their Ideas About Them." In *Three Centuries*, pp. 113-26.
Traces the influences of James Fenimore Cooper and others upon European children's literature about American Indians, especially on the works of Karl May.

B1135   JOHNSTON, BASIL. "Nanabush." *CCL* 31-32 (1983):41-45.
Analyzes the character of Nanabush, a deity in the mythology of many Algonquian tribes.

B1136   KATZ, JANE. "*This Song Remembers*: Native American Voices and Visions." *LA* 60 (April 1983):439-46.
Explores the Native American storytelling tradition as a source of literary inspiration for the young, Indian and non-Indian alike.

B1137   McHARGUE, GEORGESS. "Countering Old Myths." *American Librar-*

ies 6 (March 1975):166-67.
Surveys a number of revisionist titles portraying Native Americans and lists six myths they counter to some extent.

B1138　MICKINIOCK, REY. "The Plight of the Native American." *Library Journal* 96, no. 16 (15 September 1971):2848-51 and *SLJ* 18 (September 1971):46-50. (Reprinted in Gerhardt, *Issues in Children's Book Selection*, pp. 102-6.)
Points out common stereotypes of Native Americans in a number of well-known books and recommends titles that convey accurate information.

B1139　NAPIER, GEORGIA PIERCE. "A Study of the North American Indian Character in Twenty Selected Children's Books." Ed.D. dissertation, University of Arkansas, 1970, 126 pp., DA 31:2618A.
Examines books published between 1931 and 1966. Concludes that traditional stereotypes are not persisting, the characters are seldom presented in contemporary circumstances, the physical descriptions of Native American characters are attractive, the language they use is grammatical and fluent, and the status of the North American Indian character is acceptable.

B1140　NEWELL, ETHEL. "The Indian Stereotype Passes." *EE* 31 (December 1954):472-76.
Presents criteria for evaluating books about Indians and surveys some of the more recent nonstereotyped portrayals.

B1141　ORD, PRISCILLA. "Recent Literature for Children By and About Native Americans." *Children's Literature* 7 (1978):233-41.
Evaluates nineteen recent books of fiction, nonfiction, and folktales.

B1142　SEALE, DORIS. "Bibliographies about Native Americans--A Mixed Blessing." *IRBC* 12, no. 3 (1981):11-15.
An evaluation of bibliographies of books with Native American themes.

B1143　STENSLAND, ANNA LEE. "Indian Literature and the Adolescent." (ERIC Educational Document Reproduction Service, 1975, 17 pp., ED 124 325.)
Discusses contributions of American Indians to American culture and recommends kinds of literature that could be read by Indian and non-Indian students to enhance their understanding of its significance.

B1144　STOODT, BARBARA D., and IGNIZIO, SANDRA. "The American Indian in Children's Literature." *LA* 53 (January 1976):17-21.
Reports on a survey to evaluate children's books published from 1930 to the present in terms of their portrayal of the American Indian. A bibliography and checklist are included.

B1145　STOTT, JON C. "In Search of the True Hunter: Inuit Folktales Adapted for Children." *LA* 60 (April 1983):430-38.
Describes, through an analysis of the theme of hunting, how his study of Inuit culture has led him to reevaluate his views on literature by and about that culture.

B1146   TOWNSEND, MARY JANE. "Taking Off the War Bonnet: American Indian Literature." *LA* 53 (March 1976):236-44.

Examines the changing image of the American Indian in contemporary children's fiction. Includes extensive references and a bibliography.

B1147   TROY, ANNE. "The Indian in Adolescent Novels." *Indian Historian* 8, no. 4 (Winter 1975):32-35.

Summarizes Troy's Ph.D. dissertation, University of Iowa, 1972.

B1148   WHITAKER, MURIEL A. "Monsters from Native Canadian Mythologies." *CCL* 15-16 (1980):57-65.

Tells of the monsters of Canadian Indian and Inuit cultures, discusses how they have been handled by Canadian writers, and suggests more effective approaches.

B1149   -----. "The Raven Cycle: Mythology In Process." *CCL* 31-32 (1983):46-52.

Discusses the Raven figure dominant in Native American mythology of the West Coast of British Columbia, the Canadian Arctic, Alaska, and Eastern Siberia.

B1150   WICKERSHAM, ELAINE B. "An Analysis of Native American Verbal Images as They Are Related To Children's Literature." Ph.D. dissertation, Pennsylvania State University, 1979, 142 pp., DA 39:6371A.

Compares the verbal images used by authors of children's books portraying Native Americans, with terms used by Native American college students and the Katz and Braly List of Verbal Stereotypes. Concludes that the list is not an accurate measure of stereotypical language in literature about Native Americans.

B1151   WILKENS, LEA-RUTH C. "American Indian Children in American Picturebooks (1950-1983)." In Escarpit, *Portrayal of the Child*, pp. 167-75.

Concludes that Native American artists generally present more positive and accurate portrayals of Indian children, although this may be changing.

INDIVIDUALISM

B1152   LE PERE, JEAN M. "Beyond the Literal Level." *LA* 52 (April 1975):476-80.

Explores ways of helping children go "beyond the literal level" by looking at the theme of individualism in several books.

INFORMATIONAL BOOKS

B1153   BACON, BETTY. "The Art of Nonfiction." *CLE*, n.s. 12, no. 1 (Spring 1981):3-14.

Examines the literary characteristics of nonfiction for children, its patterns of organization, style and use of illustrations, and argues that as much good writing is to be found in nonfiction as in fiction. Cites many works she considers outstanding.

B1154   BADER, BARBARA. "Information" and "More Information." In *American Picturebooks*, pp. 88-99, 383-415.

An overview of the beginning of informational book illustration in the 1930s in the first chapter, and an account of the increasing sophistication and scope of informational books in the 1940s, 1950s and 1960s in the second chapter.

B1155 CARR, JO, comp. *Beyond Fact: Nonfiction for Children and Young People.* Chicago: American Library Association, 1982, 224 pp. (Excerpt in *Horn Book* 57 [October 1981]:514-23.)

A collection of essays on various aspects of nonfiction as literature, with sections on science writing, history, biography, and controversy.

B1156 -----. "Rousseau Reconsidered." *Horn Book* 56 (April 1980):156-60.

Traces Rousseau's relevance to children's informational book writing, emphasizing his beliefs in the importance of child development, a dynamic approach to history, the excitement of discovery, and above all the essential worth of the child.

B1157 CRAGO, HUGH. "Creation to Civilization." *Signal* 41 (May 1983):97-107.

Explores the difficulties in creating good informational books for children, particularly those focusing on the period of time from creation to civilization.

B1158 DARLING, DENNIS. "Classification and Analysis of Industrial Topics Represented in Juvenile Information Trade Books." Ph.D. dissertation, Michigan State University, 1974, 161 pp., DA 35:1475A.

Examines the representation of aspects of industry in two hundred informational books published for children in grades two through six between 1761 and 1970.

B1159 DE LUCA, GERALDINE, and NATOV, RONI, eds. "Informational Books for Children." *L&U* 6 (1982):1-97

Special issue. Includes reviews of Jill Krementz's *How It Feels When a Parent Dies* and Melvyn B. Zerman's *Beyond Reasonable Doubt*, and an interview with Anne Ophelia Dowden. Other articles have been indexed under archaeology, biography, and science in this bibliography.

B1160 DONELSON, KENNETH. "Informational Books: Of Tantalizing Topics." In *Literature for Today's Young Adults*, pp. 317-51.

Divides young-adult nonfiction into the following categories: books about the world around us, books about physical and mental health, books about sex, books about drugs, how-to books, books about work, and fun facts books (e.g., *Guinness* books). Includes a section on the new journalism and two checklists: one for evaluating informative nonfiction and a second for evaluating journalistic fiction.

B1161 DONOVAN, JOHN, ed. "Aspects of Children's Informational Books." *WLB* 49 (October 1974):144-77.

Special issue. Includes Olivia Coolidge's "My Struggle with Facts"; Dennis Flanagan's "To Each Generation Its Own Rabbits," which discusses Richard Adams's *Watership Down* and the separation between literary and scientific worlds; Zena Sutherland's "Information Pleases--Sometimes," on criteria for evaluating informational books; and Robin Gottlieb's "On Nonfiction Books for Children: Tradition and Dissent," which suggests criteria for evaluating children's biography.

B1162   FISHER, MARGERY. *Matters of Fact: Aspects of Non-Fiction for Children.* New York: Crowell, 1972, 488 pp. (Introduction excerpted in Carr, *Beyond Fact*, pp. 12-16, and in Haviland, *Children and Literature*, pp. 313-15.)

    Maintains that the author's attitude is always important and provides a framework for evaluating informational books, which she divides into the categories of (1) foundations or "topic books" for children up to age twelve (examples: books on bread, the postal system, Holland, honey bees, cowboys, and time); (2) the multiple subject, for which she has examined books on the subjects of London and atoms; (3) biography, for which she has examined numerous biographies of J.S. Bach, Helen Keller, and Abraham Lincoln; and (4) careers, for which she examined books on nursing and journalism. Includes an index to authors, titles, and series mentioned in the texts and reading lists.

B1163   FRETZ, SADA. "Why Nonfiction Books Are So Dull and What You Can Do About It." *Learning: The Magazine for Creative Teaching,* May-June 1976, pp. 68-70. (Reprinted in Varlejs, *Young Adult Literature,* pp. 362-66.)

    Summarizes the roles publishers, teachers, and librarians play in the development and use of informational books. Includes a checklist for judging nonfiction.

B1164   GOTTLIEB, ROBIN. "On Nonfiction Books for Children: Tradition and Dissent." *WLB* 49 (October 1974):174-77. (Reprinted in Varlejs, *Young Adult Literature,* pp. 381-85.)

    Examines authorities' opinions on biography, science, and social-science nonfiction for children, pointing out differences of opinion and changing views. Provides a good summary of the state of the literature circa 1974. Includes references.

B1165   HASKINS, JIM. "Non-Fiction Books and the Junior and Senior High-Schooler: Changes in Supply to Meet Changes in Demand." *Arizona English Bulletin* 18 (April 1976):78-82. (Reprinted in Varlejs, *Young Adult Literature,* pp. 356-61.)

    Examines the reasons why informational books for children and young adults became a prominent trend in the sixties and seventies.

B1166   -----. "Racism and Sexism in Children's Nonfiction." *Children's Literature* 5 (1976):141-47.

    Points out that racism and sexism in nonfiction for children are as prevalent as in fiction.

B1167   HEEKS, PEGGY. "Getting at the Facts." *TLS,* 2 July 1970, pp. 721-22.

    Points out common problems with informational books for children: too much emphasis on "fun," careless writing and editing, and lack of criticism.

B1168   HUCK, CHARLOTTE. "Criteria for Evaluating Children's Informational Books." In *Children's Literature in the Elementary School.* New York: Holt, 1961, pp. 522-39.

    Provides detailed criteria for evaluating informational books based on such categories as accuracy and authenticity, content and perspective, style, organization, and illustrations and format.

B1169　HÜRLIMANN, BETTINA. "Education through Pictures: From Comenius to the Picture-Book of Today." In *Three Centuries*, pp. 127-43.
Provides insights into the evolution of "informational books" for children.

B1170　JACOBS, LELAND B. "Hallmarks of Good Informational Books." *Reading Teacher* 12 (December 1958):115-16.
Provides a concise set of criteria.

B1171　LARRICK, NANCY. "Handsome Is as Handsome Reads: Pointers on Evaluating Nonfiction for Children." *Reading Teacher* 14 (May 1961):336-38.
Recommends careful reading of children's informational books. Many are beautiful to look at but not good to read. Often text and pictures do not fit together. It is not enough that they look nice and have been authentically attested to in introductions by scholars with Ph.Ds.

B1172　MELTZER, MILTON. "The Possibilities of Non-Fiction: A Writer's View." *CLE*, n.s. 11, no. 3 (Autumn 1980):110-16. (Reprinted as "Beyond Fact," in Carr, *Beyond Fact*, pp. 26-33.)
Explores the possibilities of creating art in nonfiction using his own experience in writing *Never to Forget* as an example.

B1173　-----. "Where Do All the Prizes Go? The Case for Nonfiction." *Horn Book* 52 (February 1976):17-23. (Reprinted in Heins, *Crosscurrents*, pp. 51-57.)
Argues for greater consideration and recognition of the literary qualities of nonfiction.

B1174　MOSS, ELAINE. "Information Books: A Few Home Thoughts about the *TES* Awards and About Television's Effect on Publishing." *Signal* 25 (January 1978):25-29.
Remarks precipitated by the awarding of the *Times Educational Supplement*'s Senior Information Book Award to Mitchell Beasley's *Man and Machines*, one of ten volumes in the Joy of Knowledge Library.

B1175　SMITH, LILLIAN. "Books of Knowledge." In *Unreluctant Years*, pp. 177-88.
Points out that it is difficult to form standard judgments of informational books because they are transient in nature, and that it is a rare book that informs, interprets, and is also a work of art. Divides informational books into those dealing with the natural world, with history, and biography.

B1176　THOMAS, JOYCE A. "Nonfiction Illustration: Some Considerations." *ChLAQ* 6, no. 4 (Winter 1981):25-28. (Reprinted in May, *Children and Their Literature*, pp. 122-27.)
Argues that illustration is probably even more important in nonfiction than in fiction, yet is often slighted by critics. Examines six books to show that good nonfiction illustration communicates feeling as well as fact. Books discussed are Peter Spier's *Gobble Growl Grunt*, Bernice Kohn's *The Busy Honeybees* (illustrated by Mel Furukawa), Hans-Heinrich Isenbart's *A Fool is Born* (photos by

Hanns-Jorg Anders), David and Maggie Cavagnaro's *The Pumpkin People*, Virginia Lee Burton's *Lifestory*, and David Macaulay's four books, *Castle, Cathedral, City,* and *Underground.*

B1177   TREMPER, ELLEN. "Grabbing Them by the Imagination." *L&U* 6 (1982):41-47.
The most successful nonfiction books are those that grab the imagination. To illustrate this point Tremper analyzes two books: Roy Hoopes's *The Changing Vice-Presidency* and Don Lawson's *The United States in the Vietnam War.*

B1178   WEISS, EVELYN R. "Writing Informational Material for Nine-to-Eleven-Year-Olds." *Publishers Weekly* 163 (18 April 1953):1678-82.
Finds that authors of informational books for ten year olds "take too little into account the limitations of the child's background information, including his store of images, his factual knowledge, his vocabulary and his familiarity with the nuances and structural forms of our language." Uses detailed examples to illustrate the problems she points out.

B1179   WENZEL, EVELYN L. "Historical Background." In *Time for Discovery.* Compiled by Evelyn L. Wenzel and May Hill Arbuthnot. Glenview, Ill.: Scott, Foresman, 1971, pp. 252-59. (Reprinted in Carr, *Beyond Fact,* pp. 16-26.)
Outlines the history of informational books for children from the eighteenth century to the present.

B1180   WILMS, DENISE M. "Out In Space: A Look at Some Recent Non-Fiction." *Booklist* 76 (15 September 1979):118-20. (Reprinted In Carr, *Beyond Fact,* pp. 34-39.)
Uses the evaluation of two recent space books to illustrate criteria for writing and evaluating nonfiction.

B1181   WILSON, JENNIFER. "Choosing Information Books." *Signal* 39 (September 1982):163-68.
Argues that informational books for children should be written in expressive language that allows the voice of the writer to come through, for that is how children themselves write.

B1182   -----. "Information Books 1983: Weeds or Flowers?" *Signal* 44 (May 1984):112-19.
Sets forth criteria for informational books, telling why so many out of hundreds she examined for inclusion in *Signal Review of Children's Books 2* were unacceptable. Criteria include: Is this book distinguishable from its predecessors? Where subject areas are combined, is the combination instructive or does it dilute each? Is the book telling the whole truth? Who is the book for? What can be learned from this book? Is the material well organized? What is the difference between this book and a textbook?

B1183   WITUCKE, VIRGINIA. "Informational Books and Their Authors." *Illinois Libraries* 64 (September 1982):853-57.
Surveys the backgrounds of writers of informational books for children.

INTERNATIONAL

B1184   CIANCIOLO, PATRICIA J.   "International Children's Literature: Trends in Translation and Dissemination." *Bookbird* 1 (1984):5-14.
An overview of trends and themes.

B1185   CROUCH, MARCUS.   "Foreign Scenes." In *The Nesbit Tradition*, pp. 86-100.
Discusses briefly some of the French, American, Australian, Dutch, Jamaican, Indian, and African books read by English children.

B1186   PELLOWSKI, ANNE.   "The Diamond and the Parrot: Aesthetics and Ideology in Children's Books." *Library Journal* 91 (15 November 1966):5683-92.
Examines the role of ideology in children's books today in a number of countries.

B1187   -----.   *Made to Measure: Children's Books in Developing Countries.* Paris: UNESCO, 1980, 129 pp.
Examines many aspects of children's literature in developing countries, including writing, illustration, editing, design, publishing, promotion, and distribution.

B1188   *Printed for Children: World Children's Book Exhibition.*   New York: K.G. Saur Publishing, 1978, 448 pp.
A catalog compiled by Rosemarie Rauter for "The Child and the Book" exhibit at the Frankfurt Book Fair, 1978, and the International Year of the Child, 1979.   Provides overviews and bibliographies of children's literature in over seventy countries.   Many of the bibliographies include both children's books and reference sources for criticism and selection.

B1189   ROOT, SHELTON L., Jr.   "A Comparison Between Works of Realistic Contemporary Fiction by Non-American and American Authors Whose Books Have Settings Other than the United States, Whose Major Characters Are Not Citizens of the United States and Which are Appropriate for Children Nine through Twelve Years of Age." (ERIC Educational Document Reproduction Service, 1977, 17 pp., ED 134 965.)
Concludes that non-American authors portrayed middle- and upper-class characters, while American authors tended to depict characters of low economic and social status in books set outside of the United States.

B1190   WOFFORD, AZILE.   "Standards for Choosing Books About Other Countries." *EE* 24 (November 1947):469-75, 494.
Discusses the standards for selecting books on other countries proposed by the Committee on Standards for Books about Other Lands of the National Council of Teachers of English.

IRAN

B1191   AYMAN, LILY.   "The Progress of Children's Literature in Iran During the Past Decade." *International Library Review* 1 (April 1969):197-99.
Despite longstanding storytelling traditions, the amount of original writing remains low in proportion to translations from English,

French, and Russian.

B1192   RAMSEGER, INGEBORG. "Persian Children's Books of Today." *Novum Gebrauchsgraphik* 44 (February 1973):44-51.
An overview, with many illustrations, of Iranian children's books of the 1970s.

B1193   SAMII, MARILYN TYLER. "Assessment of Books on Iran for Children." Ed.D. dissertation, Lehigh University, 1973, 242 pp., DA 34:5495A.
Finds that the majority of the informational books about Iran available to American children are "accurate, well-written, and informative," and that the fiction also provides "interesting information" and well-drawn, unstereotyped characters.

B1194   TAJERAN, ZARINTAJ T. "A Content Analysis of Iranian Children's Story Books for the Presence of Social and Moral Values." Ph.D. dissertation, University of the Pacific, 1979, 198 pp., DA 41:1017A.
Identifies the incidence of specific Iranian middle-class social and moral values in the content of nineteen of the most popular children's books in Iran.

IRELAND

B1195   SHARE, BERNARD. "Children's Book Illustration in Ireland." *Bookbird* 10, no. 3 (1972):70-71.
A brief overview of Irish book illustrations and publishing in both English and Irish.

ISRAEL

B1196   COOPERMAN, BERNARD DOR. "Realities and Dreams: Images of the World in Isreali Children's Literature." *Harvard Library Bulletin* 31 (Spring 1983):117-46.
Analyzes the books in the Israeli children's literature collection in the Judaica Department of the Harvard College Library.

B1197   LeBRECHT, HANS. "The Juvenile Book in Israel." *Bookbird* 41 (1965):18-24.
A brief overview, including a list of forty most frequently read books and a discussion of problems of books for Israel's Arab population.

B1198   TARSI-GAI, ESTHER. "Kibbutz Children as Reflected in Israeli Children's Literature." In Escarpit, *Portrayal of the Child*, pp. 207-17.
Finds a balance of positive and negative aspects of Kibbutz life portrayed in children's books.

ISSUES APPROACH

B1199   ADAMS, KAREN I. "Multicultural Representation in Children's Books." Ed.D. dissertation, University of South Carolina, 1981, 252 pp., DA 42:5050A
Analyzes fifty-seven classic books and Newbery-award winners for "quantity and quality of multicultural representation." Cultural groups were categorized and evaluated under headings: females, age, socioeconomic status, religion, handicaps, ethnic background, regional

culture, language, and illustration. Concludes there are multicultural books of literary worth, but no books met the acceptable criteria for all categories.

B1200 ASHLEY, L.F. "Bibliotherapy, etc." *LA* 55 (April 1978):478-81, 526.
Questions the use of "non-literary criteria" in evaluating children's books and cites articles relating to growing skepticism about the "issues approach."

B1201 CARR, JO, ed. "The Problem with Problem Books." In *Beyond Fact*, pp. 157-64.
The introductory essay examines the question of balance and objectivity on controversial issues, questions the approach of the Council on Interracial Books for Children, and calls for books that respect the reader's intelligence. Articles include Laurence Pringle's "Balance and Bias in Controversial Books"; the Council on Interracial Books for Children's "Bias in Children's Books" (reprinted from *Guidelines for Selecting Bias-Free Textbooks and Storybooks for Children* [New York: The Council, 1980], pp. 7-9, 21-23); Nat Hentoff's response, "Any Writer Who Follows Anyone Else's Guidelines Ought to Be in Advertising" (from *SLJ* 24, no. 3 [November 1977]:27-29); Ann Hildebrand's "The Bible Presented Objectively" (from *LA* 53 [January 1976]:69-75); Georgess McHargue's "A Ride Across the Mystic Bridge, or Occult Books: What, Why, and Who Needs Them?" (reprinted from *SLJ* 19, no. 9 [May 1973]:25-30); and Harry C. Stubbs's "The Impossible Book" (reprinted from *Appraisal* 4, no. 3 [Fall 1971]:1-3).

B1202 CHARNES, RUTH. "Social Justice in Children's Books: A Look at Interracial Books for Children Bulletin." *Serials Librarian* 9 (Fall 1984):17-21.
Discusses the origins and development of the Council on Interracial books for children, "the *Bulletin* it publishes, and its controversial role in the world of children's materials."

B1203 COUNCIL ON INTERRACIAL BOOKS FOR CHILDREN, RACISM AND SEXISM RESOURCE CENTER. *Human and Anti-Human Values in Children's Books: A Content Rating Instrument for Educators and Concerned Parents.* New York: CIBC, 1976, 280 pp.
Provides guidelines for evaluating books in terms of racism, sexism, agism, elitism, materialism, individualism, escapism and conformism, and literary and artistic quality. Evaluates 235 children's books published during 1975.

B1204 CUTLER, MARY AVIS. "The Book Written with a Purpose." *EER* 13 (April 1936):131-34.
Argues against books, fiction and nonfiction, with ulterior motives. There is no place in children's literature for condescension, sentimentality, sloppy, indifferent writing, or inaccuracy. "Most children are too intelligent to be taken in by the 'books obviously intended for them,' the book of fact disguised as fiction, or the made-to-order story."

B1205 DONOVAN, JOHN. "American Dispatch." *Signal* 26 (May 1978):85-89.
Summarizes some of the heated controversies that have occurred relating to "social usefulness" and "intellectual freedom," including an incident involving Judy Blume's *Forever*, the impact of Nancy Lar-

rick's "The All-White World of Children's Books" (*Saturday Review*, 1965), and the controversies surrounding Claire Huchet Bishop's *Five Chinese Brothers.*

B1206   EPSTEIN, CONNIE.   "Messages Belong in Telegrams."   *TON* 40 (Winter 1984):173-76.
Examines didactic messages in old and new children's books.

B1207   GERSUNY, CARL.   "Clienthood in Children's Literature."   *Journal of Popular Culture* 4, no. 2 (Fall 1970):444-52.
Identifies patterns in children's fiction that introduce them to "clienthood," that is, becoming clients of hospitals, schools, libraries, and other organizations.

B1208   LUKENS, REBECCA.   "Minimizing Artistry, Limiting Literature." *ChLAQ* 3, no. 3 (Autumn 1978):13-14.   (Reprinted in Dooley, *First Steps*, p. 13.)
Argues that "There is far more to literature than issues or instruction; Rudman's approach limits both the story and the reader. It minimizes artistry, and narrows significance to say nothing of boring the child."

B1209   McDOWELL, MARGARET B.   "New Didacticism: Stories for Free Children."   *LA* 54 (January 1977):41-47.
Examines *Ms. Magazine*'s "Stories for Free Children" and other similar stories designed to attack racism and sexism, in order to "yield insight into the inflexible conventions governing children's literature and into the difficulties confronting a writer who uses fiction to further an overt political and social ideology."

B1210   McVITTY, WALTER.   "If Didacticism Is Dead, Why Won't It Lie Down? or, What's the Use of Reading?"   In Robinson, M., *Readings in Children's Literature*, pp. 173-87.
Argues against didacticism in children's literature, whether old-style or new-style issues approach.

B1211   MADSEN, JANE M.   "Racism and Sexism in Children's Literature." *Encyclopedia of Educational Research.*   Edited by Harold E. Mitzel. New York: Free Press, 1982, pp. 1507-15.
A thorough review of the literature and summary of the issues, with an extensive bibliography.

B1212   PARKER, PAT.   Review.   *LA* 53 (October 1976):810-14.
Review of Council on Interracial Books for Children Racism and Sexism Resource Center for Educators, *Human and Anti-Human Values in Children's Books: A Content Rating Instrument for Educators and Concerned Parents* (New York: CIBC, 1976), Raising questions about the issues approach, its pluses and minuses.

B1213   "Race Sex and Class in Children's Books."   *New Statesman* 100 (November-December 1980).
A six part article with contributions by Marion Glastonbury (14 November):16-19; Rosemary Stones (21 November):16-18; Jill Paton Walsh (28 November):28-30; Robert Leeson (5 December):28-29; Paul Binding (12 December);19-20, and Rick Rogers (19-26 December):46-47.

B1214   "Race, Sex, and Class: A Statement from England." *IRBC* 5, no. 6 (1974):6.

        A statement by a coalition of British groups that "most children's picture books present a partial and distorted view of reality." Seven specific areas of concern are listed: sexism, racism, home life, work, class, fantasy, and responsibility for content.

B1215   RAY, SHEILA G. "Sex, Race and Class in Children's Books in the United Kingdom." *Bookbird* 15, no. 3 (1977):11-13.

        Examines the growing awareness of issues relating to sex, race, and class in British children's books. Comments on Bob Dixon's *Catching them Young*.

B1216   RUDMAN, MASHA KABAKOW. *Children's Literature: An Issues Approach*. 2d ed. London: Longman, 1984, 476 pp.

        Provides guidelines for selecting and discussing books in terms of a number of issues. Chapters cover the areas of family (e.g., the new baby, divorce, adoption); sex; gender roles; heritage (e.g., Native Americans, Afro-Americans); special needs (e.g., physical and intellectual disabilities); old age; death; and war. There is also a chapter on methodology. Each chapter includes bibliographies of references and children's books relating to the topics discussed.

B1217   -----. "Critical Reading of Issues in Children's Literature." *Advocate* 4, no. 2 (Winter 1985):102-12.

        Argues that criticizing and analyzing a book in terms of its values need not conflict with aesthetic reading. Suggests guidelines "that are concerned with issues of ethical, psychological, political, and societal import."

B1218   SCHRAM, BARBARA A. "D is for Dictionary: S is for Stereotyping." *IRBC* 5, no. 6 (1974):1-2, 6.

        Reviews several dictionaries for children and finds them perpetuating racial and sexual stereotypes. Richard Scarry's *Best Word Book Ever* is accused of erasing most of 51 percent of the population.

B1219   STEAD, DEBORAH. "A Look at Children's Magazines: Not All Fun and Games." *IRBC* 6, no. 2 (1975):1, 6-7.

        Surveys fifteen current children's periodicals, examining what they teach about race and sex roles. Concludes that children's magazines still contain racism to some extent and are "overpoweringly sexist."

B1220   THORNDILL, CHRISTINE MALTBY. "The Skeletons in the Closet: Revision of Racial, Ethnic, and Sexual Stereotypes in Series Books." *TON* 34 (Spring 1978):245-48.

        Discusses efforts to edit old stereotypes out of popular series books.

B1221   TOWNSEND, JOHN ROWE. "Are Children's Books Racist and Sexist?" In Egoff, *Only Connect*, 2d ed., pp. 382-88.

        Argues that publishers have a responsibility to children and society to consider social issues.

B1222   -----. "Didacticism in Modern Dress." *Horn Book* 43 (April 1967):159-64. (Reprinted in Egoff, *Only Connect*, 1st ed., pp. 33-40; 2d ed., pp. 55-62.)

Explores the dangers of didacticism and suggests that although "It is not irrelevant that a book may contribute to moral perception or social adjustment or the advancement of a minority group or the Great Society in general . . . there is no substitute for the creative imagination, and in criticism there is no criterion except literary merit."

B1223   WIGUTOFF, SHARON. "Junior Fiction: A Feminist Critique." *TON* 38 (Winter 1982):113-24.
Reports on a study by Wigutoff and Jeanne Bracken of areas of feminist concern in junior fiction: portrayal of family; work; sex roles; class, racial, and cultural diversity; the handicapped; homosexuals; and the elderly.

B1224   YAWHEY, THOMAS D., and YAWHEY, MARGARET L. "An Analysis of Picture Books." *LA* 53 (May 1976):545-48.
Reports on an analysis of young children's picture books before and after 1965, for racism, sexism, location, and socioeconomic status of characters.

B1225   ZIPES, JACK. "Second Thoughts on Socialization through Literature for Children." *L&U* 5 (1981):19-31.
Zipes puts forth his theory that "Literature for children is not children's literature by and for children in their behalf. It never was and never will be. Literature for children is a script coded by adults for the information and internalization of children which must meet the approbation of adults." Summarizes German writers on the topic and concludes by reviewing Lystad's *From Dr. Mather to Dr. Seuss* and Felicity O'Dell's *Socialization through Children's Literature: The Soviet Example*.

ITALY

B1226   D'ARCAIS, GIUSEPPE FLORES, and BERNARDINS, ANNA MARIA. "The Situation and Problems of Juvenile Literature in Italy in the Post-War Period." *Bookbird* 2 (1965):8-13.
An overview.

B1227   HAWKES, LOUISE RESTIEAUX. *Before and After Pinocchio: A Study of Italian Children's Books.* Paris: Puppet Press, 1933, 207 pp.
Within the context of all of European children's literature, Hawkes examines that of Italy, centering on its most popular and influential book, *Pinocchio*, discussing its precursors, its imitators, and its influences. Includes a bibliography of American translations of Italian children's books.

B1228   MOOREHEAD, CAROLINE. "Italy: The Feminist Message." *TLS*, 28 March 1980, p. 360.
Examines the impact of the women's movement on recent Italian children's literature.

B1229   POESIO, CARLA. "Children's Periodicals in Italy." *Phaedrus* 4, no. 2 (Fall 1977):32-35.
A historical survey covering the nineteenth and twentieth centuries.

B1230   -----. "Contemporary Trends of Literature for Young People in Italy, with a European Perspective." *Children's Books International 1. Proceedings.* Boston: Boston Public Library, 1976, pp. 39-43.
An overview of Italian juvenile literature.

B1231   -----. "Some Features of the Modern Italian Literature for Young People." *Children's Literature* 5 (1976):180-88.
Identifies conflict as one of the main features of contemporary Italian children's literature.

JAPAN

B1232   ABE, MEIKO. "Children's Books About Japan." *TON* 14 (May 1958):45-49.
Evaluates fiction and nonfiction designed to present Japan and Japanese people to elementary-school children.

B1233   BURRIS, MIRIAM. "Japan in Children's Fiction." *EE* 42 (January 1966):29-38.
Surveys recent children's fiction set in Japan. Books are annotated and arranged by categories: outstanding, average to mediocre, and objectionable.

B1234   CARTER, ANGELA. "Once More Into the Mangle." *New Society* (9 April 1971). (Reprinted in Tucker, *Suitable for Children?*, pp. 107-12.)
Argues that Japanese comics, with their high incidence of "death, mutilation and sexual intercourse," are decidedly not for children.

B1235   FLORY, ESTHER V., and TAKAHASHI, EIKO. "The Grimm and Andersen of Japan and other Authors of Children's Books." *Horn Book* 37 (December 1961):529-38.
A brief history of children's literature in Japan from Sazanami Iwaya (the Grimm of Japan) and Mimei Ogawa (the Andersen of Japan) through several recent authors.

B1236   HUTHWAITE, MOTOKO. "Analysis of Contemporary Japanese Children's Literature with a Focus on Values." Ph.D. dissertation, Wayne State University, 1974, 151 pp., DA 35:4148A.
Concludes that while folk literature stresses traditional values, values in fantasy and realistic fiction reveal a trend toward more democratic concepts.

B1237   MATSUYAMA, UTAKO K. "Can Story Grammar Speak Japanese?" *Reading Teacher* 36 (March 1983):666-69.
Finds that Japanese folktale story structure differs from typical Western structure, and that these differences may be related to deep differences in cultural values.

B1238   MELCHER, FREDERIC G. "Japanese Picture Books." *Publishers Weekly* 152 (25 October 1947):2092-93.
A brief but fascinating glimpse of the picture books of post-World War II Japan.

B1239   RAMSEGER, INGEBORG. "Contemporary Japanese Books for Children." *Novum Gebrauchsgraphik* 44 (September 1973):42-53.
Includes numerous illustrations.

B1240   STREET, DOUGLAS. "Kyogen for Kids: An Examination into the Adaptability of the Japanese Comic Interlude to Western Children's Audiences." *Proceedings of the Children's Literature Association* 6 (1979):188-95.
Examines a number of adaptations of the Japanese Kyogen form by Western children's playwrights.

B1241   URY, MARIAN. "Stepmother Tales in Japan." *Children's Literature* 9 (1981):61-72.
Traces the theme of the wicked stepmother in Japanese literature.

B1242   WATANABE, SHIGEO. "Post-War Children's Literature in Japan." *International Library Review* 2 (April 1970):113-24.
Finds the dramatic changes in Japanese social thought and behavior following World War II reflected in Japanese children's literature.

JEWS

B1243   ABRAMOWICZ, DINA. "Yiddish Juvenilia: Ethnic Survival in the New World." *WLB* 50 (October 1975):138-45.
Reports on the Yiddish juvenile literature available at the YIVO Institute for Jewish Research in New York. Includes extensive references.

B1244   ALTER, ROBERT. "Books for Jewish Children." *Commentary* 33 (February 1962):136-42.
Reflects upon and questions the Jewish content of a number of recent books for Jewish children.

B1245   DANIELS, LEONA. "The 34th Man: How Well is Jewish Minority Culture Represented in Children's Fiction?" *Library Journal* 95 (15 February 1970):738-45 and *SLJ* 17 (February 1970):38-43. (Also in Gerhardt, *Issues in Children's Book Selection*, pp. 90-101.)
Argues that while some authors re-create the Jewish family atmosphere of ancient cultural tradition and cultural awareness, others offer sterile characters who illustrate little more than Jewish names and celebration of the appropriate holidays. Includes an annotated bibliography of children's books.

B1246   JACOBY, JAY. "Schlemiels, Schlimazels, and Young Readers: A Perspective on Jewish Children's Literature." *Advocate* 2, no. 1 (Winter 1983):26-37.
Argues that "one need not be Jewish to read and enjoy Jewish literature," and points out features it shares with the literature of many other cultures. Includes a bibliography.

B1247   JURICH, MARILYN. "Once Upon a Shtetl: Schlimazels, Schlemiels, Schnorrers, Shadchens, and Sages: Yiddish Humor in Children's Books." *L&U* 1, no. 1 (1977):9-25.
Among tales discussed are Marilyn Hirsch's *Could Anything Be Worse?*, Yuri Suhl's *Simon Boom Gives a Wedding*, Isaac Bashevis Singer's *Zlateh the Goat and Other Stories*, and Shan Ellentuck's *Yankel the Fool*.

B1248   KIMMEL, ERIC A. "Jewish Identity in Juvenile Fiction: A Look at Three Recommended Books." *Horn Book* 59 (April 1973):171-79. (Reprinted in Heins, *Crosscurrents*, pp. 150-58.)

Finds three highly recommended books dealing with the American Jewish condition to be inadequate: Emily Neville's *Berries Goodman*, Hila Colman's *Mixed-Marriage Daughter*, and E.L. Konigsburg's *About the B-Nai Bagels*.

B1249   MENDELSOHN, LEONARD R. "The Travail of Jewish Children's Literature." *Children's Literature* 3 (1974):48-55.

"The offerings in Jewish children's literature are impressive neither quantitatively nor qualitatively." Discusses reasons for this state of affairs.

B1250   MIREL, BARBARA. "Lost Worlds of Tradition: Shtetl Stories for Suburban Children." *ChLAQ* 9, no. 1 (Spring 1984):6-9.

Examines portrayals of Jewish life in the small towns of Russia and Eastern Europe in books by American-born authors and by authors whose accounts are based on firsthand experience. Points out ways in which American-born authors' accounts fall short.

B1251   OFEK, URIEL. "The Beginnings of Hebrew Children's Literature." *Bookbird* 15, no. 2 (1977):6-9.

A brief history concentrating on development through the early years of the twentieth century.

B1252   PATZ, NAOMI M., and MILLER, PHILIP E. "Jewish Religious Children's Literature in America: An Analytical Survey." *Phaedrus* 7, no. 1 (Spring-Summer 1980):19-29.

Examines catechism/Bible paraphrase textbooks, periodicals (beginning in the late nineteenth century), books (1900-1950), and books since 1950, including holocaust books. Includes references.

B1253   POSNER, MARCIA. "A Search for Jewish Content in American Children's Fiction." Ph.D. dissertation, New York University, 1980, 338 pp., DA 41:2339A.

Examines the amount and characteristics of Jewish content in contemporary realistic fiction with Jewish characters.

B1254   SCHLESSINGER, JUNE HIRSCH. "A Comparison of the Documented Concerns of American Jewry with the Concerns Expressed in Accessible Fiction about Jewish Life Published in 1930 to 1935 and 1970 to 1975 and Suggested for Young Adult Readers." Ph.D. dissertation, University of Connecticut, 1979, 185 pp., DA 41:620A.

Finds there is greater correspondence in fictional concerns and documented concerns in 1970-75 than in 1930-35.

KOREA

B1255   YI, CHAE-CH'OL, ed. "Juvenile Literature in Korea." *Korea Journal* 19, no. 8 (1979):64 pp.

Special issue on juvenile literature. Contains an overview of Korean children's literature by Yi Chae-Ch'ol, research on Korean folktales and children's songs, and re-tellings of a number of stories and poems, folktales and folksongs.

LATIN AMERICA

B1256 CIMINO, MARIA. "New Books About South America." *Horn Book* 17
(September-October 1941):350-55.
Surveys books of the 1930s and 1940s portraying South America,
and compares them with a few older books. Includes a bibliography.

B1257 DUJOUNE, MARTA. "The Image of Latin America in Children's Lit-
erature of Developed Countries." *Bookbird* 1-2 (1982):5-10.
Finds erroneous impressions and misinformation about Latin
America in European fiction and information books for children.

B1258 PARISH, HELEN RAND. "Children's Books in Latin America." *Horn
Book* 24 (May 1948);214-23; (July 1948):257-62; (September
1948):363-66.
Part 1 covers the classics and the didactic school, part 2, fantasy
and other modern trends, and part 3, modern trends.

B1259 SCHON, ISABEL. "Looking at Books About Latin Americans." *LA* 53
(March 1976):267-71.
An overview, with criticism and praise for a selection of fiction
and biography for children that portrays Mexicans, Mexican Americans, and Latin Americans.

LATVIA

B1260 FRANKLINA, EDĪTE. "Latvian Children's Literature in Exile: A Bibliography of Children's Books and Periodicals Published Outside
Latvia from 1945-1979." *Phaedrus* 6, no. 1 (Spring 1979):44-63.
Also includes addresses of publishers and booksellers from whom
the books may be obtained.

B1261 OSMANIS, JAZEPS. "The Popularization of Children's Literature in
Latvia." *Bookbird* 3 (1981):18-20.
Surveys the status of children's literature in Latvia.

LEISURE

B1262 KINGSBURY, M.E. "Books for Special Experiences: Leisure in Children's Literature." *TON* 32 (April 1976):247-52.
Concludes that "children's fiction does not reflect the significance
of leisure available in our society."

LITHUANIA

B1263 KORSAKAITÉ, I. "The Artists of Lithuania." *Bookbird* 10, no. 4
(1972):66-71.
Surveys the work of several recent Lithuanian illustrators.

B1264 SLAVENAS, M.G. "Lithuanian Children's Literature in Exile,
1945-1978." *Phaedrus* 6, no. 1 (Spring 1979):32-40.
A historical and critical survey, including many references.
Excludes translations, compilations, readers, anthologies, and textbooks.

LOSS

B1265   KINGSTON, CAROLYN T. "The Tragic Moment: Loss." In *Tragic Mode*, pp. 124-67.
Discusses a number of children's books concerned with the theme of loss. Many indexed separately under authors' names in this bibliography.

LULLABIES

B1266   KAYYAT, S. "Lullabies of Iraqi Jews." *Folklore* 89 (Spring 1978): 13-22.
Explores the nature of Iraqi Jewish lullabies and maintains that unlike English lullabies they present a clear picture of the social milieu.

B1267   McDOWELL, M.B. "Folk Lullabies: Songs of Anger, Love and Fear." *Women's Studies* 5, no. 2 (1977):205-18.
Compares literary lullabies and the vigorous realistic folk lullabies from which they are derived. Concludes that folk lullabies "illuminate the complex love-resentment conflict universally felt by mothers toward wakeful children."

B1268   SPITZ, SHERYL A. "Social and Psychological Themes in East Slavic Folk Lullabies." *Slavic and East European Journal* 23 (Spring 1979):14-24.
Explores the motifs and images shared by the East Slavic folk lullaby and other genres of East Slavic folklore. Attempts to "discover some of the social and psychological themes these elements convey."

MADAGASCAR

B1269   RANDRIAMAMONJY, ESTHER. "Children's Literature in Madagascar." *Phaedrus* 7, nos. 2-3 (Winter 1980):4-9.
Discusses periodicals, traditional and popular literature, and the works of contemporary children's writers in the Malagasy language.

MALAYSIA

B1270   VAN NIEL, ELOISE. "Malay Folk Literature with Special Reference to Children." *International Library Review* 5 (October 1973):483-95.
Provides a summary and bibliography.

MENTAL ILLNESS

B1271   DICKERSON, FAITH B. "Patterns of Deviance in Children's Literature." *Journal of Clinical Child Psychology* 6, no. 1 (Spring 1977):46-51.
Reports on a study of deviant behavior in story characters in twenty-seven books of contemporary fiction for children nine to twelve years old, written during the past thirty years.

B1272   STROUD, JANET G. "Characterization of the Emotionally Disturbed in Current Adolescent Fiction." *TON* 37 (Spring 1981):290-95.
Finds a great diversity in books portraying the emotionally disabled. Examines a number of recent titles.

B1273 WOLFE, KARY K., and WOLFE, GARY K. "Metaphors of Madness: Popular Psychological Narratives." *Journal of Popular Culture* 9 (Spring 1976):895-907. (Reprinted in Lenz, *Young Adult Literature*, pp. 147-61.)

Characteristics of this emerging genre of the psychological narrative are identified. Concludes with a detailed analysis of Joanne Greenberg's *I Never Promised You a Rose Garden.*

MENTAL RETARDATION

B1274 BUNN, OLENA SWAIN. "An Exceptional Perspective: The Rhetoric of Retarded Children in Newbery Award-Winning Fiction." Ed.D. dissertation, University of North Carolina at Greensboro, 1978, 218 pp., DA 39:7198A.

Examines portrayals of the mentally retarded in forty-two books published since 1960.

B1275 SAPON-SHEVIN, MARA. "Mentally Retarded Characters in Children's Literature." *Children's Literature in Education*, n.s. 13, no. 1 (Spring 1982):19-31.

Praises the accurate portrayal of mental retardation in a number of children's books and points out the inaccuracies in many others.

MEXICO

B1276 De GEREZ, TONI. "A Basket of Fireflies: Quetzalcoatl and the Nahautl Poetry of Mexico." In Egoff, *One Ocean*, pp. 138-46.

Discusses Mexico's pre-Columbian literature, especially the traditional Nahautl poetry.

B1277 -----. "A Letter from Mexico." In Koefoed, *Children's Literature and the Child*, pp. 35-36.

According to de Gerez, "Right now we have such brilliant writers for adults--as Octavio Paz, Carlos Fuentes, Juan Rolfo, etc.--but no one is writing for children. No one."

B1278 -----. "The Way of Quetzalcoatl." *Horn Book* 43 (April 1967):171-75.

Describes the Aztec and Nahautl literature of Mexico.

B1279 PARISH, HELEN RAND. "Mexico's Own ABC--The Cartilla." *Horn Book* 25 (March 1949):126-28.

Describes the cartilla (alphabet book) put out by the Mexican Ministry of Education in 1944-46.

B1280 SCHON, ISABEL. "A Descriptive Study of the Literature for Children and Adolescents of Mexico." Ph.D. dissertation, University of Colorado, 1974, 109 pp., DA 35:4879A.

Surveys the limited amount of nineteenth- and twentieth-century children's and adolescents' literature published in Mexico.

MIDDLE EAST

B1281 FATTAH, ABDUL RAZZAK. "Arabian Children's and Juvenile Literature." *Bookbird* 11, no. 3 (1973):29-32.

Discusses the literature for children in the Arabic-speaking countries of Egypt, Libya, Kuwait, and Iraq.

B1282   GHURAYYIB, ROSE. "Children's Literature in Lebanon and the Arab World." *Bookbird* 4 (1981):17-19.
A brief survey.

B1283   MEYER, ANNE A. "Children's Books About the Middle East." *Horn Book* 40 (June 1964):308-12.
An overview of children's literature in the Middle East as of the early 1960s.

MISSIONARIES

B1284   KEARNEY, ANTHONY. "The Missionary Hero in Children's Literature." *CLE*, n.s. 14, no. 2 (Summer 1983):104-12.
Explores the missionary as hero in British children's books in the late nineteenth and early twentieth centuries.

MONSTERS

B1285   HANNABUSS, STUART. "A Look at Horror Monsters and Reading for Young People." *School Librarian* 30 (December 1982):301-6.
Explores monsters in children's books, discussing the influence of cinema, Frankenstein as a source book, the use of sensational language, moral influences, and the impact of Dracula and vampire stories.

MORMONS

B1286   BAUER, CAROLYN, and MUIR, SHARON P. "Visions, Saints, and Zion: Children's Literature of the Mormon Movement." *Phaedrus* 7, no. 1 (Spring-Summer 1980):30-38.
Examines Sunday School curriculum materials, periodicals, and books in categories of fiction, biography, history, inspirational, doctrine, and scripture. Includes a bibliography.

MOTHERS

B1287   BERKE, JACQUELINE. "'Mother I Can Do It Myself!': The Self-sufficient Heroine in Popular Girls' Fiction." *Women's Studies* 6, no. 2 (1979):187-203.
Reflects upon the notable absence of mothers and grandmothers in classic girls' stories.

B1288   DONOVAN, ANN. "New Mothers in Current Children's Fiction." *CLE*, n.s. 14, no. 13 (Autumn 1983):131-41.
Examines the changing portrayals of mothers in recent children's fiction.

B1289   MITCHUM, VIRGINIA. "Children of the Earth." *Reading Teacher* 34 (April 1981):756-60.
Suggests an approach to mythology centering on myths about mothers.

B1290   STANEK, LOU WILLETT. "Growing Up Female: The Literary Gaps." *Media & Methods* 13 (September 1976):46-48. (Reprinted in Lenz, *Young Adult Literature*, pp. 232-37.)
Feels the lack of mother-daughter relationships in literature is beginning to be remedied by some young adult books. Includes a

brief bibliography of paperback books portraying women as mothers.

MUSIC

B1291   ALPER, CLIFFORD D.   "Influence of Froebel's *Mother Play and Nursery Songs* on Kindergarten Song Books, 1887-1918." Ph.D. dissertation, University of Maryland, 1972, 243 pp., DA 33:344A.
Identifies "the nature and extent of Friedrich Froebel's influence on selected kindergarten song books published between 1887 and 1918."

B1292   LAMME, LINDA LEONARD.   "Song Picture Books--A Maturing Genre of Children's Literature." *LA* 56 (April 1979):400-407.
Reviews many books briefly and also discusses "What Makes a Good Song Picture Book?" and "Involving Children with Song Picture Books."

B1293   MOORE, ANNA LOUISE.   "A Study of Selected Musical Compositions and Related Literature for Children." Ed.D. dissertation, University of Colorado at Boulder, 1981, 332 pp., DA 42:3491A.
Surveys musical compositions and related children's books and provides "an in-depth look at representative examples of the musical compositions and an evaluation of the related literature."

MYSTERY AND DETECTIVE STORIES

B1294   BILLMAN, CAROL.   "The Child Reader As Sleuth." *CLE*, n.s. 15, no. 1 (Spring 1984):30-41.
Explores ways in which young people "attempt to make sense of the unknown encountered in literature" by examining how children approach children's mystery stories.

B1295   CADOGAN, NANCY.   "Girl Sleuth to Brainless Beauty." In *You're A Brick*, pp. 304-32.
Discusses the evolution of the girl detective, primarily in British serials.

B1296   DONELSON, KENNETH.   "Mysteries." In *Literature for Today's Young Adults*, pp. 238-41.
Discusses Jay Bennett, Ellen Raskin, and Paul Zindel. In mysteries for young readers "the crimes are going to be less violent . . . the 'perfect crime' is not a crime at all but instead some sort of a puzzle."

B1297   FISHER, MARGERY.   "The Sleuth--Then and Now." *Quarterly Journal of the Library of Congress* 38 (Fall 1981):277-84.
Discusses mystery and detective fiction from Nancy Drew and the Hardy Boys to Robert Cormier and S.E. Hinton.

B1298   WILLIAMS, GWENEIRA.   "Chills for Children." *Publishers Weekly* 142 (24 October 1942):1750-56.
Examines the increased demand for juvenile mysteries in the early 1940s, discusses some of the classics, categorizes three types of juvenile mysteries, and comments on some of the best.

MYTHOLOGY

B1299   CONSTANT, HELEN. "A Critical Study of Selected Greek Myths as
        Story for Children." Ed.D. dissertation, Columbia University, 1970,
        395 pp., DA:662A.
        Compares selected myths written in the original classical Greek
        with versions in English written for children. The myths are Europa
        and Cadmus, Daedalus, Bellerophon, Meleager, Atalanta, Hermes,
        Demeter, Orpheus, Prometheus, and Pandora. Comparisons were
        based on elements of plot, character, and language.

B1300   HARMS, JEANNE McLAIN, and LETTOW, LUCILLE J. "The Begin-
        ning: Children's Literature and the Origins of the World." CLE, n.s.
        14, no. 2 (Summer 1983):113-23.
        Surveys literature for elementary and middle school children that
        portrays early explanations such as biblical accounts and myths of
        many cultures, and scientific theories of the development and origins
        of the universe and people. Includes a bibliography.

B1301   LANG, J.T. "The Heroic Tradition in Children's Literature." Use of
        English 25 (Spring 1974):201-7.
        Discusses the way adaptations and interpretations for children of
        traditional mythic and epic literature reflect the times. Includes a
        brief list of recommended reading.

B1302   SIDWELL, R.T. "Rhea Was a Broad: Pre-Hellenic Greek Myths for
        Post-Hellenic Children." CLE, n.s. 12, no. 4 (Winter 1981):171-76.
        Explores scholarship establishing the matriarchal nature of early
        Greek myths, their change to patriarchal emphasis in Hellenic times,
        and the significance of all this for teaching Greek myths to today's
        children. Recommends Charlene Spretnak's Lost Goddesses of Early
        Greece.

B1303   SMITH, LILLIAN. "Gods and Men." In Unreluctant Years, pp. 64-79.
        Discusses Charles Kingsley's, Nathaniel Hawthorne's and Padraic
        Colum's versions of the Greek myths; and A. and E. Keary's, Abbie
        Farwell Brown's, and Dorothy Hosford's versions of the Norse myths.
        Kingsley's and Hosford's versions are preferred.

B1304   WOOD, JESSICA. "Unafraid of Greatness." Horn Book 32 (April June
        1956):127-36, 212-18.
        Explores the values and rewards of mythology and epic literature
        for children, citing the characteristics of various published versions.

B1305   YOLEN, JANE. "How Basic is SHAZAM?" Childhood Education 53,
        no. 4 (February 1977):186-91. (Also in Yolen, Touch Magic, pp.
        13-20. Reprinted in LA 54 [September 1977]:645-51.)
        Argues that myth fulfills four basic functions in the education of
        a child: a landscape of allusion, knowledge of ancestral culture, a
        tool of therapy, and a model for belief.

B1306   -----. "Makers of Modern Myths." Horn Book 51 (October
        1975):496-97.
        Sees children's books in terms of myth. Pays particular attention
        to Maurice Sendak's In the Night Kitchen.

B1307   -----. "The Modern Mythmakers." LA 53 (May 1976):491-95.

Modern mythmakers come from eclectic backgrounds, but they must not bear their burden lightly. Takes examples of use of myth from her own work.

NATIONALISM

B1308   MARTIN, HELEN. "Nationalism in Children's Literature." *Library Quarterly* 6 (October 1936):405-18.
Analyzes the nationalist influences in twenty-four classic children's books from seventeen countries. Provides detailed charts, statistics, and stimulating conclusions.

B1309   REID, CHRISTINE. "Children's Books in Scotland and Switzerland." In Hunt, *Further Approaches*, pp. 103-5.
Describes her research on the development of national characteristics in the children's books of Scotland and Switzerland.

NETHERLANDS

B1310   TELLEGEN-VAN DELFT, SASKIA, and BINK, ERIK. "The Netherlands." *Phaedrus* 8 (1981):70-71.
Reports on recent research. Includes a bibliography of items mostly published in Dutch.

NEW ZEALAND

B1311   GILDERDALE, BETTY. "Children's Periodicals in New Zealand." *Phaedrus* 4, no. 2 (Fall 1977):18.
A brief survey and analysis.

B1312   -----. *Sea Change: 145 Years of New Zealand Junior Fiction.* Auckland, New Zealand: Longman Paul, 1982, 300 pp.
A historical survey of fiction with a New Zealand setting. Includes sections on the Maori in junior fiction, the early settlers, fantasy, adventure stories, school stories, animal stories, books for the youngest, and books with a message. Includes references and bibliographies.

B1313   WHITE, DOROTHY NEAL. "A 'Newbery' for New Zealand." *Horn Book* 22 (September-October 1946):339-43.
Describes the establishment of the Glen award; its first recipient, Stella Maurice's *The Book of Wiremu*; and the work of Esther Glen, with comments on the state of children's literature in New Zealand in general.

NEWBERY AND CALDECOTT AWARD BOOKS

B1314   KINGMAN, LEE, ed. *Newbery and Caldecott Medal Books: 1956-1965, with Acceptance Papers, Biographies and Related Material Chiefly from the Horn Book Magazine.* Boston: Horn Book, 1965, 300 pp.
Contains acceptance speeches, brief biographical sketches of the winners, and excerpts from the award-winning books.

B1315   MILLER, BERTHA MAHONY, and FIELD, ELINOR WHITNEY, eds. *Caldecott Medal Books: 1938-1957.* Boston: Horn Book, 1957.
Includes an introductory essay on Randolph Caldecott by Miller and the acceptance speeches and biographical papers of the medal

winners. A final essay by Esther Averill, entitled "What Is a Picture Book?," provides an overview and "critical appraisal of the twenty books which have won the Caldecott Award," and distinguishes between picture books and illustrated books, both of which have won awards.

B1316   PETERSON, LINDA KAUFFMAN, and SOLT, MARILYN LEATHERS, eds. "Newbery and Caldecott Medal and Honor Books." *ChLAQ* 6, no. 3 (Fall 1981):7-31. (Reprinted in Dooley, *First Steps*, pp. 114-30.)

Includes "What If?," by Ruth Jane Roberts, discussing first Newbery-winner Hendrik Van Loon's *The Story of Mankind*; "Dorothy Lathrop and the Caldecott Medal Tradition," by Linda Peterson, which examines the first Caldecott Medal winner, *Animals of the Bible*, and compares it to Peter Spier's *Noah's Ark*; "Seeing Ourselves in Others," Janice Alberghene's discussion of the life-in-other-lands books published in the 1930s; Hughes Moir's examination of the Newbery books of the 1950s; Rona Glass's examination of Madeleine L'Engle's *A Wrinkle in Time* and Lloyd Alexander's *High King* in terms of the couples they portray; Linda Burns's examination of the Caldecott winners of the seventies for their use of folktale and traditional titles; Marjorie Reenwald Romanoff's analysis of Donald's Crews's *Freight Train* and *Truck*; Barbara St. John's exploration of the idea that "children's books reflect the society which produces them" through an examination of Newbery Medal books of the 1970s; and finally Peterson and Solt's summaries of characteristics and trends of Newbery and Caldecott books in excerpts from their book *Newbery and Caldecott Medal and Honor Books* (Boston: G.K. Hall, 1982, 427 pp.).

B1317   SHACKFORD, JANE. "Who Reads the Newbery Winners?: Children's Literary Needs and Reading Tastes." *SLJ* 23 (March 1977):101-5.

Compares reviews and children's responses to Newbery winners, as reported by librarians and teachers, in an attempt to determine what children's reading needs and tastes really are. Concludes that the following characteristics are important: (1) respect for audience, (2) authentic and convincing plot and characterizations, whether fantasy or "real life," (3) an inspiring or worthwhile theme, (4) dramatic content that provides action and suspense, and (5) relevance based on meaningful human experiences. Discussions of the individual titles are illuminating.

B1318   SOLT, MARILYN J. "The Newbery Award: A Survey of Fifty Years of Newbery Winners and Honor Books." Ph.D. dissertation, Bowling Green State University, 1973, 249 pp., DA 34:1869A.

"To survey the Newbery Award Books as a group, to recognize literary qualities, to discern trends and changing patterns, and to perceive the influence of the books singled out as the best in American children's literature was the purpose of this study."

B1319   STEWIG, JOHN WARREN. "Trends in Caldecott Award Winners." *EE* 45 (February 1968):218-23, 260.

Examines Caldecott award-winning books to determine trends in realism and choice of media. Includes a bibliography.

B1320   WEGMAN, ROSE MIRIAM, Sister. "Newbery Books Then and Now: An Appraisal." *EE* 49 (November 1972):973-80.

Compares Newbery award-winning books of the first decade to those from 1959 to 1968 and finds, among other differences, that the more recent books are stylistically superior.

NIGERIA

B1321   FAYOSE, P. OSAZEE. "A Look at Nigerian Children's Literature." *Bookbird* 15, no. 2 (1977):2-5; no. 3 (1977):14-19.
An overview.

B1322   -----. "Nigeria." *Phaedrus* 8 (1981):72-74.
A bibliography covering unpublished dissertations and conference papers and published works on Nigerian children's literature, most written in English and many published outside of the country.

B1323   ODEJIDE, BIOLA. "Adventure Books in Nigerian Children's Literature." *Bookbird* 3 (1981):13-18.
Discusses books written in English with a Nigerian setting, especially those of Dorothy Wimbush.

B1324   ODEJIDE, BIOLA, and JAMES, SYBIL L. "Nigerian Children's Books for Intercultural Understanding in the English Speaking World." *Journal of Reading* 25 (March 1982):516-24.
Surveys Nigerian children's books available in English and their contribution to cross-cultural understanding. Includes references and sources for books.

B1325   OKANLAWON, TUNDE. "Nigerian Children's Literature: Problems and Goals." *Journal of Commonwealth Literature* 15 (August 1980):30-37.
A brief overview emphasizing the roles of the schools and libraries and the status of Nigerian literature as a whole.

B1326   OSA, OSAYIMWENSE. "Contemporary Nigerian Children's Literature." *Reading Teacher* 37 (March 1984):594-97.
Provides an overview of the recent growth in Nigerian children's literature and its criticism.

B1327   -----. "A Content Analysis of Fourteen Nigerian Young Adult Novels." Ed.D. dissertation, University of Houston, 1981, 270 pp., DA 42:3420A.
Describes a composite picture of the Nigerian young adult novel based on a content analysis of fourteen representative books.

B1328   ROSCOE, ADRIAN A. "Juvenile Literature." In *Mother Is Gold: A Study of West African Literature*. Cambridge: Cambridge University Press, 1971, pp. 132-43.
Provides an overview of recent Nigerian children's literature that includes the works of major authors such as Cyprian Ekwensi and folktale retellings.

B1329   WAGNER, GULTEN. "Nigerian Children's Books: An Evaluation." *African Book Publishing Record* 2, no. 4 (1976):231-36.
A condensed version of an M.L.S. theses entitled "An Evaluative Study of Children's Books Published in Nigeria" (University of Ibadan, Nigeria).

NONSENSE

B1330   CAMMAERTS, EMILE. *The Poetry of Nonsense*. London: G. Routledge, 1925; New York: E.P. Dutton and Co., 1926, 86 pp. (Also appears in serial installments in *Junior Bookshelf* 15, nos. 1-6 [1951].)

Defines nonsense, then devotes chapters to nonsense and the child, nonsense and poetry, and nonsense in art, and concludes with a discussion of nonsense in England. Concentrates primarily on the works of Lewis Carroll and Edward Lear.

B1331   EDE, LISA SUSAN. "The Nonsense Literature of Edward Lear and Lewis Carroll." Ph.D. dissertation, Ohio State University, 1975, 166 pp., DA 36:5314A.

Provides a detailed analysis of the nature of nonsense in the works of Lewis Carroll and Edward Lear.

B1332   GRAHAM, ELEANOR. "Nonsense in Children's Literature." *Junior Bookshelf* 9 (July 1944):61-68.

Explores the meanings of nonsense and its appearance in a wide range of writing, identifying where it is and is not. Concludes that "through it always runs that sweet unreasonableness of which De la Mare has spoken."

B1333   LIVINGSTON, MYRA COHN. "Nonsense Verse: The Complete Escape." In Hearne, *Celebrating Children's Books*, pp. 122-39.

Looks at nonsense verse as rebellion against reason and the laws of nature, and as a marvelous place to escape to. Differentiates nonsense from wit and fantasy and outlines its distinguishing characteristics.

B1334   SEWELL, ELIZABETH. *The Field of Nonsense*. London: Chatto & Windus, 1952, 198 pp.

Explores the nature of nonsense in the writings of Edward Lear and Lewis Carroll.

B1335   -----. "Nonsense Verse and the Child." *L&U* 4, no. 2 (Winter 1980-81):30-45.

Attempts to analyze what is "better" or "worse" nonsense.

B1336   STEWART, SUSAN. "Nonsense: Aspects of Intertextuality in Folklore and Literature." Ph.D. dissertation, University of Pennsylvania, 1978, 370 pp., DA 39:4410A.

Focuses "upon the relationships between common sense and fiction."

B1337   THOMAS, JOYCE. "'There Was an Old Man . . .': The Sense of Nonsense Verse." *ChLAQ* 10 (Fall 1985):119-22.

Shows how even meaningless language can convey meaning.

B1338   VIGUERS, SUSAN T. "Nonsense and the Language of Poetry." *Signal* 42 (September 1984):137-49.

Viguers and Foss, the "Highly Regarded Cat Companion of Edward Lear, Celebrated Writer of Nonsense," discuss nonsense and poetry, which are shown to be more closely related than might be supposed.

NORWAY

B1339   BOZANIC, INGRID. "Contemporary Children's Literature of Norway."
         Children's Literature 3 (1974):61-65.
         Provides an overview of the development of recent Norwegian
         children's literature.

B1340   FEYDT, ASTRID. "The Best Norwegian Children's Books." *Bookbird*
         6, no. 3 (1968):34-40.
         Surveys and comments upon a number of recent, prize-winning
         Norwegian children's books.

B1341   -----. "Norwegian Books for Children." *Junior Bookshelf* 18, no. 5
         (November 1954):225-33; no. 6 (December 1954):277-83.
         A survey of recent and classic children's books.

B1342   FRASER, JAMES H. "A Comment on Norwegian-American Children's
         Literature and Language Maintenance." *Phaedrus* 6, no. 1 (Spring
         1979):41-43.
         Notes the paucity of Norwegian-American literature for children,
         and mentions children's periodicals, primarily those of the nineteenth
         century.

B1343   SCHEI, KARI. "Notes from Across the North Sea." *Signal* 25 (January
         1978):30-33.
         Discusses developments in children's book publishing in Norway,
         particularly the emphasis on series books.

B1344   SKJØNSBERG, KARI. "Norway." *Phaedrus* 8 (1981):75-77.
         A bibliography of recent Norwegian research in children's litera-
         ture; includes English abstracts.

B1345   TENFJORD, JO. "Children's Books in Norway." *Junior Bookshelf* 10
         (October 1946):103-14.
         A historical critical overview.

B1346   -----. "Children's Books in Norway." *Junior Bookshelf* 26 (January
         1962):7-12.
         A historical critical overview.

B1347   -----. "National Spirit, Landscape, and Norwegian Children's Book
         Illustration: Some Traditions and Trends." *Phaedrus* 9 (1982):17-21.
         An overview of children's book illustration in Norway from the
         late nineteenth century to the present.

NURSERY RHYMES

B1348   ABRAMS, JOAN. "How Content and Symbolism in Mother Goose May
         Contribute to the Development of a Child's Integrated Psyche."
         (ERIC Educational Document Reproduction Service, 1977, 49 pp., ED
         153 220.)
         Analyzes Mother Goose rhymes in relation to the psychological
         stages of child development.

B1349   BAKER, WILLIAM J. "Historical Meaning in *Mother Goose*: Nursery
         Rhymes Illustrative of English Society Before The Industrial Revolu-
         tion." *Journal of Popular Culture* 9 (Winter 1975):645-52.

Looks to the Mother Goose rhymes as a means of reconstructing "the life styles, the concerns, the assumptions of the English people before the coming of industrialism."

B1350   BARING-GOULD, WILLIAM S., and BARING-GOULD, CECIL. *The Annotated Mother Goose.* New York: Carkson N. Potter, 1962, 350 pp.
A heavily annotated volume that gathers together much valuable information. Includes biographical, historical, and bibliographical information as well as historic illustrations.

B1351   BODGER, JOAN. "Mother Goose: Is the Old Girl Relevant." *WLB* 44 (December 1969):402-8.
Explores the ways in which Mother Goose meets the needs of today's children. Includes references and discussions of pros and cons of various versions of the tales.

B1352   CARTER, R. "The Tao and Mother Goose." *Parabola* 6, no. 4 (Fall 1981):19-26.
Suggests that Mother Goose rhymes such as "Little Miss Muffet" express the nature of duality and the conflict between hero and monster, between good and evil within ourselves.

B1353   CHISHOLM, MARGARET. "Mother Goose--Elucidated." *EE* 49 (December 1972):1141-44. (Reprinted in Barron, *Jump Over the Moon,* pp. 69-74.)
Proposes convincing explanations of the verses "Mary, Mary Quite Contrary," "Jack and Jill," "Baa Baa Black Sheep," "Little Jack Horner," "Ring-a-ring o' Roses," "Goosey Goosey Gander," "Ride-a-cock-horse," "Humpty Dumpty," and "London Bridge."

B1354   CURTIS, DAVID. "With Rhyme and Reason." *LA* 52 (October 1975):947-49.
Discusses the use of nursery rhymes to introduce children to allegory.

B1355   ECKENSTEIN, LINA. *Comparative Studies in Nursery Rhymes.* London: Duckworth & Co, 1906. Reprint. Detroit: Singing Tree Press, 1968, 231 pp.
Traces the origins of nursery rhymes, emphasizing cross-cultural comparisons and mythic and folk elements.

B1356   EGAN, MICHAEL. "Because He Can't Work Any Faster." *TES,* 16 January 1981, p. 34. (Reply by Brian Alderson the following week [23 January 1981]:18.)
Offers a socialist interpretation of the historical and political significance of Mother Goose. Views "Simple Simon" as "a little homily in capitalist alienation." Alderson retorts, "And now it is a socialist's turn--but they will survive him too." Calls "Simple Simon" "more of a working-class joke about stupid people than an economic tract."

B1357   EZELL, RICHARD. "Mother Goose: The Rhythm of Her Rhymes." In MacLeod, *Children's Literature,* pp. 1-15.
Analyzes the meter and rhyme scheme of Mother Goose and explores their influences on later children's poets.

B1358　GUÉRON, JACQUELINE. "Children's Verse and the Halle-Keyser Theory of Prosody." *Children's Literature* 2 (1973):197-208.
　　　　　Discusses metrical analysis of French and English nursery rhymes according to the Halle-Keyser theory.

B1359　HAWKENS, ROBERTA. "Nursery Rhymes: Mirrors of a Culture." *EE* 48 (October 1971):617-21.
　　　　　Explores ways in which nursery rhymes reflect the tastes, attitudes, technology, and behavorial patterns of the societies from which they come.

B1360　HAZARD, PAUL. *Books, Children and Men*, pp. 80-85.
　　　　　Explores the nature of English nursery rhymes and comments on the ways in which they differ greatly from those of the Romance languages.

B1361　HÜRLIMANN, BETTINA. "A Magic Horn for Children: Nursery Rhymes and Songs Then and Now." In *Three Centuries*, pp. 1-20.
　　　　　Surveys the nursery rhymes of Europe, primarily those of Germany and England.

B1362　LA BELLE, JENIJOY. "William Blake, Theodore Roethke and Mother Goose: The Unholy Trinity." *Blake Studies* 9, nos. 1-2 (1980):74-86.
　　　　　Explores elements of nursery rhymes in Blake's *Songs of Innocence* and Theodore Roethke's *I Am! Says the Lamb* and *Praise to the End!*

B1363　LYNN, JOANNE L. "Runes to Ward Off Sorrow: Rhetoric of the English Nursery Rhyme." *CLE*, n.s. 16, no. 1 (Spring 1985):3-14.
　　　　　Provides an overview of nursery rhyme research and proposes that "nursery rhymes--collected as they have been from a variety of sources--were selected by and for a specific audience of both children and adults, that they remain active in the culture thanks to a similar audience and that the double nature of the audience has dictated the survival of a particular literary form. This form is characterized by compression, paradox, ambiguity, and a tension between form and content that is characteristic of genuine poetry." Includes references.

B1364　McDONALD, MARY PALMER. "Rhyme or Reason? A Microscopic View of Nursery Rhymes." *Journal of Negro Education* 43 (1974):275-83.
　　　　　Points out images of white supremacy, negative self images, and "unreal concepts" in Mother Goose.

B1365　MARY JOAN PATRICIA, Sister. "Mother Goose to Homer." *Catholic Library World* 23 (1951):75-79. (Reprinted in Robinson, E. *Readings about Children's Literature*, pp. 239-48.)
　　　　　Outlines the child's development in appreciation of literature from the simple rhymes of Mother Goose, through other childhood poets, the fairy tales and myths, to the Bible and sophisticated works of adult literature.

B1366　NADEAU, JOHN. "Mother Goose Exposed!" *Education* 80 (1960):491-92.
　　　　　Argues that Mother Goose rhymes are full of violence and cruelty to animals.

B1367   NADESAN, ARDELL. "Mother Goose: Sexist?" *EE* 51 (April 1974):375-78.
         Examines the roles of women and girls as portrayed in the nursery rhymes.

B1368   OPIE, PETER, and OPIE, IONA. Introduction to *Oxford Dictionary of Nursery Rhymes*. London: Oxford University Press, 1952, pp. 1-45.
         Discusses the quality, origins, means of transmission, and history of nursery rhymes and songs.

B1369   PETTY, THOMAS A. "The Tragedy of Humpty Dumpty." *Psychoanalytic Study of the Child* 8 (1953):404-12.
         Finds "Humpty Dumpty's" great appeal lies in its symbolizing the arrival of a sibling: the fall is the birth of the second born and the first born's fall from parental favor, "and the first-born's hostile wish that some disaster befall the sibling."

B1370   POMERANTZ, CHARLOTTE. "Little Jennifer Has Lost Her Sheep." *NYTBR*, 30 April 1978, Children's Book sec., pp. 25, 36.
         A humorous response by a modern editor to 'Ms. Goose's' rhymes. "In general, Ms. Goose, we think you have a problem with rhyme."

B1371   SACKVILLE-WEST, V[ITA]. *Nursery Rhymes*. London: Dropmore Press, 1947, 66 pp.
         Explores the significance of nursery rhymes and provides comments on many individual rhymes. "Not by history, not by mythology, not by folklore, not even by the absurdity of situations, not even by the sense of power so flatteringly suggested when by one line we can magnify a shoe into the size of a house; but by their little gift of poetry and music do the nursery rhymes abide in our heart."

B1372   SENDAK, MAURICE. "Mother Goose's Garnishings." *Book Week*, 31 October 1965, Fall Children's issue, pp. 5, 38-40. (Reprinted in Haviland, *Children and Literature*, pp. 188-95, and in Barron, *Jump Over the Moon*, pp. 62-69.)
         Surveys the history of Mother Goose illustrations, direct literal approaches and more subtle illuminative approaches; and tells which versions he likes, which he does not, and why.

B1373   SNIPES, WILSON C. "Five Ways and One of Looking at Mother Goose." *Children's Literature* 2 (1973):98-104.
         Applies biographical, sociocultural, humanistic, formalist, and psychological-psychoanalytic approaches to Mother Goose in a lighthearted manner.

B1374   THOMAS, DELLA. "Matriarch of the Nursery." *School Library Journal* 13 (March 1967):110-12.
         Reviews some of the numerous editions of Mother Goose.

B1375   THOMAS, KATHERINE ELWES. *The Real Personages of Mother Goose*. London: Lothrop, Lee & Shepard, 1930, 352 pp.
         This influential work identifies the characters of Mother Goose as historic persons and interprets the rhymes on this basis. For example, Little Boy Blue is identified as Cardinal Wolsey, and the

Cat in "The Cat and the Fiddle" as Elizabeth I.

B1376 TUCKER, NICHOLAS. "Why Nursery Rhymes?" *Where*, September 1969, pp. 152-55. (Reprinted in Haviland, *Children and Literature*, pp. 258-62.)

Explores the many ways nursery rhymes appeal to children: by their linguistic and musical genius, their appealing subject matter, and their approaches to violence and to adulthood.

B1377 USREY, MALCOLM. "Mother Goose with Tears: Fantasy and Realism in Mother Goose Illustrations since 1865." *Proceedings of the Children's Literature Association* 7 (1980):166-74.

Surveys some of the more notable illustrations of nursery rhymes.

B1378 WALKER, LOUISE JEAN. "Moral Implications in Mother Goose." *Education* 80 (January 1960):292-93.

Explores the potential of the Mother Goose rhymes for teaching good manners and behavior.

B1379 WEISS, HARRY B. "Something About Simple Simon." *Bulletin of the New York Public Library* 44, no. 6 (June 1940):461-70.

Traces the history and origins of "Simple Simon," and reproduces the complete fifteen verses from the Ryle and Paul edition of *The Royal Book of Nursery Rhymes*. Includes an extensive bibliography.

B1380 WILLIAMS, C.B. "As I Was Going to St. Ives." *Folklore* 86 (Summer 1975):133-35.

Traces "St. Ives" from Britain back to Egypt over a period of "about three thousand seven hundred years, but with few indications of the route which has been followed."

OCCULT

B1381 DONELSON, KENNETH. "Stories of the Supernatural." In *Literature for Today's Young Adults*, pp. 241-44.

Discusses characteristics of stories of the supernatural, with examples from contemporary young adult literature.

B1382 McHARGUE, GEORGESS. "A Ride Across the Mystic Bridge, or, Occult Books: What, Why, and Who Needs Them?" *SLJ* 19 (May 1973):25-30. (Reprinted in Gerhardt, *Issues in Children's Book Selection*, pp. 154-62.)

Provides a brief history and definition of occult books, and discusses various categories of the occult and its appeal for today's youth.

OCCUPATIONS

B1383 CROUCH, MARCUS. "Work." In *The Nesbit Tradition*, pp. 185-95.

Suggests that the career book "was an invention of the post-war period." Authors discussed include Richard Armstrong and Elfrida Vipont.

B1384 IVES, VERNON. "Careers for Sale: $2.00 List." *Horn Book* 19 (March-April 1943):107-12.

Lists recent books on careers and singles out those he considers excellent while commenting on qualities of the genre.

B1385 KAISER, MARJORIE M. "The Meaning of Work in Literature Popular with Sixteen and Seventeen-Year Olds." ERIC Educational Document Reproduction Service, 1980, 16 pp., ED 181 465.

Analyzes the most popular books from the 1978 Books for Young Adults poll in terms of attitudes toward work and finds they are mostly positive.

B1386 KINGSBURY, MARY. "The World of Work in Children's Fiction." *LA* 52 (October 1975):972-75, 1018.

Reports on a study of "ninety-one examples of realistic fiction published for children in the 1930s, the 1950s and the 1970s to determine the kinds of work models and work-related values and attitudes being offered to young readers."

B1387 PARIS, JANELLE. *A Comparative Analysis of Occupations Presented in Children's Realistic Fiction, 1950-54 and 1970-74.* Ph.D. dissertation, Texas Women's University, 1977, 240 pp., DA 38:5105A.

Tests the hypothesis that "there is a discernible trend toward increasing honesty and realism relating to career content in children's fiction." This hypothesis is not confirmed, however, for she finds stereotypes, inadequate information, limited views, discrimination against women workers, and many other specific complaints.

B1388 RUSSELL, PATRICIA R. "Learning about Work--A Study of Contemporary Fiction for Children." ERIC Educational Document Reproduction Service, 1977, 18 pp., ED 168 041.

Analyzes the way work is treated in 255 books of fiction written since 1970 for primary school children. Includes a bibliography of children's books with work themes.

B1389 SPLAVER, SARAH. "The Career Novel." *Personnel and Guidance Journal* 31 (March 1953):371-72.

Calls current "career novels" "sugar-coated occupational information," but finds they range from excellent to very bad.

B1390 THETFORD, MARY. "Vocational Roles for Women in Junior Fiction." Ed.D. dissertation, Rutgers University, 1974, 121 pp., DA 35:3311A.

Found that the dominant portrayal of women in children's fiction reinforces traditional stereotypes. "There is a need to write additional career fiction that portrays alternatives to these sex roles."

PAKISTAN

B1391 ALI, AHMED. "Children's Reading in Pakistan." *Horn Book* 43 (April 1967):235-38.

A brief overview.

PARTICIPATION FICTION

B1392 ALBERGHENE, JANICE M. "It's Your Choice: Reader Participation Fiction." *SLJ* 29 (February 1983):36-37.

Analyzes the characteristics of a number of recent participation books.

PASTORAL

B1393   KOPPES, PHYLLIS BIXLER. "The Child in Pastoral Myth: A Study in Rousseau and Wordsworth, Children's Literature and Literary Fantasy." Ph.D. dissertation, University of Kansas, 1977, 386 pp., DA 38:4141A.

Examines "the myth of the child as a pastoral figure in Rousseau and Wordsworth and its influence on the development of children's literature. Focuses on the work of George MacDonald, Frances Hodgson Burnett, Catherine Sinclair, Flora Shaw, Lewis Carroll, Mark Twain, Kenneth Grahame, James Barrie, A.A. Milne, and J.R.R. Tolkien.

B1394   KUZNETS, LOIS R. "The Fresh-Air Kids or Some Contemporary Versions of Pastoral." *Children's Literature* 11 (1983):156-68.

Examines Felice Holman's *Slake's Limbo* and Paula Fox's *How Many Miles to Babylon?* in terms of the way they "evoke pastoral contrasts within urban settings."

PAUL BUNYAN

B1395   RAPPORT, REBECCA TISDEL. "Paul Bunyan: Hero of the North Woods." *LA* 56 (April 1979):394-99.

Surveys the evolution, controversies, and publication history of the Paul Bunyan tales.

PEACE

B1396   LEPMAN, JELLA. "Picture Books and the Idea of Peace." *Bookbird* 5, no. 1 (1967):5-10.

Discusses depictions of the concept of peace in children's picture books, especially Munro Leaf's *Ferdinand the Bull*, Roger Duvoisin's *The Happy Lion*, Jean de Brunhoff's *Story of Babar*, and Erich Kästner's *Animal Conference.*

PERIODICALS

B1397   ALDERSON, CONNIE. *Magazines Teenagers Read: With Special Reference to "Trend," "Jackie," and "Valentine."* London: Pergamon, 1968, 127 pp.

Provides a detailed examination of the content, style, and social and moral values portrayed in three British magazines popular with teenaged girls.

B1398   CADOGAN, MARY, and CRAIG, PATRICIA. "Millgirls, Madcaps and Mothers Superior." In *You're a Brick*, pp. 125-39.

Discusses the *Girls' Friend* and other early twentieth-century periodicals designed to appeal to the young working women of the lower classes.

B1399   -----. "A Superabundance of Girls," "And Still More," and "The *Girls Own Paper* Goes to War." In *You're a Brick*, pp. 227-85.

These three chapters discuss British periodicals for girls from the 1920s through World War II. Among titles commented on at length are *School Friend*, *Schoolgirls' Own*, *Schoolgirl*, and *Girls Own Paper* (also discussed on pp. 73-76).

B1400 CAMPBELL, ALASDAIR. "The Evaluation of Magazines for Children Under Eight." *School Librarian* 17 (September 1969):233-40.
Suggests criteria for judging magazines for young children, focusing on the British children's magazines known as comics.

B1401 CAWOOD, GAYLE EALY, and GREENLAW, M. JEAN. "Juvenile Magazines in the U.S.A.: A Compleat Overview with History and Trends." *TON* 34 (Summer 1978):365-74.
Covers from 1789 to the present and includes a "Chronological Listing of the Initial Appearance of Certain U.S. Children's Magazines."

B1402 FRY, COLIN. "Picture of Perfection." *New Society* 12 (August 1971):294-95.
Explores the world of *Captain*, the early twentieth-century British boys' magazine.

B1403 JAMES, LOUIS. "Tom Brown's Imperialist Sons." *Victorian Studies* 17 (September 1973):89-99.
Traces the influences of *Tom Brown's School Days* on popular nineteenth-century boys periodicals.

B1404 JORDAN, ALICE M. "Magazines for Children." *Bulletin of the New York Public Library* 60 (November 1956):599-604.
Comments on the influences of nineteenth-century children's magazines on twentieth-century children's literature.

B1405 KELLY, R. GORDON, ed. *Children's Periodicals of the United States.* Westport, Conn.: Greenwood, 1984, 591 pp.
Detailed articles by nearly fifty experts describe numerous American children's magazines from the eighteenth century to the present. Entries include references, information on bibliographies, phies, index sources, location sources, and publication history.

B1406 KOSTE, MARGARET IRENE. "An Evaluation of Magazines Published for Children in America." Ph.D. dissertation, Ohio State University, 1962, 234 pp., DA 23:3250A.
Examines fourteen children's magazines in terms of criteria devised to determine "what constitutes a magazine of quality for children of elementary school age."

B1407 LARRICK, NANCY. "Classroom Magazines: A Critique of 45 Top Sellers." *Learning* 7 (October 1978):60-61.
Rates and evaluates the most popular children's magazines.

B1408 ORWELL, GEORGE. "Boys' Weeklies." In *Dickens, Dali and Others.* New York: Harcourt, Brace & World, 1946, pp. 76-114.
Analyzes the British boys' papers *Gem* and *Magnet*, which are then compared to a number of more recent (post-World War I) papers.

B1409 *Phaedrus* 4, no. 2 (Fall 1977):5-35.
Special Issue. Includes articles on periodicals in the U.S., Sweden, Austria, New Zealand, Canada, Denmark, Hungary, Germany, and Italy. For further information see names of these countries in this bibliography.

B1410   RANLETT, FELIX.   "Magazines for Tens and 'Teens.'"   *Horn Book* 20 (July-August 1944):271-77.
Surveys children's magazines of the 1940s, comparing them with fondly remembered favorites of the past such as *Youth's Companion* and *St. Nicholas.*

B1411   RICHARDSON, SELMA K.   *Magazines for Children: A Selection Guide.* Chicago: American Library Association, 1983, 147 pp.
Provides lengthy descriptive and evaluative annotations for periodicals published for children as of late 1982.

B1412   ROSE, ADA CAMPBELL.   "Are Children's Magazines Dying on the Vine?"   *Catholic Library World* 47 (April 1976):370-73.
Surveys the history of children's periodicals and points out recent trends and problems.

B1413   WESTERN, LINDA.   "Magazine Preferences of Fourth-and-Sixth Grade Children."   *Elementary School Journal* 79 (May 1979):284-91.
Reports on a study of children's magazine preferences.

B1414   ZOLA, MEGUIDO.   "English-Canadian Magazines for Children."   *CCL* 10 (1977-78):24-36.
Surveys and evaluates current Canadian children's magazines.

B1415   -----.   "English-Canadian Magazines for Children: An Up-Date."   *CCL* 14 (1979):41-45.
A bibliography and evaluation of current English-language Canadian magazines for children.

PESSIMISM

B1416   CARR, ROBIN L.   "From Pandora's Box: Hopelessness and Defeat in Children's Literature."   ERIC Educational Document Reproduction Service, 1978, 10 pp., ED 168 026.
Compares books that focus on the tragedies and problems of life without offering any interpretation of their meaning or any alternative to hopelessness and defeat, to those that deal realistically with "themes of darkness" while at the same time stressing the importance of the "search for goodness and victory in life."

B1417   MacLEOD, ANNE S.   "Undercurrents: Pessimism in Contemporary Children's Fiction."   *CLE*, o.s., no. 21 (Summer 1976):96-102.
Looks at novels for children that, while not openly downbeat like *The Chocolate War*, have an undercurrent of pessimism. Examines Hoban's *The Mouse and His Child*, Chester Aaron's *An American Court*, Eleanor Cameron's *The Court of the Stone Children*, and Madeleine L'Engle's *A Wind in the Door*. Concludes that children's literature, like any other, is of its time. "If the time is darkened by doubt and fear, the literature is likely to be shadowed, too, even against the intent of its creators." Letter in response from Eleanor Cameron, disagreeing with MacLeod's interpretation of her book, in

PHOTOGRAPHIC ILLUSTRATION

B1418   BADER, BARBARA.   "Photographic Books."   In *American Picturebooks,*

pp. 100-117.
Traces the use of photography as a means of illustration in children's fiction and nonfiction picture books.

B1419   FRASER, JAMES, and VOLK, ULLA. "Observations on Photographic Innovation in Children's Books: The Books of Rodchenko, Ungermann, Steichen, Martin and Boer." *Phaedrus* 9 (1982):27-34.
Examines the work of five photographic innovators in children's book illustration who were active in the early 1930s.

B1420   HÜRLIMANN, BETTINA. "Photography: A New Contribution to Education and Children's Books." In *Three Centuries*, pp. 145-51.
Discusses the development of photographically illustrated children's picture books.

B1421   OLDHAM, JEFFREY THOMAS. "A Comparison of American Photo-Illustrated Children's Books for Early Childhood Years Published in the 1950-1960-1970s." Ph.D. dissertation, Southern Illinois University at Carbondale, 1981, 134 pp., DA 41:3585A.
Concluded that in most cases "the illustrations represented exactly what was stated in the text."

PICTURE BOOKS

B1422   ABRAHAMSON, RICHARD F. "An Analysis of Children's Picture Storybooks." *Reading Teacher* 34 (November 1980):167-70.
Analyzes "Children's Choices for 1979" to find out what story structures children like best.

B1423   ABRAHAMSON, RICHARD F., and SHANNON, PATRICK. "A Plot Structure Analysis of Favorite Picture Books." *Reading Teacher* 37 (October 1983):44-48.
Analyzes the plot structures of the 61 most popular books on the 1982 Children's Choices list (*Reading Teacher*, October 1982) and suggests interesting trends and a revised system for categorizing plots.

B1424   AMOR, STUART. "A Functional Approach to Illustrations in Children's Books: The Work of František Holešovský." In Fox, *Responses to Children's Literature*, pp. 76-80.
Reports on the approach of Holešovský and other Czech structural theorists to children's book illustration.

B1425   AMSDEN, R.H. "Children's Preferences in Picture Story Book Variables." *Journal of Educational Research* 53 (1960):309-12.
Finds that children preferred light and dark colors to bright colors, and makes recommendations concerning style of illustration. Suggests areas for additional research.

B1426   ANDERSON, WILLIAM. "On Texts and Illustrators: Eight Books." *Children's Literature* 3 (1974):213-18.
Reviews eight books, including *The Juniper Tree and Other Tales from Grimm*, edited and translated by Lore Segal and illustrated by Maurice Sendak; and *King Grisly-Beard*, by the Brothers Grimm, translated by Edgar Taylor and illustrated by Maurice Sendak.

B1427   ARDIZZONE, EDWARD. "The Born Illustrator." *Motif: A Journal of the Visual Arts* 1 (November 1958):37-52.

Ardizzone expresses his views on illustration.

B1428   -----. "Creation of a Picture Book." *TON* 16 (December 1959):40-46.
(Reprinted in Egoff, *Only Connect*, 1st ed., pp. 347-56; 2d ed., pp. 289-98.)
Discusses various aspects of illustrating books, with examples drawn from his illustrations for his own writings and his illustrations for others.

B1429   BADER, BARBARA. *American Picturebooks from Noah's Ark to the Beast Within*. New York: Macmillan, 1976, 615 pp.
An immense, richly illustrated work that traces the development of American children's picture books. Many of the chapters on specific topics and individual illustrators have been indexed separately. The book is also rich in bibliographic notes and references.

B1430   BARTO, AGNIA. "Children's Response to Illustrations of Poetry." *CLE*, n.s. 10, no. 1 (Spring 1979):11-17. (Also in Fox, *Responses to Children's Literature*, pp. 81-87.)
The Russian poet comments upon children's responses to particular illustrations.

B1431   BARTON, ROBERT, and BOOTH, DAVID. "Do Swans Really Eat Fudgesicles?" *CLE*, o.s., no. 11 (May 1973):13-24.
Explores using picture books as the basis for creative dramatics with older children.

B1432   BAUMEISTER, ALEXANDRE H. "Picture Books: A Selection of International New Publications." *Novum Gebrauchsgraphik* 48 (December 1977):2-17.
An illustrated international overview of innovative children's picture books published during the year.

B1433   BERRIDGE, CELIA. "Illustrators, Books, and Children: An Illustrator's Viewpoint." *CLE*, n.s. 11, no. 1 (Spring 1980):21-30.
Suggests guidelines for criticism of picture books. "The question of the relevance of children's responses to the evaluation of books must be faced and sorted out by examining the criteria of criticism and by considering the available evidence from both marketing and academic research."

B1434   -----. "Notes Towards a Critical Method of Appraising Picture Books Produced for a Child Audience." In Hunt, *Further Approaches*, pp. 23-28.
Suggests an approach to picture-book evaluation based upon children's responses.

B1435   -----. "Taking a Good Look at Picture Books." *Signal* 36 (September 1981):152-58.
Examines the difficulties and short-comings of picture-book reviewing. Argues that a proper forum for picture-book reviewing is needed. Uses Janet and Allan Ahlberg's *Each Peach Pear Plum* as an example.

B1436   BITZER, LUCY. "The Art of Picture Books: Beautiful Treasures of Bookmaking." *TON* 38 (Spring 1982):226-32.
Art director and book designer Bitzer offers her insights into the

nature of excellence in picture books, discussing recent and classic outstanding examples.

B1437   *Bookbird* 1 (1966):3-15.
Special issue on Picture Books.   Includes František Holesovský's "The Function of Illustrations in Children's Books," pp. 3-6, which suggests a number of approaches to studying illustrations; Alfred Clemens Baumgartner's "Picture Stories Then and Now: The Problem of Comics," pp. 7-10, which distinguishes picture books and comics on the basis of history and quality; and Hans Bodecker's "Research Work in the Field of Picture Books," pp. 11-15, which summarizes recent German-language research.

B1438   BOYLE, JOAN KATHLEEN.   "Developmental Trends in Aesthetic Response to Illustrations: Children's Preferences for Varied Style of Illustrations."   Ph.D. dissertation, University of California, Berkeley, 1981, 130 pp., DA 42:3086A.
Found that younger children preferred more abstract styles in illustrations when they were presented alone, but that with the addition of oral language the differences between preferences of younger and older children diminished.   Found that the ability to focus "on the interaction between two symbol systems" increased with the child's development.

B1439   BROWN, MARCIA.   "Distinction in Picture Books."   *Horn Book* 25 (September 1949):383-94.
Presents standards and guidelines for evaluating picture books.

B1440   "Children's Books International 6:   Proceedings."   Boston Public Library, 1983, 87 pp.
Devoted to illustration.   Includes "Illustrations in African Children's Books," by P. Osazee Fayose, pp. 8-12; "In Peru . . . and Beyond," by Carlos Llerena Aquirre, pp. 13-20; "In an Old, Old World: Mongolia," by James Fraser, pp. 21-27; "In the Realms of Noma Concours," by Yutaka Sugita, pp. 28-36; "Illustrations of the Counterworld: Fantasy in Children's Literature," by Diana L. Johnson, pp. 56-59; "Reflections on Fact and Fancy," by Barbara Cooney, pp. 60-62; "to illustrate or not to illustrate: a child's eye view," by Laurene Meringoff, pp. 63-68; "Illustration and Performance, from the Book to the Stage--into Music--into Animated Film," by Emanuele Luzzati, pp. 69-72; "Visual Communications--East and West," by Ed Young, pp. 73-74; "My Floating World," by Miyuki Tanobe, pp. 75-80; "Head and Heart--What a Black Illustrator Brings to Children's Books," by Tom Feelings, pp. 81-86.

B1441   CHORAO, KAY.   "A Delayed Reply: Illustration and the Imagination." *Horn Book* 55 (August 1979):463-69.
In answer to the question, "Do illustrations rob children of the use of their imaginations?," Chorao replies, "No," giving three reasons: (1) because each illustrator draws in his or her own way, (2) because children filter art through their experiences, and (3) because there is no absolute reality in art. Uses examples from her own work.

B1442   CIANCIOLO, PATRICIA J.   "Children's Responses to Illustrations in Books: A Review of Research."   *Ripples* 6, no. 1 (Winter 1981):12-13.

Classifies the research into the following categories: content analysis, visual literacy, reading skills, oral language and written language, and preferences.

B1443   -----. "Children's Responses to Illustrations in Picturebooks." In Fox, *Responses to Children's Literature*, pp. 102-8.
Reports on two experiments concerning children's responses to illustrations.

B1444   CLIFFORD, MICHAEL. "Political Bias in Children's Book Illustration." *Bookbird* 1 (1981):8-12.
Summarizes his research for his master's thesis on the political content of children's book illustration.

B1445   COONEY, BARBARA. "The Artist at Work: Scratchboard Illustration." *Horn Book* 40 (April 1964):162-5.
Describes the technique.

B1446   -----. "An Illustrator's Viewpoint." *Horn Book* 37 (February 1961):26-31.
Reflections on illustration and design as a fine art.

B1447   CORREIA, CARLOS. "To Write, To Illustrate, and to Paginate Children's Books." *Bookbird* 1 (1984):20-24.
A Portuguese writer reflects on the role and importance of illustrations in children's books.

B1448   CRAGO, MAUREEN. "Incompletely Shown Objects in Picture Books: One Child's Response." *CLE*, n.s. 10, no. 3 (Autumn 1979):151-57.
Reports on a child's response to incompletely shown pictures in picture books and concludes that at present there is no need for publishers to change their policies. Learning to interpret the incomplete and overlapped figures is part of learning and development.

B1449   CURTIS, WILLIAM. "An Analysis of the Relationship of Illustration and Text in Picture-Story Books as Indicated by the Oral Responses of Young Children." Ed.D. dissertation, Wayne State University, 1968, 163 pp., DA 30:924A.
Found that the text was more influential in generating children's responses to a picture book than pictures alone and the combination of pictures and texts was even greater.

B1450   DAUGHERTY, JAMES. "Illustrating for Children." *Bulletin of the New York Public Library* 60 (November 1956):569-72.
Comments on the qualities he feels are necessary for the illustrator of children's books.

B1451   DE PAOLA, TOMIE. "Viewpoints: From an Artist-Illustrator." *LA* 58 (April 1981):408-9.
A brief but telling lesson about looking (really looking) at picture books.

B1452   DESPINETTE, JANINE. "Modern Picture Books and the Child's Visual Sense." In Fox, *Responses to Children's Literature*, pp. 109-16.
Explores approaches to the interpretation of book illustration for the modern child.

B1453   DOOLEY, PATRICIA, ed. "Special Section: Children's Book Illustra-
        tion." *ChLAQ* 6, no. 4 (Winter 1981-82):8-44. (Reprinted, except for
        the reviews, in Dooley, *First Steps*, pp. 133-48.)
            Includes Jane Yolen, "The Eye and the Ear" (an excerpt from
        Touch Magic), pp. 8-9, which discusses the differences in the
        stories the eye sees and the ear hears using versions of "Snow White"
        as an example. Michael Patrick Hearn, contributes "Talking with the
        Dillons: An Interview," pp. 9-11. Donnarae MacCann and Olga
        Richard discuss Selma Lanes's *The Art of Maurice Sendak* and argue
        that the book's title is a misnomer: "Sendak's illustrations . . . don't
        survive scrutiny from a fine arts perspective." Throughout the
        lengthy review they offer strong criticism both of Sendak and of
        Lanes, pp. 11-17. Jill P. May provides a brief historical overview of
        children's book illustration in "Illustration in Children's Books," pp.
        17-21. Peggy Whalen-Levitt comments on "Making Picture Books
        Real: Reflections on a Child's Eye View," pp. 21-25. Joyce A.
        Thomas comments on "Non-Fiction Fiction Illustration: Some Consid-
        erations," pp. 25-28. Karen Nelson Hoyle contributes a bibliographic
        essay on Wanda Gág, pp. 28-30. Jane Bishop Hobgood writes on
        "Walter Crane," pp. 30-33 and Selma K. Richardson on "Randolph
        Caldecott," pp. 33-37. Harold Darling reviews Fred Gettings's *Arthur
        Rackham*, p. 37, Sarah Smedman reviews Michael S. Schnessel's *Jessie
        Wilcox Smith*, pp. 37-40, Joyce A. Thomas reviews Barbara Bader's
        American Picturebooks from Noah's Ark to the Beast Within," pp.
        40-41, Louisa Smith reviews Rawle Knox's *The Work of E.H. She-
        pard*, pp. 42-43, and Maryellen Hains discusses the Addison-Wesley
        Self-Portrait series, pp. 43-44.

B1454   DOONAN, JANE. "Two Artists Telling Tales: Chihiro Iwasaki and
        Lisbeth Zwerger." *Signal* 44 (May 1984):93-102.
            Examines the way in which two artist's have met the challenge
        of folk- and fairy-tale illustration. Studies Chihiro Iwasaki's
        illustrations for H.C. Andersen's *The Red Shoes* and Lisbeth Zweger's
        for the Grimms' *Little Red-Cap*.

B1455   DRESSEL, JANICE HARTWICK. "Abstraction in Illustration: Is It
        Appropriate for Children?" *CLE*, n.s. 15, no. 2 (Summer 1984):
        103-12.
            Argues that the use of abstract art in illustrating children's books
        will probably increase and summarizes arguments for and against its
        use. Includes references.

B1456   DULLE, MARK E. "The Effect of Illustrations on Children's Interpre-
        tations of a Fairy Tale." Ph.D. dissertation, Louisiana State Univer-
        sity and A&M College, 1978, 68 pp., DA 39:5545B.
            A study of elementary school children revealed no differences in
        subjective interpretations of fairy tales in those who had seen the
        pictures and those who had not.

B1457   DURHAM, MAI J. "Some Thoughts About Picture Books." *Horn Book*
        39 (October 1963):476-84.
            A highly critical look at the picture book, faulting even some of
        the most highly praised for lack of cohesion among text, illustration,
        and page composition. Cites lack of knowledge of art technique and
        rejection of twentieth-century fine art on the part of reviewers. We
        must ask, "Is there a need for this book?" "What does this book

have to say?" "Does this book have substance in text, imagination and creativity in illustration, harmony in book design?"

B1458   DUVOISIN, ROGER. "Children's Book Illustration: The Pleasures and Problems." *TON* 22 (November 1965):22-33. (Reprinted in Haviland, *Children and Literature*, pp. 177-87.)

     Discusses what he sees as key elements in children's book illustration: the relationship of illustration to the larger world of art, to the texts illustrated, and to the child's vision.

B1459   EGOFF, SHEILA. "Picture Books." In *Thursday's Child*, pp. 247-74.

     Describes the development of the picture book, seeing Sendak's *Where the Wild Things Are* as bridging two eras--an older one of security and a newer one where children's fears are openly explored. Includes comments on wordless picture books, fantasy books, alphabet books, counting books, nursery rhymes, and therapeutic picture books. Raises serious questions about the modern picture book, which she calls "the most diverse, the most didactic, and the most debated of all forms of present-day children's literature."

B1460   EMMERSON, ANDREA. "The Significance of Book Illustration for Reading Purposes." *School Librarian* 26, no. 2 (June 1978):112-17.

     Examines the role of pictures in children's book selection and their influence on reading.

B1461   EVANS, MARGARET B. "Some Problems in Modern Book Illustration." *Horn Book* 22 (May-June 1946):176-82.

     Examines technical aspects of book illustration, considering medium and balance of form and color, among other factors.

B1462   "Ezra Jack Keats on Collage as an Illustration Medium." *Publishers Weekly*, 4 April 1966, pp. 94-95.

     Discusses collage as a technique for illustration.

B1463   FEAVER, WILLIAM. *When We Were Young: Two Centuries of Children's Book Illustration.* London: Thames & Hudson; New York: Holt, Rinehart & Winston, 1977, 96 pp.

     An amply illustrated survey containing twenty-four pages of text and 108 color and black and white reproductions with annotations covering illustrators from William Blake to Maurice Sendak.

B1464   FILSTRUP, JANE, ed. "The Fine Art of Children's Books: A Special Issue." *WLB* 55 (October 1980):97-123.

     Special issue. Includes "What is a Picture Book?" by Uri Shulevitz, pp. 99-101; "Picture Play in Children's Books: A Celebration of Visual Awareness," by Peggy Whalen-Levitt, pp. 102-7; "The Window in the Book: Conventions in the Illustration of Children's Books," by Patricia Dooley, pp. 108-12; "The Changing Picture of Poetry Books for Children," by Nancy Larrick, pp. 113-17; and "Creating Children's Books at the Rochester Folk Art Guild," by Marilyn Zwicher, pp. 118-22.

B1465   FLETCHER, DAVID. "Pictures on Paper." *Horn Book* 37 (February 1961):21-25.

     A writer expresses his views on the functions of illustrations in children's books: (1) to make an attractive package, (2) to provoke anticipation, and (3) to set the scene and aid the imagination.

B1466   FLOETHE, RICHARD. "Today's Picture Books." *Horn Book* 22 (March-April 1946):137-46.
A critical survey of picture books published in 1945.

B1467   FLOWERS, WANDA JEAN. "Pupil Preference for Art Media Used in Illustrations of Caldecott Award Winning Books." Ph.D. dissertation, University of Oklahoma, 1978, 108 pp.
First and second grade students preferred woodcuts, followed by graphics (with color), watercolor (preseparated), and tempera.

B1468   GAUGERT, RICHARD. "The Impact of Film on Picture Book Illustration." *Ripples* 6, no. 1 (Winter 1980):7-10.
Discusses ways cinematic techniques have been employed to create effective objects of art. Examples include Uri Shulevitz's *Dawn*, Caldecott's *House that Jack Built*, works by Linda Heller and Leo and Diane Dillon, Sendak's *In the Night Kitchen*, and Steptoe's *Daddy Is a Monster*.

B1469   GEIST, HANS-FRIEDRICH. "Illustrations for Children's Books/Kinderbuch-Illustrationen/Illustrations de Livres D'Enfants." *Graphis* 11 (October 1955):408-27.
Differentiates between picture books and illustrated books and comments upon the meaning of "genuine" pictures for the child.

B1470   *Graphis: International Journal of Graphic Art and Applied Art* 23, no. 131 (1967):206-318.
Special issue on children's books. Includes an introduction by Jella Lepman and discussions of trends in children's picture books in a number of countries: Arsen Pohribney on Czechoslovakia, Robert F. Klein on France, Hans A. Halbey on Germany, Judy Taylor and John Ryder on England, Bettina Hürlimann on Japan, Olga Siemaszková on Poland, Harlin Quist on the United States, Bettina Hürlimann on Switzerland, and Stanley Mason on Europe.

B1471   ----- 31, no. 177 (1975-76):10-123.
Special issue on children's book illustration. Includes an introduction by Virginia Haviland and a survey of trends in picture books in a number of countries. Jerome Snyder on the United States, John Ryder on Britain, Christine Chagnoux on France, Ingeborg Ramseger on Germany, Jürg Schatzmann on Switzerland, Tadashi Matsui on Japan, Mieczyslaw Piotrowski on Poland, Dušan Roll on Czechoslovakia, Anna Katharina Ulrich on international trends, and an article entitled "Aggression in the Children's Book," by Frank Caspar.

B1472   ----- 34, no. 200 (1978-79):478-607.
Special Issue on children's book illustration. Contains critical surveys of recent trends in children's picture books in a number of countries. Michael Patrick Hearn on the United States, Brian Alderson on Britain, Christine Chagnoux on France, H. Krahé on Germany, Bettina Hürlimann on Switzerland, Tadashi Matsui on Japan, D. Wróblewská on Poland, D. Roll on Czechoslovakia, and Anna Katharina Ulrich on the international scene.

B1473   GREENLAW, M. JEAN. "Picture Books: No Age Limit for Enjoyment." *TON* 28 (January 1972):189-97.
Reports on a successful experiment using picture books with

older children and provides detailed comments from fifth graders on three books: John Steptoe's *Stevie*, Mary Hays Weik's *The Jazz Man*, and Jacob Lawrence's *Harriet and the Promised Land*.

B1474 GROFF, PATRICK. "Should Picture Books and Young Children Be Matched?" *LA* 54 (April 1979):411-17.
Summarizes much of the existing literature concerning children's preferences in picture-book illustration and concludes that children's preferences should not be the determining factor in picture-book selection. Contains an extensive bibliography.

B1475 HALAS, J., and ALEXANDRE, A. "Picture Books 1978: New Titles and Forms of Presentation." *Novum Gebrauchsgraphik* 49 (December 1978):23-30.
Highlights innovative picture books of the year, reproducing numerous illustrations, many in color.

B1476 HAVILAND, VIRGINIA. "Illustrators and Illustration." In *Children and Literature*, pp. 169-72.
Raises several questions about recent trends in picture books in this introduction to a chapter on illustration.

B1477 HUMMEL, J. "A Descriptive Analysis of the Illustrations in Selected Showcase Books and a Study of Young Children's Responses to a Sampling of These Books Selected by Adults." Ph.D. dissertation, Michigan State University, 1977, 179 pp., DA 38:5910A.
Discusses the selections made by experts in the field of children's books in relationship with children's choices and preferences within that selection.

B1478 HÜRLIMANN, BETTINA. "Illustration and the Emotional World of the Child." *Bookbird* 7, no. 3 (1969):57-61.
Reflects upon the importance of the picture's appeal to the child's emotions in both fiction and nonfiction.

B1479 -----. "Picture Books in the Twentieth Century." In *Three Centuries*, pp. 201-45.
Provides a substantial introduction to the modern European picture book.

B1480 -----. *Picture-Book World*. London: Oxford University Press; Cleveland: World Publishing, 1968, 216 pp.
Provides a good introduction to picture books produced throughout the world.

B1481 -----. "Trends of European Picture Book Production Since 1945." *International Library Review* 3 (January 1971):51-60.
Summarizes characteristics of picture book production in England, Czechoslavakia, Poland, Yugoslavia, the U.S.S.R., France, Italy, Spain, Germany, Scandinavia, and Switzerland since World War II.

B1482 HURST, JOE B. "Images in Children's Picture Books." *Social Education* 45 (February 1981):138-43.
Presents the results of an extensive content analysis of children's picture books, considering positive and negative images and role models. Concludes that the role models present a bland, apathetic view of life and provide negative images of women and the elderly.

B1483 HUUS, HELEN. "Some Picture Book Comparisons." *International Library Review* 3 (October 1971):457-68.

Points out examples of fine picture books from countries around the world, and compares books from different countries in terms of theme, character, plot, setting, style, and illustration.

B1484 *Image and Maker*. La Jolla, Calif.: Green Tiger Press, 1984, 56 pp.

Includes the following articles, illustrated with numerous color plates: Perry Nodelman's "How Picture Books Work," pp. 1-12, which compares the effects of Trina Schart Hyman's and Nancy Ekholm Burkert's illustrations of *Snow White*; Stephen Canham's "What Manner of Beast? Illustrations of Beauty and the Beast," pp. 13-25; Helen Borgens's "Luther Daniels Bradley: Guide to the Great Somewhere or Other," pp. 26-36; Carolyn Hay-wood's "Jessie Willcox Smith," pp. 37-42; and Kenneth E. Luther's "The Great Catalogs: An Alternative Way to Study Children's Book Illustration," pp. 43-54.

B1485 JACOBS, LELAND B. "Picture Story Books at Their Best." *Reading Teacher*, February 1959, pp. 186-89.

Jacobs sets forth his criteria for evaluating picture books. Warns that "The very grandeur of simplicity in picture-story books may be, at times, deceptive." Provides a beautifully written exploration of the distinctive qualities of the genre.

B1486 JACQUES, ROBIN. *Illustrators at Work*. London: Studio Books, 1963, 112 pp.

Discusses the history and traditions of black and white illustration, the various processes of reproduction, and line-drawing for reproduction. Features reproductions of the work of a number of illustrators accompanied by their accounts of their own work. Among illustrators of children's books whose work is highlighted are Edward Ardizzone and Brian Wildsmith.

B1487 JENKINS, WILLIAM A. "Illustrators and Illustrations." *EE* 41 (May 1964):492-99. (In a symposium entitled "What Is Children's Literature?," edited by Virginia M. Reid.)

Reviews the history of illustration and gives reasons for its use in children's books: to implement the text, to give dimensions to the story, and to add pleasure.

B1488 JOHNSTON, MARGARET. "Surprised By Joy: The World of Picture Books." In Egoff, *One Ocean*, pp. 147-54.

Defines the qualities of a good picture book and then discusses briefly a number of examples.

B1489 *Junior Bookshelf* 10, no. 1 (March 1946):1-27.

Special issue on Kate Greenaway, Randolph Caldecott, and Walter Crane, marking the centenaries of Greenaway and Caldecott. Also pays tribute to printer Edmund Evans.

B1490 KEATS, EZRA JACK. "The Artist At Work: Collage." *Horn Book* 40 (June 1964):269-72.

Describes the techniques of collage, with some examples from his own books *The Snowy Day* and *Whistle for Willie*.

B1491 KIEFER, BARBARA. "Looking Beyond Picture Book Preferences."

Horn Book 61 (November 1985):705-43.

Found that three books that critics and researchers have suggested children would not like, Sendak's *Outside Over There*, Mollie Bang's *The Grey Lady and the Strawberry Snatcher*, and the Richard Kennedy/Marcia Sewall *Song of the Horse* "seemed to engender responses that extended and deepened over time."

B1492　KINGMAN, LEE.　"The High Art of Illustration."　*Horn Book* 50 (October 1974):95-103.

Examines the nature of illustration, with examples from classic illustrators.　Maintains it is as high as any art and that artists should be given time to create illustrations that will attain the rank of fine art.

B1493　KINGMAN, LEE, ed.　*The Illustrator's Notebook*.　Boston: Horn Book, 1978, 153 pp.

Thirty-five illustrators of children's books discuss their philosophy and standards of illustration, the history of illustration, its place in the arts, its place as a means of communication in today's world, and their own experiences with various illustration techniques in these excerpts from *Horn Book Magazine*.

B1494　KINGMAN, LEE; FOSTER, JOANNA; and LONTOFT, RUTH G., eds. *Illustrators of Children's Books: 1957-1966*.　Boston: Horn Book, 1968, 296 pp.

Part 1 consists of Marcia Brown's "One Wonders," pp. 2-27, summarizing accomplishments and trends of the decade; Adrienne Adams's "Color Separation," pp. 28-35; Grace Allen Hogarth's "The Artist and His Editor," pp. 36-53; and Rumer Godden's "Beatrix Potter: Centenary of an Artist-Writer," pp. 54-65. Part 2 consists of biographies of illustrators active 1957-66, and part 3 consists of bibliographies of the works of the illustrators and their authors.

B1495　KINGMAN, LEE; HOGARTH, GRACE ALLEN; and QUIMBY, HARRIET, eds.　*Illustrators of Children's Books, 1967-1976*.　Boston: Horn Book, 1978, 290 pp.

Part 1 includes Walter Lorraine's "Book Illustration: The State of the Art," pp. 2-19; Brian Alderson's "A View from the Island: European Picture Books 1967-1976," pp. 20-43; Teijiseta and Momoko Ishii's "Where the Old Meets the New: The Japanese Picture Book," pp. 44-57; and Treld Pelkey Bicknell's "In the Beginning Was the Word: The Illustrated Book 1967-1976," pp. 58-89. Part 2 consists of brief biographies of illustrators active from 1967 to 1976. Part 3 consists of bibliographies of works of illustrators and authors, and an appendix lists references for the articles in part 1.

B1496　KLEMIN, DIANA.　*The Art of Art for Children's Books: A Contemporary Survey*.　New York: Clarkson N. Potter, 1966, 128 pp.

Groups sixty-three modern picture-book artists in categories of storyteller, poetic and personal, imaginary, collage and abstraction, and specialists; provides a reproduction of a representative illustration by each artist; then comments very briefly upon his or her work.

B1497　KÜNNEMANN, HORST.　"A-B and Then What?"　*Bookbird* 8, no. 2 (1970):65-70.

Selects ten "exemplary works" that he holds to be standard books by which other picture books may be evaluated: Jürgen Spohn's *Ele-*

dil and Krokofant *and* Das Rieseross, *Leo Lionni's* Frederick, *Brian Wildsmith's* Fishes, *Janosch's* Böllerbam und der Vogel, *Walter Grieder's* Die Verzauberte Trommel *(The Magic Drum), Lieselotte Schwarz's* Dornröschen *(Sleeping Beauty), Mirko Hanák's animal books, Sendak's* Where the Wild Things Are, *Viera Bombová's Slovakian and Polynesian fairy tales, and Eleonore Schmidt's* The Endless Party.

B1498   -----. "For A Picture Book ABC--Questions, Problems, Wishes." *Book-bird* 7, no. 3 (1969):46-56.
Suggests that basic standards (an ABC), for picture books are needed and that studies need to be done on the ways in which children "read" pictures. Proposes setting up a documentation center "where all the existing knowledge and opinions relating to the field of the child's picture books could be collected."

B1499   LANDES, SONIA. "Picture Books as Literature." *ChLAQ* 10, no. 2 (Summer 1985):51-54.
Examines the way good picture-book artists go well beyond enhancing the meaning of a story by illustrating the words: they invent and develop additional story material. Takes examples from Randolph Caldecott, Rosemary Wells, and Maurice Sendak, among others.

B1500   LANES, SELMA. "Blow-Up: The Picture-Book Explosion." In *Down the Rabbit Hole*, pp. 45-78.
Provides a brief overview of the development of picture books, singling out numerous artists, and commenting on recent trends, especially "the story increasingly subordinated to art."

B1501   -----. "Picture Books: Literature, Pre-Literature, or Pretend Literature." *Ripples* 6, no. 1 (Winter 1981):1-7.
Argues for the inclusion of the best of children's picture books as literature in the highest sense, in this rather rambling discussion which touches on authors ranging from Sendak to E.B. White to Lionni and Steig, to Greenaway and E. Nesbit.

B1502   LENT, BLAIR. "There's Much More to the Picture than Meets the Eye." *WLB* 52 (October 1977):161-64. (Reprinted in Bator, *Signposts*, pp. 156-61.)
Briefly explores the nature of the picture book.

B1503   LEWIS, CLAUDIA. "Searching for the Master Touch in Picture Books." *CLE*, n.s. 15, no. 4 (Winter 1984):198-203.
Explores some clues to the success of some of children's favorite picture books, especially the "jog" of the unexpected and unfamiliar combined with the comfortable and familiar.

B1504   LEWIS, JOHN N.C. "The Illustration and Design of Children's Books." In *The Twentieth Century Book, Its Illustration and Design*, pp. 176-241. New York: Reinhold, 1967.
Surveys the illustration of school and adventure stories, animal stories, French books, revivals of classics, the works of a number of significant modern picture-book creators, the graphic design approach, and other recent trends. The emphasis of the discussion is on graphics and design rather than literary elements.

B1505   LORRAINE, WALTER, ed. "The Art of the Picture Book." *WLB* 52 (October 1977):144-73.
Special Issue. Includes "The Art of the Picture Book" by Walter Lorraine, pp. 144-47; "The Picture Book as an Art Object: A Call for Balanced Reviewing," by Kenneth Marantz, pp. 148-51; "An Interview with Maurice Sendak," by Walter Lorraine, pp. 152-57; "In Search of the Perfect Picture Book Definition," by Zena Sutherland and Betsy Hearne, pp. 158-60; "There's Much More to the Picture than Meets the Eye," by Blair Lent, pp. 161-64; and "Children's Book Illustrators Play Favorites," by Arnold Lobel, Karla Kuskin, Trina Hyman, and Tomie de Paola (they discuss their favorite illustrators and books), pp. 165-73.

B1506   -----. "The Artist at Work." *Horn Book* 39 (December 1963):576-79.
This introduction to a series of *Horn Book* articles, to be devoted to examination of the techniques of the picture-book artist, provides a concise historical overview of basic means of picture reproduction from woodcuts through "color process" separation.

B1507   -----. "An Interview with Maurice Sendak." In Egoff, *Only Connect*, 2d ed., pp. 326-36.
Sendak expresses his views about picture books in this interview.

B1508   LUCAS, BARBARA. "Picture Books for Children Who Are Masters of Few Words." *Library Journal* 98 (15 May 1973):1641-45 and *SLJ* 19 (May 1973):31-35. (Reprinted in Barron, *Jump Over the Moon*, pp. 183-86.)
Discusses the techniques of creating and printing color illustrations for children's books.

B1509   MACAULAY, DAVID. "How to Create a Successful Children's Nonfiction Picture Book." In Hearne, *Celebrating Children's Books*, pp. 97-107.
Provides a humorous account of the intricacies of illustrating children's informational books.

B1510   MacCANN, DONNARAE, and RICHARD, OLGA. *The Child's First Books: A Critical Study of Pictures and Texts.* New York: H.W. Wilson, 1973, 135 pp.
Applies principles of literary and art criticism to picture books. Sections are devoted to a historical overview, stereotypes in illustration, graphic elements, book design, literary elements, specialized texts (e.g., concept books), and the Caldecott Award. Chapter 4, pp. 47-72, is devoted to discussions of the work of thirteen outstanding contemporary illustrators: Ludwig Bemelmans, Marcia Brown, Hans Fischer, Andre François, Antonio Frasconi, Juliet Kepes, Leo Lionni, Nicholas Mordvinoff, Celestino Piatti, Nicolas Sidjakov, Bill Sokol, Taro Yashima, and Reiner Zimnik. Chapter 7, pp. 95-106 discusses key characteristics of a group of outstanding picture book-narrative writers: Theodore Seuss Geisel, Bill Peet, Maurice Sendak, Jean De Brunhoff, Virginia Lee Burton, James Flora, and H.A. Rey.

B1511   -----. "Picture Books for Children." *WLB* 56 (January 1982):368-69.
Examines some of the "best books" of 1980-81 in terms of genres and artistic standards.

B1512   MAHONY, BERTHA, ed. *Illustrators of Children's Books, 1744-1945.*

Boston: Horn Book, 1947, 527 pp.

Includes Robert Lawson's "Howard Pyle and His Times," Maria Cimino's "Foreign Picture Books in a Children's Library," Helen Gentry's "Graphic Processes in Children's Books," Philip Hofer's "Illustrators of Children's Classics," Hellmut Lehmann-Haupt's "Animated Drawing," May Massee's "Developments of the Twentieth Century," Lynd Ward's "The Book Artist: Today and Tomorrow," and biographies and bibliographies on illustrators and their work.

B1513   MARANTZ, KENNETH. "The Picture Book as Art Object: A Call for Balanced Reviewing." *WLB* 52 (October 1977):148-51. (Reprinted in Bator, *Signposts*, pp. 152-56.)

Urges that more attention be paid to the illustrator's art in picture-book reviewing.

B1514   MARCUS, LEONARD S., ed. *L&U* 7-8 (1983-84):1-193.

Special double issue on picture books. Includes "Beneath the Surface with Fungus the Bogeyman," by Suzanne Rahn, pp. 5-19, provides a detailed analysis of Raymond Briggs's *Fungus the Bogeyman*, viewed, in the context of his other books, as a plea for tolerance and a critique of contemporary civilization. "A Picture Equals How Many Words?: Narrative Theory and Picture Books for Children," by Stephen Roxburgh, pp. 20-33, demonstrates the application of narrative theory to Maurice Sendak's *Outside Over There.* "The Artist's Other Eye: The Picture Books of Mitsumasa Anno," by Leonard S. Marcus, pp. 34-46, concentrates on Anno's knack for making books that readers must complete with their own understandings, fantasies, and words.

"Invention and Discoveries: An Interview with Philomel Books Editor Ann K. Beneduce," by Leonard S. Marcus, pp. 47-63, includes discussions of Bruno Munari, Eric Carle, Anno, and the world of international co-publishing. "'Daddy, Talk!': Thoughts on Reading Early Picture Books," by David Pritchard, pp. 64-69, a parent's account of sharing first books with his child, points out some of the characteristics of the most successful of these books: animals, especially exotic ones, and detail of illustration, especially Richard Scarry's.

"Long Live Babar!," by Annie Pissard, pp. 70-77, provides a detailed analysis of the de Brunhoffs' books, commenting on responses to them by Maurice Sendak and Ariel Dorfman. "A Second Gaze at Little Red Riding Hood's Trials and Tribulations," by Jack Zipes, pp. 78-109, concentrates on the history of the illustrations of the young girl encountering the wolf in the woods, and recapitulates Zipes's interpretation of the changes made in the original tale by Perrault and Grimm.

"Remembering Caldecott: *The Three Jovial Huntsmen* and the Art of the Picture Book," by John Cech, pp. 110-19, analyzes Caldecott's style. "Caldecott might not win his own award today, but this dismissal would occur only because modern (or rather, post modern) readers have forgotten how to look--carefully, slowly, deeply into the clear, flowing pages of a Caldecott picture book." "Another Wonderland: Lewis Carroll's The Nursery Alice," by Morton N. Cohen, pp. 120-26, examines Carroll's version of *Alice* for children under five.

"Picture Book Animals: How Natural a History," by Leonard S. Marcus, pp. 127-39, examines patterns in the animal characters in children's picture books and what these patterns reveal about the authors, our society, and ourselves. "Photography in Children's Books:

A Generic Approach," by Julia Hirsch, pp. 140-55, defines and examines the types of photographs in children's books. "Idea to Image: The Journey of a Picture Book," by Elizabeth Cleaver, pp. 156-70, details her process of creating a picture book. "The Birds and the Beasts Were There: An Interview with Martin Provensen," by Nancy Willard, pp. 171-83, recounts a wide-ranging discussion at the Provensens' home.

B1515   MATTHIAS, MARGARET, and ITALIANO, GRACIELA. "Louder than a Thousand Words." In Bator, *Signposts*, pp. 161-65. (Adapted from a talk given at the Association for Childhood Education, International Conference, Chicago, 18 September 1981.)
        Describes ways in which illustrators advance a story through art in picture books.

B1516   MEYER, SUSAN E. *A Treasury of Great Children's Book Illustrators.* New York: Harry N. Abrams, 1983, 272 pp.
        Examines and reproduces the work of thirteen late nineteenth-and early twentieth-century children's book illustrators: Walter Crane, Randolph Caldecott, Kate Greenaway, John Tenniel, E.H. Shepard, Arthur Rackham, Edmund Dulac, Kay Nielsen, Edward Lear, Beatrix Potter, Howard Pyle, N.C. Wyeth, and W.W. Denslow.

B1517   MICKISH, VIRGINIA LEE. "Artistic Media, Techniques, and Styles in Children's Story Illustrations." Ed.D. dissertation, University of Georgia, 1976, 169 pp., DA 37:4118A.
        Compares the preferences of second and fifth grade students and their teachers for artistic media, techniques, and styles in story illustrations. The most significant differences were found in preferences of second and fifth graders.

B1518   MOSIER, ROSALIND. "Modern Art in Children's Book Illustration." *Library Journal* 84 (15 October 1959):3293-95.
        Analyzes the manifestations of abstract, cubist, and surreal art in children's book illustration.

B1519   MOSS, ELAINE. "'Them's for the Infants, Miss': Some Misguided Attitudes to Picture Books for the Older Reader." *Signal* 26 (May 1978):66-72; 26 (September 1978):144-49.
        Discusses the use of picture books with older children and includes a list of picture books for "The Eights and Up."

B1520   -----. "W(h)ither Picture Books? Some Tricks of the Trade." *Signal* 31 (January 1980):3-7.
        Discusses trends in picture book, publishing, ruminating on the effects of the toy books, pop-up books, and other "sports" among picture books on the genre's more traditional fare.

B1521   NESS, EVALINE. "The Artist at Work: Woodcut Illustration." *Horn Book* 40 (October 1964):520-22.
        Describes the techniques of woodcut illustration.

B1522   NODELMAN, PERRY. "Art Theory and Children's Picture Books." *ChLAQ* 9 (Spring 1984):15-33.
        Special section relating work in the history and theory of art to the work of specialists in children's literature. Includes Susan Gannon's "Rudolph Arnheim's *Psychology of the Creative Eye* and

the Criticism of Illustrated Books for Children," pp. 15-18; John L. Ward and Marian Nitt Fox's "A Look at Some Outstanding Illustrated Books for Children," pp. 19-21, which analyzes Chris Van Allsburg's *Jumanji*, Lisbeth Zwerger's *Little Red Cap*, Tomi Ungerer's *The Beast of Monsieur Racine*, Jack Kent's *Just Only John*, and M.B. Goffstein's *Me and My Captain*; Geraldine De Luca's "Art, Illusion and Children's Picture Books," pp. 21-23, which applies E.H. Gombrich's theories of art, as expressed in *Art and Illusion*, to Ezra Jack Keats's *Peter's Chair*; David Topper's "On Some Burdens Carried by Pictures," pp. 23-25, which argues that "comprehending the content and meaning of a picture is a mental process drawing upon prior knowledge of concepts"; Perry Nodelman's "Of Nakedness and Picture Books," pp. 25-30, which relates John Berger's *Ways of Seeing* to the differences in depictions of boys and girls in children's books. Devotes a fair amount of attention to Sendak's work. Sees the most common portrayals of girls as pin-ups. The section concludes with Samuel Y. Edgerton, Jr.'s "The American Super-hero Comic Strip: True Descendant of Italian Renaissance Art," pp. 30-33, which argues that the comics, even when in bad taste, follow the conventions of Renaissance art.

B1523   -----. "How Children Respond to Art." *SLJ* 31 (December 1984):40-41.
Explores the conventions of art that children need to learn to appreciate pictures properly. Uses Virginia Lee Burton's *Mike Mulligan and His Steam Shovel* as his example.

B1524   -----. "How Picture Books Work." In Nodelman, *Festschrift*, pp. 20-25.
Proposes that the successful picture book depends upon the degree of tension between pictures and texts. Analyzes examples from Burkert's and Hyman's versions of *Snow White and the Seven Dwarfs*, and comments on the works of several other modern illustrators as well. Version also in 1484.

B1525   PEPPIN, B., and MICKLETHWAIT, L. *Dictionary of British Book Illustrators: The Twentieth Century.* London: J. Murray, 1983, 336 pp.
Concentrates on illustrators of fiction and poetry whose work was first published in Britain between 1900 and 1975. Includes a brief biographical entry on each artist, a list of books illustrated, and a list of references.

B1526   PITZ, HENRY. *Illustrating Children's Books: History, Technique, Production.* New York: Watson-Guptill, 1963, 207 pp.
Provides an introduction to the history, technique and production, and professional practices of illustrating children's books. Includes a bibliography.

B1527   POLTARNEES, WELLERAN. *All Mirrors Are Magic Mirrors.* La Jolla, Calif.: Green Tiger Press, 1972, 60 pp.
Surveys and reflects upon the children's picture book, commenting on the artist-audience relationship. Examines "the realm of faerie, the relationship between pictures and words, pictures of domestic happiness, the importance of stylistic and temperamental affinity between author and illustrator, and pictures of animals." Illustrated with tipped-in color plates.

B1528   RAMSEGER, INGEBORG. "Documentary Illustration in Fiction."
         Novum Gebrauchsgraphik 46 (June 1975):34-45.
         Discusses several books of fiction meticulously illustrated as
         though they were informational books, including versions of R.L.
         Stevenson's *Treasure Island*, Michel and Annie Politzer's version of
         Robinson Crusoe, and the books of David Macaulay.

B1529   RANLETT, L. FELIX. "Books and Two Small Boys." *Horn Book* 18
         (November-December 1942):412-16.
         The quality of "gusto" is identified in several picture books by
         author-illustrators, notably those of Virginia Lee Burton, but works
         by Robert McCloskey, Ludwig Bemelmans, Hardie Gramatky, and
         James Daugherty are also discussed.

B1530   RICHARD, OLGA. "The Visual Language of the Picture Book." *WLB*
         44 (December 1969):435-47.
         Suggests criteria for evaluating picture books and itemizes compo-
         nents of art such as color, line, shape, texture, and composition that
         must be taken into consideration, as well as components of book art
         such as type, paper, and layout, and finally the artist's personal view.

B1531   ROLL, DUŠAN. "Modern Children's Books and Print Making." *Book-
         bird* 16, no. 2 (1978):61-64.
         Discusses the influence of changing techniques of printmaking on
         children's book illustration.

B1532   RUDAŠ, FRANTIŠEK. "The Influence of Illustrations on the Emotional
         World of Children." *Bookbird* 7, no. 2 (1969):65-73.
         Explores the question of children's response to modern expressive
         art, and concludes from studies of children's own art and their
         responses to art that "emotional, imaginative, and aesthetic factors
         outweigh rational and perceptive responses in the choice of pictures
         by three-to-seven year-old children." Suggests further tests of the
         hypothesis.

B1533   SALLEY, COLEEN C., and HARRIS, KAREN H. "The Bizarre in
         Children's Picture Books." *TON* 31 (November 1974):95-99.
         Identifies a trend "characterized by violence, callousness, and even
         brutality" in recent children's picture books. Picture books by Tomi
         Ungerer, George Mendoza, and Charles Keeping are singled out for
         discussion.

B1534   SAUNDERS, DENNIS. "British Picture Books Since 1960." In Butts,
         Good Writers, pp. 67-78.
         Devotes the first four pages to Charles Keeping, and comments
         on a number of other illustrators, especially Fiona French, pp. 71-72,
         Brian Wildsmith and Pat Hutchins, pp. 73-74, Quentin Blake, 74-76,
         and Victor Ambrus, pp. 76-77.

B1535   SAYERS, FRANCES CLARKE. "Through These Sweet Fields." *Horn
         Book* 18 (November-December 1942):436-44. (Also in Sayers, *Sum-
         moned by Books*, pp. 143-51.)
         Analyzes the qualities that make the best picture books and
         selects several classic examples. Appends lists of "Twenty-Five First
         Picture Books and Twenty-Five First Story Books with Pictures."
         Many of these remain popular.

B1536   SCHMIDT, NANCY. "Illustrators and Illustrations." In *Children's Fiction about Africa*, pp. 47-56.

Points out the lack of realism in illustrations of books about Africa for Euroamerican children and also in books for African children.

B1537   SCHWARCZ, JOSEPH H. "The Representation of the Child's Facial Expression in the Illustration." In Escarpit, *Portrayal of the Child*, pp. 189-94.

Finds lack of communicativeness and an impersonal mood in many of the portrayals of children's faces.

B1538   -----. *Ways of the Illustrator: Visual Communication in Children's Literature*. Chicago: American Library Association, 1982, 202 pp.

Schwarcz promotes "the examination of the illustrator's work as a means of symbolic communication." Considers topics of relationships between texts and illustration, The "continuous narrative illustration," the "interplay of the literal and the figurative," The "role of natural landscape," "The letter and the written word as visual elements," and a number of other topics. Includes a bibliography and an index of illustrations discussed. Additional topics have been indexed separately in this bibliography.

B1539   SCHWARCZ, JOSEPH, and ROTH, MIRIAM. "The 'Continuous Narrative' Technique in Children's Literature." In Fox, *Responses to Children's Literature*, pp. 117-26.

Discusses illustrations of motion in children's books.

B1540   SCOTT, WILLIAM R. "Some Notes on Communication in Picture Books." *EE* 34 (February 1957):67-72.

Reviews and discusses several picture books for the very young--ages two to four.

B1541   SELDEN, REBECCA, and SMEDMAN, SARAH. "The Art of the Contemporary Picture Book." *Proceedings of the Children's Literature Association* 7 (1980):153-65.

Surveys the work of several recent picture-book illustrators, commenting briefly on works by Sendak, Desmond Digby, Blair Lent, Leo Lionni, Ann Grifalconi, Lynd Ward, Beverly Brodsky McDermott, Jacob Lawrence, Brian Wildsmith, David Macaulay, and Nancy Ekholm Burkert.

B1542   SMITH, LILLIAN. "Picture Books." In *Unreluctant Years*, pp. 114-29.

Children "like a picture if it tells a story." Discusses Crane, Caldecott, Greeenaway, Brooke, and Potter, as well as several more recent illustrators--De Brunhoff, Bemelmans, Flack and Wiese's *Story About Ping*, Edward Ardizzone, and H.A. Rey--as examples of the type of picture book to which children return over and over again.

B1543   SPAULDING, AMY. "A Study of the Picture Book as Storyboard." *TON* 40 (Summer 1984):443-44.

Spaulding reports on her doctoral dissertation, "Closet Drama for Children: A Study of the Picture Book as Storyboard," (D.L.S., Columbia University, 1983), which studies comic book elements in picture books and relates them to Aristotle's examination of dramatic structure in *The Poetics*.

B1544   STEVENS, CAROL. "See the Children's Books. See the Taboos in Children's Books. See the Taboos Toppling in the Children's Books." *Print* 27 (November 1973):25-35.

    Explores the increasing innovations in graphics and subject matter in children's picture books.

B1545   STEWIG, JOHN WARREN. "Picture Books: What Do Reviews Really Review?" *TON* 37 (Fall 1980):83-84.

    Surveys the amount of attention reviews give to words and pictures--and finds the most attention is given to words.

B1546   -----. "Trends in Caldecott Award Winners." *EE* 45 (February 1968):218-23, 260.

    Examines Caldecott award-winning books to determine trends in realism and choice of media. Includes bibliography.

B1547   STOREY, DENISE CAROL. "A Study of Fifth Grader's Verbal Responses to Selected Illustrations in Children's Books Before and After a Guided Study of Three Styles of Art Used to Illustrate Fairy Tales." Ph.D. dissertation, Michigan State University, 1977, 477 pp., DA 39:666A.

    Finds that children's responses to three styles of illustration of fairy tales were influenced to some extent by guided study.

B1548   THOMAS, DAVID. "Children's Book Illustration in England." *Penrose Annual* 56 (1962):67-74.

    Discusses the lack of knowledge of children's reactions to the books and pictures intended for them, and explores the possibilities of establishing an aesthetic theory of illustration.

B1549   TÓTH, BÉLA. "Psychological Relationships Between Text and Illustration." In Fox, *Responses to Children's Literature*," pp. 127-30.

    Reports on a Hungarian experiment to determine the connection existing "between the text and the illustration when the child reads, how the text and the illustration compliment each other, and how the child reacts to the pictures accompanying the text."

B1550   TUCKER, NICHOLAS. "Learning to Read Pictures." *TLS*, 2 July 1971, p. 769. (Reprinted in Culpan, *Variety is King*, pp. 126-29.) Suggests that knowledge of the perceptual development of children should be taken into account in the difficult task of evaluating picture books.

B1551   -----. "Looking at Pictures." *CLE*, o.s., no. 14 (1974):37-51.

    A review of the catalog and exhibition *Looking at Picturebooks*, mounted at the National Book League in London by Brian Alderson in 1973. Tucker raises some issues concerning illustration and disagrees with Alderson in several instances. Alderson's reply is appended to the article.

B1552   VANDERGRIFT, KAY E. *Child and Story*, pp. 64-102.

    Picture books and illustrated books are differentiated. Realistic, abstract, comic-strip-type illustrations, and photography are all touched upon. End paper illustrations are discussed on pages 82-83. Toy books, including pop-ups are also mentioned. What "works" with children children is the focus.

B1553　VAN STOCKUM, HILDA. "Through an Illustrator's Eyes." *Horn Book* 20 (May-June 1944):176-84.

Presents her views on good illustration, with examples as disparate as Reginald Birch's two versions of *Little Lord Fauntleroy*, Fritz Eichenberg, Kate Seredy, Feodor Rojankovsky, and Marguerite De Angeli. Maintains that the illustrator must absorb the message and the spirit of the book and be willing to play second fiddle to the author.

B1554　WARD, LYND. "The Book Artist and the Twenty-Five Years." *Horn Book* 25 (September 1949):375-81.

Traces developments in art and technology that influenced book illustrators from the 1920s to the 1940s.

B1555　-----. "Doing a Book in Lithography." *Horn Book* 40 (February 1964):34-41.

Describes the lithographic process as used in illustration.

B1556　WATSON, ERNEST W. *Forty Illustrators and How They Work*. New York: Watson-Guptill, 1946, 318 pp..

Includes illuminating articles on Boris Artzybasheff, pp. 7-14, Robert Lawson, pp. 187-94, and N.C. Wyeth, pp. 309-18.

B1557　WAYMACK, EUNICE H., and HENDRICKSON, GORDON. "Children's Reactions as a Basis for Teaching Picture Appreciation." *Elementary School Journal* 33 (1932):268-76.

Reports on an experiment to teach picture appreciation to children. Results showed an increase in ability to analyze and appreciate pictures.

B1558　WEISGARD, LEONARD. "Contemporary Art and Children's Book Illustration." *Horn Book* 36 (April 1960):155-58.

Discusses the influences of modern art on children's book illustration.

B1559　WEISS, AVA. "The Artist at Work: The Art Director." *Horn Book* 61 (May 1985):269-79.

Provides insight into the role of the art director, who "straddles the creative and the mechanical" in the process of picture book creating.

B1560　WHITE, MARY LOU. "A Structural Description of Picture Storybooks." *LA* 52 (April 1975):495-98, 502.

Defines the picture story book in terms of external structural and internal structural features of plot.

B1561　WHITAKER, MURIEL. "Louder than Words: The Didactic Use of Illustration in Books for Children." *CLE* o.s., no. 16 (Spring 1975):10-16.

A historical overview of ways in which illustrations have conveyed didactic messages.

B1562　YOLANDA, REGINA. "The Importance of Visual Aspects in Children's Literature." *Bookbird* 2 (1981):11-14.

A thoughtful consideration of the various roles of illustrations.

PLACE

B1563 APSELOFF, MARILYN, and HELBIG, ALETHEA. "Place in Children's Literature: Introduction." *ChLAQ* 8, no. 1 (Spring 1983):9.

Introduces a special section on place, containing articles on fantasy places, home, and architectural places, and discussions of the works of C.S. Lewis, George MacDonald, Richard Adams, David Macaulay, and Virginia Hamilton, among others. Topics indexed separately in this bibliography.

B1564 CAMERON, ELEANOR. "A Country of the Mind." In *Green and Burning*, pp. 163-202.

Explores the importance of a sense of place in fiction for children, with many specific examples and quotations from important children's writers.

PLAY

B1565 HOROVITZ, CAROLYN. "Fiction and the Paradox of Play." *WLB* 44 (December 1969):397-401.

Sees reading as a form of play for children and argues that reading that appeals to them will contain elements similar to those found in children's play.

B1566 McVAIGH, BETTY LEE. "Play Orientations in Picture Books: A Content Analysis." Ed.D. dissertation, University of North Carolina, Greensboro, 1977, 121 pp., DA 38:7212A.

Analyzes sixty-four preschool and primary school books with play and game themes.

B1567 PLATZNER, R.L. "Child's Play, Games and Fantasy in Carroll, Stevenson and Grahame." *Proceedings of the Children's Literature Association* 5 (1978):78-86.

Views play as "the primary expression of the child's creative energies" in "games of word and world making, games of magic and reverie, and finally games of growing up," in the works of Lewis Carroll, Robert Louis Stevenson, and Kenneth Grahame.

POETRY

B1568 APSELOFF, MARILYN. "From Shakespeare to Brooklyn: New Trends in Children's Poetry." *Children's Literature* 5 (1976):273-85.

Reviews seven collections containing poetry written by children.

B1569 -----. "Old Wine in New Bottles: Adult Poetry for Children." *CLE*, n.s. 10, no. 4 (Winter 1979):194-202.

Surveys the works of poets for adults that are increasingly used in publications for children.

B1570 BARNES, WALTER. "Contemporary Poetry for Children." *EER* 13 (January 1936):3-9; (February 1936):49-53, 57; (April 1936):135-38, 148; (November 1936):257-62; (December 1936): 298-304.

Five articles in a series discuss contemporary poetry in terms of poetic merit and children's interest. Poets discussed include Elizabeth Madox Roberts, Frances Frost, Mary Austin, Rachel Field, Rose Fyleman, Hilda Conkling, Ilo Orleans, Nancy Byrd Turner, A.A. Milne, Dorothy Aldis, and John Farrar.

B1571   BENTON, MICHAEL. "Poetry for Children: A Neglected Art." *CLE*, n.s. 9, no. 3 (1978):111-26.
Explores the reasons why poetry for children is neglected, then offers suggestions for using poetry in the classroom. Includes an extensive bibliography.

B1572   BOGSTAD, JANICE M. "So This Poetry is Children's Poetry?" *L&U* 4, no. 2 (Winter 1980-81):83-92.
Examines recent poetry for children in terms of Stanley Arnowitz's classification of children's cultural experiences into two worlds: (1) the child is raised through institutions and socialized to structures of ownership and domination, and (2) the child's desires are followed through self-structured play.

B1573   CHAMBERS, AIDAN. "Letter from England: Inside Poetry." *Horn Book* 55 (June 1979):350-56.
Considers the nature of poetry for the young and uses "I See a Bear" from Ted Hughes's *Moon Bells* as an example. Concludes that literature needs time, "Otherwise it keeps its treasures locked up safe and tight."

B1574   -----. "Letter from England: Right for Their Time." *Horn Book* 59 (April 1983):216-21.
Compares two anthologies of poetry: W.H. Auden's and John Garrett's *Poet's Tongue* and Seamus Heaney and Ted Hughes's *The Rattle Bag: An Anthology of Poetry*.

B1575   *Children's Books International 5, Proceedings: Poetry and Drama in the International Year of the Child.* Boston: Boston Public Library, 1982, 99 pp.
Includes David McCord's "The Children's World," John Ciardi's "What Is Poetry for Children?," William Jay Smith's "Translating Poetry for Children: Problems and Rewards," and Dennis Lee's "Canadian Poetry for Children." The drama section includes Lowell Swortzell's "Introducing Drama to Children," Frank Ballard's "Puppet Drama Around the World," Margaretta Strömstedt's "Children's Theatre in Sweden," and Efrea Sutherland's "Drama in Africa."

B1576   CIANCIOLO, PATRICIA, and REID, VIRGINIA M. "Poetry for Today's Children." *EE* 41 (May 1964):484-91.
Evaluates children's poetry on the basis of rhythm, word and sound patterns, imagery, content, story element, and crystallized experiences. Suggest ways to enhance children's enjoyment of poetry.

B1577   CLARK, LEONARD. "Poetry and Children." *CLE*, n.s. 9, no. 3 (August 1978):127-35. (Also in *Proceedings of the Children's Literature Association* 6 (1979):67-77.)
Looks at the qualities of poetry from a child's point of view, with suggestions for classroom applications.

B1578   COOK, STANLEY. "The Pop Poets." *School Librarian* 24, no. 2 (June 1976):114-18.
Examines the connection between Roger McGough and other poets and pop music. Includes a bibliography.

B1579   DANBY, JOHN F. "The Difficult Poem." *Signal* 40 (January

1983):18-25.

Examines the question of teaching difficult poems to children in this excerpt from Danby's *Approach to Poetry*, first published in 1940 and now out of print.

B1580 DAVIS, ENID. "Books for Liberated Kids." *Emergency Librarian* 9 (March-April 1982):32-33.

Sees children's poetry as literature relatively free of rigid sex-role socialization.

B1581 DEMERS, PATRICIA. "Poems from Canada." *ChLAQ* 7, no. 3 (Fall 1982):60-61.

Reviews "the unrivalled anthology of Canadian poetry," *The Wind Has Wings*, compiled by Mary Alice Downie and Barbara Robertson and illustrated by Elizabeth Cleaver.

B1582 DILLON, DAVID A. "Perspectives: David McCord." *LA* 55 (March 1978):379-87.

In an interview McCord expresses his thoughts on poetry and children.

B1583 FAIRBANKS, A. HARRIS. "Children's Verse: Four Styles." *Children's Literature* 4 (1975):165-72.

Reviews Shel Silverstein's *Where the Sidewalk Ends*, N.M. Bodecker's *Let's Marry Said the Cherry and Other Nonsense Poems*, Marci Ridlon's *That Was Summer*, and Myra Cohn Livingston's *The Way Things Are and Other Poems*. Offers high praise for Silverstein and strong disapproval of Livingston's free verse.

B1584 FISHER, CAROL J., and NATARELLA, MARGARET A. "Of Cabbages and Kings: Or What Kinds of Poetry Young Children Like." *LA* 56 (April 1979):380-85.

Although primarily a survey of children's responses to poems which they rated with a star, an O.K., or a no, the relationship of poetic forms, poetic elements, and contents of the poems to the children's evaluations may have implications for the critic.

B1585 GERSHMAN, H.S. "Children's Rhymes and Modern Poetry." *French Review* 44 (Fall 1971):539-48.

Traces influences of traditional French children's rhymes on modern French poetry.

B1586 GLEASON, JUDITH. "That Lingering Child of Air." *Parnassus: Poetry in Review* 8, no. 2 (1980):63-82.

Reviews a number of recent volumes of children's poetry, providing extensive comments on the works of Lilian Moore, Judith Thurman, and Valerie Worth.

B1587 GOUGH, JOHN. "Poems in Context: Breaking the Anthology Trap." *CLE*, n.s. 15, no. 4 (Winter 1984):204-10.

Suggests that poems be presented to children in the context of the narratives or collections in which they were written to make them more meaningful. Response from Myra Cohn Livingston in n.s. 16, no. 2 (Summer 1985):121-25.

B1588 GREAVES, GRISELDA. "The Key of the Kingdom." *Signal* 30 (September 1979):159-68.

Discusses the role of poetry in children's lives by reflecting on her own experiences.

B1589   GROFF, PATRICK J. "The Most Highly Esteemed Children's Poems." *EE* 39 (October 1962):587-89.

Analyzes highly esteemed children's poems to determine if they meet the criteria favored by most anthologists of children's poetry.

B1590   -----. "Where Are We Going with Poetry for Children?" *Horn Book* 42 (August 1966):456-63.

Discusses recent definitions of poetry for children and ways of attracting children to poetry. According to Groff's precept and examples, Edna St. Vincent Millay was a better poet than Robert Frost.

B1591   HELBIG, ALETHEA. "Kenneth Koch Revisited." *ChLAQ* 9, no. 1 (Spring 1984):38-39.

Reviews a number of critical responses to the books of Kenneth Koch and suggests that the differing approaches of Myra Cohn Livingston, X.J. Kennedy, and Koch be viewed as "complementary strategies for teaching poetry rather than as contradictory arguments competing for adherents."

B1592   -----, ed. "Poetry Books for Children." *ChLAQ* 5, no. 2 (Summer 1980):9-46. (Reprinted in part in Dooley, *First Steps*, pp. 30-38.)

Includes Helbig's "The State of Things: A Question of Substance" (also reprinted in May, *Children and Their Literature*, pp. 138-47), which comments upon a number of individual poetry books and anthologies published between 1977 and 1980, and concludes, "Few of the new poetry books offer poems of integrity, that are sound, honest, and sincere, and richly and provocatively crafted." Also includes Leonard Clark's "Poetry Unfettered," (reprinted in May's *Children and Their Literature*, pp. 133-37), which explores the nature of truth and feeling as expressed in children's poetry, and argues that poems should be selected for children with these truths in mind; and Myra Cohn Livingston's "Some Thoughts on Poetry, Verse and Criticism" (reprinted in Bator, *Signposts*, pp. 211-18), which argues that serious study and criticism of children's poetry has yet to be achieved. Divides poets into three categories: those who write verse, those who write poetry and avoid light verse and versification, and those who write rhyme and light verse as well as poetry. Discusses establishing a "canon" of children's poets.

B1593   HILL, HELEN M. "How to Tell a Sheep from a Goat and Why It Matters." *Horn Book* 55 (February 1979):100-110. (Reprinted in Bator, *Signposts*, pp. 200-210.)

Argues for excellence in children's poetry and includes examples of what she considers "bad."

B1594   JACOBS, LELAND. "Poetry Books for Poetry Reading." *Reading Teacher* 13 (October 1959):45-47.

Suggests answers to the question: What can poetry do for children?, and provides guidelines for selecting poetry. Includes a bibliography of recommended anthologies and individual poets' works.

B1595   -----. "Poetry for Children." *EE* 27 (March 1950):155-57.

Suggests criteria for selecting poetry to be used in the classroom:

(1) It must produce an exhilarating sense of movement, (2) It must make commonplace experiences vibrant, (3) It must tell a wonderful story, and (4) It must bring health-giving laughter and have a lyric quality.

B1596   KENNEDY, X.J., and KENNEDY, DOROTHY M. "Tradition and Revolt: Recent Poetry for Children." *L&U* 4, no. 2 (Winter 1980):175-82.
  "In recent children's poetry one has yet to see any whole-scale turning away from the old devices and strategies." Concludes, "Both in and out of meter, many children's poets apparently need to take more pains, while awaiting the grace--if it will fall--to behold through the eyes of a child."

B1597   LARRICK, NANCY. "Poetry in the Story Hour." *TON* 32 (January 1976):151-61. (Reprinted in Barron, *Jump Over the Moon*, pp. 102-11.)
  Suggests ways of sharing poetry with children.

B1598   LEWIS, NAOMI. "Verse for the Young." *Children's Book Review* 3 (June 1973):70-72. (Reprinted in Bator, *Signposts*, pp. 194-99.)
  Reviews the Opies' *Oxford Book of Children's Verse* and ponders the nature of children's verse.

B1599   *Lion and the Unicorn* 4, no. 2 (Winter 1980-81).
  Special issue on children and poetry. Includes Robert Coles on the poetry of childhood; Terese Svoboda on oral poetry and the Nuer children of Ethiopia and the Sudan; Elizabeth Sewell's "Nonsense Verse and the Child"; Rebecca Lukens on Stevenson's *A Child's Garden of Verse*; Leonard S. Marcus on Juan Ramon Jimenez's "Platero and I"; X.J. and Dorothy Kennedy's examination of recent children's poetry; Janice M. Bogstad's "Is There Poetry in Children's Poetry?"; Edward Barrett's discussion of Kenneth Koch's *Wishes, Lies, and Dreams*; and an interview with Richard Lewis by Leonard S. Marcus.

B1600   LIVINGSTON, MYRA COHN. "But Is It Poetry." *Horn Book* 51 (December 1975):571-80.
  Discusses poetry written by children.

B1601   -----. "Not the Rose . . ." *Horn Book* 40 (August 1964):355-60.
  Explores the importance of sharing poetry with children.

B1602   -----. "Poetry--Step Child of Children's Literature: Searching Notable Book Lists, 1940-1955." *Library Journal* 99 (15 May 1974):1446-49; (15 September 1974):2222-27. Also in *SLJ* 20 (May 1974):28-31; (September 1974):36-41.
  This two part article looks at notable poetry books for children from 1940 to 1955.

B1603   -----. "Poetry: Why? and How?" *Proceedings of the Children's Literature Association* 7 (1980):17-29.
  Explores the poetry children enjoy and the problems of selecting and sharing poetry with children. Expresses hope for "knowledgeable criticism in the field of poetry children enjoy" and concludes, "I often wonder if a poem is not the nearest we will ever come to uniting the disorder of our emotions to the order of our heartbeats."

B1604 -----. "A Tune Beyond Us: The Bases of Choice." *WLB* 44 (December 1969):448-55.

Argues that the great themes of love and death should not be outside the scope of children's poetry, for after all who, as an adult, can fully comprehend those topics, but there are poems which "treat of these themes in a manner to which a child can respond."

B1605 -----. "The Voice of the Poet." *Advocate* 3, no. 1 (Fall 1983):28-48.

Discusses the importance of morality in the poet's voice.

B1606 McCORD, DAVID. "I Went to Noke and Somebody Spoke." *Horn Book* 50 (October 1974):50-57.

"Looking back over more than a century, it is easy to see that the quality and, to a greater extent, the character of verse written professionally for children has steadily strengthened." Provides numerous examples.

B1607 -----. "Poetry for Children." *Library Quarterly* 37 (January 1967):53-66.

Reflects upon poetry for children, sharing many examples he likes, and telling why.

B1608 MEEK, MARGARET, and HUNT, PETER. "The Signal Poetry Award." *Signal* 35 (May 1981):67-75.

Meek and Hunt discuss the nature of children's poetry: what they consider good and bad and the reasons why the Signal Poetry Award is not being given for the second year in a row.

B1609 MEEK, MARGARET, and PHILIP, NEIL. "The Signal Poetry Award." *Signal* 41 (May 1983):59-71.

Discusses *The Rattle Bag* edited by Seamus Heaney and Ted Hughes, winner of the Signal Poetry Award for 1982; and other books of poetry published for children and young people, notably runner-up Charles Causley's anthology *The Sun, Dancing.*

B1610 MORSE, SAMUEL FRENCH. "Speaking to the Imagination." *Horn Book* 41 (1965):255-59.

Explores distinctive qualities and fashions in children's poetry.

B1611 NODELMAN, PERRY. "The Craft or Sullen Art of a Mouse and a Bat." *LA* 55 (April 1978):467-72, 497.

Compares the attitudes toward poets and poetry depicted in Leo Lionni's *Frederick* and Randall Jarrell's *The Bat-Poet.* "*The Bat-Poet* is a challenging answer to the damaging attitudes toward poetry expressed in *Frederick* and accepted without consideration by many teachers."

B1612 PERKINS, AGNES. "Critical Summary of Recent Journal Articles on Poetry for Children." *ChLAQ* 5, no. 2 (Summer 1980):35-38.

Surveys the quantity and quality of literature on children's poetry.

B1613 -----. "A Striking Contrast: Recent British and American Poetry for Children." *Children's Literature* 10 (1982):186-93.

Examines fifteen books of poetry by British and American writers, pointing out differences in poetry-writing and attitudes toward children in the two countries.

B1614   PHILIP, NEIL, and MEEK, MARGARET. "The Signal Poetry Award."
         Signal 44 (May 1984):67-80.
             Comments on Roger McGough's *Pie in the Sky*, winner of the
         1983 Signal Poetry Award and other significant poetry published
         during that year.

B1615   SALTMAN, JUDITH. "Poetry." In Egoff, *Thursday's Child*, pp.
         221-46.
             Considers definitions and origins of poetry for children and
         discusses modern trends in realistic poetry, surrealistic, satirical and
         ironic nonsense verse, narrative verse, and picture-book poetry. Also
         discusses adult poets who write for children, and children as poets.

B1616   SMITH, LILLIAN. "Poetry." In *Unreluctant Years*, pp. 96-113.
             Emphasizes that it is the sounds of poetry that appeal to chil-
         dren. Discusses major anthologies. "Children respond to the best
         and deserve the best, but we can only be sure they receive it if we
         test what we offer them by reference to great poetry--or abide by
         the choice of those who are themselves poets."

B1617   SMITH, WILLIAM JAY. "Sounds of Wind, Sea and Rain." *NYTBR*, 2
         May 1976, Children's Book sec., pp. 23-24, 42.
             Comments on recent poetry books for children and finds too
         many that lack aural appeal.

B1618   STENSLAND, ANNA LEE. "Traditional Poetry of the American
         Indian." *English Journal* 64 (September 1975):41-47. (Reprinted in
         Lenz, *Young Adult Literature*, pp. 403-13.)
             Provides a brief overview of Native American traditional poetry,
         with some guidance on its interpretation. Includes a bibliography.

B1619   STIBBS, ANDREW; FOX, GEOFF; and MERRICK, BRIAN. "Teaching
         Poetry." *CLE*, n.s. 12, no. 1 (Spring 1981):39-55.
             Discusses ways in which poetry can be used in the classroom and
         provides insights into the applications of criticism.

B1620   TERRY, ANN. *Children's Poetry Preferences: A National Survey of
         Upper Elementary Grades.* Urbana, Ill.: National Council Teachers
         of English, 1974, 72 pp.
             Reports on a survey of children's preferences in poetry and ana-
         lyzes the most popular poems in terms of form, content, poetic ele-
         ments, and age of the poem. Found that children preferred contem-
         porary poems, poems dealing with familiar experiences, poems that
         tell stories or are humorous, poems with rhyme and rhythm, and
         poems that do not rely too heavily on "complex imagery or subtly
         implied emotions." Lists the poems selected for the survey and
         identifies the most and least liked.

B1621   WADE, BARRIE. "Rhyming with Reason." *CLE*, n.s. 13, no. 4 (Winter
         1982):188-94.
             Examines rhymes of all kinds and their role in developing chil-
         dren's understanding of and appreciation for language and literature.

B1622   WAIN, JOHN; TUCKER, ALAN; and CHAMBERS, AIDAN. "The Sig-
         nal Poetry Award." *Signal* 29 (May 1979):63-79.
             Wain discusses *Moon-Bells*, the winner of the Signal Poetry
         Award for 1978, pp. 63-66; while Tucker discusses the runners-up,

The Puffin Book of Salt Sea Verse, edited by Charles Causley, and *After The Ark*, by Elizabeth Jennings, pp. 67-73. Chambers concludes with comments on other notable poetry books published during the year, pp. 74-79.

B1623 WHITIN, DAVID J. "Making Poetry Come Alive." *LA* 60 (April 1983):456-58.
Suggests a new approach to the old and usually discredited technique of teaching poetry through memorization.

POINT OF VIEW

B1624 MANSELL, MAUREEN. "Seeing the Other Point of View." *EE* 52 (April 1975):505-7.
Discusses a number of books which can be used to develop young children's understanding of the concept of point of view.

POLAND

B1625 LEWANSKA, IZABELA. "Poland." *Phaedrus* 4, no. 1 (Spring 1977):41-42.
Summarizes current research on children's literature in Poland and provides a brief listing of recent studies (all in Polish).

B1626 MacCANN, DONNARAE. "Something Old, Something New: Children's Picture Books in Poland." *WLB* 52 (June 1978):776-82.
An overview of Polish picture books. Includes illustrations and references.

POLITICS IN CHILDREN'S BOOKS

B1627 HÜRLIMANN, BETTINA. "Politics in Children's Books: Political Influence through Classic Children's Books--Modern Children's Books with Political Leanings--Children's Books and Books for Young People in the Totalitarian States." In *Three Centuries*, pp. 173-94.
An overview.

B1628 JONES, JOAN SCANLON. "Political Socialization in Picture Books, 1972-1976." Ph.D. dissertation, University of Akron, 1979, 291 pp., DA 39:6108A.
Examines pictures and texts of books for children aged three to eight and concludes they reinforce existing political and social values, although they also tend "to value cultural pluralism and expanding roles for women."

B1629 ØRVIG, MARY. "One World in Children's Books?" In *Arbuthnot Lectures*, pp. 39-59. (Also in *TON* 28 [June 1972]:399-422.)
Urges closer attention be paid to the history and criticism of children's books from many worlds because they are important political and social influences. Extensive references, especially to criticism in foreign languages.

B1630 *Phaedrus* 8 (1981):1-37.
Contains essays on politics and ideology in children's books. Includes "The Issue of Youth Literature and Socialism," by Joachim Schmidt, a study of trends in Germany in the late nineteenth and early twentieth centuries; "Walter Crane and His Socialist Children's

Book Illustrations," by James Fraser; "Béla Balázs: A Bibliographic Note," by Bélá Tóth, which calls attention to the children's books of this Hungarian poet, essayist, and film and theater theoretician; "About Children's Literature," by Nadezhda Konstantinovna Krupskaya, wife of Lenin; "Juvenile Books in the Netherlands During the German Occupation," by Wim J. Simons; "*Snørre the Seal*: A Children's Book of the Norwegian Resistance Movement," by Kari Skjønsberg, which discusses Frithjof Saelen's book; "Gianni Rodari: An Appreciation," by Carla Poesio and Pino Boero, which emphasizes Rodari's political messages; "Politics and Comics in the Federal Republic of Germany," by Susanne Mgeladse; "Ideological Trends in Norwegian Children's Literature after 1968," by Kari Skjønsberg; "Authors in Exile," by Jan V. Le Roux, a study of South African children's literature, concentrating on three authors in exile: Ann Harries, Toecky Jones, and Joan Salvesen, and also discussing controversial author John Miles.

B1631   SUTHERLAND, ROBERT D. "Hidden Persuaders: Political Ideologies in Literature for Children." *CLE*, n.s. 16, no. 3 (Autumn 1985):143-57.
Outlines three ways in which writers express their values: the politics of advocacy, the politics of attack, and the politics of assent. Suggests examples of each from a wide range of children's literature.

POPULAR LITERATURE

B1632   BARKER, KEITH. "Attitudes to Enid Blyton and Roger Hargreaves." In Hunt, *Further Approaches*, pp. 29-34.
Explores the attitudes of critics, librarians, parents and teachers towards popular children's authors, concentrating on Enid Blyton and Roger Hargreaves.

B1633   DICKINSON, PETER. "A Defense of Rubbish." *CLE*, o.s., no. 3 (November 1970):7-10. (Reprinted in Fox, *Writers, Critics, and Children*, pp. 73-76, and in Haviland, *Children and Literature*, pp. 101-3.)
Dickinson defines rubbish as "all forms of reading matter which contain to the adult eye no visible value, either aesthetic of educational." His precise defense is based on the following premises: (1) It is important for a child to have a whole culture at his finger tips, (2) A child should feel he belongs, (3) It is important children discover things for themselves, (4) Sometimes rubbish fills a psychological need for security, (5) The diet needs roughage, (6) It may not be rubbish after all.

B1634   EGOFF, SHEILA. "If That Won't Do No Good, That Won't Do No Harm: The Uses and Dangers of Mediocrity in Children's Reading." *SLJ* 19 (October 1972):93-97. (Reprinted in Gerhardt, *Issues in Children's Book Selection*, pp. 3-10.)
Argues in favor of high critical standards and against mediocrity in children's books: "let kids have the good stuff."

B1635   JACOBS, LELAND B. "Pleasures of the Popular." *Reading Teacher* 12 (October 1958):40-41.
A spirited defense of some of the benefits of "popular" reading.

B1636   JAKOFSEN, GUNNAR. "Pop Literature for Children." *Bookbird* 11,

no. 1 (1973):30-35. (Also in Koefoed, *Children's Literature and the Child*, pp. 37-40.)
Defines "pop literature" and discusses whether it should be included in school libraries and how it might be used.

B1637 KAYE, MARILYN. "In Defense of Formula Fiction; or, They Don't Write Schlock the Way They Used To." *TON* 37 (Fall 1980):87-90.
Argues that "Adolescents have a right to the same sort of light, formula fiction available to adults." Points out distinguishing characteristics of light, escapist reading, and suggests that more is needed among all the "solid, honest, realistic" literature available to today's young people.

B1638 LANES, SELMA. "All That's Golden Does Not Glitter." In *Down the Rabbit Hole*, pp. 112-27.
Examines the phenomenon of mass-market or merchandise books for young children. Their appeal is "essentially visual rather than literary." Sees Richard Scarry as a rare example of an author-illustrator whose work has become more important than the product he has helped to produce.

B1639 McCLELLAND, DAVID C. "Values in Popular Literature for Children." *Childhood Education* 40 (November 1963):135-38. (Reprinted in White, *Children's Literature*, pp. 86-91.)
Reports on an international survey of values presented in books for third and fourth graders.

B1640 MAY, JILL. "Judy Blume as Archie Bunker." *ChLAQ* 9, no. 1 (Spring 1984):2, 14.
Suggests that Judy Blume's books provide entertainment and relaxation, present a familiar and comfortable world (just as Archie Bunker does), but are not books that touch the soul, or that raise moral questions.

B1641 NIST, JOAN STIDHAM. "Popularity in Wonderland." ERIC Educational Document Reproduction Service, 1977, 9 pp., ED 150 636. (Version also in *Advocate* 1, no. 2 [Winter 1982]:106-10.)
Urges scholars of children's literature to study not only those books that have achieved critical acclaim, but also those that have proved popular with children, for "childhood's heroes are important."

B1642 SALTER, DON. "The Hard Core of Children's Literature." *CLE*, o.s., no. 8 (July 1972):39-55.
Examines a number of titles extremely popular with British adolescents: Richard Allen's *Skinhead*, Peter Cave's (pseudonym of Richard Allen) *Chopper* and *Mama*, and H.R. Kaye's *A Place in Hell*, and summarizes critical responses pro and con.

POPULATION

B1643 MEYER, BARBARA B., and VOELKER, ALAN M. "Children's Books on Population Education." *Children and Science* 10 (April 1973):32-34.
Rates a number of children's tradebooks pertaining to population education and finds that most of them fail to deal with controversial environmental issues.

B1644 VOELKER, ALAN M. "Population and Children's Literature." *Journal of Environmental Education* 6, no. 3 (1975):57-64.
Analyzes approaches to and awareness of population problems in children's trade books published between 1944 and 1972.

PRAIRIE

B1645 WHITAKER, MURIEL. "Perceiving Prairie Landscapes: The Young Person's View of the Western Frontier." *ChLAQ* 8, no. 4 (Winter 1983):30-32.
Surveys the depiction of the prairie frontier in a number of Canadian and American children's books.

B1646 ZITTERKOPF, DEANNA. "Prairies and Privations: The Impact of Place in Great Plains Homestead Fiction for Children." *ChLAQ* 9, no. 4 (Winter 1984-85):171-73.
Analyzes the depiction of the prairie and great plains in a number of children's books.

PROBLEM NOVEL

B1647 DONELSON, KENNETH, and NILSEN, ALLEEN PACE. "The New Realism: Of Life and Other Sad Songs." In *Literature for Today's Young Adults*, pp. 181-204.
Looks at categories of concern: parent/child relationships, body and self, sex and sex roles, friends and society. Looks at *Chocolate War* and, briefly, at several other well-known modern realistic young adult novels.

B1648 EGOFF, SHEILA. "The Problem Novel." In Egoff, *Only Connect*, 2d ed., pp. 356-69.
Discusses Judy Blume, Paul Zindel, Norma Klein, and others.

B1649 -----. "The Problem Novel." In *Thursday's Child*, pp. 66-79.
Defines the problem novel as a popular, limited subspecies of realistic fiction that aims "to tell rather than show." Includes a concise checklist of common characteristics. Traces modern origins of the genre from Emily Neville's *It's Like This, Cat*, through such major practicioners as Judy Blume, Paul Zindel, and M.E. Kerr.

B1650 STANEK, LOU WILLETT. "Real People, Real Books: About Young Adult Readers." *TON* 31 (June 1975):417-27. (Reprinted in Lenz, *Young Adult Literature*, pp. 49-58.)
Analyzes stylistic characteristics of popular problem novels, categorizing the problems and exploring what they mean to adolescents.

PUERTO RICO AND PUERTO RICANS

B1651 COUNCIL ON INTERRACIAL BOOKS FOR CHILDREN. "One Hundred Children's Books About Puerto Ricans: A Study in Racism, Sexism and Colonialism." In *IRBC* 4, nos. 1-2 (Spring 1972). (Excerpted in MacCann, *Cultural Conformity*, pp. 68-72.)
Includes a survey of one hundred children's books about Puerto Rico and Puerto Ricans, a discussion of portrayals of Puerto Rico in history books, and a feminist analysis of the hundred books.

B1652 FREUNDLICH, JOYCE Y. "Fact or Fancy: The Image of the Puerto Rican in Ethnic Literature for Young Adults." ERIC Educational Document Reproduction Service, 1980, 33 pp., ED 188 150.
Finds inaccurate representation of Puerto Ricans in books for young adults published between 1950 and 1980.

B1653 -----. "The Image of The Puerto Rican in Ethnic Literature for Young Adults: A Cross-Cultural Perspective." Ed.D. dissertation, Rutgers University, 1980, 252 pp., DA 41:1456A.
Assesses the image of the Puerto Rican in young adult literature written in English between 1950 and 1980.

B1654 GARCIA, IRMA. "The Colonialist Mentality: Distortions and Omissions in Children's History Books." In *IRBC* 4, nos. 1-2 (Spring 1972). (Reprinted in MacCann, *Cultural Conformity*, pp. 73-78.)
Highly critical analysis of twelve books available in English devoted to Puerto Rican history.

B1655 NIETO, SONIA, ed. "Children's Literature on Puerto Rican Themes: Part I, The Message of Fiction," and "Part II, Non-Fiction." *IRBC* 14, nos. 1-2 (1983):4-30.
Surveys books published in the past ten years since the *IRBC* survey in 1972, and concludes more positive, accurate, and sensitive books are still needed.

PUPPETS

B1656 MICHANCZYK, MICHAEL. "The Puppet Immortals of Children's Literature." *Children's Literature* 2 (1973):159-65. (Reprinted in Butler, *Sharing*, pp. 75-79.)
Discusses both literature about puppets, for example, *Pinocchio*, and "religious overtones and philosophical implications of puppeting and children's literature" in literature written in the oral tradition to be performed by puppets.

B1657 SCHWARCZ, JOSEPH. "Puppets and Dolls." In *Ways of the Illustrator*, pp. 86-89.
Examines photographed stories of puppets and dolls.

QUEST LITERATURE

B1658 TERRY, JUNE S. "To Seek and To Find: Quest Literature for Children." *School Librarian* 18, no. 4 (December 1970):399-404. (Reprinted in White, *Children's Literature*, pp. 138-44.)
Surveys traditional and modern quest literature, available to children and comments upon its significance to them.

RACE

B1659 ALEXANDER, RAE. "What Is A Racist Book?" *IRBC* 3, no. 1 (1970). (Reprinted in MacCann, *Black American*, pp. 57-62.)
Analyzes NAACP's criteria for acceptable books and discusses good and bad titles.

B1660 DIXON, BOB. "Racism: All Things White and Beautiful." In *Catching Them Young*, pp. 94-127.
Examines racism in children's literature, especially concentrating

on Enid Blyton's *Noddy*, Hugh Lofting's *Dr. Dolittle*, and Helen Bannerman's *Little Black Sambo*.

B1661 GAST, DAVID K. "The Dawning of the Age of Aquarius for Multi-Ethnic Children's Literature." *EE* 47 (May 1970):661-65. (Reprinted in MacCann, *Black American*, pp. 169-74.)

Discusses nine approaches to the treatment of minorities in children's literature: (1) the Invisible Man Approach, (2) the Noble-Savage Approach, (3) the White Man's Burden Approach, (4) the Minstrel Show Approach, (5) the Queer Customs Approach, (6) the Multi-Ethnic Dick-and Jane Approach, (7) the Reversed Stereotype Approach, (8) the Tell-It-Like-It-Is Approach, and (9) the Remanufactured Past Approach.

B1662 HILL, JANET. "A Minority View." In Meek, *Cool Web*, pp. 309-13. (Reprinted from *Children's Book News*, May 1967.)

Argues for more care in assessing racism in children's books in Britain. Favors keeping *Little Black Sambo* on the shelf, but strongly objects to Prudence Andrew's *Ginger and Number 10* and several other books. "We shall have to become much more colour conscious about children's books . . . before we can become truly colour blind."

B1663 LONG, MARGO ALEXANDRE. "The Interracial Family in Children's Literature." *LA* 55 (April 1978):489-97.

An overview and evaluation of children's fiction relating to interracial families.

B1664 -----. "The Interracial Family in Children's Literature." *IRBC* 15, no. 6 (1984):13-15.

Examines a dozen children's books portraying interracial families.

B1665 MADISON, JOHN. "School Integration in Children's Literature." *Integrated Education* 16, no. 3 (May-June 1978):10-11.

Discusses May Justus's *New Boy in School*, Natalie Savage Carlson's *Empty Schoolhouse*, and Robert Coles's *Dead End School*.

B1666 MOORE, ROBERT B. "A Letter from a Critic." *Children's Literature* 10 (1982):211-13.

Argues that prejudices, whether conscious or unconscious, must be considered by literary critics. Uses examples from *Mary Poppins* and *Friend Monkey* by P.L. Travers and *Little Black Sambo* by Helen Bannerman.

B1667 PREISWERK, ROY, ed. *The Slant of the Pen: Racism in Children's Books*. Geneva: World Council of Churches, Office of Education, Program to Combat Racism, 1980, 154 pp.

The papers in this book are based on presentations at a 1978 workshop held in Arnoldshain, Federal Republic of Germany, sponsored by the Program to Combat Racism and the Office of Education of the World Council of Churches. The emphasis is on "white racist stereotypes and their impact on children, white and non-white alike." Includes an Introduction by Ray Preiswerk. Part 1, "Why Children's Books Are Biased, contains "The Oppressive Function of Values, Concepts and Images in Children's Books by Luis Nieves-Falcón, pp. 3-6, and "Some Typical Patterns of Argumentation Reading to Racism is Children's Books," by Jörg Becker, pp. 7-10.

Part 2 contains essays on racism in children's books in various countries: "Racism in Children's Books: An Afro-America Perspective," by Dorothy Kuya, pp. 26-45; "Children's Books in an African Context," by Bankole Omotoso, pp. 46-51; "The Ideology of Racism in Puerto Rican Children's Books," by Luis Nieves-Falcón, pp. 52-60; "Racism in Australian Children's Books," by Lorna Lippmann, pp. 61-70; "Some Specific Issues in German Children's Books and School Texts," by Jörg Becker, pp. 72-81; and "Images of Indians in German Children's Books," by Hartmut Lutz, pp. 82-102.

Part 3 contains "Racism in the Religious Instruction Textbooks of Protestant West Germany," by Rolf Lüpke, pp. 105-27; and part 4 contains "Ethnocentric Images in History Books and Their Effect on Racism," by Ray Preiswerk, pp. 131-39. An appendix includes criteria for evaluating racism in children's books and guidelines for producing anti- and nonracist books.

B1668   RAY, SHEILA; STONE, ROSEMARY; and KING, CLIVE. "Racism and Children's Writers." *Bookbird* 2 (1981):3-7.
Reports on a discussion between two British writers on race in children's books.

B1669   REES, DAVID. "Skin Color in British Children's Books: The Roots of Racial Prejudice as Depicted in James Vance Marshall's *Walkabout*." *CLE*, n.s. 11, no. 2 (Summer 1980):91.
Compares American and British treatments of racial minorities, especially questioning the attitudes depicted in James Vance Marshall's *Walkabout*. Letter in response from Stella Lees, *CLE*, n.s. 11, no. 4 (Winter 1980):203-5, strongly objecting to racism in *Walkabout*; and to Rees's defense of "that bad book." Rees replies in *CLE*, n.s. 12, no. 1 (Spring 1981):57-58.

B1670   ROCKWOOD, JOYCE. "Can Novelists Portray Other Cultures Faithfully?" *Advocate* 2, no. 1 (Fall 1982):1-5.
Explores the use of anthropological techniques in assisting a writer from one culture to portray a person from another.

B1671   SMALL, ROBERT C. "The Junior Novel and Race Relations." *Negro American Literature Forum* 8 (Spring 1974):184-89.
"Although motivated by good intentions, the authors of a large number of recent junior novels on the theme of race relations have, to a great extent, been unable to break away from narrow conventions and overt moralizing." Cites numerous examples from young adult literature.

B1672   STJARNE, KERSTIN. "A Report from Sweden." *IRBC* 5, nos. 1-2 (1974):15.
Reports on the treatment of racial minorities in current Swedish children's books.

B1673   WILLIAMS, HELEN. "The Image of Whites in Fiction for Children and Young Adults Written by Black Writers, 1945-1975." Ph.D. dissertation, University of Wisconsin, Madison, 1983, 139 pp., DA 43:3915A.
Found the predominant characteristic of whites in children's books by black authors to be "friendly social." Found a twelve to one ratio of male to female major characters.

RAIN

B1674   BAUER, CAROLINE FELLER. "The Rain in Spain Falls Mainly in Oregon: The Art of Rain in Children's Picture Books." *Pacific Northeast Library Association Quarterly* 36 (July 1972):4-14.
Examines the portrayal of rain in a number of children's picture books.

REALISM

B1675   ABRAMSON, JANE. "Still Playing It Safe: Restricted Realism in Teen Novels." *SLJ* 22 (May 1976):38-39.
Argues that despite the "hoopla over hard-hitting realism of juvenile fiction for older readers." There are restrictions that "result in books that succeed only in mirroring a slick surface realism." Conventional morality too often prevails. Discusses a number of well-known and controversial titles.

B1676   BACON, BETTY. "From Now to 1984." *WLB* 45 (October 1970):156-59. (Reprinted in Meek, *Cool Web*, pp. 129-33.)
Attacks *Tucker's Countryside* by George Selden and *Hell's Edge* by John Rowe Townsend for portraying "the world the way it ought to be" and praises *The Cay*, by Theodore Taylor, *The Little Fishes*, by Julius Lester and even Mary Norton's *The Borrowers* as realistic portrayals of survivors.

B1677   BADER, BARBARA. "Social Changes." In *American Picturebooks*, pp. 364-72.
Discusses the growing awareness and portrayal of cultural, economic, and ethnic diversity in the picture books of the 1940s and 1950s.

B1678   BURCH, ROBERT. "The New Realism." *Horn Book* 74 (June 1971):257-64. (Reprinted in Haviland, *Children and Literature*, pp. 281-87.)
Argues for realism within reason, and not to the exclusion of happy endings. "Surely in life there are as many happy endings as sad ones, so to be truly realistic, should books not average out accordingly?"

B1679   CARLSEN, ROBERT, and BAGNALL, NORMA. "Bait and Rebait." *English Journal* 70 (January 1981):8-12.
The two debate the statement "Literature isn't supposed to be realistic."

B1680   EGOFF, SHEILA. "Realistic Fiction." In *Thursday's Child*, pp. 31-65.
Considers the origins and recent development of the genre. Among examples discussed are Louise Fitzhugh's *Harriet the Spy* and books by Ivan Southall, Jill Paton Walsh, Penelope Lively, Mollie Hunter, Nina Bawden, Katherine Paterson, Robert Cormier, Bette Greene, Virginia Hamilton, William Mayne, Paula Fox, and K.M. Peyton. Ivan Southall's *What About Tomorrow* is selected to epito--mize "the best in modern realistic novels for children."

B1681   GLOECKLER, ALMA MARIE. "A Posited Basis for Criticism of Realistic Fiction for Beginning Readers." Ph.D. dissertation, Columbia University, 1969, 252 pp., DA 31:6277A.

Explores the availability of sources for a criticism of children's stories, the potential for the use of key ideas as tools for inquiry, and the nature of realistic stories for beginning readers.

B1682 GUTHRIE, JAMES. "Realism and Escapism in Children's Literature." *Junior Bookshelf* 22, no. 1 (January 1958):15-18.
Maintains that the apparent realism in much children's literature is "actually a form of escapism because it offers instead of reality a fictional shorthand which is a distortion of reality."

B1683 HADLEY, ERIC. "The Scrubbed Pine World of English Children's Fiction." *Use of English* 31 (Spring 1980):56-65.
Compares British and American approaches to handling contemporary problems and finds the British writers tend toward "escape."

B1684 HARRISON, JAMES. "Toward the Last Frontier." *CCL* 33 (1984):40-45.
Examines the handling of grief, sorrow, and unhappiness in three Canadian and one British book: Ruth Nichols's *The Marrow of the World*, Jean Little's *Kate*, Monica Hughes's *The Keeper of The Isis Light*, and William Mayne's *A Game of Dark*.

B1685 HORMANN, ELIZABETH. "Children's Crisis Literature." *LA* 54 (May 1977):559-66.
Surveys and evaluates fiction and nonfiction concerning four life crises: birth, hospitalization, divorce, and death. Includes bibliography.

B1686 JORDAN, JUNE. "Young People: Victims of Realism in Books and Life." *WLB* 48 (October 1973):141-45.
Provides a powerful argument and personal statement in favor of providing "usable, believable, practicable, desirable alternatives" to the present grim realism "in our books and in our lives."

B1687 KLEIN, NORMA. "More Realism for Children." *TON* 31 (April 1975):307-12.
Discusses her feelings and experience of writing *Mom, the Wolf Man, and Me*, and sets forth her hopes for future developments in realistic fiction for children.

B1688 LIVINGSTON, MYRA COHN. "I Still Would Plant My Little Apple Tree." *Horn Book* 47 (February 1971):75-84.
Calls for a return to the honesty and "realism" of the great novels, folklore, fantasy, and poetry of the past.

B1689 MADSEN, J.M., and WICKERSHAM, E.B. "A Look at Young Children's Realistic Fiction." *Reading Teacher* 34 (December 1980):273-79.
Analyzes ethnicity, stereotypes, and themes of a number of titles of realistic fiction for children. Includes an annotated listing of titles examined.

B1690 MERCER, JOAN BODGER. "Innocence is a Cop-out." In Meek, *Cool Web*, pp. 135-39.
Conveys the irony of adults trying to protect children and adolescents from realities they already know.

B1691   NOBLE, JUDITH ANN. "The Home, the Church, and the School as Portrayed in American Realistic Fiction for Children 1965-1969." Ph.D. dissertation, Michigan State University, 1971, 320 pp., DA 32:2918A.

Examines the ways in which these three areas have been depicted in children's contemporary realistic fiction.

B1692   PATERSON, GARY H. "Perspectives on the New Realism in Children's Literature." *CCL* 25 (1982):26-32.

Offers credibility as a guideline for evaluating the new on "ugly" realism. Argues also for more balanced approaches, including fun, beauty, and escape.

B1693   PERKINS, AGNES. "What Books Should Be Sent to Coventry? . . . A Comparison of Recent British and American Realistic Fiction." *Proceedings of the Children's Literature Association* 6 (1979):155-64. (Reprinted in May, *Children and Their Literature*, pp. 71-78.)

Compares Judy Blume's *Are You There, God? It's Me, Margaret* and Hila Colman's *Nobody Has to Be a Kid Forever* with Jane Gardam's *A Long Way from Verona*.

B1694   RINSKY, LEE, and SCHWEIKERT, ROMAN. "In Defense of the New Realism of Children and Adolescents." *Phi Delta Kappa* 58 (February 1977):472-75.

Defends the new realism and suggests books that treat formerly taboo topics in acceptable ways.

B1695   RONEY, R. CRAIG. "Fantasizing as a Motif in Children's Realistic Literature." *LA* 60 (April 1983):447-55.

Examines the motif of a character in a realistic story "who fantasizes (dreams or daydreams) to cope with some real or imagined problem or to satisfy some basic need." Sees this as a genre that has emerged since 1960.

B1696   SAUER, JULIA L. "Making the World Safe for the Janey Larkins." *Library Journal* 66 (15 January 1941):49-53.

Argues that more attention is needed to social problems in children's books, that more books like Florence Means's *Shuttered Windows* and Doris Gates's *Blue Willow* are needed.

B1697   STEELE, MARY Q. "Realism, Truth, and Honesty." *Horn Book* 47 (February 1971):17-27. (Reprinted in Haviland, *Children and Literature*, pp. 288-96.)

Despite the modern problem novels, "we still fail to level with our children." Argues that "Young minds like young bodies could profit by a little exercise." Some of today's realistic writers may be encouraging this.

B1698   STORR, CATHERINE. "Fear and Evil in Children's Books." *CLE*, o.s., no. 1 (March 1970):22-40. (Reprinted as "Things that Go Bump in the Night," in Meek, *Cool Web*, pp. 120-27, and in Tucker, *Suitable for Children?*, pp. 143-52, and in *Times Sunday Magazine*, 7 March 1971.)

Discusses difficulties of portraying evil in children's books and changing standards for fear, evil, and realism over the past three hundred years. Discusses fear and evil in adventure stories with villains, in adventure stories involving the forces of nature or impersonal villains, in stories portraying the evils of society, in comedy, in space fiction, in historical novels, and in fantasy. Concludes that horror and fear of a certain kind are necessary to children. The article stimulated extensive discussion at the 1969 conference in Exeter, England. Published with the speech in *CLE*.

B1699   WALSH, JILL PATON. "The Art of Realism." In Hearne, *Celebrating Children's Books*, pp. 35-44.
         Realism, too, is fantasy, according to Walsh, but it is often read for content alone. Argues for the right of the realistic writer to be irrelevant. Realistic works are often dismissed because "it is often felt that a child's view of reality is not really important, because it is transitory."

B1700   WESTALL, ROBERT. "How Real Do You Want Your Realism?" *Signal* 28 (January 1979):34-46.
         Sees nostalgia as "The enemy of children's realism." Discusses why he wrote the *Machine-Gunners* and talks about all the things he would like to put into children's books, things that fascinate and preoccupy children but which adults will not allow. Concludes with an in-depth discussion of Jill Paton Walsh's *The Emperor's Winding Sheet*, "a colossus in our time," pp. 43-46.

B1701   WILMS, DENISE. "Consciousness Comes to Children's Books. . . . The Veil Has Been Lifted on Divorce, Death, Sex, and Drugs; But the Decade Is Ending in a Slump." *American Libraries* 10 (June 1979):343-44.
         Summarizes trends in realism in children's books in the 1970s, but urges "greater depth" for the 1980s.

B1702   WOLF, VIRGINIA L. "The Root and Measure of Realism." *WLB* 44 (December 1969):409-15.
         Examines the use of realism in American novels for children, discussing Zilpha K. Snyder's *The Egypt Game*, E.L. Konigsburg's *From the Mixed-Up Files of Mrs. Basil E. Frankweiler*, and Eleanor Estes's *Ginger Pye* as only partially successful; and Paula Fox's *How Many Miles to Babylon?*, E.L. Konigsburg's *Jennifer, MacBeth, William McKinley, and Me, Elizabeth*, and Louise Fitzhugh's *Harriet the Spy* as more successful.

B1703   YOLEN, JANE. "Peter Rabbit . . . Say Good-bye to Snow White: You're Both Outdated but We Hate to see You Go." *Publishers Weekly* 199 (22 February 1971):79-80.
         Argues that children need and want realistic, relevant books that overcome the old taboos, but they need and want some of the old fantasy too.

REJECTION

B1704   KINGSTON, CAROLYN T. "The Tragic Moment: Rejection." In *Tragic Mode*, pp. 5-56.
         Examines the ways in which a number of books handle the theme of rejection. Individual titles are indexed separately in this bibliography.

RELIGION

B1705   BATES, BARBARA SNEDEKER. "Denominational Periodicals: The Invisible Literature." *Phaedrus* 7, no. 1 (Spring-Summer 1980):13-18.
A historical survey, with suggestions for researching this neglected field. Emphasis is primarily on the nineteenth and early twentieth centuries and is limited to the U.S.

B1706   BECHTEL, MARY. "Notes on Contemporary Evangelical Christian Literature in the United States." *Phaedrus* 7, no. 1 (Spring-Summer 1980):39-42.
"This article is a brief survey of what has come to be known as 'evangelical' books for children, books which have been produced in publishing houses in the present decade."

B1707   BREWBAKER, JAMES M. "Are You There, Margaret? It's Me, God-- Religious Contexts in Recent Adolescent Fiction." *English Journal* 72 (September 1983):82-86.
Examines religious elements in a number of well-known works of adolescent literature.

B1708   ELLEMAN, BARBARA. "The American Connection." *Signal* 39 (September 1982):191-95.
Surveys a recent crop of children's books with religious and biblical themes and explores the difficulties of evaluating them.

B1709   MILNER, JOSEPH O. "The Emergence of Awe in Recent Children's Literature." *Children's Literature* 10 (1982):169-77.
Divides children's literature into two basic views of human experience: the religious and the humanist. Reviews five books from the religious perspective: Sue Ellen Bridger's *All Together Now*, Joan Blos's *A Gathering of Days*, Boris Zhitknov's *How I Hunted the Little Fellow*, Madeleine L'Engle's *Ladder of Angels*, and Ouida Sebestyen's *Words By Heart*.

B1710   WEHMEYER, LILLIAN B. "The Future of Religion in Junior Novels." *Catholic Library World* 54 (April 1983):366-69.
Examines the nature of religion in futuristic novels for young people, and finds no mention of the mainstream religions of today.

REVIEWING

B1711   ALDERSON, BRIAN. "The Irrelevance of Children to the Children's Book Reviewer." *Children's Book News* 4, no. 1 (January 1969): 10-11.
Argues that appealing to children's tastes is often "an excuse for not seeking better books" or "for not involving oneself sufficiently deeply in children's reading."

B1712   GLASTONBURY, MARION. "Are You Sitting Comfortably?" *TES*, 20 June 1980, p. 37.
Surveys British review sources for children's literature.

B1713   HANNABUSS, STUART. "Re-viewing Reviews." *Signal* 35 (May 1981):96-109.
Provides a critical overview of British sources for children's book reviews.

B1714 HEARNE, BETSY. "Innocence and Experience: A Critical Paradox." In Hearne, *Celebrating Children's Books*, pp. 165-76.

As a book reviewer, raises the question: "How does one balance knowledge and ignorance." Argues in favor of an open mind.

B1715 KENNEMER, PHYLLIS KAY. "An Analysis of Reviews of Books of Fiction for Children and Adolescents Published in Major Selection Aids in the United States in 1979." Ed.D. dissertation, University of Colorado at Boulder, 1980, 156 pp., DA 42:81A.

Evaluates reviews of children's books in *Booklist, Bulletin of the Center for Children's Books, Horn Book Kirkus Reviews, Publishers Weekly*, and *School Library Journal* by using a Classification of Book Reviews form developed for this study.

B1716 LANES, SELMA. "Mechanics of Survival: Why Publish? Who Judges." In *Down the Rabbit Hole*, pp. 146-57.

Discusses the publishing and selling of children's books, concentrating especially on the shortcomings of the reviewing of children's books.

B1717 MAHONEY, ELLEN WILCOX. "A Content Analysis of Children's Books Reviews from *Horn Book Magazine*, 1975." Ph.D. dissertation, University of Illinois at Urbana-Champaign, 1975, 96 pp., DA 40:140A.

Finds that *Horn Book* is primarily concerned with literary rather than practical analysis of the books reviewed but more concerned with content than with formal aspects. Concludes that "better writing for children can withstand critical analysis and evaluation."

B1718 MEEK, MARGARET. "The Many and the Few." *School Librarian* 20 (March 1972):7-15. (Reprinted in part in Culpan, *Variety is King*, pp. 154-61.)

Defines four categories of reviews of children's books: the practical, the "literary," the sociological, and the child-centered. "We have to begin by understanding how children turn their expectations of books into experience of what books are."

B1719 "Reviews, Reviewing and the Review Media." 35 (Winter 1979).

Special issue. Includes Linda R. Silver's "Criticism, Reviewing, and the Library Review Media," pp. 123-30, which surveys the quality of reviews in British and American review sources and finds "a dearth of serious criticism"; Rosemary Weber's survey of seven frequently used sources of reviews, "The Reviewing of Children's and Young Adult Books in 1977," pp. 131-37; Melvin H. Rosenberg's "Thinking Poor: The Nonlibrary Review Media," pp. 138-42, which critiques eight review sources; and Audrey B. Eaglen's "The Young Adult Book Review Media," pp. 143-45.

"What Makes a Good Review? Ten Experts Speak," pp. 146-52, and "Reviews in the Academic Milieu," by Suzanne Sullivan, pp. 158-60, both tackle the question of what makes a good review. "Notes of a Book Review Junkie," by Fontayne Holmes, pp. 163-66, explores the differences between reviewing and criticism, and discusses problems and pitfalls of reviewing.

B1720 SCHUMAN, PATRICIA. "Fall Children's Book Sections and Supplements . . . Concerned Criticism or Casual Cop-Outs?" *Library*

Journal 97 (15 January 1972):245-48 and *SLJ* 19 (January 1972):2-4. (Reprinted in Gerhardt, *Issues in Children's Book Selection*, pp. 191-97.)

Examines seven general sources of reviews of children's books (*New York Times, New York Review of Books, Book World, Christian Science Monitor, Saturday Review, Commonweal*, and *Scientific American*) and finds the overall status of children's book reviewing poor.

B1721 SUTHERLAND, ZENA. "Current Reviewing of Children's Books." *Library Quarterly* 37 (January 1967):110-18.

Reports on two studies of children's book reviewing, one a doctoral dissertation and the other a master's thesis, plus reports on her own study and adds her own comments on problems, needs, and trends.

B1722 TOWNSEND, JOHN ROWE. "The Reviewing of Children's Books." In Hearne, *Celebrating Children's Books*, pp. 177-87.

Sets down principles of children's book reviewing, emphasizing the nature and the purpose of the art.

RIDDLES

B1723 PARK, ROSE. "An Investigation of Riddles of Children, Ages Five-Fourteen." Ed.D. dissertation, Columbia University, 1972, 180 pp., DA 33:905A.

Examines the structure and content of riddles and their function among children ages five to fourteen.

ROBIN HOOD

B1724 KEENAN, HUGH T. Review of David Wiles's *The Early Plays of Robin Hood* and of J.C. Holt's *Robin Hood. ChLAQ* 9, no. 1 (Spring 1984):40-41.

Finds Wiles's book tedious and his arguments tenuous, but praises Holt' "summation of twenty years research in historical and literary sources." Also mentions other recent studies of the Robin Hood legends.

B1725 KREINHOLDER, ADELINE. "A Comparison of Robin Hood Stories." *EER* 16 (January 1939):5-9.

Lists the ten most famous versions of the Robin Hood legend in the order of the author's preference. Pyle's version comes first, followed by the Paul Creswick-N.C. Wyeth version.

B1726 NAGY, J.F. "Paradoxes of Robin Hood." *Folklore* 91, no. 2 (1980):198-210.

Explores the mystique of Robin Hood, seeing him as a figure who exists "between culture and nature and several other pairs of opposed categories as well."

B1727 PEARCE, PHILIPPA. "Robin Hood and His Merry Men: A Rereading." *CLE*, n.s. 16, no. 3 (Autumn 1985):159-64.

Reflects on the power and mystery of the Robin Hood legend in Henry Gilbert's version.

B1728 ZELLEFROW, WILLIAM KENNETH. "The Romance of Robin Hood."

Ph.D. dissertation, University of Colorado, 1974, 208 pp., DA 35:5370A.

Examines one of the earliest and lengthiest literary accounts of Robin Hood, the *Lytell Geste of Robyn Hood*, published by Wynken de Worde near the end of the fifteenth or early in the sixteenth century.

ROBINSONADE

B1729   GUNSTRA, DIANE L. "The Island Pattern." *ChLAQ* 10, nos. 2 (Summer 1985):55-57.

Traces the symbol of the island as first depicted in *Adventure of Robinson Crusoe* and in a number of more recent works for children including Scott O'Dell's *Island of the Blue Dolphins*, William Steig's *Abel's Island*, and Harry Mazer's *The Island Keeper*.

B1730   HÜRLIMANN, BETTINA. "Robinson." In *Three Centuries*, pp. 99-112.

Traces the influences of Defoe's *Robinson Crusoe* on a number of European children's books.

B1731   KERR, ROSALIE. "The Desert Island Motif in Children's Books." In Hunt, *Further Approaches*, pp. 117-18.

Summarizes her research into the development of the Robinsonade from the original *Robinson Crusoe* to such modern works as *Island of the Blue Dolphins* and *Lord of the Flies*.

B1732   LINDBERG, MARY ANNE. "Survival Literature in Children's Fiction." *EE* 51 (March 1974):329-35.

A bibliographic essay covering a wide range of literature for children with the theme of survival which may be classified as types of Robinsonades.

B1733   TUCKER, NICHOLAS. *The Child and the Book*, pp. 164-68.

Discusses the great appeal of the Robinsonade for children and traces some of its variants.

ROMANCE (Young Adult)

B1734   *Advocate* 3, no. 2 (Winter 1984).

Contains three articles on the teenage romance genre.: Barbara Girion's "A Time to Write About Love," in which she describes the process of writing *In the Middle of a Rainbow*, pp. 73-81; Linda K. Christian's "The New Romances: Selling Jeans on the Outside and Femininity on the Inside," pp. 82-91, which points out the business and feminist implications of the genre, and Patti McWhorter's "Teen Romance Series: One Viewpoint," pp. 92-97, which reports on a study of adolescents responses to the books and concludes that they are more likely to have a negative effect on children aged ten to thirteen than on older children who recognize their similarity and unreality and read them purely for fun.

B1735   COUNCIL ON INTERRACIAL BOOKS FOR CHILDREN. "Romance Series for Young Readers: A Report to Educators and Parents in Concert with the National Education Association." *IRBC* 12, nos. 4-5 (1981):3-31.

The issue is devoted to the burgeoning romance series for young readers. Articles include: a discussion on the marketing of the series by Selma Lanes, and analyses of the Wildfire series by Brett Harvey, and of the Wishing Star series by Emily Strauss Watson, the Sweet Dreams series by Brett Harvey, and the First Love series from Silhouette by Sharon Wigutoff. Also includes an article an article on formula writing by Donnarae MacCann, a comparison of the Harlequin adult romances with the teen variety, and excerpts from the guidelines given to romance writers.

B1736 DONELSON, KENNETH. "The Old Romanticism: Of Wishing and Winning." In *Literature for Today's Young Adults*, pp. 205-27.
Divides the genre into adventure-romance and love-romance. *One Fat Summer* is seen as the prime example of the former; *Seventeenth Summer* and *Forever* of the latter.

B1737 JAFFEE, CYRISSE. "More Pain Than Pleasure: Teen Romances." *SLJ* 25 (January 1979):30-31.
"Nowhere is sex-role stereotyping, bias, and hypocrisy--not to mention poor writing--as blatant and prevalent as the peculiar genre known as teen romance." Analyzes briefly a number of classic and well-known titles.

B1738 JENKINSON, DAVE. "The Young Adult Romance: A Second Glance (Sigh!)." *Emergency Librarian* 11 (May-June 1984):10-13.
Explores the world of teenage romance series, finding similarities to the world of fast-food hamburgers. Includes references.

B1739 KAYE, MARILYN. "Young Adult Romance: Revival and Reaction." *TON* 38 (Fall 1981):42-47.
Defends the recent publication of teenage romance series, answering the attack upon them by Elaine Wagner in *IRBC*. Argues that the very fact that many young people want to read them justifies their existence.

B1740 KUNDIN, SUSAN G. "Romance Versus Reality: A Look at Young Adult Romantic Fiction." *TON* 41, no. 4 (Summer 1985):361-68.
"The purpose of this study is to compare the treatment of adolescent 'problem concerns' in formula romance fiction to the treatment of these problems in contemporary realistic fiction."

B1741 KUZNETS, LOIS, and ZARIN, EVE. "Sweet Dreams for Sleeping Beauties: Pre-Teen Romances." *ChLAQ* 7, no. 1 (Spring 1982):28-32. (Reprinted in Nodelman, *Festschrift*, pp. 14-17.)
Applies John Cawelti's framework (from *Adventure, Mystery and Romance*) for analyzing formulaic literature to preteen romances. Bantam Book's Sweet Dreams series books are compared and contrasted with Maureen Daly's *Seventeenth Summer*, Louise Fitzhugh's *Harriet the Spy*, and Judy Blume's *It's Not the End of the World*.

B1742 PARRISH, BERTA. "Put a Little Romantic Fiction Into Your Reading Program." *Journal of Reading* 26 (April 1983):610-15.
Explores the recent trends in romance fiction for young adults; offers definitions of the genre and suggestions for further research.

ROPE-SKIPPING RHYMES

B1743 ABRAHAMS, ROGER D. *Jump-Rope Rhymes: A Dictionary.* Austin: University of Texas Press, 1969, 228 pp.

Includes a scholarly introduction plus an extensive, annotated listing of rhymes and their sources.

B1744   BUTLER, FRANCELIA. "'Over the Garden Wall/I Let the Baby Fall': The Poetry of Rope-Skipping." *Children's Literature* 3 (1974):186-95.
An international survey of rope-skipping rhymes, pointing out common themes.

B1745   -----. "Skip Rope Rhymes as a Reflection of American Culture." *Children's Literature* 5 (1976):104-16. (Reprinted in Butler, *Sharing*, pp. 8-14.)
Examines skip-rope rhymes as a reflection of society.

RUNAWAYS

B1746   MARSHALL, KRISTINE E. "Transcending Trendiness: Treatment of Runaways in Adolescent Fiction." *English Journal* 70 (December 1981):58-62.
Compares five works, three of which she classifies as weak-- Jeannette Eyerly's *See Dave Run*, Hila Colman's *Claudia, Where Are You?*, and Gertrude Samuels's *Run, Shelley, Run!*--with two she classifies as strong: Jean Renvoize's *A Wild Thing* and Irene Hunt's *No Promises in the Wind*.

RURAL LIFE

B1747   BUSWELL, LIN. "Rural Youth: The Forgotten Minority." *ALAN Review* 11, no. 2 (Winter 1984):12-14.
Points out lack of representation of rural families in recent books.

SCANDINAVIA

B1748   DALPHIN, MARCIA. "Children of the North in Books." *Horn Book* 17 (January-February 1941):39-51.
A survey of books set in Scandinavia. Includes a reading list.

B1749   PERMIN, IB. "Current Trends in Scandinavian Children's Literature: Responsibility." In Koefoed, *Children's Literature*, pp. 41-44.
Discusses issues of censorship, truth, and responsibility, especially in Scandinavia.

B1750   *Phaedrus* 2, no. 1 (Spring 1975):3-15.
Special issue devoted to children's literature in Scandinavia.

B1751   SCHEI, KARI. "Children's Books of Today: A Scandinavian Seminar." *Signal* 15 (September 1974):136-40.
Summarizes Scandinavian debates and views on children's literature as expressed at a seminar held at the Nordic Folk Academy in Kungalv in 1972.

SCHOOL STORIES

B1752   ANDREWS, R.C. "German School-Story: Some Observations on Paul Schallück and Thomas Valentin." *German Life and Letters* 23 (January 1970):103-19.
Explores the German school-story, concentrating on two of "the

best novels to have come from Germany since the war: Paul Schallück's *Engelbert Reineke*, and Thomas Valentin's *Die Unberatenen*.

B1753   CADOGAN, MARY, and CRAIG, PATRICIA. "Jolly Schoolgirls and Bosom Friends" and "Anti-Soppists and Others." In *You're a Brick*, pp. 111-24, 178-205.
The first chapter discusses the school stories of Angela Brazil, the second primarily those of Dorita Fairlie Bruce and Elinor Brent-Dyer. Pages 227-49 discuss the periodical *The School Friend* and pages 250-62 discuss *The Schoolgirls' Own*.

B1754   CROUCH, MARCUS. "School-Home-Family." In *The Nesbit Tradition*, pp. 161-70.
Discusses the British school story. Authors include Elfrida Vipont, William Mayne, and Kathleen Peyton.

B1755   EAGLING, PETER; HANNABUSS, STUART; and LITHERLAND, BARRY. "Fiction for Children, 1970-1980: 2. School Stories: A Symposium." *CLE*, n.s. 13, no. 2 (Summer 1982):51-72.
A carefully selected list with capsule reviews of school stories published for children between 1970 and 1980.

B1756   ELLIS, ANNE. "The Misfortunes of Angela." *Junior Bookshelf* 41 (June 1977):145-49.
Points out the strengths and weaknesses of the school story as exemplified in the work of Angela Brazil.

B1757   OSBORNE. EDGAR. "In Defense of the School Story." *Junior Bookshelf* 11 (July 1947):62-69.
Traces changes in the genre as they reflect changes in society and argues that it is time to set the school story in a new direction again.

B1758   PROTHEROUGH, ROBERT. "'True' and 'False' in School Fiction." *British Journal of Educational Studies* 27 (June 1979):140-53.
Examines the authenticity of the classic British school story, concentrating on the period from 1906 to 1930.

B1759   QUIGLY, ISABEL. *Heirs of Tom Brown: The English School Story.* London: Chatto & Windus, 1982, 296 pp.
An extensive study of the genre, including chapters on Thomas Hughes, Frederick William Farrar, Talbot Baines Reed, F. Anstey's *Vice Verse*, and Kipling's *Stalky & Co.*; three school love stories: H.S. Sturgis's *Tim*, J.E.C. Welldon's *Gerald Eversley's Friendship*, and Horace Annesley Vachell's *The Hill*; Sir Shane Lesley's *The Oppidan* and Arnold Lunn's *The Harrovians*; books by P.G. Wodehouse and Hugh Walpole; G.F. Bradby's *The Lanchester Tradition*; Alec Waugh's *The Loom of Youth*; girls' school stories; popular minor writers; the school story at war; and the decline and fall of the school story. Includes references and a bibliography.

B1760   RICH, ANITA, and BERNSTEIN, JOANNE C. "The Picture Book Image of Entering School." *LA* 52 (October 1975):978-82.
Examines the images of children entering school for the first time as presented in over thirty picture books.

B1761   SAUL, E. WENDY. "The School Story in America, 1900-1940: A Socio-Historical Analysis of the Genre." Ph.D. dissertation, University of Wisconsin-Madison, 1981, 302 pp., DA 42:3481A.

Examines values and assumptions, influences, and historical and biographical aspects of the school story. Contrasts the "Brahmin" narrative, the "mass-market" tale, and the "religious story." Finally, suggests how literature on the "hidden curriculum" is useful in interpreting these tales.

B1762   TATHAM, C.S. "Yesterday's Schoolgirls." *Junior Bookshelf* 33 (December 1969):349-51.

Argues that the genre deserves more appreciation. Written upon the occasion of Elinor Brent-Dyer's death.

B1763   TUCKER, NICHOLAS. "School Stories, 1970-1980." *CLE*, n.s. 13, no. 2 (Summer 1982):73-79.

The main focus of school stories has shifted from the boarding school to the public (state-operated) day school. Tucker analyzes this trend and others in the development of the school story.

SCIENCE

B1764   ADLER, IRVING. "On Writing Science Books for Children." *Horn Book* 41 (October 1965):524-29.

Describes his goals as a science writer for children.

B1765   *Appraisal: Science Books for Children.* Boston: Boston University, School of Education and New England Roundtable of Children's Librarians. Published three times a year.

Includes numerous articles and reviews of children's science books.

B1766   BELL, THELMA HARRINGTON. "On Science Writing for Young People." *Horn Book* 38 (June 1962):248-54.

Discusses key considerations in science writing for children, among them organization of material, creation of atmosphere, accuracy of facts, clarity, and devices for maintaining the reader's interest.

B1767   BLUM, ABRAHAM. "Science Magazines for Youth in Five Countries--Different Approaches." *Science Education* 65 (January 1981):65-70.

Compares science magazines for youth in the United States, Britain, Israel, Kenya, and Zambia.

B1768   BONN, GEORGE S., ed. "Science Materials for Children and Young People." *Library Trends* 22 (April 1974):415-539.

Entire issue is devoted to the writing, editing, selecting, and evaluating of science materials for children and young people. Includes Zena Sutherland's "Science As Literature," Irene K. Logsdon's "Science Periodicals for Children and Young People," and Harry Stubbs's "The Stockpile."

B1769   CARR, JO, comp. "Science: The Excitement of Discovery." In *Beyond Fact*, pp. 43-87.

Contains an introductory essay by Carr, "Clarity in Science Writing"; Kathryn Wolff's "Reviewing Science Books for children" (adapted from "*AAS Science Books*: A Selection Tool," *Library Trends* 22

[April 1974]:453-62); Millicent Selsam's "Writing About Science for Children" (reprinted from Fenwick's *A Critical Approach to Children's Literature*); Pamela Giller's "Science Books for Young Children" (reprinted from *Appraisal: Science Books for Children* 13 [Winter 1980]:1-6); Harry C. Stubbs's "Selecting Science Books for Children" (originally published as "The Stockpile" in *Library Trends* 22 [April 1974]:477-84); Dennis Flanagan's "Science and the Literary Imagination" (originally published as "To Each Generation Its Own Rabbits" in *WLB* 49 [October 1974]:152-56); and Zena Sutherland's "Science as Literature" (reprinted from *Library Trends* 22 [April 1974]:485-89).

B1770   DAVIES, JANE. "Evaluating Books on Science." *TON* 17 (March 1961):48-52.

    Provides guidelines for evaluating science books; includes examples of ways in which books fail to live up to each of her criteria.

B1771   DE LUCA, GERALDINE, and NATOV, RONI. "Who's Afraid of Science Books?: An Interview with Seymour Simon." *L&U* 6 (1982):10-27.

    Simon answers questions about his career and his books, his views on science books for children, and science book reviewing.

B1772   DOUGHTY, FRANCES W. "Selection Criteria: Science Books for Children." *Horn Book* 41 (April 1965):195-200. (Reprinted in *Bookbird* 3 [1966]:12-14.)

    Suggests the following criteria: authenticity, timeliness, stimulation, prose style, and integration of text and illustration.

B1773   LAUBER, PATRICIA. "What Makes an Appealing and Readable Science Book?" *L&U* 6 (1982):5-9.

    Stresses the importance of good illustration, of explaining rather than of simply describing, of story line, of an overview or framework, of accuracy, and of the use of analysis.

B1774   PETTUS, ELOISE SPENCER. "A Study of The Treatment of Ecology, Air Pollution, and Water Pollution in Selected Recommended Books for Elementary Grades Published in The United States, 1960-1975." Ph.D. dissertation, Florida State University, 1977, 235 pp., DA 38:5106A.

    Studies ninety-six children's science books to determine their approach to ecology and analyze their interdisciplinary content.

B1775   PRINGLE, LAURENCE. "Science Done Here." In Hearne, *Celebrating Children's Books*, pp. 108-15.

    Examines science-book writing.

B1776   SCHNEIDER, HERMAN. "What Is a Good Science Book?" *Horn Book* 27 (September 1951):344-51.

    Presents criteria for judging science books. Includes a bibliography of recommended titles. Asks: Does the author write clearly and lucidly? Is the book clearly illustrated? In an experiment or project book, are the activities safe? Are the projects and experiments satisfying and workable? Is the book accurate? Stresses basic values to look for: total impact of the book is reassuring, permits the child to achieve a sense of participation, has a sense of human importance and dignity, stays with reality, enlarges a child's understanding of the world, has literary quality.

B1777 "Science Trade Books--Writing--Illustrating--Using--101 of 1972." *Science and Children* 10 (April 1973):19-26.
Includes Millicent Selsam's "Writing Science Books for Children," pp. 19-20, Jeanne Bendick's "Illustrating Science Books for Children," pp. 20-21, Glenn Blough's "Using Science Books with Children," pp. 21-22, and a list of outstanding science trade books for children for 1972.

B1778 *Scientific American.*
Since 1949 the December issue has contained reviews of science books for children.

B1779 SELSAM, MILLICENT. "Criticizing the Critics." In Hearne, *Celebrating Children's Books*, pp. 116-21.
Examines science book reviewing and points out the ingredients of good science books and good science book reviews.

B1780 -----. "Writing About Science for Children." *Library Quarterly* 37 (January 1967):96-99.
"To write about science for children an author needs to know science, to know children, and to know how to write--particularly to understand how to communicate with children on their level."

B1781 STUBBS, HARRY C. "The Impossible Book." *Appraisal* 4 (Fall 1971):1-3. (Reprinted in in Carr, *Beyond Fact*, pp. 198-201.)
Proposes an ideal science book that fairly treats controversial issues, but which, he admits, is probably impossible.

B1782 WUNDERHEILER, LUITGARD. "A Psychological Basis for Judging Children's Literature Dealing with Nature and Science." *Library Quarterly* 37 (January 1967):23-31.
Feels it is unfortunate that the child is frequently "introduced to scientific systems, the experimental basis of which he has never grasped." And thus the child "cannot ever challenge the scientific system." Concludes that "It may be that, if in books and conversations we could provide children with experiences that are puzzling we would be helping to do a much better job of educating scientists than insisting that they swallow logical systems that are entirely out of step with their experience."

SCIENCE FICTION

B1783 ANTCZAK, JANICE. "The Mythos of a New Romance: A Critical Analysis of Science Fiction for Children as Informed by the Literary Theory of Northrop Frye." D.L.S., Columbia University, 1979, 376 pp., DA 42:208A.
Examines a selection of science fiction for children from ages eight to fourteen that reveals "a pattern of imagery which conforms to that of the romance mode." Concludes that "In light of Frye's theory of the unity of literature's structural principles, science fiction is myth, the myth of contemporary society."

B1784 -----. *Science Fiction: The Mythos of a New Romance.* New York: Neal Schuman, 1985, 250 pp.

Based on the doctoral dissertation above.

B1785   BEREIT, VIRGINIA F. "The Genre of Science Fiction." *EE* 46 (November 1969):895-900.

Once again, covering types of science fiction, defintions of the genre, and ways in which it is "more like story or less like story."

B1786   BOVA, BEN. "From Mad Professors to Brilliant Scientists." *Library Journal* 98 (1973):1646-49 *and SLJ* 19 (May 1973):36-39. (Reprinted in Gerhardt, *Issues in Children's Book Selection*, pp. 163-67.)

Provides an overview of science fiction and its appeal to the young. "Until someone actually does invent a time machine, science fiction is the best way we have to examine tomorrow."

B1787   *Children's Literature in Education*, n.s. 14, no. 4 (Winter 1983):222-42.

Issue includes "Fiction for Children, 1920-1982: 3. Science Fiction," a symposium containing reviews of fourteen titles selected for special mention and a greater number of other critically annotated titles. Brian Earnshaw's "Planets of Awful Dread," an overview of recent children's science fiction, follows, pp. 237-42.

B1788   CROUCH, MARCUS. "To the Stars." In *The Nesbit Tradition*, pp. 48-56.

Divides modern science fiction writers into followers of Wells and followers of Verne. Discusses John Christopher, Peter Dickinson, Andre Norton, and Robert A. Heinlein.

B1789   DONELSON, KENNETH. "Science Fiction." In *Literature for Today's Young Adults*, pp. 259-65.

Contains a checklist for evaluating "imaginative literature." Discusses characteristics of science fiction that appeals to young people, not necessarily science fiction written for young people.

B1790   EAGLEN, AUDREY B. "Alternatives: A Bibliography of Books and Periodicals on Science Fiction and Fantasy." *TON* 39 (Fall 1982):96-102.

B1791   EGOFF, SHEILA. "Science Fiction." In *Only Connect*, 1st ed., pp. 384-98.

Briefly surveys the origins of science fiction and contemporary science fiction for youth. Sees youth's fascination for science fiction as a reaction to their disillusionment. They seek either a totally different world or a changed human nature.

B1792   -----. "Science Fiction." In *Thursday's Child*, pp. 130-58.

Explores the nature, origins, and recent developments in science fiction for children. Trends identified are pessimism about the future, concern with societal and sociological organization, and parapsychology. Cites Rosemary Harris's *A Quest for Orion* as a novel that has succeeded in unifying multiple subgenres of science fiction.

B1793   ENGDAHL, SYLVIA L. "The Changing Role of Science Fiction in Children's Literature." *Horn Book* 47 (October 1971):449-55. (Reprinted in Haviland, *Children and Literature*, pp. 250-55.)

Sees a science fiction for "people who are searching for touch-stones in a rapidly changing world. . . . I feel it can offer a wider perspective on reality, leading young people to view the future not with our own era's gloom and despair, but with the broader realism of renewed hope."

B1794 ERNES, ALBERT FRANÇOIS. "A Content Assessment of Science Fiction from 1947-1979 with Implications for the Elementary Social Studies Curriculum." Ph.D. dissertation, University of Akron, 1980, 401 pp., DA 41:933A.

Analyzes children's science fiction in terms of the following categories: sociology, anthropology, psychology, political science, economics, geography, and history.

B1795 ESMONDE, MARGARET P. "After Armageddon: The Postcataclysmic Novel for Young Readers." *Children's Literature* 6 (1977):211-20. (Reprinted in Lenz, *Young Adult Literature*, pp. 440-48.)

Discusses fifteen recent novels for young people that foresee "the overthrow of our way of life through socioeconomic breakdown--often coupled with ecological disaster."

B1796 -----, ed. "Special Issue: Children's Science Fiction." *ChLAQ* 5, no. 4 (Winter 1981):1-48. (Reprinted in part in Dooley, *First Steps*, pp. 54-68.)

Includes "Fantasy, Science Fiction and the Mushroom Planet Books," by Eleanor Cameron; an overview by Margaret Esmonde (reprinted as "Children's Science Fiction," in Bator, *Signposts*, pp. 284-87); "Writing for the 'Electric Boy': Notes on the Origins of Science Fiction," by Frances J. Molson; "L. Frank Baum: Science Fiction and Fantasy," by David L. Greene; "Science Fiction in the Classroom," by Carol D. Stevens; and reviews by Susan R. Gannon and Perry Nodelman of books of recent science fiction criticism.

B1797 GREENLAW, M. JEAN. "Science Fiction: Images of the Future, Shadows of the Past." *TON* 39 (Fall 1982):64-71.

Defines science fiction and illustrates essential elements with selected examples from recent literature for children and young adults.

B1798 -----. "Science Fiction: Impossible! Impossible! or Prophetic?" *EE* 48 (April 1971):196-202. (Reprinted in White, *Children's Literature*, pp. 91-100.)

Maintains that science fiction can help children interpret the issues created by the impact of science and technology on society. Considers themes of social control, respect for individual differences, and the effects of war.

B1799 -----. "A Study of the Impact of Technology on Human Values as Reflected in Modern Science Fiction for Children." Ph.D. dissertation, Michigan State University, 1970, 201 pp., DA 31:5665A.

Concludes that children's science fiction contains "significant themes and values that are a commentary on society in general and technology's impact on human values in specific."

B1800 HARTWELL, DAVID G. "The Golden Age of Science Fiction Is Twelve." *TON* 39 (Fall 1982):39-53.

Discusses science fiction fans, the status of science fiction writing, conventions, types, functions, and the relationship of science fiction to fantasy.

B1801   KETTERER, DAVID. "Canadian Science Fiction: A Survey." *CCL* 10 (1977-78):18-23.

Explores the nature of Canadian science fiction, its distinctive qualities, and the reasons for its paucity.

B1802   L'ENGLE, MADELEINE. "Childlike Wonder and the Truths of Science Fiction." *Children's Literature* 19 (1982):102-10.

Argues that often children are able to accept the truths of the wider world presented by science fiction and fantasy better than adults.

B1803   LYNN, ELIZABETH A. "Women in, of, and on Science Fiction." *TON* 39 (Fall 1982):72-75.

A feminist analysis, with brief examples from books by both men and women.

B1804   MILNER, JOSEPH O. "Oathkeepers and Vagrants: Meliorist and Reactive World Views in Science Fiction." *ChLAQ* 10, no. 2 (Summer 1985):71-73.

Compares Sylvia Engdahl's *Enchantress from the Stars*, which represents a "meliorist" or positive and progressive view of human nature, with John Christopher's *The White Mountains*, which represents a "reactive" and skeptical view.

B1805   MOLSON, FRANCIS J. "Children's Science Fiction." In *Anatomy of Wonder: A Critical Guide to Science Fiction*. Edited by Neil Barron. 2d. ed. New York: Bowker, 1981, pp. 335-78.

Provides an overview of children's science fiction beginning with Robert Heinlein's *Rocket Ship Galileo* (1947). Includes references. A critically annotated bibliography of children's science fiction follows, pp. 342-78.

B1806   -----. "The Winston Science Fiction Series and the Development of Children's Science Fiction." *Extrapolation* 25 (Spring 1984):34-50.

Explores the influence of the science fiction series published by the John C. Winston Company during the 1950s on the development of the genre.

B1807   MOSKOWITZ, SAM. "Teen-Agers: Tom Swift and the Syndicate." In *Strange Horizons: The Spectrum of Science*. New York: Charles Scribner's Sons, 1976, pp. 160-81.

Traces the history of science fiction for teenagers from the 1890s through the 1960s, concentrating especially on the Stratemeyer Syndicate and similar formula fiction. Argues that Howard R. Garis wrote the *Tom Swift* books.

B1808   MYERS, ALAN. "Science Fiction in the Classroom." *CLE*, n.s. 9, no. 4 (Winter 1978):182-87.

Argues for the use of fine science fiction in social science and science classrooms.

B1809   NIMON, MAUREEN. "SF: The Corridors of Time." *Orana* 18 (February 1982):13-19.

Categorizes forms of science fiction stories as journeys through the unknown, through time, and through new worlds.

B1810   PATTOW, DONALD J. "A Critical Chronology of Speculative Fiction for Young People." Ph.D. dissertation, University of Wisconsin, 1977, 168 pp., DA 38:7122A.
   Examines the various attitudes and projections of the future in speculative fiction for young people. Finds that most emphasize the "dark side of human nature" and "predict mankind's fall."

B1811   "Reflections on Fantasy and Science Fiction." *TON* 39 (Fall 1982):39-102.
   Special Issue. Individual articles have been indexed separately in this bibliography.

B1812   ROBERTS, THOMAS J. "Science Fiction and the Adolescent." *Children's Literature* 2 (1973):87-91. (Reprinted in Bator, *Signposts*, pp. 288-93.)
   Calls science fiction a "mode" not a "genre." Suggests that machines, aliens, sentimentality, and emphasis on the future appeal to adolescents.

B1813   TATE, JANICE M. "Sexual Bias in Science Fiction for Children." *EE* 50 (October 1973):1061-64.
   Discusses three classifications of science fiction for children: that with only boys and men as active characters, that with girls and women in leading roles, and that in which, more recently, males and females play roles of equal importance.

B1814   WEHMEYER, LILLIAN BIERMANN. "Futuristic Children's Novels as a Mode of Communication." *Research in the Teaching of English* 13 (May 1979):137-52.
   Reports on a study to apply the Westley-MacLean communications model to children's novels of the future. Found children's novelists to be more optimistic than the futurists on whose work their fiction is based, in terms of energy and fuel sources, but less optimistic with regard to system breaks, technology, and interpersonal relations; and more conservative about family structure and religious beliefs. On the whole, however, the study concludes that children's novelists have not softened the futurists' images of tomorrow.

B1815   -----. "World Future Images in Children's Literature." Ph.D. dissertation, University of California, Berkeley, 1978, 258 pp., DA 39:5301A.
   Explores utopias, pastorals, and distopias written for children between 1964 and 1977, showing the similarities and dissimilarities between science fiction for adults and for children.

B1816   WITUCKE, VIRGINIA. "The Treatment of Fantasy and Science Fiction in Juvenile and Young Adult Literature Texts." *TON* 39 (Fall 1982):77-91.
   Finds standard texts used for introducing teachers and librarians to children's literature deficient in their treatment of science fiction and fantasy.

SCOTLAND

B1817   LEODHAS, SORCHE NIC. "Scottish History Tales." *Horn Book* 43 (June 1967):323-27. (Reprinted in Norton, *Folk Literature*, pp. 139-44.)
   Argues that the Scottish history tales passed down by oral tradition should not be neglected by collectors.

SEA

B1818   CRAGO, HUGH, and CRAGO, MAUREEN. "A World Beneath the Waves." *Signal* 11 (May 1973):74-87.
Surveys the imagery of the underwater otherworld in children's fiction from 1840 to 1971.

B1819   YOLEN, JANE. "The Literary Underwater World." *LA* 57 (April 1980):403-12.
Surveys children's fiction and folklore concerning underwater forms of life such as selchies, mermaids, and mermen, and briefly discusses a number of recent works.

SERIES BOOKS

B1820   ABRAHAMSON, Richard. "They're Reading the Series Books So Let's Use Them: or Who Is Shaun Cassidy?" *Journal of Reading* 22 (March 1979):523-30.
Argues that series books not only provide entertainment but can be used to teach critical reading.

B1821   ARMSTRONG, JUDITH. "In Defense of Adventure Stories." *CLE*, n.s. 13, no. 3 (Autumn 1982):115-21.
Discusses the hold of the series adventure story on young readers and hints that the genre may be both misunderstood and undervalued.

B1822   BECKMAN, MARGARET. "Why Not the Bobbsey Twins?" *Library Journal* 89 (15 November 1964):4612-13, 4627. (Also in *Ontario Library Review* 48 [August 1964]:148-50.)
Iterates many of the standard arguments against the purchase of series books by libraries.

B1823   DEANE, PAUL C. "The Persistence of Uncle Tom: An Examination of the Image of the Negro in Children's Fiction Series." *Journal of Negro Education* 37 (Spring 1968): 140-45. (Reprinted in MacCann, *Black American*, pp. 116-23.
Finds that "Except for removing dialect, the series books are maintaining the traditional image of the Negro."

B1824   DIZER, JOHN T. *Tom Swift and Company: Boys Books by Stratemeyer and Others.* Jefferson, N.C.: McFarland & Co., 1982, 183 pp.
Examines series books, especially those of the Stratemeyer Syndicate, *Tom Swift* in particular (whom he considers the best of the series books heroes). Also includes a chapter on Stratemeyer and science fiction and another examining Stratemeyer's attitudes toward blacks. Includes extensive bibliographies of the series books and a list of secondary sources.

B1825   KINLOCH, LUCY M. "The Menace of the Series Book." *EER* 12 (January 1935):9-11.
Raises the question: Is it better for children to read series books than not to read at all? Or do they deaden the child's mentality with crude language, melodramatic situations, and commonplace vocabulary? The reader may read fifty series books without ever having to use mind or imagination after the first book in the series.

B1826   LAKE, MARY LOUISE. "What's Wrong with Series Books?" *EE* 47 (December 1970):1109-11.
         Argues that the main problem with the series books is that they do not present a true picture of life. They are full of stereotypes and false premises and provide children with a false sense of security.

B1827   LANES, SELMA. "A Series Is a Series Is a Series." In *Down the Rabbit Hole*, pp. 128-45.
         Distinguishes between good and undistinguished series, and analyzes the characteristics and appeal of both types.

B1828   MacDONALD, J. FREDERICK. "The Foreigner in Juvenile Series Fiction, 1900-1945." *Journal of Popular Culture* 8, no. 3 (Winter 1974):534-48.
         "This literature reveals a dramatic picture of race-consciousness, xenophobia, and imperialism." Documents the portrayals of various ethnic groups in series books.

B1829   MacLEOD, ANNE SCOTT. "Secret in The Trash Bin: On the Perennial Popularity of Juvenile Series Books." *CLE*, n.s. 15, no. 3 (Autumn 1984):127-40.
         Examines common formulaic elements in the books of Horatio Alger and the Stratemeyer Syndicate that may account for their continued popularity.

B1830   MASON, BOBBIE ANN. *Girl Sleuth*. Old Westbury, N.Y.: Feminist Press, 1975, 145 pp.
         Applies critical techniques to "the form and substance" of series books popular with girls. Mason's major focus is on the series book heroines as sex-role models. Major authors discussed are indexed separately in this bibliography.

B1831   MATHIEWS, FRANKLIN K. "Blowing Out the Boy's Brains." *Outlook* 108 (18 November 1914):653.
         The chief scout librarian of the United States makes a vituperative attack on the dangers of series books and "cheap reading."

B1832   NYE, RUSSELL B., ed. "For It Was Indeed He: Books for the Young." In *The Unembarrassed Muse: The Popular Arts in America*. New York: Dial Press, 1970, pp. 60-87.
         Traces the history of series books in America and their influences on the young from Horatio Alger, through Gilbert Patten's Frank Merriwell, to Edward Stratemeyer.

B1833   PRAGER, ARTHUR. *Rascals at Large*. Garden City, N.Y.: Doubleday, 1971, 334 pp.
         Personal recollections and reexaminations of popular series books, primarily Stratemeyer Syndicate publications for boys. Major writers discussed are also indexed individually.

B1834   ROOT, MARY E.S. "Not to Be Circulated." *WLB* 3 (1929):446.
         Root presents "a list of books in series not circulated by standardized libraries." An article in response, "Not to Be Circulated?," by Ernest F. Ayres, follows in March, pp. 528-29, defending the books against librarians' censorship.

B1835   SMITH, JANE S. "Plucky Little Ladies and Stout-Hearted Chums: Serial Novels for Girls, 1900-1920." In *Prospects: An Annual of American Cultural Studies* 3. Edited by Jack Salzman. New York: Burt Franklin, 1977.

Explores the rise in girls' series fiction in the early twentieth century as offering young women fantasies of independence and discovery that "paid little attention to the rewards or even the existence of domestic life."

B1836   SODERBERGH, P.A. "Florida's Image in Juvenile Fiction, 1909-1914." *Florida Historical Quarterly* 51 (October 1972):153-65.

Examines the image of Florida in early twentieth-century juvenile series books.

B1837   -----. "The South in Juvenile Series Books, 1907-1917." *Mississippi Quarterly* 27 (Spring 1974):131-40.

Explores the reinforcement of Southern stereotypes in early twentieth-century series books.

SEX

B1838   BONE, SANDRA FAYE. "Human Sexual Information, Behaviors, and Attitudes as Revealed in American Realistic Fiction for Young People, 1965-1974." Ph.D. dissertation, Michigan State University, 1977, 435 pp., DA 39:275A.

Explores the information, behaviors, and attitudes regarding human sexuality as revealed in young adult realistic fiction published between 1965 and 1974.

B1839   DONELSON, KENNETH. "Sex: Because It's There." In *Literature for Today's Young Adults*, pp. 407-11.

Summarizes conflicting views of professionals on the treatment of sex in young adult fiction.

B1840   KRAUS, W. KEITH. "Cinderella in Trouble: Still Dreaming and Losing." *SLJ* 21 (January 1975):18-22.

Traces the changes in portrayal of teenage sex and pregnancy in young adult fiction from Henry Gregor Felsen's *Two and the Town* in 1952, through Ann Head's *Mr. and Mrs. BoJo Jones* (1968), and Paul Zindel's *My Darling, My Hamburger* (1969), up to the mid-1970s. Concludes that the old double standard is reinforced by the so-called new realism, and the fiction follows a formula "as strict and uncompromising in moral tone as earlier romance novels."

B1841   POLLACK, PAMELA D. "Sex In Children's Fiction: Freedom to Frighten?" *SIECUS Report* 5, nos. 1-2 (May 1977):15-16. (Reprinted in Lenz, *Young Adult Literature*, pp. 198-204.)

Argues that much recent children's fiction dealing with sexual themes is "not free of old stereotypes about male/female relationships or misbegotten ideas about sexuality." Briefly discusses several popular works and concludes, "Our young people are being shortchanged."

B1842   WERSBA, BARBARA, and FRANK, JOSETTE. "Sexuality in Books for Children: An Exchange." *Library Journal* 98 (15 February 1973):620 and *SLJ* 19 (February 1973):44.

Wersba "would like to see more sex in children's books," whereas Frank would like to stress values and argues that there is a difference between books children are given with approval by parents and teachers and those they happen upon by themselves.

B1843   *Wilson Library Bulletin* 46 (October 1971):144-84.
Special issue on sex in children's books. Includes an introductory essay by Joan Bodger Mercer, John Newfield's "The Thought, Not Necessarily the Deed: Sex in Some of Today's Juvenile Novels," which provides detailed discussions of Annabel and Edgar Johnson's *Count Me Gone* and John Donovan's *I'll Get There, It Better Be Worth the Trip*; a guide to nonfiction by Eula T. White and Roberta Friedman; Diane Wolkstein's "Old and New Sexual Messages in Fairy Tales" (reprinted in White, *Children's Literature*, pp. 40-44), in which she analyzes "Cinderella," "Sleeping Beauty," "Twelve Dancing Princesses," and other classic tales, concluding with a discussion of Maurice Sendak's *In the Night Kitchen*, which she feels may represent a new sexuality; and Mary Ritchie Key's "The Role of Male and Female in Children's Books--Dispelling All Doubts."

SEX EDUCATION

B1844   BREWER, JOAN SCHERER. "A Guide to Sex Education Books: Dick Active, Jane Passive." *IRBC* 6, nos. 3-4 (1975):1, 12.
A survey of children's books about sex reveals that "sexist stereotypes abound and racism is implicit in the absence of characters other than whites in illustrations." Includes brief reviews of over a dozen books.

B1845   MARCELL, MICHAEL. "Sex Education Books: An Historical Sampling of the Literature." *CLE*, n.s. 13, no. 3 (Autumn 1982):138-49.
Looks at the changes in sex education books for young children from the early days of the twentieth century to the present.

SEX ROLES

B1846   AMERICAN LIBRARY ASSOCIATION. Social Responsibilities Roundtable Task Force on Women. "Women: A Recommended List of Print and Non-Print Materials." In *Mediacenter* (May 1975):36-41. (Reprinted in Varlejs, *Young Adult Literature*, pp. 256-85.)
In addition to an extensive list of materials, the article presents a list of criteria for appraising materials.

B1847   ASHBY, M., and WITTMAIER, B. "Attitude Changes in Children After Exposure to Stories About Women in Traditional or Nontraditional Occupations." *Journal of Educational Psychology* 70 (December 1978):945-49.
A study of fourth-grade girls shows that those who were read nontraditional stories "rated traditionally male jobs and characteristics as appropriate for females more than girls who heard traditional stories."

B1848   ASHTON, ELEANOR. "The Effect of Sex-role Stereotyped Picture Books on the Play Behavior of Three and Four Year Old Children." Ed.D. dissertation, University of Massachusetts, 1978, 158 pp., DA 39:1310A.

Found that exposure to sex-role stereotyped and nonstereotyped activities in picture books influenced the behavior of young children.

B1849 BARTA, PATRICIA ANN BROCK. "A Study of Children's Reactions to the Assertive Behavior of Female Characters in Books." Ph.D. dissertation, University of Minnesota, 1979, 161 pp., DA 40:3105A.
Studies the responses of pre-fourth- and pre-sixth-grade students to the assertiveness of female characters in Carolyn Haywood's *Pat and Eddie* and E.L. Konigsburg's *From the Mixed-Up Files of Mrs. Basil E. Frankweiler.*

B1850 BEREAUD, SUSAN R. "Sex Role Images in French Children's Books." *Journal of Marriage and the Family* 37 (February 1975):194-207.
Finds similar patterns of sex role portrayals (strong male bias and strict sex role stereotyping of characters) in both French and American picture books.

B1851 BERNSTEIN, JOANNE. "Changing Roles of Females in Books for Young Children." *Reading Teacher* 27 (March 1974):545-49.
Examines a number of recent books with girls and women in nontraditional, nonstereotyped roles.

B1852 BINGHAM, JANE, and SCHOLT, GRAYCE. "Didacticism in New Dress: A Look at 'Free' Stories." *TON* 32 (April 1976):253-60.
Examines children's literature as a vehicle for women's liberation. Concludes that "So far there have been very few 'free' stories and poems that can qualify as literature, that help the child to see difficult relationships, to understand complex problems, to *feel* the joy and sorrow of life as it really is."

B1853 BRACKEN, JEANNE, and WIGUTOFF, SHARON. "Sugar and Spice: That's What Children's Books Are Still Made Of." *Women's Studies Newsletter* 5, no. 3 (Summer 1977). (Reprinted in *Emergency Librarian* 5 [March 1978]:3-5.)
Finds portrayals of female roles unchanged despite the feminist movement.

B1854 CZAPLINSKI, SUZANNE M. *Sexism in Award Winning Picture Books.* Pittsburgh, Pa.: Know, Inc., 1972, 104 pp. (Based on M.A. thesis, University of Wisconsin, 1972.)
Reviews existing literature on sexism in children's picture books and the psychological literature relating to children's formation of sex stereotypes. Examines a sampling of children's picture books from the 1940s to the 1970s for portrayals of males and females and their activities and roles. Discusses as specific examples a number of well-known books and popular titles, and concludes, "Sexism or unequal treatment of the sexes does exist within children's picture books."

B1855 DANIELS, DEBORAH. "Sexism in Children's Books: An Honest Outlook." *Catholic Library World* 46 (May 1975):438-41.
Chronicles the growing awareness of the need for unstereotyped sex-role portrayals in children's books.

B1856 DIXON, BOB. "Sexism: Birds in Gilded Cages." In *Catching Them Young*, pp. 1-41.
Discusses the portrayal of female roles by Louisa May Alcott and

Susan Coolidge as well as by more recent writers.

B1857   DOHNER, JAN. "Literature of Change: Science Fiction and Women."
         TON 34 (Spring 1978):261-65.
             Feels that although "they are in short supply, there are science
         fiction books for young people that provide good female characters
         and role models." Points out good and bad examples.

B1858   DONLAN, DAN. "The Negative Image of Women in Children's Litera-
         ture." *EE* 49 (April 1973):604-11.
             This examination of nursery rhymes and folktales reveals that
         "the passive female is portrayed sympathetically; whereas the assertive
         female is portrayed unsympathetically." Discusses the evidence in
         several nursery rhymes and tales.

B1859   ENGEL, ROSALIND E. "Is Unequal Treatment of Females Diminishing
         in Children's Picture Books?" *Reading Teacher* 34 (March
         1981):647-52.
             Identifies the extent of the problem of unequal treatment of
         females in picture books selected for awards, and suggests probable
         causes.

B1860   FEMINISTS ON CHILDREN'S LITERATURE. "A Feminist Look at
         Children's Books." *Library Journal* 96 (15 January 1971):235-40.
         (Reprinted in Gerhardt, *Issues in Children's Book Selection*, pp.
         107-15.)
             Examines the portrayal of sex roles in children's books, dividing
         them into categories of "sexist," "cop-out," "positive," and "especially
         for girls."

B1861   FISHER, ELIZABETH. "Children's Books: The Second Sex, Junior
         Division." *NYTBR*, 24 May 1970, Children's Book sec., pp. 6, 44.
         (Reprinted in *And Jill Came Tumbling After: Sexism in American
         Education*, edited by Judith Stacey, Susan Bereaud, and Joan Daniels
         [New York: Dell, 1974], pp. 116-22; and in White, *Children's Litera-
         ture*, pp. 81-86.)
             This early influential article points out the lack of females and
         their stereotyped representation when they are portrayed in children's
         books.

B1862   FRAAD, HARRIET. "Sex Role Stereotyping and Male-female Character
         Distribution in Popular, Prestigious, and Sex-role Defining Children's
         Literature from 1959 to 1972." Ed.D. dissertation, Columbia Univer-
         sity Teachers College, 1976, 156 pp., DA 36:5295A.
             Compares the ratios of male and female characters to male and
         female stereotypes. Finds a predominance of male characters and
         female stereotypes in most categories of books examined.

B1863   FRASHER, RAMONA S. "Boys, Girls, and *Pippi Longstocking*." *Read-
         ing Teacher* 8 (May 1977):860-63.
             Examines responses of boys and girls to Pippi and finds both
         identify strongly with her.

B1864   GERSONI-STAVN, DIANE. "Feminist Criticism: An Overview."
         Library Journal 99 (15 January 1974):182, 184-85 and *SLJ* 20
         (January 1974):22.
             Sets forth some of the principles and aims of feminist criticism,

and includes comments on its pitfalls and dangers.

B1865   -----. "Up for Discussion: The Skirts in Fiction About Boys: A Maxi
Mess." *Library Journal* 96 (15 January 1971):282-86 and *SLJ* 18
(January 1971):66-70.
Finds that "sweeping sometimes contradictory (and often condem-
natory) . . . statements about the female sex . . . get dropped into
dialogue or inserted as undeveloped asides," and that "the girl friends
and mothers are almost always unrealized or unpleasant characters-
one-dimensional, idealized, insipid, bitchy, or castrating--while
sexually neutral characters, such as little sisters and old ladies, are
most often well conceived and likable."

B1866   GERSONI-STAVN, DIANE, ed. "Propaganda and the Sins of Omission."
In *Sexism and Youth*. New York: Bowker, 1974, pp. 163-384.
Contents: "Women in Children's Literature," by Alleen Pace Nil-
sen, pp. 163-73; "Sex-Role Socialization in Picture Books for Pre-
School Children," by Lenore J. Weitzman et al., pp. 174-95; "Dick
and Jane as Victims: Sex Stereotyping in Children's Readers--
Excerpts," by Women on Words and Images, pp. 196-208; "Run,
Mama, Run: Women Workers in Elementary Readers," by Buford
Stefflre, pp. 209-13; "Liberated Chinese Primers (Let's Write Some
Too)," by Florence Howe, pp. 214-16; "The Negative Image of
Women in Children's Literature," by Dan Donlan, pp. 217-27; "'Some
Day My Prince Will Come': Female Acculturation Through the Fairy
Tale," by Marcia Lieberman.
Louisa May Alcott: The Author of *Little Women* as Feminist,"
by Karen Lindsey, pp. 244-48; "A Feminist Look at Children's
Books," by Feminists on Children's Media, pp. 249-59; "The Skirts in
Fiction about Boys: A Maxi Mess," by Diane Gersoni-Stavn, pp.
260-71; "Feminists Look at the 100 Books: The Portrayal of Women
in Children's Books on Puerto Rican Themes," by Dolores Prida et
al., pp. 272-88; "Reducing the 'Miss Muffet' Syndrome: An Annotated Bibliography," by Diane Gersoni-Stavn, pp. 289-98; "All Preg-
nant Girls Have Boy Babies," by Carolyn G. Heilbrun, pp. 299-302;
and a number of studies of sex role presentations in text books.
Concludes with "Feminist Criticism: An Overview," by Diane Gersoni-Stavn, pp. 377-84.

B1867   GOODELL, CAROL G.   "Sex Differences in Achievement-Related
Behavior in Children's Picture Story Books." Ph.D. dissertation,
Stanford University, 1979, 204 pp., DA 41:525A.
A content analysis of sixty-seven best-selling picture storybooks
published between 1922 and 1974 for "attributes for success of the
main character and their achievement-related behaviors." The focus
is on "sex differences, with secondary emphasis on effects of age,
race, and changes over time."

B1868   GOUGH, PAULINE B.   "Non-Sexist Literature for Children: A Pan-
acea?" *TON* 33 (Summer 1977):334-43.
Discusses the influence of the revival of American feminism on
children's literature, reporting on several studies of sexism in
children's books. Includes references.

B1869   HEARN, PAMELA HINDEN.   "Images of Women in the Leisure Reading Choices of Young People."   Ph.D. dissertation, Southern Illinois
University, Carbondale, 1978, 133 pp., DA 39:643A.

Examines sex-role stereotyping and images of women in popular young adult fiction, finding that male protagonists dominate and have greater freedom of mobility, that there are few positive female role models, and that female crises tend to be limited to insanity, unwanted pregnancy, and abortion.

B1870 HENDLER, MARJORIE R. "An Analysis of Sex Role Attributes, Behaviors, and Occupations in Contemporary Children's Picture Books." Ph.D. dissertation, New York University, 1977, 164 pp., DA 38:782A.

Examines 214 picture books published during 1973-75. Concludes that "picture books published in 1975 show both child and adult characters in less stereotypic behaviors than in 1973."

B1871 HEYN, LEAH. "Children's Books." *Women: A Journal of Liberation* 1, no. 1 (Fall 1969):22-25.

An early feminist appraisal of the role of women as portrayed in children's literature.

B1872 HILLMAN, JUDITH S. "Analysis of Male and Female Roles in Two Periods of Children's Literature." Ph.D. dissertation, University of Nebraska-Lincoln, 1973, 170 pp., DA 34:2562A. (Summary in *Journal of Educational Research* 68 [October 1974]:84-88 and in "Occupational Roles in Children's Literature," *Elementary School Journal* 77 [September 1976]:1-4.)

Finds little change in male and female occupational roles depicted in children's literature between the 1930s and 1960s.

B1873 INTERNATIONAL READING ASSOCIATION COMMITTEE ON SEXISM AND READING. "Guide for Evaluating Sex Stereotyping in Reading Materials." *Reading Teacher* 31 (December 1977):288.

A set of criteria.

B1874 JEDERMAN, JEAN E. "The Sexual Stereotype of Women in Children's Literature." Ed.D. dissertation, Northern Illinois University, 1974, 99 pp., DA 34:6944A.

Examines the "social role of American Women--their marital, maternal, and occupational status--as depicted in literature for intermediate grade children."

B1875 JONES, BARTLETT C. "A New Cache of Liberated Children's Literature--In Some Old Standbys!" *WLB* 49 (September 1974):52-56.

Examines classic works of children's literature, including the fairy tales, for strong female role models.

B1876 JORDAN, ANNE DEVEREAUX. "Sugar n' Spice'n Snails." In Butler, *Sharing*, pp. 343-47.

Traces changing sex-role portrayals in children's literature, concluding that "The stereotypes of the past are falling by the way."

B1877 KAUFMAN, MELISSA MULLIS. "Male and Female Sex Roles in Literature for Adolescents, 1840-1972: A Historical Survey." Ph.D. dissertation, Duke University, 1982, 437 pp., DA 43:750A.

Concludes that stereotypes have become more, not less, entrenched as books become more modern. Finds mothers and fathers tend to be perfect in early books, and negatively portrayed in later books; girl friends are more expressive of feelings for each other than boy friends; friendships become more negative in recent books; many experiences of initiations into manhood, but initiation into womanhood limited to involvement with a man, marriage, or childbirth. The most constant attitude toward girls in boys' books is scorn and contempt; the ideal male has remained the same, while the ideal female has undergone many changes.

B1878 KARNES, ELIZABETH L. "An Analysis of Male and Female Roles in Two Periods of Award-winning Adolescent Literature." Ed.D. dissertation, University of Nebraska-Lincoln, 1975, 244 pp., DA 36:5299A.
Finds no improvement in sex-role stereotyping in recent Newbery-award winning fiction.

B1879 KELTY, JEAN McCLURE. "The Cult of the Kill in Adolescent Fiction." Paper presented at the 12th Annual Conference on English Education in the Elementary School, Cleveland, Ohio, March 1974. ERIC Educational Document Reproduction Service, ED 090 563. (Also in *English Journal* 64 [February 1975]:56-61 and in Lenz, *Young Adult Literature*, pp. 237-44.)
Considerable controversy has been generated by Kelty's claim that "Boys are conditioned via books to the cult of violence and killing as a part of their initiation into the adult world." Books discussed include Marjorie Kinnan Rawlings's *The Yearling*, Fred Gipson's *Old Yeller*, Hal Borland's *When The Legends Die*, and Robert Newton Peck's *A Day No Pigs Would Die*.

B1880 KINMAN, JUDITH R., and HENDERSON, DARWIN L. "An Analysis of Sexism in Newbery Medal Award Books from 1977-84." *Reading Teacher* 38 (May 1985):885-89.
Suggests that the portrayals of girls and women in recent Newbery books are less biased.

B1881 KNODEL, BEA. "Still Far from Equal: Young Women in Literature for Adolescents." ERIC Educational Document Reproduction Service, 1982, 7 pp., ED 217 425.
Examines the role of young women in a number of popular and highly praised adolescent novels and finds a lack of strong positive female role models. Needed are "young women with some of Nancy Drews's independence and dash, but realistically portrayed.

B1882 KNOEPFLMACHER, U.C. "Little Girls Without Their Curls: Female Aggression in Victorian Children's Literature." *Children's Literature* 11 (1983):14-31.
Argues that Juliana Ewing's "Amelia and the Dwarfs" and Francis Hodgson Burnett's "Behind the White Brick" preserve and present "brilliant satirical energies," made possible by "the indulged wish of female aggression in defiance of Victorian taboos," more fully than Burnett's later book *The Secret Garden*.

B1883 KOSS, HELEN GUEBLE. "A Comparison of Sexism in Trade Books for Primary Children, 1950-1953 and 1970-1973." Ph.D. dissertation, University of Connecticut, 1979, 176 pp., DA 40:647A.
Found the following changes in the two time periods: (1) the number of male characters decreased and the number of female characters increased, (2) the number of male main characters decreased, while female main characters increased, and (3) the number of females participating in female-stereotyped activities increased.

B1884 KRAFT, LINDA. "Lost Herstory: The Treatment of Women in Children's Encyclopedias." *Library Journal* 98 (15 January 1973):218-27 and *SLJ* 19 (January 1973):26-35.

Examines the portrayals of women in five recommended sets of children's encyclopedias in areas of women's rights and suffrage, various historical periods, cultural achievements, vocation, the family, and biography.

B1885 LA DOW, STEPHANIE. "A Content-analysis of Selected Picture Books Examining the Portrayal of Sex-Roles and Representation of Males and Females." ERIC Educational Document Reproduction Service, 1976, 59 pp., ED 123 165.

Examines the portrayal of sex roles in 125 preschool-level picture books. Concludes that females are underrepresented and both males and females are limited to stereotyped roles.

B1886 LANES, SELMA. "On Feminism and Children's Books." *Library Journal* 99 (15 January 1974):183.

Argues for a balanced approach to evaluation of children's books, maintaining that although feminist propaganda is healthy and has its place, "we will continue to look to works of true literary quality and depth" to shed light on the "great human problems."

B1887 LEVSTIK, LINDA S. "I'm No Lady!': The Tomboy in Children's Fiction." *CLE*, n.s. 14, no. 1 (Spring 1983):14-20.

"Despite the oft repeated contention that children's fiction has consistently presented a narrow and stereotypical view of the lives of girls and women, a review of books written in the 1920s and 1930s indicates a degree of dissatisfaction with the status quo."

B1888 LUKENS, REBECCA. "Girls: An Affirmation." *Bookbird* 17, no. 1 (1979):12-17.

Explores positive images of girls as heroes in children's fiction.

B1889 McBROOM, GERALDINE S. "Young Realistic Fiction, 1967-1977: Images of Adolescent Male Protagonists." Ph.D. dissertation, Ohio State University, 1979, 196 pp., DA 40:4579A.

Examines contemporary young adult realistic fiction, concentrating on male images. Concludes that the male protagonist is not much different from those in earlier young adult literature: "Despite what earlier research states this character is sensitive and displays a wide range of emotions." Suggests further areas for research and classroom applications.

B1890 "McGraw-Hill Guidelines for Equal Treatment of the Sexes." *SLJ* 21 (January 1975):23-27. (Reprinted in Barron, *Jump Over the Moon*, pp. 249-61.)

Guidelines to be employed by editors from 1975 forward in all the company's nonfiction publications.

B1891 MADSEN, Jane M. "Women and Children's Literature: We Read What We Are and We Are What We Read." In *The Study of Women: Enlarging Perspectives of Social Reality*. Edited by E.C. Snyder. New York: Harper & Row, 1979, pp. 207-27.

Reviews the research on sex-role portrayals in textbooks and storybooks and points out key characteristics of sexism. Includes references and suggested readings.

B1892 MAXWELL, A. "Sexism in the Fairy Tales of Andersen & Perrault: A
       Study." *Children's Libraries Newsletter* 12 (February 1976):20-30.
       Analyzes the depiction of sex roles in several classic tales.

B1893 MORTIMER, MARY, and BRANDLEY, DENISE. "Images of Women
       and Girls in Children's Books." *Australian Library Journal* 28 (20
       April 1979):87-93.
       Surveys sex role portrayals in Australian children's books.

B1894 NELSON, GAYLE. "The Double Standard in Adolescent Novels."
       English Journal 64 (February 1975):53-55. (Reprinted in Lenz,
       Young Adult Literature, pp. 228-31.)
       Examines five popular adolescent novels and finds stereotyped sex
       roles and situations that fail to provide positive and realistic models
       for young women. Finds that women must pay, usually by becoming
       pregnant, for stepping outside of society's bounds.

B1895 NICHOLLS, CHRISTINE. "Sexism and Children's Literature: A Per-
       spective for Librarians." *Orana* 17 (August 1981):105-11.
       Views sexism as a variety of colonialism and analyzes a number
       of well-known books in those terms. Hugh Crago responds in "Sex-
       ism, Literature and Reader-Response" (November 1981):158-62.

B1896 NILSEN, ALLEEN PACE. "Five Factors Contributing to the Unequal
       Treatment of Females in Children's Picture Books." *TON* 34 (Spring
       1978):255-59.
       Reports a decline in numbers of females portrayed in Caldecott
       Medal or Honor Books between 1950 and 1975. Contributing factors
       identified are (1) male bias in career preparation and reading materi-
       als, (2) peculiarities of the English language, (3) sexist literary
       heritage, (4) preponderance of male artists, and (5) sexuality of
       women's bodies.

B1897 -----. "Women in Children's Literature." *College English* 32 (May
       1971):918-26.
       Reports on a study of the portrayal of women in Caldecott award
       and honor books from 1951 to 1970. Finds many instances of ste-
       reotyping and asks for books portraying more independent and active
       girls and an end to the adage that boys will not read books about
       girls. Boys will not "read books about dull children--male or
       female."

B1898 NORSWORTHY, JAMES A., Jr. "In Search of an Image: The Adult
       Male Role in Picture Books." *Catholic Library World* 45 (December
       1973):220-26. (Also in *Kentucky Library Association Bulletin* 38
       [Winter 1974]:9-20.)
       Finds many picture books lack an adult male, that children
       frequently triumph over adult male wisdom, that men are depicted as
       lovable but weak, as too involved in self to understand others'
       problems, as cop-outs, and as mean. Finally, discusses a number of
       picture books that do portray strong, positive adult male characters.

B1899 PARISH, MARGARET. "Women at Work: Housewives and Paid Work-
       ers as Mothers in Contemporary Realistic Fiction for Children."
       Ph.D. dissertation, Michigan State University, 1976, 221 pp., DA

37:7730A.

Examines roles of women (housewives, paid workers, and mothers) as perceived by contemporary social scientists and as perceived by the women authors of a selected group of children's books.

B1900 PAUSACKER, JENNY, and HARPER, JAN. "Liberating Children's Literature from Sexism." In Robinson, M., *Readings in Children's Literature*, pp. 188-206.

Explores ways of counteracting sexism in children's literature, providing numerous examples from the work of the Australian organization of Women's Movement Children's Literature Co-operative.

B1901 PETERSON, C. "The Effect of Traditional and Reversed Sex-Typed Stories on the Kindergarten Child's Sex Role Perceptions." Ph.D. dissertation, University of Minnesota, 1979, 125 pp., DA 40:4884A.

Finds decreased stereotyping in the behavior of kindergarten girls who were exposed to reverse sex-typed stories.

B1902 PYLE, WILMA J. "Sexism in Children's Literature." *Theory Into Practice* 15 (April 1976):116-19.

Points out areas where changes in the images of women and girls in children's literature are needed, but also cautions against the dangers of overconcentration on nonsexist content to the detriment of literary quality.

B1903 RACHLIN, SUSAN KESSLER, and VOGT, GLENDA L. "Sex Roles as Presented to Children By Coloring Books." *Journal of Popular Culture* 8, no. 3 (Winter 1974):549-56.

Reports on a survey of portrayals of sex roles in coloring books. Finds three and a half times as many males as females are shown engaged in careers.

B1904 RAY, BECKY. "Little Boys and Picture Books." *Catholic Library World* 54 (Summer 1982):74-78.

Examines sex role stereotyping of males in picture books. "Today's little girls are learning they can do and be anything. Don't little boys deserve the same?"

B1905 ROBERTS, PATRICIA L. "The Female Image in the Caldecott Medal Award Books." Ed.D. dissertation, University of the Pacific, 1975, 509 pp., DA 36:3392A.

Examines the human, animal, and inanimate female images in the texts and illustrations of Caldecott award books. Concludes that "Caldecott winners are not free of the stereotyping of the female image."

B1906 ST. PETER, SHIRLEY. "Jack Went Up the Hill . . . But Where Was Jill?" *Psychology of Women Quarterly* 4, no. 2 (Winter 1979):256-60.

Examines picture books for three to six year olds published from 1882 to 1975 and finds stereotyped sex-role models.

B1907 SANDELL, KARIN L. "The All-Too-Wonderful World of Children's Literature: Forty Years of Award-Winning Children's Picture Books." In *Communication, Language, Sex: Proceedings of the First Annual Conference*. Edited by Cynthia L. Berryman and Virginia Eman. Rowley, Mass.: Newbury, 1978, pp. 27-40.

Findings corroborate those of other researchers on the underrepresentation and stereotyped portrayals of females in the words and pictures of children's books.

B1908   SEGEL, ELIZABETH.   "Picture Books and Princesses: The Feminist Contribution." *Proceedings of the Children's Literature Association* 8 (1981):77-83.

A critical overview of feminist criticism of fairy tales and picture books from the early 1970s.

B1909   -----.   "Picture Book Sex Roles Revisited." *SLJ* 28 (May 1982):30-31.

Analyzes a number of influential early studies of sex roles in picture books (Weitzman, Fisher, Nilsen), and concludes that despite some excesses, feminist criticism has influenced changes in picture books.

B1910   *Sexism in Children's Books: Facts, Figures, and Guidelines.* Papers on Children's Literature no. 2.   London: Writers & Readers, 1976, 56 pp.

Includes reprints of "Sex-Role Socialization in Picture Books for Preschool Children" by Leonore Weitzman et al.; "Sexism in Award Winning Picture Books," by Suzanne M. Czaplinski; "Sex-Roles in Reading Schemes," by Glenys Lobban (reprinted from *Forum* 16, no. 2 [Spring 1974]), and "The McGraw-Hill Guidelines for Equal Treatment of the Sexes."

B1911   SKILLMAN, BETTY LOU.   "The Characterization of American Women in Twentieth Century American Literature for Children."   Ph.D. dissertation, Ohio University, 1975, 200 pp., DA 36:6691A.

Compares trends in age, race, marital status, and employment status of the female population as inferred from U.S. census information, with the representation of females in children's literature.

B1912   SKJØNSBERG, KARI.   "Sex Roles in Children's Literature."   *Bookbird* 12, no. 3 (1974):3-6.

Examines sex-role portrayals in books published in Norway between 1957 and 1961.

B1913   SMITH, RONA.   "Sex-Role Stereotyping in Selected American Children's Fiction from 1950 to 1974."   Ph.D. dissertation, New York University, 1979, 239 pp., DA 40:2964A.

Examines the nature and extent of sex-role stereotyping in representative examples of children's literature.

B1914   STENSLAND, ANNA LEE.   "Images of Women in Recent Adolescent Literature."   *English Journal* 73 (November 1984):68-72.

Finds a mixed picture of women's roles in recent young adult literature and finds some themes not developed: the problems of minority women, conflicts between roles of wife/mother and career, and the problems of the single professional.

B1915   STEWIG, JOHN W., and HIGGS, MARGARET.   "Girls Grow Up to Be Mommies: A Study of Sexism in Children's Literature."   *Library Journal* 98 (15 January 1973):236-41 and *SLJ* 19 (January 1973):44-49. (Also in Gerhardt, *Issues in Children's Book Selection*, pp. 116-22.)

Reports on recent research on portrayals of females in children's literature, pointing out some of its weaknesses, and offers the results of the authors' own survey of picture books.   Concludes that "women are not depicted in the rich variety of roles in which they are engaged today."

B1916 STEWIG, JOHN W., and KNIPFEL, MARY LYNN. "Sexism in Picture Books--What Progress?" *Elementary School Journal* 76 (December 1975):151-55.

Reports on a study of women's roles in picture books published between 1972 and 1974, which finds stereotyping in women's home-making and professional roles.

B1917 STONE, KAY F. "Romantic Heroines in Anglo-American Folk and Popular Literature." Ph.D. dissertation, Indiana University, 1975, 406 pp.

Finds that the brave heroines of Anglo-American folktale collections are not as well known to today's readers as the relatively passive and helpless feminine heroines of the Grimms, Andersen, and Andrew Lang, and that the best-known were the three popularized by Walt Disney: "Cinderella," "Snow White," and "Sleeping Beauty."

B1918 STYER, SANDRA. "Biographical Models for Young Feminists." *LA* 55 (February 1978):168-74.

Suggests ways in which biographies of "women and men who have not conformed to rigid definitions of appropriate sex-role behavior" can serve as role models for children. Includes a bibliography.

B1919 SULLIVAN, ANNA MARY TOOMER. "A Comparative Study of the Sex Biased Content in Major Juvenile Periodicals Published in 1977 and the Sex-Biased Content in the Same Periodicals Published in 1967." Ed.D. dissertation, University of Southern Mississippi, 1978, 74 pp., DA 39:5507A.

Finds changes only in an increase in biographical stories about females and an increase in problem-solving behaviors ascribed to females.

B1920 TIBBETTS, SYLVIA L. "Research in Sexism: Some Studies of Children's Reading Material Revisited." *Educational Research Quarterly* 4 (Winter 1979):34-39.

Criticizes the major studies of sexism in children's reading materials as lacking well-structured research design.

B1921 -----. "Sexism in Children's Magazines." Ed.D. dissertation, University of Pennsylvania, 1979, 240 pp., DA 40:5415A.

Finds evidence of sex bias in eleven popular children's magazines based on a preponderance of male characters who are seen as independent, employed, socially active, self-sufficient, rule-makers, and protestors. Women are married or widowed, tied to the family, caretakers, and more friendly than males.

B1922 TRUMPETER, MARGO, and CROWE, LINDA D. "Sexism in Picture Books." *Illinois Libraries* 53 (September 1971):499-502.

Points out examples of sex-role stereotyping in books for young children and beginning readers.

B1923 TULLOS, TANYA. "The Role of Women in Children's Literature: What Do Books Recommended by Public Elementary School Librarians Reflect?" Ph.D. dissertation, Texas A&M University, 1979, 142 pp., DA 40:6146A.

Finds little difference in sex-role stereotyping in recommended and nonrecommended books and suggests more careful examination for stereotyping by the book-buying public. Makes suggestions for further research on the topic.

B1924 VUKELICH, C.; McCARTY, C.; and NANIS, C. "Sex Bias in Children's Books." *Childhood Education* 52 (February 1976):220-22.

Finds a predominance of subservient female role models for children.

B1925 WANG, YU JUNG. "An Analysis of Male and Female Roles in Chinese Children's Reading Materials Published in Taiwan." Ph.D. dissertation, New York University, 1980, 146 pp., DA 41:661A.

Examines sex roles in Chinese children's literature published in Taiwan. The roles were investigated in terms of frequency of presence for male and female characters, occupations engaged in, and behavior of male and female characters. The study concluded that "strong traditional-oriented attitudes toward male and female roles" continue to exist.

B1926 WEITZMAN, LENORE J.; EIFLER, DEBORAH; HOKADA, ELIZABETH; and ROSS, CATHERINE. "Sex Role Socialization in Picture Books for Pre-School Children." *American Journal of Sociology* 77 (May 1972):1125-50.

This extremely influential article analyzes Caldecott and other award-winning books in terms of their portrayals of stereotyped sex roles. Concludes that women are underrepresented and where they do appear their roles are stereotyped. Discusses the effects of these "rigid sex-role portraits" on the developing child.

B1927 WELLER, ANNA ELIZABETH. "The Portrayal of the Female Character in the Newbery Award Books." Ph.D. dissertation, Indiana University, 1977, 183 pp., DA 38:1718A.

Concludes that sex-role stereotyping has decreased in recent Newbery award books.

B1928 WIGNELL, EDNA, comp. *Boys Whistle, Girls Sing: Sexism in Children's Books*. Melbourne: Primary Education (Publishing) Ltd., 1976, 71 pp.

Includes a number of articles reprinted from *Primary Education* (Richmond) and other sources. Sexism is defined and incidences are identified and discussed in a number of well-known titles including Tove Jansson's Moomin books, B.B.'s *Little Grey Men*, Helen Cresswell's *Gift from Winklesea*, and E. Nesbit's *Railway Children*. Also examines stereotyping in textbooks, picture books, and informational books, and includes an annotated list of recommended fiction.

B1929 WINKELJOHANN, Sister ROSEMARY, and GALLANT, RUTH. "Queries: Should We Use Children's Classics that Offer Stereotypic Images of Sex Roles?" *LA* 57 (April 1980):446-50.

Includes a historical overview and responses from Carolyn W. Carmichael and Patricia J. Cianciolo as well as a list of references on the topic.

B1930 WORTH, BARBARA. "Achievement and Affiliation Motive of Male and Female Characters in Realistic Fiction for Children, 1945-1975."

Ph.D. dissertation, New York University, 1975, 159 pp., DA 38:5917A.

Examines differences between motives of male and female characters in children's fiction for two time periods: 1945-63 and 1970-75. Found little differences between sexes or different time periods.

SHORT STORY

B1931 CHAMBERS, AIDAN. "Letter from England: A Mark of Distinction." *Horn Book* 60 (September-October 1984):665-70.

In this last of his series of letters from England, Chambers discusses the short story form in children's literature, primarily in the work of Jan Mark, but also with some insightful though brief comments on Sendak's *Outside Over There* and the work of Philippa Pearce.

B1932 GROFF, PATRICK. "Short Story and Children." *Advocate* 3, no. 2 (Winter 1984):118-22.

Points out the prevalence of short stories for children and urges that they be given more critical attention.

B1933 SEGAL, ELIZABETH. "Short-Changed: Short Stories for Children." *SLJ* 26 (May 1980):40-41.

Surveys the availability and nature of short stories for younger readers and argues that more children's short stories are needed, especially from American writers.

B1934 STIBBS, ANDREW. "'Spit Nolan' and the Short Story for Children." *CLE*, o.s., no. 7 (March 1972):17-22.

Examines "Spit Nolan" from Bill Naughton's *The Goalkeeper's Revenge and Other Stories* as an example of the appeal of short stories to children.

SOCIAL CLASS

B1935 DIXON, BOB. "Class: Snakes and Ladders." In *Catching Them Young*, pp. 42-93.

Provides a British perspective on issues of class in children's books. Among writers discussed are Arthur Ransome, Geoffrey Trease, Lucy Boston, Jean de Brunhoff, and Roger Gleason.

SOUTH AFRICA

B1936 RANDOLPH-ROBINSON, BRENDA. "The Depiction of South Africa in Children's Literature." *IRBC* 15, nos. 7-8 (1984):14-22.

"A study of more than forty children's books finds that even the newest are generally inadequate, and older titles--still in circulation-- are blatantly biased." Includes an annotated listing of the books examined.

SOVIET UNION

B1937 AMOR, STUART. "Folk Tales for Children in the Soviet Union." *Signal* 16 (January 1975):46-51.

An overview of collections of tales, their handling, and their history.

B1938   BOYD, CELIA. "The Catcher in the Steppes: Soviet Adolescent Fiction in Translation." *Signal* 7 (January 1972):13-30.
Discusses the influence of Salinger's *Catcher in the Rye* on the Soviet novel for adolescents, notably Vadim Prolov's *What It's All About* (1968), Boris Balter's *Goodbye Boys* (1963), and Vasili Aksenov's *A Starry Ticket* (1967).

B1939   FOTEEVA, A.I. "For Children About the War and the Soviet Army." *Soviet Education* 18 (January 1976):87-103.
Surveys Russian children's fiction and nonfiction about World War II.

B1940   MEDVEDEVA, N. "Russian Children's Literature on the Contemporary Stage." *International Library Review* 3 (April 1971):133-40.
Summarizes recent developments in the writing and scholarly study of children's literature in the Soviet Union. This is not a study of children's theater.

B1941   MILLER, D.D.; WILLIAMS, SUSAN; and WILLIAMS, RONALD. "Children's Literature in the Soviet Union." *LA* 53 (May 1976):531-35.
A concise overview. Includes a bibliography.

B1942   MORTON, MIRIAM. "A Harvest of Russian Children's Literature." In Haviland, *Children and Literature*, pp. 374-78.
Excerpts from the introduction to the anthology of the same name. A brief overview of Russian children's literature.

B1943   -----. "The Multi-Ethnic and Interracial Children's Literature of the U.S.S.R." *IRBC* 5, nos. 1-2 (1974):1, 12-14.
Reports on the children's literature of the various ethnic groups in the Soviet Union.

B1944   -----. "Young Soviet Readers and Their Literature." In Egoff, *One Ocean*, pp. 38-59.
Provides an overview of children's literature in the Soviet Union, based on research for her anthology *A Harvest of Russian Literature* (1967) and *The Arts and the Soviet Child* (1972).

B1945   MOTYASHOV, NINA B., and NIKOLAYEVA, MARIA. "U.S.S.R." *Phaedrus* 8 (1981):80-81.
An unannotated list of recent Soviet publications concerning children's literature.

B1946   O'DELL, FELICITY ANN. *Socialization through Children's Literature: The Soviet Example*. New York: Cambridge University Press, 1978, 288 pp.
Identifies and examines the role of children's literature in the socialization of the child. Explores the organization of the production and dissemination of Soviet children's literature, and looks in-depth at text-book materials for primary-school children and the popular periodical *Murzilkla*.

B1947   *Phaedrus* 4, no. 1 (Spring 1977):3-33.
Special issue. Covers children's literature research in many of the Soviet republics and provides translations from *Detskaya Litera-*

ture, a Soviet journal of children's literature. Includes articles on the literatures of Azerbaijan, Byelorussia, Kirghiz, Tataria, and Uzbek.

B1948 PRESKA, MARGARET ROBINSON. "Humanness in Soviet Children's Literature." Ph.D. dissertation, Claremont Graduate School & University Center, 1969, 192 pp., DA 30:5417A.

Analyzes "humanness" in contemporary Soviet story books for preschoolers. Concludes that "it is difficult to distinguish contemporary Russian story books from any books representative of the children's literature produced in the technologically and educationally advanced countries of the world."

B1949 RAPP, HELEN. "Soviet Books for Children." In *Soviet Society: A Book of Readings*. Edited by Alex Inkleles and Geiger Kent. Boston: Houghton Mifflin, 1961, pp. 443-48.

Provides a concise overview of Russian children's literature as of the late 1950s.

B1950 RUDOLPH, MARGUERITA. "Children's Literature in the Soviet Union." *Horn Book* 40 (December 1964):646-50.

An overview of Soviet children's literature as of the early 1960s.

B1951 SHEVELTER, VALENTIN. "Children's Magazines in the Soviet Union." *Bookbird* 6, no. 2 (1968):56-58.

Provides an overview of Soviet children's periodicals.

B1952 SOKOL, ELENA. *Russian Poetry for Children*. Knoxville: University of Tennessee Press, 1984, 242 pp.

Traces the development of modern Russian children's poetry, concentrating especially on the influence of Kornei Chukovsky and traditional folklore. Also discusses a number of modern poets including Samuel Marshak and Vladimir Maiakovskii.

SPAIN

B1953 BRAVO-VILLASANTE, CARMEN. "Children's Literature in Spain --1969." *Bookbird* 8 (1970):17-24.

Summarizes developments in Spain's children's literature, including heroic epics, science fiction, theater, religious literature, and handicraft books.

B1954 -----. "Utility, or Art: A Fork Along the Road to Permanence in Spanish Children's Literature." *WLB* 48 (October 1973):153-58.

A historical overview of the children's literature of Spain.

SPORTS

B1955 BRODERICK, DOROTHY M. "An Open Letter to Sports Writers." *Library Journal* 87 (15 April 1962):1675-76 and *SLJ* 9 (April 1962):27-28. "A Second Letter to Sports Writers." *Library Journal* 89 (15 November 1964):4608-9 and *SLJ* 11 (November 1964):34-35.

In her first letter Broderick castigates writers of sports fiction for their "helpful hints," their "character portrayal," their "ethics," and their depiction of action and atmosphere. The second letter criticizes the too narrow scope of the sports biography.

B1956 CAMPBELL, PATRICIA. "Women in Sports in Children's Books:

Wealthy, White, and Winning." *IRBC* 10, no. 4 (1979):3-10.
Argues that though there are many recent books presenting women in sports as exciting, vital role models, even the best often contain limiting stereotypes.

B1957   CANTWELL, ROBERT. "A Sneering Laugh with Bases Loaded." *Sports Illustrated* 16 (23 April 1962):67-70, 73-76.
Surveys baseball novels for boys, especially novels by Ralph Henry Barbour and William Heyliger.

B1958   EVANS, WALTER. "The All-American Boys: A Study of Boys' Sports Fiction." *Journal of Popular Culture* 6 (Summer 1972):104-21.
Traces the evolution of the sports story from its origins in the school story, points out differences between the two, and notes common conventions and changes in the genre over the years. Includes references.

B1959   GRABER, RALPH S. "Baseball in American Fiction." *English Journal* 56 (November 1967):1107-14.
A survey of adult juvenile fiction from the nineteenth century to the present concluding, "Baseball literature has moved from the story told for the juvenile, to the fiction which attracts the intellectual to examine the game in literature for the light it sheds on American life and the paradoxes of modern existence."

B1960   LIPSYTE, ROBERT. "Forum: Robert Lipsyte on Kids/Sports/Books." *CLE*, n.s. 11, no. 1 (Spring 1980):43-47. (Reprinted as "Peddling Sports Myths: A Disservice to Young Readers," in *IRBC* 12, no. 1 [1981]:11-13.)
Castigates sports books for perpetuating myths. Argues that books are needed that "acknowledge kids' fears about sports . . . in which nice guys do finish last and it doesn't matter. In which making the team doesn't end all problems and the team doesn't win all the games. Books that integrate sports with the rest of life."

B1961   MESSENGER, CHRISTIAN K. "Sport in American Literature (1830-1930)." Ph.D. dissertation, Northwestern University, 1974, 369 pp., DA 35:6724A.
Examines the origins and development of American sports fiction, including the works of Gilbert Patten and Ralph Henry Barbour.

B1962   PRAGER, ARTHUR. "The Saturday Heroes." *Rascals at Large*, pp. 267-303.
Analyzes the treatment of sports in popular series books of the 1920s, 1930s, and 1940s, and also earlier series by Gilbert Patten (Burt L. Standish).

B1963   SAUL, E. WENDY, and KELLY, R. GORDON. "Christians, Brahmins, and other Sporting Fellows: An Analysis of School Sports Stories." *CLE*, n.s. 15, no. 2 (Winter 1984):234-46.
Points out differences in Thomas Hughes's *Tom Brown's School Days* and the American school sports story as represented by Ralph Henry Barbour and C.M. Fuess. "For Thomas Hughes, life was a battle and games a proper training exercise for service in the army of Christian soldiers. Writers of twentieth-century American sports stories have typically implied that life is a game, reversing Hughes's perception that games are like life."

B1964   SCURY, COLLEEN. "A Scorecard for Reviewers." *Horn Book* 28 (October 1952):348-51.
Sets forth criteria for evaluating sports stories.

B1965   SOJKA, GREGORY S. "Going 'From Rags to Riches' with Baseball Joe: Or A Pitcher's Progress." *Journal of American Culture* 2 (Spring 1979):113-21.
Identifies elements of the "rags to riches" theme in late nineteenth- and early twentieth-century sports stories for boys, particularly in Lester Chadwick's Baseball Joe series.

B1966   UNSWORTH, ROBERT. "Tunis Goes Down Swinging . . . Who'll Keep the Ball Rolling?" *SLJ* 25 (May 1979):38-39.
Discusses reasons why Tunis's baseball novels are now dated, and examines a few more recent titles in a declining market.

SPRING

B1967   MASTER, HELEN. "What Spring Brings." *Horn Book* 13 (May-June 1937):135-38.
Discusses spring themes in Grahame's *Wind in the Willows*, E.V. Lucas's *The Slow Coach*, Kipling's *Kim*, and Burnett's *The Secret Garden*.

STYLE

B1968   BILLMAN, CAROL. "Verbal Creativity in Children's Literature." *English Quarterly* 12, nos. 1-2 (Spring-Summer 1979):25-32.
Explores wordplay in the works of James Reaney and James Thurber.

B1969   CAMERON, ELEANOR. "Of Style and the Stylist." *Horn Book* 40 (February 1964):25-32. (Rewritten for inclusion in *Green and Burning*, pp. 137-58.)
Style is the "sound of self." Cameron explores the qualities of style, illustrating her points with examples from both children's and adults' literature.

B1970   CHAMBERS, AIDAN. "Letter from England: American Writing and British Readers." *Horn Book* 52 (October 1976):532-38.
Discusses differences in American and British literary style and its relationship to the British class system. Compares William Mayne and Paul Zindel.

B1971   CHURCH, ELIZABETH, and BEREITER, CARL. "Reading for Style." *LA* 60 (April 1983):470-76.
Describes a technique for heightening students' awareness of literary style.

B1972   COHEN, DOROTHY H. "Word Meaning and the Literary Experience in Early Childhood." *EE* 46 (November 1969):914-25. (Reprinted in Barron, *Jump Over the Moon*, pp. 418-34.)
Points out several ways in which writers for children help make the meanings of their words clear without losing the quality of the story as a story. Examples from twenty-two children's books illustrate nine different techniques, including piling up examples, detailed

description of a process or function, meaningful context, and contrast and comparison.

B1973　GARDNES, G., and LOHMAN, W. "Children's Sensitivity to Literary Styles." *Merrill-Palmer Quarterly* 21 (April 1975):113-26.
Reports on a study to determine children's sensitivity to literary style at various ages, provides a summary of existing research, and suggests further studies.

B1974　GUTTERY, JEAN. "Style in Children's Literature." *EER* 18 (October 1941):208-12, 240. (Reprinted in White, *Children's Literature*, pp. 172-78.)
Discusses style in children's literature and how it differs in some respects from style in books for adults: (1) often takes an informal, intimate approach, (2) more reliance on visual detail and color, (3) uses figures of speech, such as similes suitable for children, (4) expressions of time, size, and distance are often more concrete, (5) appreciates children's sensitivity to rhythm and repetition, and (6) repetition is used to foreshadow.

B1975　HEARNE, BETSY. "The American Connection." *Signal* 33 (September 1980):151-59.
Bemoans the tendency of American writers for children to take short cuts in developing character, plot, and style. Concludes, "Living is new to children, it's minutiae marvellously fresh. A writer with less than the same unjaded awareness of common details combined with the experience to craft them into a rich story can't live up to writing for children."

B1976　HUNT, PETER. "The Cliché Count: A Practical Aid for the Selection of Books for Children." *CLE*, n.s. 9, no. 3 (Autumn 1978):143-50.
Proposes that the number of clichés found in the language of a book may indicate the author's authenticity and originality.

B1977　HUNTER, MOLLIE. "The Limits of Language." In *Talent is Not Enough*, pp. 103-23.
Reflects on the uses of language by the creative writer, particularly the writer for children, commenting on dialect, poetry, diction, rhyme, and magic.

B1978　MOIR, LEO HUGHES. "A Linguistic Analysis of Certain Stylistic Elements of Selected Works of Literature for Children and their Relationship to Readability." Ed.D. dissertation, Wayne State University, 1969, 175 pp., ERIC Educational Document Reproduction Service, ED 048 251.
Concludes that semantics and grammatical complexity influence reading difficulty, that the ease with which a reader can identify the syntactic context of a passage influences understanding, that there is a great variation in consistency and complexity of style among authors writing for the same audience, and the literary content of a passage influences the reader's interaction.

B1979　NEUMEYER, PETER. "What Makes a Good Children's Book?" ERIC Educational Document Reproduction Service, 1977, 16 pp., ED 146 632.
Defines a "good" book as one "that is rich and dense in texture and that draws on many authorial resources." Examines the use of

individual words in a story by A.A. Milne, in Beatrix Potter's *Peter Rabbit*, in Paul Zindel's *I Never Loved Your Mind*, and in E.B. White's *Charlotte's Web*.

B1980   PEDDICORD, MARY H.   "Linguistic Stylistics and Children's Literature."   Ph.D. dissertation, University of Southern Mississippi, 1980, 293 pp., DA 41:4700A.

Identifies syntactic variations of basic sentences used by fourteen Newbery Medal winners and concludes that "the difference in complexity between literature for children and for adults lies not in the kinds but in the degree of complexity."

B1981   PICKERT, SARAH M.   "Repetitive Sentence Patterns in Children's Books."   *LA* 55 (January 1978):16-18.

Illustrates two patterns of repetition common in children's books: sentence repetition in a repetitive plot and sentence repetition in a cumulative plot.

B1982   TOOTHAKER, ROY EUGENE.   "Rhetorical Devices in Literature for Children."   Ed.D. dissertation, University of Arkansas, 1969, 115 pp., DA 31:1126A.

Examines the "incidence, extent, order and character of eighteen rhetorical devices occurring in one-hundred trade books for children in primary grades." Found devices of sound ranked first, devices of comparison second, of composition third, of contrast fourth, and of association fifth.

SWEDEN

B1983   ANDREWS, SIRI.   "Children's Books In Sweden, 1750-1950."   *Horn Book* 42 (June 1966):328-29.

Reviews Eva von Zweigbergk's survey, of Swedish children's literature, *Barnboken i Sverige, 1750-1950*.

B1984   HAMRIN, MARGARETA.   "A Study of Swedish Immigrant Children's Literature Published in the United States, 1850-1920."   *Phaedrus* 6, no. 1 (Spring 1979):71-78.

Examines "the role of literature for Swedish-American children and young adults in at first maintaining the native language and then later failing to maintain it."

B1985   KÅRELAND, LENA.   "Sweden."   *Phaedrus* 8 (1981):76-77.

A bibliography, annotated in English, of recent books, catalogs and studies of children's literature.

B1986   LUNDQUIST, ULLA.   "Some Portraits of Teenagers in Modern Junior Novels in Sweden."   In Escarpit, *Portrayal of the Child*, pp. 117-24.

Examines the problems and conflicts faced by teenagers in modern Swedish fiction.

B1987   ØRVIG, MARY.   *Children's Books in Sweden 1945-1970: A Survey.*   Vienna: International Institute for Children's Literature and Reading Research, 1973, 51 pp.

Provides a concise overview of children's literature in Sweden, especially since World War II. Includes discussions of books for the youngest, fantasy, adventure stories, historical fiction, realistic fiction, and children's literature scholarship.

B1988   -----. "Eight Women Who Write Books in Swedish for Children." *Horn Book* 49 (February 1973):17-23; (April 1973):19-27. (Reprinted in Heins, *Crosscurrents*, pp. 248-60.)

Discusses the works of Astrid Lindgren, Tove Jansson, Irmelin Sandman Lilius, Edith Unnerstad, Britt C. Hallqvist, Anna Lisa Warnlöf, Maria Gripe, and Gunnel Linde. Includes a bibliography.

B1989   -----. "Saga: Swedish Publishers of Children's Books." *Horn Book* 36 (August 1960):318-25.

An overview of sixty years of publishing by Saga, "the only publishing house in Sweden devoted exclusively to children's books."

B1990   "Some Views from Sweden." *Bookbird* 3 (1984):9-18.

Reprints discussions of criticism of children's books from the Swedish newspaper *Svenska Dagbladet*. Includes articles by Ying Toijer-Nilsson, Vivi Edström, Lena Kåreland, Hans Peterson, Carl Hafström, and Anna Lena Wirk-Thorsell.

B1991   STRÖMSTEDT, MARGARITA. "The Swedish Debate." In Koefoed, *Children's Literature and the Child*, pp. 48-50.

Discusses issues of censorship and realism in contemporary Swedish children's books, including arguments about the controversial author Sven Wernström.

B1992   SVERSSON, SONJA. "Children's Periodicals in Sweden." *Phaedrus* 4, no. 2 (Fall 1977):11-16.

Mentions the few secondary sources that exist about Swedish children's periodical literature and examines the periodicals themselves from early days to the present.

B1993   VESTERBERG, BERNT. "Swedish Folklore and English Versions for Children." *Orana* 17 (November 1981):149-52.

An overview.

SWITZERLAND

B1994   SENFT, FRITZ. "Children's Literature in a Changed Switzerland." *Bookbird* 9, no. 4 (1971):13-16.

A brief overview of trends in Swiss children's literature since World War II.

B1995   SHAFFER, BLANCHE WEBER. "The Bread of Home." *Horn Book* 24 (September 1948):351-62.

A survey of Swiss children's books including a bibliography and a list of prize-winners.

B1996   VON STOCKAR, DENISE. "From Toepffer to Delessert: The Picture Book Illustrators of French-Speaking Switzerland." *Phaedrus* 9 (1982):35-40.

Calls attention to the contributions of several often-overlooked illustrators from French-speaking areas of Switzerland.

B1997   -----. "A Selection of Swiss Picture Books in American Translation." *Horn Book* 56 (June 1980):274-82.

Surveys classic and recent contributions of Switzerland to the picture book.

B1998   -----. "Switzerland." *Phaedrus* 8 (1981):78-79.
         Reports on recent Swiss research in children's literature.

TEACHERS

B1999   DAVIS, HAZEL K. "The Teacher in Selected Fiction for Adolescents."
         Focus: Teaching Language Arts 3, no. 2 (Winter 1977):4-15. (Also
         in ERIC Educational Document Reproduction Service, ED 157 082.)
         Reports on a study of the image of the teacher in adolescent
         fiction written since 1966 and finds most of the images negative.

B2000   GOODHOPE, JEANIE. "Love, Hate, Manipulate: How Teachers Rate
         in Young Adult Fiction." *English Journal* 73 (November 1984):52-53.
         Concludes that whether the images of teachers in young adult
         fiction are real or fantasized, they are assigned strong feelings and
         pivotal roles.

B2001   KAUFFMAN, MELVA GRACE. "An Analysis of the Teacher as Por-
         trayed in Modern Juvenile Fiction." Ed.D. dissertation, Columbia
         University, 1962, 311 pp., DA 23:4244A.
         Analyzes the portrayal of teachers in books written for children
         in grades six through nine, published between 1945 and 1956.

B2002   LOCKE, DUNCAN ALLAN. "Teachers as Characterized in Contempo-
         rary Juvenile Fiction." Ph.D. dissertation, University of Oregon,
         1979, 111 pp., DA 40:3001A.
         Argues that the portrayal of teachers in contemporary juvenile
         fiction is primarily a negative caricature, overgeneralizing and
         exaggerating teachers' foibles and vulnerabilities.

B2003   MUCKLE, JAMES. "Images of the Teacher in Stories for Soviet Chil-
         dren." *Compare* 9, no. 1 (April 1979):59-64.
         Examines the portrayals of teachers in a collection of short
         stories for children as illuminating official Soviet attitudes toward
         education.

B2004   PINNEY, REBA. "Reading Teachers in Children's Books." *Orana*
         17 (August 1981):90-91.
         Discusses the images of reading teachers in children's books.

B2005   RYGIEL, MARY ANN. "The Image of the Teacher in Adolescent Fic-
         tion." *ALAN Review* 9, no. 1 (Fall 1981):12-15. (Also in ERIC
         Educational Document Reproduction Service, ED 208 419.)
         Discusses fifteen books by thirteen authors, examining the traits
         of teachers that are portrayed positively and negatively. Characteris-
         tics identified are imagination, insight and involvement, talent, and
         adherence to standards.

B2006   WINTER, RYOKO Y. "The Role of the Teacher as Depicted in Ameri-
         can and Japanese Literature for Children and Younger Adolescents."
         Ed.D. dissertation, University of San Francisco, 1983, 148 pp., DA
         44:747A.
         Concludes that the roles played by teachers in America and in
         Japan are different and the fictional portrayals reflect this difference.
         American books were more negative.

TELEVISION--INFLUENCE

B2007 EPSTEIN, CONNIE C. "A Nutritious Backhand." *Children's Literature* 10 (1982):199-203.

An editor muses on the possible influence of television, particularly animation, on recent children's books.

THAILAND

B2008 BUNVANICH, CHANTIMA. "An Analysis of Selected Studies of Thai Folktales as Applicable to Elementary English Reading Programs." Ed.D. dissertation, University of Northern Colorado, 1976, 96 pp., DA 37:4184A.

Includes commentaries and analysis of twelve Thai folktales, translated by the author, for use in an elementary English reading program in Thailand.

TIME

B2009 AERS, LESLEY. "The Treatment of Time in Four Children's Books." *CLE*, o.s., no. 2 (July 1970):69-81.

Discusses Ronald Welch's *The Gauntlet*, E. Nesbit's *The Story of the Amulet*, Philippa Pearce's *Tom's Midnight Garden*, and Alison Uttley's *A Traveller in Time*.

B2010 CROUCH, MARCUS. "Experiments in Time." *Junior Bookshelf* 20 (January 1956):5-11.

Briefly touches on various approaches to time in a number of children's books.

B2011 LIVELY, PENELOPE. "Children and Memory." *Horn Book* 54 (February 1978):17-23; (April 1978):197-203. (Reprinted in Heins, *Crosscurrents*, pp. 226-33.)

Stresses a need for both historical and personal memory in children's books, a need for developing a sense of the past in children, and an awareness of time, if only to make up for the twentieth-century loss of oral narrative tradition and lack of personal contact with the old.

B2012 MEEK, MARGARET. "Speaking of Shifters." *Signal* 45 (September 1984):152-67.

Maintains that "children come to understand very complicated notions of time both by telling stories and by reading those specially written for them where time is the author's chosen theme." Discusses Pat Hutchins's *Clocks and More Clocks* and Philippa Pearce's *Tom's Midnight Garden* and *The Way to Sattin Shore*.

B2013 SHANNON, GEORGE. "All Times in One." *ChLAQ* 10, no. 4 (Winter 1986):178-81.

Examines the motif of objects which hold a memory in four works of fiction: Sharon Bell Mathis's *The Hundred Penny Box*, Doris Gates's *Blue Willow*, M.B. Goffstein's *My Noah's Ark*, and Alan Garner's *The Stone Book*.

B2014 WOLF, VIRGINIA L. "The Cycle of the Seasons: Without and Within Time." *ChLAQ* 10, no. 4 (Winter 1986):192-96.

Analyzes the way the cycle of the seasons provide form and

meaning in four novels: E.B. White's *Charlotte's Web*, Laura Ingalls Wilder's *Little House in the Big Woods*, Eleanor Estes's *The Moffats*, and Louise May Alcott's *Little Women, Part I*.

TOY BOOKS

B2015 ABRAHAMSON, RICHARD F., and STEWART, ROBERT. "Moveable Books--A New Golden Age." *LA* 59 (April 1982):342-47.
Reviews the recent crop of pop-up books and includes a section on how to make them. Also includes a bibliography.

B2016 BADER, BARBARA. "Cloth Books and Toy Books." In *American Picturebooks*, pp. 235-40.
Traces the evolution of American cloth and toy books in the 1930s and 1940s.

B2017 CAROTHERS, MARTHA, and SOMMESE, LANNY. "Nostalgia: Children's Toy Books." *Novum Gebrauchsgraphik* 52, no. 8 (1981):48-56.
A lavishly illustrated survey of historical toy books from the collection of Herbert H. Hosmer.

B2018 HAINING, PETER. *Movable Books: An Illustrated History*. London: New English Library, 1979, 141 pp.
An illustrated history of "Folding, Revolving, Dissolving, Mechanical, Scenic, Panoramic, Dimensional, Changing, Pop-Up, and other Novelty Books from the Collection of David and Brian Philips." Includes a bibliography.

B2019 HEARNE, BETSY. "The American Connection." *Signal* 37 (January 1982):38-42.
Examines recent trends in toy books--pop-ups, boardbooks, shaped books, and others.

B2020 HOGARTH, GRACE ALLEN. "Toy, Play, and Game Books for Indoor Days." *Horn Book* 19 (January-February 1943):21-26.
Discusses those books that are not really books but "things in book's clothing." Includes a list of recommmended toy and play books.

B2021 McGEE, LEA M. "Books with Moveables: More Than Just Novelties." *Reading Teacher* 37 (May 1984):853-59.
Comments on characteristics of movable books and ways in which they can be used to teach reading. Includes an annotated list of books.

B2022 OPIE, IONA, and OPIE, PETER. "Books That Come to Life." *TLS*, 19 September 1974, p. 1055.
A brief history and overview of mechanical devices in books.

B2023 VANDERGRIFT, KAY. *Child and Story*, pp. 84-96.
Provides extensive comments on modern and antique pop-ups, cloth books, story dolls, shape books, scratch and sniff, and other varieties of "toy books."

TOYS

B2024 MENDELSOHN, LEONARD R. "Toys and Literature." In Butler, *Sharing*, pp. 80-84.
Explores the role of animated toys in children's literature.

TRAGEDY

B2025 KINGSTON, CAROLYN T. "Exemplifications of the Tragic Mode in Selected Realistic Fiction for Eight-to-twelve-year-old Children." Ed.D. dissertation, Columbia University, 1970, 426 pp., DA 29:2216A.
Found that although children's stories deviated from classical tragic form, the "underlying tragic feeling" remained the same.

B2026 -----. *Tragic Mode.* New York: Teachers College Press, 1974, 177 pp.
Examines a number of books for children and young adults in terms of their tragic themes. Individual titles have been indexed separately in this bibliography.

TRANSLATION

B2027 BELL, ANTHEA. "Children's Books in Translation." *Signal* 28 (January 1979):47-53.
Discusses issues in the translation of children's books. Reviews the proceedings of the 1976 symposium of the International Research Society for Children's Literature, edited by Göte Klingberg, Mary Ørvig, and Stuart Amor (see below).

B2028 -----. "Ten Years of Parcels." *Signal* 31 (January 1980):20-28.
A free-lance translator of children's books discusses a number of issues relating to translation and internationalism in children's literature.

B2029 CRAMPTON, PATRICIA. "Will it Travel Well?" *Signal* 17 (May 1975):75-80.
Expresses the concerns and considerations of translating.

B2030 EGOFF, SHEILA. "The European Children's Novel in Translation." In *Thursday's Child*, pp. 275-96.
Provides an introductory overview of translated classics and comments on differences between recent English-language writers and Europeans especially in their depiction of war. Also comments at some length upon Maria Gripe's Josephine and Hugo trilogy.

B2031 FENTON, EDWARD. "Blind Idiot, or, The Problems of Translation." In *Children's Books International 2. Proceedings and Book Catalog.* Boston: Boston Public Library, 1977, pp. 50-60.
Discusses the problems of the translator, particularly the problems of the translator of children's books.

B2032 GOTTLIEB, ROBIN. "On the Translation of Children's Books: A Selective Bibliography." *TON* 30 (June 1974):369-71. (Also in *Bookbird* 12, no. 1 [1974]:26-28.)
An annotated bibliography on topics relating to the difficulties and importance of translating children's books.

B2033   KLINGBERG, GÖTE; ØRVIG, MARY; and AMOR, STUART, eds. *Children's Books in Translation: The Situation and the Problems: Proceedings of the 1976 Symposium of International Research Society for Children's Literature.* Stockholm: Swedish Institute for Children's Books, Almquist & Wiksell, 173 pp.

Includes Richard Bamberger's "The Influence of Translation on the Development of National Children's Literature," pp. 19-27; Jörg Becker's "The Internationalism of Children's Books: Translations and their Ideological Deformations in the Federal Republic of Germany," pp. 28-45; Carmen Bravo-Villasante's "Translation Problems in My Experience as a Translator," pp. 46-50; Wolfgang Bussewitz's "The Role of Soviet Children's Literature in The GDR," pp. 51-59; Lars Furuland's "Sweden and the International Children's Book Market: History and Present Situation," pp. 60-76; Hannes Huttner's "The Share of Translations in the Reading Matter of GDR Children," pp. 77-80; Elvira Ivanova's "Foreign Literature as Read by Soviet School-children," pp. 81-83; Göte Klingberg's, "The Different Aspects of Research into the Translation of Children's Books and its Practical Application," pp. 84-89; Izabela Maria Lewanska's "Problems in Connection with the Adaptation of the Classics in Poland," pp. 90-96; Igor Motyashov's "The Social and Aesthetic Criteria Applied in Choosing Children's Books for Translation," pp. 97-103. Mae Durham Roger's "Translation--Art, Science or Craft," pp. 104-12; Norman Shine's "The Translation of Children's Literature: A Case Study of English Children's Books Written between 1800 and 1900 and at Some Point in Time Translated into Danish," pp. 113-29; Birgit Stolt's "How Emil Becomes Michel--on the Translation of Children's Books," pp. 130-46; Torben Weinreich's "International Book Production for Children Related to the Children's Local Experiences and Local Consciousness," pp. 147-58; Muriel A. Whitaker's "Canadian Indian and Eskimo Legends as Children's Literature," pp. 159-67; and Yuri Yarmish's "The Children's Literature of the People of the USSR and Foreign Countries in the Ukrainian Translation," pp. 168-73.

B2034   ØRVIG, MARY. "Children's Books in Translation: Facts and Beliefs." *SLJ* 19 (November 1972):23-27. (Reprinted in Gerhardt, *Issues In Children's Book Selection*, pp. 185-90.)

Examines important issues in the translation and international exchange of children's literature today. Includes a bibliography of works concerned with translating.

TRENDS IN CHILDREN'S LITERATURE

B2035   BAMBERGER, RICHARD. "Trends in Modern Literature for Children and Young People." *Bookbird* 8, no. 3 (1970):3-15. (Reprinted in *Reading and Children's Books*, pp. 5-17.)

Identifies five trends in modern children's literature: (1) the trend toward a world literature, (2) the trend toward world orientation and national understanding, (3) the fantastic story or the breakthrough of the irrational, (4) the attempt to overcome the "cultural lag" in form and content, and (5) away from formulas: freedom of form and content. Identifies many titles exemplifying each trend.

B2036   BUTLER, FRANCELIA. "Children's Literature: The Bad Seed." *Virginia Quarterly Review* 56 (Summer 1980):396-409. (Reprinted in Bator, *Signposts*, pp. 37-45.)

Proposes several reasons why children's literature has been

ignored by English departments: it is "regarded as shallow and silly," "it is associated with women, and it stirs up an unconscious resentment in adults of those who will succeed them."

B2037   -----. "Preface: The Editor's High Chair." *Children's Literature* 1 (1972):7-8.

In this preface to the first volume of *Children's Literature*, Butler suggests reasons for the neglect of children's literature by humanists and critics, and suggests areas of concern for humanists.

B2038   CHAMBERS, AIDAN. "The Child's Changing Story." *Signal* 40 (January 1983):36-52.

Reflects on the way the great changes in human life in the twentieth century have changed our stories: the theory of relativity, space, gender, and nuclear fission. Provides examples from many contemporary children's books.

B2039   -----. "Letter from England: Keeping Up with the Critics." *Horn Book* 57 (August 1981):463-67.

Points out the number of new titles appearing in the field of criticism of children's literature. Quotes Auden on the function of the critic, urging that critics of children literature examine carefully their motives for writing.

B2040   CIANCIOLO, PATRICIA J. "Iconoclastic Literature for Young People Has 'Arrived.' ERIC Educational Document Reproduction Service, 1976, 21 pp., ED 120 813.

Identifies three types of modern themes that have become increasingly prevalent in children's literature: existentialist, surrealist, and impressionist. Includes a bibliography of relevant children's books.

B2041   DAVIS, DAVID C. "Who'll Kill the Mockingbirds?" *Horn Book* 39 (June 1963):265-71.

Complains of "mockingbird writers" in children's literature who sing the same refrain over and over, repeating both themselves and the "successes" of other writers instead of pursuing the difficult paths of true integrity and originality. Names examples of respected and well-known writers whom he feels have fallen into the trap.

B2042   EAKIN, MARY K. "Trends in Children's Literature." *Library Quarterly* 25 (January 1955):47-57.

Comments on the children's books, fictional and informational, of the 1930s, 1940s, and 1950s. Finds there has been an increase in quantity and in attractiveness, but not necessarily in excellence of content.

B2043   EGOFF, SHEILA. "Beyond the Garden Wall: Some Observations on Current Trends in Children's Literature." In *Arbuthnot Lectures*, pp. 189-203.

The metaphor of the garden wall describes children's literature of the 1930s, 1940s, and 1950s and earlier: "The wall represents its seclusion, protection, confinement, the garden--order serenity, aesthetic delight." Since the 1960s, however, the walls have come tumbling down. Leaves the reader with the question--has children's literature gained the whole world but lost part of its soul?

B2044   -----. "Precepts and Pleasures: Changing Emphasis in the Writing and Criticism of Children's Literature." In Egoff, *Only Connect*, 1st ed., pp. 419-46, 2d ed., 405-33.

Surveys children's literature from Caxton to the present, emphasizing varying critical positions and trends in writing, especially in recent years.

B2045   EPSTEIN, JASON. "Good Bunnies Always Obey: Books for American Children." *Commentary* 35 (February 1963):112-22. (Letters in response in *Commentary* 36 [August 1963]:169-71. Reprinted in Egoff, *Only Connect*, 1st ed., pp. 70-90; 2d ed., 74-94.)

Maintains that "Children's books have increasingly become part of a bureaucratically administered sub-culture, largely cut off by a dense fog in conventional and irrelevant theory from the best literary and scientific culture of the community at large." Attacks recent Newbery award winners and the positions of Josette Frank and Nancy Larrick, and laments a bowdlerization of *Peter Rabbit* (whence the title).

B2046   FREY, CHARLES, and GRIFFITH, JOHN. "College English Courses in Children's Literature: A Sampling." *EE* 10 (February 1979):183-85.

Reports on response to a survey of college English departments regarding the teaching of children's literature.

B2047   GAY, CAROL. "The Onus of Teaching Children's Literature: The Need for Some Reappraisals." ERIC Educational Document Reproduction Service, 1975, ED 108 219. (Also in *ADE Bulletin* 47 [November 1975]:15-20.)

Suggests that children's literature should be taught in English departments in universities because that is where the subject properly belongs, that there is a great need for further research into the "cultivated, artistic, historic, psychological, and philosophical significance of children's literature," and that "active innovative" graduate courses leading to postgraduate degrees are needed.

B2048   GERHARDT, LILLIAN N. "An Argument Worth Opening." *Library Journal* 99 (15 May 1974):1425 and *SLJ* 20 (May 1974):7.

Suggests that children's literature is not part of the mainstream of literature but rather the last bastion of values, standards, and techniques that occurred in adult literature twenty years previously. Responses included those by E.L. Heins in *Horn Book* 51 (August 1975):355.

B2049   HAVILAND, VIRGINIA. "Current Trends in Children's Literature." *International Library Review* 5 (July 1973):261-67.

Discusses new criteria for evaluation, new themes, new attention to minorities, trends in graphics and in paperbacks, and changes in the status of children's literature emerging in the early 1970s.

B2050   -----. "A Second Golden Age? In A Time of Flood?" *Horn Book* 47 (August 1971):409-19. (Reprinted in Haviland, *Children and Literature*, pp. 88-97.)

Agrees with Townsend that a second Golden Age of children's literature has arrived while questioning the "narrowly centered case-study stories" that "tell it like it is."

B2051   HUNT, PETER. "Children's Book Research in Britain." *Signal* 25 (Jan-

uary 1978):12-15.
Summarizes trends in research in children's literature in England.

B2052   MOSS, ELAINE. "The Adult-eration of Children's Books." *Signal* 14
(May 1974):65-69. (Reprinted in Meek, *Cool Web*, pp. 333-37.)
Decries the increasing sophistication or "adulteration" of picture
books and teenage fiction. The challenge is to "maintain proven
standards" and still appeal to "the broader mass of young readers."

B2053   NIST, JOAN STIDHAM. "Children's Books: Current Trends." ERIC
Educational Document Reproduction Service, 1980, 9 pp., ED 192
366.
Mentions the increase in new texts on children's literature and
the emergence of new scholarly periodicals. Also summarizes trends in
children's literature, including the celebration of traditional America,
emphasis on ethnic materials in picture books, emphasis on grace of
language, and increase in media translations of children's books.

TRICKSTERS

B2054   ABRAMS, DAVID M., and SUTTON-SMITH, BRIAN. "The Development of the Trickster in Children's Narrative." *Journal of American
Folklore* 90 (January 1977):29-47.
Examines the response of children to trickster tales, particularly
those in *Bugs Bunny* cartoons, and their ability to construct their
own trickster tales.

B2055   MOSS, ANITA. "Versions of the Trickster in Children's Literature."
Advocate 2, no. 2 (Winter 1983):106-15.
Examines the role of the trickster in a wide range of classic and
recent children's literature and suggests stories for sequences on
tricksters for various age groups.

TURKEY

B2056   WALKER, BARBARA K., and AHMET, URPAL. "Folk Tales in Tur-
key." *Horn Book* 40 (February 1964):42-46.
An introduction to oral and written Turkish folktales.

UKRAINIA

B2057   WYNAR, CHRISTINE L. "Ukrainian Children's Literature in North
America." *Phaedrus* 6, no. 1 (Spring 1979):6-21.
Describes "the current status of Ukranian children's literture in
North America." Includes "Ukrainian language fiction, stories, poems,
legends, and national tales and nonfiction books for children to about
age 14" and also textbooks, language instruction books, periodicals,
reprints of classics, and some English language books with Ukrainian
themes. Contains a bibliography and a list of organizations.

UNCLES

B2058   MASTER, HELEN ELIZABETH. "Here, Then, Are Uncles." *Horn
Book* (August 1933):137-39.
A response to an earlier *Horn Book* article on aunts, describing
some well-known uncles in children's books.

UNITED STATES

B2059   AVI. "Children's Literature: The American Revolution." *TON* 33 (Winter 1977):149-61.
Traces the history of American children's literature, maintaining that it has from its beginnings been rooted in a realistic, serious, moral, and instructive mode. "Even American fantasy has it roots in realism." Concentrates on the nineteenth century.

B2060   BELLON, ELNER C. "Content Analysis of Children's Books Set in the South." Ed.D. dissertation, University of Tennessee, 1973, 208 pp., DA 34:6936.
Analyzes the content of thirty-six books of children's realistic fiction set in the South and draws inferences about the influence these books might have on readers.

B2061   EGOFF, SHEILA. "Children's Books: A Canadian's View of the Current American Scene." *Horn Book* 46 (April 1970):142-50. (Reprinted in Heins, *Crosscurrents*, pp. 128-36.)
A Canadian's view of the United States as presented in current realistic fiction for children.

B2062   HAVILAND, VIRGINIA. "The American Scene." In Koefoed, *Children's Literature*, pp. 14-20.
Summarizes trends in American children's books at the beginning of the 1970s, especially changes in readers and books in response to social changes, the impact of the children's paperback book, and increased focus on children's literature as a part of mainstream literature.

B2063   KELLY, R. GORDON. "Children's Literature." In *Handbook of American Popular Culture*, vol. 1. Edited by Thomas M. Inge. Westport, Conn.: Greenwood, 1978, pp. 49-76.
Provides a chronological and bibliographic survey of American children's literature, emphasizing references, sources, research collections, and historical criticism.

B2064   -----. "Children's Periodicals in the United States." *Phaedrus* 4, no. 2 (Fall 1977):5-10.
Reviews research on early American and recent periodicals for children, and concludes that the study of the children's periodical in America "is a neglected area within the relatively neglected field of children's literature."

B2065   LEVSTIK, LINDA SUZANNE THOMAS. "Refuge and Reflection: American Children's Literature as Social History, 1920-1940." Ph.D. dissertation, Ohio State University, 1980, 339 pp.
Examines American historical and realistic fiction for children in the period 1920-40 in relation to social, intellectual, and literary trends of the time.

B2066   LYSTAD, MARY. "From Dr. Mather to Dr. Seuss: Over 200 Years of American Children's Books." *Children Today* 5 (May-June 1976):10-15.
Provides a concise summary of the history of American children's literature.

B2067   OFEK, URIEL. "Tom and Laura from Right to Left: American Books Experienced by Young Hebrew Readers." In *Arbuthnot Lectures*, 1978, pp. 167-85.

       Describes the past and present American books read by young Israelis in Hebrew translation.

B2068   SHAW, JEAN DUNCAN. "An Historical Survey of Themes Recurrent in Selected Children's Literature Books Published in America Since 1850." Ph.D. dissertation, Temple University, 1966, 325 pp., DA 28:1059A.

       Identifies the popularity of themes in six categories during various periods: (1) the search for values, (2) problems of growing up, (3) travel and understanding people in foreign lands, (4) lives of heroes, (5) fun and fairy tales, and (6) the urge to know.

B2069   SMITH, DORA V. *Fifty Years of Children's Books, 1910-1960: Trends, Backgrounds, and Influences.* Champaign, Ill.: National Council of Teachers of English, 1963, 149 pp.

       A concise survey of American books for children, divided into four periods, with each period subdivided by discussions of particular trends, topics, and genres. Includes selections of illustrations from the books discussed and extensive notes, bibliographies, references, and sources of additional information.

UTOPIA

B2070   CARPENTER, HUMPHREY. "Epilogue: The Garden Revisited." In *Secret Gardens*, pp. 210-23.

       Explores the differences between the utopian themes of writers of the "Golden Age" (pre-World War I) and more recent writers of children's fantasy. Examines the works of J.R.R. Tolkien, C.S. Lewis, Mary Norton, Alan Garner, Philippa Pearce, and others. Concludes "We do not, it appears, live any longer in a society in which adults turn to child readers to work out their private dreams on a scale of a River Bank or a Never Never Land. The Enchanted Places, the Secret Gardens, were created in an age when society, the child, and the author stood in a certain relationship to each other which has now broken down. We may revisit those Enchanted Places ourselves, but we cannot create new ones."

B2071   DONELSON, KENNETH. *Literature for Today's Young Adults*, pp. 272-75.

       Discusses the appeal of books with utopian themes for young adults.

VALUES

B2072   ARKSEY, LAURA. "Books, Children, and Moral Values: A Subliminal Approach." *TON* 34 (Summer 1978):375-86.

       Argues in favor of allowing children's literature to "exert whatever impact it may have without the help of the moral educator." Also discusses the applications of Kohlberg's theories of moral development to children's literature.

B2073   BIRD, KATHY. "The Value of Individualism." *EE* 50 (May 1973): 707-14.

Examines the ways in which the American ideal of individualism has been reflected in children's literature. Among books discussed are Fred Gipson's *Old Yeller*, Elizabeth Speare's *The Witch of Blackbird Pond*, Esther Forbes's *Johnny Tremain*, Robert McCloskey's *Homer Price*, Madeleine L'Engle's *Wrinkle In Time*, Louise Fitzhugh's *Harriet The Spy*, and Mary Weiks's *The Jazz Man*.

B2074 BISKIN, DONALD, and HOSKISSON, KENNETH. "Moral Development through Children's Literature." *Elementary School Journal* 75 (December 1974):152-57.
Discusses using children's literature to help develop moral awareness.

B2075 BLOUNT, MARGARET. "The Moral Tale." In *Animal Land*, pp. 42-60.
Traces the use of animals in moral tales from early times through the twentieth century.

B2076 BRODERICK, DOROTHY. "Moral Values and Children's Literature." *SLJ* 18 (December 1971):42. (Reprinted in Gerhardt, *Issues in Children's Book Selection*, pp. 35-39.)
Provides a concise summary of Kohlberg's aspects of moral development as they might be useful to the critic of children's literature.

B2077 -----. "A Study in Conflicting Values." *Library Journal* 91 (15 May 1966):2557-64. Reply by Deane S. Smith in 91 (15 December 1966):5006.
Examines the role of conflicting values in the selection and evaluation of children's books, citing a number of examples of controversial books.

B2078 CAMERON, ELEANOR. "Art and Morality." *Proceedings of the Children's Literature Association* 7 (1980):30-44.
Compares the positions of critics Susan Sontag (morality has no place in a criticism of a work of art) and John Gardner (the artist's expression of morality cannot be separated from art), siding with Gardner. Takes as examples her own *To the Green Mounains*, Ursula K. Le Guin's works, Jill Paton Walsh's *Unleaving*, and Cormier's *Chocolate War*, *I Am the Cheese*, and *After the First Death*. She finds Cormier's books bleak and grim and calls them a "trilogy of despair."

B2079 CARMICHAEL, CAROLYN WILSON. "A Study of Selected Social Values as Reflected in Contemporary Realistic Fiction for Children." Ph.D. dissertation, Michigan State University, 1971, 224 pp., DA 32:3296A.
Examines the extent to which the values of "justice, work, obedience and knowledge, and the corresponding value-themes of belief in equality of opportunity for all people, acceptance of responsibility, obedience to laws and recognition of the importance of an education and knowledge were expressed in contemporary realistic fiction for children . . . from 1949 through 1969."

B2080 CHAMBERS, DEWEY. "An Exploratory Study of Social Values in Children's Literature." Ed.D. dissertation, Wayne State University, 1965, 110 pp., DA 26:4324A.

Finds children's fiction lacking in the social values identified as important for the developing child between ages of five and nine.

B2081   CIANCIOLO, PATRICIA J. "Children's Books Can Reflect the American Style of Living." *EE* 41 (November 1964):773-77, 822.

Identifies books that (1) dignify humanity, individuality, and freedom, (2) respect truth and rule of law, (3) show how individuality contributes to the welfare of the group, (4) depict children having a well established place, (5) acknowledge likenesses and differences in people, (6) face the realities of life, (7) welcome change, and (8) depict democratic living in an open society. Includes a "Bibliography of Children's Books Which Reflect the American Style of Living."

B2082   COLLINSON, ROGER. "The Children's Author and His Readers." *CLE*, o.s., no. 10 (March 1973):37-47.

Explores ways in which authors communicate values and appropriate ways for publishers, critics, teachers, and librarians to respond.

B2083   COUGHLAN, MARGARET. "Guardians of the Young: Being a Strange and Wonderful Relation of How They Have Striven to Distinguish 'The Firm Ground from the Boggy Mire'; or, Why There Has Never Been--and Probably Never Will Be--Intellectual Freedom for Children." *TON* 33 (Winter 1977):137-48.

Surveys trends in the guardianship of the morals and values of the young in the literary world over the past 100 years. Includes references.

B2084   DORNELLES, LENY WERNECK. "The Creation of Children's Books and Cultural Values." *Bookbird* 12, no. 3 (1974):25-31.

Argues that children's books should come from deep roots in traditional culture.

B2085   GARVEY, JOHN. "Voice of Blume: That Doesn't Recognise Itself." *Commonweal* 107 (July 1980):392-93.

Argues that new realistic books such as Judy Blume's and Norma Klein's are presenting the assumptions and values of upper-middle-class white liberals and do not realize how orthodox and didactic they are.

B2086   GIBLIN, JAMES CROSS. "Aesthetic or Functional, Saccharine or Shocking? An Editor Looks at Values in Children's Books." *CLE*, n.s. 8, no. 3 (1977):120-26.

Identifies values in children's books as (1) artistic or aesthetic, (2) social and cultural, (3) functional, and (4) commercial. Traces changes in values as reflected in changes in advertisements in *Horn Book* for 1947, 1957, and 1967. Concludes that the frequent heated debates in the field of children's literature over what is valuable and what is not, reflect a great value placed on children's literature.

B2087   GOSA, CHERYL. "Moral Development in Current Fiction for Children and Young Adults." *LA* 54 (May 1977):529-36.

Surveys recent literature for children in grades kindergarten through third, fourth through sixth, fifth through seventh, and eighth through twelfth in terms of Kohlberg's stages of moral development, and finds that the books are filled with moral dilemmas beyond the ability of their readers.

B2088   GUPTON, SANDRA LEE. "Moral Education as a Part of the Study of Children's Literature: An Inservice Model and Case-Study." Ed.D. dissertation, University of North Carolina at Greensboro, 1979, 237 pp., DA 40:2011A.

Explores the use of children's literature to teach moral education, pointing out advantages and disadvantages.

B2089   HANNABUSS, STUART. "The Moral of It All." *Junior Bookshelf* 40 (June 1976):131-34; (August 1976):185-87.

Surveys the tendency from earliest times to the present to mingle entertainment and instruction in children's picture books and books for older readers.

B2090   HEARNE, BETSY. "Timely and Timeless Children's Books as a Mirror of Society." *Catholic Library World* 54 (July-August 1982):18-20.

Discusses recent trends in values in children's books.

B2091   HIET, SHARON LEE. "Dealing with Moral Issues in Fiction." *ALAN Review* 11, no. 1 (Fall 1983):40.

Discusses the handling of moral dilemmas in three books for young adults in terms of Kohlberg's theories of moral development: Pat Frank's *Alas Babylon*, Paul Zindel's *The Pigman*, and Lois Duncan's *The Killing of Mr. Griffin*.

B2092   HIPPS, G. MELVIN. "Adolescent Literature and Values Clarification: A Warning." *Wisconsin English Journal* 20, no. 2 (January 1978):5-9.

Warns that attempts to use literature to teach values clarification may distort the literature. Attacks the reasoning in Jean McClure Kelty's "The Cult of the Kill in Adolescent Fiction."

B2093   HOSKISSON, KENNETH, and BISKIN, DONALD S. "Analyzing and Discussing Children's Literature Using Kohlberg's Stages of Moral Development." *Reading Teacher* 33 (November 1979):141-47.

See also "Using Children's Literature to Foster Moral Development," by Arlene M. Pillar, pp. 148-51, in this same issue.

B2094   INGLIS, FRED. "The Awkward Ages; or, What Shall We Tell the Children?" In *Ideology and the Imagination*. Cambridge: Cambridge University Press, 1975, pp. 140-61.

Examines the intersection of values and art in literature, particularly children's literature. Sees in children's literature a last bastion of morality or "goodness."

B2095   -----. "The Lesser Great Tradition: Carry On Children." *CLE*, n.s. 9, no. 2 (Summer 1978):73-77.

Argues for "a sense of responsibility" in children's novels, for books that "return a credible meaning to such great names as 'honour, love, obedience, troops of friends.'"

B2096   JAN, ISABELLE. "Didactic Influences." In *On Children's Literature*, pp. 18-29.

Discusses the role of didacticism and especially Rousseau's influence on the development of children's literature, particularly in France.

B2097   KELLY, R. GORDON. "Literary and Cultural Values in the Evaluation of Books for Children." *Advocate* 4, no. 2 (Winter 1985):84-100.

Argues that the critic's "evaluation based on conventional literary values may mask what is truly at issue--a critic's acceptance or rejection of the moral and social implications of an author's fictive world."

B2098   LUECKE, FRITZ J., ed. *Children's Books, Views and Values.* Middle-town, Conn.: Xerox, 1973, 86 pp.

Reprints the following articles: "A Feminist Look at Children's Books," by Feminists on Children's Media, pp. 3-20; "Peter Rabbit . . . Say Good-Bye to Snow White," by Jane Yolen, pp. 21-26; "The New Realism," by Robert Burch, pp. 27-40; "The Dawning of the Age of Aquarius for Multi-Ethnic Children's Literature," by David K. Gast, pp. 41-50; "If Not Busing How About Booking?," by Barbara Glancy, pp. 51-60; "Violence: Factors Considered By a Children's Book Editor," by James C. Giblin, pp. 61-70; "Death in Children's Literature," by Judith P. Moss, pp. 71-78; and "Morals, Morals Everywhere: Values in Children's Fiction," by William D. Eisenberg, pp. 79-89.

B2099   MOIR, HUGHES. "If We've Always Had Books That Taught All These Virtues, Why Is Our Society in Such Lousy Shape?" *LA* 54 (May 1977):522-28.

Explores the applications of Kohlberg's theories of moral development to the study and teaching of children's literature.

B2100   MOYNIHAN, RUTH B. "Ideologies in Children's Literature: Some Preliminary Notes." *Children's Literature* 2 (1973):166-72.

Discusses the ways in which children's literature reflects the dominant values within a society, with examples from L. Frank Baum, A.A. Milne, Watty Piper's *The Little Engine that Could*, Virginia Burton's *The Little House*, and Dr. Seuss's *Horton Hears a Who!*

B2101   NEVILLE, EMILY. "Social Values in Children's Literature." In Fenwick, *Critical Approach*, pp. 46-52.

Discusses the handling of social values in a number of classic and recent works of children's literature.

B2102   PATERSON, GARY H. "Adults, Children, Didacticism, and the Modes in Children's Literature." *CCL* 14 (1979):14-23.

Examines the ways in which certain repeatedly upheld values are portrayed in children's literature. Argues that "Writers often associate the level of normality, deservability, or achievement with the children's world, while the level of dullness, ineptitude, and austerity is relegated to the adults."

B2103   RIHN, BERNARD ANTHONY. "Kohlberg Level of Moral Reasoning of Protagonists in Newbery Award Winning Fiction." Ph.D. dissertation, Stanford University, 1978, 137 pp., DA 38:7141A.

Investigates "how the nature of a passage and the characteristics of a judge act jointly to influence the assignment of a 'stage of moral reasoning' score to the solutions of dilemmas faced by protagonists in Newbery Award Winning Fiction."

B2104   ROSENHEIM, EDWARD W., Jr. "Children's Reading and Adults' Values." *Library Quarterly* 37 (January 1967):3-14. (Reprinted in

Egoff, *Only Connect*, 1st ed., pp. 17-32; 2d ed., 39-54.)

Urges that the same standards of judgment be applied to juvenile as to adult literature, not preconceived adult notions of what juvenile values should be.

B2105　RYDER, MARY STEPHENS. "Personal Values and Values Identified in Newbery Medal Books by Students and Children's Librarians." Ed.D. dissertation, University of Denver, 1978, 157 pp.

Compares seventh grade students' and librarians' perceptions of values expressed in Newbery Award books published between 1971 and 1975.

B2106　SCHARF, PETER. "Moral Development and Literature for Adolescents." *TON* 33 (Winter 1977):131-36.

Applies Kohlberg's theory of stages of moral development to teenagers' responses to literature.

B2107　SCHWARTZ, SHEILA. "Using Adolescent Fiction that Deals with Current Problems and Lifestyles to Explore Contemporary Values." ERIC Educational Document Reproduction Service, 1976, 17 pp., ED 119 199.

Argues that contemporary adolescent fiction be used to teach humanistic values.

B2108　SHACHTER, JAQUELINE. "Themes and Values in Selected Children's Literature." ERIC Education Document Reproduction Service, 1979, 13 pp., ED 173 866.

Suggests ways to stimulate discussion of ethical values and moral issues in four books: Virginia Hamilton's *The Planet of Junior Brown*, Scott O'Dell's *Island of the Blue Dolphins*, Madeleine L'Engle's *The Arm of the Starfish*, and Katherine Paterson's *The Great Gilly Hopkins*.

B2109　SHACKFORD, JANE W. "Dealing with Dr. Dolittle: A New Approach to the 'isms.'" *LA* 55 (February 1978):180-87.

Suggests using Kohlberg's stages of moral development as a basis for discussing moral dilemmas provoked by racist and sexist fiction. Illustrates the technique with Lofting's *The Voyages of Dr. Dolittle*.

B2110　SORIANO, MARC. "Children's Books and Human Rights." *Prospects* 7, no. 2 (1977):204-25.

Explores ways in which children's books have been used to teach values and suggests ways in which a conscious effort might be made to create new books that incorporate positive statements about human rights.

B2111　UFFMAN, BARBARA ELIZABETH. "Responses of Young Children and Adults to Books with a Lesson." Ph.D. dissertation, University of Minnesota, 1981, 183 pp., DA 42:119A.

Concludes that young children (first graders) do not consider lessons important in stories, and that teachers should focus on literary elements, appreciation, and enjoyment of literature.

B2112　WOOD, T. "A Comparison of Values Found in Preschool and Primary-Aged Children's Books and Values Held by Adults." Ph.D. dissertation, Michigan State University, 1976, 117 pp., DA 37:5593A.

Examines shifts in values as expressed in children's picture books and as held by adults during the years 1960, 1964, and 1968. Finds a lack of correlation between adults' values and those expressed in children's books.

B2113   ZWEIGBERGK, EVA VON. "Aims and Ideals Reflected in Children's Books." *Bookbird* 6, no. 3 (1968):3–14.
Surveys the history of children's books in terms of the values they have presented.

VIETNAM

B2114   MORTON, MIRIAM. "Children's Books and Vietnam." *IRBC* 4, no. 3-4 (Winter 1972-73):10.
Reviews three books of Vietnamese folktales, the only Vietnamese literature available to children in the United States at that time.

B2115   NGUYEN, HAANG. "Literature for Young People in Vietnam." *Bookbird* 1 (1984):24–26.
An overview.

VIOLENCE

B2116   BLATT, GLORIA T. "Children's Books: X or PG?" *TON* 32 (November 1975):61–66.
Examines violence in children's books and children's response to it. Concludes that arguments for censorship are without foundation.

B2117   -----. "Violence in Children's Literature: A Content Analysis of a Select Sampling of Children's Literature and a Study of Children's Responses to Literary Episodes Depicting Violence." Ph.D. dissertation, Michigan State University, 1972, 358 pp., DA 33:2316A.
Analyzes violence in children's realistic fiction published between 1960 and 1970. Finds historical fiction more violent than books with contemporary settings.

B2118   GIBLIN, JAMES. "Violence: Factors Considered by a Children's Book Editor." *EE* 49 (January 1972):64–67.
Among criteria suggested are appropriateness of treatment, realism, honesty, emotional depth, and thoughtfulness.

B2119   LEACOCK, STEPHEN. "Mother Goose--Step for Children." *Horn Book* 14 (May-June 1938):175–78.
Defends the old unexpurgated fairy tales and the blood and violence of adventure tales. The terror and bloodshed represent "the way in which little children, from generation to generation, learn in ways as painless as can be followed, the stern environment of life and death."

WALES

B2120   KEYSE, FRANK, ed. *Loughborough 1983. Proceedings. Sixteenth Loughborough International Seminar on Children's Literature.* Aberystwyth, Dyfed, Wales: Welsh National Centre for Children's Literature, 1984, 140 pp.
Concentrates on Welsh children's literature. Includes Raymond Garlick's introductory "Once Below a Time," pp. 3–12; Gwyn Thomas's "The Four Branches of the Mabinogi," pp. 13–22; Bedwyr

Lewis Jones's "Gladly Would We Have a Tale," pp. 23-32; Mairwen Gwynn Jones's "Un tro . . . Once Upon a Time . . . A Remembrance of Books and Children Past," pp. 33-47; C. Davies's "Byd Sali Mali: Publishing in a Minority Language," pp. 48-52; Robin Gwyndaf's "A Story Without End: The Folk Narrative Tradition of the Children of Wales," pp. 53-71; Alan Garner's "The Edge of the Ceiling," pp. 72-76; Lloyd Alexander's "A Recorded Message to Loughborough 1983," pp. 77-78; Susan Cooper's "My Links with Wales," pp. 79-81; Gweneth Lilly's "The Deep Streams: Welsh Folklore and History as a Sense of Inspiration," pp. 82-90; Nancy Bond's "Landscape of Fiction," pp. 91-99; Alison Morgan's "Morgan Country," pp. 100-108, and Aeronwy Thomas-Ellis's "Christmas: When Dad Showed Goodwill Towards Children," pp. 109-11.

B2121   KIEFER, BARBARA Z. "Wales as Setting for Children's Fantasy." *CLE*, n.s. 13, no. 2 (Summer 1982):95-102.
     Looks at the Welsh setting in the fantasies of Lloyd Alexander, Alan Garner, and Susan Cooper.

WAR

B2122   BARKER, KEITH. "The Glory of the Garden: Evacuees in Children's Literature." *School Librarian* 32 (June 1984):102-7.
     Discusses a number of children's books portraying the children evacuated from London and other urban areas during World War II.

B2123   CADOGAN, MARY. *Women and Children First: The Fiction of Two World Wars*. London: Gollancz, 1978, 301 pp.
     Examines the experiences of women and children in the two major wars of the twentieth century as presented in English fiction for children and adults. There are chapters on the girls' and boys' literature of World War I, chapters on the juvenile fiction of the 1940s, and on postwar children's fiction about the war.

B2124   FOX, GEOFF. "Pro Patria: Young Readers and the 'Great War.'" *CLE*, n.s. 16, no. 4 (Winter 1985):233-47.
     Examines poems written for young readers during World War I, many of them drawn from the *Boy's Own Paper*.

B2125   GARRISON, JEAN WOOD. "A Comparison of Selected Factors in Children's Realistic Fiction Having War-Related Plots Published in England and the United States during World Wars I and II." Ed.D. dissertation, Temple University, 1981, 193 pp., DA 42:1930A.
     Finds that, contrary to theories, over three hundred books with war-related themes were published for children during World Wars I and II in England and over four hundred were published in the United States. Categorizes the plots as follows: (a) home front, (b) home front in other countries, (c) evacuation, (d) flying, (e) sea action, (f) spies, (g) land fighting, (h) animals, (i) sabotage, (j) girls in action, (k) training, and (l) miscellaneous or undetermined. Finds few books of quality and few now still in print. Finds no significant differences in the English and American books.

B2126   HEARNE, BETSY. "U.S. Children's Books on World War II--An Overview and Representative Bibliography." *Bookbird* 3 (1980):23-25.
     Surveys American children's books about World War II.

B2127   JAMES, DAVID L. "Recent World War II Fiction: A Survey." *CLE*, n.s. 8, no. 2 (Summer 1977):71-79.
A critical review of fourteen recent novels, including detailed analysis of Robert Westall's *The Machine-Gunners* and Nina Bawden's *Carrie's War*.

B2128   JOHNSON, NICHOLAS. "What Do Children Learn from War Comics?" In Tucker, *Suitable for Children?*, pp. 93-102. (Abridged from an article in *New Society*, 7 July 1966.)
Considers the "presentation of nationality" and "evidence on some of the probable effects of reading war comics."

B2129   KINGSTON, CAROLYN T. "The Tragic Moment: War." In *Tragic Mode*, pp. 93-123.
Analyzes the treatment of war in a number of books for children and young adults. Many titles have been indexed separately in this bibliography.

B2130   LAUBENFELS, MARY JEAN. "A Study of the Theme of War in Selected Literature for Junior High Readers (1940-1975)." Ph.D. dissertation, Ohio State University, 1975, 176 pp., DA 36:3547A.
Compares the attitudes toward war expressed by writers depicting World War II and more recent conflicts.

B2131   MacCANN, DONNARAE. "Militarism in Juvenile Fiction." *IRBC* 13, nos. 6-7 (1982):18-20.
An overview of the changing treatment of war in children's fiction. Includes references to other criticism on the topic.

B2132   MANESS, MARY. "War Is Glorious: War is Hell: War Is Absurd." *LA* 53 (May 1976):560-63.
Finds highly diverse treatments of war in children's literature.

B2133   MELAMED, LISA. "Between the Lines of Fire: The Vietnam War in Literature for Young Readers." *L&U* 3, no. 2 (Winter 1979-80):76-85.
Reviews four books on the Vietnam War for young readers and finds them lacking.

B2134   MILLER, ROGER. "Up Front with the Comics." *Southwest Review* 57 (Autumn 1972):288-300.
Examines attitudes toward war expressed in American comics during World War II.

B2135   NIST, JOAN STIDHAM. "Perspective on World War II." *Children's Literature* 9 (1981):203-9.
Reviews six books on World War II: Sheila Burnford's *Bel Ria*, pp. 208-9; Bette Greene's, *Summer of My German Soldier*, pp. 207-8; Hans Peter Richter's *Friedrich*, pp. 205-6; Yevgeny Ryss's *Search Behind the Lines*, pp. 206-7; Robert Westall's, *The Machine-Gunners*, pp. 204-5; and Alki Zei's *Petros' War*, pp. 203-4.

B2136   ØRVIG, MARY. "War in Books for Young People." *Bookbird* 5, no. 2 (1967):3-16.
Surveys old and new children's books with war and its aftermath as their theme. Includes a bibliography of children's and adults'

books discussed.

B2137 PRAGER, ARTHUR. "Beating the Boche." In *Rascals at Large*, pp. 169-213.

Analyzes the treatment of war in popular series books of the 1920s, 1930s, and 1940s.

B2138 RAJALIN, MARITA. "The Second World War in Finnish Juvenile Literature." *Bookbird* 1 (1980):13-16.

Discusses eleven Finnish and eight Bulgarian books for children and young people.

B2139 RIFAS, LEONARD. "'War Makes Men' Is Message from Comic Books." *IRBC* 14, no. 6 (1983):8-12.

An analysis of over 200 war comics reveals five common prowar themes: (1) war makes men, (2) war is necessary, (3) war defends freedom and democracy, (4) war improves race relations, and (5) war is the ultimate sport.

B2140 SODERBERGH, PETER A. "The Dark Mirror: War Ethos in Juvenile Fiction, 1865-1919." *University of Dayton Review* 10, no. 1 (Summer 1973):13-24.

Surveys the handling of war themes in popular American juvenile fiction.

B2141 SHUTZE, MARCIA, and GREENLAW, M. JEAN. "Childhood's Island Receives a Gift of Myrrh: A Study of Children's Books with World War II Settings." *TON* 31 (January 1975):199-209.

Examines trends in juvenile books set during World War II, based on a study of twenty-two books written from the time of the war itself up into the 1970s.

B2142 TAYLOR, ANNE. "A Comparative Study of Juvenile Fiction Dealing with the Second World War." *Emergency Librarian* 11 (November-December 1983):13-21.

Surveys a range of children's fiction dealing with World War II, analyzing various themes and approaches. Includes a bibliography grouped according to the country in which the story is set.

B2143 "World War II Reflected in Children's Books." *Bookbird* no. 3 (1979): 3-17; no. 4 (1979):8-16.

Issue 3 includes Winifred Kaminski's "The Depiction of War and Nazism in West-German Children's and Juvenile Literature," pp. 3-7; Lucia Binder's "World War II in Books Read by Austrian Children," pp. 8-13; and Sheila Ray's "1979--40 Years After World War II: Children's Books in Great Britain," pp. 14-17. Issue 4 includes Genevieve Humbert's "The Second World War in French Books for Adolescents," and Yoshiko Kogochi's "The Depiction of World War II in Japanese Books for Children."

WEST POINT

B2144 ADAMS, TIMOTHY DOW. "The Long Gray Lie: West Point in Children's Fiction." *CLE*, n.s. 12, no. 3 (Autumn 1981):151-59.

Examines the unrealistic way in which series writers handle moral and ethical problems in the West Point setting.

WESTERNS

B2145   DONELSON, KENNETH. "Westerns." In *Literature for Today's Young Adults*, pp. 234-38.
Points out that the conventions of the western are "similar to those of the young adult novel."

WILLOW PATTERN

B2146   McCLARY, BEN HARRIS. "The Story of the Story: The Willow Pattern Plate in Children's Literature." *Children's Literature* 10 (1982):56-69.
Traces the development of the story from its origins with the plate's creation in 1780 up to the present.

WORDLESS PICTURE BOOKS

B2147   BADER, BARBARA. "Wordless Picturebooks." In *American Picturebooks*, pp. 539-43.
Discusses the nature and development of the wordless and almost wordless picture book.

B2148   CIANCIOLO, PATRICIA JEAN. "Use Wordless Picture Books to Teach Reading, Visual Literacy and to Study Literature." *TON* 29 (April 1973):226-34. (Reprinted in White, *Children's Literature*, pp. 163-71.)
Suggests ways to use a wide range of wordless picture books to teach reading, visual literacy, and many aspects of literature. Includes a bibliography of wordless books.

B2149   GRASTY, PATRICIA ELAINE. "The Status of Wordless Picture Books, 1960-1976." Ed.D. dissertation, Temple University, 1978, 124 pp., DA 39:2049A.
Examines the mechanics and content of wordless picture books published between 1960 and 1976 and identifies major characteristics and trends.

B2150   GROFF, PATRICK. "Children's Literature Versus Wordless 'Books.'" *TON* 30 (April 1974):294-303.
Argues against Cianciolo's thesis (see above) that wordless books can be used to teach children to read and appreciate literature.

B2151   KAUFFMAN, DOROTHY MAE. "An Identification of Wordless Picture Story Books for Children Published in the United States from 1930 to 1980." Ph.D. dissertation, University of Maryland, 1981, 222 pp., DA 42:3478A.
Describes the literacy, visual, and formal aspects of a sample of 127 wordless picture story books. Concludes that the wordless picture book is literary as well as visual, that its narrative art is comparable to verbal storytelling, and that it will continue to be published as a type of children's book.

B2152   LARRICK, NANCY. "Wordless Picture Books and the Teaching of Reading." *Reading Teacher* 29 (May 1976):743-46.
Explores the responses of young children and their teachers to a number of wordless picture books. Some highly praised by adults

were not enjoyed by the children.

B2153 OMOTOSO, S. "Responses of North Floridian American and Western Nigerian Seven-year Olds to Wordless Picture Storybooks: A Cross cultural Analysis." Ph.D. dissertation, University of Florida, 1976, 166 pp., DA 37:6352A.

Found that Nigerian subjects told longer but less grammatically complex stories than the Americans. Concluded that "wordless picture story books might provide a vehicle for children raised in an oral storytelling tradition to develop both awareness and stimulate language development" and that "Children raised in a literary [book] culture might be encouraged to 'tell' stories to wordless picture story books as a bridge to oral storytelling of original stories."

B2154 SCHWARCZ, JOSEPH H. "The Textless Contemporary Picture Book: A Minor Art Form." *Phaedrus* 9 (1982):45-50.

Defines textless picture books and categorizes them according to content and structure: collections of objects or scenes, conceptual challenge books, pictorial fiction, and framed sequences. Also discusses pseudotextless picture books and the role of the textless picture book. Includes references.

YOUNG ADULT LITERATURE

B2155 ABRAHAMSON, RICHARD. "*Nowhere Runner*: A Study in the Creation of a Novel for Adolescents." Ph.D. dissertation, University of Iowa, 1972, 204 pp., DA 38:2026A.

Includes an original novel, *The Nowhere Runner*, written for a teenaged audience, the author's journal written during the creation of the novel, and a list of "ten conclusions about the creative process as it pertained to one writer during the creation of a novel for adolescents."

B2156 AGEE, HUGH. "Hackneyed, Acned, or Just Plain Good: Perceiving Quality in Young Adult Fiction." ERIC Educational Document Reproduction Service, 1980, 20 pp., ED 185 549.

Discusses the application of Stephen Dunning's rating scale for young adult fiction to Maureen Daly's *Seventeenth Summer*, M.E. Kerr's *If I Love You Am I Trapped Forever?*, Robert Cormier's *The Chocolate War*, and Alice Childress's *A Hero Ain't Nothin But A Sandwich*.

B2157 ALM, RICHARD S. "The Glitter and the Gold." *English Journal* 44 (September 1955):315-22, 350.

Discusses the rise of fiction centered on the personal concerns of teenagers. Among flaws pointed out are the "sugar puff" approach, oversimplification, and inconsistencies and lack of development in characterization. Among writers he praises as substantial are Anne Emery, Betty Cavanna, H. Gregor Felsen, Maureen Daly, Mary Stolz, Mildred Walker, Rumer Godden, and Harmon Bro. Also singles out Esther Forbes's *Johnny Tremain* and Marjorie K. Rawlings's *The Yearling*.

B2158 -----. "A Study of the Assumptions Concerning Human Experience Underlying Certain Works of Fiction For and About Adolescents." Ph.D. dissertation, University of Minnesota, 1954, 1044 pp., DA 16:2343A.

Concludes from a study of books by ten recommended and ten not recommended authors that both contain false and valid assumptions about human behavior, that recommended novels in general contain a truer representation of human experience, and that they contain more valid assumptions than the not recommended books.

B2159 AUBIN, PATRICIA. "The Young Adult Novel in American Schools, 1930-1980." Ed.D. dissertation, Boston University of Education, 1980, 174 pp., DA 41:3502A.

Finds the young adult novel has developed "from romanticism to realism, from stereotyped characterizations to multi-faceted protagonists, and from pedantic problem solving to problem posing." Recommends that teachers acquaint themselves with the wide assortment of young adult novels, especially from the 1970s, that they listen to their students, and take into consideration "the developmental nature of appreciation and understanding in literary experience."

B2160 BABBITT, NATALIE. "Between Innocence and Maturity." *Horn Book* 48 (February 1972):33-37. (Reprinted in Varlejs, *Young Adult Literature*, pp. 140-44.)

Says teenaged fiction is not needed. "Teenagers do not need a fiction of their own: they are quite ready to move into the world of adult fiction."

B2161 BACHELDER, LINDA; KELLY, PATRICIA; KENNY, DONALD; and SMALL, ROBERT. "Looking Backword: Trying to Find the Classic Young Adult Novel." *English Journal* 69 (September 1980):86-89.

An overview of the development of the young adult novel with a listing of those from the seventies whose status approaches "classic."

B2162 BEASLEY, WALLACE. "The Self as the Source of Knowledge: A Philosophical Study of the Identity Theme in the Adolescent Novel." Ed.D. dissertation, University of Tennessee, 1980, 204 pp., DA 41:3395A.

Examines identity searches in nine adolescent novels: Lynn Reid Banks's *My Darling Villain*, Gunnel Beckman's *That Early Spring*, John Bowers's *November . . . December*, Hila Colman's *Sometimes I Don't Love My Mother*, Charles P. Crawford's *Letter Perfect*, Alice Hoffman's *Property of*, Irene Hunt's *William*, Norma Klein's *It's Ok if You Don't Love Me*, and Ursula Le Guin's *Very Far Away from Anywhere Else*. Concludes that the search for identity in these novels contains "the same kinds of universal human concerns and experiences that were dominant in past philosophical, religious, and literary movements."

B2163 BLEICH, LINDA LEE. "A Study of the Psychological and Social Characteristics of Adolescence in Adolescent Literature, 1945-1975." Ph.D. dissertation, 1980, 206 pp., DA 41:2542A.

Analyzes and compares the portrayal of stages of adolescent development in young adult novels published between 1945-60 and 1960-75.

B2164 BURTON, DWIGHT L. "The Novel for the Adolescent." *English Journal* 40 (September 1951):363-69.

An influential early survey of adolescent fiction. Among novelists discussed are Maureen Daly, Paul Annixter, Betty Cavanna, John Tunis, and Madeleine L'Engle.

B2165   -----. "Pap to Protein? Two Generations of Adolescent Fiction." *Texas Tech Journal of Education* 7 (Winter 1980):15-24. (Reprinted in Bator, *Signposts*, pp. 310-18.)

Surveys development of the junior novel between 1951 and 1980.

B2166   CAMERON, ELEANOR. "McLuhan, Youth and Literature: Part III." *Horn Book* 49 (February 1973):79-85.

In the third part of this article (the first two parts dealt primarily with Roald Dahl's *Charlie and the Chocolate Factory* and E.B. White's *Charlotte's Web*) the focus is on young adult literature, which on the whole she finds lacking, although several titles she considers excellent are discussed briefly.

B2167   CARLSEN, G.R. "Criteria for Excellence in Adolescent Literature." ERIC Educational Document Reproduction Service, 1978, 10 pp., ED 155 670.

Identifies the following characteristics as common to adolescent novels: a tone implied by diction and syntax, themes that relate to adolescent concerns, a predilection to convey a message, and an atmosphere of realism that presents life as it is through the use of details in setting, characters, and plot.

B2168   *Children's Literature in Education*, n.s. 15, no. 3 (Autumn 1984):157-85.

Includes "Fiction for Children 1970-1984: 4. Growing Up," pp. 157-70, a critically annotated list of recommended books on growing up; and Mary Hoffman's "Growing Up: A Survey," pp. 171-85, which argues that in the 1970s children's literature itself has grown up, and comments on books classified as "problem novels," books handling race, sexual identity, and family roles, and new themes and new stereotypes arising in the 1980s.

B2169   CLARKE, LORETTA MARIE. "A Critical Approach to Four Novels of Adolescence." Ph.D. dissertation, University of Iowa, 1970, 131 pp., DA 31:4758A.

Examines four adolescent novels "exclusively from the viewpoint of literary criticism": Paul Zindel's *The Pigman*, John Tunis's *His Enemy, His Friend*, Chaim Potok's *The Chosen*, and John Knowles's *A Separate Peace*.

B2170   COHEN, PHYLLIS. "A New Look at Old Books: Coming of Age." *Young Readers' Review* 1, no. 1 (September 1964):12.

Discusses *And Now Miguel* and *Onion John* by Jospeh Krumgold, and *Call It Courage* by Armstrong Sperry as examples of the initiation rite archetype.

B2171   COMPTON, MARY F., and SKELTON, JUANITA. "A Study of Selected Adolescent Problems as Presented in Contemporary Realistic Fiction for Middle School Students." *Adolescence* 17 (Fall 1982):637-45.

Finds the characters in contemporary realistic fiction positively portrayed as realistically confronting difficult problems.

B2172   COOPER, B.W. "The Adolescent in Contemporary Fiction." *School Librarian* 19 (June 1971) 118-24.

Analyzes the portrayal of adult-child relationships, adolescent friendships, and self-awareness or self-identity in fiction for adolescents.

B2173   COPELAND, JEFFREY S. "A Refreshing Breeze in Young Adult Literature." *TON* 41 (Winter 1985):147-50.
A humorous look at changing trends in young adult fiction from
the 1940s and 1950s to the 1980s.

B2174   DAVIS, JAMES E., ed. "Fiction for Adolescents: Theory and Practice."
Focus: Teaching English Language Arts 3, no. 2 (Winter 1977):85 pp.
(Also in ERIC Educational Document Reproduction Service, 1977, 85
pp., ED 157 082.)
The entire issue focuses on the study and teaching of adolescent
fiction. Articles on Robert Cormier, Judy Blume, M.E. Kerr, Norma
Klein, and Paul Zindel have been indexed separately in this bibliog-
raphy.

B2175   -----. "Recent Trends in Fiction for Adolescents." *English Journal* 56
(May 1967):720-24.
Compares characteristics of novels for adolescents before and
after 1959.

B2176   DE LUCA, GERALDINE. "Taking True Risks: Controversial Issues in
New Young Adult Novels." *L&U* 3, no. 2 (Winter 1979-80):125-48.
Discusses five recent young adult novels where conventional
morality does not always prevail. Sandra Scoppetone's *Happy Endings
Are All Alike*, Walter Dean Myers's *It Ain't All for Nothin'*, M.E.
Kerr's *Gentlehands*, Robert Cormier's *After the First Death*, Aidan
Chambers's *Breaktime*.

B2177   -----. "Unself-Conscious Voices: Larger Contexts for Adolescents."
L&U 2, no. 2 (Fall 1978):89-108.
Argues that just as *Catcher in the Rye* is a descendant of *Huck-
leberry Finn*, the modern young adult novel is a direct descendant of
Catcher. After outlining clichés found in most young adult fiction,
which are traceable to Salinger, De Luca analyzes three novels which
do not follow the pattern and which she feels are "worth an adoles-
cents time and attention." These are Mollie Hunter's *A Sound of
Chariots*, Betty Smith's *A Tree Grows in Brooklyn*, and Judith
Guest's *Ordinary People*."

B2178   DERING, ROBERT H., Jr. "Ego Identity in Adolescent Literature."
Ed.D. dissertation, Rutgers University, 1980, 146 pp., DA 41:3923A.
Analyzes the characters from four popular adolescent novels using
a psychosocial index based upon Erik Erikson's theories of adolescence.

B2179   DONELSON, KENNETH, and NILSEN, ALLEEN PACE. *Literature for
Today's Young Adults*. Glenview, Ill.: Scott, Foresman, 1980, 484
pp.
Essentially a text book for teachers and librarians. Chapter 2,
"Literary Aspects of Young Adult Books," provides a good overview
of the field. Individual topics and authors are indexed separately in
this bibliography.

B2180   -----. "Young Adult Literature Comes of Age: Growing Up Real."
WLB 52 (November 1977):241-47. (Reprinted in Lenz, *Young Adult
Literature*, pp. 58-67.)

Provides a capsule history of young adult literature from the 1940s to the 1970s and identifies four themes in adolescent novels today: (1) humanity's loneness, (2) our need for love and companionship, (3) our need for hope and the search for truth, and (4) our need for laughter. Concludes that adolescent literature is coming of age.

B2181   DONELSON, KENNETH, ed. "Adolescent Literature, Adolescent Reading and the English Class." *Arizona English Bulletin* 14, no. 3 (April 1972):156 pp.
Includes a wide range of articles on many aspects of young adult literature, many indexed separately in this bibliography. Includes bibliographies.

B2182   -----. "Evaluation, Yes! But According to Whose Standards and For What Purposes?," and "Writing About and Critiquing Young Adult Literature," in *Literature for Today's Young Adults*, pp. 387-99.
Examines problems of balancing interest to young adults and literary quality, and raises other issues pertinent to critiquing young adult literature.

B2183   DUNCAN, FRANCES. "The Young Adult Novel: One Author's Response." *Horn Book* 57 (April 1981):221-28. (Reprinted in Bator, *Signposts*, pp. 324-30.)
Argues against a separate category called "young adult," maintaining that much excellent writing is hidden there and that "all these young adult novels are being written not for today's young adults but about yesterday's adolescents, by yesterday's adolescents."

B2184   DUNNING, ARTHUR STEPHENSON. "Definition of the Role of the Junior Novel Based On Analysis of Thirty Selected Novels." Ph.D. dissertation, Florida State University, 1959, 356 pp., DA 20:2641A.
Analyzes thirty selected junior novels.

B2185   EAGLEN, AUDREY. "Writing the Teen-age Soap Opera." *SLJ* 25 (April 1979):24-27.
Explores the nature and excesses of the teenage problem novel.

B2186   EDWARDS, MARGARET A. "How Do I Love Thee?" *English Journal* 4 (September 1952):335-40.
An overview of the rise in the 1940s of adolescent fiction concerning love and marriage, designed to appeal to teenaged girls.

B2187   ELLA, COLIN. "Forum: Teenage Literature--Drawing that Line." *Children's Literature in Education* 13, no. 1 (Spring 1982):44-47.
A teacher discusses the difficulties posed by explicit young adult books for classroom use.

B2188   ELLIS, W. GEIGER. "Adolescent Literature's Changes, Cycles, and Constancy." *English Journal* 74 (March 1985):94-98.
A personal view of recent trends in the writing and criticism of adolescent literature.

B2189   ENGDAHL, SYLVIA. "Do Teenage Novels Fill a Need?" *English Journal* 64 (February 1975):48-52.
Views the designation "teenage" as reflecting a book published by a children's book department of a publishing house. Disagrees with

Babbitt (above): feels there is a need for a separate category for young adults and that the distinguishing characteristics of the genre are complexity and point of view.

B2190   -----. "Why Write for Today's Teenagers?" *Horn Book* 48 (June 1972):249-54. (Reprinted in Heins, *Crosscurrents*, pp. 144-49.)
Feels that young adult literature allows the writer a more optimistic outlook than is acceptable in adult novels.

B2191   FORMAN, JACK. "Young Adult Books: 'Watch Out for #1.'" *Horn Book* 61 (January 1985):85-87.
Compares the approaches of Judy Blume and Alice Bach to social problems and finds more consciousness in Bach of the effect on other people of the consequences of actions.

B2192   FRENCH, JEFFREY A. "Rock On, Read On: Music in Young Adult Novels." *TON* 38 (Summer 1982):360-63.
Looks at rock music in young adult novels and finds there is not much. Discusses nine books briefly.

B2193   FULLER, LAWRENCE B. "Literature for Adolescents: A Historical Perspective." *English Education* 11 (February 1980):131-41.
Provides a historical overview of the development of young adult literature. Includes extensive references.

B2194   GAUCH, PATRICIA LEE. "'Good Stuff' in Adolescent Fiction." *TON* 40 (Winter 1984):125-29.
Explores, within the context of young adult fiction, the distinction between great literature (the "good stuff") and literature that is primarily entertainment (the "good read").

B2195   GRANITE, HARVEY R. "The Uses and Abuses of Junior Literature." *Clearing House* 42 (February 1968):337-40.
Argues that most books classified as adolescent literature are popular, slickly written, stereotyped, and do not qualify as literature worthy of study in the English classroom.

B2196   HENTOFF, NAT. "Fiction for Teen-Agers." *WLB* 43 (November 1968):261-65.
Briefly discusses the writing of his own *Jazz Country*, then writes about what he feels is being left out of literature for young adults and suggests additional possibilities. An article entitled "Where Hentoff Left Off," by librarian Lyle Wilson Warwick, follows, pp. 266-68.

B2197   -----. "Tell It As It Is." *NYTBR*, 7 May 1967, Children's Book sec., pp. 3, 51.
Argues in favor of more realism in books for teenagers.

B2198   HIGGINS, JOHN. "Evaluating Novels for Young Adults: All that Glitters is Not Literature." *English Record* 32 (Winter 1981):22-23. (Also in ERIC Educational Document Reproduction Service, ED 199 714.)
Attacks the lack of artistry, poor characterization, and lack of narrative control in many of the books listed as "classics of the genre," while praising Virginia Hamilton's *M.C. Higgins, The Great* and Richard Peck's *Father Figure*.

B2199   HINTON, SUSAN E. "Teen-Agers Are for Real." *NYTBR*, 27 August 1967, pp. 26-29.
A plea for integrity, honesty, and reality in writing for young adults.

B2200   HOLLAND, ISABELLE. "What Is Adolescent Literature?" *TON* 31 (June 1975):407-14. (Reprinted in Lenz, *Young Adult Literature*, pp. 33-40.)
Contends that there is no such category, that adolescent literature is any story that appeals to "people within the ages of about twelve and nineteen."

B2201   HUTCHINSON, MARGARET. "Fifty Years of Young Adult Reading, 1921-1971." *TON* 30 (November 1973):24-53. (Reprinted in Varlejs, *Young Adult Literature*, pp. 39-69.)
Reports on a survey of the field of young adult reading based on an examination of articles indexed in *Library Literature* under the headings Young People's Reading, Youth's Literature, Youth's Reading, Young Adult's Reading, and Young Adult Literature, from 1921 to 1971. Includes a bibliography.

B2202   JOHNSON, JAMES WILLIAM. "The Adolescent Hero: A Trend in Modern Fiction." *Twentieth Century Literature* 5 (April 1959):3-11.
Examines the increasing importance of the adolescent hero in modern literature, primarily in works for adults.

B2203   JONES, VICTOR H., ed. "Focus on Literature for Children and Young Adults." *Indiana English Journal* 7, no. 4 (Summer 1977):47 pp. (Also in ERIC Educational Document Reproduction Service, 1977, 47 pp., ED 144 095.)
Articles in this issue devoted to adolescent literature include Ken Donelson's "Keeping Up-to-Date with Adolescent Literature," a bibliographic essay that mentions key articles from significant journals, articles on current issues in young adult fiction, changes in portrayals of the family, and the use of comics and transactional analysis in teaching literature.

B2204   "Junior Novel--Pro and Con." *TON* 17 (May 1961):19-28.
Two librarians, Alice Krahn and Marjorie Hoke, argue against the young adult novel, and two writers of books for teenagers, Anne Emery and James L. Summers, argue in its favor.

B2205   KAYE, MARILYN J. "Trappings of Morality: Didacticism and the Young Adult Novel." In *New Directions for Young Adult Services.* Edited by Ellen V. LiBretto. New York: R.R. Bowker, 1983, pp. 73-80.
Explores the new didacticism in today's young adult fiction.

B2206   KLEIN, NORMA. "Thoughts on the Adolescent Novel." *TON* 37 (Summer 1981):352-59.
Discusses her realistic books and those of Judy Blume and argues that more realistic books for the young are needed. Argues for writers and teachers to have the courage to tackle difficult themes.

B2207   KRAUS, WILLIS KEITH. "A Critical Survey of the Contemporary Adolescent-girl Problem Novel." Ph.D. dissertation, Southern Illinois

University, 1974, 118 pp., DA 35:7910A.

Surveys adolescent fiction published for girls since 1969 and finds that during the sixties the "safe" books of the 1940s and 1950s were superseded "by novels of more serious consequence."

B2208   KURTH, ANITA. "Biting the Hand that Feeds You: Parents in Adolescent Novels of the 70s." *SLJ* 28 (April 1982):26-28.

Analyzes the portrayal of parents in young adult fiction of the 1970s and finds a preponderance of unhealthy family situations.

B2209   LaCAMPAGNE, ROBERT J. "From Huck to Holden to Dinky Hocker: Current Humor in the American Adolescent Novel." *L&U* 1, no. 1 (1977):62-71.

The best of humorous adolescent novels "satirize the exaggerated importance that adolescents give to certain passing issues in their lives while at the same time recognizing that their pains are real and legitimate."

B2210   LENZ, MILLICENT, and MAHOOD, RAMONA M., comps. *Young Adult Literature.* Chicago: American Library Association, 1980, 516 pp.

Contains a wide-ranging collection of previously published essays on various aspects of young adult literature, many indexed separately in this bibliography.

B2211   *Lion and the Unicorn* 2, no. 2 (Fall 1978).

Special issue. Includes articles on Robert Cormier, Paul Zindel, Judy Blume, Leon Garfield, M.E. Kerr, John Donovan, and Rudyard Kipling, as well as a subject-oriented article on poverty, and an article by Geraldine De Luca delineating the development of the genre young-adult fiction as originating with J.D. Salinger.

B2212   LYSTAD, MARY. "The Adolescent Image in American Books for Children: Then and Now." *TON* 31 (June 1975):407-14. (Reprinted in Lenz, *Young Adult Literature*, pp. 27-33, and in *Children Today* 6, no. 35 [July-August 1977]:16-19.)

Describes changing concerns of books read by adolescents over the past two hundred years.

B2213   McBROOM, GERRY. "Young Adult Literature: Research: Our Defense Begins Here." *English Journal* 70 (October 1981):75-78.

Review recent research, including reading interest surveys, developmental stages of adolescents, characterizations in young adult novels, and approaches to using this literature. Includes a bibliography.

B2214   MacQUOWN, VIVIAN J., and WESTPHAL, VIRGINIA. "The Teenage Novel." *Library Journal* 89 (15 April 1964):1832-33 and *SLJ* 11 (April 1964):34-35.

The two authors offer a defense (Westphal) and a critique (MacQuown) of the young adult novel, especially of the teenaged girls' romance as written by Betty Cavanna.

B2215   MAGALIFF, CECILE. *The Junior Novel: Its Relationship to Adolescent Reading.* Port Washington, N.Y.: Kennikat Press, 1964, 116 pp.

Provides chapters on the background of the junior novel, the role of the junior novel in adolescent reading, and an evaluation of the junior novel. The major part of the book consists of chapters summarizing and evaluating the works of six writers for young adults: Betty Cavanna, pp. 25-37, Stephen Meader, pp. 38-51, Phyllis Whitney, pp. 52-61, Mary Stolz, pp. 65-77, Rosamund du Jardin, pp. 78-88, and Henry Gregor Felsen, pp. 89-99. Bibliographies of primary sources and excerpts from reviews are included for each author.

B2216   MARZANO, ROBERT J., and DISTEFANO, PHILIP. "Literary Characteristics Which Constitute 'Quality' in the Junior Novel: An Empirical Approach." ERIC Educational Document Reproduction Service, 1977, 15 pp., ED 136 301.
         Reports on a study to determine what constitutes quality in young adult fiction. Concludes that quality is a function of style, plot, setting, and theme, while characterization, literary devices, and "within-and-between-sentence modification were less important."

B2217   MATTHEWS, DOROTHY. "Writing About Adolescent Literature: Current Approaches and Future Directions." *Arizona English Bulletin* 18 (April 1976):216-19. (Reprinted in Varlejs, *Young Adult Literature*.)
         Categorizes writing about adolescent literature into three types: (1) articles that stress reader response, (2) articles that are functional, and (3) articles that center on the books themselves. Also focuses on various critical approaches to the books as literature. Suggests more close analysis.

B2218   MEADE, RICHARD A., and SMALL, ROBERT C., Jr. *Literature for Adolescents: Selection and Use.* Columbus, Ohio: Charles E. Merrill, 1973.
         A textbook-style compilation of previously published articles, many from *English Journal*, grouped around the topics of literature in the classroom, the why of adolescent literature, themes in literature for the adolescent, the literary quality of books for adolescent readers, and classroom use of literature for the adolescent.

B2219   MERTZ, MAIA PANK, and ENGLAND, DAVID A. "The Legitimacy of American Adolescent Fiction." *SLJ* 30 (October 1983):119-23.
         Identifies ten characteristics of adolescent fiction in an attempt to define the genre.

B2220   MERTZ, MAIA PANK. "New Realism: Traditional Cultural Values in Recent Young Adult Fiction." *Phi Delta Kappan* 60 (October 1978):101-5.
         Argues that the new realism in young-adult fiction tends to uphold standard American mores.

B2221   MORGAN, LINDA O. "Insight Through Suffering: Cruelty in Adolescent Fiction About Boys." *English Journal* 69 (December 1980):56-59.
         Examines the cruelty adolescents frequently inflict on each other as portrayed in Robert Lipsyte's *One Fat Summer*, Cormier's *The Chocolate War*, S.E. Hinton's *The Outsiders*, and Mildred Lee's *The Skating Rink*.

B2222   MULLER, AL. "The Adolescent Novel in the Classroom." *Media and Methods* 10, no. 8 (April 1974):32-33.
         Essentially a list of popular young adult novels, categorized by the various literary techniques they employ: for example, flashbacks, interior monologues, symbolism, literary allusions, irony, etc.

B2223   -----. "The Currently Popular Adolescent Novel as Transitional Literature." Ph.D. dissertation, Florida State University, 1974, 336 pp., DA
35:1056A.
Concludes that "despite the growing sophistication of the adolescent novel, the genre conforms to the traditional characteristics of
transitional literature."

B2224   -----. "New Reading Material: The Junior Novel." *Journal of Reading* 18 (April 1975):531-34. (Reprinted in Varlejs, *Young Adult
Literature*, pp. 124-28.)
Maintains that his study of thirty-one junior novels reveals that
increasing sophistication in subject matter has been matched by
increasing sophistication in literary techniques.

B2225   -----. "Thirty Popular Adolescent Novels: A Content Analysis."
English Journal 63 (September 1974):97-99.
Finds the problems depicted in the novels are more controversial
than those found by James E. Davis in his 1967 article "Recent
Trends in Fiction for Adolescents" (see above).

B2226   NEWFIELD, JOHN. "Young Adult Propaganda and Change." *ALAN
Review* 10, no. 3 (Spring 1983):1-2.
Answers the question of why he writes for young adults.

B2227   NILSEN, ALLEEN PACE. "Bottoms Up in Young Adult Literature."
TON 40 (Fall 1983):62-67.
Examines the influence of popular forms such as romance fiction,
formula, occult, and religious themes on mainstream young adult
fiction.

B2228   -----. "Rating, Ranking, Labeling Adolescent Literature." *SLJ* 28
(December 1981):24-27.
Reports on a survey concerning the definitions and preferences
for using the terms adolescent literature, junior novel, juvenile
fiction, and young adult literature. Young adult literature was the
preferred term.

B2229   NILSEN, ALLEEN PACE, ed. *English Journal* 73 (November 1984).
Special issue on young adult literature. Includes the editor's
comments, "The Rites of Passage for Adolescent Literature," p. 21;
Robert G. Carlson's "Teaching Literature for the Adolescent: A
Historical Perspective," pp. 28-30; Don Gallo's "What Should Teachers
Know About Young Adult Literature for 2004?," pp. 31-34; and
Susan M. Nugent's "Adolescent Literature: A Transition into Future
Reading," pp. 35-37. Several other articles, including discussions of
specific themes and authors, have been indexed separately in this
bibliography.

B2230   ORTIZ, MIGUEL A. "The Politics of Poverty in Young Adult Literature." *L&U* 2, no. 2 (Fall 1978):6-15.
Discusses three novels: *A Hero Ain't Nothin But a Sandwich*,
by Alice Childress; *Daddy Was a Number Runner*, by Louise Merri-
wether; and *Nilda*, by Nicholasa Mohr. Praises the first for its
aesthetic and political point of view, and finds the other two disappointing.

B2231 PATTERSON, EMMA L. "The Junior Novels and How They Grew."
English Journal 45 (October 1956):381-87, 405.
Traces the development of the "junior novel" and poses challenges
concerning its future.

B2232 PECK, RICHARD. "In the Country of Teenage Fiction." *American
Libraries* 4 (April 1973):204-7.
Expresses concerns about young adults' needs and the books being
written for and about them. Argues that more middle ground is
needed between "sex-violence-social problems on the one hand, and
Tolkien fantasy on the other."

B2233 -----. "The Invention of Adolescence and Other Thoughts on Youth."
TON 39 (Winter 1983):182-90.
A rambling personal statement about adolescents--what they like
and what writers offer them. Provides some memorable insights into
the nature of young adult literature and Peck himself. Example:
"The great work thus far produced in Young Adult literature is Robert Cormier's *The Chocolate War* because it tells a truth too strong
for its own readers: that the great threat comes to the young not
from the world or their parents. It comes from their peers. But
readers, young and old, don't reward writers for the truth. People
don't read fiction to be informed or challenged or change."

B2234 PETITT, DOROTHY. "A Study of the Qualities of Literary Excellence
Which Characterize Selected Fiction for Young Adolescents." Ph.D.
dissertation, University of Minnesota, 1961, 380 pp., DA 24:1889A.
Attempts to establish literary criteria for judging fiction for
younger adolescents. Concludes that "the limitations imposed on such
fiction by the immaturity of its readers result in artistic simplicity,
rather than complexity, but literature need not necessarily be complex."

B2235 RADNER, REBECCA. "You're Being Paged Loudly in the Kitchen:
Teen-Age Literature of the Forties and Fifties." *Journal of Popular
Culture* 11 (spring 1978):789-99.
Examines the ways in which Maureen Daly and other popular
writers of the 1940s girls' books influenced young women, not always
for the best.

B2236 RAMSEY, JOSEPH. "The Initiation Theme in Adolescent Literature."
Clearing House 52 (January 1979):210-13.
Explores the theme of initiation as a means of unifying the study
of adolescent literature.

B2237 RAY, SHEILA. "Trends in the Teenage Novel." *School Librarian* 25
(March 1977):19-23.
Traces the development of the young adult novel in the 1960s
and 1970s, identifying key events, basic qualities of the books, and
treatment of topics of interest to teenagers.

B2238 RITT, SHARON ISAACSON. "Journeys: Another Look at the Junior
Novel." *Journal of Reading* 19 (May 1976):627-34.
Analyzes thirty-nine junior novels in terms of "journeys" made by
the central characters, "journeys concerned with the broad themes of
maturing, searching for self-definition, clarifying values, and relating
to others."

B2239   ROXBURGH, STEVE. "The Novel of Crisis: Contemporary Adolescent
         Fiction." In Lenz, *Young Adult Literature*, pp. 141-47. (Reprinted
         from *Children's Literature* 7 [1978]:248-54.)
             Discusses Judy Blume's *Forever*, Norma Klein's *Hiding*, Penelope
         Farmer's *Year King*, Isabelle Holland's *Hitchhike*, Paul Zindel's
         Pardon Me You're Stepping On My Eyeball, and Robert Cormier's *I
         Am the Cheese* in terms of identity crisis.

B2240   SCHWARTZ, SHEILA. "Adolescent Literature and the Pursuit of Val-
         ues." *Media & Methods* 12 (March 1976):20-25.
             Argues that adolescent fiction offers a "means of developing in
         our students the humanistic values that offer the promise of a better
         world."

B2241   SEARSON, MARILYN. "Adolescent Culture in Junior Novels: A Con-
         tent Analysis of Selected Junior Novels Recommended in the 1972,
         1973, 1974 Supplements to the *Junior High School Library Catalog*."
         Ph.D. dissertation, Florida State University, 1975, 170 pp., DA
         36:4827A.
             Analyzes the characteristics of American adolescent culture as
         portrayed in sixty selected junior novels.

B2242   SEVERIN, MARY SUSAN. "Applying a Schema for Studying the
         Instructive Techniques Employed by Authors of Four Novels for
         Adolescents." Ph.D. dissertation, University of Iowa, 1976, 195 pp.,
         DA 37:5022A.
             Examines the lessons communicated by the authors of four recent
         adolescent novels.

B2243   SMALL, ROBERT C., Jr. "The Junior Novel and the Art of Litera-
         ture." *English Journal* 66 (October 1977):56-59.
             Proposes use of young adult fiction as "working models" to teach
         elements of literature.

B2244   STANEK, LOU WILLETT. "Adolescent Formula Literature and Its Pro-
         miscuous Progeny." ERIC Educational Document Reproduction Ser-
         vice, 1974, 19 pp., ED 102 573.
             Identifies the following characteristics of the "formula" for
         adolescent novels: (1) after the protagonist is introduced, the
         problem is dramatized by a brief episode; (2) some event destroys the
         precarious equilibrium of the protagonist and precipitates a crisis; (3)
         the protagonist reacts with increasing frustration and does not
         approach the solution to the problem; (4) just as a point of hopeless-
         ness seems to have been reached, an accident of the sudden interven-
         tion of a transcendent character brings illumination and insight to the
         protagonist; and (5) the problem is solved by the protagonist and
         appropriate action is taken. A brief synopsis and possible teaching
         approach are outlined for each of three adolescent formula novels:
         Watership Down, *A Hero Ain't Nothing But a Sandwich*, and *The
         Chocolate War*.

B2245   -----. "The Junior Novel: A Stylistic Study." *EE* 51 (October
         1974):947-53.
             Discusses Hope Campbell's *Why Not Join the Giraffes?* as an
         example of "a conventional formula novel with much action and
         visual description"; *I Never Loved Your Mind*, by Paul Zindel, as

experimental, "perhaps a parody of formulaic fiction and more serious novels about adolescents"; and Mary Stolz's *The Seagulls Woke Me* as a classic that "holds up the whole spectrum of human life with no quick and easy solutions to serious problems." Analyzes the style of each. Includes references.

B2246   -----. "The Maturation of the Junior Novel: From Gestation to the Pill." *Library Journal* 97 (15 December 1972):4046-51 and *SLJ* 19 (December 1972):34-39. (Reprinted in Gerhardt, *Issues in Children's Book Selection*, pp. 174-81.)
Examines a common formula of young adult fiction to see how it has reflected changing adolescent culture and how it has changed and been adapted. Closely examines Zoa Sherburne's *Too Bad About the Haines Girl*, Henry Gregor Felsen's *Two and the Town*, Ann Head's *Mr. and Mrs. Bo Jo Jones*, and Paul Zindel's *My Darling, My Hamburger*.

B2247   -----. "Real People, Real Books: About YA Readers." *TON* 31 (June 1975):417-27.
Examines books popular with teenagers, looking at what they like and why.

B2248   STEVENSON, DINAH. "Young Adult Fiction: An Editor's View Point." *ChLAQ* 9, no. 2 (Summer 1984):87-88.
Explores reasons why fewer young adult books are being published and attempts to define the changing genre.

B2249   STRAUSER, ATHA MAXINE TUBBS. "Archetypal Analysis and the Teaching of Adolescent Novels." Ph.D. dissertation, University of Texas at Austin, 1978, 197 pp., DA 39:2042A.
Proposes the use of archetypal analysis, based on the work of Mircea Eliade, to teach adolescent fiction, emphasizing "a search for identity within a social structure that lacks a cohesive community," or the "attempt to find a meaningful existence in a chaotic world."

B2250   SUTTON, ROGER. "The Critical Myth: Realistic Young Adult Novels." *SLJ* 29 (November 1982):33-35.
Argues that the realism in most teenage fiction is not "hard-hitting," "shattering," or "tragic," just "sad." "Truly challenging realism" is not often presented, but "we have talked and written ourselves into believing it is so."

B2251   SUTTON, WENDY K. "Developing Literary Appreciation via Contemporary Adolescent Literature." ERIC Educational Document Reproduction Service, 1977, 15 pp., ED 158 265.
Maintains that by examining the wide range of increasingly sophisticated literary techniques used in popular adolescent fiction, teachers can help make connections between juvenile and adult literature.

B2252   THOMPSON, SUSAN. "Images of Adolescence." *Signal* 34 (January 1981):37-59; 35 (May 1981):108-25.
The first part of this article discusses "how youth is represented in a small sample of novels, and then looks in more detail at the treatment of sexuality." The second part concentrates on "the search for independent identity" and considers "the potential of teen-age fiction and the limitations of a didactic approach."

B2253   TUNIS, JOHN R. "What Is A Juvenile Book?" *Horn Book* 44 (June 1968):307-10.
Objects to the term "juvenile" as a "product of a merchandising age."

B2254   UNSWORTH, ROBERT. "Holden Caulfield, Where Are You?" *SLJ* (January 1977):40-41. (Reprinted in Varlejs, *Young Adult Literature*, pp. 120-23.)
Argues that there is a need for more "rites of passage" fiction for adolescent boys.

B2255   VARLEJS, JANA. *Young Adult Literature in the Seventies: A Selection of Readings.* Metuchen, N.J.: Scarecrow, 1978, 452 pp.
Contains dozens of articles on all aspects of young adult literature: historical perspectives, reading interests, censorship, minorities, genres, selection, and use. Individual topics and authors have been indexed separately in this bibliography.

B2256   WEISS, M. JERRY, ed. *From Writers to Students: The Pleasures and Pains of Writing.* Newark, Del.: International Reading Association, 1979, 113 pp.
Interviews seventeen writers for young adults who talk about what it is like to be a writer, the way they work, their aims and influences: Sue Alexander, Judy Blume, Vera and Bill Cleaver, Julia Cunningham, S.E. Hinton, Isabelle Holland, Mollie Hunter, M.E. Kerr, Norma Klein, Norma and Henry Mazer, Milton Meltzer, Nicholasa Mohr, Richard Peck, Mary Rodgers, Barbara Wersba, Laurence Yep, and Paul Zindel.

B2257   WIGUTOFF, SHARON. "Junior Fiction: A Feminist Critique." *L&U* 5 (1981):4-18.
Discusses three findings of her research on sex-roles portrayed in young adult fiction: (1) parents (especially mothers) are the "heavies" in junior fiction, (2) there are frequently wonderful friendships between young and elderly (usually grandparents), and (3) there is a paucity of good new books about Third World children and their families that are both nonsexist and nonracist. Cites many specific titles.

B2258   YATES, JESSICA. "Controversial Teenage Fiction." *School Librarian* 32 (September 1984):206-13.
Discusses a number of recent controversial books and the problems of censorship that they precipitate.

B2259   YODER, JAN MILLER. "The Rites of Passage: A Study of the Adolescent Girl." *News from ALAN*, Fall 1976, pp. 3-5. (Reprinted in Varlejs, *Young Adult Literature*, pp. 24-31.)
Examines the treatment of three phases of initiation rites in adolescent fiction: separation, transition, and incorporation. Books discussed include Honor Arundel's *The Blanket World* and *The Terrible Temptation*, Jean George's *Julie of the Wolves*, Carson McCullers's *A Member of the Wedding*, and Donia Mills's *Long Way Home from Troy*.

YUGOSLAVIA

B2260   KAMENETSKY, CHRISTA. "Folklore Revival in Slovenia: A Quest for Cultural Identity." *Library Journal* 99 (15 May 1974):1441-45.
Provides a detailed account of Slovenian children's books and their emphasis on folk heritage.

B2261   PRIBIC, RADO. "Blue Jeans Fiction of Yugoslavia." *Journal of Reading* 26 (February 1983):430-34.
Describes characteristics of a new subgenre of adolescent literature currently popular in Eastern Europe. Includes a bibliography and sources of English translations.

Appendix:
Resources in Children's Literature

Annotated lists of reference materials and major journals related to children's literature.

REFERENCE WORKS

CARPENTER, HUMPHREY, and PRICHARD, MARI. *The Oxford Companion to Children's Literature.* New York: Oxford University Press, 1984, 587 pp.
Contains entries on individual authors and illustrators, titles, characters from children's fiction, fairy tales, and many aspects of children's culture.

CECH, JOHN, ed. *Dictionary of Literary Biography. Vol. 22, American Writers for Children, 1900-1960.* Detroit: Gale, 1983, 412 pp.
Provides signed essays and extensive bibliographical information on forty-three writers.

Children's Literature Abstracts, May 1973-.
Published quarterly in England by the International Federation of Library Associations and edited by Colin Ray. Abstracts articles about children's literature. Cummulative indexes are available for nos. 1-28 (May 1973-March 1980) and for nos. 29-44 (June 1980-March 1984).

Children's Literature Review: Excerpts from Reviews, Criticism, and Commentary on Children's Books. Detroit: Gale, 1976-.
Covers writers whose work is currently "being critically evaluated for its suitability or appeal for present day young readers."

COMMIRE, ANNE, ed. *Something about the Author: Facts and Pictures about Contemporary Authors and Illustrators of Books for Young People.* Detroit: Gale, 1971-.
A standard continuing multi-volume source of information on juvenile authors and illustrators. Entries include biographical data, bibliographies, and critical comments.

FORDYCE, RACHEL. "Dissertations of Note." *Children's Literature*, 1972-.
An annual annotated listing.

HAVILAND, VIRGINIA. *Children's Literature: A Guide to Reference Sources.* Washington, D.C.: Library of Congress, 1966, 341 pp. *First Supplement,* 1972, 316 pp.; *Second Supplement,* 1977, 413 pp.

Critically annotated guides to the entire field of children's literature. Includes sections on history and criticism, individual authors, illustration, bibliography, teaching, storytelling, libraries, and international and national studies.

KIRKPATRICK, D.L., ed. *Twentieth-Century Children's Writers.* 2d ed. New York: St. Martin's, 1983, 1024 pp.
Includes biocritical essays and extensive lists of authors' writings for both children and adults, for over 700 English-language children's writers.

LEIF, IRVING P. *Children's Literature: A Historical and Contemporary Bibliography.* Troy, N.Y.: Whitson, 1977, 338 pp.
Includes numerous master's theses in addition to an assortment of books and articles pertaining to children's literature.

Literature, Literary Response, and the Teaching of Literature: Abstracts of Doctoral Dissertations Published in "Dissertation Abstracts International." ERIC Educational Document Reproduction Service.
An ongoing semi-annual series providing abstracts of recent doctoral dissertations, many relating to the study and teaching of children's and young adult literature.

LUKENBILL, W. BERNARD. *A Working Bibliography of American Doctoral Dissertations in Children's and Adolescents' Literature, 1930-1971.* Occasional Papers, no. 103. Champaign: University of Illinois, Graduate School of Library Science, 1972, 56 pp.
Attempts to identify dissertations in "almost all areas of children's literature, including reading interests and pedagogical techniques." A bibliographic essay includes subdivisions on types of literature and history and criticism.

MacDONALD, RUTH. "Proceedings: An Index to the First Five." *ChLAQ* 8, no. 4 (Winter 1983):46-48.
An author, title, and subject index to the proceedings of the Children's Literature Association's conferences five through nine, 1978-82.

MEACHAM, MARY. *Information Sources in Children's Literature: A Practical Reference Guide for Children's Librarians, Elementary School Teachers, and Students of Children's Literature.* Westport, Conn.: Greenwood Press, 1978, 256 pp.
Describes standard selection tools for children's books, sources for book reviews, and specialized guides to the field.

MONSON, DIANE L., and PELTOLA, BETTE, comps. *Research in Children's Literature: An Annotated Bibliography.* Newark, Del.: International Reading Association, Association, 1976, 96 pp.
Includes dissertations and ERIC Documents from 1960 to 1974 and research published in journals between 1965 and 1974.

Phaedrus: An International Journal of Children's Literature Research, 1973-.
Each issue includes extensive bibliographies of critical articles, books, and dissertations relating to children's literature, as well as critical essays centered around themes or geographic areas. Indexed in *Library Literature.*

RAHN, SUZANNE. *Children's Literature: An Annotated Bibliography of the History and Criticism.* New York: Garland, 1981, 451 pp.

Covers criticism of numerous writers for children from earliest times to the present, as well as articles grouped according to broad topics.

ROGINSKI, JIM, comp. *Newbery and Caldecott Medalists and Honor Book Winners: Bibliographies and Resource Materials through 1977.* Littleton, Colo.: Libraries Unlimited, 1982, 339 pp.
Provides listings of awards, primary and secondary sources, media, collections, and exhibitions.

SARKISSIAN, ADELE, ed. *Children's Authors and Illustrators: An Index to Biographical Dictionaries.* 2d ed. Detroit: Gale, 1978, 251 pp.
Covers approximately 15,000 authors and illustrators who are cited in about 150 reference sources.

–––––. *Writers for Young Adults: Biographies Master Index.* 1st ed. Detroit: Gale, 1979, 199 pp.
Covers sources of biographical information on writers of interest of high-school students.

SHANNON, GEORGE W.B. *Folk Literature and Children: An Annotated Bibliography of Secondary Materials.* Westport, Conn.: Greenwood, 1981, 124 pp.
Covers materials published from 1693 through 1979 that are concerned with the combination of children and folk literature.

SMITH, ELVA S. *The History of Children's Literature: A Syllabus with Selected Bibliographies.* Revised and enlarged edition by Margaret Hodges and Susan Steinfirst. Chicago: American Library Association, 1980, 290 pp.
Covers English-language criticism of an international array of children's writers up to the beginning of the twentieth century. Includes listings of primary and secondary materials.

WHITAKER, MURIEL A., ed. *Children's Literature: A Guide to Criticism.* Edmonton: Athabascan Publishing Co., 1976, 64 pp.
Includes sections on bibliographies and general reference guides, and lists materials relating to the history of children's literature, myth, and folklore. Has a brief section devoted to criticism of individual authors.

WHITE, VIRGINIA L., and SCHULTE, EMERITA S., comps. *Books about Children's Books: An Annotated Bibliography.* ERIC Educational Document Reproduction Service, 1979, 49 pp., ED 176 333.
Lists 145 sources of information on children's literature in categories of bibliography, biography, criticism, history, indexes, research, teaching methods, and textbooks.

"Year's Work in Children's Literature Studies: 1982. *ChLAQ* 8, no. 4 (Winter 1983):42-45.
Lists 161 articles from a number of journals, by critic name and category.

In addition to the above sources, computerized and manual searches of the following indexing and abstracting services yield numerous citations relating to children's literature in a wide range of sources: *Education Index, Current Index to Journals in Education, Resources in Education, Dissertation Abstracts, Psychological Abstracts, Library Literature,* and the *MLA* and *MHRA* bibliographies.

JOURNALS

Advocate, 1981-.
Published three times yearly by Southeastern Advocates for Literature for Young People and the Center for the Study of Literature for Young People. Includes practical and scholarly articles on literature for children and young adults.

ALAN Review, 1973-.
Published three times yearly by the Assembly on Literature for Adolescents of the National Council of Teachers of English. Devoted to young adult literature.

Bookbird: Literature for Children and Young People, Problems of Juvenile Reading, Best Books from All over the World, 1963-.
Issued quarterly by the International Board on Books for Young People (IBBY) and the International Institute for Children's Literature and Reading Research. Indexed in *Library Literature*.

Canadian Children's Literature, 1975-.
Published quarterly. Devoted to "the literary analysis, criticism, and review of books written for Canadian children." Indexed in *Canadian Periodicals Index* and *Children's Literature Abstracts*.

Children's Literature, 1972-.
Published annually by the Children's Literature Association. Edited by Francelia Butler. Includes scholarly articles, reviews of significant scholarly works, and a section of varia that includes an annotated listing of dissertations (see Fordyce under Reference Works). Indexed in the *MLA Bibliography*, Vol. 11 (1983), contains an index to volumes 6-10. Twenty-six articles from the first ten years have been reprinted in *Reflections on Children's Literature*, edited by Francelia Butler and Richard Rotert (Hamden, Conn.: Shoe-String Press, 1984), 281 pp.

Children's Literature Assembly of NCTE. Bulletin, 1975-.
Formerly called *Ripples*, this is the newsletter of the Assembly. Occasionally contains substantial articles.

Children's Literature Association Quarterly, 1976-.
First published as a newsletter, the *Quarterly* contains extensive articles devoted to critical analysis of children's literature. From 1983 the through 1986 the proceedings of the annual conferences of the Association were published in the winter issue. See "Books of Criticism Indexed" for the complete list of separately published proceedings.

Children's Literature in Education, 1969-.
Published quarterly by Agathon Press in New York, but originates in England. Includes scholarly and practical articles. Indexed in *Current Index to Journals in Education* and *Education Index*.

English in Education, 1966-.
Published three times yearly in England. Devoted to the teaching of English. Includes articles on children's literature.

English Journal, 1912-.
Published eight times yearly by the National Council of Teachers of English for junior high and high school English teachers. Occasionally

devotes an issue or an article to young adult literature. Indexed in *Education Index* and *Current Index to Journals in Education.*

Horn Book, 1924-.
Published six times yearly. Includes reviews of children's books and lengthier, in-depth articles on many aspects of children's literature. Indexed in *Library Literature* and *Current Index to Journals in Education.*

Interracial Books for Children Bulletin, 1966-.
Published eight times yearly by the Council on Interracial Books for Children (CIBC). Includes reviews and in-depth articles examining and criticizing racial, sexist, agist, and elitist biases and stereotypes in children's books. Indexed in *Education Index.*

Journal of Popular Culture, 1967-.
Published quarterly by the Popular Culture Center of Bowling Green State University. Includes numerous articles on aspects of popular culture that overlap children's literature, especially comics, series books, folklore, and highly popular authors such as L. Frank Baum and Edgar Rice Burroughs. Indexed in *Humanities Index.*

Junior Bookshelf, 1936-.
Published six times yearly in Yorkshire, England. Bears some resemblance to *Horn Book* with its long publishing history and mix of reviews and in-depth articles. Indexed in *Library Literature.*

Language Arts, 1924-.
Previously entitled *Elementary English* (1947-75), and *Elementary English Review* (1924-46). Published by the National Council of Teachers of English for elementary school teachers. Usually has one issue every year devoted to children's literature, and occasional articles at other times. Indexed in *Education Index* and *Current Index to Journals in Education.*

The Lion and the Unicorn, 1977-.
To be published twice yearly by Johns Hopkins University Press beginning in 1986. Edited by Geraldine De Luca and Roni Natov. Each issue centers on a theme or genre. Indexed in the *MLA Bibliography.*

New York Times Book Review. Features a special children's book review section twice yearly, usually in November and in April or May.

Orana: Journal for School and Children's Librarianship, 1976-.
Published quarterly, this Australian journal was preceded by *Children's Libraries Newsletter*. Includes numerous critical and scholarly articles on children's literature.

Phaedrus: An International Journal of Children's Literature Research, 1973-.
See annotation under "Reference Works" above.

Reading Teacher, 1947-.
Published nine times yearly by the International Reading Association for elementary school teachers. Coverage of children's literature has varied over the years. Indexed in *Current Index to Journals in Education* and *Education Index.*

School Librarian, 1937-.
> Published quarterly by the the School Library Association in Britain. Includes a series of articles entitled "Writers for Children" and occasionally other articles on children's literature. Indexed in *Library Literature.*

School Library Journal, 1954-.
> Until 1975 published as part of *Library Journal.* Devoted to library work with children and teenagers. Occasionally contains important articles on children's literature. Indexed in *Library Literature.*

Signal: Approaches to Children's Books, 1970-.
> Published three times yearly by Thimble Press in England. Includes scholarly critical articles on children's literature.

Times (London).
> The *Times Educational Supplement* frequently features articles relating to children's literature and also contains some book reviews. The *Times Literary Supplement* features special children's book sections two or three times a year.

Top of the News, 1942-.
> Published quarterly by the Association for Library Service to Children of the American Library Association. Includes book reviews and a wide range of articles on children's and young adult literature. Indexed in *Library Literature.*

Use of English, 1951-.
> Preceded by *English in the Schools.* Published by the Scottish Academic Press, Edinburgh. Throughout the 1960s and 1970s contained numerous articles on children's literature. Indexed in *British Education Index.*

Wilson Library Bulletin, 1914-.
> Published monthly. Every one or two years features an issue devoted to a particular aspect of children's literature. Monthly reviews of picture books by Olga Richard and Donna Rae MacCann are also worth noting. Indexed in *Library Literature* and *Education Index.*

Index of Critics

Elkins, Hilda Arnold, B695
Ella, Colin, B2187
Elledge, Scott, A2523
Elleman, Barbara, A2083; B76, 444,
 1708
Ellis, Alec, A33, 1790; B77, 289,
 709, 803
Ellis, Anne W., B803-4, 1756
Ellis, James, A1396
Ellis, John M., A1085
Ellis, Margery, A658
Ellis, Sarah, A614, 1235, 1290, 2416;
 B280-81
Ellis, W. Geiger, B2188
Ellison, Carolyn, B805
Ellison, Shirley, A1146
Elms, Alan C., A2379
Ely, Amanda, Sister, B5
Elzea, Rowland, A1970
Emberley, Barbara, A827
Emberley, Ed, A827
Emery, Anne, B2204
Emenyonou, Ernest, A822
Emmerson, Andrea, B1460
Engdahl, Sylvia, A831; B1793,
 2189-2190
Engel, Rosalind E., B1859
Engen, Rodney K., A487, 692
England, A.W., A1671
England, David A., B2219
English, Gladys, A1917
English, J., B2229
Enright, Elizabeth, A2275-76; B998
Epstein, Connie C., B1206, 2007
Epstein, Jason, B1005, 2045
Erisman, Fred, A194, 219, 2062-63,
 2548
Erlich, Richard D., A1491
Ernes, Albert François, B1794
Escarpit, Denise, B319
Esmonde, Margaret P., A859, 1483,
 1491; B1795-96
Espeland, Pamela Lee, A1996
Estes, Eleanor, A834, 2225
Ets, Marie Hall, A840
Evans, B. Ifor, A2043
Evans, David, A1137, 1876; B327
Evans, Ernestine, A940
Evans, Eva Knox, B211
Evans, Gwyneth, B1125
Evans, Joan, A1799
Evans, Margaret B., B258, 1461
Evans, Murray J., A2517
Evans, W.D. Emrys, A1630, 2390
Evans, Walter, B1958
Eyre, Frank, B266
Ezell, Richard, B1357

Faben, Aline Sidney, A1655
Face, Andrea, B372
Factor, June, A375, 1691
Fadiman, Clifton, A1044, 2171, 2464;
 B360-61, 445
Fairbanks, A. Harris, B1583
Fardell, Joyce, B1081
Fargnoli, Betty Ann, A664
Farjeon, Eleanor, A1738
Farmer, Lillah, B78
Farmer, Penelope, A860-61; B838
Farmer, Philip Jose, A457
Farrell, Diane, A1266, 2238
Farrell, Jacqueline M., A980
Fatchen, Max, B126
Fattah, Abdul Razzak, B1281
Faust, Wolfgang M., B378
Fava, Rita, A2603
Favat, Andre F., B417, 446, 729
Fayose, P. Osazee, B19, 1321-22,
 1440
Feaver, William, B1463
Fee, Margery, B282
Feeley, Margaret P., A1366-67
Feelings, Tom, A870-71; B1440
Feiffer, Jules, B379, 393
Feldman, Sari, A1579
Fell, Christine, E., A100
Feminists on Children's Literature,
 B1860
Feminists on Children's Media,
 B1866, 2098
Fenner, Phyllis, B1082
Fenton, Edward, A2636; B2031
Fenwick, Sara Innis, A900; B362
Ferns, John, A689
Feydt, Astrid, B1340-41
Fiedler, Leslie A., B312, 380
Field, Carolyn, A1729; B447
Field, Elinor Whitney, B1315
Field, Rachel, A874
Filstrup, Jane Merrill, A163, 1036,
 2053; B1464
Fincke, Kate, B806
Fine, Gary Alan, B922
Finnes, Ern, B547
Fish, Helen Dean, A1443, 1610
Fisher, Aileen, A54
Fisher, Anita, A1327
Fisher, Carol J., B1584
Fisher, Clyde, A2078
Fisher, Crispin, A1455
Fisher, Elizabeth, B1861, 1909
Fisher, Emma. *See* Wintle, Justin.
Fisher, Laura, B1127
Fisher, M.F.K., A122

Index of Authors, Titles, and Subjects

1542, 1979, 2045
Potter Thompson, A995
Poverty, B2230
Prachatická, Markéta, A523
Prairie, A2561; B1645-46
A Prairie Boy's Summer, A1419;
B281
A Prairie Boy's Winter, A1419;
B281
Praise to the End!, B1363
Preschool books. *See* First books
Preussler, Otfried, A1966
Price, Evadne, A707
Pride and Prejudice, A41-42
The Prince and the Pauper, A2468
Prince of Annwn, A1630-31
"The Princess and the Frog," B794
The Princess and the Goblin, A1546,
1659, 2145; B883
"The Princess and the Pea," B763
Printmaking and picture books,
B1531
The Prisoners of September, A960
Problem novels, B1647-50, 2168,
2185
Progressive era, A194, 219
Prolov, Vadim, B1938
Prometheus, B1299
Propaganda. *See* Politics
Property of, B2162
Provensen, Alice, A1967
Provensen, Martin, A1967; B1514
Prydain series. *See* Chronicles of
Prydain
"Psyche's Art," A40, 68
Psychoanalytic criticism, A185, 189,
721, 792, 1450, 1451, 1735;
B547. *See also* Fairy tales,
psychological interpretations
of Barrie, A199, 203, 205
of Baum, A215, 218
of Carroll, A510, 527
of nursery rhymes, B1369, 1373
Psychofantasy, B855
Psychological criticism, B545
Psychological fiction, B517
Psychological significance of chil-
dren's literature, B526
Puck of Pook's Hill, A1371,
1373-74, 1388-89
Puerto Rico and Puerto Ricans,
B1651-55, 1667, 1866
The Puffin Book of Salt-Sea Verse,
A551; B1622
Pulga, B318
The Pumpkin People, B1176
Punch and Judy, A1145; B671

Puppets and puppet plays, A261;
B1575, 1656-57
"Puss 'n Boots," A1968; B763, 775
Pyle, Howard, A1969-72; B1027,
1512, 1516, 1725

The Queen Who Flew, A897
Queenie Peavy, A432
The Quest for Orion, B1792
Quest literature, A179, 2292; B1057,
1658
A Question of Harmony, B222

Rabbit Hill, A1446-47
Rabbit Island, A2299, B318
Rabbits in children's books, B77
Race, A780
Race in children's books, A780;
B943, 1001, 1659-73. *See also*
Ethnic groups; names of con-
troversial books; names of races
A Racecourse for Andy, A2614,
2616; B982
Rackham, Arthur, A1973-80; B1516
Radio Boys series, A560
Radio Patrol, B411
Ragged Dick, A56, 451, 69; B323
Raggedy Ann books, A1099-1100;
B965
Rags to Riches, A1145
Rags to riches theme, B1965
Railway books, A173
The Railway Children, A1793; B1928
Rain, B1674
The Rain Maker, A823
Ralph Fairbanks series, A560
Ramée, Marie Louise de la, A1846;
B110
Ramona and Her Father, A1861
Ramona books, A611
Rand, Paul, A1981
Rank, Otto, A2219
Ransom for a Knight, A1911
Ransome, Arthur, A1982-91; B75,
1935
"Rapunzel," A163, 1992; B738, 752
Raquel of the Ranch Country,
A1679
Raskin, Ellen, A1993-95; B1296
Rasmussen, Halfdan, A1996; B646
The Rattle Bag, B1574, 1609
Raven cycle, B1149
Ravensgill, A1704, 1711
Rawlings, Marjorie Kinnan,
A1997-2005; B1257, 1879
Reader response criticism. *See*
under Critical theory; Picture

WITHDRAWAL